DUES

The Coming of Allie Cohen

Dr. Arnold Heller

Library of Congress Control Number:		2017919395
ISBN:	Hardcover	978-1-5434-7390-2
	Softcover	978-1-5434-7389-6
	eBook	978-1-5434-7388-9

Print information available on the last page.

Rev. date: 01/29/2018

To order additional copies of this book, contact:
Xlibris
1-888-795-4274
www.Xlibris.com
Orders@Xlibris.com
770219

To my late wife, Sue Auerbach Heller, who heroically supported my effort to develop and write this novel. Her love and magnificent spirit inspired and supported me in completing a book that has been over *thirty-eight years* in the writing.

Also to my son, Sasha Heller, who grew up during the early drafts. As a small child, he used to sit on my lap and model his dad by pecking away at the typewriter keys. Today he is a journalist and editor for a major newspaper group.

ACKNOWLEDGMENT

I thank my special friend Patty Morrison for providing me the support and encouragement needed to dust off this novel after twenty-five years of marinating and finally complete it.

*What if God sent a messiah to teach
the people how to live in peace and they
failed to exalt him?*

Book I

"A child is coming—a child is coming to you."

—David Crosby, Paul Kantner, Grace Slick

Chapter 1

January 1, 1946

God, in heaven, stared down at his chosen people struggling to establish the new Jewish state of Israel. Gabriel, His special angel, joined the Lord Almighty in His perch over Jerusalem.

"Happy New Year's, Hashem. It's the first day of a new year. Why so pensive when we should be celebrating a fresh start for the world?"

Yahweh smiled at Gabriel. "My special angel, I did not call for you today to exchange New Year's greetings. I need your help."

"How may I be of service to You, oh omnipotent One?" Gabriel flapped his wings to express great joy and pride.

"Yes, Gabriel, I know that, when called upon, I can bear all the burdens of the earth. Unfortunately, when I do, I usually spread myself thin, and few challenges are aptly met. For the next two years, I must focus on moving heaven and earth to redeem the children of Israel in their new nation. It is time for Jews to end the wandering, return home to Zion, and dwell among themselves in their own state."

"Yes, it is. Sadly, their neighbors will war against Israel for the next forty years, and then Iran and jihadist terror groups will haunt them. So, Hashem, what job do You have for me?"

"With this catastrophic world war finally over and the ashes of the Holocaust having cooled, the people must learn to make peace and live together. This new atomic bomb will set off an arms race so terrible that the planet will be threatened with annihilation. I will soon send a prophet to teach the people how to bind their fissures and build a lasting and prosperous peace."

"I gather, eternal One, that You want to focus on redeeming Israel and need me to tell the people about the prophet and help him touch their hearts to succeed." Gabriel realized.

"Yes, Gabriel, all the people may *behold* the prophet, but they must sincerely *exalt* him to usher in a first coming. If *awe* is not the common state, then they will wait decades more to be saved."

"I will get right to work, Adonai, educating the people with all my heart and soul and being there for the prophet as he needs me."

"You have your work cut out for you, Gabriel, for it is hard to get people's attention these days. With the invention of radio and now television, the people have been shaped to think all important news and information comes from a stupid box with knobs."

Chapter 2

February 22, 1946, 9:30 PM, Newark, New Jersey

My second child is due any minute, thought Barney Cohen as he finished assembling a crib. *Dr. Weiner told Janet that he thinks it's a boy by the way she's carrying the baby. I already have a beautiful daughter, my five-year-old Carla, so please, God, make it a boy, and I'll never ask You for anything else again.*

"Barney, the nursery is almost ready for this baby." Janet smiled. "A *boy*, God willing." She fixed a sheet to the mattress, dropped a folded blanket on it, and adjusted the mobile while Barney fastened it to the sideboards.

"Barney, we need a couple of more pictures over the crib."

Janet picked up a small hammer and three nails from the gunmetal-gray tool chest. She squeezed herself between the crib and the wall, placed a nail between her fingers, and drove it into the plaster.

"Please, Janet." Barney worried. "I don't think it's a good time to be hammering nails. There's enough art and photos on the wall already."

"Barney, I'm so ready for this baby that I almost pray that my water will break."

Janet stretched to hang a picture of Mickey Mouse and Donald Duck and heard a soft pop. Water trickled down her thigh and then turned into a gusher. Janet showed her husband the huge stream of fluid pouring out from deep inside her. Barney looked down to observe the puddle spreading outward on the beige wool area rug.

3

"Barney, call the hospital to tell them that we're on our way. Please get my bag and clean up this mess too. Thank god Carla is sleeping over tonight at her grandmother Pearl's place."

"Honey, let's go *now*." He preferred to play it safe. "I'll deal with this mess later."

Barney helped Janet in to the car, put her bag on the back seat, and drove carefully to Beth Israel Hospital. He thought about how fortunate they were as he turned right from Bergen Street onto Lyons Avenue.

Janet and Barney both had jobs when they married in 1935. He made $25 a week managing a grocery store; she earned twenty as a secretary so they got through the tough time better than most. Barney was really lucky to make serious money during the war years that funded his wholesale deli distributorship, which now included monthly provisions for two hundred accounts. The Cohens were about to pay ten grand cash for a two-bedroom house in the Galloping Hill section of Union.

Life is good. *Dear God*, prayed Barney, *life will be perfect if you send us a healthy and happy little boy to play in the big backyard. A sandbox, a bike, and a baseball bat for my son will make me the happiest man alive.*

The Cohens arrived at the hospital's entrance, where an emergency room attendant met them and asked Mrs. Cohen to please sit down in the wheelchair.

"The orderly will take you right to delivery. Mr. Cohen, the waiting room for expectant fathers is just down the hall to the left."

For the next hour, Barney routinely paced the floor back and forth or sat down for a few minutes, only to get up and pace again. Finally, he sat down.

"Let me close my eyes for a few minutes."

He napped for an hour until one minute after midnight, when Dr. Weiner stuck his head out of the delivery room door.

"Mazel tov, Mr. Cohen. You're the father of a handsome eight-pound boy who, I swear, was *smiling* at me as I pulled him out of his mother."

Prematurely bald, Barney sprung from his chair and jubilantly cut the air with a punch, the force of which messed his hair island, the last strands left across the top of his forehead.

"A boy." He rejoiced. "A boy! I have a son! Thank you, Doc, and thank you, God!"

Dr. Weiner opened the delivery room door. "Barney, it's all right to go in and see how your wife is doing."

Janet lay on a gurney, holding her newborn son. "Barney, his name is Allan Arthur Cohen, but we're going to call him Allie. Please call Ma and Pa to let them know that we're fine and doing well." Janet held up Allie. "Here, Barney, take a good look at your future partner in New Jersey's best deli diner."

"I can't believe that Allie already has more hair than me. You gave me a beautiful son, Janet. He's perfect. My god, look at him smile. I love you so much, honey."

"Barney." She radiated sheer happiness while saying, "Allie's been smiling at me the whole time I've held him. I swear he's the most adorable and happy infant I've ever seen. When the nurse brought Carla to me, she cried like I was the wrong mother."

"I remember. I love my pretty Carla, but she's not the easiest kid in the world to raise."

"I'm exhausted, Barney, and need to close my eyes."

Barney blew her and his newborn son a kiss as the nurse took Allie back to the baby dormitory. "I'll call Ma and Pa. You rest, sweetheart."

Barney approached the pay phone and dialed his father-in-law's number. In a sunny four-room apartment a block away from West Side Park, seventy-seven-year-old Aaron Abraham, with a full head of soft white hair and rimless glasses, picked up the receiver on the third ring.

"Hello," said the gentle, loving father of three sons and two daughters, who had enriched him with a dozen grandchildren.

"Pa, it's a boy. His name is Allan Arthur Cohen, but we plan to call him Allie."

"Another grandson," he called out to Ruchel, his wife of fifty-seven years, standing nearby, and then told Barney, "Allie Cohen, I like it. Allan Arthur Cohen. You know that his Hebrew name is *Avram Aron*."

"Avram Aron? Okay, Pa, I wasn't even bar mitzvahed, so whatever you say. Anyway, I'll be sure to tell Janet tomorrow. She's asleep, and I'm headed home to clean up a wonderful mess."

Aaron spoke in a voice of absolute fulfillment. "Barney, Allie is my *thirteenth grandchild* and a very special blessing from God. Someday when the time is right, I will tell you and Janet why."

Chapter 3

Two Years Later

Hashem, in heaven, was perched over Brazil. The angel Gabriel appeared and beheld the Almighty looking down at the world below.

"Holy One," Gabriel kidded, "I think You're teasing the Brazilians again."

Yahweh's light smiled lovingly at His special angel. "No, I'm not, Gabriel, but they do go around a lot saying *God is a Brazilian*."

The light of the Lord frowned; Gabriel expected a concern to be forthcoming.

"Gabriel, I am worried about the people of the earth, particularly the children of Israel."

In a flash, the Master of the universe and Gabriel were over Tel Aviv.

The Lord pondered, "I made the seed of Israel strong, gave them their land again, so when did that strength become a stiff neck?"

"Name." Gabriel understood well. "You've been complaining about that for three thousand years. *Ma nishtana*, why do You expect different today?"

"You're right, it's true. Gabriel, you have been following My little prophet for two years now. Do you think his parents have an idea yet of how special Allie is?"

7

"His parents sense Allie is very special but just want him to be a normal kid. The masses, Hashem, are clueless that the prophet or teacher exists. Their political masters use the little box to lie and manipulate them. Truth is a casualty, and fear rules their world."

"I know. I constantly worry that the people are thickheaded enough to actually destroy themselves."

I always love to discuss the fate of humankind with Hashem.

Gabriel, excited, questioned, "Isn't the Messiah's challenge, Adonai, to awaken the people so that they may change their ways?"

"Yes, of course, Gabriel, but you are not getting my point. Our little teacher is very different from what the people have been taught to expect of a messiah. You know too that his origin as a thirteenth grandchild of the lost tribe I redeemed and fused into the Ashkenazim Jews of central Europe will be an issue. Allie is also part Christian. That's two strikes against him."

"Yes." Gabriel remembered. "The lost tribe that had degenerated into Chazers, and You had to save them. Still, I will never forget the scene of Echutz, their tribal leader, telling Moses that *his people did not break the Egyptian pharaoh's chains only to be enslaved by a Hebrew pharaoh and his 613 chains.*"

"Yes, and because of his leadership in their rebellion, the Jews do not know that I brought thirteen tribes out of Egypt, Mitzrayim. For their rejection of Moses's 613 laws and my gift of Zion, I banished all mention of the tribe of Echutz in the holy books and any thought of them from Hebrew people's minds. They never existed and still don't."

"After the charismatic Echutz led the tribe to peace and freedom on the Anatolian plain, Adonai, they honored him by declaring that his name and the word *king* and the names of all future kings will be Echutz forevermore."

"Yes, Gabriel, they survived ninety-two generations of Echutz's until I saved them from the Christian and Muslim armies and redeemed them as Jews after two thousand years. Since the great migration into central Europe, there have been forty generations of Avram Aron's, though a precious few have known this."

The light of the Lord darkened; Gabriel asked, "What is wrong, Hashem?"

"Gabriel," the Redeemer sighed, "there are so many rules to thwart appearances of prophets or messiahs in case they are false. The people seem too fearful and divided to place their faith in My *Einstein* of human relations research. How can they listen in awe when they foolishly treat their presidents as prophets because their voices come from the authoritarian little box with knobs?"

The Creator paused. Gabriel waited. "Christians compound the matter too with their apocalyptic visions of Armageddon that must happen before some rapture, cataclysm, and select survival."

"What are you trying to tell me, holy One?"

"I am tired of religions claiming that My wrath will destroy mankind on some faith's judgment day."

"I assume that you are referring to *Revelation*: He will emerge from the sea that constantly rages—politics—and turn brother against brother until there are no more."

"Yes, Gabriel, the Antichrist belief. No, My plan has always been to send a prophet who will speak the truth, educate the people, and show them how to live in peace. Without tranquility, too many good people will face only want and suffering."

"I sense, Creator, that You are starting to worry that the teacher may fail in his quest."

"Well, he is a little boy and two years old today. My birthday gift to him is My blessing and a big sandbox."

The benevolent One and Gabriel watched Allie happily playing with three other little cousins in his big new sandbox.

Allie enchanted Gabriel. "Look, Lord, how his cousins adore him, and the adults keep kissing him. He already expresses a sense of fairness and justice that resembles King Solomon when he was a child."

"Yes, Allie does remind Me of Solomon, My little Shlomo with his huge pet eagle. Unfortunately, Gabriel, Allie's life will not be an easy one growing up. But as you have witnessed, his heart is good, his will strong and unyielding, his aims for mankind pure as new snow."

"Eternal One, I share your concern that the people will fail You."

"Yes, sadly, he may come and go without them realizing it. Worse, they will not know of their loss."

"Name," Gabriel carefully advised the Almighty, "You know very well that You can *shortcut* the process if You want to."

The Redeemer looked at His special angel as if he should know better.

"No, Gabriel, the people must *earn* redemption to win My ultimate blessing. Until then, let us pray that the people behold the prophet and exalt him and his teachings and then follow in awe."

"How long, holy One, is the messiah's time on earth to achieve all of this?"

"Forty years. Moses built the nation of Israel in forty years of Sinai wanderings. The people of Israel built a nation in forty years after Herzl's call. The teacher should not need more."

"Only forty years? Why not more, Adonai? That's just two generations."

"In the wired and connected world of today, Gabriel, forty years should be enough time."

"O eternal One," Gabriel differed, "I fear You are setting the teacher up to fail."

"Gabriel, either the prophet's light will shine upon them in forty years or the people will choose darkness, until I, the Name that they dare not say, lifts the veil."

Chapter 4

The Origin: The Anatolian Plain of Turkey, AD 1188

Adonai sent me once a century to check on the wayward thirteenth tribe to see if they were ready for redemption. Their short limited exposure to Judaism did not take strong root and quickly faded. The first generation on the plain, without the restraints of religion, quickly dissolved into a swinish lot who soon became known as the *Chazers*.

I swear that, over the centuries, they looked less and less Jewish. I must grant them this: they were the freest living and happiest people who may have ever graced the earth.

For two millennia, Chazers tilled, herded, or hunted food on the fertile plain and made a steady living supplying caravans crossing from Europe to Asia with food and goods. Chazer traders also plied the Silk Road to sell their highly valued pork, lamb, red barley wine, and unique handcrafts in the busy marketplaces.

The seminomadic Chazers drifted with the change of seasons to search for more trade or to enhance security. They took refuge in the nearby low hills from the summer heat and herded in the green river valley during winter to wait out the snows. The tribe's route and annual range of movement, forty miles back and forth, was richly planted with a variety of crops and sizable herds of farm animals that they tended to. Horses were raised for defense and plowing; cows, pigs, sheep, goats, and chickens for eating; and many camels for heavy transport on the Silk Road.

On this particular visit for the Almighty, a strong cold wind from the north pushed hard against tens of thousands of sturdy Chazer tents spread out on both sides of the river. The nomads inside their warm tents ignored the howling frosty air as just another wintry night and pursued their earthly pleasures.

12

Thousands of red-hot braziers, as far as the eye can see, filled the encampment's air with endless columns of smoke. The smell of roasted meats and seasoned rice tonight was everywhere.

Inside the tents, men and women drained large gourds full of sweet red barley wine or smooth, cloudy beer. Dancing girls in states of nakedness entertained the men while musicians' drums, horns, and lutes encouraged them on.

Loving grandmothers nurtured small children and sat between oversexed teenagers. The grandparents shielded the children's eyes from their parents' lustful coupling under thick woolen blankets and goatskin pillows.

The Chazer gods were their *oversized appetites* that naturally burst from their souls, hearts, and loins. They loved music and dance and freely consumed abundant food, drink, and sex.

Many Jews, Christians, and Muslims who traded with the Chazers thought them godless, shameless, and vulgar. The pretty Chazer women dressed immodestly and the handsome men flamboyantly, and their children ran around naked all summer long.

Jews, including me, were bothered by the Chazers' child-rearing practices or lack of them. Their Christian and Muslim neighbors reviled the Chazer encampment as Sodom and Gomorrah on the plain.

I was always amazed at how the Chazers loved their hard but hearty lives and how brazenly they defied moderation. They lived every day as if it might be their last and freely let fly loud farts and big belches. To them, even the women, a rippling fart was a sign of a good meal, a hearty belch that one had drunk well.

I noticed that Echutz, the ninety-second king of the Chazers, was not partaking in the nightly festivities, nor was he giving much thought to what the three great religions on the plain thought about him and his people. Echutz just canceled his sixtieth birthday celebration with his three pretty wives and seven children. He looked not at his plate of roasted pork ribs and prized custard cakes, which lay uneaten, or the large silver chalice still filled to the brim with the finest red barley wine.

Echutz dismissed the pretty naked, dancing girl with a gentle shake of his hand. She bowed her head and quietly disappeared into the evening throng frolicking outside his tent.

The king rubbed his big belly with his hands. *My stomach aches not from indigestion but from dread and terror. The survival of my two-thousand-year-old people is at stake, and their fate lies in my hands. Chazer scouts have reported to me that the tribe has crossed paths with a Christian crusader army headed to the Holy Land and Saladin's Muslim army waiting to stop them. Each army is roughly two hundred thousand men, a standoff is possible, and my four hundred thousand Chazers will tilt victory into the hands of one or the other.*

The Christian forces demand from me, 'Join us to slay the Muslim infidels, or we will slay you along with them.' Saladin and the Muslims counter, 'Join us to slay the Christian infidels, or we will slay you along with them.'

He put his hands on his head. *Joining one or the other is suicide, and I have racked my brain for a plan or strategy. The Council of Elders is convening in the morning, and I am expected to advise them on what to do. It is late, and hopefully, a plan or strategy will come to me in a dream. Maybe some fermented mare's milk will help me fall asleep.*

Echutz extinguished the burning sensation in his belly with a big gourd of the thick, creamy mare's milk. Sleep arrived surprisingly fast, and he lay in a deep dark slumber.

Morning neared, and Echutz dreamed of cruel armies slaughtering his people. Deep red rivers of Chazer blood flowed off in all directions from gleaming Christian and Muslim swords. Endless rows of long spears killed tens of thousands; deadly arrows rained down like cloudbursts of giant stabbing needles and killed even more. In the valley, there was no place to hide from either.

Hashem has accompanied me for the first time in two thousand years. Concentric rays of light and a harp playing soft music suddenly replaced the slaughter and eased the king's fear. A calming, holy voice—Adonai—spoke from blue and white rings that drifted off into the night.

Echutz, king of the Chazers, I am Yahweh, God of the Hebrews. I will redeem and save your people from the Muslims and Christians, but you must receive My instruction with solemn and eternal devotion. Do you promise to *obey* Me, Echutz, the ninety-second king of the Chazers?

I know two important things about the powerful Hebrew God. Yahweh drowned *the Egyptians and* smote *the Philistines.*

Yes, "Yahweh," he answered, "I promise to honor and obey You."

"The Chazers," the Creator commanded unto Echutz, "must embrace Me as their one true God and promise to become good Jews. If they do this, I will lead them to safety in the great European cities to the north and make you the Moses of your people. King Echutz, are you worthy?"

"Yahweh," assured Echutz, "I will do anything to save my people, even give up their name and become Hebrews, but I must express a very grave concern."

"What is that, Echutz?"

"The Jewish people do not like Chazers and think that we are an inferior, aimless, and gluttonous tribe, but what hurts me most is that they think we are bad parents too. We love our happy

15

children just as much as they do. Where we differ is that Chazers treasure our children's freedom, and are not our children healthier and happier than theirs?"

"Yes, Echutz, I understand, and the Jews can be a stiff-necked people, believe Me, but the Jews in the northern cities are not fruitful and multiplying to My satisfaction. Your people with their vibrant appetites will infuse a vital and fresh strain of seed into the Jewish being. The Chazer people, in time, will learn to become good Jews, strengthen their family bonds, and value education."

"So, Yahweh, Chazers—whom the Jews call pigs—are expected to become ascetics overnight? Don't you think the Jews will laugh at us when we claim to be one or, worse, will have nothing to do with us?"

"Echutz, it will take time, but I will transform your people. Your fate is to leave your past on this plain and forever more be Jews. Your people will live accordingly to the laws of Moses and the Ten Commandments. Be a wise and forceful king, and I will reward you and your people. Remember, you have a choice, Echutz."

"And that choice is Yahweh?"

"Better to be a live Jew than a dead Chazer. I think that fate will persuade your Council of Elders tomorrow. This day will be the last in the history of the Chazer people. You have been reborn and redeemed as the Jews of Anatolia."

Echutz recalled. "Many years ago, a lost Maronite Christian trader from the Lebanon wandered among us and told me that he thought the Chazers were a lost tribe of Israel. This one tribe of thirteen, according to his friend, a rabbi in Jerusalem, rejected the laws of Moses as oppressive. The tribe headed north and supposedly settled on the Anatolian plain two thousand years ago. Neither I nor any other Chazer remembers such a thing."

"The trader's story is true, Echutz. The Chazers believed the Ten Commandments were a blessing but Moses's six hundred and thirteen laws were enslavement. Their leader, the first Echutz, declared Moses to be a Hebrew pharaoh, and his tribe made him king upon his safely leading them to freedom on this plain. Now I have come to make you and your people the Jews they should have become when I took you out of Egypt."

"That trader, Yahweh, was so sure of this fact that he always made me wonder if the story was really true."

"That's because the trader was my special angel Gabriel, who also came to you as a Muslim sheikh, an elderly rabbi, a Christian farmer, and a dozen other disguises telling the Chazers the same truth—efforts that were always lost on you until this emergency. Now you know, so go and leave this forsaken plain and follow the North Star and the Danube to Europe. From there, I will melt your people into the Jewish communities, which will absorb you."

"Yahweh, it will be very hard for my people to become Jews again and live only among them."

He nervously rubbed his short trim beard from stress.

"I understand, so for the time being, I will ease your challenge by demanding slavish devotion to only *six basic commitments*."

Echutz beheld Hashem's magic as a mysterious quill wrote the six commitments down on a lamb parchment as listed by the holy One, blessed be He.

1. Circumcise and bar mitzvah your sons.

2. Marry but one wife at a time and honor her.

3. Study the Torah and let the rabbis guide you.

4. Educate and treat your daughters well.

5. Raise smart and resourceful children.

6. Swear off the swine, drink moderately, and keep kosher.

"Echutz, I promise that if your people do all this, life will be good, and the Jews will eventually embrace and absorb you."

"Thank you, God, but what if the Christians and Muslims reject our decision and draft the new Anatolian Jews in to their divisions?"

"I have already taken care of that. Vicious strains of bubonic plague and cholera are shooting through the enemies' ranks. Both armies are too preoccupied with burning their dead to bother with you, so your exit is arranged. Now, King Avram Aron, get to work in securing your exit."

"Excuse me, God?"

"Yes, you are now to be addressed as *Avram Aron*, king of the Anatolian Jews, the thirteenth lost tribe of Israel."

Echutz awakened from his dream and began his first day as King Avram Aron and an Anatolian Jew.

I wonder if Adonai has already changed me in any way.

He sat down to breakfast and a naked servant girl brought his usual plate of barley biscuits, a slice of cold lamb, and a smear of pig fat. His new appetite allowed a biscuit, some lamb, and a cup of tea.

My first test and sign. The smear sickens me. The sight of nakedness, for no reason, suddenly offends me too. "Henceforth," Echutz instructed the naked young maiden, "all female servers will bring me my meals fully clothed."

Chapter 5

The cold north wind blew dense clouds of brazier smoke that stung the eyes of the elders as they entered the Great Tribal Tent. Clearing the land for agriculture and keeping tens of thousands of daily campfires lit for two millennia decimated the plain's once vast forests of black pine and kermes oak trees.

With the trees long gone, the Chazers smartly grew and harvested tall grasses that were dried and tied into logs before burning. The smoldering fuel cooked the food and lit the night but filled the air with thick and smelly smoke.

The Chazer elders were normally a loud and shifty lot, a tough bunch to control, but they were gathered today for an emergency meeting and sensed from King Echutz's solemn aura that they needed to be very serious and listen. Echutz smiled to show his appreciation for their interest and unusual focus. He was fond of saying that two Chazer elders can express three opinions on the same subject.

Echutz had their attention and spoke. "Venerable elders, let me be clear. Today we face the most terrible peril in Chazer history, one so great that it will require us to transform ourselves."

Buzzing spread throughout the Great Tribal Tent. Echutz raised an eyebrow, and silence followed, so he presented the Christians and Muslims demands, stated that they can join forces with neither, and advised, "A neutral outcome is our only option."

The broad-shouldered and able Moades possessed the largest flocks of sheep and goats that produced the richest milk. The best maker of cheese and curds and the second most powerful clan chieftain questioned his king, "Echutz, what do you advise us to do if taking up arms is unwise? The Chazers have won battles against Christian and Muslim armies in the past. We can field sixty thousand strong-backed warriors."

Echutz nodded but advised, "Moades and esteemed elders, our brave soldiers are lambs before the slaughter given the combined size and power of these two armies. Therefore, please listen carefully. I believe that our only way out of this grave danger is to become Jews."

The Chazer elders are stunned; some laughed openly, others scoffed, and most said nothing and awaited more details from Echutz.

"Yahweh," Echutz explained, "our new God, has saved us from joining forces with either foe. Both sides are offering us safe passage in moving north by following the Danube. After we are gone, the two armies will slaughter each other without us."

Morritch grew the finest red barley that the sweetest wine and the smoothest and most potent of cloudy beers were made from. The profane and selfish chieftain of the largest, richest, and most influential clan asked the obvious question.

"Echutz, are you serious about Chazers becoming Jews? The few Jews whom I have met think we are the most vulgar and disgusting people on the plain, and I won't argue with them, for I know not of their ways, nor do I want to."

He spit twice on the ground for emphasis. Echutz needed Morritch's support more than any other clan leader.

"Yes, Morritch, it is a great challenge for a Chazer to live like a Jew. But unfortunately, we have no choice. Today we must cease being Chazers and forevermore be Hebrews. It is God's will. He told me in a dream last night."

Morritch exploded with laughter. "God's will, eh?" He held his side and mocked, "He told you this in a dream, and we are to believe it? Echutz, we Chazers don't have any gods. What, the god of cloudy beer came to you?"

The tent rocked with laughter. Echutz let it play out but spoke sternly.

"Morritch, it is the will of Yahweh, God of the Hebrews. Two thousand years ago, the Chazers and the first king Echutz rejected the laws of the prophet Moses and made their way to this plain. Our Jewish selves were lost during ninety-two generations. Here and now, Yahweh has come to both redeem and save us from the two opposing armies of religious fanatics. Let me be clear, Morritch, the condition is that we turn our back on our Chazer ways and finally become good Jews."

Moades, whose clan power nearly equaled Morritch's, put his arm on the clan leader's shoulder and counseled him. "Morritch, the way I figure, is it not better to be a live Jew than a dead Chazer, especially if we used to be Jews, like Echutz says?"

Echutz seconded that and pointed his finger at Morritch. "Those were Yahweh's own words. So, elders," the king commanded, "have your clans pack up their belongings, for the wagons will roll with the morning sun. We will follow the North Star and the river Danube to cities where large Jewish communities already live and thrive."

The elders acknowledged the instructions and sensed more important news forthcoming.

"And, elders, one more thing, from this day on, all are to address me as Avram Aron, king of the Anatolian Jews, the thirteenth lost tribe of Israel. Say that to yourselves over and over until you get used to it."

Morritch felt Echutz was acting rashly and loudly protested over the elders' buzzing, "Look, King Aron Avram or whatever this Yahweh calls you, Chazers have won great battles, grown the fattest animals and richest crops. Hunger has not known us for ages."

Echutz acknowledged his claims. Morritch further pressed his case.

"You now proclaim that we are expected to cease being proud Chazers and become observant Jews, live as pious tailors and merchants in big cities full of violence and poverty. And you command that we do this because the Hebrew God supposedly cares about lowly Chazers. Sorry, Echutz—excuse me, Avram Aron, but that is too much to believe and ask."

Borchern owned huge colonies of bees that filled six big vats with clear golden honey. The father of three beautiful daughters and the third most powerful clan chieftain wondered about his girls' future.

"So our *fate*, Avram Aron, is to become the *despised* among *the chosen*?"

"Borchern," Avram Aron pleaded with all his heart, "the Hebrew God has reached out to save us by, again, making us one with His children of Israel. We must accept and follow Him, or we will surely perish on this plain."

Borchern bowed his head. "I understand. We have no choice."

"Good, so as of this moment, the Chazers no longer exist, nor will our people make mention of our past again. Today we are Jews once more, forevermore. So help us God, and may Yahweh bless us."

I'm not sure what shocked me more. King Avram Aron realized. *That I just said those words or that the Chazer elders accepted them at face value.*

The elders conferred among themselves while solemnly leaving the tent to round up their clans and prepare to leave. Suddenly, the elders beheld the commotion of a dozen mounted riders approaching them on galloping white steeds that pulled up and stopped right before them. A westward wind blew the cloud of dust the horses stirred up into the elder's faces.

The great Redeemer and I gathered a dozen leading rabbis from Vilnius, Vienna, and Warsaw to tutor the new Anatolian Jews. The elderly rabbi Hyman Auerbach—the grand rabbi of Vilnius, Lithuania—with his long white beard and black frock coat dismounted and approached the astonished elders, who wiped dust from their eyes and mouths.

"Avram Aron, king of the Anatolian Jews, and esteemed elders, we are Hashem's rabbis for His new flock. By the time we reach the river Danube, Adonai will have your people able to read some Hebrew prayers, speak a little Yiddish, and start living a Jewish life."

"On behalf of our people," King Avram Aron said, "I thank the Lord Almighty and His distinguished rabbis for leading us onto the path to salvation as Jews."

"You're welcome, King Avram Aron. However, it will take forty years for the too loud laughter to die down or the coarse appetites to moderate. It is up to the Creator to determine how much of Chazer history, lore, and ways will survive, and I frankly think it will be very little, probably none."

Avram Aron viewed the rabbis as the second miracle of the Chazer exodus. First, Yahweh spoke the answer to him; now the Lord provided teachers to help them become Jews. Avram Aron smiled from the parallel with the prophet Moses leading the Hebrew slaves out of Egypt.

Perhaps I will someday be revered as the third Hebrew prophet.

Adonai and I made Avram Aron remember his pact with Hashem—no word of the Chazer world is to be spoken of again. *Echutz* no longer existed as a word or kingship.

The new Jews from Anatolia quietly streamed into hundreds of Hebrew ghettos located across central and western Europe. They marched westward into Germany and Austria and eastward into Russia, Ukraine, and Hungary.

Large numbers reached the Baltic north and clustered in the larger cities of Poland, Lithuania, and Latvia. The infusion of the vital new seed from Anatolia transformed the Ashkenazim Jews of central Europe into a fruitful and multiplying people.

Chapter 6

As Yahweh planned, the Jewish population of central Europe doubled in the fifty years after the Chazer Exodus and quadrupled in a century. The dramatic population increases threatened Christian domination and caused church-led reactions from concerned or insecure Christians. Periodic religious campaigns and violent pogroms against the fast-growing Jewish communities were designed to *put* and *keep* the surging Jewish population in its place.

At first, the Chazers repulsed the local Jewish communities they settled in with; and in quick fashion, local rabbis questioned the Anatolian Jew and last lost tribe identities. The former Chazers fervently believed and stated that their new Anatolian Jew heritage was the will and Word of God. They were the lost tribe of Israel and had been redeemed by Yahweh, and they were.

The Jews of central Europe did not know what to do with the huge mass of primitive and vivid creatures with two identities that shook up their well-ordered world. Synonyms for Chazer and Anatolian Jew quickly formed and were referenced in the Yiddish lexicon for pig, vulgar, loud, excessive, and disgusting.

In time, though, as the Lord Almighty promised them, the Chazers became good Jews. Their absorption was accelerated by Jewish boys' attraction to pretty Chazer women with their big breasts, spirit in bed, and amazing fertility. Jewish girls were drawn to the Chazer men's virile, good looks, lust for life, and enterprising ways. Jewish fathers and mothers learned to live with it.

Two centuries later, the word *Chazer* ceased to be an identity and became more a code of behavior or etiquette. The Chazers' coarseness and excessiveness was rubbed away by centuries of Jewish civility and sensibility. Yahweh rewarded the Chazers for keeping their promise to Him. When left alone by the Christians, life was good.

As Hashem's rabbis predicted, Chazer lore, customs, and history virtually disappeared; and by the tenth generation, all proof and remembrance of their origin was gone, and they'd become a myth.

Sometimes Adonai and I discuss, verifying the Chazers as the thirteenth lost tribe of Echutz; tell the people that the Chazers existed, and get used to it. We hold back because it may confuse the people and divert them from exalting the prophet.

In 1204, Avram Aron's body was buried in a little Jewish cemetery just outside Linz, Austria. His kin took the name Abraham and, over the centuries, multiplied and spread across the eastern half of the country.

Most of the Abrahams became skilled furriers and made decent livings making fine garments for the Christian elites. Some survived as chicken and vegetable farmers, others by trading bolts of cloth or new or used furniture.

There was, however, one keeper of Chazer identity. Avram Aron, on his deathbed, told his thirteenth grandchild that he was a king of the Chazers until Yahweh redeemed them as Anatolian Jews, but he instructed him never to tell anyone.

That child, on his deathbed, was to summon his thirteenth grandchild and tell him the same. Avram Aron's hope was for the Abraham family line to be fruitful and multiply, and so it was. Thus the secret of Echutz who made the pact with Adonai was passed on from one thirteenth grandchild to another for forty generations.

Seven centuries after the assimilation of the Chazers and Anatolian Jews, the Austro-Hungarian Empire's designs on the Balkans conflicted with the nationalist stirring of a greater Serbia. A secret war to exterminate Serbian rebels was failing.

The Austrian emperor Franz Joseph drafted Jews for ten years and trained them to infiltrate the Serbian underground. None came back; all were caught, castrated, and hanged from lampposts.

Twenty-five-year-old Aaron Abraham, a descendant of Avram Aron and a thirteenth grandchild, was drafted despite being married and the father of two and supporting his two younger brothers.

I am surely headed for Serbia, and since I care not to die or return a ghost, I must flee to America.

The night before catching a train to Hamburg for a ship to New York, Aaron held his young bride in his arms and reassured her, "Ruchel, don't worry, if anything happens, my brothers, Kappy and Baruch, will look after you."

Ruchel bathed Aaron's face with loving kisses as he spoke. "You'll see, three years will go by very fast. I will find a job as a furrier and bring the family over as soon as I can afford to. Now I must go or miss my train. Kiss Yussel and Miriam goodbye for me. I love you so much. Shalom."

Between 1880 and 1910, thirty million Europeans immigrated to America. Aaron Abraham arrived in 1895 and proceeded through the Ellis Island Processing Center, hoping that he would not be rejected and sent back. The United States did not take everybody; 10 percent were refused entry because of criminal records, disease, or apparent mental deficiency.

When Inspector O'Malley certified Aaron, his mind raced with dreams for his family.

O'Malley knew some Yiddish, so Aaron asked, "I'm a furrier and need a job to bring my family over."

"Try Berliner's Fur Corporation," recommended O'Malley. "It's located on the Lower East Side. My Jewish brother-in-law is

27

their bookkeeper and told me they're hiring for the busy fall and winter seasons."

Aaron got the job, and a fellow worker invited him to share his L-shaped room with seven other occupants. The Hebrew Immigrant Aid Society (HIAS) formed to help the waves of immigrants like Aaron who were streaming into the country; they found the immigrants jobs, alleviated crowded living conditions, counseled families in crisis, and petitioned businesses to reform dangerous work conditions.

HIAS appealed to Berliner's to transfer Aaron and a dozen other workers to their Newark, New Jersey, branch and found him an airy apartment too. Aaron worked hard, saved his money, and managed to reunite his family a year ahead of schedule, Kappy and Baruch too.

Kappy became an agitator and organizer for a Communist labor union and barely made a living. He and his high-strung wife, Bertha, fought every day of their sixty-year-long marriage. They fought in front of relatives visiting them, and if they felt like it, they would turn on their guests and fight with them too.

Baruch started as a night clerk in the fancy Essex House Hotel in Downtown Newark. He vacationed in Miami in 1934, decided to stay there, and changed his first name to George. He soon found a job managing a motel and bought a small hotel on South Beach before World War II and then a bigger one after the war. Finally, in 1960, he built one of the first upscale hotels on Fort Lauderdale Beach.

Aaron Abraham, on his eightieth birthday, took stock of his life. *I never made it big in America like my brother Baruch. He'll never be George to me. No, my mission in life was to get everybody over here from Austria, and I did because if I hadn't, we would have all wound up in Hitler's ovens.*

Maybe Aaron's lack of success was due to his easygoing nature, old-world ways, or mild heart condition at fifty. However, his shrewd wife, Ruchel, made up the difference by running a small mom-and-pop grocery store for over twenty years to supplement Aaron's meager and seasonal earnings at Berliner's.

Yussel, Aaron's eldest son, Americanized quickly and changed his name to William in elementary school. He built a thriving real estate management firm, supported Aaron and Ruchel after the store closed, and replaced his father as patriarch of the family when he turned fifty.

"Yussel was never really a kid as a child, and he's more than welcome to it."

Chapter 7

January 27, 1949

Aaron was up very early on a snowy morning and out the door before Ruchel awakened. Wednesday was his favorite day of the week because he visited his daughter Janet and son-in-law Barney Cohen. American-born Janet, his baby, was the first child to move to the suburbs.

Aaron boarded the no. 17 Clinton Hill bus, sat down, and thought how his shrewd son-in-law Barney made a small fortune selling black market meat during World War II. The government exempted him because he was a family man, and the nation needed workers to grow, process, or distribute the food supply.

In Barney's case, it was the meat distribution trade. When customers exhausted their meat-rationing coupons before the end of the month, Barney knew where more meat could be found for an under-the-table premium. If the order was for hot dogs, corned beef, or pastrami, the premium doubled because of their lower production priority.

The Cohens were trying to sell their house to help finance Barney's buying the new Mogen Zion Kosher-Style Meats franchise for New Jersey. All of Barney's accounts would go with him if he made the move; they'd drop him if he didn't.

I'm certain, Aaron thought, *that my son-in-law is going to make it big as Mogen Zion's kosher-style deli lines are the best around.*

Aaron Abraham transferred at the Irvington Center Station to board the bus for the Galloping Hill section of Union and settled into his seat. Last week, Barney told him that, after selling the house, he planned to move the family into the new 1,100-unit Stuyvesant Village Garden Apartments in Union that spilled over into Irvington and Maplewood. Barney and Janet dreamed of building a home in Millburn or Short Hills after the business took off.

A few miles away, his grandson Allie, three years old next month, got out of bed. "Look how hard it's snowing." He noticed and excitedly ran down the stairs to tell his mother, who was in the kitchen cursing the Dugan's bread deliveryman.

"Dammit, the bakers left out the salt again. I swear, everything the Christians bake is tasteless. Pa will probably choke on this pap. Oh, good morning, Allie."

Janet bent down to kiss her darling little boy.

"Ma," asked Allie, "do you think Grandpa will still visit today? Look how deep the snow is already."

"It looks so beautiful out there, Allie." Janet admired. "But I worry for my eighty-year-old father walking a long block in a heavy snowstorm."

"So you think Grandpa *will* come."

"Yes, I think so, Allie, because after sixty years of marriage, a man will probably do anything to get out of the house."

Allie laughed at his mother's joke and climbed on the dining booth to scan Lenni-Lenape Terrace.

"Ma, I think I see Grandpa. There's a man with an umbrella coming."

"Pa must be exerting himself something awful. Thank god that he only has one more hill to cross."

Five minutes later, a cold and wet Aaron entered Janet's side door, kicked off his galoshes, and hung his coat on a hook. As

31

usual, he hugged his thirty-five-year-old baby daughter and kissed her on the cheek. He smiled at Allie, his special blessing from God, and pinched his grandson's cheeks. Aaron typically followed that up with tussling Allie's dark brown hair and kissing his forehead. Allie always laughed and his grandpa loved him even more for it.

Janet's concern melted faster than the snow on Aaron's cuffs. She opened a can of Campbell's tomato soup for her father and made scrambled eggs for Allie. With the sleight of hand of a magician, Janet threw the bread into the garbage and buried the bacon deep into the freezer section.

Aaron observed Janet and Allie as they spoke and ate. *Of all my family, the Cohens are the most comfortable in this new America, a land that still seems strange to me after fifty-five years here. Maybe they're too comfortable*, thought Aaron. *My baby just hid the bacon from me.*

They moved to the living room after lunch and chatted until Carla came home from school early because of the snow. Aaron threw out his arms to Carla to hug her; Carla returned her grandpa's gesture a bit stiffly.

"Carla, give your grandfather a proper hug."

Carla hugged Aaron more warmly, gave him a sweet kiss, and skipped away to play outside in the snow, which had stopped falling.

Janet asked how Aaron's brothers were doing. The intermediary between the deeply alienated Abraham brothers shared the one great sadness of his life.

"Ehh, the pension fund for Kappy's union is going broke, and he's scared of being put out on the street. Two years ago, Baruch sold his Miami Beach hotel to buy and renovate a bigger and fancier one two blocks north."

"Maybe, Pa, we should all pay him a visit down there this winter."

"I don't think so, Janet. Baruch left his family behind when he changed his name, especially after he married a rich Christian woman. I'm sad to say that I haven't heard from him in over a year."

"I didn't know that, Pa."

"What can I tell you? I have two brothers—one's a Communist, the other's rich—and they haven't said a word to each other in over fifteen years. And to think they were so close growing up as boys."

"It happens in a lot of families."

Aaron was a decent tennis player in his thirties and tossed a ball to Allie to see if he could catch yet. Allie caught the ball with one hand and tossed it back to Aaron with very good form for a child his age.

"Allie, you're a natural baseball player. Your daddy taught you well."

Aaron stared as his grandson with a loving smile. *Of all my family spreading across New Jersey and Brooklyn, I can't help loving my thirteenth grandchild the most.*

"My baby girl," Aaron said as he looked directly at his daughter, "it's time for me to tell you something important."

"Sure, Pa," said Janet, who'd always felt closer to her father. "What is it?"

Aaron whispered so that Allie couldn't hear him. "Janet, would you say that Allie is different or, uhm, special in any way?"

33

Aaron's question surprised her. "He's a good kid, and I enjoy him. That's enough. But since you asked, he has your disposition, Barney's drive, and my common sense, but all I want for Allie is to have a normal life."

Aaron nodded, smiled, and then looked down.

"What, Pa? I can see that you really want to tell me this."

Aaron described an incident from his childhood. "When I was only a few years older than Allie, my father, Chaim, took me to a small village in the country. My grandpa Moshe was dying and asked as a last wish to have me, his thirteenth grandchild, brought before him. The old man started telling me about the Abrahams being descended from kings, which sounded like a lot of foolishness to me."

Is it possible, Janet wondered, *that Pa is showing the first sign of dementia?* "Pa, this is crazy talk."

"No, it isn't."

Aaron was firm about this because I put the strong words in his mouth. Adonai wants Janet to know that Allie *is* special; also, Aaron can be *too* easygoing.

"Chaim held me up in front of Grandpa Moshe, who told of a Chazer king's pact with God that redeemed them as the Jews of Anatolia, a lost tribe of Israel. Their king Avram Aron led them to Austria and beyond. Moshe looked into my eyes and told me that I was a king and that my thirteenth grandchild was destined to be a king too."

"Papa, are you telling me that you and Allie are Chazer kings—excuse me, the Jews of Anatolia? Seriously, Pa?"

"Janet," the uncomplicated Aaron said and shrugged, "I quickly put that story out of my head. I didn't want to go through life knowing that."

"I don't blame you. It's absolute nonsense, that's why."

I made Aaron stick to the story. "Trust me," Aaron said to Janet. "Allie is my thirteenth grandchild. If, as Moshe said, I was a king, then what kind of king could this adorable little boy be? You don't think that maybe Allie will be the first Jewish president of the United States, do you?"

Janet, stunned, remained dismissive. "Pa, I think that story is nothing but the deliriums of an old sick man."

"Isn't Allie's Hebrew name *Avram Aron*?" argued Aaron. "Isn't he also a *cohen*, the line of Jewish priests descending from Aaron in the Bible?"

"Yes, that's all true, Pa. And frankly, I've heard enough about this Chazer stuff. First, Avram Aron is his Hebrew name because his first and middle names start with *A*—Allan Arthur Cohen, that's all. Second, there's absolutely no way that the Abrahams could be descended from kings or that you're a king."

Aaron and I were insistent. "Janet, darling, his first and middle names starting with *A* has nothing to do with his Hebrew name. Avram Aron is my Hebrew name too, and in our family line, according to Grandpa Moshe, for forty generations, it's been the Hebrew name of the thirteenth grandchild."

"C'mon, Pa." Janet refused to believe it. "I mean, Ma is from peasant farming stock and you a line of furriers. I promise you, Pa, I will go to my grave with this ridiculous story. Allie will never hear a word of this or anyone else. What a tale, the Abrahams descended from kings, vulgar Chazer kings no less."

She emphasized the word *vulgar* by holding her arms up and shaking them and then joked, "So how do you explain your two brothers? For sure, they're no princes."

Allie ended the discussion and laughter by switching on the Cohens' floor-model DuMont TV and sat up close to the ten-inch screen. Aaron let the subject go and observed his grandson entranced by a cartoon featuring stick mice getting out of a car, running around, and disappearing over a horizontal line drawn across the screen.

"Janet, have you ever wondered about the effects of TV on my grandson's mind? I heard Milton Berle say the other night that TV is just *home vaudeville on a ten-inch screen*, so it's no big deal."

Janet defended TV. "Pa, I think Allie is more advanced because of the information and visual images he gets from TV. If you think of it, he's one of the first kids of his generation—in fact, the whole world—who will watch TV growing up. I have to admit that, once in a while, it comes in handy as a babysitter too."

"So," her old-world father asked, "whatever happened to playing with children?"

"Come on, Pa, I've already taught him to print all the letters of the alphabet, and he is very close to reading. It's just that TV is a lifesaver when you have housework to do or dinner to cook."

"My god, Janet, Allie's not even three, and he can almost write and read already. He is a very smart little boy."

Carla skipped into the room and teased her pleasingly chubby little brother. "Hey, little tubbo, how are you doing?"

Janet's stare made Carla back off, and she went upstairs to decide which of her many pretty dresses she might wear to school the next day.

"Janet," Aaron wondered, "do you think Carla is like that because she was born before people had televisions?"

Janet laughed. "It's simply a matter of temperament, Pa. She's really a sweet girl and good student, and I love her just as much as Allie. It's just that whatever you give her, she usually wants more. Now Allie, in contrast, never asks for anything and loves whatever you give him."

Aaron changed the subject back to TV. "Kappy, my Communist brother, thinks television is a capitalist trick to make the people stupid and keep them down. I don't know from such things and don't want to."

After dinner, Barney drove Aaron back to Newark. Early the next morning, though, a heavily sobbing Ruchel called with shocking news delivered in her thick accent and gravelly voice.

"Janet, it's Ma. Papa died in his sleep last night."

Janet almost dropped the phone and began crying heavily too. "Oh my god, Ma, I can't believe Pa's dead. Oy vey, I hope his walking in the snow didn't cause it."

Janet broke down sobbing; Ruchel was almost hysterical.

"My Aaron had a heart attack and was gone in a second. Thank the Lord he didn't experience any pain or suffering. Can you imagine, Janet? He died *smiling*."

Janet considered. "After unburdening himself of the Chazer story, maybe Aaron was ready to meet his Maker."

Her mother confirmed it. "I think he was ready to go, and God took him. Janet, I'm crying so hard I can't talk. Darling, I have to say goodbye."

"I'm so sorry, Mom. Does William know yet?"

"Yes, he's already making all the funeral and burial arrangements and will be in touch with you about the details. I love you, Janet, but I have to get off and go lie down. I don't feel so good. Sixty years of marriage is over just like that. Goodbye, sweetheart."

Janet put down the phone and thought how strange it was that Aaron's grandfather also died after telling him the same story.

I think it best to give that story no more thought and let it go to the grave with Papa.

I can't make you believe Aaron's story, Janet, but your son Allie *is* the prophet, so please deal with his and your family history.

Chapter 8

"I miss my grandpa Aaron."

Allie remembered him on his fifth birthday. What Allie missed was Aaron's way of spoiling him with love and affection, and he treasured the memories of his only grandfather.

Over the next five years, Allie developed a passion for baseball and dreamed of becoming a great Jewish ballplayer. Unfortunately, young Cohen's desire exceeded his modest size and athletic abilities.

"I don't need baseball to make a good living," Allie was fond of saying, "because one day my dad and I are going to own the largest deli distributorship and best Jewish-style restaurant in the state of New Jersey. Barney says that, by the time I'm old enough to drive a truck, we'll have over two thousand accounts."

At age five, Allie began helping Barney in the store on most Saturdays; his first job was putting six hot dogs in a cellophane bag and vacuum-sealing it. Allie loved being with Barney as he drove from place to place to collect from his accounts.

Five years later, Allie was watching the Yankees play the Red Sox in Boston. It was the bottom of the ninth, the game was tied, and the bases were loaded. Young Cohen, unable to see the Yanks lose, got up to look out the window and saw what the ruckus was in the street.

Holy cow, there are a lot of people milling about, and some are holding their heads. It looks like there's been a car accident, and the police have blocked the street off, causing traffic to build up in both directions.

Allie saw dozens of hot dogs strewn from one side of the two-lane road fronting his apartment house to the other. He remembered that his dad was supposed to bring home four dozen frankfurters for the Goldstein family in apartment number 3 for a birthday party, but he didn't want to make the connection.

Allie overheard a phone call from his downstairs neighbor Marsha Miller to his mother.

"Janet, hurry, there's an emergency outside. I think Barney's been hurt."

Janet threw on a jacket and ran down the steps and into a growing crowd that encircled a victim on a stretcher. Allie watched from the second-floor window; a tall burly policeman spoke to his mom. Janet gasped and cupped her hands over her mouth. The attendants finished placing the stretcher in the ambulance, Janet climbed in, and it rushed off to nearby Maplewood General Hospital.

Marsha Miller stayed with Carla and Allie during Janet's absence. She said very little the whole time, remaining so calm to almost give them the impression that nothing bad had happened. For three hours, she encouraged Carla and Allie to watch TV in the hope that it would keep their young minds off their father's fate.

The Cohen children remained in a fog of sorts until their mother returned after midnight. The front door burst open, revealing a ghostly-looking Janet, who stood in the doorway crying and shrieking.

"He's dead! Daddy was hit by a car driven by a seventeen-year-old boy, and he died of a fractured skull!"

Carla cried hysterically; Allie froze, his young head and heart unable to fathom what had happened and how his life had changed.

Are they trying to tell me that my dad—who spoiled me with love, toys, comic books, and baseball cards—is dead? I don't want to believe that he's not coming home anymore.

40

Each day for months after Barney's death, Allie walked to school trying to understand what happened to his family.

Mom tries hard to run Dad's business and keep a normal home too. Each day, though, that she passes that bad spot in the street where Daddy died takes its toll on her.

Janet kept from Carla and Allie her manager's constant demands for a pay raise and the parent company's squeezing her cash by demanding that she buy expensive refrigerated trucks. Janet, going through probate, was forced to sell and accept a lowball offer. Allie's delicatessen future ended with a fire sale that freed him to become a social studies teacher instead.

Allie's carnival-managing grandfather catered to the senses. Allie's delicatessen-owning father catered to the taste buds and stomach. Allie hoped to cater social science information for the brain, an amazing pattern spanning three generations of Cohen males.

It's mainly the constant reminder of the tire marks from the car that killed Dad that's driving Mom to move us back to Newark. Her mom, sister Rosie, and brother William still live there.

Carla, however, felt she was moving down in life, from a middle-class garden apartment in the suburbs to a transitional neighborhood in the city. She was especially put off by the existence of Aunt Rosie's luncheonette in her apartment building with the three-family units. Apparently to Carla, the store's existence represented a form of poverty to her.

Allie, more easygoing, understood that his mother's broken heart was healing faster by being near her family. He also loved having full freedom to go behind Aunt Rosie's soda fountain to help himself to a milkshake, malt, or ice cream soda.

Barney's untimely and tragic death nearly destroyed Janet, who said as her husband's casket descended into the ground,

"Twenty years is not enough time to fulfill a marriage. It only assured Barney being the love of my life."

Ten years would pass before her first date, twenty years before she could even consider the thought of remarriage.

Chapter 9

Allie adapted fairly well to the rougher streets of Newark, though his educational achievement level suffered a bit. He remained a good student throughout junior high, but in high school, his academic drive slackened and limited choices of colleges. Janet occasionally called him her *very social street kid* and urged him to *study more* but was grateful that he rarely got into trouble and had many close friends.

When Allie turned seventeen, Janet asked William to please sit down with her son for a heart-to-heart career talk. Allie wanted to be a social studies teacher since the third grade, but nobody encouraged him because everyone worried about his ability to make a living.

"Janet," William assured his sister, "I told you the day after Barney's death that I'd underwrite Allie's future, and nothing's changed."

Uncle William, the family patriarch, took some time out of his busy schedule on the morning of November 22, 1963, to meet with Allie over lunch. Young Cohen left Weequahic High School at 11:00 AM to ride the Public Service Clinton Hill bus downtown and settled in for the thirty-five-minute ride to Park Place and the Park Central office building.

Few teenagers have well-defined goals at seventeen, and Allie was no exception. Three years earlier, Pres. John F. Kennedy, in his famous inaugural address, planted a seed in Allie's young brain.

"Ask not what your country can *do* for *you* but what *you* can *do* for your country."

That seed sprouted into a value conflict: should he seek riches in business or become service-to-society-oriented?

Allie rode the elevator to his uncle's sixth-floor suite with a nagging feeling inside. *While I love, respect, and admire Uncle William, I don't really identify with him.*

Abraham Realty Management Inc. rented the entire floor. The elevator door opened, and he was greeted by Estelle Washton, Uncle William's lovely and efficient receptionist and personal secretary.

"Welcome to Abraham Realty, Allie." The slim brown-haired Estelle briefed him on his duties. "Here, let me show you the advanced features of this brand-new IBM Selectric typewriter."

William heard Allie's voice and signaled from behind his desk for Estelle to send his nephew into his office. The newest and youngest employee sat himself down in a chair to William's left and patiently waited for his uncle to conclude a phone call with his son, Stanley, a respected surgeon.

"Stan, did you read in this morning's *NY Times* about what the CIA did to Patrice Lumumba in the Congo? I mean, helping a guy to jump from a jeep at seventy miles an hour is a bit much, don't you think? Yeah, yeah, I know the guy was a Marxist but still."

Uncle William put up his finger to signal Allie that he was nearly done.

"By the way, we got a letter from your sister, Rona, and her beatnik husband yesterday. They're now living in Mexico, La Huaca or something like that. I'll leave you with this: you don't have to be a *kanaker* to live in La Huaca. Ha, ha! You know, *kanaker*, a big deal. Hey, be sure to kiss the wife and the little one for me, okay? See you."

William shook Allie's hand, and they took the elevator down to a sandwich shop on the ground floor of the Park Central.

Allie ordered a hamburger and Coke, William his usual peanut butter and cream cheese on whole wheat bread with a glass of milk.

The waitress served them just as Uncle William got down to business.

"Allie, as you know, my son, Stanley, spurned my firm to become a surgeon. Since you're the smartest of my nephews, this part-time job is a first step toward your being groomed to take over the company, but you first have to obtain the right kind of education to prevent running the firm into the ground."

"What kind of education is that, Uncle William?"

His having to ask annoyed William, who sighed and answered, "Allie, you need a business administration degree with a foundation in accounting."

"Why?" Allie asked and threw William for a loop. "Does a slumlord have to major in accounting?"

That description got under William's skin, and he protested that he wasn't a slumlord, but Allie held William's feet to the fire.

"Ma says you are and once told me that you got rich by buying old tenements for next to nothing and charged the mostly poor black tenants high rents for crummy apartments."

"Granted," William defended himself. "I do own some inner-city properties, but I've since added quite a few suburban apartment complexes and downtown office buildings, including this one. Now listen, I started as an accountant, and it was the smartest thing I ever did."

"My dad had an accountant. Couldn't I hire one too?"

"That's just part of my requiring you to get a business degree. Allie, Abraham Realty did not become one of New Jersey's biggest out of sheer luck. It took lots of good planning, guts, and old-fashioned know-how."

"Look, Uncle William, I do appreciate your advice, and thank you. But lately, I've been thinking about being a lawyer and not corporate law, so why accounting?"

"Allie," William cautioned, "stay away from the law because I've already promised your uncle Irwin that I'd throw my legal business to his son, Robert, who just graduated from Columbia. So don't hang out a shingle because I can't do anything for you and predict you'll starve to death in six months."

"Uncle William, you might be selling me a bit short."

"Look, Allie, I promise you that you'll never regret taking over for me. I guarantee you making a million and retiring by sixty, if you want. Now tell me, nephew, what's so bad about that?"

It's dawning on me that Uncle William doesn't know me very well. Let me educate him in a hurry.

Allie spent the better part of an hour sharing recent thoughts of joining the Peace Corps after college or maybe being a social studies teacher or perhaps a defense lawyer but made it clear to his uncle.

"Don't get me wrong, Uncle William, I have a healthy regard for money. My compassion for the poor does not translate into solidarity with them."

William, the family patriarch, laughed and acted like a father to his nephew. William, the realtor, had a prized property to close on in an hour and bargained, "Allie, please do this for me."

"Sure, Uncle William, fire away."

"Just give business administration a chance. If you think you've made a mistake, then at the end of your freshman year, change your major to whatever you want, okay?"

Allie was about to say "fair enough" but never got the chance. Dorothy, their sweet heavyset waitress, was bawling like a baby as she handed William the check. Before he could ask what was wrong, flaming-red-haired Dorothy announced to all the patrons in the restaurant through a flood of tears.

"Everyone, there's been an assassination attempt against President Kennedy in Dallas. Mo, in the kitchen, said part of his head might have been blown off. The doctors are working on him, but for all we know, he might already be dead."

Allie idolized JFK; William, a strong supporter, raised substantial sums of money for the 1960 New Jersey Democratic campaign. Both were shocked by the heartbreaking and unthinkable news and much too sick inside to discuss future plans. Allie thanked William for his very generous offer and the time he'd taken with him, but both had to go home and watch the news.

"My guess is it's the Cubans or Russians, Allie, but get home safe."

William and Allie shook hands, and then his uncle hugged him for the first time and gave him a pat on the back too. Allie went home to watch the TV coverage of the assassination and mourn his first political hero and martyr. Sadly, it was not to be his last.

Allie owed it to Uncle William to at least give business administration a chance and enrolled at Park Row College in Lower Manhattan but missed orientation day to undergo a draft physical for the army. It was 1964, and Pres. Lyndon Johnson was greatly expanding the Vietnam War and needed fifty thousand soldiers immediately; two hundred thousand more would be drafted over the next two years.

Instead of listening to deans welcome him to Park Row, Allie reported to the Selective Service building, General Lewis Hershey's cavernous processing center on Broad Street in Downtown Newark and waited with two hundred mostly poor and black males and two hundred mostly middle-class white guys while an intimidating huge black officer shouted at four hundred scared souls.

"Okay, gentlemen, strip down to your underpants and shoes. Negro men, that includes your prized hats. Relax, guys, the locker area is guarded by a soldier with live ammunition, only joking to get your attention, but the lockers are secured, trust me."

Allie was untouched by drugs or hippie values and, despite growing pot use all around him, remained a fairly straight young man. His hair was short, parted, and with whitewalls around the ears—pure Ivy League look. Unaware of growing resistance to the war that was becoming a movement, he pulled no stunts.

At the urine analysis station, Allie noticed a white guy with longish hair dropping two sugar cubes into his cup, his intent obviously being to appear diabetic and unfit. The young man was caught and told that he'd be dead if his urine had that much sugar.

At the X-ray station, he observed another white guy with longish hair covertly spreading iron filings across his chest to show that his lungs had holes and that he was unfit. He was quickly caught because he'd be dead from such extensive lung damage.

At the hearing test station, a white guy with longish hair acted stone-deaf to appear unfit. The sergeant dropped a $5 bill on the floor to test him.

"Is it yours?"

The kid, who'd pretended to hear nothing, picked it up and was caught.

At the psychological station, another white guy with longish hair jumped across the desk to plant a big wet French kiss on the shrink to show he was queer.

Funny, I think the dude may get away with it.

The word *gay* has not yet been widely adopted by the homosexual community; *queer* was still the major word in public use.

Allie heard a psychologist tell the sergeant, "One of the guys swallowed LSD to appear mentally ill. He's not going to get away with it. We placed him in a hospital for an overnight to come down."

Allie was very curious. *Why are so many young white guys trying so hard to get out of the draft? Also, why do they all have longish hair? The black guys just think those white dudes are strange, even fucked-up.*

The sergeant called out the names of all the young men who passed the physical and then directed them to report back in a month with pajamas and a toothbrush to be transported to Fort Dix, New Jersey. Cohen felt proud that he was considered fit but very anxious about serving.

I don't know what to do. I'm supposed to start college today, so let me ask the sergeant.

The officer was busy filling out multiple copies of federal forms and didn't bother to look up at Allie while answering his question.

"Son, go to your registrar, fill out your verification of enrollment form, proceed according to draft regulations, and you shouldn't hear from the army again until 1968."

Most of the two hundred white guys followed those instructions and went off to college. Most of the two hundred black guys weren't college bound, got drafted, and were part of the first wave of fifty thousand Charlie Company troops. From that, Allie learned that being white and middle-class meant different strokes for different folks.

The prophet received a 2-S deferment, a military exemption for college attendance and because his mother was a widow and supposedly in need of his part-time job income. Adonai and I have more important plans for Allie than fighting in Vietnam.

By the spring of 1965, Accounting I and Cohen were not hitting it off; credits and debits felt foreign to him. In contrast, his social science classes were interesting and helpful in better understanding the world. Allie's concern about living his life for others or pursuing an education that was not well-rounded ate at him.

His day of reckoning happened the next day in class. Professor Eng, his portly Chinese accounting teacher, decided it was time to weed out all the weak and uninterested students.

"Class," the laconic Eng instructed, "please take out last night's homework for me to check." Professor Eng waddled around the lectern and headed straight toward Allie in the back row. "Mr. Cohen, I'll start with you."

Allie self-consciously opened his notebook for the professor to check, and Eng scanned the long rows of numbers.

"Mr. Cohen," Eng said to him, "your figures do not match. You are aware of this discrepancy?" Cohen nodded yes. "Mr. Cohen, you do realize that the most elementary rule of accounting is to *balance* the columns, yes?"

Almost grateful for the interrogation, he answered, "Yes, Professor Eng."

"But yours aren't close, Cohen. How come?"

Cohen had no quarrel with Eng, did not want to appear disrespectful by saying that he didn't care, and simply said, "I don't know."

"Please," Eng next asked Cohen, "tell me what goes through your mind when you calculate your columns."

Cohen was very tempted to say "naked women" but just politely shook his head and told Eng, "I'm not sure, Professor."

Eng got to the heart of the matter. "Only sheer indifference could produce such shameless work, yes?"

Allie remained evasive, but his guilty eyes affirmed Eng's assessment. "Mr. Cohen, have you ever considered switching to another major? You strike me as a student who might be happier in social science."

Eng's words ended Cohen's burden. "Professor, I think you're exactly right."

The professor put it bluntly. "I recommend that you pay the registrar and the bursar immediate visits. You can still get some money back. Frankly, I do not predict success for you in the business world."

"Thank you, Professor Eng. I am very grateful for your insightful advice."

Allie sensed, as he exited, that his mind had been given back to him and unshackled to develop freely. The real Allie Cohen surfaced, and he industriously used the next three years to study history and economics, pursue culture, and prepare for teaching high school social studies.

Park Row's specialty was business and accounting education, but Allie fortunately discovered that it also had an underrated school of liberal arts, for many of his professors also taught at Columbia, NYU, Penn, and Princeton. The campus location was a virtual laboratory for urban life; every day, some group picketed the city hall. The whole city was Allie's real campus; some of the professors actually inspired him, and he sought out students who resisted the pressure to conform to the culture of business.

A second transformative moment occurred one day in April at the end of English class. Jose Rodriguez, a brilliant Puerto Rican classmate, and Allie walked to the cafeteria for lunch. They ate and hung out for half an hour and then left and headed out the Park Row entrance across from the city hall.

Jose whispered to Allie, "Let's smoke a joint. I have some really good stuff."

"I've never smoked pot," Cohen confessed. "I don't know how."

Jose, amazed, said, "Well, let me show you. Is it okay?"

Cohen felt he was ready and took a first hit and then a second and third. "I like this." They finished the joint, smiled, and laughed at how stoned they were.

Jose shared that, earlier that morning, he'd met with Puerto Rican congresswoman Dona Battista.

"Allie, I've been selected as a Young Puerto Rican Leader of the Future. Dona Battista is transferring me to Yale immediately. I just want to tell you that you've been my only friend at Park Row, and I'm going to miss you."

"Congratulations, Jose, and I'm going to miss you too, man. Being groomed by a congresswoman, eh? Nice work if you can get it."

Jose laughed at his funny line, but both had to get home— Allie to Newark, Jose to the Bronx. They hugged, wished each other well, and walked off into their futures.

Cohen's routine commute became an adventure as he took the Independent Subway System up to Port Authority and then boarded the no. 107 bus that, thirty-five minutes later, dropped him off on Chancellor Avenue and Leslie Street. From there, he walked two blocks to his apartment house and found every inch of the way home fascinating; boredom seemed impossible.

My body and senses are heightened. Feelings of peace, love, and happiness seem more than a mantra. Why can't the world feel like this all the time?

The young prophet sensed that the United States was changing fast; his huge boomer generation had altered every institution they passed through. Thousands of schools were built, and universities expanded to educate the boomers; clothing styles, TV shows, and cars were designed for them.

"The boomers," the young prophet vowed, "are coming of age. It's our time, and we're going to transform the nation and the world, and I want to be in the vanguard of the sweeping change that seems inevitable. America is rich. If we invest more money in the poor and middle class, we can eliminate poverty and ignorance.

LBJ's Great Society legislation and programs promised a utopian society to me and my generation, and we expect him and the country to deliver on that damn promise."

Chapter 10

Allie, in his sophomore year, began questioning America's expanding war in Southeast Asia. Murray Ross, a Rutgers student and friend, influenced him.

"Allie, this war is illegal, a disaster in the making, and will sap the positive change being unleashed by the new social welfare programs. LBJ fears the energies he's released and wants to redirect it as support for the war. Vietnam is a total waste of money and has to be stopped, and it's up to all of us to start trying."

"Murray, how do you know all this?"

"I heard Norman Mailer say it last week at a Columbia University sit-in."

Murray persuaded Allie to join Students for a Democratic Society (SDS), which was formed in 1962 in Port Huron, Michigan, by Tom Hayden and other left-leaning students. By 1965, SDS was a national organization that provided Allie with training to counsel guys on how to avoid the draft. SDS and Cohen's hope was if young men defied the draft, the war machine would grind to a halt.

Over the next five years, Allie helped twenty-three friends, cousins, and strangers avoid Vietnam by advising them to see Ann Stanford, a NY psychiatrist who taught how to fake paranoia and schizophrenia. He also taught guys how to use the appeals process to delay the induction process for up to three ninety-day periods or urged young men to become teachers in the inner city to obtain the 2-S deferment. A severe shortage of teachers in urban areas was being filled by the government's offering military exemption.

Vietnam and the draft was the reason Allie and his fellow college graduate friends met on the night of September 4, 1968, in front of the Burgerama Diner on Chancellor Avenue. For several hours that evening, the Kuhlman-style diner with excellent burgers became a temporary draft resistance center.

Cohen and his comrades against taking up arms had spent the weekend at Loch Arbor Beach near the exclusive Deal, New Jersey, getting stoned and laid. The draft notices waiting for them when they got home were a real bummer and led to Allie counseling seven buddies in the main dining room while the waiters fumed at him for monopolizing three tables.

"Allie, I've heard," Mike Schwartz proposed, "that some guys are escaping the draft by starting businesses in Toronto or Montreal. We could open one of the first jeans boutiques. My dad's in the garment business and can provide a steady supply of high-quality product."

The waiter decided that enough was enough. "C'mon, guys, you're killing my tips." Mike told Stinky, the waiter's nickname, for apparent reasons to fuck off.

The rags merchant option was a last resort. Mike's parents, Holocaust survivors, were ready to finance their only child's share. Uncle William, pushed by Janet, promised to underwrite Allie's half.

Cohen made it clear to the group. "Draft dodging is equivalent to desertion and makes one ineligible to return, so going to Canada means leaving family and friends behind. People who have shown up at their parents' funerals have been arrested by the FBI."

The nervous young men sitting in the blue vinyl booths surrounded by orange and white tiling believed that an inner-city teaching deferment was preferable to exile. New Jersey winters were brutal, Canadian winters unthinkable.

"No one," Allie emphasized, "knows whether the draft board will defer or induct us, and we can expect a decision tomorrow."

Unimaginable at that moment to Allie and his buddies was a peanut farmer from Georgia coming out of nowhere nine years later to pardon the draft dodgers and welcome them back home with open arms.

The roll call, after Allie and Mike, included Rick Samuels, a UCLA business and media major; Lenny Meltzer, a fledgling DC architect; and Terry Winkler, working in advertising. Two of Cohen's first cousins, Ira and Larry, were both in sales.

Three obtained teaching deferments—Mike, Rick, and Allie. Ann Stanford helped Lenny obtain a 4-F mental deferment for anxiety, while Larry, Terry, and Ira were forced to join the National Guard at the last minute.

Allie wrapped up the session. "Again, does everybody understand how to use the draft board's appeals process to indefinitely delay induction?" Everybody raised their arm *yes*. "Good, oh, by the way, General Hershey and the army have caught up with Ann Stanford. When I hear of another psychiatrist stepping up, I'll let you know."

The meeting adjourned, and Rick, Mike, Lenny, and Allie got into Terry's car after the meeting and drove into Manhattan. Lenny dedicated a joint to Ann Stanford, and they passed it around while grooving to the car's FM radio.

A deejay announced that there were still some seats left for the midnight Jefferson Airplane concert at the Fillmore East concert hall. They all yelled "yeah." Allie passed tabs of mescaline to each, and all swallowed trustingly while barreling over to Second Avenue and the box office.

This night was a turning point of sorts for Allie. When the Airplane sang "Up against the Wall, Motherfuckers" from "We Can Be Together, *Volunteers* album, their mescaline peaked. When the Airplane finished with "A Child Is Coming", Allie's vision for a new and better America crystallized.

"Maybe it's the mescaline, but I swear, an angel whispered into my ear, 'Allie, don't ever sell out if you want to achieve your dream for America and the world.'"

Allie was right; an angel did whisper into his ear, "Believe what you feel, Allie, in your heart and soul, and stay the course."

The concert ended at 3:00 AM. Lenny brought them down from their hallucinogenic heights by donating quaaludes to ease the descent. Allie walked into his mother's apartment at four, ready to get some sleep, and heard Janet talking to Carla on the phone.

"Look, we did it because you didn't need to know. He drank and was a louse to Pearl, your poor grandmother. Carla, how the hell did you find out anyway?"

"Joel and I attended an Abraham family cousins club tonight in Staten Island. I was talking to cousin Mandy, who suddenly blurted out, 'That was so brave what your grandmother did. I mean, it must have been around 1910, and nobody did that back then.'

"I told her, 'Sorry, Mandy, I don't consider my grandmother particularly brave or even smart. Now what the hell are you talking about?'

"Mandy shrugged and explained, 'Well, Carla, to marry out of your faith back then, c'mon, people just didn't do that, so yes, your grandma Pearl was *very brave* in my opinion.'

"'Marry out of her faith?' I said, stunned. 'Mandy, what the *fuck* are you talking about?'" I assure you that Carla strived to be a lady at all times and almost never used the *F* word.

"Mandy realized and apologized. 'I'm sorry, Carla, I didn't know that I was giving away a family secret.' Mandy shared that she'd learned it from her mother-in-law Adele—you know, Pearl's younger sister."

"Adele always had a big mouth, goddamn her."

Janet spat angrily.

"Mandy said Grandma was a knockout, had blue eyes, blond hair, and a very cute little figure. Her husband, Grandpa, was supposedly a handsome Mennonite from Allentown. I believe he converted and was circumcised at age twenty-four because my great-grandpa refused to let him marry her until he did. Can you believe being *circumcised* at twenty-four, Ma? Now that's real love."

"Everyone says how much he must have loved her, Carla, maybe. For Christ's sake, he sure didn't show it from what your father told me."

"Anyway, Mom, Joel and I were in a state of shock all the way home and called you the second I entered the house."

Now I have to explain to Allie why all over again. Janet sighed. "I gather that you want to know what we were discussing at 4:00 AM, Allie."

"Yeah." Allie laughed and asked, "Mom, what's going on?"

Janet told Allie the story and the reason. "Your dad and I and his brother David and your aunt Jill were married within a few months of each other. Jill and I swore that we'd never tell our children about your grandfather Alvin, whom you are named after."

"Why did you do that? Because he's a total blank to me?"

"We were worried that you'd feel too comfortable marrying outside your faith. Since he wasn't a nice guy, you and Carla did not need to know about him."

A light bulb went off in Allie's head. "Aha, now I understand why you and my aunt Jill would stop talking about

Grandpa Alvin. I could ask questions all day long about this relative or that one, and you two would answer everything. Then when I got around to Alvin, suddenly, you had to cook or iron or do whatever."

"I am glad, Allie, that you are taking it better than your sister."

"No, Ma, I'm not. I'm just as mad at you as Carla. You had no right to manipulate our identity like that. Dammit, Ma, you and Aunt Jill could have worked for the CIA with the way you kept secrets."

Another bulb went off. Janet looked at him. "What?"

"Ma, while we're at it, is there any other secret you're keeping from me that I should know about, another family history tidbit that's been withheld?"

I'm tempted to tell him the story of King Avram Aron, Janet thought. *Maybe if he knows that he's descended from kings, it will be good for his self-esteem. Perhaps I'm being selfish. His dad died, though, and life hasn't been easy for him growing up, so why burden Allie with that crazy story?*

"No, Allie, just your grandpa's Mennonite background, that's it."

"That's not true." He challenged. "What about the Chazers and Anatolian Jews and me supposedly being a king of them or something? Avram Aron, right? You know, throughout Hebrew school, I always wondered why I had two Hebrew names, and both were of prophets."

"My god, you heard Grandpa tell me. Only three years old and you can remember that crazy story. Pay it no attention because it's too bizarre to be true."

"I'm inclined to believe that, Ma, because they have about as many jobs today for kings as for shepherds."

Janet laughed and reminded her son, "You know, Allie, Jill will kill you if you tell Ira about his grandfather, David too."

The first thing next morning, Allie called Ira to let him know. This infuriated Jill and David, who called him back to loudly complain.

Allie stood his ground. "You guys lacked trust in your own children. You lied to us our whole lives about this, and that's wrong."

Cohen's Christian ancestors, Joachim Kanne and his five sons, supposedly migrated from German-speaking Switzerland and landed in Philadelphia in 1740. The Pennsylvanian colonial government drove the Lenni-Lenape Indians out of the northeastern corner to open the area up to settlement. Joachim and his five sons moved in and set up the first trading post and farm. In 1766, the Kanne family moved fifteen miles west to help establish a new settlement and built the town of Pen Argyl.

In 1904, Alvin lost his job in a Hellertown pencil factory, and no jobs were to be found. Alvin heard that new factories were opening up in Newark, moved there, and quickly found a job with a carnival. He also found the beautiful blond, blue-eyed Pearl, fell in love, and married her. Upon conversion, Alvin and Pearl changed their name to Cohen to make life simpler.

Alvin managed a carnival that regularly traveled up and down the East Coast. Because he was away from home for long periods without Pearl, he suffered chronic loneliness, tended to drink and philander, and finally demanded that Pearl place Barney and David with relatives in Buffalo and East Stroudsburg to join him on the road. The boys were separated from their parents and each other for months at a time. Neither had the stability to receive a proper Hebrew education and to progress to bar mitzvah.

Alvin caught pneumonia one night in Lawrenceville, Georgia, a small town northeast of Atlanta. He ignored the aggressive bacterial pneumonia and worked all day with a high fever and vomiting, and it killed him that evening. Pearl brought his body back to Newark and buried him in a Jewish cemetery on the west side of town.

He was forty years old.

Chapter 11

Teaching deferments arrived three days later on September 7—Allie was assigned to the drab, old, and underachieving Twentieth Street School. Mrs. Ratner, the tough blond-haired assistant principal, escorted him to his new class of *thirty-six* poor and black third graders and introduced the class's third teacher in five days. Chubby Vladmir, the lone white student and Puerto Rican, seemed comforted by the presence of another white person.

"Hello, class, this is Mr. Cohen. He is your new teacher and will be with you for the rest of the year—I hope."

Cohen scanned the sea of babyish brown faces that were his responsibility. The students scrutinized Allie for signs of vulnerability.

Mrs. Ratner left, and Sanford sailed a paper airplane from the back of the room. Tough rawboned Edith stood up to punch chubby, little Ronald sitting behind her, who cried, and then she slapped off his glasses, and he cried harder—she smiled. Cohen sensed that he better take charge quickly or become the class's fourth teacher in six days.

Allie saw a math book sitting on his desk and announced, "Class, I need to assess your math skills and levels."

He, in five minutes, filled two blackboards with fifty simple addition, subtraction, and multiplication problems; division was yet to come. The pupils wrote and answered each problem as best they could and appeared to be getting comfortable with their new twenty-two-year-old white male teacher, who had long dark hair and a mustache, just like the Beatles.

Allie followed with a spelling lesson and filled the boards with fifty words for the students to learn and write in a sentence. *I expect this lesson to last until lunch and buy an hour to think up the afternoon lesson plan. Oh shit, Mrs. Ratner just stuck her head in the door to see how things are going. From her face, it isn't a pretty sight.*

In an annoyed voice, Mrs. Ratner directed Cohen to come to the door for a conference.

"Mr. Cohen, we always do reading first in the morning, not math."

"It's my first day, Mrs. Ratner, and I'm trying to assess their skills. By the way, isn't spelling a reading lesson too? Just look at the board."

"If that's so, then why didn't you first diagnose their reading skills? Improving reading helps improve math and spelling and leads to better test scores overall. Furthermore, a dozen examples are sufficient. You put a week's worth on the board."

"I'm sorry, Mrs. Ratner. I must have gotten carried away."

"Why are you doing spelling on Wednesday? We start new spelling units on Monday and test on Friday. Mr. Cohen, how about if we simply cancel your lesson and start assessing their reading abilities right now? That is how to best familiarize yourself with each student."

Mrs. Ratner, a woman as hard as woodpecker lips, left Allie with the impression that he better get his act together and fast. He did and tried hard to be an effective and caring teacher without writing out elaborate daily lesson plans.

Thirty-six kids, though, was a big class and hard to control; corporal punishment, hitting students, was permitted and commonly applied by the staff. Cohen worked like a dervish in the classroom to keep their attention and avoid falling into the *slap 'em upside the head* syndrome.

Because Cohen was much bigger than the students, his best asset was a youthful athleticism that captivated the boys. The girls appreciated Allie's being a strong role model who made the boys behave properly toward them. Despite typical rookie mistakes, most of his students advanced more than a year above level on the Iowa Test of Basic Skills.

The school year, overall, was beneficial to Allie and his students. They learned a lot from him, and he grew from giving a lot of himself to them. If discipline was necessary, he visited families to tell parents about their child's need for improvement. That follow-through usually kept the students in line because the parents beat their asses if they heard from him more than once during the school year.

Allie summed up his first year. *Many of my students were smart, sweet, and loving kids, save for a few already damaged from regular exposure to random violence or family pathologies. A decent life is very reachable by a large majority if they don't succumb to the lure of the streets.*

Twentieth Street School—a dumping ground for the inexperienced, incompetent, and maladjusted—was a place to leave. Allie went from bad to worse by being transferred to First Street School, a seething cauldron of resentment, personal agendas, and despair.

The greatest source of tension was from the Black Nationalist poet Imi Jaraka. The head of the PTA's declared goal was "If it's the last thing I do, I'm going to get rid of all twenty-three of you dope-smoking, draft-dodging males."

Allie became the unofficial leader of the *notorious twenty-three.*

Cohen shared with a colleague; "Although I don't like hearing Jaraka say it like that, twenty-one white and two black males, average age twenty-two, paying off their note to Uncle

Sam by teaching in a K-5 African Free School magnet program is unprecedented. In all fairness to Jaraka, twenty-three males, white or black, teaching at one elementary school in grades two through five is probably undesirable."

Jaraka's method to get rid of the twenty-three was to make them feel unwanted and build cases for their dismissal. Jaraka's green-robed women followers invaded classes to take copious notes. They called themselves the Sisters; their mission and criteria to check for degree of African culture worked into the curricula, for example, building an arithmetic problem around the Nigerian Kwanzaa, a tribal holiday during which no meat is consumed for thirty days. As the Kwanzaa neared, the Jarakians pressed the school to substitute soybeans for meat in all lunches. When Cohen registered his students' complaints to have meat restored, and it was the next day, the Sisters took notes.

The Jarakians next packed Cohen's vocabulary lists with Swahili words and phrases until he quickly protested that students' chances for scoring well on the Metropolitan Achievement Test and California Achievement Test were being compromised. The Sisters again took more notes.

Allie's fairly smart and small class was his shield against the aggressive Afro-Islamic cult. His students' average verbal and math scores advanced two years in one, the highest increase in the school, and kept the humorless bunch at bay. Ultimately, the Jarakians ideology that all whites were devils drove Allie away, the type of young teacher they should have been trying to hold on to.

For three years, Cohen begged the system for a high school social studies position. Jaraka packed the Newark Board of Education with his black power disciples, who always told Allie that no social studies jobs were available yet quietly hired blacks only for the social studies positions that did open up.

After three years of rejection, Cohen jokingly thought, *The Jaraka-dominated school system would turn the fucking Messiah*

Himself away because He was white. I will have to find a social studies job somewhere else.

It was difficult to assess what Cohen accomplished in his three years in Newark. The worst scar was rejection based on skin color in a northern city. Allie was sure that he influenced lives but saw no proof as the neighborhoods became more violent. Since there was more to life than sex, drugs, and rock 'n' roll and surely Newark, New Jersey, it was time for Cohen to move on.

Teaching was to have been a means to an end—avoid getting drafted and going to Vietnam. A high number, though, in the 1971 lottery put the draft and the war permanently behind Allie, and he faced a critical juncture. Life strangely has a way of turning a detour into a highway.

Cohen conveniently picked up a master's degree in social studies, and graduate school was where he met Professor Aronin, the district administrator for twenty-seven district one schools. Dr. A. sympathetically heard Allie's pleas to escape Newark and placed him in the East Third Street School located on the Lower East Side.

Newark's loss was to be New York City's gain. Cohen crossed the Hudson River into New York, but he did not leave the problems of poverty, junkies, or collapsing tax bases behind. The sole change was that his students were mostly Puerto Rican instead of black.

With school out for the summer, Allie toured Europe like a birthright. A strong dollar aided his quest to cover the entire continent in ten weeks, and he discovered that traveling was his greatest joy in life. Rick, Lenny, and Allie traveled so fiercely with their prepaid Eurail passes that, after a month of cannonballing around the northern countries, fatigue caught up with them in Paris.

Despite Lenny and Rick also being exhausted from the grueling late-night ride from Denmark, they dragged themselves out of bed to go stand in line at the Louvre.

"You guys go without me," Allie told them. "I prefer to take it easy and read this book given to me by that friendly tall Swede who shared a compartment from Copenhagen to Brussels with us."

As a token of appreciation, the Swede—me, Gabriel, who always loved my time spent with Allie and his friends—gave Cohen a copy of Jean-Paul Sartre's autobiography. I sensed that Allie would benefit from reading it while lounging in a Left Bank Hotel, a stone's throw from the existential philosopher's favorite café, where he held court with his lover Simone de Beauvoir.

That afternoon, Sartre became Allie's mentor in a search for understanding.

"I am struck," thought Cohen out loud, "by the numerous parallels between me and Sartre. My dad and Sartre's father were both members of the meat trades and apolitical members of the middle class. The early deaths of our beloved fathers freed us from being molded in our dad's images and assuming their careers."

The middle-class security provided by a small inheritance and supportive family members permitted Sartre and Cohen to pursue a life of exploring ideas instead of accumulating wealth. This exemption from want allowed common left-leaning hearts to beat in reaction to the times they lived in.

The holes in the prophet's identity and sense of self were filling in nicely, and he was nearly ready to make his way in the world.

Chapter 12

Cohen returned to New York in September and settled into the rhythms of the school year, looking forward to a long and fruitful career with a relatively high-paying system. Allie quickly fell in love with his bright group of Puerto Rican and black students, who worked very hard for him.

Allie realized that he'd finally grown into the role of teacher because, now and then, he'd even break down and write a lesson plan to please an administrator. His first evaluation declared him to be a *thoughtful* and *effective* teacher.

Allie spent his weeknights with the pretty dark-haired Nancy Newman, a second-grade teacher whose classroom was directly above his. What Allie liked most about Nancy was that she gave really good head, and her daddy owned thirty shopping centers.

Allie also spent his weekends with the cute raven-haired Sarah Kartzman, a senior special ed major at West Long Branch College who rented a beach apartment. Allie delighted in long walks by the ocean's edge with Sarah, also in her long legs and delicately voluptuous body.

Allie liked his job, enjoyed his bachelor status with two pretty girlfriends, and felt relatively content. Blessed with number 352 in the draft lottery and with most of the troops home from Vietnam, the war was finally behind him.

Challenging the government's prosecution of the war left him antiauthoritarian. For palpable reasons, his life advanced more rapidly than the men who served. With God's grace, Allie avoided being one of the fifty-eight thousand victims' names on the chilling black memorial. Cohen concluded that he was at least a secondary victim of the turbulent antiwar era.

Cohen was clearly a primary victim of the openhanded John Lindsay years that led to the first breakdown of New York's finances in the early 1970s. The accountant mayor Abraham Beame inherited fail-safe borrowing practices and unorthodox record keeping from the Lindsay administration. The fallout from the city's financial crash buried Allie's last hope of a life in the city.

Allie's Big Apple world officially fell apart on December 4, 1971, when he received a message instructing him to report to Principal Dr. Alfredo Gonzales's office. Allie liked the dapper administrator who was under attack from the local Hispanic pressure group, the Young Lords. Cohen wondered why the group so badly wanted to fire Gonzales, a PhD who got along great with the mostly Jewish staff and spoke perfect English.

"That's it." Cohen figured it out. "Gonzales isn't authentically Hispanic enough for them. They want somebody who speaks broken English and gives the Jewish teachers fits, just like Jaraka and his green-robed sisters."

The intense short Gonzales welcomed Allie into his office. *Hmmm, Alfredo's acting very anxious, and that makes me really nervous.* Cohen noticed.

"Allie, it's good to see you again. Sit down, please. You know, your teaching license will expire February 1. Normally, that's nothing to worry about. But with the city's fiscal crisis, well, I don't know anymore."

Cohen suspected that his life might be turning upside down again and nervously asked why the expiration was such a big deal.

"Allie," Gonzales informed, "renewal is normally automatic for certified teachers, but your status is probationary, so you will have to be retested."

"Well, I volunteer to take the test as soon as possible."

"You can't." Gonzales made it painfully clear. "Your name has to go to the end of a very long list, of which only portions are tested at a time. Furthermore, hiring and testing have been frozen indefinitely."

"So you're telling me that there's no way I can take this test."

"Yes, Allie, I'm afraid that I will have to let you go as of February 1, 1972."

Allie felt dizzy and confused. "This is Catch-22 madness, Dr. Gonzales, isn't there any way around this? Aren't I doing a good job?"

"Allie, you are doing an excellent job. Your students love you, the parents praise you to the skies, and I wish I had thirty more of you. I'm sorry, but it looks like I'm really going to have to release you."

"Release me?" questioned a shocked Cohen. "Who the hell are you going to replace me with, Dr. Gonzales?"

"I'm embarrassed to tell you"—Gonzales looked down at his feet and then out the window—"that I've been stuck with a dud previously transferred by two other principals."

Alfredo closed his eyes—he could not bring himself to look at Cohen.

"I find it ironic, Allie, that you're active in a union whose idiotic work rules are responsible for you losing your job to an— Jesus, I can't believe I'm saying this—to an *incompetent*."

Gonzales's soul ached. *I expect Allie to vent like hell, and who can blame him? Not me. I'm forced to do the dumbest fucking thing that I may ever do in my life.*

70

"Lose my job to an *incompetent?*" Cohen tried to comprehend that. "My class is doing nine lessons a day, and you are replacing me with an *incompetent?*"

He stood up, walked around his chair, and then shouted, "You are going to kill learning for twenty-six terrific kids! Shame on you, Dr. Gonzales and the whole damn system. This is unfair to the children, the parents, and the school and stupid as all hell!"

Gonzales again apologized. "I feel terrible, Allie, but there is nothing I can do short of setting off a system-wide strike. I encourage you to see Dr. Aronin, your last hope of holding on to this position."

Cohen called Aronin right after the meeting with Gonzales and was told that his hands were tied by mayoral edict and union work rules.

"Allie, I'm sorry, but I risk a system-wide strike if I keep you on after February 1, so obviously, there's nothing I can do or anybody else."

"Doc, this system's fucked-up! It's killing education for twenty-six terrific kids who love learning. I swear, the fucking union and system could replace the Messiah Himself with an incompetent."

"That's a funny line, kid. I'm going to share that with my wife tonight. What can I tell you, Allie? You were a pleasure to teach, kid. Good luck and goodbye."

This was the second time in less than a year that Adonai and I put that line in Allie's mouth, our purpose being to inform the Newark and New York school systems that they moronically discriminated against or fired the messiah and replaced him with an incompetent—classic examples of acting thickheaded to use Hashem's description.

71

Allie left feeling that merit meant nothing in New York. Fun City's policy for hiring teachers was like the army's; Brooklyn needed seventeen thousand warm bodies, Manhattan twelve thousand more fodder, and so on. Cohen still wanted to be a social studies teacher, and now New York was out of the picture too.

I'm ready to peddle myself to some other metropolitan area, possibly Boston, Washington, or LA. He thought outside the box for a second. *Maybe Atlanta too, they just elected a Jewish mayor and received national attention as a progressive pocket. My problem's that I have two lovely girlfriends and like both of them.*

Translation: Allie didn't love either; the words *marriage* and *dumb* were interchangeable to him at this stage of his life.

Nancy was beautiful and rich but a bit whiny like a JAP and probably wouldn't follow Allie anywhere.

She was planted in Westchester, where she belonged—with her shopping center family. JAP's an acronym for Jewish American princess, a super-entitled young lady who believes it's all coming to her and that the husband better provide it, or he is unworthy of her love. She, in her mind, *is* that special.

Sarah, in comparison, was cute and more free-spirited, just graduated, and can't find a teaching job in recession-wracked Jersey. Her brother Jerry lived in Atlanta, and she seemed more likely of the two to relocate with Cohen.

Sloe-eyed Nancy was starting to fall in love with Allie and worried to him at the holiday assembly. "Should I spend Christmas vacation skiing in Gstaad, Switzerland, with my family or stay home and hang out with you?"

I influenced Allie, who reassured her, "You love to ski, and it's quality time with your family. I'll be here when you get back." Nancy was just a pretty fling for Allie.

"Okay, you talked me in to it."

Nancy appreciatively pulled Allie into a nearby utility closet and gave him a blow job, which would serve as a sweet parting memory.

I admit I interfered, but it's only because I believe that Sarah is the right girl for Allie. She is smart, good, and strong and can stand the test of the fires of life that Allie, a prophet, will face.

New York terminated Allie right before he happily passed two weeks with Sarah in Miami Beach and Key West. The great getaway drew Sarah and Allie closer, and they stopped in Atlanta on their way back up north to spend New Year's Eve with her brother Jerry and his friends and to check out Atlanta for opportunity and livability.

"My view of America," admitted Allie while driving around with Sarah and Jerry and exploring their new city, "is similar to the old joke about liberals. The United States consists of California and New York connected by United Airlines."

"Well, Atlanta," Jerry told him, "is one of the pockets of civility in between. What I like most is that it's a big city that's booming economically but is still laid-back. The city somehow preserved a sense of graciousness and lets you be."

"Atlanta," Sarah commented to her brother, "is very hilly and green and blessed with an incredible tree cover."

"Sister, you ain't seen nothing yet." Jerry snickered. "You should see the place in spring, when the dogwoods and azaleas bloom. Man, Atlanta is a riot of color and possibly the most beautiful place on earth the first two weeks of April. There are four distinct seasons with short mild winters too. What more can you want?"

"What about salaries, Jerry?" Allie inquired.

"My experience," extolled Jerry as they drove down Roswell Road toward Buckhead, "is that salaries are definitely lower, but you still gain. You have much lower rents and living expenses. In my opinion, the place is a virtual paradise for the middle class compared with New York."

Sarah and Allie joined Jerry and fourteen of his friends to celebrate New Year's Eve at the Ambassador Restaurant on Roswell Road. To Allie, young Atlantans appeared prosperous, confident, and content. The men exhibited an audacious streak, and the women were pretty by any city's standard.

A hint of sex was in the air. At five minutes to midnight, the big group got ready to welcome in 1972.

Suddenly, Harriet, a slinky twenty-year-old dark-haired native Atlantan in a tight white dress, walked up to Allie and drawled, "I find northern Jewish men irresistible."

Harriet grabbed Allie's cock right in front of Sarah, who warned the bold little slut, "Well, that scene sure shatters my stereotype of sweet southern belles." She looked at Harriet sternly. "Girl, you better let go of Allie's schlong, or I'm going to kick your ass to the Belt Parkway and back."

Matchmaker, matchmaker, sing me a song. Sometimes it's fun to be a special angel.

Chapter 13

Two thousand miles away in Malibu, California, Carole Herman, America's most popular Jewish movie and singing star, stepped out of a hot shower refreshed. The former New Yorker towel-dried her hair and stared into the full-length mirror.

Not bad for a woman on her thirty-seventh birthday, felt the five-foot-two-inch, one-hundred-pound actress with curly light brown hair. *I think I look pretty damn good for a woman my age, no plastic surgery yet either. When I started out at eighteen, producers called me ordinary looking right to my face. I'm one of the few who can truly say that their talent got them there.*

It was true. Carole's become much prettier and sexier; men and movie critics were taking notice too. Normally, looking good made Carole feel great, but tonight was different. Her personal life was a bit of a mess, and she felt a little unfulfilled in her career too.

I'm starting to play it too safe. I need to take bigger artistic risks, stretch my acting skin more, and explore more areas of music too.

She checked her legs. *Uucch, gross, let me shave these stubby dark hairs.*

She creamed up the right one and bent over to shave it. David Conte, her horny erect lover, snuck up and selfishly entered her from behind. He stuck it in a little too hard; the force drove the razor blade into the skin above the ankle and cut her.

"Christ!" shouted Carole, ballistic. "What are you, a schmuck? Didn't you see me shaving? My god, I'm bleeding like a pig."

"I'm sorry, I did something dumb. Forgive me."

"Jesus, this was more than dumb. It's almost abusive."

"You don't have to harp on it. Look, I'm horny and lonely and tired of jerking off. I impulsively figured that a little spontaneity might help. You know, I'm wondering if you still like having sex with me."

I can't bring myself to tell him that our sex life has died. She shaved the other leg. *The problem is David's dick. It works well enough, but it's simply too damn big for me.*

Carole, before David, was intimate with very few men, all with relatively normal-size penises. At first, David's erections were exciting, and she treated them like a new toy to be played with in every conceivable manner. Well, there are only so many ways to fry potatoes too, and of late, a recurring pain during intercourse limited frequency.

Carole, a third-generation Jewish American, has rediscovered her religious and ethnic roots during the filming of *Dora*, the story of a Latvian immigrant girl who made it big in the old Yiddish theater. Broadway beckoned, and Dora became a music and dance star.

From the stage, Dora moved to Hollywood, where she faced an identity crisis—Hollywood box office success or regaining her lost Jewishness? In the end, Dora married an Orthodox rabbi and lived happily ever after.

I'm having a hard time letting this role go, Carole reflected with a glass of Merlot. *It's crawled into my psyche, and I swear, it's making me wonder what to do about David, which makes no sense at all because he grew up in a Jewish neighborhood, uses Yiddish words constantly, and acts even more Jewish than my ex-husband, Myron, whose family is Brooklyn Orthodox.*

Just the thought of breaking up with David and searching for a new man all over again left Carole cold. She rationalized that better an inert relationship than none at all, for in three years,

Conte had brilliantly managed Carole into being a top-grossing actress and queen of the Billboard charts.

What Carole loved most about David was how good he was to her, better than any other man in her life except her late father.

I wish I could return it. He deserves it, but my well is almost dry.

David brought her back to reality by continuing to press the issue of sex.

"Come on, Carole, be honest with me. You don't enjoy sex with me anymore, do you? You used to but certainly not lately. I'm a big boy, babe. I can handle the truth."

I know he can't *handle the truth.*

She raised a different subject.

"I think I really took it out on you, David, for booking that fucking concert for Reagan at the Kennedy Center. Frankly, I'm surprised that the White House went for your lame idea. I mean, I was only a few places behind Paul Newman on Nixon's enemies list."

"Babe, we stand to get millions of dollars of free publicity for *Dora*. The news coverage will help sell more albums of the film's soundtrack and also raise a lot of money for your favorite charity. Besides, Reagan's not so bad. In fact, he's a pretty nice guy."

Carole sat in front of the vanity as she tweezed her eyebrows. "What did you do to pull this one off, shtup Nancy in the Rose Garden?"

Conte laughed, though her irreverent humor made him a little nervous.

"No, Sam Minkowitz hooked us up with the White House because Caspar Weinberger supposedly pissed off the Jewish community by sounding too pro-Arab. The White House sees your performance as a means to appease the Yids."

"Weinberger was instrumental," she reminded him, "in sentencing Jonathan Pollard to life in prison."

She plucked a hair from her eyebrow and then saw that David had no idea who Pollard was or what he did. "That, my man, was for Pollard giving Israel, an American *ally*, vital information that we should have been sharing with them anyway. By the way, did the White House use the word *Yids*?"

"Of course not. Come on, Carole, put yourself in my place. Would you have turned down the president of the United States if he called you up and asked you to sing?"

"I sure as shit would have. Sorry, David, I haven't sung in public in two years and feel a cold coming on. Look, can't you just call the White House and reschedule it?"

"Please, Carole, every GOP big shot is coming to a thousand-dollar-a-seat concert that sold out in minutes, so cancelling is definitely out of the question. If you want to put down Reagan, that's one thing, but depriving special children of five hundred thousand in therapy money—well, let that be on your conscience."

"My god." His tone and message stunned her. "Can you ever lay on the guilt? I swear, you're better than my mother who is the world champ."

She smiled at him through clenched teeth but wearily relented. "Don't do this again without first asking me, okay?"

David imitated Señor Wences who performed on the old *Ed Sullivan Show* 259 times, more than any other act. "'S'okay? Is okay."

David had the voice and hand motion down pat and made her laugh happily.

She decided. *I swear, that was so good I have to forgive him. You know what, I'll give him a blow job. I bet that'll keep him happy for a few days.*

That's a winning wager, Carole.

Chapter 14

Over on the west side of Atlanta, just off the Bankhead Highway, the muscular Eddie White groped the pretty Farrah Wilson's little tight behind. The black eighth graders humped ever so slowly to Lionel Richie and the Commodores in a darkened corner of Juanita Blood's finished cellar.

Farrah's two best friends, sisters Andrea and Sharon Johnson, sat in the well-lit area and judged Farrah.

"Jesus, she's sure making a terrible mistake. I mean, he's a loser, straight and simple."

The dance ended, and Farrah returned to her friends' corner. The very pretty and bright Sharon did not mince words.

"Tell me, Farrah, what in god's name do you see in him? I'll be kind and just say he isn't good-looking. Since I have English with him, I know he isn't smart."

Andrea agreed. Sharon continued. "As far as I can see, football's his only saving grace, and he can't get along with the gym teacher. So, girl, why are you grinding on him like that?"

"Sharon's right, Farrah," Andrea chimed in. "Eddie's dark as shit, got lips as thick as steaks, and has an awful temper. So tell me, girl, what do you like about him?"

That was a good question.

I can't admit to my friends that Eddie turns me on. They'll get all over me. Instead, she said, "I think he has a gentle soul."

That evasion drove Andrea to laugh and get personal. "Gentle soul, my ass. C'mon, be honest. It's sex. You want to fuck him, right?"

Farrah realized. *I do want to fuck him.* She didn't answer.

Andrea let it go, but Sharon struck a nerve. "Honey, you keep grinding in the dark corner with him like that, and he's gonna tag you good."

Sharon's choice of word bugged Farrah. "What you mean by *tag?*"

"You know, get you pregnant and make you a welfare mother living in the Bankhead Estates housing project or, worse, the Perry Homes. There's no way that's happening to me. I'm going to college to become a clothing designer. Farrah, you got the brains to be somebody too, that is, unless you let yourself get slack, girl."

Andrea shared her low opinion of Eddie White.

"Shit, the thought of being stuck with him for a lifetime make my flesh crawl. Oh, oh, Farrah, here he comes again to take you back into the dark corner. What you gonna do, girl?"

Farrah turned Eddie down, looked away from him, and did not acknowledge his existence for three cold and long years.

Chapter 15

As of February 1, 1972, the New York City Board of Education stopped acknowledging Allie's existence. Cohen visited the school three days after his termination date to pick up a last check—Allie's moving money—and say goodbye to his students.

Cohen approached the door to room 201 and looked in first to see how his students were adjusting to Mr. Gorin, their incompetent new teacher.

He gritted his teeth. *Juan, who in five months advanced a year and a half in his reading series, is running up and down the aisle like a jerk. Even Julie, who normally does an extra half hour of homework, is carrying on. This entire class that loves learning is misbehaving. What the hell is that idiot Gorin doing while this travesty is happening?*

The dense fifty-year-old fool endlessly fumbled with mysterious papers behind his desk. *This fuck face resembles a man who's had nervous breakdowns. Oh shit, Jose and his 128 IQ just fell asleep at his desk. I can't take it anymore.*

Cohen entered and was overrun the second the students saw him. They told him they missed him and that they were bored out of their minds and begged him to return.

"Why did they take you away from us?" Math whiz Milton Lopez had to know. "We were learning so much. This guy is so out of it that he drooled on himself yesterday while taking attendance."

"Yesterday," Juan reported to Cohen, "we played tic-tac-toe all day while Gorin filled out racing forms. Tell me, do you think he's on drugs?"

Cohen choked up; tears formed in his eyes. *I can't let the students see me cry.*

Allie hugged them all before saying goodbye. The children's pitiful cries followed him down the steps and out the door.

"Mr. Cohen, please don't leave us. Why can't you be our teacher anymore? We love you, Mr. Cohen."

The children did not lead the way in New York's schools. Allie's delightful class has been sacrificed on the altar of teacher union work rules.

Allie drove back to New Jersey with a hole in his heart. New York, for the first time, looked seedy and ugly to him. Huge numbers of people required giant bureaucracies to provide basic services, and occasionally, some people—including he and his third-grade class—fell between the system's cracks.

Allie began looking forward to his upcoming interview with the Atlanta Public Schools, and a week later, he and Sarah flew down there and stayed with Jerry. This time, the numbers game worked for them. The interviewers informed the migrants that Atlanta needed every white teacher they could find, and they were hired on the spot.

The interviewer elaborated, "The city's desegregation mandate required staff racial composition to be in balance and strictly maintained. Since desegregation, the system had hired so many black teachers that they were far out of compliance. The judge extended a deadline for six months while threatening to impose massive fines."

Sarah and Allie felt they were not quite ready to live together, and each rented separate luxury apartments three times the size of an L-shaped Manhattan room and at a third of the cost. Allie's salary dropped from $13,800 to $9,500, and his standard of living improved dramatically.

On February 20, Cohen kissed his mother goodbye and steered a seventeen-foot U-Haul van out of the parking lot. Sarah followed in his 2002 BMW coupe and waved goodbye to her prospective mother-in-law. Like modern-day carpetbaggers and so many before them, they had high hopes and a little money and were headed southward toward golden opportunities.

Chapter 16

If Atlanta proved less than a promised land, it did provide Allie and Sarah a chance to break in and start their lives together. Since the Big Peach's beginning in 1835 when two railroad lines crossed, the city's been wide open to newcomers and welcomed migrants' skills and energy to help build the New South colossus.

The interviewer assigned Allie his first elusive social studies job at 99 percent black Bankhead High School, where 30 percent of the students went on to college. Sarah's entry-level position was teaching fourth graders at the Asa Waterman School in Vine City built in 1884 to provide the first legal education for blacks in Georgia.

Atlanta is a city of neighborhoods; Vine City is one of its poorest. Sarah's practice teaching in exclusive Rumson–Fair Haven, one of New Jersey's richest communities, did not prepare her for the challenge of teaching poor kids, many from welfare families. They tested her for the first few days until Allie taught her a few discipline tricks.

Sarah persevered, became a beloved teacher, and enjoyed two fruitful and pleasant years in Vine City before winning a reading coordinator position in fast-growing DeKalb County, where whites fleeing integration and blockbusted by unscrupulous real estate agents were moving to in droves.

I have an important new job and a master's degree, she thought. *Now I'm ready to tackle the subject of marriage. Allie and I are both from families who have experienced little divorce, and we hope to avoid becoming a statistic.*

Similar to many other young couples in the 1970s, Allie and Sarah lived together for a year to learn if they were compatible. On February 14, 1973, Sarah's mother, Rebecca, called to tell him it was time to get married.

Rebecca asked Sarah to let her speak to Allie, and he took the phone.

"Allie, you've been living with my daughter for nearly a year and have tested the limits of my liberal ways. It's time to make my daughter a good woman and marry her."

"Sure, Mrs. Kartzman. I love Sarah and want to spend the rest of my life with her."

"Allie," said Rebecca, thrilled, "that's wonderful. Please call me Mom and my husband, Harvey, Dad. I promise you guys a June wedding at the Estate, a beautiful event facility in West Orange, New Jersey. This is going to be a memorable wedding, a beautiful ceremony, and a fabulous party."

"Thank you, Mom. Give Dad my best. Here's Sarah."

Sarah said goodbye to her mother and put down the receiver. Allie put his arms around Sarah, kissed her lips, and slowly removed her clothes and she his. They skipped the foreplay and made urgent love on the living room floor.

My present to Allie and Sarah on their wedding day was a seventy-eight-degree temperature in June and a cloudless blue Jersey sky. I smiled every time someone told Allie or Sarah that it was the best wedding they'd ever been to.

The night before the affair, Terry Winkler, Allie's best man, scored seventy-five doses of synthetic marijuana that was lifted from a University of Chicago research lab. Terry conducted a line of Cohen's cousins and friends, male and female, that stretched from the bride's dressing room all the way up a hundred-foot-long spiral staircase.

The Cohens spent the summer honeymooning on Martha's Vineyard Island off the coast of Massachusetts for two terrific months. That was my other wedding present to Allie and Sarah.

The local realtor gladly rented them a lovely cottage for seven weeks in the Menemsha fishing village up the hill from the beach and pier for a fraction of the normal rate. My greatest power may be friendly persuasion.

Allie and Sarah returned to Atlanta in late August to start a new school year and build a great permanent union. Both quickly acquired reputations as exceptional educators and pursued advanced degrees at Southeastern State University (SSU) in Downtown Atlanta.

Both found adjusting to Dixie a bit arduous; being northerners, they cared more about *ends* than *means* in getting a job done well. Southerners preserve graciousness by stressing means as well as ends. The Cohens were occasionally perceived as aggressive New York Jews, a cultural difference that affected Allie more than Sarah.

The adjustment that Allie experienced in moving South was best described by a witness to the Atlanta race riot of 1906. David Yampolsky, a Russian immigrant to Atlanta by New York's Lower East Side, observed white policemen rushing into the black community to *beat and kill as many blacks as possible.*

A white woman complained to the police that a black man had been *rude* to her on a streetcar. Yampolsky thought the riot to be worse than any pogrom that he'd witnessed in Russia.

In New York, Yampolsky worked in a sweatshop textile company and shared a room with three men. In Atlanta, he owned a fabric shop on Peters Street and rented a four-room sunny apartment. He reasoned that in New York, he had a *soul* without a body. In Atlanta, he had a *body* without a soul.

By the end of his third year in Atlanta, Allie Cohen was recognized as a master teacher and creative curriculum developer; but like Yampolsky, his body was much more comfortable than if he'd stayed up North. The downside was Atlanta's blandness made for a less nourished soul, the quality of deli, pizza, and Chinese food lagging badly in comparison. Harry Baron's Deli in Phipps, Gigi's and Everybody's Pizza, and the Lotus Garden Chinese Restaurant on Buford Highway paled in comparison to what he'd been used to.

If the few rough edges of Cohen's northern Jewish personality ruffled a few administrators, his New York shtick and energy level was eaten up by his students. So many signed up for his classes each semester that the registrar regularly had to come in and reassign dozens to other teachers with emptier classes.

Sharon Johnson and Farrah Wilson, two of his brightest pupils, took two classes a day from Cohen. Atlanta's corporations were starting to recruit young blacks like Sharon and Farrah and groom them for executive status. Although Eddie White had been named to the all-city football team and was doing much better work in class too, Cohen was concerned about Farrah and Eddie dating exclusively again.

Melvin Meacham, Bankhead High's principal, combined pugnacity, insecurity, and limited intelligence—not a good combination for running a high school. Meacham disliked Eddie White and was looking for one more infraction to kick him out of school. Meacham gave Eddie another chance after a serious incident occurred during spring practice. The football coach, Clarence "Pops" Green, kept getting on Eddie about not picking up his blocks. Finally, Eddie snapped and threatened to shut Pops up if he didn't stop. Two beefy linemen friends held Eddie back, and he quickly calmed down and apologized. Meacham suspended him for two weeks, causing him to fail English.

I think it odd, Cohen mused, *that the better Eddie does, the more Meacham distrusts him. Eddie's earned a good chance of getting a football scholarship to a small black college that will put him on the right path in life. Pops told me at lunch the other day that Miles College in Alabama recently scouted him.*

The temperature during the last week of school languished in the high nineties, and Bankhead wasn't air-conditioned. The heat and humidity made both teachers and students a bit nutty, and only the thought of summer vacation was getting the school through it.

Sweat dripped from Allie's brow as he wrote a homework assignment on the blackboard for his international relations class. He dropped his chalk when Farrah walked in late for class wearing a maternity blouse. Her belly had popped, and she could no longer hide it.

Farrah fell from grace with Allie right there by breaking his sacred commandment—maximize one's human potential and achieve working- to middle-class status; at a minimum, be a contributor and not a dependent. He repeatedly taught economics lessons on the purchasing power of *two paychecks* versus being a *single provider.*

Allie gleaned. *I give my heart to improve my student's condition and am determined that they will graduate and be imbued with a love of learning. My goal for every one of them is that they live a meaningful life, be inspired to leave the block, and travel their country and even the world.*

Cohen lamented. *I can no longer bear to watch the bellies of 70 percent of mostly smart black females pop and trade off their lives for a welfare check. To me, that is the ultimate devil's bargain, and I will apply for a transfer to another school.*

Cohen looked at the clock. *Shit, Eddie is already five minutes late. I'm really pissed off at the future father. Let me walk to the door and look up the hall to see if he's coming.*

Allie turned his head to the left. *Holy shit, Eddie just passed three glassine envelopes filled with white powder to Danny Hall.*

Danny was the son of a school kitchen worker who washed heavy pots for a living. Mrs. Hall, a devout Jehovah's Witness, and

Cohen always exchanged pleasantries as he moved through the cafeteria serving line.

There's bantam rooster Meacham coming down the hall.

He watched Danny turn and scat right into the arms of his principal. Meacham pinned Danny down on the hall floor and directed Cohen to go to the office, call the police, and send for the other assistant principals.

Allie took off as directed while Eddie White ran out the side door and right into the arms of Marcus Miller, a three-hundred-and-fifty pound, six-foot-six-inch giant of an assistant principal who managed to fend off a flurry of very hard punches from the powerful seventeen-year-old, bear-hug White to the ground, and finally subdue him.

"I don't deal drugs!" Eddie screamed at Miller. "I just held it for him for a little while and was giving it back!"

"C'mon, Danny, tell the truth," he pleaded to his friend with tears in his eyes. "Tell 'em that it's yours. I don't deserve this. Meacham's gonna throw me out of school unless you fess up."

Cohen noticed Danny staring at Eddie to advise him to shut up, like he might cut Farrah with a knife if he didn't. The police arrived and charged Eddie with selling and Danny with receiving. White ceased shouting, looked down at the floor, and wept quietly. Meacham informed the police that Cohen was a witness to the transaction.

"Officer, I clearly saw the transfer take place but need a clarification. Does it make any difference if a person was just holding the dope for a while and not involved in the actual sale or transaction?"

"No." The cop shook his head. "It's illegal to have possession for any reason."

"Atlanta Public School policy," Meacham cited, "applies zero tolerance of hard drugs on campus. Expulsion is usually mandatory for heroin."

"Mr. Cohen." The officer pointed at him. "You do understand that Mr. White has broken the law and Board of Education policy, right?"

"Officer," Allie assured him, "I fully respect the law and board policy."

Eddie glared at his teacher. "That's the first time in three years that I ever saw you two agree on anything. Cohen, I can understand Meacham screwing me. He's a dumb-ass piece of shit, but you know better. You care about your students, so why are you letting them fuck me over?"

"Eddie, I do feel badly for you." Cohen looked Eddie in the eye. "And I know it seems very unfair, but you broke the law, and school policy is clear and rigid. I hope and pray that you can come back from this disaster and turn your life around. Good luck to you, and I really wish you the best."

Meacham unfortunately zinged, "And good riddance."

"Someday," Eddie, enraged, swore, "I'm gonna get even with you, motherfuckers."

The cop cupped his mouth, pushed him into the back seat of the police car, and took him down to the local precinct. Eddie was booked and kept overnight until Farrah bailed him out the next day with money borrowed from Danny Hall.

Eddie earned his high school equivalency degree by attending adult education courses at night at Atlanta Vocational and Technical High School (Vo-Tech). During the day, he worked as a garbageman, lifting smelly cans and yelling "yoh" over and over.

He married Farrah the week after their first child, Arvida, was born, who was followed a year later by Dennis, a colicky baby boy. Economically, they barely made it from month to month; and thanks to Farrah's strength, their one achievement during this difficult time was to keep the family together.

Chapter 17

Allie moved on to Buckhead High, a showcase school with a highly regarded performing arts magnet program. No one got pregnant at Buckhead High; 85 percent went to college, the rest into the arts, military, or trades.

Cohen found a home at Buckhead High and finally achieved self-actualization as a social studies teacher. He capitalized on Buckhead's growing reputation by building a speaker series that became an important forum in the city of Atlanta. Allie invited politicians, artists, media members, athletes, and prominent businesspeople to Buckhead, and most of them accepted.

Rebecca and Harvey visited from Brooklyn one weekend and over Sunday morning breakfast with Sarah and Allie. Harvey pulled out a blank check, wrote it to Allie for $5,000, and handed it to the Cohens over the bagels and lox.

Harvey, a great restaurant manager and designer who always wanted to own his own place, was also a great father-in-law. "Here, Allie, you and Sarah use this for a down payment. It's time you two have a house so I can play with my grandkid in the backyard. Mother and I did very well in the stock market this year."

Sarah and Allie bought a split-level home in suburban Sandy Springs, and she got pregnant just about the time he received his PhD and started writing a novel. On Thanksgiving weekend of 1980, on a cold rainy Sunday night, ABC News blared in the background while Cohen tried to squeeze in a couple of more sentences. Sarah's familiar whine to stop and come up to the bedroom was met by his usual plea.

"Please, honey, just one more minute, babe."

That minute, as usual, stretched into ten as he rewrote the first sentence to chapter 2. Cohen contemplated how to introduce his antagonist, a smooth college professor and Nazi sympathizer who had written a disturbingly popular book claiming the Holocaust was a Zionist hoax.

The words came to him: "Ralph Helms adjusted the knot of his tie and complained, 'Christ, I hate these fucking mandatory faculty parties.'"

"Come on, it's late," Sarah complained. "You know I don't have kids like yours."

"I'll be right up, babe." Allie was experiencing first-novel hell—hold down a job, maintain family commitments, and write during every spare minute after work and on weekends, holidays, and summer vacation. He turned off the outside lights and walked up the steps leading to the master bedroom.

"I'm curious," Sarah said to him, "what you're going to teach your students tomorrow."

"I have handouts," he rattled off, "from Schermerhorn's *Comparative Ethnic Relations*, the five intergroup sequences of global ethnic interaction, followed by Kramer's *Ethnic Assimilation Model*, the four transitional stages and dependent conflict variables—birth, life chances, allegiance to family, and so on."

"Allie, your teaching such high-level stuff to high school kids amazes me. God, I don't think you could have taught that at Bankhead."

Cohen felt differently but didn't pursue it. "Babe, I'm experiencing writer's high and know I'm going to keep you up unless I go downstairs to the den and relax for a while."

He put his ear to her very pregnant belly and then kissed his son in there. "I am a lucky man to have such a pretty and sexy wife."

She smiled. "Don't stay up too late. I love you."

"I love you too, honey."

Allie retired to the den, put a soft jazz album on the stereo, and sat down in a heavily padded gray leather chair. He lit a joint; the pot's tranquil qualities and the mellow sounds of Grover Washington Jr. lilting out of the powerful speakers soon furnished a reflective atmosphere for stream-of-consciousness thinking. *I'm thirty-four years old now and a respected teacher in three social science disciplines. My doctoral dissertation, an international education process, is being applied in selected school systems in England and Australia.*

The problem is I'm not a traditional scholar and resist grinding out journal articles needed for tenure or sitting through endless committee meetings.

The Reagan era too is breaking, and getting rich is in again. Cohen occasionally gives thought to leaving the classroom for administration to earn more, but the truth is he loves teaching too much.

Let me roll the story around in my head again. Seymour Umansky, my protagonist, is such a strong worker that he survives thirteen death camps. Seymour becomes alarmed by the acceptance Helms's book receives. A second big lie is forming, and it must be stopped. Seymour kidnaps Ralph and takes him to an abandoned building, where he teaches Helms a lesson, the title of the book.

Every gruesome Nazi torture technique that Seymour witnessed, received, or heard about is applied to Helms. Acts such as slicing off much of Ralph's skin and making a lampshade from it torments Seymour's soul, and he fears he has not achieved enlightened self-sacrifice. Instead, he has practiced barbarism. I'm unsure of how to end the story. Should I kill Seymour off out of moral necessity or let him live out his days as if he has done the world a favor?

Allie had six more chapters to write, so why lose sleep over it? He walked upstairs, got into bed, and promptly fell out. Five hours later, the unforgiving alarm clock pierced his brain. Cohen had the constitution of a jazz man and hated getting up so early in the morning, but the fear of the bank taking away his mostly paper wealth got his butt out of bed and moving as always.

Sarah and Allie dressed, ate, and drove off to work in opposite directions. Cohen mused while maneuvering his Toyota Celica out of the modestly affluent subdevelopment,

From SDS to suburbia. Well, at least the houses don't all look alike.

Allie switched on the car radio; Eastern Air Lines touted a new low rate to the West Coast.

I'm tempted to visit Rick Samuels in LA as it's been at least five years since I last saw him. We are way overdue to get together.

Rick and Allie both grew up fatherless and roamed the streets of Newark as a rat pack with working mothers.

I recall our last time together. Cohen turned right from Roswell Road on to Habersham Road. *Samuels was struggling to establish a commercial photography business, and he seemed to be getting by.*

Monday morning blues often made Allie wonder if he should have listened to Uncle William. In terms of personal evolution, he was right on schedule in achieving professional goals. Regarding everyday life, though, mounting financial pressure was getting to him.

One hundred and eighty days a year, four or five times a day, Allie poured out a steady stream of entertaining lessons. Cohen's special talent was presenting meaningful structures of information that incorporated facts, concepts, or stories all told in his inimitable manner.

Allie employed an arsenal of jokes, impressions, and sound effects and was almost never boring. Imagine George Carlin looking like Al Pacino as your social studies teacher.

Someone once told me that if I'd been born poorer or less academic, I might have become a comedian instead. Not possible, I have too much difficulty pretending and cannot bear playing a fool, no matter how highly paid.

Cohen exemplified the middle-class curse of seeking total credibility and, moreover, a sense of purpose.

The fate before me, though, is to do the same thing for thirty more years. Both Barney, my dad, and Alvin, my grandpa, died at forty. Might I too?

Social marginality gnawed at Allie's ideal of social commitment. Society's misplaced priorities limited the sustenance he needed to stay happy in a position he was tailor-made for. In a mean world, Allie felt that life boiled down to the warmth of commitment versus the freedom of cold cash.

Despite his crying need for more money, a battle for Allie's heart, mind, and soul was *not* commencing. I was steering him to his destiny and clearing the path.

Chapter 18

Rick Samuels fiddled with his wide-angle lens. He achieved perfect focus and the correct ASA and rearranged the background for his new account, *Speed & Chicks*, a raunchy, sexy biker magazine.

This month's centerfold—ha ha ha!—is taking a big step. Chicks sitting on the cycle spread their legs to showcase their vaginas. Times are changing, and bare breasts and butts aren't enough anymore. Readers want to see pussy too.

The work, Rick appreciated, paid very well, much better than sweating beer can photos he was shooting when Allie and Sarah last visited. He didn't have to make do with cardboard boxes for furniture anymore too.

Rick now rented a lovely three-bedroom villa from Jeffrey Picker, a record company executive. The U-shaped home was lined with French doors that led out to a small heated pool, a hot tub, and a gazebo.

Samuels earned commissions from *Playboy*, *Penthouse*, *Gallery*, *Hustler*, and many lesser known brands. His reputation in the industry was built on tastefulness—give sex and nudity a hint of elegance. The term *flesh peddler* didn't faze him either; he was very proud of the fifty grand he'd net after taxes this year, almost twice his teacher pay.

Rick, who graduated from UCLA and returned to LA after seven years in the Newark school system, looked back.

The first three years out here were really tough. I honed my craft by outworking the competition for less money. That's how you get a foothold in the market.

In terms of women, love, and sex, there were occasional empty one-night stands; but since he moved into this place, the models were coming on to him, one beautiful sex goddess after another. His current life, producing male sexual fantasies, was a hell of a lot of fun but about as satisfying as three meals a day of ice cream and chocolate cake.

He pined. *I'm ready to meet a nice, cute girl like Allie's Sarah and settle down, someone I can introduce to my mother.*

The doorbell rang. Samuels opened the front door and gaped at an exquisite blonde of near Amazonian proportions. She looked inside.

"Wow, Rick, cool house."

"Thank you. It's not mine, belongs to Jeffrey Picker."

Man. He silently sized his new model up. *Will you look at this beautiful lady wearing the shortest of shorts and briefest of spandex halter tops? Ooh, is she hot.*

"What's your name, sweetie?" he asked while escorting her over to the set.

Out of blazing white teeth framed by full bloodred lips came "Greta Person."

Rick watched Greta walk and delighted in the view.

That fucking body and bubble butt could make Einstein do stupid things. Her name rang a bell. *Now I remember I once saw her with David Conte at a small Italian restaurant in Malibu. I swear, they couldn't keep their fucking hands off each other in a very public place. Carole Herman has got to know all about them.*

Samuels improvised. "Greta, I'm going to take advantage of your ability to enter a room and dominate its space. You're going to act out an erotic fantasy, a tantalizing Hells Angels' groupie who *loves to make men happy.*" Rick emphasized with his hands.

"Make men happy, eh?" She giggled. "Okay, ready."

"Greta, please take three exaggerated steps forward, and then hit your mark, and slowly strip off your top. Once removed, seductively drape your gorgeous 36-23-35 body over that beige sofa, slowly remove your denim minishorts, and reveal your G-string panties. Don't worry about the pubes showing." She followed him perfectly.

Rick sketched for her. "Now wriggle out of your G-string, put your left leg over the cycle, and the other leg down on the floor. Yeah, very good, now give me that straight-line shot to show off that legendary bubble butt of yours."

Unfortunately for Greta, that asset was her major calling card in life, and it closed as many doors as it opened. She would soon come to grips with this issue and benefit from it.

"I'm not exaggerating, Greta. Your modeling reputation precedes you. Okay, now bend over, sweetie. Yeah, excellent. Arch your back to capture the magical V shot, uh-huh, ooh. 'Got it, perfect. Wow, can you hold a pose."

"Is that it, Rick?"

"Nah, here comes the big finale. Please sit on the cycle seat, and straddle your legs up in the air. Excellent. Now on my command, pull them as far apart as you can. Yeah, yeah, hold it a little longer like that. Okay, beautiful."

She held the pose while Rick clicked away with a wide-angle lens.

"'Got the money shots. You are so good. I bet you'll make those 350,000 biker readers take themselves in hand. Christ, can you believe that ridiculous circulation size? Fucking amazing."

Rick directed Greta through a dozen more sexual contortions for filler—hands on breasts, hands on butt, and several different facial expressions, pouty, smiling, and alluring.

"That's it." He ended the shoot. "Fantastic job, Greta. You are the best damn model I've ever shot, and I look forward to working with you regularly. I can easily guarantee you a hell of a lot steadier income source than what you're earning as an actress."

Greta appreciated Rick's professionalism, manners, and generous offer.

I think I've finally found the perfect photographer for me. Rick is a gentleman, knows how to direct me, and makes me look beautiful and special, and he's kind of cute too.

The still naked Greta whispered seductively into Rick's ear, "Let me show you a little appreciation, Rick, for being the nicest guy I've ever posed for."

Greta hugged Rick and gave him a little kiss on the lips and then a long warm kiss. She placed Samuels's hands on her natural C-cup breasts. Rick grinned like a happy idiot as he kneaded away.

"I like you Rick." She put his hand on her vagina. "You're not a pig like so many of the horrible, mean assholes in this business." Greta fondled him. "Ooh, you're hard, good."

Rick's crying need to meet a nice girl took a back seat. Greta pulled Rick's jeans down, gave him a great blow job, and then fucked him like he was the last man on earth.

I'll worry about my prostate tomorrow. Today I'm fucking David Conte's gorgeous girlfriend, and man, that's as good as it gets.

You have met your first queen, Rick, but you don't know it yet.

Chapter 19

Dr. Allie Cohen of Buckhead High in Atlanta was not busy fornicating with starlets. He was busy conducting one of his periodic killer tests, this one an eight-part essay on key historical, political, and economic components of Soviet Communism.

Mrs. Bonner, the school secretary, stuck her head in the doorway midway through the class to inform him, "Dr. Cohen, you have an important phone call in the main office. Dr. Nolan Craig of Southeastern State University needs to tell you something. I'll watch your class in the meantime."

Nolan was the SSU provost's nephew and a strong supporter of Allie's international education treatment. Allie and Nolan cowrote a grant proposal to jointly put a selected number of Georgia public school teachers through Cohen's human relations process. Cohen entered the office and picked up the receiver.

"Yes, Nolan?"

Nolan kept screaming, "Allie, we got it! We got it! We got it!" The gangly Vanderbilt grad calmed down to provide details. "Wait, it gets better. SSU wants to expand the symposium into an international summer festival theme too."

"Incredible, Nolan, but why are the trustees suddenly so hot for this?"

"Allie, SSU," explained Nolan, "wants to break the mold of being a commuter college forever. Downtown can feel dark and foreboding at night, and the crime fears of prospective enrollees limit our growth. State's new thirty-year development plan is to use the festival as a first tiny step toward creating an on-campus environment that feels safe and fun."

"No kidding?"

"Uh-huh, SSU is bringing in the chamber of commerce and the mayor's office to work together on boosting summertime tourism with a focus on after six at night. The chamber will raise the money to expand the program from thirty teachers to one hundred. All will be housed in a new boutique hotel and fed at several cooperative restaurants near the university. The teachers provide the diverse mass of bodies in which to schedule ambitious cultural events and block parties around."

"Nolan, please thank the trustees for me. Sorry, I have to return to my students. Thanks and take care."

Cohen put down the phone and returned to his classroom just before the dismissal bell rang. His students dropped off their tests on the desk as they passed him on their way out.

He drove home and went up to his mailbox and found an important letter sandwiched between the bills from Visa and Mastercard.

Excellent, it's from Dr. S. K. Kapoor, the noted British ethnologist and my colleague with whom I've been corresponding the past two years.

Allie ripped open the letter from a man he'd never met but had the greatest respect for.

Dear Dr. Cohen,

Congratulations, our offer to Hahnes Bros. Pub. Ltd. has been accepted. I am happy to say that Hahnes Bros. is sincerely committed to promoting your *international education treatment* and process in commercial book form.

I very much look forward to personally delivering your $2,500 advance this July 7. Yes, I am coming to Atlanta and then onto Washington DC, and New York. It is good that we will finally have a chance to meet and work together.

As you say in America, I've saved the best for last. The Greater London Social Science Council has budgeted £25,000 to facilitate a combination symposium of workshop and festival for 350 British teachers the following summer. Your stipend is £1,000 plus expenses.

The Thatcher government, embarrassed somewhat by recent urban riots involving alienated youth and minority groups, is predisposed to initiating your program on a small-scale basis. The application's *statistical validity* is the main selling point.

Perhaps we may be able to help reduce nativist-immigrant tensions and, with God's blessing, produce the means by which England peacefully evolves into a pluralistic society.

Yours sincerely,
S. K. Kapoor

Cohen looked at the letter again and expressed his delight by yelling "hooray" and jumping up and down. After landing, he opened the Visa and Mastercard charge invoices; both cards were nearing credit limits.

Shit, I'm not going to receive my tax return this year until June and the advance till July. I know, I'll apply for a new home equity line of credit and figure we're sitting on top of about twenty-three thousand.

Sarah arrived home from work at the moment Allie and his feet returned to the earth. He told her the good news, and she jumped up and down too.

"Allie, I'm going to prepare us a fancy meal to eat in our newly remodeled kitchen and dining room."

By ten forty-five, they were in bed and making love. Screwing during pregnancy for Cohen was an accomplishment. Sarah, seven months pregnant, looked as sexy to Allie as an eggplant, so arousal for him required the concentration of a bean counter, but like a good husband, he got her off, and they rested silently on the bed.

I'm complicated sexually. Allie compared. *Sarah, in contrast, is as free as a bird. Nothing bothers her.* "Sarah," he asked her, "how many more times do you expect to make love before birth?"

She matter-of-factly said, "Oh, about thirty or forty."

Cohen cracked up, laughing. "Sarah, honey, we'll be lucky to do it a half-dozen times."

"I'm less than thrilled with your honesty, Allie. Okay, come share a bath with me, and we'll talk about it."

They soaked in the tub, and he told her, "Honey, I haven't seen Rick in years, and I'd really like to visit him during our spring break."

His intonation, she thought, *about going alone bothers me.*

"That's not fair, Allie."

"Life's not fair, Sarah. We're teachers, so we know better than most how unfair life is, so please get used to it."

"Okay, you have my permission. You guys should have some time to hang out."

"Thanks, honey, I'll call Rick tomorrow to make the necessary arrangements."

"Allie, let's stop calling each other *honey*. Everybody calls each other that."

"Okay, Sarah, what do you have in mind?"

She cackled. "*Money*, everybody loves money. 'I love you, money. Hey, mon.' Yeah, I like that. From now on, we call each other money."

Allie laughed, put his arms around his funny wife, and kissed her cheek. "I love you too, *money*."

Sarah is an angel, Allie, a true gift from the eternal Giver.

Chapter 20

"Greta, sweetie, thanks for helping me out at the last moment with these two retakes."

She said while putting on her clothes, "No big deal, Rick."

She did not share with him but thought, *The real big deal is that my fucking lover suddenly canceled our date and left me with nothing else to do. He's too goddamned busy organizing Carole's White House performance.*

"Here, sweetie." Rick tried to boost her spirit. "Let me show you some appreciation with a dozen new record albums hot off the studio promo lists. Take 'em. They're yours. I'm sure that Jeffrey will never miss them."

Greta flipped through the stack of albums. "Wow, Rick, the new Billy Joel, Prince, Elton John, Whitney, and Carole Herman releases and a bunch of other good ones too."

She hugged Rick, picked up the stack, and headed out to her car.

Rick remembered something as she opened the door.

"Greta, I almost forgot, are you available April 12 for a shoot?"

"Is it a daytime shoot?" He nodded yes. "Okay, but I have to be done by 5:00 PM because Reny and I are invited to a private screening of Carole Herman's latest film, *Dora*. David and a lot of suits like Sam Minkowitz will be there. Maybe one of them will give me a big part."

"I promise that you'll be done in plenty of time for the party."

"Great, who's the shoot for?" She stared at him.

"I'm a bit ashamed to admit, Lenny Martin's *High Lifers*. It's his latest magazine and probably a new low for him."

"I don't know, Rick." She shook her head back and forth. "He's one of the worst. I mean, he's beyond scatological."

Rick laughed at her description and then recalled Reny. "Your roommate, Reny, she's an adorable little brunette, right?"

"Yeah, Rick, so what?"

"I need for the two of you to do this job together."

"I'm uncomfortable with that. Lesbian photos could cost me a lot of daytime soap opera work. What's the pay?"

"Seventeen thousand five hundred, sweetie. I'll give the two of you half for two hours' work, maybe a little longer."

"My dad is a lay preacher back home in Bismarck, North Dakota. I got to think."

Greta realized that she'd won only three decent film and TV roles the past year, earned $8,200 after her agent's cut and taxes, and could earn half of that for two hours' work for Lenny "Think Pink" Martin.

"How explicit, Rick?"

"Some intimate touching and simulated sex. I promise to protect you all I can, hand in the way, hair cascading down to cover more hard-core stuff, convenient airbrushing."

She thought, *I really need the money and my dad no longer speaks to me because of David.* "Okay, Rick, I'm only doing this because I trust you, also because of Reny, who's done a lot more of this type of work than me."

She looked at her watch. "Sorry, Rick, I have to split." She kissed Rick's cheek and surprised him. "Let me thank you by inviting you to the screening too. You can be Reny and my escort. David owes me big-time."

Rick's eyes opened wide; a happy smile followed. "Are you sure, Greta?"

"I've been raving to David how great you are to work for, so he's interested in you taking some stills of Carole for her new album. The screening's a good place for the two of you to meet and come to terms."

Rick hugged and kissed Greta as she left and walked to her car. "Thank you, sweetie. I've wanted to break into that market forever."

She smiled warmly at him and left. He thought, *I love that hot white smile of hers that she flashes.*

She drove off. Rick's head was spinning. *Taking stills of Carole Herman. Next stop: Malibu.*

The phone rang and snapped him out of his fantasy. Rick picked up the receiver. "Hey, Rick, it's Allie."

"Allie, I'm glad to hear your voice. Man, it's been way too long."

They exchanged regrets over having lost contact, tried to catch up, and shared past and current successes.

"Allie, I'm in absolute awe of your research. Wow, a prejudice reduction treatment. My friend, the *scholar*."

"Well I'm astounded by what you're doing for a living. I told you years ago that *tits* and *ass* paid a hell of a lot better than sweating beer cans. Anyway, who's the record producer whose home you're renting?"

"Jeffrey Picker. Why, you know him?"

"Amazing, he's the only one out there that I do. Is Jeffrey still the recycling king of rock 'n' roll?"

"Yeah, and Jackie Kahn is still working for him, ferrying those has-been rock groups around the country in a vain hope they'll connect one more time with the public."

"Rick, is it okay if I come out for spring break? Sarah's pregnancy is too advanced for her to come too, so it's just me."

"Of course, we're going to have a blast. Send me the dates, time, and flight number."

"I'll mail you the information tomorrow. Take care, Rick."

Samuels retreated to the rectangular white kitchen with big windows and a direct view of the Sunset Strip below. He poured himself a small glass of orange juice and sipped it as he looked out the window.

Ah yes, I just remembered that I have another photo session. He flipped open his appointments book to check the model's name., *Mamie Lee. I bet she's Chinese. I love beautiful Asian women.*

Samuels watched a blue Toyota Corolla enter and park in the driveway. *I assume that's Mamie because a gorgeous petite Chinese American girl in her early twenties just got out and is headed for my front door.*

Enchanted so far, Rick opened the door and was instantly mesmerized by Mamie's exquisite features. *Man, her body defines the word* nubile.

"Hello. Mamie, right?"

She smiled, and he took her hand and escorted her over to the set. Mamie's demure body language grabbed hold of him as no woman had before, and he babbled a bit while encouraging her to relax and acclimate.

Mamie is so hot dressed in those tight black jeans and little white tank top. I think life has played a cruel joke on me. She's the sweet, nice girl I could bring home to meet Ma. Instead, I have to take raunchy pictures of her for Lenny Martin's smuttiest product. I don't know how to start the photo session.

He talked the next hour away and learned that she was an unemployed art teacher and was laid off because of declining enrollment. After six months, her money had almost run out.

"Rick, I can't bear to ask my parents for any more help. My dad's an unemployed aerospace engineer, so he and my mama are struggling too."

"I understand."

"Rick, let me get to the point. The week before, Lenny Martin walked by my Marina del Rey apartment pool and spotted me in a string bikini. He walked right up and offered me fifteen thousand to pose for his magazine."

"You have to admit that Lenny pays very well."

"Yes, he does. Anyway, he tells me"—she emphasized by holding her arms out and shaking them—"'Baby, beautiful Asian women like you are the *hottest thing in the business* right now. Lenny here can make you a *star*.'"

Rick bent over, laughing. "You nailed that imitation of Lenny perfectly. You are so cute, Mamie Lee."

"Thanks. Well, at first, I rejected his offer until Lenny told me that you were shooting the photos for him and showed me some of your work. I have to say that I was impressed by the tastefulness and gave right in."

"I'm glad that you did, sweetie."

"Well, I needed the money that badly, and at least you don't degrade your models. Jesus, I live in dread of my parents learning what I'm doing, my dad especially."

How come Rick seems so reluctant to start shooting? I have to ask him if anything's wrong.

She coughed before asking, "Rick, do you always take an hour to talk to your models like you are with me?"

"No, not really, I usually get right to it."

He silently agonized. *Man, I wish I was taking her out for dinner instead.*

Samuels dragged himself off the sofa and over to the equipment and set. Mamie pulled the tank top over her head and revealed breasts that were way up high and all her own and then dropped her jeans and underpants.

Oh, man, her naked body is perfect under the lights, taut and with skin smooth as silk. I'm having trouble, though, pulling the trigger. Mamie's trying to be casual about her nakedness but is rigid before the camera. I think her Asian modesty is making me feel guilt from her shame. Man, before Mamie, I couldn't have imagined wanting a beautiful, sexy woman to keep her clothes on.

"Mamie." Samuels tried to relax her while expecting three hours of mixed emotions ahead of him. "I'll protect you to the best of my ability. Direct views of your vagina will be few, with most obscured by soapsuds, sheets, or sheer cloth."

Afterward, both were uncomfortably silent while Rick wrapped up the shoot and broke down the set. Mamie beat up on herself.

What did I do? I know this is a mistake. What the hell? Let me tell him.

"Rick, I like you more than any guy I've met in a long time and don't know what to do about it."

"I like you too, Mamie," said Rick, pretending to play dumb. "So what's the problem?" He smiled innocently.

"Be honest, Rick. Nice girls aren't supposed to take their clothes off before cameras, especially for Lenny Martin."

Thank god I have the perfect answer. He gratefully looked up at the sky and then at her. "Well, the world's not supposed to be shitty to sweet, pretty ladies like you." He held Mamie in his arms and whispered in her ear, "I'm crazy about you, Mamie."

He nuzzled her neck and sweetly kissed her cheek and then her lips. Regarding the corruption part, he whispered, "Just see me as a working stiff lucky enough to get a preview of your outstanding body."

Mamie's worry ended, and she smiled happily.

"Hey, sweetie," he offered, "let me take you out for dinner and a movie. I haven't seen the new *Star Wars* film yet. Have you?"

He's so sensitive. I think I'm aroused. She pressed her still naked body up against him. "You know, Rick, this work can make you feel sexy."

I hope I've found the girl of my dreams. Rick looked up at the sky again. *I guess I'll find out as time is usually the test of dreams and reality.*

Yes, it is, Rick, for you have now discovered your second queen.

Chapter 21

In the main Kennedy Center dressing room in Washington DC, Carole Herman rolled up a $20 bill and snorted two thin lines of cocaine.

Hopefully, she wished, *a quick little buzz will get me up for a gala for one thousand Republican bigwigs.*

Carole almost never needed anything to get going, even coffee and especially cocaine, but tonight too many things had ganged up on her.

"Christ," David Conte preached, "why the hell are you getting coked up? You're too great a talent and star to do that and one of the real professionals."

"Please stick your advice and praise up your ass because it's *your* fault I'm doing coke."

He protested with both hands gesturing and mouth squinched up. "How the hell is it my fault, please?"

"It was your fault to book this gig, it was your fault to schedule a red-eye flight to DC, and it was you, asshole, who refused to reschedule. I think I might prefer to throw up than perform for a thousand Republicans."

I can put up with her complaints, but I'm not going to let her call me an asshole.

The stage manager knocked on Carole's door before he could defend himself. "Mrs. Herman, showtime is less than a minute away."

"Fuck it, I'll massage her neck and shoulders to ease her unusual preperformance jitters."

She looked at him and smiled. "How did you know that was exactly what I needed?"

He flashed a smile of appreciation. She acknowledged her bad attitude.

"David, I apologize for calling you names." She fondled him for a few seconds too, and he flashed another happy smile and massaged away.

"Your muscles are so damned tight. Jesus, I'm sorry, Carole, that I caused this physical stress that you're dealing with, so please go and make all those right-wingers eat right out of your hand."

Carole eased her nerves with a wisecrack. "Christ, an entire audience that's in opposition with everything I believe in. Jimmy Carter was almost fun compared with this crowd."

"Ha ha! Babe, I swear that you are more beautiful and sexy than ever."

She gave him a warm kiss on the lips and walked onstage with her white chiffon gown flowing. The spotlight found her, and the staid audience of government officials, GOP VIPs, big business leaders, military brass, and the Supreme Court justices politely applauded.

Carole warmed the crowd up with a big smile and then respected the Reagans.

"It's my very great honor and pleasure to perform for the president and the First Lady tonight and good to be back in Washington again."

The audience cheered and clapped loudly; the spotlight found the Reagans and the president and Mrs. Reagan stood, smiled, and waved to the audience.

The once divorced Carole plugged *Dora* and an upcoming TV special before moving into her first number, "I'll Always Love the First Man More." The medium-slow ballad, her current hit, had been on the Billboard charts for two months.

She finished. *Now let me move into a short medley of three of my biggest hits and end with 'Tortuga Flats,' my first platinum record.*

She rocked the GOP out of their stuffiness. *Good, the establishment is breaking out of their controlled shells a bit and starting to rock with me. Now that I have the crowd in hand, I can stop for a few minutes to catch my breath and kibitz with the audience.*

"Hmmm, I don't see or smell any funny cigarettes out there. Is it because you're all Republicans, or has Ed Meese packed the place with narcs?"

Atty. Gen. Ed Meese publicly pledged to bring new energy to the War on Drugs with the slogan "Just say no." President Reagan cracked up, the First Lady laughed hard too, and the crowd ate it up.

Three youthful pranksters in the close-in rows each threw a joint onto the stage, and they rolled right up to Carole's feet. The audience saw and gasped.

Carole stared down at the joints and then out at the audience. "You know, I think Caspar Weinberger can use them a lot more than me."

While the audience roars, I'll scoop the joints up and throw them back at the young guys who got the idea.

The audience held its breath, waiting for her next wisecrack.

117

"You sweet guys, please run them right over to the Pentagon pronto. It'll do Caspar a world of good."

She put her hands together to pray for Secretary of Defense Weinberger. *I killed them with that.*

She left the stage for a five-minute break and costume change and returned wearing a sequined denim suit and then swayed the crowd with a couple of progressive country tunes and soft California folk-rock ballads.

The audience provided her with a standing ovation for each of her inspirational closing numbers, "God Bless America" and "America the Beautiful." The Republicans clapped and roared their approval, and despite many calls for an encore, she did not return.

David, waiting for her in the wings, raved on and on about the smash performance he'd just witnessed.

"You were fantastic, babe. They love you. *You* transcend politics."

"Thanks for pushing me, David. You were right again. In fact, I'm actually pleased by how well it went and now very glad that I did it. They were a good crowd after all and surprisingly a lot of fun."

A secret serviceman knocked on the door. David opened, and the agent officially informed them, "Ma'am, the president and Mrs. Reagan are on their way to congratulate you on a great performance and personally thank you for doing the show. We just need a minute to clear the way."

Carole worried. *My world is show business, not politics. David's is show business, sex, and drugs, not real political either, but the Reagans are from show business, so I guess I can relax.*

The president and the First Lady entered, exuded warmth and good cheer, and offered one compliment after another. The president said, "Mrs. Herman, you are a very funny woman and my favorite female singer." The First Lady stated, "Carole, you are so beautiful and funny and sing like an angel."

I think I'm starting to like the Reagans very much. They are so nice to me. The president seems sharper and more engaged than people perceive. The First Lady generates real warmth and kindness and seems much softer and sweeter than her image.

President Reagan looked Carole in the eye as he spoke to her.

"It's late. You're probably very tired, and as a fellow Californian, I know all too well that flight you took this morning, so I promise to be brief. Ms. Herman, you are a national treasure, and your talent is universal. It touches every type of person on earth. Therefore, you're a natural ambassador for this country, and I would be grateful if you were to represent the United States of America abroad, performing concerts in selected countries. You and David will work with the White House and State Department to set up your tour and assist you with whatever you need."

The president's offer stunned Carole; her jaw dropped.

I wonder if Reagan remembers my long history of supporting Democrats and liberal causes in general. She had to know though. "I'm curious, Mr. President, are there any countries in particular that you might want me to visit?"

"Good question. Currently, there are a number of nations that we have strained relations with—first, the Russians, of course, and then to a lesser extent, our Israeli allies. From there, I think Egypt, France, and maybe Chile, Argentina, and Brazil and if you still have strength left, perhaps China and South Africa."

Carole felt overwhelmed and apprehensive of Reagan's generous and exciting proposal. She experienced qualms about politically bolstering the president, but he was providing her a great opportunity to see the world.

She was already thinking by the time the president finished, *Whom will I trot the globe with? David is not an appropriate cultural ambassador.*

"Mr. President," she responded to Reagan's proposal, "I'm extremely honored and flattered. I just wonder if I'm equipped for this. Five years ago, I was at Frank Sinatra's party for the king of Italy and was frazzled at the moment and told the king, 'Excuse me, Your Majesty, but I'm all screwed up tonight.'"

Reagan laughed warmly. "That's part of your appeal, Carole. You're so real and down-to-earth and lovable. Look, it's late, and we've taken enough of your time. When you're ready, call the White House and ask for Ted Bell, an intern we recently took on for projects like this."

"Good night, Mr. President and Mrs. Reagan, and thank you very much."

"Good night, Carole, and thank you, David. You did a great job putting this concert together and for a good cause too."

The Reagans departed, leaving Carole and David stunned. David, the less speechless of the two, said, "Wow, that was some offer Reagan made you. Are you going to take him up on it? I sure hope so."

"The Reagans are lovelier and much more tolerant than I'd given them credit for." She looked at David. "That offer is so incredible that I have to think about it for a while."

She thought, *I know David doesn't fit, and I have to start letting him know.*

"David, try to understand that I started performing almost every night from age sixteen on and got out of high school by the skin of my teeth. I was so desperate to pass U.S. history that I considered sleeping with my teacher to graduate. Luckily, I didn't have to. But since then, I've been immersed in show business, and it's all you and I know or ever talk about.

"The whole word is show business today, sweetheart."

"Be real. What are we going to talk about with all of those country's leaders? Man, you're even worse than Myron about talking Hollywood movie crap all the time."

"We'll throw ourselves into this." David turned to a salesman. "This guy Bell will brief us."

"When's the last time you read a newspaper editorial page? Man, the only thing I see in front of your face is the *Hollywood Reporter.*"

David sounded troubled. "Are you saying, babe, that you'd actually go without me, really?"

"Dear David, after Myron hurt me, you helped me heal, and you've easily been the best thing that's ever happened to me, but—"

Shit, I'm fucking worried that I'm losing her.

David then said out loud to her, "But . . . but what, babe?"

"Jesus, David." Carole sighed deeply. "You and I have kids from previous spouses, and it's doubtful we'll ever blend and marry. We also have some issues that I'd rather not get into right now." *She's floored me.*

He spoke emotionally. "Carole, the time apart might cause us to become strangers. Surely, you can't expect me to stay faithful while you tour the world for months at a time."

He knew the second he said it she was going to make him regret his words.

"Christ, you haven't been faithful for quite a while now. I know damn well that you've been sleeping with Greta Person again. I've just let it go because I admit I've not taken care of you lately."

"I appreciate hearing that, babe."

"Look, can we drop all this stuff for now? I'm tired as hell and just want to get back to LA to see my kids. They're home from school on break."

Chapter 22

In Westfield, New Jersey, Janet Cohen Kamensky dialed Rebecca Kartzman's Brooklyn phone number. Allie's mother, an old Roosevelt liberal, still dyed her hair dark brown and kept herself thin and well-informed.

In Sheepshead Bay, cheerful light-haired Rebecca picked up the receiver. "Rebecca, its Janet Kamensky."

"Janet, it's so good to hear from you."

"I hope things are great with you, guys. Max and I want to invite our terrific fellow in-laws to dinner next Saturday night."

Rebecca, a warm, loving earth mother, was renowned for invisibly slicing up full bowls of fruit that magically appeared in mere seconds. Allie swore that Rebecca once sliced up a bowl of fruit while carrying one of his luggage pieces up the front steps.

"We look forward to it, Janet," Allie's sweet short mother-in-law answered. "What time should we come?"

"Seven o'clock. Rebecca, you know, it's taken me years to accept that life in the South is far more promising for Allie and Sarah, your pretty and smart daughter."

"Thank you, but we think it's far more promising for us too."

Janet, surprised, asked, "Why? It sounded to me, last time we talked, that Harvey was building restaurants all over New York."

"Yes, but Harvey's also tired of bribing crooked building code inspectors hundreds of dollars to open each project on time. Worse, the other day, a check for a diner he built in Queens bounced. Try collecting a bad check from Johnny Dio and the Mafia."

"My god, a rubber check from the mob, that's really scary, so what are you going to do?"

"We're going to move to Atlanta to be near the kids and just sold our home and took the first bid, a real lowball offer too says Harvey."

"It's a brick row house, right?"

"Yes, a single dentist plans to convert it into a joint office and residence. We settled for less money than hoped for, but we're just glad to be getting out of New York."

"I'm very happy for you guys, but, Rebecca, have you found jobs yet or rented an apartment?"

"No, Janet," said Rebecca, amazing her. "We'll worry about jobs and a place to live later. Our aim is solely to be closer to the kids and soon-to-be-born grandson, we hope."

"I can't wait for the whole family, Rebecca, to gather in Atlanta for the birth of Allie's first child."

The front door of the first-floor garden apartment opened and distracted Janet. "Rebecca, it's Max returning from his adult education class. Every day he comes home hungry with low blood sugar, so I have to get off the phone and fix him lunch. Regards to Harvey. Bye now and love you, guys."

Max Kamensky, seventy years old, immigrated to the United States when he was eight. He was a very different man from Allie's father, now dead for a quarter of a century.

It's taken time for me to grow close to Max, thought Janet as she prepared his dish, *a man who's known only hard work his whole life. He does not warm my heart like Barney did and never will. We're good companions who have the same grandchildren and manage to make this arrangement work.*

She set the dish down on the table. *My biggest worry in life is that both of my children inherited their late father's extravagance. Carla lives a high-roller lifestyle, Allie merely beyond his means. Neither can save a dime. Barney's laxity over paying bills forced me to assume the role of handling family accounts. Max set me up for life, and I like the security and freedom from bill paying.*

Max—depressed after the death of his lovely first wife, Rosa—almost went mad from grief, so Carla kept hinting that Max should date her mother, and he finally did to escape his funk. The visits grew more frequently, and they were married a month after the unveiling.

Max owned a profitable meat market, invested wisely, lived frugally, and accumulated a modest fortune. Lately, Carla and Joel's fantastic borrowing against residential equity threatened his lifetime of savings and scared the crap out of him.

He occasionally said to Janet, "They can wipe me out just like that"—and he usually snapped his fingers—"by saving them from crashing and burning."

Max, it pains me to say, views Carla's spending as an insatiable debt creation machine and his son as a weak man unable to control his wife.

Janet dropped a big glop of sour cream on Max's mashed potatoes and told him of the Kartzman dinner engagement. She happily shared with Max how excited she was about seeing her new grandchild in two months.

Max, busy shoveling in his Polish gruel, said between mouthfuls, "Sure, Janet, anything you want."

Max developed a temperamental stomach in his late teens, and potatoes and sour cream bothered his stomach less than anything else. Janet stirred her saccharine-laced coffee and informed Max of the phone conversation with Allie the night before.

"His novel is starting to shape up, and he has so many other projects going. I tell you, Max, he never used to have such discipline. It's a miracle."

"Allie's grown up," said Max, who liked to give opinions. "He's accepted responsibility and found a nice girl. Unfortunately, they had to move far away to realize their dreams."

Max's perceptive remark almost brought tears to Janet's eyes.

"Max, the wandering Jew still exists. Back in the Old World, the Jews migrated to countries that permitted them to survive in shtetlach or ghettos. In America, the Jews move to cities where they can earn their best living or simply one at all. The way I see it, Max, is that very little has changed over the centuries."

You're right, Janet, but nothing will change until the people exalt your son, the prophet. Awe will empower Allie to lead the people, and they will hopefully follow him—or not.

Chapter 23

Rose Herman sat in a deck chair on her Malibu Heights condo porch high above the Coast Highway across from the beach.

Too bad my Sol didn't live to share this view of the Pacific Ocean with me. I was nineteen when we married and gave birth to Carole at twenty. The whole world has told me that I look like Carole's elder sister.

Sol and Rose spent forty happy years living on Batchelder Street in Sheepshead Bay.

I was shameless how I bragged about Sol—a small plumbing and heating contractor—*that he never gave me a hard moment and made a comfortable enough living to spend two weeks each winter at the Eden Roc Hotel in Miami Beach.*

Ironically, they lived around the corner from Rebecca and Harvey Kartzman and never met. Sarah Kartzman Cohen lived four blocks from her dear friend Riva Klein Forman. They were in the same grade, attended the same schools, graduated the same year, and never met until they both moved to Atlanta—tyical New York City story.

Rose looked at her watch. *Carole's late again, though I don't mind. I'm in no rush. The sun is warm and feels good on my face.*

The lone dark spot in Rose's mind was Carole's disorganized life. Her bright big spot was Sharon, her younger daughter, who was married to Dr. Lloyd Kaufman, a Westchester orthodontist, and had three lovely children.

My only wish is for Carole to settle down with a stable Jewish man like Lloyd.

The muffled roar of Carole's Porsche 928 revved up the driveway and shook Rose from her memories. She put away her aluminum folding chair and, as always, kvetched about Carole's car.

"Every time, I nearly break my back getting into this damned Pischer."

Carole corrected her mom as usual. "It's a Porsche, Mom, and I love this car almost as much as my kids."

Carole smiled at Rose while leaving the Coast Highway and turning onto Santa Monica Boulevard and then asked, "So, Ma, how are you doing today?"

Rose said "fine" and nothing more, her way of delivering a message to stop being late.

Carole heard her loud and clear. "I apologize for getting tied up in script revisions."

"You're forgiven."

"Ma, how come you don't take more advantage of David's beach bungalow? You have a key, you know, so use it once in a while."

"I did a few times but stopped going because of the sight of famous actors getting dead drunk in the afternoon. Can you believe it, Carole, world-famous men acting like assholes in the sunlight? It's so depressing. Several times, I've been tempted to give back the key, but the easy beach access does make it worth keeping."

"Still has to beat sitting in the Fontainebleau's shadows for twenty years." Carole cracked. "I don't recall once getting tan during all those winter vacations in Florida."

Rose didn't laugh. "Where are we going? I thought you and I were supposed to have lunch by the beach in Santa Monica? We're headed toward Beverly Hills."

128

"Change of plans, Ma, we're meeting an old friend of mine on Rodeo Drive."

She made a left onto it and drove into the valet parking service area. She and Rose got out of the car.

"You know, Mom, it's been two years since Papa died, and he always said that life was for the living. You're now out West for six months. It's time to start seeing someone nice, start dancing again too. That's where I get my love of dance from, Mom, from you. I remember you dancing to Broadway show tunes while dusting."

"I don't know, Carole, dancing is starting to hurt my feet. I think my dancing days may be over."

An Atlanta family with a darling seven-year-old boy was also waiting in the valet station. Carole couldn't take her eyes off him.

"My god, are you cute." She struck up a conversation, and he happily engaged her.

"My name is Shane. I'm Jewish, just skipped the first grade, and like Los Angeles a lot. When I get older, I want to come out here to live."

"Is that so?"

"I want to be a big movie star like you, and I like your new music video."

Shane's parents had tried to be inconspicuous and not bother Carole just because she was a big star. The father explained that they were rewarding Shane with a trip to California for skipping the first grade.

"One of these days," the father kidded, "Shane will break out of his shell."

Carole and Rose laughed hard. The movie star bent down to give Shane a hug and a kiss on the cheek.

"You are so adorable and smart. I can imagine how proud your parents are of you."

"Can I please have your autograph, Mrs. Herman?"

Carole smiled from Shane calling her Mrs. Herman and his use of the word *please*, a sign of respect. She took out a pen and wrote, "To Shane with love, Carole Herman."

Rose watched and took note. *I've seen Carole play the gracious-movie-star part many times before, but this time, I'm truly touched. This little boy really is adorable.*

As they walked out of the garage, Carole shocked her. "Ma, if God could guarantee me a kid like Shane, I'd get pregnant in a minute."

Rose was glad to hear Carole add a qualifier. "Relax, Mom, but it is time that you start sharing your life with a nice man."

"Carole, honey," Rose protested as they headed to the boutique hotel where the café was, "I'm not ready to date yet. I have friends. We go out. I just don't stay home. I'm also content to babysit my grandchildren when you're on location or touring."

"No, you aren't, Ma. You're only fifty-seven and too young to be alone. It's time for you to have a good man in your life again."

The Iranian-born maître d'hôtel sat them at a table in the café's back corner to shield them from attention. Sam Minkowitz was waiting and waved to them. Carole briefed Rose as they walked toward Minkowitz.

"Ma, Sam runs Global Media Enterprises Inc. (GMEI), the largest entertainment conglomerate in the world. He's one of the most powerful men in Hollywood and has his fingers in nearly everything."

"And he's single, Carole?"

"Yes, Sam was married thirty-seven wonderful years to Eleanor, a lovely lady who'd died of cancer ten months ago. It was Sam, Ma, who brought me out to Hollywood, who financed *Dora*, and who has been a kind of father to me."

Carole kissed Sam on the cheek and introduced him to her mother. Carole sensed an immediate chemistry between them when Sam smoothly kissed Rose on the cheek.

"Carole, I never knew you had such a young and pretty mother. My god, she could be your sister."

Sam looked into Rose's eyes and held her hand. "Rose, it is my great pleasure to meet you. I swear you look like Betty Bacall's daughter."

Rose's breath slowed from the comparison to Lauren Bacall; her pulse quickened from his attractiveness and didn't let up throughout lunch.

Sam fascinated Rose with his tales of big deals in the works, with the projects he was saving for Carole, and with whom he was just conferring.

"Carole," said Sam, surprising her, "I was speaking with Ronnie Reagan yesterday, and he told me about the State Department trip. Sweetie, let me know how I can help. We have apartments in almost every big city in the world that you can use."

Rose thought, *He calls him* Ronnie *Reagan and has apartments around the world. This guy is single? Did Carole have Central Casting send him over?*

They spent the better part of an hour schmoozing. Sam, who lived in Bel Air, excused himself—he had a meeting.

"Please forgive me, ladies. There's a producer at my house ready to arrange financing for his new film."

Sam kissed Carole on the cheek, hugged Rose, and kissed her on the cheek too.

"My mother"—Carole nudged Sam—"is a very good dancer, and I think it's time for her to dance again."

Sam looked deeply into Rose's eyes. "Rose, it'd be my pleasure to take you dancing. Carole, if I ever remake *Fiddler on the Roof*, I'm casting you as Yente, the matchmaker. I'll be in touch, Rose."

Rose's eyes smiled as Sam departed. Carole saw it. *Ma's blushing like a schoolgirl, and that makes me happy.*

"To think a nice man of that caliber is available." Rose marveled. "He could easily have a woman half his age."

"Sam needs a mature woman, someone he can really talk to, someone—"

"Enough with Sam and me, darling," Rose cut her off. "What's happening with you?"

"Ma, you'll be the first to know when there's a change in status."

"Honey," said Rose, penetrating her daughter's wall, "I don't like to meddle, but I feel it's time for you and David to either marry or go your separate ways. You're living in sin for three years. That stuff is for college kids, not mothers of twelve- and ten-year-olds, even if they are away at boarding school much of the year."

"I know, Mom, all right. One thing, a kind of Jewish renewal has come over me. The role sparked it."

Rose, using psychology, said, "Darling, are you thinking of marrying an Orthodox rabbi too? Dora was a make-believe character." And she sat back and held her tongue.

Carole stroked her chin while contemplating out loud, "Mom, I've made a wonderful life for myself in California and have no desire to ever live in New York again. Oddly, the type of man I need is probably living in Manhattan."

Rose wanted Carole to describe this mythical man and pressed her.

"Okay, a highly intelligent and successful man who will challenge me intellectually and spiritually, someone I can't dominate."

Carole reached Rose's condo, parked in the driveway and finished the conversation. Carole saw in her mother's face that Rose was sad.

"You're thinking about Myron, aren't you, Mom?"

Rose nodded without looking at Carole and spoke from her heart.

"Honey, no one was sorrier than me when you threw him out. Looking back, you should have given him another chance. Men are different from women that way, except your father, of course."

Rose's words dredged up remembrances of Carole's early years with Myron.

"We struggled, but we were happy, Ma, and then my career boomed. His languished, and reporters and waiters addressed him as Mr. Herman and not Silver, and he couldn't take it. I came home early one day and found him in bed with a nineteen-year-old model named Turkish. Years later, I still believe that he forced me to break up the family."

Rose changed the subject. "I'm mystified by Reagan's State Department tour. Is it possible that Reagan is overlooking your being on Nixon's enemies list?"

"I don't think he cares, but it is nuts, Ma, I know. I guess the president simply likes me and my act and thinks I'll create a lot of goodwill for the United States."

The Lord and I influenced President and Mrs. Reagan to impulsively visit Carole's dressing room and, in the name of bipartisanship, offer her the world tour. Carole Herman would play her role of a lifetime—an angelic peace advocate for Adonai.

Rose started to get out of the car but first urged her daughter, "Do your self a favor and end it with David today."

"Today's not the right time, Ma, but it might be soon."

"Good, well at least the first step has been taken, Carole."

That got Carole's attention. "What step is that?"

"Carole, dear"—Rose leaned in—"you are finally ready to have someone new walk right into your life and zap you."

Rose looked up at the sky. "God, please, no more handsome tall Christians. For me, Rose, send a cute, smart little Jew, and make it quick too."

We hear you, Rose, and he's on the way.

Chapter 24

Cohen looked up from his desk. *Ah, my sixth-period economics class has filtered in, and they're almost all here. I can't wait to leave for California, and thank god there's only an hour until Easter break. Time to start the lesson with a joke for the motivation.*

"It's Popeye's birthday today, class. Guess how old he is."

Carl Smalls, the son of a Coca-Cola executive, did a fine Ed McMahon impression. "How old is he?"

Allie delivered the punch line. "It's Popeye's fiftieth. Now he has to have his spinach strained." An unfunny groan echoed across the room.

Allie smiled and then announced, "Class, today's lesson is to evaluate how effectively Reaganomics is working. Reagan's supply-side theory is really trickle-down economics, which has been around longer than old geezers Popeye and Reagan."

The class laughed from his absurdly lumping Popeye and President Reagan together.

"Okay, let's put the president's performance to test to see if supply-side theory is just so much spinach or baloney. So far, we've had almost a year of deep recession."

Ed Mayfield, the brilliant son of a millionaire carpet manufacturer, sought a clarification.

"Doc, the theory *is* that if you cut taxes for the rich, consumers will go out and spend so much more that tax revenues will actually increase, the Laffer curve theory, correct?"

"Yes, that's the primary claim. Very good, Ed."

"And if you free producers of goods from regulations, Doc, they will be more efficient and productive. Innovation will thrive from freer markets, competition will lower prices, and the consumer will be rewarded."

"Yes, that's the secondary claim, Ed."

"Besides failing in the 1920s, Doc, as the Mellon tax cuts and leading to the depression, it's failing again and feeding the very sharks who take advantage of deregulation."

"That's all true, Ed, very good knowledge base, though a bit cynical. However, fraud and other unscrupulous actions *do* tend to increase when regulations are weakened."

"Social welfare programs," Amherst-bound Teddy Williams deduced, "have been cut badly, defense spending has skyrocketed, and interest payments on the national debt are soaring. That sounds to me, Doc, like we're paying just as much but getting less back from the government than before."

"That's a very interesting view, Teddy." Allie kept to him self that he strongly agreed.

"Doc," Diana Rubin, a shapely blond daughter of a pediatrician who got an early acceptance at Yale, questioned, "how come the media's not painting the same picture?"

Her friend Stacy Sanders summed it up for her. "The press, Diana, has been easier on Reagan than Carter, and the recession's made the public more tolerant of him, but I believe that most Americans genuinely like the Great Communicator."

Some pupils believed Reagan to be a great president; others thought him to be an amiable dunce. Cohen guided the debate by mostly sitting back and listening, and for a social studies teacher, this was as close to educational nirvana as it gets—a smart class of good kids practically teaching themselves.

The bell rang, and the students wished Allie a nice vacation and quickly left the room to start theirs. Cohen tried a new way home that day, and it took a little longer. He pulled up to his mailbox and separated three letters from a pile of junk mail.

Ah, the first correspondence is from Elliot Shapiro, a sociologist friend who's the education director of the St. Louis Antidefamation League. Very good, Shapiro's relaying information concerning Ralph Helms, my fictional antagonist, who is roughly based on a real-life person.

Dear Allie,

I'm sorry, but there is very little background on Professor Kicklighter. He is a mystery, even to his colleagues at the Missouri State University School of Agriculture. They report that he is a loner, that when he shows up at faculty parties accompanied by a female, he will be rude to her. I have spoken to students of his who say that he is one of the few professors who will not return a hello.

As far as personal data is concerned, we know that he comes from Omaha, that he is of German background, and that his father was with the Nebraska Board of Education. Kicklighter is in his late forties and lived shortly in New York as a boy. I wouldn't be surprised if he was scarred by youthful experiences in NYC during the traumatic WWII era, but this is pure speculation. There is no proof to suggest that he may be Jewish.

I wish I could be more helpful in providing you with insight concerning the character for your well-meaning novel. Take care, Allie.

Sincerely,
Elliot Shapiro

Allie had hoped for more because he'd learned some of this on his own, but it was still very helpful. The second letter was from Donald Merchant, President Reagan's deputy chief domestic adviser.

Merchant is responding to my senior-level sociology class's collective design of an urban reorganization plan that extends urban boundaries to the suburbs' limits to end white flight. Merchant thanks my class for submitting their detailed National Defense Metropolitanization Act (NDMA).

The third letter is from Paul Householder, the assistant secretary for urban affairs, who also thanks the class for their interesting proposal to Donald Merchant and hard work on behalf of their fellow Americans. Householder informs the class that NDMA requires massive federal intrusion at the local level and is out of step with the Reagan administration's policies that are committed to less interference from Washington, not more.

Householder admits NDMA, though anachronistic, has merit because it's a great educational project. Urban Affairs is proud to submit an example of exceptional teaching and student achievement to the congressional subcommittee for consideration.

He ends by frankly admitting that the NDMA proposal will probably wind up in Congressman Morris Winters's filing cabinet. The Urban Affairs Committee chair ironically represents a rural West Virginia district of mountainous hollows that has no town over two thousand.

I appreciate Householder's respect for my student's plan. It's my belief, though, that all the politically brain-dead Republicans know is no.

After dinner, Allie retired to his study to put things in perspective. *Two types of people generally migrate down south, the ambitious and the struggling. The former usually improve their situation. The latter survive a little easier.*

Sarah and Allie were ambitious ones because, over the next three weeks, an airline and a consortium of banks donated $22,500. With a surge of support from the business community, Cohen's original request for $2,700 for thirty teachers expanded to $47,500 for one hundred educators.

Cohen reviewed his novel's altered plot. *Manny Kaplan, a tough New York street kid, taunts and humiliates young Ralph Helms. The provocation feeds anti-Semitism caught from Helms's bigoted father. His hatred is nurtured by a perverse intellectual curiosity that manifests in writing that the Holocaust is a Zionist hoax.*

Sarah and Allie got into bed early. Allie watched the Playboy Channel for the first time; the cable installer had turned the home erotica on that afternoon.

I need arousal help these last six weeks of pregnancy. He rationalized. *Sarah's not ready to abandon sex yet, and the channel may help a little and give her hope for a few more times.*

Early the next morning, Sarah drove Allie to the airport. He begged her to please leave him in front of the terminal and skip the trip to the gate. Sarah smiled and kissed him goodbye, and he disappeared into the world's busiest airport.

An hour later, Allie was flying over Memphis, and a recurring thought came to him. *California's a place where the inhabitants come from somewhere else to be something different from what they were. The state is so damn seductive that, each time I visit, it almost makes me want to stay.*

Welcome to Hotel California, prophet.

Chapter 25

Look at that huge orange sun hanging languorously in the dusky sky over the blue Pacific.

Carole thought while admiring the sunset and turning the Porsche off the Coast Highway and onto Malibu Canyon Road.

Hey, that's a pretty good lyric for a folk-rock ballad I'm working on.

She pulled into her garage and thought about New York as she got out of the car and entered the kitchen. *California's natural beauty is, for me, the best part of living here. Just the thought of Manhattan's crowded sidewalks starts to bring out tensions in me.*

Carole thought about her old neighborhood. *The community I grew up in, Sheepshead Bay, has dissolved into a world full of strangers, mostly Russians, Asians, blacks, and Hispanics now from what Ma's told me.*

This modern circumstance, according to me, Gabriel, was created by the Jews' drive for upward social mobility and success. The community's young American Jews grew up in dissolves, and they must make their career and lives somewhere else. I differ with Carole and think that her old neighborhood is thriving because of the new ethnic groups.

Malibu, ironically, has become my home or whatever that means out here.

During the filming of *Dora*, David built Carole a magnificent eight-thousand-square-foot contemporary house on six acres of enclosed canyonlike land that faced and opened to the ocean. The materials were natural and beautiful—light adobe brick, exposed wooden beams, vast expanses of glass, lots of tile, and special wood and ceramic inlays imported from all over the world. The house was also solar heated, elaborately landscaped with desert vegetation, and richly decorated with soft earth tones.

Conte, with his exquisite taste, personally supervised the construction and interior decoration and brought it in for a shade under thirty million.

David, astride a golden palomino pony and wearing a collarless white shirt, his long brown hair blowing in the wind, rode right up to Carole. He descended the horse and tied it to the hitching post.

He's so fucking handsome he could have been a movie star too. Funny he hates acting and directing but surprisingly enjoys editing a lot. Go and figure.

David loved most the deal-making part of the business and the ideas and energies that flow from it.

David approached Carole to kiss her. "Darling," he suggested, "why don't we sit on the back patio, drink some Chardonnay, and watch the sun set over the ocean?"

He has so many fine qualities. Carole assessed. *If only I could cut off half his dick, this might still work.*

She laughed at what had just popped into her brain and made conversation. "Isn't it wonderful how Sam and Rose are getting it on? I'm so happy for my mother."

"Rose," David commented, "is a smart lady. After all, she's your mother."

Carole braced for the business talk that usually followed the flattery.

"Sweetie, I heard that Noel Seymour wants you for his latest comedy. I think it's a good role for you. So you think you'll do it?"

"Maybe." Carole shrugged. "I don't know."

She gave it a second thought. *I'm well aware of David's uncanny knack of knowing what's right for me. I also expect him to push me to do it.*

"Carole, there must be ten million women out there going through the same changes as the chick in the Seymour script. Noel's comedies are big box office. If you pass, Jane Fonda or Bette Midler will probably scarf it up."

I won't answer him. My silence will probably say everything.

He got it and more. "So you are going to take that trip without me, and that's why you're being so evasive."

"Yes, I think so." She wondered why she could never keep anything from him. "David, I invited my mother to join me in Israel along with the kids. Why don't you also meet up with us?"

Rose predicted that she'd weaken, and she was right.

David considered the invitation before answering, *I'm not thrilled by the offer, especially with Rose and the damn kids.*

"I don't know, Carole, Israel must be hot as hell in the summertime. Let me think it over." He changed the subject. "Want to smoke some sinsemilla with me? Peter Bates laid it on me, and man, it's easily the best shit I've had in a long time."

"You're depressed, aren't you, David? You always get stoned after learning of news that you don't want to hear."

"No, you're wrong. Seriously, look at this bud."

David pulled apart the half-foot-long resinous bud, the flower of the most powerful female plants. He broke it up, rolled a joint, lit it, and held the smoke in his lungs.

Further communication is unlikely, acknowledged Carole. *The setting, though, is so lovely that I think I'll join him and take a hit or two.*

She took three hits, felt nicely stoned, and suggested to her housemate, "David, why don't you grill some fish and sweet corn and I make salad and garlic toast and open another bottle of wine? Doesn't that sound good? Then let's fuck the night away."

He held her hands. "Darling, I'd love nothing more. But unfortunately, we can't."

"How come, David? My god, you must be horny as hell." She was stunned that he'd turned her down.

"Sweetie, we have plans with Peter and Daria Kelsey to go to Nate'n Al Deli in Beverly Hills. They'll be over soon, so maybe you want to wash up and change."

"I thought the two of us could use a night together, not with Peter, whom I don't trust, and Daria, that name, I'm almost tempted to call her diarrhea."

"They are always very nice to you," said David, defending his friends. "So what do you have against them?"

Carole chose silence over disputing his friend's sincerity and examined Peter Bates's life, one of Hollywood's leading actors. Bates had made only thirteen films in twenty years, seven of which were monster hits. He invested smartly, was reportedly worth fifty million, and had screwed most of his leading ladies and dozens more, his pattern being to grow bored after a hot one- or two-month fling and then drop them.

She finally answered him, "Okay, David, I admire Peter's looks and talent, but his scruples and attitude disgust me."

"C'mon," David differed. "Tell me one thing he ever did to you."

"Okay, Happy Trails, remember last year when he dropped over with a movie deal and you went riding off shortly after?"

He nodded yes. "As soon as you were up the beach, Peter jumped into my shower, *naked*. Man, I was so outraged that I took a sandalwood soap by the string and knocked him right in the nuts. That stopped him, and when I threatened to tell you, to ruin his deal, he left that second. You get it now why I don't trust him."

David drolly asked, "Is that all he did?" She eyed him. "Seriously, I'm sorry that happened to you, and thanks for telling me. What can I tell you, Carole? He's Peter Bates, and the rules are different for him."

They both laughed, and she dressed quickly and finished David's joint to tune out Peter and Daria's talk. During the drive to Beverly Hills, Peter presented David with a two-picture deal with screenwriter Bob Urban, who'd recently clashed with Conte over contractual differences.

"Sorry, Peter, I won't work with Bob again. The cocksucker sued me last month."

"David, be straight with me. You shook on a deal and then reneged on it. That's called breach of contract. Bob had already lined up financing. You're liable. Be reasonable."

"I don't think I am. I just met with my lawyer, and he's preparing a case against Bob. We're deciding whether to sue the prick for more money than he's suing me. Fuck him."

At the table, Peter positioned himself next to Carole while urging David to put the past conflict with Bob behind him and both to drop their lawsuits. She removed Peter's hand from her inner thigh before the pickles arrived. Not ten seconds later, he put it on her other thigh, and she again removed it.

Carole studied the menu. *The pot's given me the munchies, so I think I'll order the night's special, stuffed cabbage, though I never liked my mother's version, which my sister Sharon swears is Rose's best dish, and Ma is a very good cook.*

Daria volunteered how she broke into show business. "I began an affair with Billy Diamond, the neurotic Jewish comic actor, but I wouldn't fuck him until he gave me the leading female role in his new film. I guess we had such good sex that he also starred me in his next two films."

Everyone always describes Billy as a neurotic Jewish actor. Carole viewed Diamond's public image. *He's actually very rational, hardworking, and not neurotic at all. He wasn't bar mitzvahed and don't think he ever saw the inside of a shul one day in his blessed life.*

Carole shared, "Daria, I also dated Billy a few times, and he currently rents my Central Park East apartment. I am still good friends with him. In fact, he's confirmed for *Dora's* screening. As much as I like him, though, I could never bring myself to sleep with him. He's one of the funniest men I know but just not sexy to me."

Carole wondered if maybe she was being too hard on Peter, but not for long though. His hand soon squeezed her behind.

I must remove it before he feels I'm encouraging him. She gave Peter a discreet look to cool it.

After dinner, Peter and Daria invited Carole and David back to their beach house.

"Hey, guys, let's swallow some ecstasy, the new *love drug* everybody's doing."

David's eyes lit up, but Carole declined. "I'm sorry, Peter, but the stuffed cabbage was a dumb choice and has badly disagreed with me. I think I need to go home and sleep it off. We'll take a rain check on that. Good night."

David and Carole hardly spoke to each other during the ride back to Malibu. As soon as they arrived home, he questioned her, "Why'd you lie? You don't have a stomachache."

Truth has liberating qualities, and Carole didn't hesitate. "Actually, the stuffed cabbage *is* bothering me, and I've been making silent farts since we dropped them off, but that's only reason number two."

He asked, "So what's reason number one?"

"I simply wasn't in the mood, David, for swimming in the nude with them and swinging in the bedroom."

David defensively said, "C'mon, Carole, you know damn well that I would never let something like that happen."

"That's bullshit, David. After some ecstasy and sinsemilla, Peter talks us all into taking off our clothes. They both come on to us, and we head to the hot tub to start fondling and fucking right in front of each other. I'm telling you, that script was written."

David strongly disagreed. "How can you be so sure of that?"

"Because tonight his hands were all over me in the restaurant, and he almost wore me down. Tonight I might have relented if I was high enough, but sorry, not going there." Carole turned and walked away from him.

"Where are you going, babe?"

"To the bathroom. I'm a little nauseous from that shitty stuffed cabbage. I should have played it safe and ordered a corned beef or turkey sandwich. You live and learn."

Chapter 26

"Shit!" cursed Greta, who was spending the afternoon of April 11 in the back of a Burbank TV studio, growing more depressed by the minute.

The fucking bitchy gay casting director switched my position from first to last, and I have to get over to Rick's soon.

Greta was competing against five talented young actresses for an important part in a prime-time soap opera. With each girl's audition, she felt a good, cathartic role slipping further away from her.

She called Rick, who picked right up. "Rick, this little gay prick of a casting director is tormenting me. I think that I'm going to be pretty late."

"Don't worry, sweetie, I'm headed to the airport to pick up an old buddy flying in from Atlanta. We'll shoot the scene this evening, and good luck with the part."

"You're a doll, Rick, thanks. I'll pick Reny up on my way over to Laurel Canyon."

"'Sounds great, Greta, and thank you."

Allie is going to love watching these two ladies in action. I'm eager for Allie to meet Mamie too. Our relationship has developed so nicely the past month or so.

Mamie and Rick waited while Allie deplaned and headed toward the baggage claim. The old friends saw each other and embraced.

"Rick, it's great to see you again, and who is the lovely lady?"

"Allie, this is my girlfriend, Mamie. We're first going over to her place for a homemade Chinese dinner, and then I have special surprise for you this evening."

While Mamie prepared the meal, Allie praised her to Rick.

"'Have to tell you, man, Mamie is the whole package—beauty, intelligence, and refinement. You did well, my friend, and the delicious smell coming from the kitchen tells me she can cook too."

Mamie set before them an exquisite spread of spareribs, crispy fish, and sautéed asparagus and mushrooms with rice. The three of them consumed the spareribs until Mamie's younger sister, Libby, joined the group. Mamie passed the plates of the fish, rice, and vegetables around the table while introducing her sister.

"Rick, Allie, this is my sister Libby who, believe it or not, is not my twin. She's fourteen months younger than me. Trust me, we are as different as two clones could be."

Libby sat down close to Allie and immediately put her hand on his thigh just below his left ball. Cohen, surprised, looked at her, his mind racing. *She's sure not modest or demure like her sister.* He channeled his nervousness into telling a Jeffrey Picker story.

"Jackie Kahn, Sarah, and I were lounging around Jeffrey Picker's house when an incredibly built and beautiful girl named Greta stopped over to make it with Jeffrey."

Libby put her hand on Allie's dick and gently rubbed it. He looked at her, dumbfounded, but continued talking.

"Well, Greta's neckline plunged below her nipples and intimidated my modest Sarah, who is very sexy in her own way. I think Greta worked for David Conte as a model. He owned a dress factory back then."

Rick was watching the interplay between Libby and Allie and laughed.

Allie just looked at Libby, dumbstruck again, but he's enjoying himself too much to stop her. Mamie's eyeing her sister to stop. Libby's ignoring Mamie and rubbing Allie harder. Man, is he loving it.

Allie savored his good fortune. *Wow, I'm only in LA two hours, and a gorgeous Chinese chick is playing with me right at the table. Who could imagine such a thing happening? Fuck the rest of this story. No one really cares that I smoked a joint with two of the Eagles.*

Mamie eyed her sister to cease because Allie did not know what to do.

Should I stop her? Cohen thought. *I don't want to, but Mamie's face is frozen. Rick is smiling his ass off. Damn, Libby's the hottest and most sexually aggressive Asian girl I've ever met. She just unzipped my fly, worked her way through my underpants, and is stroking my penis.*

Let me get Allie out of here before he embarrasses himself. Rick pulled Allie up by his arm.

Libby removed her hand but whispered in to Cohen's ear, "I love the power and control that gives me—you know, make men hard and pull the fucking come right up out of them."

"Shame on you, Libby," Mamie scolded. "Give it a rest. Jesus."

Allie smiled and scratched his head. "That's very interesting, but I believe you just really like pleasuring men."

Libby smiled and then let loose a loud laugh. "Funny. I guess I do like pleasuring men. I always thought I was just trying

149

to be the opposite of my sister, who was the perfect little Chinese girl growing up. I like being crazy because it's a lot more fun."

"And a lot more trouble," said Mamie, adding her two cents, "which is something you've certainly given Mom and Dad in spades. This *was* a nice meal until you came in and literally assaulted Allie, who was a stranger. You seem to need sex all the time. Maybe you should do porn and get paid for it since you hardly work and contribute to the rent."

Libby just sat there listening and smiling while Mamie scolded her. After Mamie finished, Libby shocked them.

"Porn star, eh? You know, that makes a lot of sense given my love of sex and exhibitionist nature in general. You know, big sister, I can break in giving hand jobs and gradually advance to bolder shit. Seriously, I need to think about this."

The sister's frank exchanges amazed Rick and Allie. Mamie apologized for her sister as she escorted them to Rick's car.

"Allie, Libby's a dominant and likes to take over a situation and means it when she talks about controlling men like that. After doing that to a couple of guys last year, I put my foot down, and she promised never to do it again and has been pretty good lately. She has a thing, though, for guys who look like Al Pacino, and you're almost a double. I know that it sounds nuts, but I'm sure it triggered her."

"Mamie, it's strange. I both want to apologize to you and thank Libby for being so *friendly.*" He coughed. Mamie and Rick laughed.

"Have a good time with Greta and Reny tonight," teased Mamie. "And try not to corrupt Allie too much. My sister already did a pretty good job."

"How'd you know about tonight?" said Rick, his brow showing a sweat bead or two.

"You left your appointments book open the other day, and I couldn't help glancing at it," said Mamie slyly. "My god, what a job, Rick, envisioning sexual fantasies all day long and producing them right in your own living room. That's pretty damn good work, if you can get it."

Allie bent over laughing. "That's one of *my* regular lines." They drove away and headed back to his place.

Rick shared with Allie during the drive, "You can see why I'm crazy about Mamie. I'm a little concerned, though, where we're headed."

"What do you mean?"

"You heard Libby talk about porn. Well, Mamie's nude photo spreads for me are breaking circulation records. She's already the highest-paid model in the business, and publishers are throwing offers and money at us. I can't help it, but it puts ideas in my head of these two gorgeous Asian sisters maybe doing porn and me producing them. Triple-X video sales and rentals are exploding, and I'm a purist doing tasteful nudity. Maybe I'm missing the fucking boat."

"I understand, but you're a great photographer. Is it possible to be a great pornographer?"

Rick considered that. "I think the better question is, can I produce high-quality hard-core video? I believe yes if the girls are gorgeous enough, the guys can act, and you have high production standards."

"I see your vision, Rick, but know that you will soon be bothered by exploiting the girls sexually. I suggest that you develop a stable of four and make them your partners. Help them get rich too. That's the only justice in porn, Rick, to get rich, and it's not the girls who own the big mansions in the valley."

"That's a good idea, Allie, and you're right. I will hate myself if I become a pig like so many of the big pornographers."

"Yo, Mamie hinted at some corruption thing. Please tell me about it, ol' buddy."

Rick described the shoot while turning into his street. "I'm doing a layout for a *Penthouse*-type rip-off that does even uglier things with women's pussies. The best that I can do, in this case, is to make them less ugly, but with these two girls, it's easy. Guess who one of them is."

He smiled impishly. Allie shrugged ignorance. "Greta Person, uh-huh. 'Bet you're surprised, and her friend Reny, she's a hot little brunette. Ooh ooh, you're really gonna like her."

"Frankly, Rick, I doubted you could continue forever making a good living doing only tasteful soft-core."

"Until today, Allie, I thought I really could, even though Lenny Martin makes it very hard for me. He throws tons of money at me, tells me he loves me, and then makes me shoot ever raunchier stuff. I tell him that, at some point, even I can't make the picture tasteful. It's funny. Today I suddenly feel like, why fucking bother anymore?"

"I'm weeping for you. Do I have orchestra-level seats for a sex scene tonight?"

"More like at the fifty-yard line with the coach."

They both laughed hard as Rick pulled in to the driveway.

"Rick, I think I see Greta and Reny waiting for us in the garage and wearing—well, it's not enough material to describe it as an outfit, is it?"

"They're in work clothes, Cohen, and $17,500 is at stake here, so let's get going, man." They both giggled.

Allie made himself comfortable in a director's chair right by the camera while Rick directed the girls.

"Here is the script, ladies, that you'll act out in fourteen photos spread across eleven pages. The two of you meet in a hot tub, become attracted to each other, and make it with a member of the same sex for the first time."

Greta experienced difficulty getting into the role. "This is a little hard for me, Rick. Reny and I are straight."

"I understand, sweetie, so take your time to find your zone. Your face tells me you're trying to hide that the bitchy gay casting director dismissed you without an audition and that you're still trying to get over it. It's his loss, the stupid little prick."

"Thank you, Rick. You're always so understanding and supportive."

Allie watched Greta and Reny use a method-acting trick to get into the role. They failed, so Reny lifted her block with four tiny toots of coke, twice in each nostril. Greta borrowed the spoon and followed suit. Allie passed the joint to the girls, who each took two big hits and were ready for action.

"Okay, girls," Rick coaxed, "let's try a couple of bisexual clutches. We'll consummate your new exploration of the joys of lesbianism. Now give me some exaggerated heavy petting . . . Now more tender petting. Yeah, that's good. Now pretend to touch each other down there and hold the hand maybe a quarter inch away. Nice, it's always such a pleasure to work with you, ladies."

"Okay, my beauties," Rick commanded, "it's time to get naked."

Cohen's breathing slowed down, and then he got up to follow Samuels around as he clicked away on his trusty Canon.

Rick's focusing his camera on the girls' vaginas is making me horny. I don't think I can resist temptation tonight. I'm too fucking aroused from watching Reny perform oral sex on Greta.

Rick wrapped up the shoot. "Allie, roll another joint please."

Cohen smiled at Samuels, who passed around a plate with four tablets of ecstasy. Everyone swallowed a tablet as if taking a vitamin pill. Cohen completed his rolling task while Greta's left breast settled against his arm. Reny sat on Allie's lap, and he passed the joint to her, the nudity a heady brew.

Let me fire up this joint and rub Reny's tight little ass.

She smiled at his touch, and that encouraged him to fondle her beautiful full breasts and arouse her nipples. Reny guided Allie's finger into her vagina and moved it in and out, and she quickly became very wet and hot.

Greta gave Allie a look that screamed "hey, man, I'm missing out on some good action here."

Allie took care of Greta with his other hand, a manic glee driving him. Rick replaced Allie's finger with his own middle digit. Greta opened wide to receive him.

Rick quipped to Allie as he led Greta into the bedroom, "It's good to be ambidextrous. Thanks for warming her up for me."

Reny and Allie enjoyed a half hour of saturated sex until Rick and Greta returned. Rick passed around another joint, and then the partners swapped and shared the waterbed.

Greta, Allie thought while fucking, *is the largest woman I've ever experienced. Although a treat, I prefer smaller women like Reny - or Sarah. I've been a good husband during pregnancy, and I'm rationalizing that I'm being rewarded with an incredible release. Shit, I better focus on Greta or risk going soft.*

Both couples experienced powerful orgasms within minutes of each other, after which Greta and Reny quickly opened up to Rick about how men had used them sexually their whole lives.

"If this is our fate in life, Rick," Greta reasoned, "why not make it really work for us? My daddy always said to turn a negative into a positive."

Reny cracked up. "My mother always said that too. Anyway, Rick, when I turned thirteen, every time in class, when I walked up the aisle to get a test or sharpen my pencil, boys started grabbing my ass, and it's been like that ever since. Yet if it weren't for this job tonight, I couldn't make rent, and I don't want to live like that anymore. Greta, what do you think, girl? What, we have three, maybe five smoking hot years left?"

Greta nodded that that sounded right. Reny continued. "Greta and I need to get rich now and think we're ready to do porn, and we need you to be our producer and partner."

Rick hugged them both. "There must be a convergence happening. I was just saying the same thing to Allie on the way over here."

Rick suggested to Reny and Greta, "Ladies, I have two beautiful Asian dolls in mind to join in this venture and believe the four of you, magnificent women, will take the business by storm and revolutionize it."

The party ended at 1:00 AM; the girls excused themselves, and Rick and Allie sat around drinking single-malt Scotch for a couple of hours and covered a lot of ground.

"I think, Rick, I've acclimated to California as all thoughts of Atlanta and home are vanishing from my consciousness. My body time is 6:00 AM, and it's catching up to the time zone. I think I'm ready to go to sleep."

Rick suddenly remembered. "Believe it or not, but I'd forgotten to tell you. Greta has gotten us invited to a screening party at Carole Herman's home tomorrow night."

Allie's eyes lit up. "Now that's what I call exciting. A private screening at a movie star's house like Carole Herman, man, Samuels, you're connected big-time. You know, Rick, David Conte is a fucking magician of sorts."

"Why?" He sipped some more Scotch. "Because I absolutely agree with you on that."

"Although I've always admired Carole's talent, I felt that she was a bit too middle-of-the-road for my taste. Conte retooled her career a few years back, gave her a hipper image, and even made a fan of me. My sister, Carla, has loved Carole since her early Broadway show tunes days. My mother just thinks she sings loud."

Rick, in between sips of Scotch, said, "Well, like your sister, I'm a fan of hers from the get-go and love her more than ever. Conte *has* worked miracles. I'll tell you, man, I'm dying to do her next album cover."

"I know, Rick, even teens dig her now. She's probably become the biggest Jewish star in the world today, and we're going to preview her new movie. That's really cool."

Yes, it is, Allie. Carpe diem. Seize the day, prophet.

Chapter 27

Greta turned onto Sunset Boulevard to access the Coast Highway.

"Reny, I have to meet you-know-who, so where do you want me to drop you off, sweetie?"

"The Comedy Store. Terry is scheduled to do the last show. I'll go home with him. He's lusting after me like a rat in heat."

"That's okay, Reny, Terry's a comedian whose career is really taking off. I hear a TV show is in the works, so you know what, you could do a lot worse."

"And you, Greta, could do a lot better. Christ, he's never going to leave Carole when you hop right into bed with him every time he snaps his little finger." She snapped her finger. "Forget him already. You're only hurting yourself."

"Jesus, Reny, you're hardly the one to play 'Dear Abby.' Look, I know you're only saying that for my own good, but what can I do? I love him, and I simply pray he'll do something to make her throw him out."

Greta deposited Reny in front of the Comedy Store; Terry Cunningham's name headed the marquee.

Reny left Greta with "I'm sorry if I was a little hard on you, girl. I mean, who am I to judge you? Me who's ready to do porn."

Greta stared straight ahead. "It's time to grow up. I'm not going to win any Oscars and can barely pay the rent too. Funny, sometimes the smart thing to do isn't the right one."

"For me, Greta, it's Rick. I trust him to act in our best interest. I can't work for a pig that only sees me as a piece of meat, calls me slut and that shit, feels it his right to come in my fucking mouth or eyes. No, I need someone who, at the end of the day, still sees me as a person and values what I did for him. I think that's Rick."

"I agree, Reny, but by taking this step, we have to get really fucking rich so we can easily take care of ourselves, also be able to start over new in an open place like San Francisco, Seattle, or even New York. I'll never be able to go home to North Dakota again, that's for sure. My dad already prays for me every day."

"My pa," Reny revealed, "raped me when I was in the eighth grade. He stuck his finger in me and tried to make me suck his cock and fuck him, said it was his right to have me first since I was probably putting out already. My ma saw him, got his gun, and shot him dead. They sent her to prison for thirty years because he was a cop, even though she saved me from a rapist, my fucking pa. I hardly got any family to go home to anymore or anywhere."

"I didn't know. Jesus, so sorry that happened to you. Look, Reny, I'm running really late and have to head out to Malibu. Bye."

Greta roared down the strip and out to the Coast Highway.

"Shit, I'm an hour late and he's going to be pissed. Better step on it and hope I don't get a ticket."

She plotted silently. *He's supposed to be doing last-minute editing changes, so time is precious. This hit-and-run shit makes me feel used, and I swear I'm going to give him crap for it.*

Greta parked next to David's Land Rover, skulked around to the back of the bungalow, opened the door, and was chastised instead of greeted.

"Christ, Greta, you're late again. Thanks to you we only have a lousy hour to get it on, so hurry and take off your clothes because I'm horny as hell."

What a miserable shit. I'm going to bust his balls good for that.

158

She set him up by speaking sweetly. "I need some music to get in the mood. Where's the stereo? I want to play this new album."

"The hell with the music!" he yelled. "C'mon, let's get it on already!" She looked disapprovingly at him. "Okay, it's in the bedroom." He pointed the way.

A minute later, when Carole's voice boomed out of the speakers, he bolted over to the turntable and smashed the record against the wall.

"You think you're pretty cute, don't you, Greta? Well, I didn't dig that at all."

"You didn't dig it?" His obnoxious behavior freaked her out. "Well, fuck you because I'm out of here."

She pulled down her sweater, the denial of sex frustrating him.

"Come on, Greta, chill out, okay? I'm sorry, all right?"

Greta found the courage to demand he show more respect for her. "Christ, you don't even talk to me anymore. You just expect me to jump into bed, get you off, and get lost. Well, I've made up my mind. Move in with me tonight, or it's over."

"I can't. The timing is bad. C'mon, babe, just give me six more months."

He's humiliated me for the last time with that line.

Greta ranted, "My god, it'll always be another six months. Sorry, I've run out of patience."

He tried to calm her by kissing her on the lips. "Fuck you, David, leave me alone."

159

"Please, Greta," appealed David. "You know this isn't the right time, and we're wasting every precious moment."

He pulled up Greta's sweater and began sucking on her nipple. He instantly aroused her, but she pulled away.

"Wait, you son of a bitch, there's something I want you to do for me."

"As long as it's reasonable, I'll be glad to."

"I have a single nonnegotiable demand. I want to attend tomorrow night's screening with three guests."

He took his mouth off her nipple. "That's not reasonable. We already have over forty people coming, and there's no more room."

Greta pulled down her sweater. David started to lose his erection.

"Okay, you win, but be cool around me, you hear?"

Oh my god, that's the first time he ever gave in to me on anything.

She seductively removed her clothes and fell into bed with him. Their quarrel heightened their urges, and the makeup sex was better than ever.

No other man makes me feel as complete. With him, I don't need drugs or hot tubs or whatever to get off. If only I can get him to leave her.

David thought, *Greta's body is virtually sculpted to fit mine. No other woman has ever turned me on sexually like her. If only she were smarter and more talented, I'd actually consider marrying her.*

Chapter 28

Rose and Sam enjoyed a lavish dinner party with three other GMEI executives and their wives. The golden-aged sweethearts glowed like they hadn't since the deaths of their beloved spouses. Both were reliving the wonder and pleasure of enjoying the company of another person and caring for them.

Sam put down the top of his white Rolls-Royce for the cruise back to Rose's Malibu condo, the delightful warm breezes sweeping Rose's hair back.

It's been a long time since I felt romantic and alive like this. She swooned. *Sam has proved himself a gentleman, and I'm ready to open my heart to him.*

Rose moved close to him and rested her hand on his thigh.

"I don't want this evening to end yet, I know." She impulsively suggested, "Instead of going back to my place for cake and coffee, let's use David's bungalow to sit by the ocean. The full moon and the sea air will be nice."

"I love your idea." He impressed her with "Please open the glove compartment."

She did and found a bottle of Dom Pérignon champagne. "I brought along a little bubbly to celebrate our first month together."

He's so good, she thought, *even better than my Sol in some ways, and God broke the mold with Sol.*

Rose nestled in even closer to Sam and rubbed his thigh. *I can't wait to get two wineglasses and a bottle from the kitchen and snuggle on the patio love seat. I may even touch him a bit down there to show him how much I like him.*

They pulled in the bungalow's driveway. Rose freaked out.

"Sam, the bungalow is supposed to be empty, so why are two cars parked here? I recognize David's Land Rover. Why isn't he in the studio editing film? Who does this purple VW convertible belong to also? Sam, I don't like this."

Rose impulsively got out of Sam's car and walked around to the back entrance. In a forceful whisper, she said, "This is bad, Sam."

Sam figured fast. *I know what Rose is going to find, and I have to try to stop her.*

"Rose," he whispered back out through his side window, "why don't we take a rain check? Cake and coffee at your place are fine too."

"No, Sam, something wrong is going on here, and I have to find out."

Sam nervously watched her. Rose turned the key and mumbled, "The door's unlocked. I'm dumbfounded. How could they leave such a valuable property open?"

Rose walked inside and toward a shimmering red light in the master bedroom. She stuck her head inside the dimly lit room; her heart pounded when she saw two large naked bodies having very physical intercourse.

Their moaning sickens me. David is grunting like a pig, and who the hell is the blonde on the bottom receiving him? It sure isn't my Carole.

David and Greta climaxed and jolted Rose, who fled from the cottage.

Sam saw her exit and called out to her. "Rose, are you all right?"

"Who does that little VW convertible belong to?" she asked Sam.

He sighed. "I've used Greta Person in a few small parts as a favor to David."

Sam thought, *I fear a volcanic reaction and must choose my words carefully.*

"Rose, please use caution here. Carole might not want you to expose him."

"Sam, maybe in the past but not anymore. Please, how long has this been going on?"

Sam shrugged and sighed again. "Three years ago, they were a hot number until David got out of the dress business and moved in with Carole. About a year ago, they began fooling around again. I suspect that Carole and David are having sexual problems, but that's really none of my business."

Sam's Rolls quietly chugged up the steep hill leading toward Rose's townhouse. He pulled in the driveway and turned the car off to talk.

"You say that you love Carole," said Rose, trying to understand Sam's behavior. "How could you let this go on for a year?"

"Rose, I know you won't like my logic, but if you live long enough in LA, you learn that many people out here openly deceive themselves. If you want to keep friends, don't step on their dreams or delusions. If you do, they may hate you for it."

"Sam, I know you're leveling with me, but your logic is lost on me, a simple woman from Brooklyn. I'm sorry, darling Sam, that such a beautiful evening has to end on such a disturbing note." Her voice cracked.

"I know and share your disappointment." Sam put his arm around Rose and brought his lips to hers. "Hey, Gene Kelly invited us for dinner this Sunday night at his place. I was hoping that you could make it. I've told Gene all about you."

He wrapped his other arm around Rose and kissed her.

She kissed him back and hugged him. "How can I stay mad at a man who's taking me to dinner at Gene Kelly's, one of my favorite performers of all time?"

Rose almost buckled at the thought of telling Carole about David's adultery. She gave Sam another nice kiss and then drew back from him and smiled as he got in the car and drove away. Rose entered the living room, stared at the phone for nearly thirty seconds, and finally found the strength to pick up the receiver and dial.

"I hate David for causing this trouble."

Carole, asleep, answered on the fifth ring.

Rose stammered, "Hello, Carole, honey, it's Ma. Uh, is David there?"

That's strange, my mother calling so late and asking if David is home. She asked why. "No, he's in the studio, editing. How come you want to know?"

Rose bled inside trying to get the words out. "Honey, something awful happened tonight. I'm so sorry that I have to be the one to tell you this."

"Ma, did anything bad happen between you and Sam?"

"No, things are fine with us. You know how you told me to use the bungalow more?"

"Yeah, I guess you went there with Sam tonight. Did he get fresh with you?"

"Yes, sweetie, we went there, but Sam can never be fresh with me because I really like him. Enough with me. Tonight I saw David with another woman. I walked in on him having sex with a big blonde."

Rose's words hit Carole like a two-by-four to her head. She sat motionless on the side of the bed. Rose sensed how her daughter was reacting.

"Carole, I'm so sorry that I've caused you this pain."

"Ma, don't worry, you did the right thing."

"Carole, do you have any idea who the girl is?"

"Her name's Greta. I've looked the other way because I'd given him so little sex lately, but you seeing him bone her is plain unforgivable. He's gone as soon as he gets home."

"You deserve better, Carole, and you will get it."

"That took a lot of courage. Thank you, Ma. You tried to protect me from my own lack of judgment, and I appreciate it."

"It's the milieu, Carole. Even friends lie to each other. Sam knew."

Carole thanked Rose for setting her straight and said "good night." She poured herself a big glass of cold Chablis and sat down in a rocking chair in the living room. She quietly rocked and sipped wine for the next half hour and waited for the confrontation.

David entered with a reel of film under his right arm and a plastic smile on his mouth. Carole ignored his greeting and started to interrogate him with the steely voice of a prosecutor asking for the death penalty.

"Where were you tonight, and who the hell were you with?"

"What are you talking about, Carole?" he protested. "Please give me a break. I've been at the studio for hours, editing, and I am tired as shit."

Carole opened the can; it was empty, no reel. "You just added lying through your teeth to your growing list of crimes. Please confess."

She's staring at me like I'm a piece of shit. Conte wised up. *I think I totally fucked up this time, better not bullshit her.*

"Carole," he pleaded, "I beg you to understand that I'm only fucking her because we aren't connecting at home. She means nothing to me. Please forgive me, babe."

David, with folded arms and head bowed, sat on the couch a few feet away from Carole. With finger pointed, Carole scorned him.

"My mother saw you banging Greta tonight. Sorry, unforgivable, so adios, amigo. Go pack your bags, and get the fuck out. As of this moment, I'm a single woman again."

His eyes and hands pleaded for one more chance. "I don't want to fucking hear it. You could wear a hair shirt and a crown of thorns and be crucified with a cross and a Jewish star, and I still couldn't forgive you."

He continued to stand silently pleading for forgiveness, tears streaming out of his eyes. Carole said, "Cry all you want, I swore that, after Myron, no man would do that to me again. The party tomorrow night will be our last act as a couple."

166

"Please don't break us up, Carole. You and I are a fantastic partnership."

"We *were* a fantastic partnership. Sorry, it's over. Before the screening, the two of us will begin dividing up all joint business assets and property to save us millions in legal expenses. Herbie, our business manager, will help us do this tomorrow. Now go to your stupid blond bitch. The two of you deserve each other."

David left without uttering another word. Carole went to bed alone and cried herself to sleep. It was over.

Chapter 29

Allie opened his eyes and looked at the clock next to the bed—10:00 AM.

Don't want to sleep the day away. I need to call Sarah, and then maybe I'll start a search for a West Coast agent to represent my novel.

In Atlanta, Sarah interrupted her conversation with her mother to take a call.

"Hello, Allie, it's so good to hear your voice. How was the flight?"

"It was okay."

"And Rick, how's he doing?"

"Rick's doing very well. He's renting Jeffrey Picker's house. 'You remember? The rock 'n' roll recycling king."

"Good for Rick, no more cardboard boxes for him. Is Jeffrey planning Delaney and Bonnie's fifteenth comeback tour yet?"

They both laughed hard from her joke. "So what did you two do last night?"

"Oh, we ate Chinese and then spent a quiet evening at home discussing old times. I was tired from the flight, and today I'll test interest in my book. Tonight I understand that we've been invited to a private screening of Carole Herman's latest film—at her house."

That was big news in Atlanta. Sarah yelled across the kitchen to her mother.

"Guess what, Ma! Allie's going to party with stars tonight!" She swiveled and hoped for him. "Allie, maybe you'll meet a big shot tonight who'll want to make a movie of your novel."

"I should be so lucky, Sarah. Hey, I think Rick's gotten up. He has to eat breakfast when he wakes up just like me, so I'm going to have to say goodbye, babe."

"Sure, no need to call again until you get home, that is, unless you just miss me and want to hear my voice. I'll pick you up in baggage. Now be a good boy. 'Love you. Bye."

"'Love you too, money. Bye."

Allie walked out on the front porch to check out the weather.

Amazing, it would be pure blue sky without the smog, but I am glad to be shirtless and warm. The sun is already so hot that maybe we should forget about business and hit the beach instead.

Rick joined Allie on the steps overlooking Laurel Canyon Boulevard and also saluted the day's warmth.

"Hey, Allie," he recommended, "why don't we take the Lee sisters to the beach today? Then tonight we'll go to Conte's place with Greta and Reny. How does that plan sound to you?"

"Fine with me, Rick. You know, the Lee sisters sure aren't like that old joke back in Newark, the -ly sisters, ugly and very ugly."

Rick laughed at that old joke. "Are you feeling guilty, Allie? You realize that I'm not trying to help you cheat, just thought you could use letting off some steam, correct?"

"I'm okay, Rick, and thank you, my man, but yes, I'm experiencing some guilt."

After breakfast, Rick and Allie headed over to Mamie's apartment. The foursome decided to sit by the pool and skip the beach. Cohen scanned the pool area.

Incredible, Mamie's complex seems like a concentration camp for beautiful blondes and brunettes. Perhaps half is topless too.

They schmoozed, joked a lot, and enjoyed themselves immensely; three hours passed quickly. This being Cohen's first sun exposure in four months, he began to burn. Libby, in her microbikini and taut body, winked that she and Allie had unfinished business.

Libby volunteered to apply Elta body lotion to Allie's more pinkish areas and guided him to her apartment and bathroom. She sat him down on the toilet seat, rubbed his reddish shoulders, and then massaged her way down from the neck to his lower back.

Libby moved around to his chest and started from the neck too and kept going lower and lower and reached his waist. She looked Allie cutely in the eye and then shoved her hand right down his bathing suit. She stroked his penis and made him erect in a second.

Cohen hesitated. *Sex with Libby seems too much too soon and can't be right, even if this is California. Libby, though, is too beautiful and hot not to give in.*

She led him to her bed, got on top, and slipped him into her. She sensually moved up and down and told him to sit back and let her take them both over the rainbow.

She delivered twenty minutes of bliss and a memorable orgasm. Libby shared the afterglow as she lay in Allie's arms for a few minutes and then suddenly sat up and brushed the hair from her eyes.

"I normally don't do older guys," she confided to Cohen. "But you are so cute and fun that, from the second I met you, I had to do a thing with you. It's probably best for both of us, though, if this ends now. Don't you think so, oh clone of my god Al Pacino?"

Allie smiled self-consciously, put on his trunks and shirt, and nodded yes.

"I need to be a good boy for the rest of my trip, but, Libby Lee, you sure will be one sweet and pretty memory."

Libby gave Allie her power-over-men smile, fondled him once more for old time's sake, and left to meet up with friends. Allie realized, at that moment, that his marriage could not survive a moral one-way street, and he was not comfortable with heavy traffic coming in the other direction either.

The cooler late afternoon breeze cued Rick. "I think it's time to leave and get ready for Carole Herman's party tonight. You know, Allie, for two guys from Newark, this is *big*."

Yes, it is, Rick, and it is about to get much bigger.

Chapter 30

"While you were fooling around with Libby," Rick related to Allie on the ride back to Laurel Canyon, "Mamie and I had a frank talk. She told me that her teaching prospects are dead and that she's giving some thought to her and Libby being the first Asian sister act in porn. They need to get rich so they can be secure, also escape their parents' shame someday, and want me to help them produce their own product as partners. This is shaping up just like I hoped."

"Now you have your stable of partner beauties, the Lee sisters and Greta and Reny, your four queens of porn so to speak. Be good to them, and they will make you very rich."

"Four Queens of Porn Productions, thank you, I like that. Their introductory gig will be three sequential posters like Farrah Fawcett's, except nude—one featuring the Lee sisters; the other Reny and Greta, your classic cute little brunette and beautiful tall blonde; the third the four queens of porn. My target market is the private offices of horny dentists and doctors across America."

They turned into Rick's driveway, and Allie spotted Reny and Greta emerging from the VW Cabriolet.

"Rick, will you look at our lovely escorts dressed in their littlest of black dresses, push-up bras, and G-string panties covered by sheer black netting, leaving almost nothing to the imagination or eye?"

Allie changed into a black and white checked sport jacket with white shirt and black slacks; Rick put on a three-piece rust-colored suit that contrasted nicely with his blond curly hair. They left the house with Reny's arm through Allie's and Greta's through Rick's, all glowing from expectations of consorting with the rich, famous, and powerful.

The four fringe guests piled into Jeffrey's brown Mercedes sedan, Greta in the front with Rick, Reny in the back with Allie, who pinched himself.

Man, I'm sharing this space with a nearly naked sex pistol of a darling on my way to a film premiere.

All the way to Malibu, Reny sensually fondled Allie, who pleasured her, his left hand covering both cheeks while the right stroked her soft pubic hairs and vagina.

I know I have to stop this, but I can't. Am I a sex addict? No, I'm not. Opportunities are everywhere because of Rick's peculiar profession and stream of life. This only happens out here like this because of the film and porn industries. Elsewhere, it happens very occasionally at best. I plead guilty, though, to being a major-league Chazer.

Greta reckoned with them just as they reached Carole's Malibu estate.

"I can't put off telling you guys about last night any longer. Carole's mother walked in on me fucking David and then ran home and told Carole, who threw him right out."

Reny gasped. "No shit? Wow, that's huge. Now he has to come to you or lose you."

"We'll see, Reny. Right now, I'm more concerned that, with Carole mad at him, we're all still invited."

That last phrase drew an unhelpful remark from Reny. "Greta, how unbelievably stupid."

Greta, with hands placed against hips, gave Reny a "what kind of friend are you" look.

Rick ordered both to make nice to each other. "Ladies, take a deep breath. I'm hoping to leave the party tonight with a prestigious commission."

Allie seemed removed from the tension between them. Greta knocked on the front door and shocked them.

"David's never going to marry me. He doesn't think I'm smart or talented enough."

"How do you fucking know that?" asked Reny, stunned by the revelation. "Did he ever say such a thing to you?"

"No, it's just the way he looks at me sometimes. Christ, I swear I heard him think it last night, right after a fabulous orgasm too."

Reny looked at Greta as if she was nuts and rolled the line around in her head.

She heard *him* think *it?*

"You'll see, Greta," said Rick, trying to raise her spirits. "Conte will do right by you. Trust me too about Carole. She's a lady and won't make a scene."

Cohen looked around as they waited and then commented on the architecture and property, "The home's understated, but still, grand design impresses me. This is the most beautiful physical setting and desert landscaping that I've ever seen, and I gather that the land, location, and house must be worth anywhere from twenty to forty million easy."

"I've been inside twice," shared Greta. "The place is an art deco showcase with lots of high-tech mirrors. Intimate levels and nooks are almost everywhere. Too bad it's in her name."

"I'm just a little old social studies teacher from Atlanta, Georgia," said Allie self-consciously. "I wonder what I'm going to have to say to these people."

"Cut the humility crap, Allie," said Greta, not wanting to hear it. "Try to sell them your novel. These guys are always interested in a good story. Most of them are nicer too than you'd expect."

They were still waiting, Greta rang again, and a drinks server finally opened the door and led them to the living room, where the reception was being held.

"Greta," Allie said, curious, "what's Carole like in real life?"

"As much as I hate to admit it, Allie, she's a nice person and cool lady who deserves better from David too. She's so down-to-earth that you easily forget that you're with the biggest star on the planet today."

Cohen took in the scene. *The major merchants of the world's most important dream factory are circulating and drinking in this large raised living room. This is easily the most beautiful home I've ever been in—wide floor-to-ceiling windows with spectacular views of the mountains to the east and Pacific to the west. The sun's setting over the ocean and bathing the room in a golden light. Magnificent.*

Carole praised David, both busy in the bedroom working out their division of assets.

"I really appreciate how you're cooperating with me to divide the property without lawsuits and doing it quickly too. Thank you, David." She gently touched his cheek.

"I appreciate hearing that from you. You're the best thing that ever happened to me."

"Me too, you really were. And for that, you can have the beach bungalow and horses, all the cars except the 928, my Texas Hill Country property, and fifteen million bucks for your half share of this property. You did an extraordinary job in acquiring this land and built me my dream house on it. You changed my life in countless ways for the better, and I thank you for the three best years of my life. May we always remain good friends, and please don't fuck that up."

He smiled. "It's a deal, Carole, and you can keep the little mountain. Texas and I don't get along that well."

They both laughed and agreeably shook on it.

Sam and Rose subbed as official greeters. Goosebumps appeared on Greta's arms when Rose eyed her disapprovingly.

"What's Greta doing with these two cute Jewish guys, especially the one in the black and white sport coat? He's very interesting looking."

The affable Sam introduced himself, shook hands with Rick and Allie, kissed Reny and Greta on the cheeks, and had drinks brought to them. Rick and Allie shadowed their escorts, who quickly struck up conversations with balding studio executives.

The handsome Peter Bates, blessed with thick, wavy hair and of medium height, spotted Greta and walked over to say hello. They'd dated a few times before she met David and remained friends of sorts.

Peter affectionately stroked Greta's tush as he spoke. "Greta, you look as hot as ever. I've always loved your bubble butt."

Greta smiled at Peter as she removed his hand. "Thanks, Peter, but my stomach is churning, and you know why."

Peter intimately rubbed her bare shoulders to relax her. "David will do the right thing. I'll put in a good word."

"Peter, do you remember Reny?"

He removed his arm from her shoulder and resorted to long-term memory.

I think I recall casually balling Reny a few years back at a beach party.

He finally said, "Yeah, we're old friends." He hugged Reny and began rubbing her butt.

"And Rick Samuels, the photographer I've been doing most of my modeling with lately."

"Samuels, yes, I like your work. Hey, are you interested in shooting some stills of Daria, my fiancée?"

He took his hand off Reny's butt and wiped a smile off her face; she liked the attention from him.

Rick, thrilled, answered him, "Sure, I'd love to, Peter." Bates and Samuels exchanged business cards. Bates told him to call next Monday.

Greta introduced Allie. "Peter, Allie's writing a Holocaust-related novel. Perhaps you'd be interested to hear what it's about."

Allie gratefully smiled at Greta and then encouraged Bates that the world was ready to deal with the subject of the Holocaust. Bates considered that for a few seconds.

"The Holocaust, hmmm, sure. Please describe it, Allie."

Allie excitedly presented a short synopsis and admitted, "I'm still searching for a suitable ending, but I feel the timing is right for a Holocaust-themed book and movie." He cautioned himself not to talk money yet.

Cohen heard the three magical words that any writer wished from the first important person to learn of their work.

"Allie, I like it. Actually, I like it a lot. Seymour's extreme moral outrage is a good role for someone utterly decent like Jack Lemmon or with the extreme credibility of a Gene Hackman, no porkpie hat, of course." Everyone laughed at his joke.

Bates came up with an ending; Allie's heart fluttered.

"Allie, what do you think about this for a conclusion? Seymour flies to Israel and jumps off Masada. His symbolic suicide atones for his unspeakable atrocities and redeems him as a martyr for the Jewish people. You like?"

"Yes, I do, and Lemmon or Hackman are both fine actors, though to add some comic relief I also like Gene Wilder too. So, Peter, are you interested in producing it?"

His stomach churned. *Bates can empower me with one word—yes.*

"Let me get with Bob Urban tomorrow." Cohen's hope rose. "I want to find out how much of the gruesome lampshade scene can be filmed. That's the story's turning point. Seymour crosses a line and cannot return to his regular life."

Allie, happy that Peter had written his ending for him, saw Daria romping over to Peter. She interrupted them.

"Peter, you have to come and meet my sister, who's out here trying to get into acting too."

"Okay, Daria, but please wait a second. Allie, where are you staying at in LA?"

"At Rick's, you have each other's cards."

Daria tugged at Peter's arm. "I'll call you at about eight o'clock tomorrow night."

Peter shook Cohen's hand and conversed with Daria's sister.

Allie contemplated *The Lesson* becoming Bates's eighth straight hit that he acted in, directed, or produced until Sam brought Billy Diamond over to meet Allie and Rick.

Minkowitz kibitzed. "I'm trying to segregate all neurotic New Yorkers from mellow Californians."

Allie volunteered. "I'm a former Jersey guy who moved to Atlanta a decade ago. Regardless, it's a pleasure to meet Billy Diamond, one of my favorite comic actors."

Cohen noticed that Diamond wore ultracomfortable clothes in real life just like in his movies.

He has to be the only guy in LA wearing a baggy gray corduroy suit in ninety-degree weather.

"Allie, please call me Billy. You know, Atlanta's always reminded me of a giant peach."

Cohen laughed and played straight man. "What do you mean?"

He spoke with his arms and hands when emphasizing key words, timed to set up the punch line.

"You drive here and take a bite of the big peach, and then you drive over there and take a bite. Atlanta is a huge gentile still-life painting."

Cohen laughed. "I love the description, Billy, but I'm not sure what it means."

Carole emerged from her bedroom, saw Billy, and made a beeline for the group. "Man, I'm so glad to see you, Billy."

David appeared shortly after her and headed straight for Peter and Daria to seek advice.

Peter listened and told David, "I know why you hesitate to marry Greta. I think that it's only fair that you be straight with her and move on."

"I'm not sure I want to do that just yet."

Peter, annoyed, grimaced. "See what I mean?"

Carole pressed Billy to make her laugh. "Please, Billy, say something funny for me. I desperately need to laugh."

Diamond studied his landlord's face. "Jesus, Carole, you know that I hate to be put on the spot and can't tell a joke without a cue card. Man, you really are down, aren't you? Holy shit, your face could be a lyric for a Mississippi delta blues song. How's this for a blues title? 'Blind Lemon Carole's Hound Dog up and Died.'"

Carole laughed from her belly. Billy remembered to introduce Allie.

"Carole, this is Allie Cohen. Peter Bates just told me he's a budding novelist from Atlanta. God, I hate that word, like his arms are going to turn into black-eyed Susans."

Carole's blues had lifted enough to kid back, "Since Allie's from Georgia, perhaps his arms will turn into black-eyed peas."

Billy booed and scolded, "That line was so bad that I wouldn't tell it to my ex-wife, either of them."

Cohen again played straight man for Billy. "Is that all?"

"It's so bad that I'm thinking of casting Carole as the lead in my new film, *The Martha Raye Story*."

Allie and Carole were in stitches; she looked at Allie. "I can see that we're both old enough to remember one of TV's first great comediennes, Martha Raye, a truly gifted woman and clown."

"You're right, Carole, she was a kind of Jewish Lucille Ball, just not as pretty and sexy."

"That's a good description, Allie."

She stared at Allie and liked what she saw. *Christ, he's really cute and looks very interesting.*

I, Gabriel, put those thoughts in Carole's head and took jokes from Allie's friend Phil Brodsky, a public speaker and master storyteller, and also put them in Allie's head. This stand-up routine was Allie's life-changing moment—the prophet found his beholding angel.

"I just heard some funny jokes from my friend Phil." Cohen then realized. "I did?"

Diamond got in one more joke. "Hey, when did I become an opening act? I'm going to have to fire my manager."

They all laughed again, and I passed their attention back to Allie, for I have a front row seat watching a star being born. Phil Brodsky's jokes and hand movements began pouring out of Allie.

"There's this group of condemned men at Sing Sing who try to get through each crummy night by telling the same lousy jokes over and over again. That gets old real quick, and for a change, they assign numbers to the funniest ones, for example, number seven, ha ha ha, number nine, ho ho ho." Carole was laughing already.

181

"One day a new prisoner is brought to death row. The murderers call out numbers all night long, and the whole cell block laughs so hard they all cry tears. The new prisoner's puzzled. 'I can't figure it out,' he tells the aged serial rapist in the next cell. 'What the hell's going on?' The old guy ignores him."

Carole was laughing tears from *aged serial rapist* but gagged Billy, who was also laughing hard but anticipated the punch line.

"Understandably, the new prisoner wants to be one of the guys. That night the prisoner waits until it's real quiet and yells number four, usually a killer of a joke."

Cohen stifled short spasms of laughter, which made the group laugh louder. "To his surprise, no one laughs, not a chuckle. The poor guy's perplexed and shouts, 'Number seven,' always a screamer, but for him, he gets deafening silence."

By now, the group was waiting on Cohen's every word. "The guy's desperate and bangs a metal cup against the wall and yells at the old serial rapist, 'Hey, fuck face, why is this place quieter than the morgue when I tell one?'"

His use of words *fuck face* cracked Carole and Billy up. "The old guy, on death row for thirteen years, had heard each joke hundreds of times. He scratches his head for a few seconds and answers, 'Well, young fellah, some guys can tell 'em, and some can't.'"

Rick roared, Billy bent over howling, and Carole staggered around the room, holding her sides. The whole group kept repeating the punch line, each time bringing new spasms of laughter. Carole stole a line from Richard Pryor.

"Wow, that couldn't have come at a better time. I was so down today that I had to bend over to look up."

Billy asked Allie, "Are you planning to tryout at the Comedy Store?"

Cohen threw a one-liner. "No, I'm an unhappy Pisces and just flew out here to have the sign change operation."

That got them roaring again. *I'm on a roll. People all around me are looking at me like I'm Rodney Dangerfield and ready to do stand-up. I'm a social studies teacher and not Shecky Greene, but the crowd wants more, so I'll give it to them.*

"Okay, a couple of newlyweds are on their honeymoon, and the husband's a male chauvinist pig." Carole was already laughing. "He decides that now is the time to get across who's the *boss* in the family. Right before making love for the first time, he tosses his trousers at his wife and orders her to put them on.

"'I can't,' she protests. 'They're too big."

"'That's right,' he says. 'And I want you to remember that for as long we're married.'

"Not to be outdone, the wife goes into her overnight bag, takes out a tiny pair of lace panties, and tosses them at her husband. 'Here, get into these.'

"He protests, 'I can't. They're too small.'

"She tells him, 'You're right, and you *won't* unless you change your attitude.'"

They were still laughing, if a little less hard, but the next joke set them off roaring again.

"A flasher walks up to three little old ladies sitting on a park bench and opens his raincoat. He stands stark naked and massively erect right in front of them. This sight causes the first little old lady to have a stroke. The second little old lady also has a stroke. The third little old lady—well, her arms were a little too short to reach."

They were wiping tears from their eyes again. Allie deadpanned in the best tradition of Myron Cohen, the king of one-liners and no relation.

"We Jews are a very old people. In fact, we're such an old culture that when the Anglo-Saxons were in caves eating berries, we Jews already had diabetes."

That set off a new spasm. Rose and Sam were also part of Allie's audience. Carole's mother was pleased and charmed.

I'm glad that this guy Allie is cheering my daughter up. I wonder if Carole thinks he's as cute and intelligent looking as I do.

The next logical conclusion for Rose was *This guy Allie is probably too good to be single. Things never work that easy for my Carole.*

Cohen, on cloud nine, spat out a Henny Youngman one-liner; "I got a dog for my wife yesterday. It was a great trade."

He made Rose a bit nervous with that one, but his roll continued because of his delivery and timing. Still, he knew to quit while ahead and left the crowd wanting more.

"Your timing," Billy Diamond complimented him, "is flawless and delivery excellent. I'm serious. Did you ever consider stand-up? You could be big."

"Sorry, man, I'm a civilian," said Allie, extremely flattered but dismissive of the idea. "Thank you, Billy, but I enjoy *being* funny and not *having* to be funny."

"Well, how about being a comedy writer for me? That's how I got my start in the entertainment business."

"Billy, you've made my day with your offer, but I don't think so. I'm too serious a person to have to grind out dozens of jokes on demand, and I can't do thirty minutes when the refrigerator light bulb goes off too."

Billy and Carole both smiled from Allie's use of that old Jerry Lewis insider joke about professional hams.

"Allie," Carole recommended, "why not at least consider Billy's proposal? He makes two movies a year, uses his comedy writers to help develop the scripts, and gives them cowriter credit. That's a very nice springboard for a successful career, trust me on this."

Rick stepped up for Allie. "Carole, try to understand that Allie's a kind of intellectual and academic Martin Luther King. He just developed an educational treatment for prejudice reduction and received an advance from a major publisher."

"Really, Rick?" She looked at Allie, smiled, and then commented, "That is a very impressive achievement indeed."

Rick followed up with "Allie's also writing his Holocaust novel and is one of the best social studies teachers in the country."

Allie appreciated Rick's support and joked to lighten the mood. "Thanks, Rick. Hey, how'd you like to be my agent?"

Rick looked at Carole to see her reaction. *Fuck, she's staring at Allie in awe as if she's been looking for someone just like him. I may be crazy, but I think Carole is actually falling for Allie. This is very weird.*

Rick tensed up at the thought of the publicity factor. Carole checked her watch to see if it was time to show the film yet. It was and told everyone to move to the screening room.

"People, *Dora* starts in five minutes, so take your seats please."

Carole stunned Allie and everyone else by locking arms with him as if he was her escort for the evening.

The guests buzzed. "Who the hell is that guy with Carole?"

Behold the prophet Allie Cohen teaming with his angel Carole Herman to help engage the master teacher with the entire world.

Chapter 31

Rick watched Carole lead Allie by the hand into the theater and seat him beside her in the middle of the first row.

Holy shit. Samuels worried as he sat down in the center row with David, Greta, Reny, Peter, and Daria. *Carole's coming on to Allie threatens to make him an instant public figure with the first AP photo. Christ, he could be the* National Enquirer *headline tomorrow. Oh, Sarah.*

Allie, meanwhile, sat tongue-tied for a minute, trying to figure out how he came to be seated with Carole. I ended his pregnant pause by again putting words in his mouth, and he finally looked Carole in the eyes and complimented her.

"Ms. Herman, has anyone told you lately that you are now a more *beautiful* and *sexier* lady than ever?"

His timing was perfect and fully endeared him to her. Carole held Allie's hand and tenderly caressed it.

"Please, Allie, call me Carole."

I encouraged Allie's opportunistic nature to take over by wiping fear from his brain. The prophet needn't bother about kisses or sensual touches transforming him into an *instant public figure*, to use Rick's words, for I was covering him. It was Adonai's proviso that Allie bond with Carole, his caveat to the world, his beholding stepping stone.

Billy Diamond distracted them with a straight-line question. "Allie, what do you think of Los Angeles?"

Allie volleyed back. "Oh, so that's what LA's name means. I'd thought it meant 'lots of avocadoes.'"

Billy and Carole cracked up laughing again, so he followed with another. "Billy, I love that LA line of yours about hating the mellowness out here. It makes you start to feel like an overripe cantaloupe."

Allie imagined Sarah's amusement at watching him kid around with Billy Diamond. That ended when Carole stroked his fingers. Allie felt a tingle and grasped Carole's left hand in his, held it, and stroked it with his index finger.

The last time I experienced this was during my first date with Sarah. Ironically, I took her to a Carole Herman movie playing at a big Brooklyn movie palace. We were sitting in the balcony. I was wearing a peasant-style Indian pullover, and some guy named Sal, thirty rows away, yelled, "Nice shirt!"

Carole leaned up against Allie's jacket and heard a crinkling noise. She, needing to go to the toilet, asked, "Allie, what's in your pocket?"

"I hoped," he half-fibbed, "to explore opportunities out here and brought along a résumé to run off at a copy center. Unfortunately, we didn't pass a Kinko's on the way over. Hey, I'm not looking for a job, mind you."

Carole, not knowing the real reason, laughed and snuggled up to Allie, who put his arm around her when she whispered, "Allie, I have to pee and love to read in the john. Please give me your résumé to help me pass the time."

Allie did, and she took it with her. Carole set herself down on the basin and scanned Allie's life listed in four typed, single-spaced pages. One page in, she was amazed by his range of accomplishments and uncanny specialties for her areas of immediate need.

After completing the vita, she sized Allie up.

My god, he's a one-man think tank, very well traveled, expert on international relations, economics, and U.S. history. I really like his having written a Jewish American curriculum that's used by the reform branch to teach converts to Judaism. Is it possible for a man with Allie's qualities and age to still be single and without children? I doubt it.

She turned back to the top of the cover page, looking for marital status and cursed to herself.

Shit, there it is. He's fucking married. Damn it, nothing ever comes to me without problems. He probably has a kid, is a poor fucking teacher pushing a novel. The public could skewer me for taking another woman's man away.

How unfair, she thought. *Twenty-four hours after I threw out one of the two great loves of my life, Rose's* cute little Jew *shows up* married. *Shit, my men haven't exactly been off-limits to other women, so why should I be expected to honor the rules of the game when no one else does?*

One reason, Carole—your mother, Rose, and the public could skewer you. Carole flushed, buttoned up her pants, and washed her hands.

"Forgive me, Mrs. Cohen, for what I am about to do."

Inside the theater, Rose experienced unease at Carole's absence and left the theater room to knock on the bathroom door.

"Carole, darling, are you okay?"

Through the door, she replied, "Come in, Mom. I have to talk to you."

Those ever-troublesome familiar words. Rose cringed. *"Ma, I have to talk to you." That always gets my guard up.*

189

She turned the knob and was greeted by Carole handing her Cohen's vita.

"Here's the idealized cute little Jew you wanted for me. Well, he's a PhD and not an MD, so I guess he's almost ideal."

Rose quickly read the vita and specified, "Such distinctions mean little to me, Carole. Smart is smart. Holy cow, his credentials are incredible. He's practically a Hanukkah present. There must be something wrong. He's too good a catch not to be married. Yep, says right here."

Thunder and lightning crashed inside Rose's head and made her slump down on the toilet seat. She put on her glasses and scanned the vita again. Cohen's exceptionality and Rose's desire to see her daughter happy forced her to think atypically.

"Honey, he's so adorable and accomplished that, while I can't approve, I do understand. I'm sorry, Carole, but that's the best I can do."

Rose looked at her daughter and lovingly stroked her cheek with her hand. "You really like him, honey, don't you?"

"Ma, I'm grateful for your tempered approval, but I also need your blessing to take the Reagan tour with Allie. After that, we can sit down and talk."

"Carole, your glossing over obvious complications makes my head spin." Rose buried her face in her hands while identifying the more obvious ones. "What about your children? Can you bring yet another man into their lives and not create problems?"

"We'll see."

"Wake up! Do you think a teacher can run all over the world with a movie star and return to his job and wife? Have you given any thought that his face could be on the cover of *People Magazine* tomorrow? What then?"

Carole nodded that she hadn't. Rose sighed. *My daughter's problems are wearing me out.* Rose urged Carole to be prudent. "Please, darling, first experience Allie for the next week before inviting him to move in or trot the globe with you. By the way, sweetie, who's the stunning tall blonde who came with him?"

"I really don't want to go there." But she did. "Greta, she's a model who poses for Rick, Allie's friend."

"You left out David's mistress."

"I know."

"How could you let David's mistress in your house?" Rose scrunched up her face.

"Ma, get over it. Look at the good that came out of it. I met Allie."

Carole kissed her mom, again thanked Rose for her understanding, and took her seat next to Allie. Within seconds, Carole was leaning into Allie as if he were her darling.

Allie's 1982 salary, $32,000, and Sarah's $30,000—$62,000 in combined gross family income—was very comfortable. Cohen's stake in his life with Sarah was enormous, and he hesitated before reciprocating.

His id, though, signaled that a movie goddess was making a play for him and that he must stop acting like a lox. Adonai and I suspended Allie's powerful sense of morality to bond and consummate a special friendship as partners for humanity's welfare.

Fuck it. Allie fatalistically kissed Carole on the lips, and his courage emboldened her.

"I'm thrilled, Allie, by the sweetness of our kisses, and I'm very excited."

They held each other tightly and then kissed and intimately touched each other passionately. Rose ignored the steamy love scene being played out a few rows in front of her and fixed her gaze on the screen.

Billy Diamond, sitting next to the lovebirds, was aggravated by the intense display of raw lust two feet from him.

"Hey, you guys, cut it out. What's this, a drive-in movie? Go to the goddamned bedroom if you must."

The lovers, amused by Billy's annoyance, stopped. Carole, short of breath and very aroused, suggested, "Allie, since we're making everybody around us uncomfortable, why not split to my bedroom and finish what we started?"

Cohen, riding an exciting tidal wave of risk, inarticulately responded, "Far fucking out."

Carole and Allie rose and strolled out of the minitheater arm in arm, leaving all guests, except Rose and Rick's whole row, still wondering, *Who the hell is he?* or *What the fuck is she doing with him, whoever he is?*

They would learn when Hashem wished for them to know.

A California king bed with a shiny brass backboard and white and beige furry throw rugs and pillows dominated the master bedroom. The lovers said few words, for they had come to communicate with their bodies.

192

Allie kissed Carole's face tenderly while she pulled him down on the bed to make love to her. He unbuttoned her blouse while she unzipped and removed his pants. Their clothes fell away, and the lovers merged into one.

"You're a perfect fit," she whispered in to his ear. "It's almost like I punched your specs into a computer, and out came a customized little Jew."

They laughed, Allie taking pleasure in her absurdist sense of humor. Their intense hunger for each other was quickly satisfied as both came together after five glorious minutes of hot sex.

"As much as I'd like to make love all night," Carole wisely recommended, "we can't, but we will later this evening."

She rested in his arms for a few minutes, basking in the afterglow of great lovemaking and marveled. "I experienced orgasm with you tonight like no other man before."

Carole's size, weight, bone structure, and body movements are eerily similar to Sarah's. I swear that they both have the same delicately voluptuous body and pretty face. Allie realized.

"Even though that was a fabulous fuck, Allie," she advised, "I think we ought to get dressed and back to the theater."

"That was more than just fantastic sex for me too, Carole. You're an exquisite lady."

The actress told the teacher, "It is incredible how my defense mechanisms melted in minutes after meeting you. In my whole life, I never made love to a man *ten minutes* after an introduction. It usually takes me at least ten days. David took a month, Myron too."

Adonai and I are eager to move this partnership along.

193

That bolsters my confidence, Allie pondered. *But am I simply a tourist who got lucky or her new boyfriend?*

I put these words into Carole's mind and mouth. "Allie, I'd like you to return after the screening and spend the rest of your week in LA with me."

Before answering, Cohen contemplated the possible consequences of a six-day love affair with the most bankable female movie star.

On the seventh day, will I still be able to go home to Sarah, who's due to bear me a child in six weeks?

I steered Allie to pursue this. "Carole, I'd love to spend this next week with you. Should I bring all my clothes?"

"No, come naked." she barked, and they cackled all the way back to their seats for the film's last half hour. Allie did not see Rick give him the same look when they were teenagers and when one had just done something really stupid.

The screening ended, and the audience applauded the schmaltzy little film. Rick and Allie left first because they were blocking the driveway. Greta and Reny left earlier with two young producers who snowed the girls with phony promises of big parts for them in their new film; that was bullshit. This would be the last straw for Greta and Reny.

Samuels was silent until he reached Sunset Boulevard. "Well, Allie, I hope you're prepared to accept the consequences of your risky actions."

Cohen tried to reason with one of his closest friends. "You know, Rick, there are consequences for *not* taking an action too. Look, pal, I'm not sure how I got myself into this, but I have to spend this week with Carole to find out if this is just a one-night stand or something much more. It's absolutely amazing how my physical chemistry and communication with Carole is virtually the same as with Sarah."

"It's not that easy, Allie. This screening was a fucking media orgy. Some schmuck might be feeding this story into the AP wire right now. With your luck, in ten minutes, Sarah will hear about this scene coming through her TV screen. How do you think she's going to feel, pregnant no less?"

"I understand, Rick. Still, I have to explore this possibility, so please forgive me for spending the rest of the week with Carole instead."

"See, I'm in the same boat as Sarah. You're an opportunistic prick who sees a better deal, a veritable Sammy Glick."

Allie shuddered; the Sammy Glick reference hurt. Author-director Budd Schulberg's striving fictional character in the play *What Makes Sammy Run?* achieved great success at the expense of forsaking all who loved him in his pursuit of power and fortune.

"Look, Allie, good memories are like good clothes," quoted Rick, hoping to reach Cohen. "They always fit well and never go out of style."

"Great quote, Rick, but what the fuck's that got to do with Carole?"

"Allie, I got a hot poster scene with the Lee sisters waiting for us back at the house and another with Greta and Reny scheduled for tomorrow night. I beg you to forget about Carole and stay with me. I promise you that you'll never regret it because these posters are going to make so much fucking money that you can quit teaching and publish your own goddamned book."

"Rick, I appreciate the offer *and* concern, but if I turn my back on Carole, I'll regret it for the rest of my life. Besides, I really like Carole, maybe even love her a bit and have to find out."

The Lee sisters let themselves in and were busy oiling their bodies for the photo session when Rick and Allie arrived. Cohen's eyes locked on Mamie and Libby arousing their nipples into a state of erotic symmetry.

Coach Samuels barked out plays to his team. "C'mon, ladies, let's produce the kind of great poster art that will hang in the private bathroom of every horny dentist in America."

Allie silently observed Mamie. *I noticed that she has lost her shame and now exhibits a detachment similar to top strippers, the professionalization of nudity syndrome.*

"You know," Rick commented, "the amount of money to be made from even soft-core porn is outrageous. I tell you, it's a sick society."

Mamie commented while combing her pubic hairs: "The really sick thing is that all four of us started out in education."

Rick and Allie both nodded *yes* and were affected.

"Being rich and pretty," asserted Libby, "means that I don't have to take shit from any man. Money gives me the power to play with any fucking dick I want."

That included mine. Cohen recognized and then envisioned. *Porno films are next. Rick will not bring Mamie home to meet his mother or marry her. The riches will inevitably lead to disillusionment or disgust, but it will be a really huge sum of money, almost too much to fucking walk away from.*

He hugged Rick, blew kisses to the well-oiled Lee sisters, and then borrowed Samuels's Corvette to drive to Carole's. Allie headed back to Malibu and felt a life force pulling him as he turned onto the Pacific Coast Highway.

Destiny is a word that keeps popping up in my head like a silly old pop song.

The Redeemer and I have shaped your destiny, Allie, since you were born, and now, prophet, you have taken the first great step in your beholding.

Chapter 32

The bartender Wiley Jackson poured a double Scotch. *Man, ain't nothing goin' to drown Eddie White's Bankhead Highway blues tonight.*

Eddie looked over in the back corner and recognized a droopy prostitute in a tight lime-colored dress playing a monotonous Joe Simon record on the jukebox.

"Fuck me. Holy shit, that's Jacquida from high school. I once pinched that big ass as it swayed up the aisle to pick up one of Mr. Cohen's tests."

Jacquida, like too many others, graduated with a Grady baby instead of a diploma. Grady Hospital is the city of Atlanta and Fulton and DeKalb Counties' primary hospital for the black poor.

Jacquida swayed up to Eddie and saucily offered, "You interested in a little brown sugar tonight, Eddie?"

Wiley laid down the law to Jacquida. "Bitch, I told you twice not to bother the customers, so you see that door? Well, don't let it hit your fat ass on the way out."

Eddie ignored Jacquida and sipped his drink. Wiley apologized to him. "Sorry about that, man."

Eddie, unfazed, replied, "Don't worry about it. It's cool."

Wiley studied Eddie for a few seconds. "What's the matter, man?"

"What you mean, Wiley?"

The balding, paunchy very dark-skinned Wiley asked, "Why you drinking so hard tonight, my man?"

Eddie looked down into his glass and just said, "I got problems, Wiley."

"Well," Wiley probed, "you ain't gonna get no solutions from Teacher's Scotch."

White tried to brush Wiley off. "And you ain't gonna make no money if you keep driving off the customers."

"Eddie, that's my problem. Now what's yours already?"

"Okay, I'm a nigger."

Wiley laughed hard from the belly and then told Eddie, "That's nonsense. What you mean you're a nigger? Shit, man, you ain't sayin' nothin'."

Eddie seemed to have an all-too-convenient answer. "Okay, I'm a nigger garbageman who can't stand his slave no more. That should tell you plenty."

"Then quit."

"Quit?" said Eddie, who looked at Wiley like he was out of his mind.

"Yeah, quit."

"You must be kiddin', man. I can't afford to quit, so I just lift them smelly fuckin' cans and yell 'yoh.' Take-home pay barely makes the rent and hardly puts decent food on the table. I tell you, Wiley, workin's guaranteed poverty."

"You're young. If you're that miserable, you can quit, trust me on this."

"'Can't afford to quit and can't afford not to and don't know what to do neither. Farrah's one of them proud niggers who won't take the welfare. Dumb-ass bitch claims our kids need a daddy more than we need a check. She probably right too, but I sure ain't no model father."

"What about the union?"

White almost fell of the barstool, laughing. "The union is worthless, ain't no help at all. Every time they strike, the mayor just fires the whole damn lot. And the next day, a thousand jobless niggers line up for our slaves. The mayor sucks wind for whitey."

"Hey, man, the mayor's black."

"So what? He's a nigger too."

"How can you say that, Eddie?" argued Wiley as he washed and dried glasses. "The mayor is a famous and powerful man."

"Shit, the white man can take his power away in a minute." He snapped his finger.

Wiley did not have Cohen for a teacher. "How is that?"

"Man, I'm surprised that I even have to explain it to you. Okay, all they got to do is move the city's boundaries so far out that the niggers will become a minority again. Once they do that, niggers won't count for shit no more."

Wiley couldn't bear Eddie's constant use of the word *nigger.* "Enough with this nigger shit already, man. Ain't you ever heard of the words *black, Negro, Afro-American,* even *colored*? Besides, whitey can't get away with that shit no more. The blacks are too well organized to have to give up the power."

"Bullshit," mocked White, who imitated a pompous black bourgeoisie.

200

"Now look here, brothers and sisters, we gots to do what's best for the big A or lovely Atlanta. The city needs more taxes so the white man can do more for the Negro race. We're all in this together, black and white. Well, bullshit to that! Man, this is one nigger who's up to his eyes in pig shit and drowning fast too."

"Eddie, you are too young a man to be so bitter. You kill your soul that way. All that liquor you're drinkin's hell on the stomach and liver too."

Eddie summed up his life as he rose from the barstool to pay his bill and leave.

"Wiley, can you imagine being twenty-six years old and already wishing you were dead?"

Chapter 33

Allie Cohen's life, in comparison, over the past thirty-six hours had taken on a surrealistic quality. The two most fantastic opportunities in Allie's life just happened, and both demanded that he gamble away his marriage and educational career. Despite the high stakes, Allie had already anted up for a bet that made Carole a croupier and Bates his paymaster and prayed he would not crap out.

He neared Carole's home, and the Rolling Stones' "Tumbling Dice" blared from the radio as he made a left onto Carole's property and pulled into the garage. Carole greeted him from the doorway leading to the kitchen wearing only a blue denim shirt and nothing else and happily hugged him.

"For a while, I was scared that you'd punk out. I guess you're as crazy as me after all."

Allie passionately kissed Carole on the lips and aroused her as fast as turning up the thermostat.

"My god, I'm amazed by how you can sexually ignite me in a second, but believe it unwise to linger in the garage, so please follow me into the kitchen."

Once inside, he took her in his arms and started to kiss her naked flesh all over.

I can't believe I'm kissing Carole Herman's cookie in her kitchen.

As much as Carole wanted him to, she stopped him by placing her hands on his cheeks and made him pay attention to her.

"Allie, I want to make love just as much as you, but you're still a stranger to me. You told me a bunch of jokes, and we jumped into bed. So why don't we save making love for later and spend the next few hours getting to know each other?"

"That sounds fine to me." Carole poured two glasses of Cabernet. Allie joked to fill a silence. "Hey, did you hear about Reagan coming out against the electric chair?"

She played along. "No, I thought he was for it."

"Of course, he is, but there are so many guys on death row that now he wants to replace Old Sparky with electric bleachers."

His funny line made her laugh *and* worry.

He's probably a liberal and might refuse to work with the opposition in an official status. Reagan's right-wing administration might also bar him from the entourage. Let me feel out Allie's degree of hostility to Reagan.

"What is your opinion of President Reagan and the job that he is doing?"

Cohen took a second to organize his response. "I'm mystified, Carole, by the public's affection for him because his policies overtly hurt the poor and help the rich. Americans don't hold him accountable for his failures and celebrate his congeniality. Worst of all, he's made greed and venality popular again."

Man, he's way out in front of the public, but his oversized sense of social justice makes it hard to enlist him without insulting his integrity. I'm unsure of where or how to start, so I'll refill his glass to buy some time.

Carole sipped from her own glass and then put it down. She paced back a forth a few times while relating some of her recent changes and ultimately got to Reagan's offer. Allie, aware of her political background, appeared thrown for a loop.

I see conflicting expressions crossing Allie's face.

Cohen's eyes, to her, radiated delight at the chance of visiting countries he might never be allowed to or afford. His mouth, though, suggested dismay at the idea of representing Reagan, a man he just dissected as a congenial failure.

Cohen took for granted. *Until this moment, I've reveled at simply being in Carole's company—a beautiful woman, a great star, and a celebrated liberal who likes me a lot. For a second there, I wondered if Carole had suddenly become conservative similar to Frank Sinatra or Charlton Heston.*

"Look, I'm in the same boat as you, Allie." Carole stated, "I know it's weird to work with a Republican administration, but you have to admit that our opportunities are extraordinary and exciting."

"It is strange, Carole, but I guess I can get over it. There is a much more important issue to be faced—Sarah, my wife."

"Allie, I'm sure that your wife is lovely. She is, isn't she?"

He thought, *I feel guilty at how quickly I'm not keeping Sarah in mind.*

But Allie was straight with her. "Believe me when I tell you, Carole, our relationship is not due to any lack in my marriage. Sarah's a great wife."

I'll take some credit for your marriage with Sarah, Allie, and all the credit for Carole Herman, your new partner in the world's beholding of you. Sing praises to Hashem, prophet, who blessed me to guide you. See your two exquisite women as your left and right arms in life and treasures from the Master of the universe. Trust me, we will figure out a way to make this unique arrangement work, Allie.

Carole gently stroked Allie's cheek with her fingers. "Are you willing to risk it all by having a relationship with me?"

It's not lost on me that I'm dealing with a movie star's ego. Taking too long to answer her questions might hurt her feelings and cause Carole to kick my ass out of her house. He answered without blinking, "I'm here, aren't I?"

"Allie," said Carole with the breathless voice of a salesperson readying her best pitch, "if I were to search the entire world, I would not find a more ideal person to take the world tour with me."

He thanked her by nodding that he understood. "Of course, Allie, I realize it's for Reagan, and that compromises your ideals a bit, but please also think about Uncle Sam opening doors up to us worldwide. Imagine the best of France, Israel, Russia, China, South Africa, Chile, and Australia, wherever the United States thinks we can do the most good."

"I see your point."

"Admit it, you almost have to like Reagan for taking a chance on me. That was a big stretch for him, and he should be recognized and appreciated for it. So if *I* can do this, *you* can do this, and *we* can do this together."

Cohen agonized. *I want to say yes so badly my lips hurt. There are two hesitancies. I don't want to publicly humiliate Sarah or carry water for the Gipper.*

Indecision caused Cohen's face to wrangle up in a knot. His contorted face reminded Carole of a clenched fist, and she cracked up laughing.

"Allie, your scruples are so pure they cause pain. I think you need a little time to digest all this, so I'll let it go for the time being."

"I think making love is better than talking at the moment."

He pulled Carole down on the floor to make love. Their sex was exciting and conversation easy and nearly constant. They were becoming a couple.

Chapter 34

Five-year-old Arvida White wasn't saying much, nor was she eating her cheese-flavored grits like a good little girl should. Arvida's attention focused on a rerun of *The Jeffersons*, and she tapped her spoon to the beat of the show's raucous theme song.

In this episode, a former teacher of George's walked into his cleaning store. A series of flashbacks occurred, during which the then troubled teenage George was helped by his teacher-mentor. In the end, George credited the teacher with his moving on up.

Arvida, whose parents had only moved sideways, still hadn't touched her grits. The cute, smart light-skinned kindergartner watched her mommy wash and dry the dishes and put them away.

I'm curious, Arvida wondered, *if my mommy had a special teacher in life like Mr. Jefferson.*

"Mommy, who was the best teacher you ever had?"

Farrah, busy cleaning the stove, matter-of-factly answered, "That's easy, baby, Mr. Cohen, my social studies teacher back in high school."

"Why, Mommy?"

She started eating her grits. Farrah saw it. *I'll encourage her to eat by talking.* "Mr. Cohen, honey, was the hardest teacher I ever had, and I often studied until 2:00 AM to pass some of his tests. He taught us a lot and tried his best to prepare us for life too."

Arvida, waiting for more, kept eating. "Unfortunately, a lot of us were young and foolish and didn't listen enough to what he was saying."

Arvida was close to finishing her grits. Farrah sighed. Her daughter asked, "Why so sad, Mommy?"

"Mr. Cohen expected me to go to college and become a professional. Let's just say that life didn't turn out that way."

Farrah flashed on a memory. *I was young and built and used to sit back in my seat and pretend that I was yawning, and then I'd thrust my big bust out and almost never fail to catch Cohen's eye.*

Arvida snapped Farrah out of her memory. "Mommy, did Daddy have Mr. Cohen too?"

Her plate was clean.

"Uh-huh," said Farrah. *I hope to God that Arvida doesn't display any more interest in her father's academic achievements and Mr. Cohen.*

"Did Daddy do well too, Mommy?"

Farrah flinched before fibbing, "He did okay, honey."

Eddie came home a minute later and sat down at the table without washing his hands. Farrah sensed trouble when he snatched up a slice of spongy white bread and coarsely shoved it into his mouth.

Uh-oh, she thought. *He must have stopped off at Wiley's and had too many beers.*

She watched him sullenly grab another slice and clumsily spread margarine across it. *Shit, he's fucking drunk. I better get Arvida out of here.*

Farrah directed her daughter. "Arvida, sweetie, please go and watch TV in your bedroom for a little while. Please look after your brother too. Mommy and Daddy need to talk."

Arvida got up from the table but had to know. "Daddy, did you like Mr. Cohen too?"

His judgment was clouded by alcohol. "No, I hated the dude."

"Why, Daddy? Mommy liked him."

"Cohen's a racist. That means he hates niggers." He shoved more bread in his mouth.

Farrah hushed him; that fueled his belligerence. "Let me give you a lesson in life, baby. There's an old ghetto saying. 'If you're *white*, you're all right. If you're *brown*, hang around. But if you're *black*, get back.'"

"Eddie, please don't go there."

He went there. "Well, baby, take a good long look at your daddy because God sure did make me black and hold me back. You lucky girl, you got your mommy's light skin, so you're going places in life."

Farrah shushed him. "Eddie, she's only five years old."

Eddie mumbled, "Bitch."

That pissed Farrah off. "You know, Eddie, there's another old saying. 'Beauty is skin-deep, and ugly is to the bone.' Well, your ugly go right to the marrow."

Farrah's put-down set a blood vessel high on Eddie's forehead percolating like an old-time coffeepot. Their sharp words and exchanges made Arvida cry, and she ran off to her room. The sight of his own firstborn running from him made Eddie stop and regain control. Farrah saw the sadness in his face and figured that he couldn't be all bad.

"I'm sorry, my man," she said, apologizing. "We got to stop hurting each other like this. Just because our life is shitty right now don't mean we got to brutalize our children too. Frankly, we're damn lucky that the streets ain't made them hard and mean yet."

Farrah put her arms around Eddie to comfort him, not for long, though, because she raised a taboo subject.

"You got to stop blaming Mr. Cohen for everything that's happened to us. We made our own bed, Eddie, and we're sleeping in it too."

The blood vessel started percolating again. "Yeah, well, I blame that motherfucker for everything bad in my life."

She begged him, "Let that thing go. It's just going to eat you up inside."

"He's the reason I'm a nigger garbageman, and he's the reason I ain't playing fullback for the Falcons or some other team this Sunday, so how can I just let it go?"

"Eddie, there was nothing Mr. Cohen could do."

"Give me a fucking break, Farrah."

Farrah lost patience with Eddie's stubborn refusal to own up to his mistake and get on with his life.

"Grow up, Eddie. A real man takes responsibility for his actions, and it's time that you did too."

Her words, though well-meaning, angered him. He wagged his finger and warned her, "You better watch your mouth, woman."

That pushed Farrah over the edge. "Why, you gonna hit me? Real men spoil their wives, not bang them out."

That baited him, and he got up to wash his hands. "You're too smart for your own good."

With that, he pissed Farrah off. "Are you threatening to leave me, Eddie? Nah, you know you ain't gonna do that because

I keep you the tiniest bit respectable. If it wasn't for me, you'd probably be in jail right now."

Farrah just told me I ain't shit.

With no self-esteem and only his pride left, White put on his jacket and headed for the door.

Oh shit, he's going to Wiley's to piss away a half day's wages.

She backed off. "Eddie, I apologize. Please stay."

He obstinately ignored her and left for Wiley's.

Chapter 35

Out in Malibu, California, Allie and Carole made love twice that evening before falling asleep in each other's arms. Cohen opened his eyes in the morning and lay there for a few minutes, wondering if he was dreaming. He looked at Carole to make sure that he wasn't fantasizing and then scanned the room.

Yes, I am in her bedroom, in bed with a beautiful, sexy, famous movie and singing star worth a reported $135 million.

The thought of being this very special lady's lover gave him a hard-on. Carole was sleeping on her stomach, so Allie entered her doggie-style and started a slow grinding for a few seconds.

She awakened, smiled, and cooed to him. "You sexy little devil you. I haven't had it in the morning in two years or doggie-style either, oooh, ahhh."

They eventually came for the third time in seven hours. "That, Allie, is a personal record for me. I think I'm hitting my sexual peak, and you brought it out of me."

Carole's and Sarah's sexuality is totally similar. Neither is complicated, and both like a lot of foreplay. Great sex the night before or in the morning also bequeaths sweetness and light at the breakfast table.

Carole and Allie spent a leisurely first day together exploring the canyon's trails and swimming naked in her kidney-shaped pool. They smoked a joint on the patio, watched the sun set over the ocean, and engaged in a quickie before showering, dressing, and heading out for dinner.

Carole handed Allie the keys to the Porsche. "What are you in the mood to eat?"

"Rick told me about an Italian restaurant in Studio City that specializes in a calamari steak with lemon butter sauce that's to die for."

"It's Monte's Trattoria. I was last there maybe ten years ago when it opened. It's very nice, good choice."

They opened the sunroof and headed south on the Coast Highway. Carole turned on the radio, and Mick Jagger's "Beast of Burden" blared from the speakers. She lit a joint as soon as Allie safely entered the Ventura Freeway. Unfortunately, they got stuck in a traffic jam just as they were about to get nicely buzzed for the meal.

Suddenly, gawkers recognized Carole. The driver of the car next to her asked for an autograph, and she ignored him. The car on Allie's side asked him for his autograph, and he signed it.

The driver looked at the signature and then right back at Allie and cursed, "Who the fuck is Allie Cohen?"

Cohen laughed at the dude. "You'll probably know soon enough, man."

The traffic jam finally broke up, and they whooshed away from the public.

Allie shared a fervent wish. "I pray, Carole, that Sarah does not hear of our relationship until I break it to her. She's been a wonderful wife and deserves a personal explanation. Just in case, let's construct a cover story that supports why I'm living in your house."

While she thought about it, he offered, "How about my being a Jewish education consultant to provide a crash course in preparation for your upcoming trip to Israel?"

"I can do better," said Carole. "How about I'm interested in buying your book too? We spent a week developing a treatment to obtain studio underwriting, also publication as a novel. I'm offering a half million for the screen rights, 50 percent up front, because I want to play Seymour's wife. The marketing concept is to rush the paperback into circulation to create interest and release the movie right before Passover."

"Your plan is *much* better, babe."

Carole honored him up by singing "Tortuga Flats," an act of generosity she bestowed on precious few souls. The professional songstress encouraged the partially tone-deaf Cohen to join her. "Come on, Allie, sing with me."

"Sorry, babe." He resisted at first. "Singing with you is like getting in the ring with a young Muhammad Ali."

Allie gave in and impressed her by hitting an occasional note. They pulled up to Monte's, parked the car in the lot, and walked inside.

Monte, owner and maître d, recognized Carole immediately and placed her and Allie in a corner booth in the back. He brought them a bottle of his most special white wine and personally sautéed the tender calamari steaks. Monte served them with angel hair and white clam sauce, an antipasto salad, and garlic bread.

"We have to pretend," Carole reminded Allie, "to be engaged in a business deal, so outward displays of affection are limited."

Peter Bates dampened Carole's dessert by arriving with her canoli.

"Okay," said Peter as he sat down beside Allie. "I did happy hour with Bob Urban, who says we can film a lot of that lampshade scene through trick photography, mostly shadows on walls and stuff. He wants Rod Steiger as Seymour, but I think Rod is too old. Maybe Gene Wilder would be a good choice. What do you think?"

Carole asked, "How the hell did you find us?"

"I drove out to your place, saw you guys leaving, and followed you out here. I've been on my car phone, though, the past hour with this deal and a few others."

I need to know his purpose too. Allie realized. "Peter, talking about the lead before the terms is kind of premature, isn't it?" He held his breath.

"You're right, Allie. Okay." Bates delivered transformational news. "Bob and I only needed ten minutes to talk Sam Minkowitz into paying $940,000 for film rights and another nine forty to publish the book and build the property for exhibiting the film."

"Oh my god," stated Carole. "That's fantastic."

"God," insisted Bates, "had nothing to do with it. Sam, Bob, and I feel that the world is finally ready for a powerful story like this and paid for the rights to both."

Wrong, Peter. Adonai and I influenced Sam to underwrite Allie to unite him with Carole, and let me tell you, he is not an easy man to sway. But yes, the timing is right.

"Peter, that's a life changer," declared Allie. "And I'm incredibly grateful."

"You could, of course, Allie, peddle each separately and maybe get a little more, but remember, Sam is forking over nearly two million with half of it up front on an unknown and untried writer."

Peter pointed his index finger downward to emphasize that he was ready to start production in a month or two. Allie vigorously shook Peter's hand.

"Thank you, Peter, I appreciate your confidence, and I'm going to work my balls off to make this a great book and movie."

Bates passed the cashier's check for $940,000 to Allie, who stared at the incredible numbers.

"As Dr. Allie Cohen back home in Atlanta, I'm one of the highest-paid public school teachers in the entire South, yet it would take me over twenty years to earn this much money, and I'd be ready to retire."

Carole hugged and kissed Allie. "Your story is in good hands with Sam, Peter, and Bob behind it."

"Save your words for the typewriter, Allie," Peter told him. "You've got two months to finish your book."

"No problem, Peter, all that's left is the fleeing to Israel and Masada suicide scenes."

"Allie," Peter inquired, "would you mind if I brought in Elie Wiesel as a Holocaust consultant?"

"No, not at all, he's a survivor and an authority. That shows me how serious you are in treating this subject sensitively."

Peter smiled. "I like hearing that." He laughed and zinged Carole, "I think you finally picked a man with substance."

"Tell me," she jabbed him back. "Is that supposed to be a compliment?"

Any comeback line was weak compared with Peter's topper.

"Oh, by the way, call Rose and congratulate your mother and Sam on their getting *engaged*." He smiled wickedly.

Carole's mouth opened for a few seconds before reacting. "Sam must have told you before Rose could share the incredible news with me. That wasn't fair, Peter."

Bates flashed another wicked smile and then left. Carole asked Allie if he felt changed by sale of his novel.

"Yeah, $1.9 million is liberating. I don't have to hold down a steady job anymore, and best of all, I can do a lot more for my family."

Carole interpreted. "I guess you'll be leaving education. Do you think you'll miss teaching?"

"Of course, I will, but it'll be impossible to continue in that job and meet my new responsibilities. I loved teaching high school kids, but I'm deliriously happy over becoming a professional writer—strike that, an author."

When Allie was three years old, his daddy noticed that he had independent ways. A concerned Barney Cohen picked up his spirited and stubborn little boy, sat him on his lap, touched the tip of Allie's nose with his finger to get his full attention, and taught him an important life lesson.

"Son, for every lion, there's a lion tamer."

It was never in Allie's nature to obediently follow. His whole life seemed to him a series of awkward accommodations to a higher authority. Since most systems usually reward those it can control and punish those it can't, a price of success is often conformity.

For Allie, each new success demanded an uncomfortable trade-off, and his latest and greatest success required a *sellout*— leaving Sarah.

It doesn't feel right, and I don't think I can live with myself. I need to figure out how to keep both Sarah and Carole in my life.

Allie and Carole spent the last night of Easter vacation enjoying a casual dinner with Rose and Sam. Rose served a delicious veal dish, and Sam entertained them with hilarious blooper stories of past cinematic stinkers. I am partial to Sam's stories and his manner of telling them with funny hand gestures.

While Rose and Carole cleaned up, Sam and Allie sipped Grand Marnier from beautiful handblown snifter glasses.

"You got to admit it, Allie, it's astonishing that the media still hasn't picked up on you and Carole yet."

"You're not kidding," said a grateful Cohen.

The Lord Almighty and I were trying our best to keep the media storm at bay until Allie can tell Sarah personally. Keeping talent or prized properties secret, though, was not in the best interest of Sam's media business.

"Let me say, Allie, that you're not invisible anymore to the people who run this business. In less than a week, you've become viewed as a major new talent."

"None of them, Sam," Cohen pointed out, "have read a single word of my lone incomplete work of fiction."

"Allie, you should be proud that people appreciate your art, even if they haven't read it yet." Cohen smiled at that line and let it pass. "Every once in a while, a new talent like you and Elia Kazan appear and push the envelope with fresh themes."

"Thank you, Sam, that's very good company."

Minkowitz described how Hollywood devoured talent.

"Today we grind writers up like so much chopped liver." He held his hands apart to illustrate. "While this is not the golden age of moviemaking, the business is bigger than ever, namely, the *Star Wars*– and *ET*-type grosses."

"Sam, what are you trying to tell me?" He sipped some Grand Marnier.

"Okay, today good scripts are hard to find, Allie. So between the movies and TV, there are barely five great concepts a year to produce big profits." He spread the fingers of his right hand. "With the rise too of the independents, movie studios are being reduced to releasing institutions."

"Okay, but every industry changes structurally over time."

"You're right, but agents now crank out ideas for their stars who often want to produce too. They then hire a writer to produce a script or novel from it. In GMEI's case, our film, TV, and publishing units all try to make money off the same concept."

"That makes sense."

"Frankly, I love your book, even if I haven't read it yet. I sense that there are a lot more great ideas inside you and want to give you the chance to tap them. I think you and GMEI can make a lot of money together, eh, boychick."

Cohen got the drift, finished his liqueur, and then asked, "Sam, are you making me an offer?"

"Yeah, I am and a package deal too."

"Nice and straight, Sam," said Allie appreciatively and then asked, "What do you have in mind?"

Sam, master of the deal, laid his cards on the table.

"Three print projects to be made into movies over the next five years. For you, there's $3.5 million in it with a quarter-of-a-million payment up front. You got all the standard clauses for weeks on the best-seller lists, plus 2 percent of all movie profits. With just moderate hits, the payoff to you is $5 million. With blockbusters, your share tops $10 million or more. So Allie, what do you say?"

"It sounds fantastic. Just one question, please clarify *print projects.*"

"No problem, first, a reworking of a Noel Seymour comedy that I purchased a while back for Carole. She claims it's too tame for her, and maybe she's right. Since you're younger and hipper than Noel, maybe you can give it some more bite."

"I don't know about reworking Seymour's crap."

"Noel is a respected author. Please don't call his stuff *crap.* There's nothing wrong with being *popular.*" Cohen acknowledged that. "Second, a six-hour historical miniseries for ABC's '87 season. They pick the subject and are thinking about Thomas Jefferson, Lincoln, FDR, or JFK."

Allie figured before speaking, *I prefer not to rewrite other author's scripts or tailor a miniseries around Burger King or Ford. I just want to write novels, but everyone has to start somewhere, and Sam is opening the door widely.*

Allie thanked Sam, who graciously brushed it aside. "The third project is anything you want. 'Got anything in mind?"

"Lately," Allie revealed, "I've been thinking of a story my grandfather told my mother when I was three. They thought I was watching cartoons when my grandpa Aaron told my mother that he and I were descended from kings."

"You're shitting me?" Allie told Sam the details and how his mother hid the story from him for over thirty years. "Allie, that's the wildest Jewish tale I've ever heard."

Allie illustrated it to Sam. "Until now, I didn't want to think of it because it was a burden. Plus, no one knows if the Chazer people actually existed. They might have been a lost tribe of Israel, according to some historians."

"I like it and think it has dramatic and humorous elements. I suggest we bring in Billy Diamond to help shape the comedic parts."

Hashem and I would later wash this idea from Sam's mind because the world was still not ready to deal with Chazer existence. Israel would squawk the loudest about the recognition undermining Jewish claims to the Holy Land, especially Judea and Samaria. The production would not happen, and Allie would replace it with a very successful African adventure story and do a terrific job updating the Noel Seymour comedy, which did big box office.

"Allie, you're a talented novice who can benefit from having the resources of a Fortune 500 company behind you." Sam emphasized, "GMEI has the ways and means to groom you into becoming another James Michener, Saul Bellow, Herman Wouk, or Alex Haley. As I see it, Allie, you're still a young man learning your craft, and a little seasoning can't hurt."

"I appreciate hearing that, Sam."

"You'll see, Allie, GMEI and I will do right by you."

"I'm sure you will, Sam."

Minkowitz expressed a concern. "Allie, forgive me for possibly being out of line, but I sense the issue is not artistry or integrity but instead *guilt*. Tell me, and please be frank. Are you guilty over leaving your wife for Carole?"

"Guilt is literally dripping from my pores," admitted Allie. "I even feel it in my molars. First, I have to draw a line at writing crap. Creativity and freedom to follow through on ideas is at risk of compromise. Second and more importantly, I need to keep Sarah in my life too and must figure out a way."

Minkowitz, an artful negotiator, promised, "Okay, I'll add an option to buy a second concept from you if you agree to do the Seymour script and TV miniseries. The deal is now for $4.5 million for the four projects over five years."

"That sounds fair enough, Sam."

"So, Allie, since you don't plan on leaving your wife, how would you make this thing with Carole work?"

"I'm not sure yet, Sam. All I know, at the moment, is that I need both Carole and Sarah in my life."

Sam put his arm around Allie's shoulder just the way his uncle William did when he was seventeen.

"Kiddo, I'm a rich old man who has very little family and plans to marry Rose, and you know that Carole is like a daughter to me. My son just turned thirty-five and is a confirmed bachelor and wants no kids."

"I understand."

"I'm also comfortable with you and would like to see you make Carole very happy."

"Sure, Sam."

"Good. Rose constantly worries over the lack of stability in Carole's life, and I don't blame her, and since you're a smart guy, you should understand that anything that makes Rose and Carole happy also makes my life that much easier. That's not so hard to understand, is it?"

Allie sheepishly answered, "No, it isn't."

"Fine, now let me give you some good advice."

"Sure, Sam, what?"

Sam looked Allie in the eye while stating one of his prized proverbs. "Allie, nobody ever got poor by taking."

That line went over easily enough with Allie, though it was still unclear to Cohen how much more taking would cleanse his guilt—or add to it.

Rose and Carole returned from the kitchen, and Sam informed them of the deal he'd struck with Allie.

"That's fantastic, Allie, and thank you, Sam."

Carole hugged Sam. "Allie, let's go home. I know exactly how to celebrate this."

They went straight back to her place to make love. Physically contented and reasonably secure that Allie was moving in with her, Carole fell right to sleep.

Cohen was not so lucky, for he lay in the dark for two hours, contemplating what he'd say to Sarah when he got home.

I'll take a sleeping pill. Maybe it'll smother my brain and let me get some shut-eye.

After a few hours of restless sleep, he awoke to the same nagging questions that were beginning to haunt him.

How does someone become something different in only six days?

How does a husband tell his wonderful and pregnant wife that he's been paired with a second woman?

What if it's a boy? Do I just take off after the bris and miss his development?

Will I be able to live with myself?

Sure, if I'm a selfish fucking bastard.

Chapter 36

Cohen got out of bed and went to the kitchen to make some coffee.

Where's Allie's ass? I can't find it.

Carole awoke to find no buttocks or Cohen. She put on her robe and also headed toward the kitchen. Allie, drinking from a mug and staring into space, was so deep in thought that he didn't hear her speak to him from just a few feet away.

"Allie, what's wrong? Why are you up so early?" Carole tried again, but this time she yelled, "Allie, what the hell is wrong?"

He heard her. "I'm sorry, Carole. I guess I just have a lot on my mind."

"From your look," she voiced, "I suspect that you're wrestling with the big decisions that you're facing. I'm right, aren't I?"

He probably shouldn't have said, "So you're right, Carole. That doesn't make it any easier for me."

Carole, annoyed, let him know it. "Hey, you're thinking of yourself. Why is this only hard for you?"

She's right. He got it. *It's a big adjustment for her too. Look at the risk she's taking by inviting me to move in with her. By all accounts, I should get down on the ground and kiss her feet.*

"My problem, Carole," he joked, "is that I'm Jewish and must agonize over every good thing that comes my way. Why can't I be guiltless like Johnny Carson, a true WASP, who leaves his wife if she gets a stretch mark?"

Carole, who had met two of Carson's ex-wives at awards and women's functions, laughed hard.

Allie apologized to her. "I'm sorry, sweetie. I do love you and plan to take that trip with you, but now that we're a couple, I must warn you that life for me is congenitally problematic."

His last two words brought a sunny big smile to her face.

"You're incapable of just saying 'it's *complex*,' 'it won't be *easy*,' or 'with me, it's *never simple*.' No, you have to say *congenitally problematic*. Come here. I love you."

He held her in his arms and kissed her cheek. "It bothers you that I feel like a heel, doesn't it?"

"I guess," answered Carole wistfully, "I'm like a child who wants the candy bar all to herself. In your case, though, I'm willing to share you for a while. I realize that it will take some time to gracefully extricate yourself from Atlanta, and I expect you to move in with me before the month is up. Does that sound fair to you?"

"A month seems unrealistic, and the birth factor is a big wild card. Sarah needs a lot of support. Let's play this *moving in* thing by ear."

That should buy me some time to figure out how to include Sarah in all this.

Cohen packed up his clothes to return Rick's car and hop a ride to the airport. Carole came up from behind and put her hand down his pants to fondle him.

"Come on, Allie, let's have sex one more time, just a quickie."

He gently removed her hand from his pants and urged, "Carole, honey, please realize that I've barely enough time to get back to Rick's and to the airport to catch my plane."

"You and Rick came with Greta and Reny." She had to know before he left. "Did you do both of them too?"

He figured that it was smarter to confess than lie and told her *yes.*

"Holy shit," she teased. "You really had one hell of a trip out here, didn't you?"

Allie flashed a memory of Libby Lee and broadcast a solar smile. Cohen didn't tell Herman that he also did Turkish, the girl she caught screwing her ex-husband Myron Silver. Cohen, Turkish's high school practice teacher, boned her standing up in an IND line subway car on her eighteenth birthday and his last day of practice teaching.

Allie kissed Carole. "I love you, babe. I'll let myself out of the house."

He hurriedly started the Corvette and raced back to Rick's place.

Samuels, waiting for Cohen in the driveway, was instantly ready to go and snidely commented as he took over the wheel, "Gee, Allie, it was nice of you to leave your ol' buddy Rick a whole six or seven minutes to see you off."

Rick's clever sarcasm forced Allie to laugh. Rick passed a message from Sarah.

"Your wife—remember her?—will meet you in the baggage claim area. I covered for you but was uncomfortable being a part of your conspiracy."

Adonai told me to put an idea in Allie's head, for the Lord did not want to break up Allie's marriage, only assign him an angel to engage the world. In Jewish American culture, though, the angel seems to have to fall in love and have sex with the prophet to justify the relationship with her mother and sustain the partnership with him.

Allie bounced an idea off Rick as he entered the freeway.

"I plan to *co-live* with Sarah and Carole."

"Co-living, what the hell is that? Does that mean you're only *half-leaving* your wife?"

"Look, Rick." Cohen defended his action. "Nobody can accuse me anymore of hiding in the classroom my entire life. I'm taking my best shot, and if people want to condemn me for it, well, that's their problem."

"Allie, that's a load of shit."

"Man," Cohen snapped back, "I'd have to be nuts or stupid to turn down an offer that will make me a major author and millions of dollars."

"You see what I mean? You're a whore like everybody else out here."

"We all have a price, Rick, and some of us come cheaper than others. Given that teachers are the most timid people in risk-taking, they sell out for less than everybody else."

"That's a gross rationalization," ridiculed Samuels. "And you know it."

"So what, Rick? If Sarah and I are really meant to be, it'll be, the same with Carole."

"Oh, man, now you're resorting to fatalism, kismet shit."

"Come on, Rick, give me a break. I struggle from one pay period to the next. Now I don't have to worry about money for the rest of my life."

"I guess you don't, Allie. Man, what a week. We both experienced life-changing situations. You got published big-time, and I got my four queens. Six incredible days transformed us both into players, and now you face the challenge of making two formidable women happy. I guess I got four now to keep happy."

"Rick, Sarah will have to trust me that somehow, in some way, I will do right by her. Carole will have to accept that I must be shared with Sarah, or I'm no good to her either."

"Good luck with that. Proud, strong women like Sarah and Carole agreeing to share you is, at best, temporary, and I predict that someone is going to get shortchanged. Given your deals out here, I suspect it'll be your Atlanta family."

They reached the Delta terminal. Cohen got his bags out of the trunk and checked them with a porter. The alert young black male attendant recognized Allie from a photo he'd just seen on CNN.

"Hey, you're Allie Cohen, aren't you? Can I have your autograph?"

"Oh shit, Rick, the stardom thing is starting. Better race home to tell Sarah before she hears it from somebody else. I'm lucky that she never watches CNN. Please, Lord, make her into a good long novel like *War and Peace*."

Allie signed the autograph, thanked the young man, and turned to say goodbye to Rick.

"What can I say, Rick? You've been great."

229

Rick winked before sentimentalizing. "Some week, eh?"

"Yeah, Rick, absolutely incredible. I owe you big-time for this week, and I hope I live through the next one."

"Allie, I've always been amazed by your capacity to live on the edge. You know, you might just do it all by forty. I've got to concede. You have pretty good odds now."

Allie emotionally hugged Rick for a few seconds before making a run for the circular Delta terminal and arrived at the gate after everyone had boarded. Cohen attempted to act inconspicuously while taking his seat and looking away from the aisle.

I have a mess waiting for me in Atlanta, and it's my job to clean it up before leaving. The price of my success is a host of good and bad changes coming to my loved ones.

Prophet, you can kiss *grace*—the special Atlanta ambience—goodbye for quite a while.

Chapter 37

It's after 11:00 PM. Farrah White sighed. *I'm tired as hell and, I swear, could fall out right now.*

Farrah slid the covers back to get into bed and turned on the TV to watch news. Her nightly habit was to ignore the TV until the meteorologist gave the next day's weather and temperature. She could then fall asleep because she'd know what to wear tomorrow for Atlanta's changeable weather.

Farrah believed ardently in the old saying "If you don't like Atlanta's weather, wait a minute, it'll change."

This evening was different, however; an extraordinary news item grabbed her attention and riveted her. The *Eleven Alive* "Eye on Atlanta" segment focused on a familiar name from the past.

"Dr. Allie Cohen, a Buckhead High School social studies teacher, has written a novel that will be published by Global Books this summer. Cohen's story, *The Lesson*, will also be made into a major motion picture scheduled to be released by Global Pictures next year. The really big news is a rumor circulating around Hollywood that Dr. Cohen"—his picture was flashed—"is romantically linked to actress-singer Carole Herman." A picture of her also appeared on the screen. "Well, well, talk about a local guy making it big. Now a commercial message from our sponsor."

Farrah, excited by her old teacher's success, hailed Eddie, who was in the kitchen finishing off a four-pack of Steel Reserve malt liquor.

"Eddie, come here. I just heard incredible news."

Eddie, fairly intoxicated, slowly rambled into the bedroom and slurred his words.

"For Chrissake, what's the big deal?"

231

Farrah enthusiastically forwarded the news. "Mr. Cohen from high school is now a rich and famous author. His novel is being published and made into a movie. But dig this. He's doing Carole Herman, the movie star."

Eddie's pronounced feelings of obscurity limited him to "So?"

"I'm sorry I bothered," said Farrah, understanding his reaction but still disappointed. "Jesus, Eddie, is that all you can say, *so*?"

Farrah examined Eddie and what he'd become almost nine years after getting his general education diploma at Vo-Tech.

Christ, if self-esteem was motor oil, he'd be three quarts low.

Eddie switched the setoff, yelled at Farrah, and cursed Cohen.

"Yeah, that's all I can say! What, you expected me to be happy for the motherfucker?"

Farrah thought before letting it fly. *I may be making a mistake by not dropping it, but fuck it.*

"Mr. Cohen was a brilliant man, Eddie, and much too cool to be a teacher his whole life."

"Cool, my ass."

"Eddie, I beg you to put that behind you already. I swear, you're going to kill yourself over a stupid mistake you made years ago. Please, baby, let it go."

"I don't know why you don't buy his hatin' niggers, Farrah."

232

"Well," she angrily but unwisely pointed out, "then Cohen must have hated you because you're acting like the dumbest fucking nigger of all time."

She cupped her hands over her mouth. "I'm sorry, Eddie, I shouldn't have said that."

It was too late. Eddie, his pride deeply wounded by Farrah's reply, whacked her hard with the back of his hand. The powerful smack knocked her off the bed and onto the floor, where she sprawled half-conscious.

"Woman," he warned, "don't you ever talk to me like that again."

He put on his coat and headed to Wiley's.

We can't save Eddie until he's ready to turn himself around, but thankfully he is close to hitting rock bottom.

Chapter 38

Cohen's plane landed at the same time as the "Eye on Atlanta" broadcast. Sarah and her parents happily waited for in him in baggage instead of gnashing their teeth at the TV. Harvey spotted Allie approaching and his luggage arriving almost at the same time.

"How come his luggage," Harvey questioned, "is always waiting for him or the first one up? I never saw anything like it. You'd think he was the chief of the Atlanta Baggage Handler's Union."

Allie's being the prophet had nothing to do with his luggage always being available. Trust me, he was just lucky that way.

Rebecca noticed. "Allie, you look marvelous, so tan and healthy looking."

Allie opened an eye toward Harvey, who seemed to notice too.

I wonder if my father-in-law is peeved from my California tan and his pregnant daughter's deep winter paleness. How high will his bile rise when he learns of truly unjust acts? I hate having to prepare lines of bullshit and program my face into a public mask, but what else can I do? The truth has to wait until a better moment than baggage claim.

Allie and Sarah embraced with hugs and kisses. "I'm so glad to see you, Allie. Please tell us all about your trip, especially any publishing deals."

He answered the trio's questions with stock answers. "Anyway, a model friend of Rick's got us invited to a screening at Carole Herman's house."

They said they already knew that. In chorus, they stated, "Get to the good parts already. For example, what's she like?"

"I didn't get a chance to talk to her very much. She had to entertain a bunch of studio suits and their wives, but she is more real and down-to-earth than you might suspect."

Sarah was curious if he met any other famous people. "Uh-huh, I got to know Billy Diamond, Peter Bates, Daria Kelsey, and Sam Minkowitz. They've become friends. The rest were basically studio executives who, except for making films, weren't special."

"I can't stand Billy Diamond." Rebecca sneered. "Papa likes the jerk and keeps dragging me to his movies."

Sarah sided with her father as they drove away from the airport and onto I-85 north.

"I disagree, Ma, Billy Diamond's one of the funniest men alive, isn't he, Allie?"

Now I'm an authority. He laughed to himself but added, "Sarah, he's funnier in real life than in the movies, and I actually did shtick with him. At one point, I was on such a roll that he tried to hire me as a comedy writer."

"Wow, I'll bet his offer made your day." Allie smiled to reflect that it did, and she kissed him. "My celebrity, I can just imagine you and Diamond standing around trading lines about how life is a bad Jewish joke."

Allie gulped hard from her remark but was thrilled that he'd made it through the airport unnoticed. He realized a new need for limos waiting for him everywhere, a first step toward isolation from normal life.

Harvey rode up front with Allie and switched on WGST, a news channel.

Cohen panicked. "Dad, could you please turn off the radio? I have a little headache from the flight. There was a lot of turbulence."

Harvey did. Allie thanked him and disclosed selling his book. "The other night, I had dinner with Peter Bates, and he bought my book."

After a few seconds of speechlessness, he added, "Peter's going to make it into a movie too. Sam Minkowitz and Global Pictures are publishing the book and producing the movie and gave me a huge advance to complete it for an August rollout. This may be hard to believe, Mom and Dad, but Sarah and I are now millionaires."

He handed Sarah the cashier's check for nine forty. "That check is 50 percent good-faith money. I also negotiated a contract for four more projects over the next four years for a minimum of $4.5 million. We're rich."

Sarah stared at the cashier's check and then shrieked. "Allie, you did it. You did it! I knew that you had it in you. My god, I'm so proud of you I could cry."

"My son-in-law, the novelist," Cohen's mother-in-law proudly boasted through tears of joy. "I had faith that you'd be a great success, and God rewarded us, right, Papa?"

Harvey stared at the check too. He had worked hard his whole life and made dozens of men rich without becoming wealthy himself. Harvey liked being able to help Allie and Sarah now and then, but the shoe was on the other foot now. Harvey tried to bury his feelings of devaluation by Allie's sudden riches.

Cohen loved the Kartzmans and long prided himself on not telling in-law jokes. He reciprocated for their past support, particularly the down payment on his mortgage.

"Mom, Dad, I'm going to be spending a lot of time out in LA on business from now on. There are some beautiful condos being built in Sandy Springs, and nothing would make me happier than to buy you one. This way, you can be closer to Sarah and the baby."

"Allie," said Rebecca, crying from happiness, "you're the most wonderful son-in-law imaginable. For years, I've bragged to my friends what a smart man my Sarah married, and now you've made her life like a fairy tale. God bless you, Allie."

Sarah wrapped her arms around Allie, who was agonizing internally, and then she suddenly remembered important news.

"Allie, from August 14 to 22, the National Institute of Education (NIE) is sponsoring a human relations seminar in Washington, and you're one of the top ten specialists they selected. This is an elite NIE research project, so all our expenses are taken care of, along with childcare services. Won't that make a fabulous vacation?"

Allie forced a smile, weakly nodded yes, and then almost choked when his mother-in-law proposed to join them.

"Ooh, Harvey and I haven't been to Washington since he got out of the army in 1945. Hey, why don't we meet you two and take in all the sights during the day while Allie's attending his conference?"

Sarah, ever the devoted daughter, replied, "Ma, I love it. Allie, doesn't that sound like a lot of fun to you?"

Allie politely nodded yes again. *Now I actually have a headache. That's what I get for lying. Fortunately, we're nearly home, and I can take an aspirin for relief.*

Allie got his luggage from the trunk and seemed unusually quiet to Sarah while lugging his suitcases upstairs to unpack. Sarah kissed her parents goodbye and became sentimental while helping her husband put his things away.

"Allie, do you remember what you said to me on our third date?"

"Is that the one when we borrowed Terry Winkler's apartment to make love?"

"Uh-huh, you promised me that you were a shrewd dude who had a ton of good ideas and that one of them would bust it open for us. And, man, have you delivered on that promise. I'm so damn proud of you I'm going to cry."

Sarah cried tears of joy. Allie put his fist into his mouth and chewed on it.

Dammit, no combination of magical words exists to soften the impact.

He continued to appear oddly withdrawn to her. Sarah thought, *Maybe he's just tired from the flight. I want to make love.*

Sarah playfully snuck up from behind him, put her hand down his pants, and fondled his penis until it was hard. Allie appreciated her affection.

I hate to put it like this, but I sense a moral obligation to make love to Sarah right now.

He began caressing her oversized breasts. "Money, your boobs are like milk jugs."

"I wish you hadn't noticed. Remarks like that do a hell of a lot for my self-confidence about my physical appearance in late pregnancy."

Thus began an endless period of foreplay to stoke some level of eroticism. Allie eventually mounted Sarah and courageously tackled fifteen to twenty minutes of Olympian sexual gymnastics. Amazingly, his arms held out long enough for both to achieve orgasm.

Sarah Cohen, while making love, meditated that Allie and she were on the threshold of realizing all their dreams. Soon the house would be filled with the laughter of a happy and healthy baby born to a rich and vibrant young family. Sarah's only sadness was that her saintly grandmother did not live long enough to become a great-grandmother.

"You know, Allie." She interrupted her flashback to comment, "Living with you is never boring. One never knows what's coming from you next."

Chapter 39

There's your lead-in, Allie, and although I know that you don't want to go there, you're obliged to tell your angel of the hearth.

"Sarah," he said with a downbeat tone, "you may be more of a visionary than you care to imagine."

His tone bothers the hell out of me.

Sarah put her hands on her hips and asked, "Why'd you say that to me, Allie. What do you mean?"

Allie sighed three times; no turmoil was expelled. He groped for a gentle introductory phrase; none existed. Allie lit a joint and slowly puffed four times.

Allie's silence is not a good sign. She worried. Cohen spoke deliberately.

"This is the hardest thing that I have ever had to say to you, but you once made me promise that if something like this happened, I'd tell you immediately before you heard it from someone else. We both swore that neither of us would keep this from the other."

She thought, *He's making me nervous and annoyed.*

"Stop babbling, Allie, and get to the point."

"Babe." He sighed again and mentioned the unmentionable, "While out on the coast, I had an affair, and a certain person fell in love with me."

Sarah's body language expressed hurt and shock, and she quivered for a few seconds.

240

"Who fell in love with you out there, and why is that even important?"

Allie sensed the absurdity of it all and sighed once more before saying the unimaginable.

"Carole Herman. I've spent the last six days with her."

Sarah, stupefied, took a long hard look at Allie. She tried to take his words seriously. Was there something in his face that she'd not seen before?

"Carole Herman, the movie star, loves you? You've had an *affair* with her for a week? You're kidding me?" He shook his head no. "Hasn't she been living with a handsome tall producer?"

"Her mother caught him screwing another woman, and she threw him out. I showed up the next day, and—boom—it happened, that fast too."

"This is totally outrageous. Christ, Carole Herman, why you, my little teacher? Well, I guess you're now a novelist too."

Allie analyzed. "Carole is experiencing a sea change in life. David and she have had problems for a while, and when he humiliated her, he was toast."

"They say timing is most everything in life."

"Her last film role changed her direction in life. Now she wants to fill in some intellectual and travel gaps. Reagan just offered her an around-the-world tour to entertain people wherever. She likes me, and I have the background to satisfy her new needs and wants."

Sarah, still too stunned to cry, put two and two together. "So that's the attraction to you. You're a brainy, cute little Jew who likes to travel?"

"Ha ha! I guess so, but there is one more thing. It's rumored that David Conte has a ten-inch dick. Imagine someone your size receiving him." Sarah's eyes crossed at the thought of a ten-inch penis entering her. "Uh-huh, it killed sex for them."

"So your organ being a little more than half his size made the difference?" He nodded yes. She had to know. "Is sex better with her, Allie?"

Tears formed in her eyes and began rolling down her cheeks. He wiped them away with a tissue and made clear to her.

"No, it's unbelievably the same. You and Carole could be clones sexually. You're the same size and have the same bones and movements. I'm not nearly as comfortable with her yet as I am with you."

"Is that a compliment? Is that supposed to be a consolation and make me happy? That my husband is having an affair with one of the most famous women in the world? That being similar sexually is somehow a positive? Sorry, I'm having trouble with that one."

He didn't say anything; she did. Sarah comprehended. "My god, this is all over TV, Allie, isn't it?"

He again nodded yes and then warned her, "I have to prepare you, Sarah. It just started today. CNN and 'Eye on Atlanta' have broadcast it, and a tsunami of publicity is revving up, including Global's promoting the book and film."

Now she was crying hard. "I'm going to be humiliated worldwide. Relatives in Israel and South Africa will turn on their TV sets and hear this. How could you do this to me?"

"That's why I had to tell you tonight because, by tomorrow, you'll probably read it in the newspaper or hear it on the radio or TV. I thank the Lord I was able to tell you first."

242

Yahweh and I are both glad that we held back the media onslaught for Sarah's sake but sad too that our linking Carole with Allie hurt her. It will be hard for Sarah, but she will come to understand that Carole is our beholding *angel* for Allie's mission, and Sarah's angelic role is to be his *rock* and sustain the family.

"This is the type of shit," mused Sarah, "that you read about in the *National Enquirer*. Think about it. I'm going to see myself in headlines at the supermarket checkout counter. That's really awful, man."

"That *is* really awful, Sarah, but someone once said that with *riches come fame, and fame is a fuck*."

Sarah buried her head in her hands and slowly rocked. "Carole Herman said that in the movie you took me to on our first date. You remember Sal, the guy who yelled 'nice shirt' from thirty rows away?"

"Ha ha! Yes, I do, Sarah. That could happen only in Brooklyn."

They had a good laugh before Sarah started to cry again. "My family and friends and millions of strangers are going to read that I couldn't hold on to my husband, that he cheated on me a month before giving birth to his child, and how he traipsed around the world with an actress."

"Please, Sarah." He held out his hands.

She bawled, "Allie, how could you do this to me?"

"Sarah, I didn't plan for this, but I'll do my best to protect you from the media crap as much as possible. Frankly, though, my living more in LA may intensify the fishbowl effect a bit."

"So you're moving in with her and abandoning me and the baby?"

"No, Sarah, I'd never abandon you and the baby. I'm going to take good care of everybody and try to be there for both of you as much as I can."

"Allie, can't you do everything from here?"

"Not really, these are huge projects that require more of my time being out there. And the Reagan tour gives me a chance to affect change in all the places that need it. This opportunity is setting all of us up for life and allowing me a chance to realize my most fervent goals."

"You working behind the scenes for Reagan bothers me."

"I assure you, Sarah," Cohen pleaded, "that I'd much prefer to tour for a Democrat, but America elected the Gipper."

"I get it."

"Money, there are forty-five wars raging in the world, so the tour provides a safe means of repairing the world as much as I can. I'm just sad that it won't be with you."

"Listen to him," she complained. "He's sad. Isn't that too bad? Well, buddy, you may be sad. But for me, it's a nightmare."

"Yes," Allie agreed. "My words are terribly inadequate, but what can I tell you Sarah? That's the truth. All I can say is that I'm very, very sorry."

"Please don't leave. Isn't our life rich and full enough now? Look at all the good things that are happening to you professionally. That should be sufficient."

"True, Sarah, but the pursuit of mission, power, and wealth demands more time on the West Coast and on the road."

"You're my husband," Sarah pleaded one more time, "the father of my child. I'll change if you need me to."

"Money." Allie held Sarah in his arms. "You don't have to change at all. You're perfect as you are and didn't do anything wrong. I love you."

"I'm glad that you still do and that you feel that way."

"Sarah, try to understand this. I'm not leaving you. I'm *co-living* with her. We'll see what the future brings."

"So," Sarah said, skeptical, "you're co-living with me and her, but it sure seems to me like you're going to be living with *her* a lot more—that whole travel thing, for instance. I assume you're expecting me to let you get this thing out of your system and come back."

"Yes, Sarah, very possibly, but I all I can promise is that, if you trust in me, in five years, we can have $10 million in the bank. Plus, I can be a global teacher for millions of people around the world."

She pushed him away. "I'll live and even manage fine without you." Another wave of crying started. "What will I tell my parents?"

"Whatever, just tell them first thing in the morning before they hear it from the media."

"Right, Allie, basically, you're leaving me for a better deal but keeping this door open. Following through actually has never been a strength of yours."

She pointed to her big belly.

"That hurts, Sarah."

"Too bad, you know you're also dropping about a half-dozen academic projects on cosponsors, Cohen, and running off to something even more ego gratifying."

"That hurts too." Tears welled up in Allie's eyes. "I understand how you see things like that, Sarah. All I ask, though, is that you trust in me. I love you, Sarah, and I love you a lot more than Carole. You're about to bear me a child, who is already dear to me, and I intend and hope to return home at some time in the future. Please work with me in this important mission."

"How can you be so sure," Sarah countered, "that I'll still be available?"

He rubbed her belly. "I can't, but that bun in the oven is ours. We're tied to for life, and I love that. You've been a perfect wife and still are."

"I like hearing that, Allie."

"*Tikkun olam*, Sarah. Repair the world. I have an unprecedented opportunity to make a difference. Please have faith in me, and I will make it up to you. I realize that I could lose everything that is precious and dear to me."

"For money and fame too. You're a Chazer, Allie. You deserve to lose everything."

Allie took it, so she tried another strategy. "Wait, Carole hasn't had to put up with your allergies like that sinus problem that causes you to sneeze a lot or make that disgusting sound with your throat or the gassy stomach that makes you belch *and* fart out loud."

"You fart too. Patoot, patoot, toot, little farts." They both laughed, and Allie confided to her, "I've thought about things like farting out loud. Sometimes my stomach aches before I can sneak one out. You're the only woman in the world whom I can comfortably fart out loud with."

"Thanks, Allie."

"Hey, that's important."

Both laughed from his half-assed compliment, and he held her hands. "Sarah, I want you to learn how to be a rich woman. Get on with your PhD, and stop putting it off. I insist that you visit all those places that I had already been to before you and made you go elsewhere. Start with seeing Paris, Amsterdam, Spain, and Italy."

"I prefer to travel with you."

"Sarah, the world changed today, and nothing will be the same again."

"It's true that money is the root of all evil. It took you away from me, Allie."

Cohen squirmed, looked at the floor, and finally answered, "Well, Carole is a fantastic woman, very smart, and funny and—"

"Oh, shut up, you sound like Montgomery Clift talking down to Shelley Winters in *A Place in the Sun.*"

He threw up his hands to say that he didn't know what else to say or do. Sarah sat herself down in a hot bath to relax and fall asleep. Allie followed her into the steaming white porcelain tub and held his arms around her enlarged waistline.

"Who needs you in here?" said Sarah, half in jest.

"Sarah, I've decided to ask our friend Sandy Forman to be my business manager and provide you a thousand a week allowance. That should suffice. I assume that, given how much you've loved your work in the past, you'll return to it after six months."

"Why did you pick him, Allie? Sandy can be a little compulsive."

"I've thought this through. He's a damn good accountant and has a good head for business, but most of all, he's honest and very responsible. Bringing good friends along for the ride will help me from getting too puffed up when the phonies out there keep telling me I'm a blooming genius."

"I see what you mean."

"Dig it. Nearly everyone out there has told me in the same breath that they think it's a great book, but they haven't read it yet. Think about that."

"Now that you mentioned that, maybe it is a good idea, after all, to hire Sandy."

Chapter 40

Sarah finally fell asleep at 2:00 AM. Allie's body, still on West Coast time, revved a bit, so he went downstairs to the kitchen to nosh. Cohen stared into the refrigerator, found nothing desirable to eat, and decided to call Sandy and hire him.

Forman, normally a light sleeper, did not appreciate Cohen's calling at 2:16 AM. "Who the hell is this?"

"Sandy, I apologize for calling so late but have urgent business to discuss."

"Allie, are you crazy? Whatever it is can wait till morning."

"I realize the hour is outrageously late, Sandy, and promise to be brief."

Sandy opened his eyes. "So how did the West Coast trip go?"

Cohen described the contract he'd signed and the dollar amounts per project. "I need a business manager and am offering you the position."

"Sorry, I've just taken a job with Sony as a regional comptroller."

"How much is Sony paying you?"

Forman qualified his base. "They're offering forty-seven five and a car."

"I'll make it sixty-five thou, a BMW 3 series, and 25 percent cut in building my asset base."

"It's a deal, pal, so how will I be serving you?"

"Look after Sarah." Allie quickly outlined Sandy's role. "Coordinate all my gigs, and manage and grow our expanding pile of money. Basically, protect me. Try to understand that I'm now a rich and visible literary figure who'll be squiring a famous actress and singer around the world for Reagan."

"I'm wondering about the squiring-the-famous-actress part and how Reagan and Sarah fit into all this."

"Look, I'm co-living with Carole Herman and will maintain a second residence at the Malibu ranch. I'll be coming and going as needed, and that's all that we should get into at this hour of the night. Go and get some rest, my friend, and give my best to Riva."

Sandy's hanging up stirred Riva. "Was I dreaming, or were you just talking to Allie at two thirty?"

Sandy made her wait for the really big news. "Crazy Allie just hired me to be his business manager."

"That's ridiculous. What the hell does a teacher need a business manager for?"

Sandy smiled as he played with Riva's mind. "To manage the fortune he made from selling his book. He offered such a lovely financial package that I think we can get very rich from this too."

"I'm ecstatic for Sarah, and thank god he sold it already. Allie placed such an intolerable load on Sarah that sometimes I wondered if she might leave him."

Sandy chuckled while cleaning her clock. "That's funny because Allie's left Sarah for Carole Herman. Excuse me, he's *co-living* with both."

"Holy shit, how did he hook up with her? My god, one week in LA and he's shacking up with the biggest Jewish star in the world."

Sandy turned over on his side. "I don't know. We'll have to wait to tomorrow for the next episode of this new soap opera, Allie's life."

Cohen smoked a joint at two forty-five and then called Carole to see how she was doing.

"Oh, Allie, I miss you so much. I'm lying here naked, sweetie, and wish we were doing it right now. You miss me?"

"Of course, I miss you, but please stop with the sexy talk. You're making my nuts ache."

She laughed but changed the subject. "Are you at home now? Did you tell Sarah?"

"Yes, and overall, I guess Sarah's taking it pretty well. What's helped the medicine go down was my telling her that we're all co-living together. This way, she doesn't feel abandoned. It also helps her deal with our relationship that you are my mission angel, and she is my angelic rock."

Adonai and I recognized that Carole's stature may prevent her from sharing, so we bent her measures of self-esteem and values to forge a great personal compromise.

"Allie, co-living means you're not leaving her for me. You intend to go back and forth and ultimately decide. Sarah, with child, will always hold the trump card."

We helped Allie organize his words so that his explanation finalized their arrangement.

"Sorry, baby, that's the best I can do and am thrilled that Sarah hasn't been crushed by all this. Give her a break, Carole. She's due to give birth in three weeks. I'm excited by what waits ahead for us, but I have to do this right, or I won't be any good to you either."

We massaged Carole's attitude and influenced her to change the subject.

"All right, Allie, I understand that." She changed the subject. "Dig this. Peter's promoting you as the next prophet of this generation."

"People thinking I'm a prophet, Carole, because I wrote a book is scary. That's a designation better left to the Lord. Please tell Peter a *sage* is plenty generous. They piss fewer people off. Frankly, prophets are prone to assassination, so their life insurance premiums are sky-high."

She bent over laughing. "I really think you're funnier than Billy Diamond and a lot better looking too. Anyway, Peter's placed a full-page ad in the trades hyping the book's theme and message as the star of the movie. The role of Seymour will be played by a relatively unknown named Alex Harel, a middle-aged Israeli actor who just won a Golden Globe Award. How do you feel about that?"

"I have no complaints, except maybe missing your tush."

She laughed while preparing him. "Starting tomorrow, Monday morning, you will be packaged and sold like any other commodity. The studio is betting ten million of advertising on you."

"That's fantastic but a bit odd in that they're spending over five times more money to *market* me than they're *paying* me."

"Sam was telling me today that your book is one of the most powerful themes ever to hit the screen. So to use your phrase, you've busted it, Allie. I just hope that you're glad. Well, are you?"

"I'm surprised that you had to ask. Hell yeah, I'm glad. And believe me, Carole, I will handle it all because I have you by my side."

"I love hearing you say that. Oh, I almost forgot. We have our first meeting with Ted Bell at the White House on Thursday. Planning for the tour has begun."

"That's great news." He yawned; fatigue finally settled in. "Sorry, babe, jet lag just hit, and I need to get to bed but sure look forward to seeing you."

He made her nervous by sounding too formal. "Allie, I love you very much."

He reinforced her. "I love you too, sweetie."

Allie brushed his teeth and then prayed, *Lord, give me the strength to make it through next week. I will have to quit my teaching job, renege on many commitments, and disappoint old friends who've gone out on a limb for me.*

Allie got into bed and tried to fall asleep. He tossed and turned for the next three hours until the alarm clock drilled him at 6:20 AM.

Sarah heard him mutter, "Fucking alarm clock."

She shared a thought. "I have to tell you something."

"What?" He yawned.

"Since I'm entitled to 50 percent of you, I'm going to quit work too. If you could walk away from everything, so can I."

"Okay, if that's what you want. Fair enough."

He dragged himself out of bed and accidentally stepped on the TV remote. Maria Shriver of *The Today Show* reported that Hollywood might be witnessing another Arthur Miller–Marilyn Monroe romance. Cohen argued at the TV set.

"Hey, I'm a year younger than Carole. The writer-actress thing is different."

Sarah freaked out. "My parents watch that show every morning."

She immediately called Rebecca and Harvey. "Mom, Dad, are you, by any chance, watching *The Today Show*?"

Rebecca sounded like a shock victim to Sarah. "Yes, we are. Is it really *our Allie* that they're talking about?"

"Yes, Mom, it is. Look, I need to get off and will call back later."

She went straight to the toilet to throw up. Cohen couldn't comfort her because the producer of the CBS morning show called from New York to invite him to be on the show the next morning. Allie apologized that he was unavailable and placed the receiver down; it rang again instantly, and he picked up.

It was Jack Richards, Cohen's tall husky, balding principal.

"Allie, I know that it's unusual for me to call at this hour, but we need to talk. Are these reports true? Are you still expecting to be a classroom teacher? If you are, well, you're going to have to run a media gauntlet."

"Don't worry, Jack," assured Cohen, getting the message. "I'm coming in today to resign. I understand that my success is a disruptive force to the school, even one with a performing arts magnet. You've been a good boss, Jack. Can I at least come in and say goodbye to everybody personally?"

Jack, very protective of his school, had trouble even with that.

"Allie, how about if you just say goodbye to your best friends? If the celebrity thing makes the kids wild or the media further disrupts the school, you'll have to leave immediately, all right?"

Allie agreed, told Jack he'd be in an hour, and went down to the kitchen to pour himself a cup of coffee. Before he had a chance to sip, Sarah tried to get under his skin.

"Tell me, it really won't bother you if I actually sleep with other men?"

"Sarah, is it necessary to discuss this at 7:00 AM? Frankly, I expect a few of my so-called good friends to try to get in your pants six weeks after you've given birth and I'm in LA on business."

She viewed his remark as cavalier, and it damned him in her eyes.

"I hate you, Allie, and didn't consider our lives as teachers to be a middle-class trap, but thanks to you, everything we built together has been crapped on. Don't you think that was a hell of a price to pay for success?"

"Sarah, try to understand that few people are in a position to state their terms for making it, and I'm not one of them."

"That's bullshit, Allie," said Sarah, unimpressed. "What you did was extreme and unfair. Yes, those words, *extreme* and *unfair*, fit you to a tee."

Allie's intuition told him not to touch her line, but his empathy forced him.

"Sarah, a host of events came together this past week that changed our lives forever. The sooner we deal with it, the faster we'll get on with things."

She replied, "Fuck off."

Allie realized it was getting late, so he kissed Sarah on the cheek, took his briefcase in hand, and headed to Buckhead High. For the first time, the ride did not seem long enough. Cohen adroitly pulled into the high school parking lot, turned the engine off, and crossed the asphalt.

Barbara Benson, the beautiful brunette daughter of a top Atlanta lawyer, called across the parking lot. "Dr. Cohen, congratulations."

Allie smiled, nodded, and disappeared into the modern red brick facility. He approached the glass-enclosed main office and saw trouble.

Shit, Jack's standing over the sign-in book trying to shoo away two reporters.

Richards saw Cohen and signaled with his eyes to hide in the nearby boys' bathroom until he got rid of them. Allie took refuge in the scurrilous water closet once identified in a school newspaper headline as the "bathroom of death."

Maybe, Allie foresaw; *this is a sign of where I'm going to wind up some day.*

A few minutes later, Jack pushed open the door a few inches.

"It's safe now to come out." He held his nose. "Uccchh, I'm going to have the janitor fumigate this place."

"No, for this, you need Marvin the Torch, the king of Jewish fires."

Allie followed Jack to his office and, as always, sat down in the same heavily padded leather chair across his desk. He settled in to listen to Richards, who seemed to speak in a rehearsed manner.

"Allie, you are one the best teachers that I've ever known and have brought a dynamic quality to this school that can never be replaced. Nearly everyone at Buckhead High, including me, is going to miss you. However, as much as it pains me, I have no alternative but to ask you to please leave the grounds as soon as possible."

"I understand, Jack."

"I feel bad about doing this, but the school," described Jack, "is crawling with reporters and photographers hunting you down like vultures. Worse, virtually the whole student body is inventing reasons to get out of class."

"I'm sorry to hear that, Jack."

"I've already suspended two kids who cut first-period class to loiter by your room in an attempt to get discovered for movie roles. Lily Rosen, a new English teacher, claimed she overheard four senior girls conspiring to have group sex with you. Now put yourself in my place. What would you do?"

"I'd ask me to leave the building ASAP," said Cohen, telling Richards what he needed to hear. "And my new business manager will exercise power of attorney to expedite all resignation forms and pension termination papers. Finally, I shake my boss's hand and tell him he was the best principal I ever worked for."

Cohen hugged his former boss and thought, *Buckhead High was a fantastic place to teach in, but I've already closed this sweet chapter of my life.*

By the time Cohen reached the front doors, he was singing as a refrain, "Bye, bye, Buckhead High."

Chapter 41

Cohen closed the doors to his Buckhead High career and walked out into his new future.

Dammit, a local TV station's mobile van is lurking in the parking lot, trying to obtain an exclusive first interview.

The news team spotted Cohen getting into his peppy Celica hatchback and tried to tail him. Cohen tracked them in his rearview mirror and floored the gas pedal, made a quick right and then left, and lost the lumbering truck.

He motored over to the Virginia-Highland area to meet with Sandy, who opened the door and barraged Allie with questions.

"Are you really having an affair with Carole Herman? How'd it happen? What's she like? Is she as pretty in real life as on the screen?"

Cohen deflected Forman's questions for later by first stating his plans for them.

"Sandy, literally overnight, I've become a credible venture capitalist. I need a good detail man and technician to roll over ideas into tangible properties, and I've always said that you were a damned good accountant."

Riva entered the room, kidding, "No, I've always heard you say that Sandy was the most *libidinous* accountant you'd ever met. Besides, it sounds to me like you're really looking for a sixty-five-thousand-a-year Jewish mother."

The cute, buxom short Riva opened a bottle of French Bordeaux to celebrate Cohen's incredible success. After a toast, Allie provided a slightly sanitized version of his West Coast adventure. When Cohen's tale covered co-living with Sarah and Carole, Riva's face stiffened.

Cohen noticed. "Riva, what's wrong?"

"While I'm happy for your new success and empowering Sandy to keep you together," she explained in a mixed tone, "Sarah is one of my best friends, and I hurt badly for her. I simply have trouble accepting your new arrangement and probably will for a while. Can you understand that?"

Allie did and nodded so.

Sandy expressed his gratitude. "Thank you for saving me from the fate of corporate auditing."

"Sandy." Riva grounded her husband. "Corporate auditing is not a *Godzilla* movie. Gentlemen, I have something to do in the kitchen and will leave the two of you alone for a while."

"You know, Sandy, taking care of me might take a lot more than forty hours a week."

Forman thought about that and then answered, "'Doesn't matter to me. In your business, it's often hard to tell where work leaves off and the play begins. In corporate accounting, I assure you, they don't blur, and there isn't any play."

Cohen understood and joked, "Put a clause in your contract for excessive coast-to-coast travel. Your bonus will be visiting Rick Samuels's sets."

"Very stimulating rewards system, and by the way, Libby just posed for *Penthouse* and Mamie for *Playboy*."

"Somehow that sounds very appropriate. Next time you're in LA, see Rick Samuels, who by the way calls *Penthouse* and *Hustler* the ugly vaginas people."

Allie and Sandy spent an hour jointly planning for taking care of Sarah, getting first ventures in the pipeline, and answering

259

questions about Carole. He left and headed back home and arrived just as Sarah finished talking with her parents.

Cohen studied her long face. "From your expression, it seems to me that your parents took it reasonably well."

Sarah sighed heavily and spoke from the heart. "You know my parents. Naturally, they're terribly disappointed. Both feel that we have a good marriage, though, and your thing with Carole is a real mind fuck."

"I can imagine."

"You're right. I guess that they did take it okay. I think my mother was the saddest. She'd taken pride that both of her children were happily married because so many of her friends' kids have been divorced."

"And your dad, how'd he handle it?"

"My father was his usual stoic self. He hopes the affair will burn itself out because, with all the money, things should be better than ever. They really love you, Allie, and still want us to make it, no matter what."

I know I'm going to make Allie uncomfortable but have to know if Carole is just a fling. She asked him, "Allie, do you think it will burn itself out?"

I don't really know what to tell her. He looked quizzical. "Burn itself out, Sarah? To be frank, babe, in most ways, it hasn't even started yet."

"I'm terribly sorry to hear that." She cried again. "I just want to be your wife and mother of your child. We're a great partnership."

She's making me feel miserable.

He put his hands on her shoulders and held her. "Sarah, we still are a great partnership and always will be. Our relationship has enlarged to nearly unlimited. It's our world now."

The phone rang; he was almost glad for the interruption but not after the frantic caller identified himself.

"Allie, it's Steve Hamall, Global's Atlanta publicity director. I've booked you three TV interviews scheduled for tonight. Tomorrow you will fly to Washington and, on Thursday, do two spots on *AM-DC* and *Washington PM.*"

"Oh shit," Cohen cursed out loud. "It's starting to happen, and I'm not sure that I can handle it yet."

"What's already starting?" wondered Hamall. "Is something wrong?"

"Nah, I'd hoped to slowly ease into this celebrity trip and need some more time to develop a public face."

"That is plainly unacceptable to me and the studio. Try to understand that we have target dates to meet and that the studio is betting big bucks on you and must have your fullest cooperation. Please try to see it from our point of view too."

"You're right." Cohen compromised. "Look, how about this? If you cancel those interviews, I'll submit to a mass press conference on the eleven o'clock news live from my driveway tonight, a sort of coming-out party."

Hamall, less than pleased, gave in. "Despite such formats having limited publicity value, I'll let you go this time. However, from now on, please let me do my job."

Cohen confused Hamall. "Steve, can a snake only shed half his skin?"

"Allie, what the hell are you talking about?"

"Never mind, bye." He instructed Hamall to, from here on, work through Sandy Forman.

Sarah glared at Allie as he hung up. He anxiously looked in the refrigerator to eat something and quell his nerves. She sorted out her feelings while munching a banana.

"I think I can actually deal with an affair—excuse me, co-living, but this publicity stuff is such bullshit. I bet you thought you'd peddle a few profitable ideas and then sit back and enjoy a rich, laid-back lifestyle. You obviously overlooked the goddamned media part haunting you."

"Frankly, Sarah, I'm terrified of an unstoppable attention from the media."

"Hah." Sarah scoffed. "The media will make you a prisoner before it lets you be mellow. I promise you'll be an old nobody first."

Her mean prediction sent a chill down his spine. Sarah saw that Allie preferred not to discuss this subject, so she put him on notice.

"Look, I know that you have plenty of apologies to make, especially to Kapoor in England and Nolan at Southeastern State, so I'm getting out of here until all this bullshit cools down and will hang out at Sheila Weiss's up the street. If anybody needs me, they can call me over there."

Allie realized that his prejudice reduction research was doomed to a slow death, and only Sarah could save it.

"Sarah, I beg you to sub for me in the upcoming symposiums. This can provide you with professional exposure and help us from drifting apart."

262

Cohen stooped down to one knee to beg her. "Please, money, only you can stop my human relations research from disappearing into the library card catalog. Besides, you're excellent at workshops, even better than I am."

"Christ, you really do want your cake and eat it too."

Sarah considered his proposal. *He's probably right about the work keeping us closer. I also find the subject matter fascinating and adaptable to my own specialty.*"Okay, Cohen, but remember, I'm not you and will need a free hand to modify your approach to fit mine."

"Fine," he assured her. "I love you very much for this."

"Don't build me up so much. There's self-interest on my part too. I can apply your process to special ed for my own dissertation and postdoctoral applications too."

"That's cool. Believe me, I'm very grateful."

"Shit, Allie, I just saw a reporter lurking up the hill, so now I need to go out the back." She crossed the yard and neighboring property and safely snuck over to Sheila's.

Cohen marched up to his office to write the multiple letters of explanation.

This is too time-consuming. It makes more sense to simply phone people.

Allie dialed Elliot Shapiro first; the Antidefamation League Education director picked up. Cohen greeted Elliot and started to talk.

Elliot cut him off, "Allie, I've already heard the good news about *The Lesson*. Global has placed ads and stories in all the

Jewish weeklies, with some even purchasing serialization rights after the general paperback release."

"Elliot, between you and me, I haven't finished the book yet."

"Well then," said Elliot, "I better not take any more of your time. Now you get right to work, my friend. Ha ha! Good luck with the book and take care, Allie."

Allie then called his mother. Janet Kamensky was warmly surprised.

"Allie, it's so good to hear your voice. How was your trip to California?"

Janet, always well-informed, had yet to see the daily newspaper or turn the TV set on. She listened quietly and, when he'd finished, reacted as expected; she shamed her wayward son.

"Allie, although I'm very proud of your big success, I'm upset by this co-living thing. My god, leaving a pregnant wife. Oy vey, the next time I see Harvey and Rebecca, I'm not going to be able to look them in the eye."

"But, Ma," he pleaded, "Carole's a wonderful woman—"

She cut him off, "Don't *but, Ma* me or sell Carole Herman either. She just sings loud. You were lucky to find a girl like Sarah, and what's with this co-living crap? What are you, Brigham Young, the Mormon? Trust your mother on this. You can only make one woman at a time happy."

"I'm not sure that's true, Ma, but I'll see you next week when I come to New Jersey."

Chapter 42

It's only a matter of time until Mom softens, or Carole wins her over, Allie thought, downplaying his mother's negativity.

Josh Bradley of WGGA-TV called a second later. The roving reporter for the local NBC affiliate unsuccessfully lobbied for an exclusive interview.

Allie said brusquely, "Sorry, Josh, not ready yet." He hung up.

Man, I hate this shitty siege mentality forming up in me. Dammit, the fucking phone's ringing again.

Cohen angrily picked it up and was greeted by an enthusiastic Nolan Craig. The SSU professor and co-organizer of Cohen's symposium shared a stunning development.

"Allie," raved Nolan, "Peskin, Otis, and Meriwether—three of the top experts in this field—have all agreed to appear."

That excellent news made him feel worse. "Nolan," said Cohen, trying to find the right words, "I, uh, have, uhm, some bad news."

"Like what?" Cohen described how plans had changed and said that he could only attend one of the sessions.

Craig, an introspective type, didn't relish the leadership role. "Allie, you're being incredibly unfair."

Cohen, in desperate need of Craig's goodwill, compromised. "Nolan, how about if I open the symposium and then fly back for Kapoor's symposium? Sarah's willing to sub for me, and that should take a big load off your back too. Well?"

"Sarah's skill and involvement does help a lot, Allie. However, you're the main figure, and it's not fair to the participating teachers who signed up on the strength of your reputation or to the business community who dug deep into their pockets to support your concept or to me who already has a summer school class to teach."

"I understand, Nolan. I'm sorry again, and please stay in touch."

"Don't bet on it, Allie." He hung up.

Cohen worried. "Man, if Craig's that angry, how will Kapoor react?"

The operator connected Cohen's transoceanic call to the depressed industrial midlands of England 3,500 miles away. After several rings, the gentle scholar with a soft British accent marveled when Allie introduced himself.

"Dr. Cohen, it is a pleasure to finally speak to you."

Cohen appealed to the other most respected researcher in the field of prejudice reduction treatments and provided Kapoor with a quick overview of the recent changes in plans. The brilliant and unflappable Kapoor understood but expressed deep concern.

"You are a creative fellow, Dr. Cohen, so when you mentioned that you developed a commercial property, I sensed that material success might interfere with our ambitious objectives. I admit to being a bit anxious and require assurances."

"I swear," promised Cohen, "that we will yet achieve our mutual dream. I think we will have enough time in Atlanta to initiate a global application."

"The process requires necessary inputs of time, energy, and intelligence, Dr. Cohen, but not money so much. Frankly, I fail to see how you can live up to your part."

"Trust me, Dr. Kapoor," Cohen said, bargaining. "It will take a little longer, but we will realize our mutual vision."

"I'm not one to knock success. I just worry about your new schedule. Will it permit the six-week-long London Festival, or is that in jeopardy too?"

"Yes, that too," disclosed Cohen. "I will attend whenever possible, and my wife, Sarah, will sub for me the rest of the time. Please forgive me for these compromises."

Kapoor, a patient and trusting fellow, rededicated his loyalty.

"You do seem to have a knack for making a big splash. Therefore, I am still confident that we will persevere. It will just take a little longer."

Cohen thanked Kapoor, said goodbye as he put down the phone, and thought about the professor and his parents' emigrating from India when he was a little boy. Kapoor's parents slaved in the Leeds textile mills, and he endured intense prejudice in working-class grammar schools. The fierce anti-immigrant attitudes the family confronted motivated Kapoor to identify and expose the origins and nature of British racism.

Kapoor's research connected with Cohen's, and through correspondence, they tweaked the treatment for portability to modify prejudice anywhere. The process was partly based on Kapoor's theory that to prove one race less intelligent than another, 105 life variables must be controlled and accurate data collected for three generations to prove all hypotheses. Since much of the data was unobtainable, thus making the proof or desired outcomes impossible, it was questionable why one wanted to make the effort.

Adonai teamed Cohen, our prophet and Einstein of prejudice reduction treatments, with Kapoor, who laid the procedural groundwork in Australia and planned a global application when he was done with the UK and the *colonies*.

Cohen and Kapoor's joint mission scientifically taught the people of the world how to better understand and live together. The social scientists would achieve their goal by providing statistical validation in lieu of metaphysically walking on water, flying around, or hurling lightning or thunderbolts.

Cohen completed his chores by the time the press conference was to begin. A small army of media personnel stood in his driveway, jockeying for position. Allie was expected to stand in front of the garage door, face the floodlights, and answer questions.

Cohen's neighbors were mystified by the scene occurring in their sleepy cul-de-sac. An excited mob of late-night dog walkers, joggers, and suspicious homeowners congregated near Allie's mailbox. Cohen viewed the scene as the greatest community spectacle of the past ten years—a decade earlier, a rich redneck torched a home he'd heard was being rented by two gay guys who threw wild parties.

Allie spotted Evelyn Wilson, his next-door neighbor and a sweet and helpful friend who headed the Neighborhood Watch Force, the subdevelopment's first line of defense against burglars. Evelyn was bewildered by the big crowd in his driveway. She pushed her way through the crowd of reporters.

"Allie, was there a burglary? I've never seen so many reporters cover a break-in before."

"Sorry to disappoint you, Evelyn. Nope, I'm holding a press conference."

"You're holding a press conference? Why?"

Evelyn, with her South Carolina, low-country accent, stretched *why* into three syllables.

"You really don't know, Evelyn?"

"No, I stopped reading the paper and watching the TV news years ago, too depressing with all the murders and robberies."

He knew that. "Evelyn, the media is here because I sold my book for more than I ever dreamed of."

"Fantastic, congratulations. Hey, where's Sarah? Why isn't she celebrating with you?"

"She's hiding out at Sheila Weiss's house. She likes the money but hates the publicity, and come to think of it, I do too."

"Dr. Cohen," a sound engineer stated, "your microphone is active. Please speak in a moderate voice when the red light goes on. Thank you."

Josh Bradley introduced himself as moderator and then Allie.

"Dr. Allie Cohen is a local high school teacher and writer whose first published novel has been received as a critical and commercial success."

As a favor to Steve Hamall, who organized the interview session, Bradley added, "*The Lesson*, published by Global Books, will soon be made into a big-budget movie to be produced by Global Pictures."

Rhonda Edwards of WPAT-TV asked the first question. "Dr. Cohen, please describe the theme of your novel, and is there a message?"

Rhonda's basic note pleased Allie, who smiled at her.

"My book contends that the world may waver in the face of the big lie that the Holocaust is a Zionist hoax. Seymour Umansky—a multi-death-camp survivor, including Auschwitz— taught the ultimate doubter the truth by grisly applications. Those interested in what he did and how the story ends can find out by paying $14.95 or so at the local bookstore unless you care to wait for the cheaper paperback edition, and if you don't read, see the movie."

"Now that you've successfully published your book," Joe Petty of WSOU-97 radio inquired, "will you continue to teach high school and run the Atlanta International Summer Festival (AISF) at SSU?"

"No," Cohen announced. "My new commitments necessitate my retirement from teaching and also reduce my festival involvement level. My most able wife, Sarah Cohen, and Dr. Nolan Craig will co-organize and direct the conference. Regardless, AISF is still a progressive step forward for multicultural Atlanta, and I am sure that Sarah and Nolan will do an excellent job."

Barbara Chase of WAC-90 FM got right to the nitty-gritty.

"Dr. Cohen, an undisclosed source has leaked to the press that you'll be accompanying actress and singer Carole Herman on an around-the-world goodwill tour for the White House. Can you verify that?"

The source, a tight-lipped Cohen thought, *must be David Conte.*

He admitted, "Yes, but only as a private consultant to Ms. Herman and with no association with the White House whatsoever. I hope I made that very clear."

Allie made the *no White House association* up, but this will ironically become the case.

Ms. Chase pursued the lead. "I'm not sure that you clarified anything at all, Dr. Cohen. Can you please elaborate?" *A rule of thumb for a press conference is if you don't say it, it can't hurt you.*

Allie answered, "No, I can't, Ms. Chase. I'm sorry."

May Moore, an amiable *Atlanta Journal-Constitution* (*AJC*) morning columnist, asked, "There have been rumors out of Hollywood, Dr. Cohen, that you are romantically linked with Ms. Herman. Can you substantiate that?"

The amazed neighbors buzzed with excitement. Cohen took refuge in vagueness.

"Ms. Herman and I are collaborating on several professional projects."

The media here are viewing me as a scoundrel. The neighbors just tried to bust through their lines to get my autograph, but the reporters and photographers, holding the higher ground, pushed them back.

May Moore probed, "Dr. Herman, are you and Ms. Herman planning to live together?"

Annoyed that only one question so far dealt with his book and he was already fending off questions about Carole, Allie avoided the subject with a quip.

"Ms. Moore, isn't this a family-friendly news program? Can we please keep the subject focused on my book and upcoming movie of it?"

May brushed Cohen's deflection aside. "Is that an evasion, Dr. Cohen?"

"No, Ms. Moore, it's a plea." Allie sensed it was wise to conclude his electronic debut. "Sorry, that's all I have to say. Thank you for your attention and good night."

Most of the media packed up and left. A couple of journalists lingered behind to add depth to their print pieces.

Jimmy Barnes, a popular and funny columnist, predicted, "Dr. Cohen, I imagine that, after tonight, you and this cul-de-sac will never be the same."

Cohen reacted with hand gestures signifying *helplessness* and *what price success.*

Sarah returned and slipped by them and in to the house. Cohen noticed the perceptive Barnes catching sight of Sarah's wounded look and braced himself.

"Pardon me," drawled Jimmy. "But how come Mrs. Cohen reminds me of a bear that wants to hibernate for six months until the public's interest wanes?"

Cohen acknowledged that Sarah was not yet comfortable being in the public eye and excused himself. "Thanks for covering this, Jimmy."

The neighborhood calmed down in a few minutes and settled in for the evening.

"I must say," said Sarah, scorned, "that, for a rookie, you handled yourself okay."

Her tone switched to understated melodrama. "Uh, Allie, do you have a spare straight razor that I can slash my wrists with? Or is slitting my throat neater? Messy suicides are so nowhere, you know what I mean?"

"Please, Sarah, I didn't enjoy that any more than you did. Global expects me to support the product they're lavishly marketing."

A dam broke in Sarah, and she tried to beat his chest with her fists. "You bastard, Allie, how can I ever look a neighbor in the eye again?"

He held her hands. "Sarah, I made no admission of an affair with Carole."

"I don't care, Allie. You still disgraced me."

The day drained Sarah, and she went to sleep.

At 4:30 AM, the *ABC Morning News* woke her up to ask Allie to be on their show, and she verbally passed the message.

"David Hartman is sending over a limo to take you to the airport. From there, you will fly to New York for an 8:30 AM interview session. The producer says to be ready in a half hour."

"Like hell I am." Cohen took the receiver and told scheduler Bill Stewart, "Don't bother, and I'm not doing any more interviews until the end of the week."

He hung up. "Sarah, I am in hiding for the next three days to complete the last forty pages of the book. I need to write ten to twelve hours a day and for you to diligently protect me."

Writing previously caused tensions. Sarah recalled. *I often felt bored, neglected, and frustrated by his writing every spare moment. I worked full time, assumed the bulk of the household chores, and deserved a rich social life too. Not so long ago, we haunted flea markets together.*

Allie, in parallel thinking, thought, *Until one is published, they remain a writer. If unpaid, the pursuit is soon viewed as a form of private madness. I've surely driven Sarah crazy during the three years of researching and writing this book. Now I'm an author and a handsomely paid one too.*

Chapter 43

Sandy Forman, in his first official act as Allie's business manager, commented positively and extensively on three particular offers selected from a dozen or so companies with deals and then switched gears.

"Allie, we need to talk. Publicity's complained to Sam that you're not cooperating with the program. You know what Minkowitz's golden rule is—the *bottom line*. Everyone does their best to sell the product and make money." Allie promised to do better.

"From now on," pressed Forman, "you do just about everything they demand of you, some even degrading in your opinion. Do you get the message, Cohen?"

"Now I know how a bronco feels when it's been busted. Okay, I'll give more of myself. I promise."

"Glad to hear that."

"Is there anything else, Sandy?"

"Yeah, I'll be back out in LA next week. Please give me Rick's number."

"You devil you, I'll bet it's the Lee sisters you're interested in."

Sandy wrote the phone number down and then requested, "Sam says not to get too many irons in the fire. If you only succeed with the four projects, they'll still call you the new boy wonder of Hollywood."

"I hear you."

"Remember, Allie, the entertainment world only cares about big box office receipts and high Nielsen numbers."

"Okay, Sandy, enough with that crap. Look, I need you to buy Rose and Sam expensive engagement presents. Also, please send my mom a floral bouquet."

"That's being a good politician. You're learning. Bye."

Allie put the phone down and reflected. *It's apparent that Sam Minkowitz has replaced Jack Richards in creating hoops for me to jump through. A system exists whether a public school or a media company. Control is crucial to stability and planning.*

Allie fleshed out an adult African adventure concept for his first project for Sam; the Chazers were history. The idea took root on a flight from LA to Atlanta, where he observed rich, urbane blacks saying that they were going to Lagos and Nairobi. All were revered social activists, professionals, or government dignitaries.

The story had an elite black group surviving a plane crash deep in the African interior. The highly urbanized New Yorkers and Californians were challenged to survive the rigors of the dense bush. They managed to cross a broad veld and rugged mountain chain and battled with lions, rhinos, poachers, and indigenous tribes.

With the plot well-formed, Allie piddled with the title. "Hmmm, *Déjà Vu*. That's not bad. I think that I may have been on this journey before. Yeah, *Déjà Vu Odyssey*. Sweet."

Cohen's mother, in the meantime, wrestled with her emotions.

Allie's actions have depressed me.

Janet eased her angst by smashing steaming hot boiled potatoes still in the pot. Her daily task, preparing Max's peasant lunch, was normally no big deal. Today, though, the potatoes and sour cream reminded Janet of mounds of smelly paste.

Max sat down to eat his cementlike concoction. She spoke while he rhythmically shoveled in mouthfuls of carbohydrates and fats.

"Max, I feel awful."

"Nu," he emitted in between chomps. "What's the matter?"

"I want to call Rebecca Kartzman, but to tell the truth, I'm too ashamed. Carla says I should call, that it's the right thing to do, but it's my son who's half-walking-out on her pregnant daughter."

Max took a breath. "I think you're overreacting, Janet, and is it really that simple?"

"No, it's not. On the other hand, he has achieved most of his big dreams in life. I may have helped him with some tuition and a little money here and there, but he essentially did it on his own."

"He's done great. The smartest thing Allie ever did was to marry Sarah and move to Atlanta."

"Max, Allie reminds me of a story I once heard about a mother who's extremely proud that her son has become a millionaire. She's also tormented that he'd made his fortune by embezzling from the bank he worked for. I know it's crazy, but that's how I feel. What can I tell you?"

Max chuckled while empathizing with Janet's mixed emotions of joy and embarrassment. For a change, he posed the right question.

"Why not call? How would you feel if you made such a big move and then *bam!*" His right fist smacked his left palm.

"You're right." Janet summoned the courage to call the Kartzmans and told Max while waiting for some one to pick up in Atlanta, "I think that Carla is finally proud of her brother. To show how crazy life is, she almost seems like the moderate one now. My god, Carla must be dying for Allie to bring that loud singer around, not me."

In a North Atlanta apartment that was as severely clean as Janet's, Rebecca Kartzman picked up. "Hello, who is it?"

"Rebecca, it's Janet. How are you and Harvey doing?"

"Eh, we're okay. Actually, Harvey's out looking at a piece of land to build and open the first great deli in Atlanta. Allie's financing it."

Janet cupped the receiver with her hands and mentioned the hot news to her husband; for ten years, he was a former corned beef and pastrami pickler with a North Jersey deli chain.

Max, introspectively; *Am I missing out on something big?*

The glint in his eye ignored a tired body that craved retirement, and he lost his appetite for Warsaw grits. Janet encouraged Rebecca to tell her all about it.

"They're calling it Allie Cohen's Sit-In, a combination Carnegie Deli and northern diner with an incredibly broad menu. A customer can get the best of everything twenty-four hours a day, from hot pastrami to lobster and aged steaks to breakfast and great baked goods made on the premises."

"My god, Rebecca, that's a big operation."

"Harvey's the managing partner, Janet, and thinks this is his last great chance in life to get rich."

Janet thought, *The Sit-In news allows me to feel a little better about my Allie.*

To Rebecca, she said, "I hope the Sit-In is a great big success."

"Thank you, Janet. I'm surprised that I don't miss working, although my pharmacy wants to hire me as a prescription assistant. Right now, it's enough to be there for Sarah."

"I understand. When you're ready to work, you'll find something."

"Can you imagine, Janet? With only three weeks to go, Sarah's been admitted into a doctoral program, and she's also assumed direction of Allie's symposiums. My daughter is really trying to make this co-living thing work."

"She's amazing. My god, how she finds the energy and time."

Janet got to the hard part. "Rebecca, I need to tell you how truly sorry I am. Big fortune or not, I don't approve of what my Allie is doing."

"I'm glad to hear your sentiments. Of course, we're all disappointed. Strangely enough, Allie's made so much money and interesting projects available. That has kind of distracted us. Maybe I'm a foolish old woman, but I still believe that Allie loves Sarah and will return to her someday. But you know life. Who can really say for sure?"

"My son is fortunate to have such wonderful in-laws. It sounds like you can more easily forgive him than his own mother."

Rebecca moved the conversation along. "Anyway, he's finished his novel and left for Washington today. I think he's to meet with people from the White House tomorrow about conducting her tour."

The words *her tour* drove Rebecca to express her sense of powerlessness with Janet.

"Can you believe that my Sarah has to fight Carole Herman for Allie? Ves es mere, what is this world coming to?"

The mother-in-laws were on the same wavelength. "I don't care how big a star she is." Janet judged. "She did wrong by stealing a man away from his family. I do have to admit that she is a very good actress."

Rebecca pined. "Oddly enough, I love her voice too and think she's my favorite performer of all time."

On this, the mother-in-laws were not on the same wavelength. "She sings too loud. I'd have been happier if Allie had stayed a teacher. This is unreal."

"I know," agreed Rebecca. "My son-in-law the doctor of education was more than enough for me."

"I don't remember him being so driven to make a big fortune, though he always seemed to expect it."

A clue unfolded to Cohen's mother. "That's it, Rebecca, society did not reward his teaching accomplishments enough. If they'd paid him a lot more, I bet all this insanity wouldn't have happened."

"Maybe." Rebecca shrugged. "Who knows?"

"Look, once again, I'm sorry."

"Please," demanded Rebecca, "stop apologizing. It's not your fault."

"Thanks, well, anyway, we love you both and look forward to seeing you. With God's blessing, we'll all be gathering soon for a bris. Well, take care, and tell Harvey that we wish him the best of luck with the Sit-In."

The Sit-In would be a great success because the Great Provider strongly believes that high-quality Jewish delicatessen is partly necessary for the sustenance of the Jewish soul, and the food maven Harvey Kartzman was a one-man preservation society. The prophet married into a very wonderful family.

Chapter 44

Pres. John F. Kennedy once described Washington DC, as a city of Northern charm and Southern efficiency. During the term of Pres. Jimmy Carter, Cohen often felt that JFK's depiction fit.

A major reason for Allie's moving to Atlanta was that the days of past segregationists, such as Lester Maddox, were numbered. Governor Carter, in contrast, impressed Cohen as a prototypical New South leader and politician.

Unfortunately, the year Carter left office to run for president, he gave the teachers a 0.5 percent raise during a year with a 6.0 percent inflation rate. As a result, Sarah and Allie became 5.5 percent *poorer*, and that lessened his enthusiasm for Carter's candidacy. After that raise, Cohen began referring to Carter as Peanut Breath but still hoped he'd win, and of course, Jimmy did.

Cohen looked back. *I seemingly missed the boat. Perhaps if Carter had awarded us a 6 percent raise, I might have walked into his campaign office and joined the Peanut Brigade. Upon helping the governor win the Democratic nomination and presidency, I might have landed a position in the Department of Education or maybe the White House. But I didn't, while dozens of other Georgians who helped propel Carter into the White House were selected to run the federal government.*

Although highly political and interested in a career of government service, Cohen always had limited connections and less luck. When Allie graduated from college, Republicans Richard Nixon and Spiro Agnew were minding the store, and he wanted no part of them.

In 1980, Cohen felt the campaign choice of Carter and Reagan to be dismal. Carter appeared politically spent, and former actor Reagan did not seem adequate to lead the free world. In the end, he thought that better a Democrat than a Republican and voted for Carter. America thought differently and elected Reagan.

Allie deplaned and entered the baggage claim area, where Carole waited for him. Her smile drove home the reality that he'd better learn to break bread with the Reaganites.

Allie hugged and kissed Carole. "I missed you so much, babe."

"Me too, but," she warned, "we dare not dawdle. I bribed an airline employee 250 bucks to send the press to the other side of the terminal. Come on. If we hurry, we can get out of the terminal before they spot us."

She pulled his arm and beat a path to a waiting limo. *I'm getting a taste of what life with Carole Herman is like.*

She brought him up-to-date. "My kids and I have fallen in love with Washington. We've been to most of the monuments and Capitol Hill buildings and must have walked a million miles all over town."

"'Sounds like you guys have had a lot of fun."

"We have, and oh, Ted Bell told me he's sending a car for us tomorrow morning at ten. We have to work out an itinerary that crams in one foreign policy objective, or initiative, for every location."

"Where are your kids, Carole, and how old are they?"

"Martin is twelve, Caryn ten, and they're waiting in the hotel suite, watching their favorite music videos."

She noticed his exceptional gifts for her kids. "Why did you bring them such expensive presents? It's not necessary to bribe them."

He just smiled while ignoring her. *I've taught many rich children over the years and know better but won't tell her that. Sandy Forman located for me the world's best baseball mitt for Martin and largest stuffed animal for Caryn. My hope is for the impressive toys to jump-start the bonding process.*

"Allie, I got in touch with your old friend Lenny Meltzer. His architectural firm is now the fifty-second largest in the country."

"I didn't know he was that big, Carole, and that's just from doing interiors."

"Allie, he's a prince. He showed us his firm's latest projects and took us to the Old Ebbitt Grill, where George Washington once ate."

"It's not the same Old Ebbitt Grill. It's the third one and anchors a small mall. I don't think Washington *shopped* there."

"Ha ha! That was very clever line. For tonight, Lenny's made dinner reservations for the five of us at a French restaurant overlooking the Georgetown Canal that he designed and owns. He said we should dress casually. Doesn't it sound great?"

Allie answered by hugging and kissing her. The cab pulled up in front of the L'Enfant Plaza Hotel. The driver got out to unload Allie's luggage, and a bellhop took it and led them to their suite.

Carole stuck a computerized key card into the electronic lock, opened it, and introduced Cohen to her kids. Both were sitting on the floor, engrossed in the new Michael Jackson *Thriller* video.

She tried to get their attention, but three minutes were left in the spectacular half-hour-long production. Allie and Carole stood there invisibly until Jackson released the kids from his spell.

Martin and Caryn finally turned toward Allie, and he studied their facial expressions. *They seem indifferent. Maybe I should have worn one white glove or beat it.*

Cohen remembered to offer his presents. *I think my gifts are special enough to slightly dent the detached hearts of two of the richest children in California. I want to create an opening and realize that it will take a great deal more to win them over.*

Caryn—pretty, slim, and with dirty-blond curls like her mother—smiled shyly, touched the bear, and said, "It's so big and soft."

She smiled and touched it again. "Thank you, Allie. Please excuse me, I'm going to watch a video of my favorite all-girl band, the Go-Go's."

Cohen focused on Martin, who looked like his dad, Myron, and was tall for his age and very handsome and tanned.

"Martin, Mom tells me that you're a loyal Dodgers fan."

Martin smiled. "Yeah, oh, by the way, thank you for the glove. It's really cool. The leather is incredibly soft, and the workmanship is unbelievable."

Allie softly tossed a ball to Martin—they easily threw it back and forth for a few minutes.

Martin asked, "Mom says you're a doctor. What kind?"

Allie, glad that Martin spoke to him, answered, "I'm a PhD, not a medical doctor."

Martin, unfamiliar with the title, wanted to know, "Is that a foot doctor?"

"No, Martin." Allie chuckled while correcting him. "I'm a specialist in education."

"Who says so?"

Martin stared at Allie, whose eyebrow rose from that question and figured Martin to become a lawyer.

Allie said, "Southeastern State University in Atlanta does."

"My dad says they're not so smart down South."

Chapter 45

"I assure you, Martin"—Cohen laughed loudly—"that each region and state has more than their fare share of ignorant people. Look, I promise not to be your teacher." He changed the subject back to the Dodgers. "When's the last time that you went to a game?"

Martin loosened up. "David used to take me whenever I was back from school and the Dodgers were playing at home."

He looked at his mother to see if he had said something dumb or wrong.

"It's okay, Martin." Carole supported her son. "David was a part of your life these past three years, and I understand that he's still your friend."

"Next time," Allie offered, "you're back from school and the Dodgers are at home, I'll be glad to take you."

"Thank you, Allie, and thanks again for the glove too. If you'll excuse me, Caryn's watching a Judas Priest video, and they're my favorite heavy metal group."

Cohen looked at Carole. "How big a hit do you think I was?"

"I know my kids, but let's go into the dining room to talk." They did. "Allie, you may have a different impression, but I must tell you that things went fairly well. I mean, I was prepared for a really bad scene."

"I'm very relieved, Carole, but for the sake of insight, how about bringing me up to date with your children?"

"Okay, Caryn was the apple of her daddy's eye and has never forgiven me for throwing him out. As you just saw, she punishes me by acting aloof and unaffectionate. Martin's gun-shy, figuring the men in my life aren't his daddy and that I probably won't marry them, so why bother to care? Look, honey, they're not taking you seriously until absolutely sure you're their new stepdad and that you're not just passing through."

They both laughed. He appreciated her advice, gauged that he worked his way perhaps a half-inch into their hearts, and reminded himself not to push too hard. *Running off with Carole to see the world, I sense, is going to be a lot more emotionally demanding than I anticipated.*

Allie felt time was passing too slowly in the hotel room. *I know that the kids are going to bum out waiting another two hours for Lenny to pick us up. Despite rush hour starting, I think I'll give them a tour of the city. Let me hire a van taxi through the concierge to take us around town while I entertain Carole and the kids by sharing my knowledge of DC.*

Allie so delighted the Herman family with a treasure chest of stories as the taxi zipped throughout the District of Columbia that I put a dozen more vivid stories into his head to fill two full hours amusing two children who had serious issues with their mother. They all liked the history of a hot-pink stucco mansion on Connecticut Avenue that was owned by an old Latin American dowager and practically a retirement home for exiled dictators from Central and South America.

Martin loved statistics; items like how many thousands of El Salvador refugees per square mile lived in Adams Park or how Washingtonians now consumed more whiskey per capita than even Mississippians, the national champ for a century, fascinated him. Carole loved Allie's accounting of the two slightly different color granites used during the construction of the Washington Monument.

The pope donated the rock to thank the United States for accepting so many Irish immigrants in danger of starving from the potato famine. The Know-Nothings—an anti-immigrant, anti-Catholic, and anti-Semitic party of its day—hated the Catholic rock. They snuck in under the cover of darkness and threw the remaining stones in the Potomac River. The monument remained half-built until the 1880s, when a quarry in Vermont, presumably Protestant granite that virtually matched, was tapped to finish the top half.

After the tour, Caryn clutched Allie's hand in the elevator ride up to the suite.

"Even though we like you, Allie, what's more important is we understand why Mom does. You know what I mean?"

A tear formed in Allie's eye, and he responded in his sincerest voice, "Caryn, it was wonderful to hear you say that, and I like you very much too." He stooped to Caryn's height and kissed her on the cheek. "Ooh, you are so cute."

Martin also warmed up to Allie. "That tour was the best time I've ever had while learning so much. Allie, how do you remember all that stuff?"

"Martin, except for my writing ability," Cohen joked, "my garbage-can-sized memory is my only bankable skill."

They all laughed. Allie felt things were going better than expected and saw the kids were happily mesmerized by a Survivor video, *Eye of the Tiger*, the theme from *Rocky III*. Cohen took advantage by sneaking into Carole's shower and going down on her. She moaned luxuriantly, and he entered her.

"Ah, Allie, this is the first sex we've had since the coast, and I missed you so much. I swear, you're the best lover I've ever had."

She started to go down on him. "You're also the first man I've ever wanted to perform oral sex on too. The rest I just gave an occasional blow job to keep them happy, but with you, I love giving you good head."

Cohen thought; *Man, she is good to her word too.*

Allie and I agree that Jewish women are vastly underestimated in their pursuit of the joys and pleasures of oral sex.

Chapter 46

The doorman buzzed the Herman-Cohen party. "Mr. Lenny Meltzer is waiting to pick your group up."

Meltzer parked his black BMW 325 coupe by the hotel entrance and took stock of his past fifteen years.

Business flourished; his two marriages did not. Pauline, his first shiksa goddess, pleaded mental cruelty and cried to the judge that his superior decorating and cooking skills reduced her to uselessness. She had to leave him to find herself.

Halle, his second wife and named for a Cleveland department store, also told the judge that he had no need of her. *The stupid bitch,* he thought, *was damn right and lucky that she had a smart lawyer who kept the useless slut from testifying how she strayed frequently, lied constantly, and abused painkillers and cocaine.*

Lenny was ready for another shot at marriage if he can meet the right woman. At the moment, he was happy expanding his booming interior design business that served mostly Crystal City defense contractors and federal and corporate offices. Meltzer's second revenue stream is redeveloping old Georgetown warehouses into plush office space and residential lofts and town houses. His tasteful Cleveland Park house was recently displayed in the *Washington Post*'s "Home Living" section.

The sight of Allie leading the Herman family through the wide brass doors made him smile. Cohen's most creative and elegant friend hugged him.

"Your success has boggled my mind, Allie, and I'm happy as hell for you."

"Thank you, Lenny. It sounds like you are doing very well yourself."

Lenny headed across the Key Bridge to Georgetown and parked in front of his contemporary bistro called Le Canard, French for "duck." The party of five entered the café full of skylights, hanging plants, and singles on the make.

Cohen pointed to the dozen poster-sized prints of tabloid headlines translated from French to English that efficiently covered a long exposed brick wall.

"Carole, Martin, Caryn, these prints are copies of a small but influential French investigative weekly's top stories. *Le Canard* is famous for digging up political scandals that have brought down the conservative Gaullist government of Giscard d'Estaing in the 1970s and recently forced the haughty Socialist prime minister François Mitterrand to resign. For the record, I was the one who turned Lenny onto *Le Canard*, the name taken from the old saying 'If it walks, sounds, and acts like a duck, it's a duck.'"

Lenny sat them at his private table. "The menu is more eclectic continental than French, and I recommend any of the veal dishes, the freshly made pastas, or the roast duck with cherry *or* orange sauce. The menu also includes mesquite-grilled fish, basic American favorites, and a nightly vegetarian entrée. Tonight's special is duck potpie."

Martin and Caryn each chose the duck potpie. Three patrons recognized Carole before she could order, and she politely signed their paper cocktail napkins. Word of her presence spread through the place, and normally blasé Washingtonians lined up in droves. Lenny ended the assault on her person and privacy by moving the group into his office.

Two waiters sat the party around Lenny's desk and brought platters of roast duck, grilled sea bass, fried potatoes, duck potpies, and salad to feast on and a carafe of Beaujolais to wash it down.

Carole shared a recurring nightmare while they all munched away.

"I'm crossing a Midtown Manhattan side street, and a speeding taxi runs me over. I'm flat on my back, bleeding to death, and am silently screaming for help. My fans can see the condition I'm in, but they still line up for my autograph. Naturally, I die at the end of the dream. Nice, huh?"

Her description of the insanity of celebrity status made Lenny shudder and Allie introspective. Carole looked out the floor-to-ceiling window and stared at a beautiful stand-alone town house. Meltzer took notice while changing the subject to Cohen's absurd White House involvement.

"Christ, Allie, you're the last person on earth I'd figure for selling ol' bozo Reagan abroad. Frankly, your radical zeal pissed me off at times and occasionally made me feel like a bourgeois pig instead of the urban social ecologist that I prefer to see myself as."

They all laughed at Lenny's little joke, though his uncalled-for advice annoyed Carole, who didn't appreciate his protecting Allie's political virginity. She caught Lenny looking at her to gauge if she was mad at him. Carole put the remark behind her and purposely smiled.

Martin and Caryn picked up on their mother's strategizing. "Mom," Caryn told her, "we've had a great meal. Please excuse Martin and me to visit the mall down the corridor and have some fun."

"Sure, sweetie. Do you need money?"

Martin shook his head no.

Carole waited for them to leave before starting in on Lenny.

"I agree, Lenny, it's a terrible thing I'm doing to Allie. My god, making him fly down to Rio and Buenos Aires at Christmastime when they have summer—horrible. Tell me, do you think Allie can stand watching all those bikini thongs on Ipanema

Beach, or should I subject him to one important government official after another falling all over him?"

Lenny and Allie employed basketball's time-out hand motion; she wasn't done.

"So do you think I should schlep him to all those places where he can affect positive change? I mean, why would I ever want to do that to him?"

This is the strangest situation Allie has ever gotten me into. Meltzer half-smiled. *I love Sarah and hope to find someone just like her. Mostly, I don't want to rock Allie's tightrope act. And frankly, I'm a fan of Carole too and don't want to alienate her.*

"Look, Carole, let me give you a good example," said Lenny, recalling a prime moment. "Imagine Allie and sixteen other May Day demonstrators barging in on me at 6:00 AM. While I'm sleeping with my girlfriend, he and fifty thousand other radicals were evicted from the White House ellipse by fifteen thousand federal troops armed with bayonets in their rifles."

"May Day, eh? The Communist's international holiday, hmmm."

"Yep, all seventeen, wired from LSD and dancing all night long to a half-dozen rock groups, walked up Connecticut Avenue through a mile-long cordon of troops and metropolitan police forces lining the boulevard. I saw army intelligence officers photographing them from across the street as they entered my apartment. Now that's how radical he was."

Lenny's description of that exciting time in his early manhood made Allie nostalgic.

Meltzer reconsidered. "On second thought, I got to give it to you, Allie. Ripping off Ronzo and the Republicans for free travel is sweet revenge for aging sixties radicals."

"Allie," Carole added, "it's just safer and more convenient to let the government organize the trip, sort of like federal travel agent. My input is to sing a few songs here and there to show some gratitude. Now what's so terrible about that?"

"Nothing." Cohen conceded. "I now love the idea that Reagan is picking up the tab."

"Now promise me," Carole demanded, "never to complain about subversion of your integrity. If you do, I'll call old Ironhair Reagan and cancel the trip, okay?"

"With Lenny as my witness, I pledge."

"Then it's settled, Allie. We are going, and that's that, right?"

"Yes, we are going, Carole," he answered her, hoping it was his last dummy response.

Meltzer, glad to change the subject, directed their attention back to a four-story townhome perched on a low hill across the restaurant.

"I built my perfect townhome, but by the time it was completed, the costs had soared to the point where I could no longer afford it. How's that for a kick in the head?"

"You're an experienced architect, Lenny. How could that happen?"

"Easy, the labor union's rates and building material costs rose much faster than expected. Almost all the builders in DC were hurt by the sharp increases. Price increases on my other projects further squeezed me."

"Lenny," propositioned Carole, "I like Georgetown's ambience and am intrigued by the idea of acquiring this property. Allie, this could be our East Coast base of operations."

She impetuously asked Meltzer, "Can we see it?"

"Yeah," seconded Allie. "I'm always eager to see your latest project."

Martin and Caryn conveniently returned with Italian ices in hand, and the group moved across the street.

"My real estate holdings include the Malibu ranch, a Central Park East penthouse apartment that I lease to Billy Diamond, and fifty undeveloped acres in the Texas Hill Country. With the beach bungalow now belonging to David, I need to buy a new property for tax reasons," Carole said.

"I have an option," proposed Lenny, "on the lots on both sides of the place. A small fortune can be had by putting up two more units just like this one."

"Lenny, you can stop selling. I've already fallen in love with the place. You won me over with the soft blue and beige furnishings with pale red and yellow highlights set against those lightwoods. They contrast very nicely with the brick walls that you painted white and varying shades of gray."

"How do you like the large kitchen all done in stainless steel, butcher block, and granite countertops?"

"Beautiful materials. I might even break down and cook one year." They all laughed.

Lenny showed them the third-floor gym and sauna and the fourth-floor rooftop with a small heated pool, hot tub, and patio garden. The elevator in the two-car garage in the cellar accessed all floors, including the roof. The place was the ultimate proof of how costs can escalate when one seeks heaven under one roof in the heart of the city.

They drifted back down to the second-floor study with its view of the Georgetown University campus. Carole leaned up against Allie and spoke quietly while rubbing the nape of his neck.

"I really like this place, Allie. How about you?"

"What's not to like? But—" She put her finger to his lips to shush him.

"No buts about not being able to afford this place. Look, Herbie, my accountant, said buy something or give the government four million this year. Better me than them."

Cohen's smile showed that he understood. "There, I'm buying it because it's a smart thing to do."

Lenny appeared, and Carole asked him, "Okay, Lenny, how much for the place?"

Lenny must have hemmed and hawed for two seconds. "I can let you take it off my hands for only $1,150,000. I know that sounds like a lot, but it's actually a steal."

Cohen flinched at the price; Carole did not. "Lenny, it's a deal, and please start construction of the other two."

"If Mondale makes it," joked Lenny, "rich Democrats will pay through the nose for these two babies."

Chapter 47

Nobody laughed, and Allie said why. "Greed isn't funny to real Democrats."

Allie, Carole, and her kids left and returned to the hotel.

While waiting for the elevator, Carole mentioned to Allie, "You know, it's ridiculous that I've never seen my Texas Hill Country property."

"For many reasons, I can't see you in the Hill Country, although I'm fond of the place."

"It's a classic Hollywood financing tale, Allie. A few years ago, I did a favor for Sam by taking a small and unflattering part to give a boost to a flat film. At first, I put Sam off because Herbie told me I couldn't make any more money that year, and it was only July. So Sam appeased Herbie with a loophole that allowed me to own a whole little mountain he'd bought while filming a Western in an area just outside a place called Sattler."

Allie had been there. He described it for her. "Carole, they damned a river and created Canyon Lake that's so blue it looks like a small Mediterranean Sea. It's located halfway between Austin and San Antonio near San Marcos and New Braunfels and close to the top of my list of future retirement locations."

"That's music to my ears, Allie. How'd you like to start about thirty years sooner and help me develop it?"

Everybody went to bed happy that night, especially Lenny. The next morning, a White House limo arrived at nine forty-five to take Carole and Allie to their first meeting with Ted Bell.

"Carole," he whispered to her, "I feel like a *Doonesbury* character visiting the White House, probably Mike."

297

The limo motored past the front gate and up the driveway to the west wing, where the guard directed them to the Executive Office Building next door, a location that reeked of lowly status within any administration.

"Bell's rung is so low," Cohen kidded to Carole, "that if the government was a bowl of cherries, he'd be in the pits."

A White House guard led the new U.S. tour group down a dank dark hallway and into a nondescript office. The nerdy tall, thin Ted Bell greeted them.

"Ms. Herman, Dr. Cohen, it is my great pleasure to meet you both, and please let me introduce Robert 'Chip' Allwood, an intern from Dartmouth."

Allwood, a short, plump preppy from the exclusive Chicago suburb of Kenilworth, shook their hands. Bell, on loan from Stanford, displayed dork humor.

"Chip and I are WHIMPs. That's White House Internship Model Program. Ha ha!"

Chip smiled, said he had some things to do, and left. Ted briefed them on their broad and exciting itinerary while Allie sat back and listened intently until he became distracted. *There are aspects of Bell that don't appear to be kosher. He has the right early sixties haircut and preppy clothing, but he doesn't seem to fit with this Reagan crowd.*

He continued staring at Ted almost to the point of rudeness. *There's a glint in Bell's eyes that I do not see in the others, and I'm trying to put my finger on it.*

Allie signaled that he'd figured it out by slapping his knee. Carole gave him an even stranger look than Bell, who excused himself to use the bathroom.

"Bell's eyes," Allie whispered into Carole's ear, "reveal the soul of a victim, so he must be Jewish. Check out Chip's eyes, not a trace of victimization, nada."

Bell returned and made Allie and Carole laugh by relating how the White House chain of command passed the assignment on down to him.

"Nobody else had the time or inclination, and I'm obviously not in the position to decline duties sent my way. There's no one below me to delegate to."

I planned it that way Ted. The president followed my lead in assigning the tour to you, but there were protocols to consider.

Carole inquired about Bell's background. "Ted, what other missions have you performed for President Reagan?"

"None," he said. "This is my first major task in the three months that I've been on board. Mostly, I've answered the phone, opened mail, and helped write a few reports. Let me say, though, that I'm very excited by the challenge, and you can count on me to be supportive in any capacity that you may require."

Cohen incorrectly surmised that, while Reagan napped, the buck was passed by each tired official until the memo filtered down to Bell.

Allie, I put Ted Bell's name in President Reagan's mind when he offered the cultural ambassadorship to Carole because Ted will become a disciple of yours. President Reagan forgot Bell's name the second he said goodbye to Carole.

Bell described his measures of sponsorship. "I promise to see you through this world tour, and here are the vouchers guaranteeing full support through March 1985, also State Department directives. You guys leave for Russia two weeks from the day."

Bell held a file in the air as he spoke. "I've saved the bad news for last and am sorry to say that we do have one problem that is, uh, political in nature—Dr. Cohen's liberal democratic advocacy. Now what I'm going to say next is strictly off the record and between you and me."

Allie leaned in; Carole tensed. "Although I have no problem with Dr. Cohen's political values, be aware that this administration aggressively enforces an *unofficial policy* requiring all Americans representing the government abroad to have a uniformly conservative ideology."

Cohen sarcastically challenged Bell. "It's not policy if it's *unofficial*. It's discriminatory, repressive, and illegal government behavior."

Carole looked at Allie unhappily as if he shouldn't feel a need to add or clarify."

"Look." Bell sought reassurances. "This policy is quite sensitive. Please keep in mind that the admittance procedures for foreigners invited to speak in the United States is equally restrictive. So I trust that no one will embarrass the government or wreck my career."

Allie needled Bell. "Ted, would you mind if I examine that frighteningly thick folder Uncle Sam has on me? It'll only take a minute. Just a little peek inside is all I need."

Bell appreciated his humor and smiled before turning him down.

"I'm sorry, Dr. Cohen. I'm not at liberty to release it to you. You may petition under FOIA, the Freedom of Information Act, to examine your file."

"No way. The minute you petition, the IRS audits your taxes for the past seven years and probably for the next seven too."

"Dr. Cohen," cautioned Bell, "you're getting carried away. There have been only a few isolated incidents of that happening."

"Yes, Ted, and I'll be the next one."

He begged Bell for at least a small word picture, and Ted gave in and listed a usual litany of leftist sins.

"There must be a dozen photos of you attending antiwar rallies, including a May Day concert. You were the executive director of your SDS chapter in college, and you engaged in extensive draft resistance counseling. Furthermore, you participated in a Central Park smoke-in to call for the legalization of marijuana."

Cohen's question expressed mirth and relief. "That's all?"

"No, we know you once subscribed to the *Guardian*, a known Marxist tabloid."

"Stuart Alboum," he protested, "a Marxist college friend and son of a prominent New York psychiatrist bought me that subscription without my knowledge."

Bell acknowledged, "That's true."

"You know that too?" Cohen was both surprised and impressed.

"Yes, Dr. Cohen, the FBI vetted it and cleared you. Let's see, you also helped lead a teacher's union strike in Newark, government records show that you were a McGovern campaign worker in Georgia of all places, and you also ran as a Kennedy elector in 1980 and lost badly in your own Sandy Springs district. Dr. Cohen, I could go on but believe I've already said more than I should." Bell closed the file and put it in his desk drawer.

Allie asked him, "Might the file's contents limit the role I'll play during the tour?"

301

"Yes," said Bell. "Government provisions allow for Ms. Herman to bring one person with her. We will pick up your expenses, but it is imperative that you constantly specify that you are traveling as a private citizen and guest of Ms. Herman and not as a representative of the Reagan administration."

Allie loved hearing Bell say that and smiled. Bell's specifications made him happier.

"Failure on your part to make clear that you are not affiliated with the White House will result in your dismissal from the tour. The government also reserves the right to deny your existence, if necessary. If that sounds harsh, I'm sorry, but I don't make policy as you can see."

Cohen thought; *Bell, you made my day. I might be so incognito during the tour that nobody could prove I took it.*

With the meeting's aims accomplished, Carole and Allie got up to leave. Bell escorted his guests to the front door, whereupon Allie hurled a question at him.

"Mr. Bell, are you, by any chance, of the Hebrew persuasion?"

Bell paused, became pale, and hesitantly responded, "I'm not sure."

"You're not sure if you're Jewish—you know, like me?"

Bell phumphed out of the side of his mouth, "I think there may have been someone on my mother's side."

Cohen did not back off. "You mean, like, maybe your mother?"

Bell pursed a tense smile, sweated, and said nothing. Allie appeared to let it go, but truth was Carole dragged him out of there.

302

"Please," she begged. "Stop trying to get leverage on this sweet, helpful young man, and be grateful for what he's doing for us."

Allie learned right there that he can't put anything over on her and that he'd have to either get better at it or cease trying. What pleased him—the Central Command's farming the tour out to Bell with his minimal status—Carole saw as a slap in the face.

Carole cooled down during the ride as visions of exotic locales danced in her head and made her happy. They were starting on a fantastic journey, a once-in-a-lifetime travel experience for both.

Upon their return to the hotel, Carole needed a nap, Allie some fresh air and time alone, so he walked around the area. Cohen called Sandy Forman from a pay phone in the plaza, quickly updated him about the trip and town house, and then instructed him to find out if Bell was Jewish.

"Is this blackmail," asked Forman, cutting to the chase, "or hardball? There's a big difference."

"It's hardball, so please hire a private detective to investigate his ancestry. I need to create some more wriggle room."

"I'll get right on it."

Cohen walked around Georgetown for an hour, stretched his legs, assessed his situation, and returned to the suite. Allie remembered that he was due in New Jersey in a few hours and needed to tear himself away from Carole and then head up I-95 to Westfield to deal with his mother's and Carla's interrogations.

"Come on, Allie," begged Carole, yearning to hear some live blues at a local club. "I feel like boogying on down to the Cellar Door tonight to listen to Georgie Tyler. Let's smoke some weed, go drink some good Scotch, listen to Georgie and his band, and get up and dance. You can go to Jersey tomorrow."

"I can't. I promised my family that I'd be in tonight, and there's a Hertz in the lobby to rent a car. I also have to visit my old friend Mike Schwartz. I'll just be gone two days."

He hugged and kissed her and then disappeared into the elevator. His independent nature made her sigh.

I normally dominate my lovers, but I don't think that's going to be the case this time.

Carole, you are partners in a great mission for Hashem, not husband and wife.

Chapter 48

The lanky Antonio Willis walked into Wiley's Bar and ordered a beer. Eddie White, who was nursing one, called out to him.

"Yo, Antonio, what's happening, my man?"

Willis, glad to see his old high school buddy, called back.

"Eddie White, my main man, far fucking out! Jesus, I ain't seen you since Bankhead High."

"That's right, so what you been up to? Let's see, last time was Mr. Cohen's class, right?"

"Yeah," Willis replied. "Mr. Cohen, man, that dude sure was a hard motherfucker."

"Yeah," Eddie agreed. "He was a motherfucker, all right."

"You know, Eddie," shared Antonio, "if it weren't for Mr. Cohen, I'd probably be dead or in jail today."

"No shit? Why's that?"

Antonio remembered as if it were yesterday and rapped away.

"He told me I was fucked-up and going nowhere, and he was right. You remember how he caught me in the back of the room showing my dick to Linda Gray, who was underage, and trying to get her to touch it?"

Eddie chuckled as he nodded yes. "Well, he told ol' shithead Meacham that maybe some time in jail might shape me up. Of course, pea-brain Meacham loved that idea and called the cops."

Eddie, spellbound by Antonio's story, said, "Yeah, I'll bet."

"Well, I spent two days locked up with murderers, rapists, and bad robbers—dudes that'd kill you for nothin'—and it fucking scared me straight. Mr. Cohen heard how I was at risk and got me out of jail and felt I'd learned my lesson, and he was fucking A right. After that, I kept my cool the last month in school and graduated, and my uncle Julius got me a job as a sleeping car porter for Amtrak. Mr. Cohen may have saved my life."

"Cohen saved your life, huh? Wow, go on."

"A couple of years later, I got picked to manage an Economic Opportunity Atlanta crew that paints murals on urban walls. I got that through my smart cousin Sandra, who works in the Bureau of Cultural Affairs. You remember Sandra, don'tcha?"

"Uh-huh, yeah, Sandra was smart as hell."

"Dig it, Eddie. My job is to prepare the budget, procure the supplies, and make sure everybody gets what they need so things go smoothly. I'm kind of like my own boss, and the pay's not so bad either. Hey, you remember Juanita Blood?"

"Yeah, she was real cute. I remember those eighth-grade parties in her finished cellar."

"Yeah, good times, man. Anyway, we got married four years ago and now have two little boys. We also just put a down payment on a nice ranch house in East Point."

"Now ain't that something." Eddie kicked that around. "East Point is letting niggers in."

Antonio no longer thought of himself as a nigger nor said the word anymore too. Willis changed the subject to Eddie's post-Bankhead existence.

306

"So what you been up to, man?"

White resorted to his usual lines. "I been liftin' garbage cans with all the other niggers and can barely keep a roof over Farrah and the kids."

"I'm sorry that things didn't work out better. You were some kind of fullback. I swear, you could have made the pros."

"Yeah, well." White had his pat excuse ready. "Motherfuckin' Cohen took care of that."

Antonio saw a chance to help his old friend. "We go back to kindergarten together. You're the closest thing on earth I can call a brother. I love you, man. Do you get it?"

A tear welled up in Eddie's eye. "I get it, man. I love you too, bro, and it's been too long since we hung out."

"Then listen good, Eddie. The incident was a long time ago. It's past and done, and you need to move on."

"I know, Antonio." Eddie looked down at the floor and brushed a tear from his eye. "Farrah's been telling me the same thing for years, and I think I finally heard right for the first time. I think they call that breakthrough, don't they?"

"Trust me, Eddie, Mr. Cohen was never the source of your problems, and he would have gladly helped you like he did me. We all should have listened more to Cohen. Most of us should have gone to college too like he wanted for us."

"I know, Antonio, I fucked up bad, and I finally need to own my mistake."

"Frankly, you put Cohen in a tight corner, especially when you went after him and got kicked out. You should be apologizing

307

to the smartest man we ever met and not cursing him anymore. You dig, bro?"

Hearing Antonio say it instead of Farrah was the turning point in Eddie's life. A mentor would soon appear and help him finally make his place in the world.

"Eddie," Willis inquired, "you interested in another job, man?"

Eddie answered Antonio like he'd asked a stupid question. "Does fat meat make grease?"

Willis laughed at his friend's Marcus Miller imitation, the enormous assistant principal who bear-hugged Eddie out of Bankhead High.

"Anyway, we need a painter's assistant. The pay's only a little more, but the work sure smells a lot sweeter."

Eddie only needed to say, "When do I start?"

Willis briefed him. "I got to tell you that Reagan's been cutting the budget for the past three years, so you never really know when the goddamned money will dry up. We got four walls left, though, which should keep us busy for at least a year."

"Antonio, after lugging garbage, a year sounds good to me."

"Maybe, Eddie, but by that time, it could be something new. We'll see. It's all politics and connections. Sandra's been dating the mayor's chief aide, so right now, I got a pretty good grapevine."

"Antonio, my man, tell me more about the job."

"Okay, we beautify old downtown buildings by painting a scene on an ugly but visible wall. For example, yesterday we finished up a train coming out of MARTA station that was painted on the side of an old firehouse near Georgia Tech. Next week, we begin a black hero's scene on the side of a black bank on Courtland Street."

"That sounds easy enough."

"Bullshit," said Antonio, who knew better. "That job's gonna be a real pain in the ass. Every civil rights organization and leader gonna be telling me I got to put this one in, take that one out, and get nasty about it too."

"Well, the brothers just want some input. It is a community mural."

"That's naive. Reagan ain't funding any black revolutionary shit. Black pride and heroes are cool but nothing to make the brothers restless."

Eddie nodded that he got it. Antonio briefed Eddie on the main problem.

"The guy painting the mural belongs to a really heavy group that's pushin' hard for a wall showing white crimes against blacks. Dude calls himself Lesotho Xeranga, son of a bitch used to be known as Richard Sampson."

Eddie seemed more impressed than intimidated, so Antonio grounded Eddie.

"You'll see how heavy he is when he and his people get in your face and call you names."

Eddie laughed. Antonio gave him the information.

"You start Monday morning at nine o'clock in front of the Citizens Union Bank. Hey, Wiley, pour another round for me and my man, Eddie." They celebrated.

For the first time in years and because he was finally dealing with his Cohen thing, White went to sleep feeling good inside. His old friend Antonio returned to him the gift of hope and a second chance in life.

Yes, Eddie, Antonio has given you a second chance in life. Now make the most of it, and be better to your wife and children too, and the Lord will begin rewarding you.

Chapter 49

Westfield-bound Allie left Washington and its politics in the rearview mirror. His family up ahead was possibly a tougher nut to crack, especially since so much had changed since he moved to Atlanta.

Allie pulled off the turnpike and onto the parkway. *I've always hated the fucking drive from Washington to New Jersey, a real meat grinder of high-tension driving and pocket-emptying pay tolls.*

This was well before the coming age of E-ZPass. Cohen exited the parkway and drove into the Maple Gardens apartment complex and headed for quadrangle H. He parked, got out, and walked into a U-shaped courtyard with six four-family adjoined buildings.

Cohen found his mother's unit, 3901, and knocked twice. Janet opened the door and was overjoyed to see her son.

"My boychick, the big shot. It's so good to see you, Allie."

She kissed his cheek with the force of a plunger, took his hand, and led him into the kitchen. The first course in his welcome-home feast was a nice smoked whitefish chub.

Max made do with his Polish gruel but promised Allie, "It will be my pleasure to supply the Sit-In with the choicest smoked fish available."

Allie thought, *I haven't the heart to tell Max that Harvey will soon begin smoking his own fish in the Peachtree Corners prep facility—salmon, sturgeon, sable, and whitefish chubs too. I'm also not going to tell him how we plan to pickle corned beef in forty-five-day brine and dill baths and make handmade pastrami. I'll just smile appreciatively.*

Janet next served cold, homemade beet borscht laced with a dollop of sour cream and garnished with a thick slice of crusty pumpernickel. A favorite dish of golden brown potato pancakes, *latkes*, preceded a slice of creamy cheesecake and coffee.

Allie thought it a good time to bring up the forbidden subject—Carole. Maybe her rigid middle-class morality had softened a bit.

"Ma," he appealed, "it's time you meet Carole already."

Janet's twinkling eyes turned an icy gray; the beaming smile switched to creased cement, and she typically said, "I can wait."

"Please give her a chance, Ma. You're not being fair."

"Look who's talking. To show you I'm a lady, I won't say what I'm thinking."

He dropped that and tried another approach. "I have two extraordinary women in my life now. I'm not saying it's right, but it's happened. Carole is a whole other half of my life, and I want you to be a part of my other world too."

The subject tired her. "Allie, I'm not ready yet. Give me a little more time, please. If you're still together in six months, then I promise, okay?"

"How about one month?"

"I'll split the difference, three months."

He let it go and discussed politics with his mother, an old FDR New Deal liberal.

"Allie, I'm for Mondale, but a shocking amount of my friends say Reagan isn't doing such a bad job. Can you imagine that? The man is wrecking the country. It's very disturbing."

Cohen wondered if the White House was listening in on their conversation, so he looked out the window. He didn't see any nondescript panel trucks parked nearby and felt comfortable enough to kid around with her.

"I know, Ma. I think old Ironhair is showing signs of Alzheimer's, and Republicans are talking about putting him up on Mount Rushmore."

Janet laughed and gave him her rundown on the candidates.

"I'm not so crazy about Gary Hart, a real skirt chaser. And that Jesse Jackson, him I don't trust at all. With this Farrakhan and all the anti-Semitism, I'm very worried. Jackson should apologize to the Jews, don't you think so?"

It's obviously where I get my political genes from. Max's one issue is to stop giving welfare to the blacks and make them work.

They spent the rest of the night catching up on family matters until midnight and slept well.

After a breakfast of bagels, cream cheese, lox, and sweet onions, Allie and Janet drove to a Jaguar dealer and purchased for Carla a black luxury coupe with silver gray interior. The rest of the plan was for Sandy Forman to schedule a UPS delivery to Carla's home that was timed to Allie's arrival; a truck unloaded a Honda all-terrain vehicle and a reduced-by-half-scale Volkswagen Beetle convertible too.

Max followed in Allie's rental. Janet scolded her son too for being so extravagant.

"Allie, you are overcompensating for a past lack of money and acting very nouveau in the process."

"Wow, Mom, did you ever learn a lot of schlock psychology when I was in college." Janet laughed. "Anyway, for one time only, I am being Carla's idealized brother, the one she always wanted me to be."

"Why bother, Allie? She's so jaded that the impression will last about five minutes."

"You'll see, Ma. I have something to prove and think it'll work."

"Bull." Janet doubted. "You're proving something to yourself."

"So," said Cohen, "you, I'm planning to send to Israel or any country you want to go to."

Janet hugged him. "Thank you for Israel. I'm not so interested in seeing others. My eyesight is getting worse. Travel's not so much fun after your vision begins to dim a bit."

Max followed Allie into Carla's driveway; the UPS truck was right behind him with the ATV and mini-Bug. Carla, an attractive forty-two-year-old blonde who looked thirty and was blessed with an incredible energy level, spotted her family from her kitchen window and ran out to greet them. As usual, she was exquisitely dressed and wore four striking rings, each a different colored rock that was big enough to refract sunlight.

"You of all people, Allie," she stated, "I can't see in a Jaguar. I think you're more of a BMW or Saab Turbo kind of guy."

He let it sink in. "Actually, I bought it for someone I owe a lifetime worth of gifts to." Carla's jaw dropped; he confirmed it. "Yep, it's yours, big sister."

She hugged and kidded him, "Boy, did you quickly learn how to spoil." Allie smiled. "My god, Allie, you'll probably buy your kid a real fire truck."

Carla again hugged and congratulated Allie. "Success really agrees with you, and frankly, it couldn't happen to a nicer guy."

She stuck out a cheek to kiss; he took Carla's hand. "Let me show you the four-wheeled ATV and the VW Bug."

The gifts for her sons staggered Carla. "As much as I hate to admit it, Allie, even I must accuse you of overdoing it."

Allie, Janet, Max, Carla, and her sons Stephen and Brent all piled into the Jaguar and headed to a fine Italian seafood restaurant in Millburn Center. Carla's husband, Joel, met them there straight from work, and during dinner, Joel couldn't resist needling Allie about his past liberalism.

"I can see you're not content anymore, Allie, educating the black race for the rest of your life. I also wonder how you're going to endure all of that filthy materialism."

Allie enjoyed Joel's good-natured tease. "I appreciate your concern, brother-in-law, but I'll manage somehow."

He refilled Joel's wineglass; Carla lobbied for a meeting with Carole.

"Hey, brother, when are you going to introduce me to her already? You, of all people, must know what a great fan of hers I am."

"I'm planning to invite you and Joel to have dinner with us in two weeks, when we pass through New York on our way to Moscow, but if that's not convenient, we can always reschedule for another time."

"Allie, don't you dare kid around with me like that. My god, I can't wait. If you don't hurry and marry Carole, you're both stupid and crazy. You must know that I'm dying to become her sister-in-law."

Janet disapproved. "Carla, I can see that you're really praying for this affair to burn itself out."

She ignored her mother. "Allie, listen to me, she's the number one star in the world. Get her pregnant as soon as possible."

"Enough," Janet told Carla.

Carla again ignored Janet. "Mom, of course, wants you to do the right thing, Allie, like go back to your snobby little teacher of a wife."

"Too much red wine," scolded Janet, "is unloosing your tongue and brain. A person cannot forever crap on morality. Sooner or later, it catches up to you. Now please stop."

With dramatic hand gestures, Carla drove home her point. "Ma, people don't give a damn about what's right, only what you can do for them. You and Allie should both grow up, and then you wouldn't be so disappointed when the world dumps on you."

Both Janet and Allie stared at Carla to change the subject, but she had one more thing on her mind.

"Most years, I was lucky to get a card from him, and today he drops a Jaguar on me. He can do a lot more with the stroke of his money in one day than he can from the classroom in twenty years."

"Please, Carla," they begged.

"Allie, you'll get in the history books faster being Carole Herman's husband than you will from teaching a brotherhood class or even writing a best-selling novel. That's your peculiarity, isn't it, to get in the goddamned history books?"

"No, Carla," said Allie firmly. "I just want to help people understand how to come together and work for peace. That's the mark that interests me."

Well said, prophet, in an understated way.

Carla rested her case; Janet glared at her daughter. Allie estimated that Carla was ripe for her lesson—do not expect him to shower her with any more expensive presents. She and her children were simply to love Allie because he was her brother and the kids' uncle Allie.

"Carla, for the past fifteen years, I've felt as much endured as loved." Although her face showed disgust for that comment, he used a quote to get through. "Henrik Tikkanen once said, 'People who lose their money are not dumb, but what they have to say is worthless.' I felt like I'd made it halfway into your family's hearts."

Carla acknowledged that they all could have been more demonstrative and contested, "My kids were always, and still are, crazy about you. That's because you had summers off and played ball with them, swam with them, taught them about life. I know what you invested in my kids, so don't downplay it."

He acknowledged her argument but let his money make a statement. After generously tipping the waiter, Allie gave each of Carla's children $200. Twelve-year-old Steven and ten-year-old Brent ecstatically thanked and hugged him.

"Man, Uncle Allie, an ATV, a miniature Beetle, and now two hundred bucks. Even Grandpa never gave us gifts like these. Man, you're the greatest."

"And guys," Uncle Allie promised them, "if you learn your haftarah perfectly, I'll give you both five thousand for your bar mitzvah presents."

Steven and Brent went gaga and raved, "Wow, did you hear that, Mom?"

Carla's face stiffened. "Yes, Steven, yes, Brent, I heard it."

Steven drove Allie's lesson home by again raving, "Isn't Uncle Allie the greatest, Mom?"

Allie read Carla's face. *She's grateful that I'm not rubbing her nose in it.*

Janet, glad that the conversation had cooled down, dared to get one last good dig at her provocative daughter.

"All right, Allie, you know there's a limit to how much truth Carla can take at one time."

Carla playfully stuck her tongue out at her mother and graciously invited everyone back to her house for cake and coffee. Small talk about Reagan and future destinations prevailed for the rest of the evening. Steven, Brent, and Allie shared a bedroom, talked much of the night away, and became closer than ever.

At breakfast, Allie found it hard to talk to Carla and asked why. Her reply sounded like it was formed late the night before.

"Because, Ayatollah Cohen, you always display your aggravating moral superiority, and it bugs the hell out of me. I mean, I'm supposed to be the elder sister, yet you always manage to show me up. Can you understand where I'm coming from?"

He did and let her know it. "I'll grant you, Carla, that I deserved that, but I sincerely feel that you now recognize and

318

accept we're different and love me regardless of what I can do for anybody."

"Why did you get all the brains?" She smiled; he did too.

"Come on, you were a talented copywriter out of college and a merchandising executive by the time you were twenty-five. Don't sell yourself short. Look, I have to split for Mike Schwartz's place and will leave you with this."

"What, pray tell?"

"We were born five years apart and were almost from different generations. You, Carla, were Jackie Kennedy and her pillbox hats, and I was Bob Dylan with his blue denim work shirts."

"Ma used to joke that you wouldn't have worn a work shirt if you'd really had to wear one for a living."

Allie laughed and added, "Daddy's death also made us rivals for Ma's attention and more limited resources. Foolishly, we were tough on each other too."

"Allie," said Carla, needing to know, "is there still a gap?"

"Nope," answered Allie firmly. "There's no more gap."

"Allie, the problem of scale now belongs to me. And if you were expecting a car for your birthday, I'm afraid that I'm going to disappoint you."

Allie enjoyed a good belly laugh, kissed Carla goodbye, and left her with magical words.

"I'll call you as soon as we land in New York and make plans. I think you and Carole will really like each other."

Carla's feet hardly touched the ground while walking Allie to his rental. Her moist eyes produced a tear.

"Take care, little brother, and please remember that I love you very, very much."

Chapter 50

Carole's children returned to boarding school, and she stayed in Washington to explore Georgetown and the Capitol on her own. Washington, in the past, was a city she avoided; now she was falling in love with the place. With Allie in New Jersey, the free woman made a date with Lenny to have lunch.

Carole was in a fine mood as the taxi darted in and out of federal district traffic and dropped her off in front of Le Canard. She looked up at the sky. The weather was warm and sunny, and after lunch, she planned to check out Georgetown's many cute shops.

Lenny met Carole at the door, welcomed her with a hug, and instructed a waiter to serve a bottle of Pinot Noir and two glasses in his office. Carole picked up vibes that Lenny was about to lay bad news on her.

"Carole, you won't believe what an unsettling incident happened to me this morning. I was visiting two Roslyn jobsites that were close enough to walk between. While strolling over to the second job, I thought I saw an old girlfriend following me."

"So what's the big deal?"

"Carole, I spun around. And sure enough, it was June Merrick, a freelance journalist. She noticed that I was aware of her and snuck into a coffee shop to hide. I chased and caught up to her and demanded that she tell me what she was up to. She came clean thankfully and said she was trying to run into me in order—"

Carole completed the sentence for him. "She's trying to get at Allie and me. What else? Shit, the fucking media comes at me in any way possible."

Lenny searched for the right words to convey a degree of seriousness.

"June has written for the *Times, Post, Harper's, Atlantic* and has—"

"Lenny," interrupted Carole, "it doesn't matter who June's written for. Reporters are all the same. They only care about their story, and June's just a little more intellectual."

"That's not it, Carole. June's gorgeous, sexy, and amoral. We dated a few years back, and I loved her and thought she loved me too. Well, one night we're at a White House cocktail party, and she's introduced to Peter Bates, the movie star—"

"Lenny," Carole interrupted him again, "I know Peter Bates very well, so I can imagine where this story is going."

"Yeah, you may know Peter, but you don't know June. I was busy refilling our wineglasses when Bates hinted to June that if she came across with sex, he'd submit to an exclusive interview. By the time he finished his sentence, she was leading him into the men's room by the hand and fucked him in the stall. I cried while watching them brazenly go right in, and it took me about a couple of minutes to find the courage to walk in and stop it."

"Did they stop?"

"No. June told me to get the fuck out. She hadn't come yet, and I was holding back her orgasm. I left that second and had no contact with her until this morning."

Carole, bothered, folded her arms. "So this fearsome sexual animal is stalking my Allie at this very moment?"

"Yes, sexually stalking attractive men may be her greatest talent in life, *and* she's a pretty good writer too."

Lenny's waiter interrupted their laughter by serving French onion soup garnished with toasted minibaguettes and celery stalks filled with hummus. Carole picked at her meal before getting up from her chair with a long face.

"I'm sorry," said Lenny, assuming blame, "that I ruined our meal and your day."

Carole sweetly touched his cheek. "You meant well, Lenny. Friends sometimes have to pass on bad news. That's the way it is."

"When's Allie due back from New Jersey?"

She guessed while standing in the doorway. "Some time tomorrow night, I believe."

"Hey." He suggested, "Why not come by for lunch again tomorrow? There's an art gallery around the corner that I'd love to show you. Let me make today up to you."

"Sure. In fact, that's a good idea. Thank you, Lenny."

She left to buy gifts for her children and Rose and Sam.

About 250 miles north, Cohen carefully followed Mike's directions to his home. The ride took an hour, and he had time to think.

Mike and Allie grew up together in the Weequahic section of Newark. The once great Jewish community produced a disproportionate number of professionals, intellectuals, business leaders, and bookies. That was until the Jews relocated to the suburbs with the other white ethnic groups running from the blacks sweeping across the city. Cultures that spoiled their women were naturally in conflict with others capable of terrorizing meek elderly ladies.

One example was Cohen's aunt Rosie and uncle Harold, who owned the corner luncheonette in his apartment building. Harold, a night-shift plumber at a Newark Airport motel, was part of a five-man crew of older maintenance workers. They were all beaten into comas one night by black burglars who broke in and pistol-whipped the defenseless older men.

After getting out of the hospital, Harold and Rosie shopped around for a business to buy and built the old candy store into a thriving luncheonette and kiosk—cigarettes, candy, newspapers, pinball machine. Sadly, the beating administered to Harold led to the deterioration of every organ in his body and eventual heart failure.

Rosie ran the store with the aid of her drug-addicted son, Fred, and despite Fred's stealing her blind to support his habit, she managed to hang on.

One night, though, four burly black robbers held Rosie up, beat her senseless, and left her to die on the floor. Ironically, her life was saved when Fred broke into the store to hit up the register for a fix and discovered his diabetic sixty-year-old mother lying in a pile of empty cigarette cartons.

Janet stayed with Rosie the whole time in the hospital. After the robbery and beating, she told her son over the phone, "The blacks just don't rob you, Allie." She made it very clear. "They also have to beat you up, little old ladies too."

A second incident happened five days after Rosie left the hospital. Janet bought Allie a brand-new convertible for a college graduation gift. The reward was not for his going away to college but for commuting to Park Row for four years, which saved about $25,000.

On his fifth day of ownership, Allie discovered that a robber had forced a foot-long screwdriver into his ignition to start it up and steal it. The ignition jammed, the car wouldn't move, and he watched the tow truck drag away the shiny first step in his American dream.

Crime was what caused the exodus of a great Jewish community into the vast anomic sprawl of North and Central

Jersey. A month after the attack on his car, Allie moved Janet to a suburban garden apartment in Irvington.

Mike Schwartz, the tough, cynical child of Holocaust survivors, taught in the Newark school system with his wife, Marla. Most of Mike's students were uninterested in learning math and granted him a peace of sorts if he didn't work them too hard. He was trying to be a great math teacher and trying to survive the day too.

White flight pushed up suburban home prices so steeply that Mike and his wife moved halfway to Pennsylvania to find a house they could afford. Allie imagined how tired they must be from the seventy-mile round-trip commute that took almost an hour each way.

Cohen recalled. *I know that feeling of pressure from the cost of paying for a middle-class standard of living. It begins to scare you. The predictability of everyday life starts to wear you down too, and if you're not careful, you can become a broken shell.*

Mike's cute petite very pregnant wife, Marla, opened the door and welcomed Allie into their modest split-level home.

Mike saw Allie and joked, "Hey, Allie, let's go get high. I know you're coming from the house of your sister, Carla, and a night at her place is like a night in the Ukraine."

I might have laughed harder, thought Allie, *if not coming from such a tender scene with Carla.*

"I got to hand it to you, Allie." Mike slapped him on the back. "I just read a *People* magazine article on you, and I'm in awe of your success."

"Did you complete it while reading it in the john? All their stories, Mike, are written short enough to be scanned during a bowel movement."

Mike laughed and then sentimentalized. "We must go back twenty-five years already. We've had some good times, man."

"Yeah, man, we sure did." They nodded in agreement.

"Allie, I need a favor."

The politics of friends, thought Cohen but asked, "What Mike?"

"It's a beautiful day," Schwartz pointed out. "Let's walk around the lake, and I'll tell you while strolling."

"I like that, Mike. I recall it being a pretty lake with a sweet little beach and short pier."

Mike unbuttoned himself as they strolled. "Allie, I've read all about your movie deals and figure that you might have some connections by now. Would you mind listening to an idea for a novel or screenplay?"

Allie felt that he at least owed it to his friend to listen. "Sure, Mike, shoot."

Mike related a heartbreaking tale of a born loser, Jody Wilder, a thirty-year-old hairdresser from Jersey City who lived a bleak existence. Allie's loser cousin Fred lived a bleak hairdresser existence in Jersey City too, so Cohen immediately empathized with Jody's woeful situation and life.

Mike continued. "Jody is poor, plain, divorced, and going nowhere. She luckily enjoys a fairy-tale breakthrough with a Hawaiian prince and experiences love and a happy marriage."

"This doesn't end happily, does it, Mike?"

"Not at all." Mike knowingly giggled. "A brain tumor makes him crazy, and he beats her repeatedly and ultimately throws her out on the street. Jody's one chance at happiness is trashed even worse when the next night, after taking refuge in a cheap Honolulu hotel, she is brutally gang-raped by four big Samoan brothers and winds up back in Jersey City cutting hair but in much worse shape."

"Holy shit, Mike, that is a powerful story. I like its potential. The story line is guaranteed to leave even hard-hearted persons with lumps in their throat. Women who read that book will be crying in airports and on beaches. The part sounds like a good, meaty role for a lucky young actress."

"The most amazing part, Allie, is the story is mostly true. Marla knows the chick, and she recently developed breast cancer too."

"Stop it. I can't take it anymore." Then he said the magic words. "So I guess the favor is to help sell the concept, correct?" Mike nodded yes, to which Allie, the pro, questioned, "Have you outlined the concept for either a novel or a movie script?"

This time, Mike shook his head no. "Okay, Mike, then is your ending Jody wallowing in self-pity for the rest of her life in Jersey City, or does she join a convent or develop early Alzheimer's? What?"

After a good laugh, Mike stated, "Early Alzheimer's brought on by the shock of the gang rape, yes, that's the perfect tragic ending, thank you very much."

Allie grounded Mike into reality. "I'm glad, but who's going to write it, Mike? To be honest, I'm overobligated for a while."

"Allie," said Mike, nominating himself, "I'm ready for a challenge like this and need a year to grind it out. I feel strongly that I can write but have never had the proper motivation or enough pressure on me. This could be my only chance in life to make it, and I realize that there's no margin for failure."

Allie's heart wanted to do it, but his head wondered if Mike had the right stuff. He looked into Mike's eyes and saw a hungry streak, and with Marla expecting to give birth any day like Sarah, Allie ventured that Mike would get it done. Cohen never forgot how Peter Bates took a chance on an unknown social studies teacher from Atlanta with an unfinished story and a pregnant wife and helped change his life.

Mike's eyes blazed happiness when Allie agreed to try to sell it.

"Here's a title, Mike, *Jane Wilson: Portrait of a Born Loser* or whatever name or title that you prefer. Keep it short, maybe 170 to 220 pages or about forty-five thousand to sixty thousand words. I'll put you in touch with my editor, Harland Cooper, who'll expect a rough draft in three months and a fairly powerful second draft in seven months. He'll keep your nose to the grind—"

A cream-colored Mercedes sedan literally drove right up to Cohen's feet, and he stopped in midsentence. A stunning thirtyish woman with long blond hair clad only in a skimpy, clinging, sheer white jogging suit and running shoes got out of the car. She bent down to pick up a can of film she'd dropped, and magnificent breasts spilled out of her low-cut top.

"What was I saying, Mike? Eh, forget it."

He noticed the tools of the working press—a camera and tape recorder hanging from shoulder straps. June Merrick, in Allie's presence long enough to raise his blood pressure a bit, introduced herself.

"Dr. Cohen, I presume?"

Allie coolly answered yes, his inflection encouraging June to state her intentions.

"I'm June Merrick and a freelancer for the *Washington Post* Sunday magazine. I want to interview you, and I'll be candid. Outside several guarded radio and TV spots, you've yet to sit down for a comprehensive interview. I'm going to be writing five thousand words on you whether you cooperate with me or not, so please do us both a favor and say yes."

Allie did not care for June's be-damned attitude and turned the tables on her.

"Ms. Merrick, since you plan to present me as you wish, you might as well go ahead and write whatever you want. Now if you'll excuse me, I have an important favor to do for an old friend. Good day, Ms. Merrick."

He turned his back to June. "Mike, I'm ready to make that phone call."

They began walking up the hill to Mike's house. June Merrick was frantic, and they heard her outburst from frustration.

"Christ, I have driven too fucking far to blow an interview opportunity like this."

She ran after Allie. "Dr. Cohen, I didn't mean it the way it sounded. If I offended you, I'm sorry. Please wait up."

Allie and Mike stopped to let her catch up. She tried to make it very clear.

"What I meant to say was that if you refuse, I'll have to resort to filler rather than personal quotes. My references will be limited to what's already written about you instead of describing the *real you* for the first time—"

Cohen cut her off with a tease. "Well, since I only got discovered a little while ago and have pretty much kept my mouth shut, there ain't a whole helluva lot to sort through yet now, is there, Ms. Merrick?"

Good, the media is starting to behold the prophet.

Chapter 51

"Dr. Cohen," Merrick politely requested, "please call me June."

"That's cool." He tested her research skills. "June, what do you know about me?"

"I know that you and Mike are friends since you're eleven, that you wrote half a dozen innovative curricula, and that you pioneered a scientifically valid prejudice reduction treatment that has been very well received. Most importantly, I know that you were a master teacher who'd affected the hearts and minds of countless students."

Allie nodded to communicate "good job"; she added, "And now you've written a powerful work that, overnight, is propelling you into literary-champ status. That's the Allie Cohen I want to present to the world—who Allie really is, how Allie got here, and where Allie's probably going."

"June, you passed that part of the test with flying colors. Next hoop for you to jump through is proportion and perspective. There's no way that a single novel qualifies me as a major writer. It's true my book's been appreciated, but we shouldn't get carried away."

"Please, Allie, a book of this stature only comes along every couple of years. Your novel has already been nominated for a Man Booker Prize for Fiction, and because of record demand, a second printing is planned even before the first one's sold out."

"I didn't know that." Her news puffed him up a bit.

"Global, Allie, is heavily marketing you as a must-read for the mass market. Frankly, you can retire on easy street from what you'll eventually earn from this one property."

He pondered that while she reminded him that they had a friend in common who gave them their first big break—Peter Bates.

"I didn't know that. How interesting. June, please drive us back to Mike's house."

She did, and halfway up the hill, he complimented her. "I have to admit it, you did your homework like a true professional. We can start by driving back to Washington together. That's four or five hours at least."

"Very good. Thank you."

"How do you feel about taking a tour through Newark? I want to trace my family's roots from Prince Street downtown to the Weequahic neighborhood and beyond. That would add one or two more hours to talk."

Merrick was extremely appreciative and then inquired, "Thank you, Allie. Now what about the subject of Carole?"

"That is mostly off-limits, only when absolutely pertinent to the subject." She pouted a bit. "The last thing I want to do is add to Carole's media hell."

June acquiesced with a smile and shrug. Marla opened the door and looked shocked by June's unexpected appearance and anxious from her raw sexuality. She called Mike into the kitchen for an explanation.

June and Allie heard Marla forcefully whisper to Mike, "Where'd you pick this chick up? My god, she's not wearing any underwear. What, is she a porn star? That sweat suit is more of a see-through negligee from Victoria's Secret than gym clothes."

June and Allie laughed nervously. Cohen excused himself to call Sam. June tagged after Cohen and heard him describe the

Jody Wilder plot to Minkowitz, who liked it a lot for the same reasons and naturally asked the big question.

"So who's writing this, kiddo? You're booked solid."

"My friend Mike is."

"Look, Allie, since Mike isn't my illegitimate son-in-law, why should I take a chance? I'll be glad to give your friend a creator's fee for thirty-five thousand, but I need a seasoned pro to make sure it gets done right. You're one in a million, boychick. That's the best I can do, sorry."

"I appreciate that Sam, but Mike is really the guy to tell this story. He's a smart fellow and has the necessary fire in the belly."

Cohen heard Sam sigh loudly into the phone. "Okay, Allie, make me a deal."

"You advance Mike fifty-thousand with a quarter-of-a-million payoff upon completion. If he fails to deliver a professional manuscript a year from the day, I'll reimburse you the fifty grand. Voila, you got nothing to lose. Either way, you make money from a relatively inexpensive investment and project."

Allie, Sam thought, *is not getting it that I don't have to make Mike's life easier, but he is making me a good deal that is stupid to turn down.*

Sam agreed with a comment. "All right, Allie, it's nice the way you believe in your buddy. But from now on, please write and travel, not wheel and deal anymore."

"Thank you, Sam, I'm extremely grateful."

He was also relieved. June looked at Allie in awe.

"You going out on a limb for your friend like that was heroic."

Mike and Marla stared at Allie in awe too. Cohen teased using his best southern accent, "What's the matter, y'all?"

Mike had trouble composing himself. Marla, who appeared ready to drop a baby any minute, had tears in her eyes.

"With one phone call"—Mike snapped his finger—"you changed our lives for the better, just like that. I promise you, Allie, that I'm going to write day and night to produce a work that you'll be proud of. Allie, is it really this easy?"

Cohen chuckled and then answered, "No way. Most people have to die a little before they connect, but even Sam would have told me to get lost if the idea was no good, and a lot of the people out there like Sam do know if it'll work. Excuse me, guys, I have to call my business manager. And if you don't mind, I need some privacy."

Allie called Sandy, who excitedly reported, "Allie, I got the dope on Bell you've been looking for. Guess what, he is Jewish. His father, Leo Bellinsky, a struggling lawyer, left Brooklyn after WWII for Southern California and set up an Orange County practice."

Allie pumped his fist. "I knew he was Jewish. What else?"

"Leo changed his last name to Bell and prospered, along with the growth of Anaheim, as a Jew who made himself useful to the big boys. Supposedly, he got himself involved in state GOP politics and even played cards a couple of times with Richard Nixon when he was still a congressman representing Orange County."

"Holy shit, Bell's dad was a political fixer."

"Legendary political fixer. Some say Leo was the greatest in California history, did a lot of work for Democratic governor Pat Brown too, and peaked when Reagan appointed him to head the Department of Transportation when Ronzo was governor of California. Leo unfortunately developed a bad habit of seeking kickbacks for contracts he was authorized to give out."

"So Bell's dad took bribes too."

"Yes, and it earned him a few years in the slammer, where he died of a heart attack."

"Man, that's heavy and also tells me a lot about Ted, his son. Is there any more?"

"Ted landed the White House job through a Stanford law professor. The word was given to wallpaper the White House with some young Yids to appease rich Republican Jews. Bell supposedly was the only conservative Jewish law student the professor could find, or at least they think he's conservative. Basically, Bell is honest, hardworking, and nerdy. In my opinion, the report sounds like it fulfills your request and needs perfectly."

"That report bolsters my ability to maneuver better in Reagan world. Excellent, Sandy, I'll call you tomorrow."

Forman got in a few more words before saying goodbye. "Allie, Sam just called me, and he means business about you revving down to just meeting the terms of your contract. You can't keep popping good projects on Sam and put him on the spot like that. So what are you going to do?"

"I can't be constrained for these reasons. Let's look into starting our own production company and make it a division of AlCoCorp, the Allie Cohen Corporation."

"I'm warning you, Allie, Sam might not like that. Consequences are possible."

"Big ideas are coming fast, and we have the resources and means to make them happen. We can't risk letting Sam veto great projects just because he thinks I'm too busy."

"Okay, I'll get right on it."

Mike raved while walking June and Allie to their cars, "What can I say, man? That fifty-thousand advance was almost as much as I made the past two years. I'm going to work my balls off too for that quarter of a mil."

"Remember, Mike," Cohen counseled. "The advance is more like thirty-six thou after taxes, and the big money is conditional. You could wind up paying me back for years. You've also never written a novel, which William Faulkner once said is like—"

June sweetly finished the quote for him. "Like a one-armed carpenter putting up a chicken shack in a hurricane."

Mike smiled and professed, "Allie, both of our wives are ready to give birth any minute. I look forward to our kids being friends too as they grow up."

"I like that, Mike, and we'll make it happen."

Allie hugged and kissed Marla goodbye and told June to please follow him to a Hertz rental card drop-off lot on Route 80. June did, and Allie took the wheel of her car and headed down Route 80 to Newark. He passed the parkway connector and got off deep in the inner city of Newark to locate the old tenements that his grandparents first settled in at the turn of the century.

An hour later, Allie realized that a funny thing happened on the trail from Cohen family ground zero on Prince Street to suburbia. Everything had been torn down; not a trace existed anymore. His dad's delicatessen on Lyons Avenue and Aldine Street was also torn down for a freeway that bisected and degraded the Weequahic neighborhood. The cityscape looked third-worldish and fearsome.

June empathized. "This devastation brings to mind that old Tom Wolfe quote about not being able to go home again. In your case, there's almost no physical trace that you ever lived here."

Allie's high school, once the fifteenth best in the country, resembled a detention center. The Burgerama Diner was rubble; the Indian Pizzeria was an empty lot; the Bunny Hop, famous for its steak sandwiches and hot dogs fried in oil, had become a shoeshine parlor; and Syd's Hot Dog Haven, the best boiled dog ever, was a hole in a crumbled wall.

"Allie," inquired June, "where do people dry-clean their clothes or buy decent food? There seems to be no place to simply fill a prescription or eat out other than Shabazz Steak and Take."

"June, even Keer Avenue, once a pretty classy residential street, has declined. Had enough of this?" he asked as they approached an entrance to an expressway leading to I-95 south.

"I'm ready, Allie. I'm afraid that I've witnessed as much poverty and social disorganization as I can bear for one day. I'm ashamed to admit that I'm close to overdosing on reality."

The ride back to Washington proved to be quick, pleasant, and surprising. The conversation never ceased as June peppered Allie with incisive questions.

There was one series of questions, though, that irked him. "What exactly are your politics, Allie? You mainly strike me as an aging Kennedy liberal."

"Fair enough, June, but as I get older, ideology becomes less important than viable solutions. My wife has told me that."

Allie intuitively knew that an opening happened and entitled June to ask several nosy questions about his marriage.

337

"Here's the deal, June. I'll grant you two homelife queries, and that's it."

"Fair enough," she answered and asked her first question. "Are you officially separated from your wife?"

Allie realized that journalists will now report his next statement as fact.

"I am co-living with Sarah and Carole, and the arrangement is working out all right despite occasional challenges."

June laughed richly. "That's a new one, co-living, maintaining your marriage and your lover equally. You're a very lucky man to have your cake and eat it too."

He let that one pass. "Okay, next question, June."

"Last week, I again interviewed Peter Bates to learn how he'd hooked up with you to produce your novel. We're at a Thai restaurant in Encino when Rick Samuels walks in with the Lee sisters, the two most beautiful Asian women I've ever met. While Rick and Peter talk, I strike up a conversation with Mamie and Libby, who tell me that they'd just finished a porno that's matching *Deep Throat*'s grosses, *Casting Couch Revolt* or something like that."

"I guess I am sorry to hear that but knew it was coming."

"Allie, that's really depressing, those beautiful, smart girls exposing themselves like that in front of a camera."

"Well, they each own 15 percent of their own production company and are about to make a shitload of money, so they aren't being exploited."

Cohen boldly delved in. "Just curious, how much money would it take to get you to blow a guy in front of a camera?" Before the words were out of his mouth, Cohen knew he'd given June another serious opening.

"I wouldn't do porn, Allie, for all the money in the world. My husband's a billionaire, but I love oral sex even more than intercourse. If you like, I'll get you off right now at seventy miles an hour."

Before Cohen could blink, she was across the seat and pulling his zipper down. June stuck her hand inside Allie's underwear and fondled away to get him hard. The harder she made him, the heavier he sweated because they were driving through the long Baltimore Harbor Tunnel, and he felt unsafe.

Just as June wrapped her warm mouth around his penis, he pulled her head up and hand away from it.

"June, I think it best that we keep the relationship professional. Sex can only get in the way."

June smiled as she let go of his penis and questioned his decision. "Okay, if that's what you want. I really thought we could mix business with pleasure, but if you can't handle it, fine with me. Still, if you're ever in the mood to get it on, you know where you can find me."

Chapter 52

Carole was alone in a strange city, listening on her Walkman to seven new songs from a soon-to-be released album and getting ever more bored by the minute waiting for Allie to return. She was aware of Georgie Tyler's playing the Cellar Door in Georgetown and had never seen him perform before or experienced the club and figured it was about time that she did.

Carole showered, dressed, and walked over to the nightclub on a warm spring night. The streets were full of college students, young professionals, and government workers walking everywhere.

In LA, we don't walk anywhere—for me, only on the beach. I'm thrilled that no one is recognizing me and letting me stroll.

The musician in Carole led her down memory lane as she moseyed to the nightclub. Herman and Tyler were old acquaintances, but she mainly knew him through her long friendship with Charna Daniels, Georgie's ex-wife and a beautiful, sexy blues and jazz singer. Carole rated Georgie as the best blue-eyed soul singer alive who also performed great blues and rockabilly.

Carole arrived, still unnoticed; paid her admission; ordered a glass of red wine; and sat in one of the few empty seats still left in a dark corner. The place was packed with a lot of kids wearing George Washington, American University, and Georgetown sweatshirts.

I feel a nice vibe because of all the college kids. Ah, Tyler's starting his set with old standards that these kids obviously know most of the words to. They're already singing along. He just spotted me and smiled. I'll smile back and hope he sings a few more songs before he outs me to the crowd. I'm digging on his music tonight and think I'm hearing some piano notes I'd like to steal from him.

Georgie played three more songs—blues, rockabilly, and country hits—and then introduced Carole by shaming the audience.

"I can't believe no one here is aware that we're graced tonight by the presence of the best female singer in the business, maybe the world. Oops, I just got myself in trouble with my ex-wife, Charna."

The club rocked with laughter. "Carole, please come up on the stage for a short duet with me. I've always wanted to sing with you."

At first, Carole begged off but gave in when the audience applauded and kept clapping and wouldn't stop. *We're an unusual pairing,* she thought. *But I do occasionally like to sing soul, blues, and rockabilly.*

On this night, Georgie and Carole clicked; 275 music lovers witnessed rock 'n' roll magic happening. The surprising highlight was an Alabama blues number made famous by Mississippi Fred McDowell and later the Rolling Stones.

"You gotta move. You gotta move. You gotta move, child. You gotta move. Oh, when the Lord gets ready, you gotta move."

After singing it with the crowd, Georgie and Carole followed it up by performing dueling harmonicas to the song and then dueling pianos. Both artists filled the club with happy, beautiful music, and no one had more fun than the two of them.

What started out as a short duet extended into a long set. Southern-fried boogie music weirdly wailed from the lips of a Brooklyn songstress and a Carolina rebel. They warmed the hearts of the audience with progressive country hits such as "Can't You See," "Georgia," "Tupelo Honey," and "Will the Circle Be Unbroken?"

Carole also joined Georgie in his blue-eyed soul set that included a short medley of old Motown rhythm and blues hits. It was half past two when the lucky crowd left with affection for the two performers and a memorable musical evening. As the crowd filed out, Carole and Georgie sat on the stage thanking each other for a night that musicians dream of and many live for.

They left the club together, the streets noticeably emptier. Carole kidded, "Georgie, I think Georgetown has closed down and betrayed us rockers who are still on a musical high. Why don't we smoke a little grass at my house just a few blocks from here? It'll be a safe place for us to come down and chill out."

"That's a good idea, Carole. I'm feeling a bit of coke itch, and some pot will safely help me ease it."

They walked back to her place talking, laughing, and singing. She rolled joints for them to smoke as they talked for two hours, mostly about how hard drugs came between Georgie and Charna and caused their divorce.

Georgie, a handsome big guy, was healthy and coherent for the first time in years. Carole, feeling a growing attraction for him, fired up another joint, and they smoked it while singing one of Georgie's slow love ballads.

Carole stared into Georgie's eyes. *I'm horny*, she thought. *And he's ready to jump on me. I went from David to Allie in one day. Fuck it.*

Carole touched Georgie's face with her hand. He put his arms around her and kissed Carole, she kissed him back, and they began undressing each other. It was 5:00 AM, so they didn't bother with a lot of foreplay and just fell into bed and enjoyed good hard sex.

After climax, Carole and Georgie lay in each other's arms for a few minutes. She was surprised that she felt no guilt or regret; in fact, she thought this episode a perfect, titillating tidbit to include in her memoirs.

Carole stood up Lenny by sleeping till 1:00 PM with Georgie and breakfasted when most Washingtonians had returned from lunch. Georgie got an idea.

"This is my last show at the Cellar Door before moving on to Lexington, Kentucky, tonight for a university concert. My tour bus leaves after the performance, so I got an hour before I have to gather my stuff and head for the nightclub. Babe, are you up for a one-for-the-road quickie?" He smiled cutely.

Carole laughed and figured, "Sure, why not?"

She assumed a mission position with the six-foot-four-inch Tyler, who quickly pumped her hard and made her come in a couple of minutes. He didn't and kept pumping, and she was about to climax again.

At that moment, Allie got out of June's car and said goodbye to her. He opened the door, entered the town house, looked around to find Carole, and didn't. Allie walked toward the bedroom and opened the door.

Holy shit, is that Georgie Tyler banging Carole? Man, she's moaning louder than I recall her ever doing for me. Fuck, she's about to come.

Allie felt like a man who'd been punched in the gut. Carole saw Allie staring at her and gasped. Confused and angry, he ran out of the room and staggered over to the living room couch, where he sat and stared into space.

Carole, in a mad dash, stepped all over Georgie, who was very embarrassed, and stood before Allie less nude than naked.

"Allie, please give me a chance to explain before you go crazy on me. I'm so sorry."

"It's funny, Carole. June tried like hell to suck me off going through the Baltimore Harbor Tunnel. Can you imagine? I refused, and now I'm sorry I didn't give in. You created a new sexual calculus and can bet your ass that, sooner or later, I'm going to even the score."

"Look, Allie, I'm sorry for smashing the rules before we really formed any."

He brushed off the incident. "Carole, if a new set of rules are needed, the burden is on you to define them."

"I'm just thankful that you're not making a scene. I guess you'd be entitled to, wouldn't you?"

Her luck ran out as he started to make an awful scene.

"You're damn right! I'm entitled to be pissed as shit, but I'm mostly bothered about you needing even more sex than I've been giving you. What, you couldn't go two nights without getting laid?"

Cohen quickly calmed down and regained control. "Look, I understand that you went straight from David to me in a single day and had no time in between to experience other guys. I also understand how it could happen with an attractive guy like Georgie Tyler."

Georgie appeared, smiled, and self-consciously apologized.

"I'm sorry, Allie. I hope I didn't cause any trouble. It's just something that happened between two old musicians who were lonely and needed some TLC. You're a very lucky man, Allie. I will, for the rest of my life, remember my one night with Carole

344

Herman, and you have this fantastic lady's heart twenty-four seven. You sure are one lucky man, Allie Cohen. Peace, brother."

Georgie sweetly flashed Allie the peace sign, smiled, fist-bumped Cohen, picked up his bags, and quietly left with his gear.

Cohen almost regretted seeing him go. *I always liked Georgie's music, and it would have been nice to smoke a joint with him and schmooze for a while.*

I understand the weaknesses of human beings, especially the matters of the heart and sex, and give them much leeway. Carole's artistic nature caused this lapse, and Adonai will not let it end His plan for Allie. They are both partially right too; he's hurt, and she, a musician, let her emotions sway her.

Carole rolled a joint, lit it, and passed it to Allie, who toked away. Carole hoped to make up for her disaster and show Allie that she loved him as much as ever. She did this by opening his zipper and passionately deep-throating him.

I always massage lovers the same way. Carole pulled the prophet down on her to make love, and in a matter of seconds, it was almost as if nothing had happened.

Chapter 53

Across town, though, two White House aides who had no love for the other were working late again. The snotty Chip Allwood, the son of a conservative Republican banker, finished up his work. The voiceless Ted Bell, the son of a deceased California jailbird, intended to put in two more hours.

Allwood stared at Bell. *I don't trust Ted anymore*, thought Chip. *I'm picking up hints he's a closet Jewish liberal.*

Bell felt Chip's dislike. *I'm concerned what this toxic Pillsbury Doughboy is up to.*

Chip put on his coat on his way out the door and then summoned the courage to finally pop the big question to Ted.

"Bell, are you, by any chance, a Jew?"

Bell had put up with Allwood's hostility since day one and felt Chip needn't know his religion. He only said, "There might have been someone on my mother's side."

Chip's response was the only thing he had in common with Allie Cohen. "Oh, sure, like maybe your mother, eh?"

The consistent Bell pursed his lips tightly as usual. *I'm waiting for the political litmus test Allwood's about to subject me to.*

"Bell, the Central Command is betting that Mondale will win the nomination. Now this is off the record. We have a mole planted in old Mush Breath's campaign who heard that *whine on harvest moon* picked Geraldine Ferraro to be his veep—"

Bell cut him off, "I heard that yesterday and have to admit that it was a bold but foolish move on Mondale's part. The polls

346

show that 58 percent of wives will vote for the president just like their husbands."

Chip was enraged. "Bold, my ass. Putting a liberal mafiosa a heartbeat away from the presidency is outright terrifying. I swear that liberal Democratic slime threatens to destroy this great republic. Don't you think so?"

Bell tried to pacify Chip by using a *Conan the Barbarian* analogy.

"Chip, last time around, Carter painted the president as Reagan the Barbarian. This time around, my guess is that Mondale and the Democrats will trot out Reagan the Destroyer."

Bell's creative analysis of Arnold Schwarzenegger's *Conan the Barbarian* film series changed Chip's view of him.

"You know, Bell, in my time in the White House, that's one of the smartest things I've heard come out of anybody's mouth, even ol' Dutch Reagan, our national treasure."

Bell smiled proudly. His smile disappeared. *Uh-oh, Allwood's spotted Cohen's file and is hurriedly thumbing through it. Better brace for trouble.*

A half minute of silence ensued until Chip closed the folder and looked up.

"Bell!" yelled Chip. "No way that you're letting this commie pinko Cohen out of the country with Carole Herman. I mean, if you want to see shit hit the fan, just try it! You hear me, asshole?"

Bell warned Chip that he was out of order. "Please pipe down, Chip. This is the White House, well, the Executive Office Building, but security cameras and the Secret Service are still everywhere, including this room."

Bell pointed to it. Chip regained control.

"Good," praised Bell. "Now listen, the law states that Ms. Herman can be accompanied by one person of her own choice and who is not a registered Communist. The FBI vetted Cohen and found no tangible links. The law is the law."

"Fuck the law! This is politics. In the White House Bell, politics trumps the law."

"With an attitude like that, Chip, you sound like the perfect candidate to create another Watergate scandal."

"Look, Bell, there's no way that I'm going to let this dangerous Socialist roam around the world on Uncle Sam's dime. My god, you added Chile to Cohen's list."

"So what, Chip? Please stop being hysterical."

"'So what?' he says. Jesus, what if Cohen organizes street demonstrations in Chile to pressure Pinochet? You're leaving Dutch vulnerable to the charge that the Republican Party cozies up to elites and dictators."

Ted perceived Chip as acting near borderline paranoid and reduced the issue back to applying common sense.

"I think you underestimate the Chilean people, Chip. Why in the world would they march with Allie Cohen?"

"I don't know," Chip admitted, but common sense still eluded him. "It doesn't matter, Bell. Sending Cohen to Chile is like giving heroin to a junkie. Bell, sometimes I wonder about you . . ." His voice trailed off.

Bell addressed the pudgy preppy. "Okay, Chip, what are you trying to say?"

Chip said very intensely, "Bell, it's my impression that you are a liberal Jew and a crypto-Democrat."

Chip took that premise to the next illogical conclusion. "You're forewarned that your name will be given to White House Security. I'm worried that you're a Democratic mole and must protect Dutch from leaks or sabotage."

"Chip, that's preposterous, and besides, you're not acting like a good Republican, and your action will backfire on you. Despite your silly charges, I'm looking out for your own best interest."

The words "you're not acting like a good Republican" worried Chip enough to ask, "Bell, what are you're trying to say?"

Ted's explanation, a put-down, passed right over the thick ideologue's head.

"Chip, by asking security to investigate another Republican will result in your not displaying the correct drowsy harmony, clubbiness, or yes-man mentality a corporate type must always exhibit."

As he expected, Allwood actually took that seriously.

"I don't know, Bell, maybe you're right. Okay, I won't turn you in, but I'm still going to be on your ass for laxity on Cohen. Nobody risks the Reagan revolution's mandate and gets away with it."

"Chip, please stop overreacting already. If Cohen makes a nuisance of himself, we'll just bring him home and even terminate the tour, if necessary."

"For Chrissake, Cohen's a rich author. How are you going to bring him home? Have the CIA kidnap him or Navy SEALs shoot him? You know we can't get away with that shit anymore, though I sure would love to ship Cohen's commie ass straight to Russia."

Bell reasoned with him. "Chip, Dutch and the First Lady love Carole's music and ignore her politics. Therefore, you better also. Remember, you can't cancel this tour unless Cohen starts a revolution or civil war, so relax."

"All right, Bell, but you better keep Cohen in line because your nuts are on the chopping block." Chip, down the hall by now, shouted, "Remember, if pinko Cohen carries on just once, I'll see that you won't get a job as a law clerk in Harlem!"

Ted perused the file for the source of Allwood's fury. The top two pages were letters Cohen wrote to the Carter and Ford administrations.

The first correspondence was an idea to metropolitanize all major U.S. urban areas, the aim being to fix central city boundaries at the suburban edge so that no commuter could reasonably live beyond its centralized taxing authority. All provision and distribution of civil services were regionalized to share costs.

The Carterites noted on the letter, "Most intelligent, available solution for urban problems and suburban sprawl but politically untouchable, especially in the South."

The other concept was born out of the flood of federal monies released by the Ford administration to celebrate the 1976 bicentennial to honor and study the country's ethnic groups and their heritages and contributions to American society. Cohen proposed that a nationwide consortium of ethnic culture centers be established to support the integration of ethnic studies into the framework of the country's educational infrastructure.

The Ford administration passed Cohen's proposal on to the Carterites, who liked this idea too. Hamilton Jordan, though, feared that it would dredge up the old *Playboy* magazine ethnic purity remark that had gotten Jimmy Carter in so much hot water during the 1976 Democratic primaries and tabled it.

Ted rated Cohen's two ideas as fascinating, brilliant, and extremely divisive. The National Defense Metropolitanization Act (NDMA), as he saw it, if ever implemented, might provoke a civil war. The Ethnic Culture Center Act (ECCA) could foster resurgent tribalism, the antithesis of what U.S. assimilation structures were designed to achieve.

Bell figured that if the Carterites considered Cohen's ideas too progressive, then they were as heretical as Marxism to Chip and the Reaganites. Ted felt trapped between political bookends Cohen and Allwood.

Although I'm product of a political family, I never developed my own worldview. Reaganism was literally thrust on me as a career opportunity, and I haven't evaluated it. In comparison with Cohen's bold, forward-thinking visions, Reaganism seems shallow, misguided, and reactionary.

Alarmed, Ted Bell went right home to work out his evolving political belief system that exposure to Allie Cohen inspired.

Chapter 54

Across the Key Bridge in Georgetown, Allie and Carole enjoyed a relaxing evening at home, watching a cable movie, reading magazines, and falling asleep early. Sam Minkowitz called Allie at midnight to brief him on a public appearance.

"Allie, sorry for calling you so late, but I needed to go over some things with you and finally got a chance to talk. Peter and I are flying into DC tomorrow morning in the GMEI company plane. Our limo will pick you up at noon and take you over to the Hilton on Connecticut Avenue. Please dress appropriately to appear before the very important National Book Distributors Convention."

"Suit and tie?"

"If you wish, but sport coat and shirt with collar is okay too, and please prepare well to answer their questions regarding your best seller. While that might not sound important to you, winning these guys over can result in doubling the sales of your book."

Cohen, half-asleep, said "How is that?"

"Where the outlet presents the book, Allie, will determine its ability to solidify the current number one spot in the market. If you wow them tomorrow, they'll rush the book to the front of the store."

"That's good, Sam."

"If you're truly excellent, they'll give your book its own display case at the entrance."

"That's even better."

"If you're only so-so, Allie, your book will get lost in the inventory and be off the best-seller list in a few months."

"Is it really that cut-and-dried, Sam?"

"Of course, that's an exaggeration, but visibility and presentation generally increases the range from three to seven million units. Over forty thousand books get printed every year, so you need these guys more than they need you."

"I'll do my best, Sam."

"Wonderful, and if you like, you and Carole can hop a ride on my plane that will be returning to LA right after the conference. So, kiddo, get a good night's sleep, and knock their socks off tomorrow."

The next morning, like a good soldier, Cohen entered the side door of the hotel where John Hinckley shot President Reagan. Allie shared the dais with his friend and a former editor Harland Cooper, Global's new publisher; Sam; and two major chain store owners.

Sam served as emcee and welcomed everyone. He acknowledged the presence of major booksellers in the audience, announced Harland Cooper's promotion to publisher to many cheers including Allie's, and emotionally expressed his reaction to *The Lesson*.

"Seymour's martyrdom shamed me into becoming a more vigilant protector of the Jewish people. Dr. Cohen's intent was clear. The continuing threat to Jewish existence necessitates that modern-day Maccabees step up to selflessly defend the Jews."

The audience applauded; Sam took a drink of water. "More importantly, the despicable horrors perpetrated by the Nazi butchers, unequalled in human history, must never happen again— never again."

Minkowitz, ever the super salesman, paused to calm himself; his intensity, the hype, was saluted by some merchants clapping.

"In my opinion, Dr. Allie Cohen has written a landmark book that depicts what civilized people whose lives are ruthlessly violated or degraded will do to protect an illusory peace."

Allie was very pleased by how hard Sam was working to make his novel successful but wondered where Sam was going with the buildup.

"*The Lesson*," bellowed Sam, "is the most powerful and important book of our time and is a must read for the mass audience."

The biggest chain bookstore owners enthusiastically clapped.

"*The Lesson* should be institutionalized as a literary classic." The smaller book chain owners joined in.

"*The Lesson* should be included in all mandated college reading lists."

The full audience applauded very loudly; some whistled.

I'm very happy, thought Cohen. *But Sam has praised me enough.*

He watched Sam take another sip of water and deliver his closing pitch.

"*The Lesson* must be made widely available to all humanity. *The Lesson* must be sold from its own display counter at the store's entrance."

The audience clapped louder until Sam held the book in his hands.

"*The Lesson* must be *up front* so *never again.*"

Sam put the book down and affected a cheerleader chant.

"Let's hear it now. Up front so never again."

The enthralled audience responded with a loud chorus answer. Sam demanded more from them.

"I can't hear you. Everybody, louder now. Up front so never again!" The distributors topped themselves with a much louder chant. Sam brought it home.

"That's better. One more time now as loud as you can." Sam pumped his arms with each syllable. "Up front so never again!!" they shouted louder yet.

Sam held a marketing display in his arms with the book's title that got their attention.

"Good, now go home to your communities and stores, and put this display with copies of this important novel in the entrance for sale, and you will have done your job in alerting the world."

The distributors gave Sam a prolonged standing ovation. Many clapped wildly and whistled while some ran up to Minkowitz to tell him that "Up front so never again" was the greatest merchandizing slogan they'd ever heard.

"I'm absolutely stunned." Cohen's head spun; the phrase rang in his ears. The retailers' enthusiasm bothered him, and Sam's exploiting the Holocaust disturbed him, but he was greatly benefiting from every one of them.

Cohen buried his confusion when Sam lavishly introduced him to the convention.

"It's my pleasure and honor to present the next great mind and writer of our age, our newest prophet, Dr. Allie Cohen."

Cohen's nerves eased; the book retailers rose from their seats to award him an absurdly short standing ovation. He used his prophet-and-sage joke to warm them up.

"Thank you, Sam, for the generous introduction, but please, a *sage* is plenty. Being a prophet these days can be dangerous. Simply being a sage will save me a small fortune on life insurance premiums."

Most in the audience laughed; he was no Jackie Mason but the line worked again. The literary critics warmed up to him.

Jonas Marion, the *NY Times* literary editor, led off with what sounded like the simplest of questions but was often the hardest.

"Dr. Cohen, why did you write this book?"

"Good question. I created the gentle but vigilant Seymour to represent a fairly typical organizational Jew. This Hymie, to quote Jesse Jackson"—the audience laughed at his cheap shot—"is driven to an extreme, even monstrous action to save his people from another enemy of the Jews."

"Is he modeled on anyone?"

"Yes, his real-life model, a man I'll call Chaim, lived through Auschwitz and a dozen other death camps. The only reason he's alive today is that he was too strong a worker for even the Nazis to senselessly waste."

Neal Cartwright, from the *New York Review of Books*, expressed concern. "Dr. Cohen, don't you feel that Seymour acted uncharacteristically, even in a non-Jewish manner?"

"Neal, what do you mean by non-Jewish?"

"Okay, Jews traditionally have been peaceful and cultured and never practiced barbarism. Therefore, are you justifying the use of Israeli violence in cases such as the West Bank, Gaza, and Lebanon?"

"No," Cohen emphatically denied. "While I believe in nonviolence, I am not a pacifist. In a nutshell, the media was allowing itself to be used by Helms. The barely literate viewing audience started believing Helms, thus whitewashing the Nazi crime. Seymour recognized the striking parallels and took action before the big lie became mainstreamed and viewed as fact."

Jordan Balaban of *Harper's* expressed, "Dr. Cohen, isn't Seymour messianic and perhaps overreactive too?"

"Our final weapon to deal with threatened barbarism," Cohen crisply responded, "may be to use the same tactic."

Sonia Calloway of the *Atlantic* said, "Dr. Cohen, I'm interested in your perceptions of Jewish life in America."

Cohen employed a stock answer. "Bellow has said that, in Israel, everybody is Jewish, and no one is the Jew. Malamud's been quoted as saying, 'If you ever forget you're a Jew, a gentile will remind you.' Israel is obviously the best place to be a Jew, but Zion is still a challenging environment. The United States is definitely the second best country, but Jews face the economic and social pressures of assimilation and absorption."

Sonia started to interrupt. "I'm not finished, Sonia. Jews are no longer considered an American out-group, no more quotas and affirmative action programs for us. We're now a fortunate

357

establishment group like Presbyterians and Episcopalians. For example, university positions and scholarships that used to go to Jews now go to blacks, Hispanics, Asians, and women." He finished; Sonia sat down.

Coincidentally, Joanna Cassidy of the *Atlanta Journal-Constitution* and a Cox publication followed.

"Dr. Cohen, many Jews own newspaper chains and TV networks, so is it feasible that the media would spread Helms's lies? Might you ironically be aiding the false slur of Zionist control of the media to rise again?"

"Ms. Cassidy, I find your question ironic because Cox Enterprises has no Jews at the highest levels of management. Perhaps your media group deserves a pat on the back for doing their part in preventing the Zionists from seizing the global media."

Scattered laughs were heard, and then a loud rumbling of laughter rolled across the room, causing Cassidy to roll her eyes to insinuate that Cohen's charge was unfair.

"Ms. Cassidy, that fact was published last month in *Atlanta* magazine. Look, I'm only saying that the commercial media, seeking higher ratings, can invite aggression by aiding Helms spin his myth. That's a form of violence against a Holocaust survivor, yet the media provided him access to the airwaves to spew his bilge."

Cohen's publisher, Harland Cooper, viewed the exchanges positively.

"Allie's strong opinions and broad perspectives have impressed a fairly jaded group, and I think he's succeeded in enhancing the novel's credibility."

U.S. News & World Report claimed that the novel's effect on the public was comparable in the changing of intellectual attitudes to Solzhenitsyn's *Gulag Archipelago.*

"No longer did an intellectual portray wooziness to the Holocaust just as the *Gulag* destroyed the last vestige of attraction to Marxism."

The Israeli public embraced Cohen's book as a searing work that justified Ze'ev Jabotinsky's concept of the fighting Jew.

The Gush Emunim (Bloc of the Faithful), an ultraorthodox and right-wing political movement, claimed it as yet another reason that the West Bank must not be *Judenrein* or Jew-free.

Israeli's assistant defense minister Yossi Gavron, in an interview explaining an Israeli pullback to Lebanon's southern border, mentioned that he had just finished reading Cohen's book.

"A people who do not remember have lost their souls. *The Lesson* will help Israel to always remember."

The novel, over the next five years, was translated into thirty-one languages and sold seventeen million copies. An estimated fifty-two million persons eventually shared the powerful and haunting reading experience. I am one deeply appreciative reader who will never be counted in that number.

Cohen ended the very successful conference with an announcement. "I will soon be visiting Russia, Israel, Egypt, and South America. In Chile, I hope to start work on a political thriller."

Allie, in Chile, you will be living your political thriller and have no time to write, nor afterward either.

Cohen remembered. *Sarah is due to give birth any minute. Shit, I've been swallowed whole so quickly. Indeed, money, I'm thinking less of you every day. How does one stop the merry-go-round?*

Peter Bates, the first person to congratulate Allie, asked him if he was as stunned as Bates was from Sam's "Up front so never again" line.

"By now, Peter, I'm even able to laugh at it. You sure have to admire Sam's power of salesmanship."

Peter laughed and slapped Allie five. "Sam is outrageous," praised Bates. "And you did a very good job too."

He slapped Cohen five again and then smiled and dangled car keys.

"June Merrick is waiting for you in a hot tub, so get your ass over to McLean, and muff-dive into that delicious flesh."

Allie looked around to see where Sam was; Bates read his mind.

"Don't worry, Sam's busy bullshitting Neil Jerome, who owns forty-eight outlets in California and Oregon. Next, he'll collar Bill Williamson, who owns 60 percent of the airport book market, so go jump on June. She's worth it, believe me."

Allie hesitated. Bates advised in his usual straight-forward manner.

"Hey, June is twice as good-looking as Carole and three times as sexy."

"You have a point there, Peter."

"So relax, Allie. June's old man has a billion bucks, so she ain't leaving him for you. He just likes to watch through his video-taping system. I know he'll want her to give you good head. And, man, she's got the most amazing tongue."

"Peter, please keep this between you and me."

360

Peter bent over laughing. "You're going to fuck a journalist." He laughed even harder. "And you're asking me to keep it a secret? Think about that. On second thought, don't. So come on, beat it already."

Chapter 55

Allie slithered out of the conference room and located the car Peter rented for him. It was a forty-five-minute drive to McLean, an exclusive Washington suburb in northern Virginia.

Carlton Merrick has lived among the fox-and-hound set and a couple of Kennedys too. Cohen parked in the driveway, rang the bell, and peeked in through the door's window.

This tall ruddy man with insincere gray hair coming to greet me must be Carlton.

Carlton acted like he expected Allie. "Oh, I believe you are my wife's interview subject. Please let me show you the way."

Cohen analyzed. *Carlton seems strangely aloof and acts more like an event planner, or maybe a butler, than a husband.*

Carlton escorted Allie into the kitchen, where June, wearing a blue bathrobe, mixed drinks. Carlton disappeared.

June noted her husband's generosity. "Allie, did you know that Carlton donated the entire sum to build the local Jewish community center?"

Cohen thought Carlton to be such a queer figure that he just cracked a weak smile of gratitude. Allie's Scotch tasted too warm to his liking, and he helped himself to more ice cubes from the tray in the freezer. He reached in and somehow caused a small avalanche of ice cubes to tumble onto the floor and begin melting.

Cohen spotted a sink sponge, grabbed it, and began cleaning up the mess. June watched in horror at his inappropriate kitchen etiquette—use of the sink sponge for cleaning the floor. She asked him if his father was a Communist.

He was rocked by her question. "June, I didn't know my breach was a foundation of Marxist-Leninist doctrine." She laughed hard. "A good day for Barney Cohen, my dad, a small businessman who detested politics, would have been selling a big order of corned beef and hot dogs to the czar *and* Stalin."

June laughed even harder and then walked arm in arm with Allie out to an enclosed deck where a king-size spa bubbled away. She dropped her robe to the ground and descended into the steaming water. Allie beheld her majestic figure and large firm breasts in awe.

Thank you very much, Peter. You did me a solid to the second power.

Allie quickly removed his clothing and followed her into the hot, swirling water. He wisecracked as a jet shot a warm stream up his butt.

"I guess I got it made." He blurted, "I have a beautiful naked woman before me and hot water shooting up my ass."

"This beautiful naked woman wants to make one thing perfectly clear, Allie. I have no intention of interviewing you tonight. We're here to suck and fuck."

June floated Allie on his back, so his penis stuck up out of the water. She took him whole into her silky mouth and tongued away, deep-throating him over and over, kissing his balls, jerking him with both hands, tonguing the tip, slowly building his eruption.

Bates was right again. Her tongue is so magical I can't hold it back any longer.

He shot come all over her breasts and lay in her arms with eyes closed for a few minutes. Cohen opened his eyes and squinted. A video camera was aimed right at him.

Carlton, he realized, was spying on them through the house's security system. Cohen tightened up and pondered what to do about it.

Fuck it. He decided. *In this case, it's all right to ask an unsexy question to a hot lady about her marriage.*

He spoke quietly. "Forgive me, June, but I've been wondering how you deal with this situation."

"What situation?"

She pretended not to know what he was talking about, so Cohen pointed to the video camera and smiled at her.

"What can I tell you?" She confided, "The only way Carl can climax is to watch me have sex with a famous man or a pretty boy. You qualify as both, so Carl was very excited about you paying me a visit. Take pity, Allie. Let's see how well you get it up when you're seventy-two."

"I'm not judging you. I simply feel a bit compromised."

"Compromised, huh?" June purred. "Well, you have all of me." She mounted him. "Isn't this sex great, Allie? Do you still feel *compromised?*"

Although slightly uptight, he was frenzied enough to engage her in three positions before coming deep and hard.

June swooned and asked, "Now wasn't that worth it?"

"I'll tell you after I read your article. Sorry, I'm not crazy about your husband getting his jollies off by watching me, and I don't think that's unreasonable either. Well, well, here comes Carl wearing a matching blue robe."

"Christ, Cohen, I openly share the favors of my gorgeous, sexy wife, and you have the gall to deny me a mere electronic image humping across a twenty-inch screen."

"Sorry, Carl, that's my image, and I don't want anybody else turned on by it. I suggest that you call your cable TV company and subscribe to the Playboy Channel."

"Why, you little—" The phone rang before Merrick could complete his expletive-filled statement regarding the legitimacy of Cohen's birth and left to answer it.

June, while floating on her back in the tub, decided that Cohen was right after all.

"You know, Allie, this is a sick marriage. I'm going to leave Carlton tomorrow."

The thought of June as a sexual moose on the loose made Allie a little nervous.

Merrick returned and snidely announced, "Cohen's famous mistress called to give him a message from his pregnant wife, whom he wantonly ran out on."

Allie brushed off Merrick's shot to speak to Carole, who verbally lashed out at him. "Man, you sure didn't waste any time getting even. Shit, you jumped right on her."

Cohen wondered how she'd found him but instead said, "Carole, don't you think that you're a bit out of line lecturing me about faithfulness? Give me a break. You did it twice with Georgie over the course of two days, so it wasn't exactly a heat-of-the-moment thing. Am I correct or what?"

"I agree. I'm sorry, Allie."

"Now I assume you're finished busting my chops, Carole. If so, please tell me what is happening with Sarah."

"Okay, Sarah's water broke, and your neighbor Evelyn drove her to the hospital in plenty of time. However, she's hardly dilated at all, so there's probably sufficient time to get to Atlanta for the birth."

"Great, I'm leaving here right now. I'll see you in a half hour."

Allie bid June farewell and raced back to Georgetown. Carole, to save time, had packed his bags and booked him a flight on Delta. She seemed unusually quiet while driving him to National Airport, so he sensed that something was bothering her.

"Be honest with me, babe. What's going through your mind?"

"Okay, Allie, I'm happy that you're going to be a father but sad that it's not mine."

"Come on, sweetie, you can't make a baby in a month. Besides, we have lots of time."

"Allie, that's not what's disturbing me. I know that its nuts, but I have this fear that you won't be coming back to me."

"That's crazy, babe."

"Maybe," she admitted. "But I can't picture you kissing a darling baby boy or girl goodbye. Be honest. You grew up without a father and know better than most how hard that is."

"Well, yeah."

"Is your fate to be the unknown dad who missed the joys of a first step or word or hitting a baseball or maybe, best of all, a

366

hug? Well, Allie, if it isn't, then please don't blame me twenty years from now."

All four—first step, hitting a baseball, a hug, and first word—affected Cohen, but he did not know what to say, so he wisely said nothing.

Carole gathered from his silence. "I'm right, Allie, aren't I?"

He sighed and asked her, "Sweetie, why are you trying to make me feel like a selfish shit?"

"I'm sorry, Allie." Tears welled in her eyes and rolled down her cheeks.

"What?" he asked, though he wasn't sure that he wanted to hear.

"It's my fault. My mother was right." She cried harder.

"What do you mean? How was your mother right?"

"She said that I'd be creating another David, so I have to decide."

Allie found dragging information out of Carole exhausting, but he kept his patience.

"Why and what do you have to decide?"

"Whether to say goodbye to you right now and never see you again or . . ."

He held his temper. Carole, through a mess of tears, declared, "Fuck it, I love you, Allie, and we're going to take that damn tour come hell or high water."

Allie rejoiced. "Praise the Lord. So, Carole, darling precious, what are you going to do while I'm in Atlanta becoming a father?"

"Would you mind if I recorded some songs with Georgie Tyler for my next album?"

"Not at all, baby cakes. You're a free woman, but I need to know one thing, and please be honest with me. Has a little disillusionment set in yet? Sarah predicted that it would occur when my bad stomach began ripping off farts or I sneezed on your hand during an allergy attack. Please be up-front with me."

Carole laughed hard for several seconds. "Allie, we have something very special, and the most fabulous experiences in the world are awaiting us. Now go to Atlanta and be a mensch for the next week."

Allie kissed Carole goodbye and philosophized while walking into the terminal.

What my lover calls being a mensch will be seen by my wife as being a louse. I just hope that the Lord doesn't nail me good for this contradiction.

You need not worry, Allie. Adonai is good; you know that.

Chapter 56

Sandy was in LA on business, so Riva picked Allie up at the airport and drove him to the hospital before the blessed arrival. Delta arranged for him to leave the plane first, and he bombarded the placid Riva with questions.

"How's Sarah, and how far along is she? What's happened so far?"

"Sarah is fine, Allie, except that she's only dilated three centimeters and might require a C-section if she doesn't get to ten real soon."

"A C-section is safer than a normal birth, Riva. That's good."

Riva let him out in front of the hospital, and she parked the car. Allie saw a waiting elevator, tore through the lobby, and just made it before the doors closed. He got off at the second floor and hunted down room 206.

Cohen did not go right in though. He stood outside for a moment to think of the right words to say to his vulnerable wife. He felt glad Sarah exuded a rosy, healthful glow and appeared to be in excellent condition.

Cohen sucked in his gut, entered, and found Sarah busy collecting her thoughts. His appearance surprised her as she'd just written an insightful comment.

"The difference between *united* and *untied* is where you dot the *i*."

Sarah balled it up, threw it into the wastepaper basket, and stared straight ahead. She mechanically waved to him, and he braced for shit to hit the fan.

"Hello, Sarah." He gave her a sweet short kiss on the lips. "How are you feeling, money?"

"Me? Ehh, I'm okay. I'm only having a baby, big shit."

A straight answer he was not going to get from her. He ignored her and tried again.

"Please, Sarah, how are you doing?"

"I have to admit, Allie. Carole is awfully sweet, a true angel. You have no idea how miserable that makes me, Cohen. I mean, I'm trying real hard to hate her, but I'm not able to, and it bugs the shit out of me because it means that I'm actually accepting this co-living thing."

"Sarah, would you please tell me how far apart your contractions are and to what extent you have dilated?"

Sarah responded in a rehearsed, blasé manner. "Okay, about every two minutes and four centimeters." That was all the information she would give Allie and set him up for another put-down.

"Hey, Cohen, how long are you planning to stay around?"

Cohen realized that was a loaded question that she'd zap him regardless of how he answered it. Allie flashed on a scene where Sarah nails him to a huge wooden Jewish star and forces him to lug it throughout the hospital's corridors Jesus-style. He hoped his answer would not give her too much ammunition to use against him.

"I plan to be here, Sarah, until everything supportive of mother and child is functioning."

His afterthought was *I stand damned the second I said it.*

"Well, Allie, it's apparent that you're not including the role of father in the support systems you claim to be giving mother and child, now are you? By the way, you still haven't told me how long you plan to be around."

"I plan to be in town for seven to ten days, Sarah." He thought, *She's going to have a field day with that.*

"Seven to ten days, huh?" she mocked. "So that's fatherhood, seven to ten days for you and eighteen years for me. Boy, Cohen, have you got balls! You must really be counting on a son too, aren't you?" Allie hedged; Sarah didn't. "And of course, Cohen Junior must be welcomed into the tribe of Abraham and Moses, right?"

"Yes, a bit sarcastic, Sarah. But otherwise, well said."

"You're in luck, Cohen. The doctor thinks it's a boy. They can tell by the heartbeat. Males are slightly weaker than females."

"And that usually signifies a boy?"

"Most of the time, it does." She appeared to be easing up on him.

"I'm very excited, a boy. Sarah, that's wonderful. Of course, if it's a girl, no difference."

Sarah gave him a look that suggested he was full of shit. A long sharp contraction stopped the wisecracks and forced her to reach out to him.

"Cohen, we have unfinished business and need to get it done fast. You're aware that you left before we had a chance to settle on a name. Well, I've been thinking that if it's a girl, I'd like the child to be named after my late grandmother. And if it's a boy, he would be named after your maternal grandfather because I like the name Andy."

"I'll compromise, Sarah, if you change the boy's name to Ari."

"I don't know, Allie, it sounds too much like an Israeli fighter pilot."

"I hope that he never has to be one, but if the crunch comes—anyway, it sounds intelligent and forceful, Ari Ben Cohen, Ben after my father, Barney."

Allie saw Sarah's contractions worsening and becoming very painful and reached out to comfort her.

"Come here, Cohen. I need you. Hold my hand. I'm scared, Allie. I don't think I could survive if anything went wrong again."

He scanned a bureau full of religious items. "I think you have everything covered, money. Let's see. There's a little Jewish star, a hand of God, and a Mr. Mazel ministatue. The only thing missing is the Wailing Wall."

Sarah's painful giggle melted her concern. "I hope so, Allie. One good thing is that it's a dry birth."

"That means no chance of aspiration, right?"

The pain limited Sarah to just nodding. A nurse entered the room to see if she had dilated further.

"She hasn't," said the nurse. "The decision to perform a C-section is automatic."

Sarah and Allie summoned Dr. Horowitz to confer with and schedule the operation for two to three hours from that moment. Allie sized him up. *Horowitz appears competent enough and likes to flash a big smile.*

Sarah handed Riva a list of items. "Riva, this is what's still needed to finish putting the infant's room together."

Riva and Allie managed to take care of everything and still squeeze in a dinner at a nearby mall restaurant. His attempt at rationalizing away guilt over being a half-absentee father bothered Riva.

"Allie, are you planning to be attentive through the showering of expensive gifts or time on the job? They aren't the same, you know."

"Are you saying that either you're a father who's there every day or you're just bullshit?"

"We know that a child benefits from both quality and quantity of time with its parents."

"I plan to be there as much as I can, Riva. That's what co-living is for."

"Does that mean that you'll be getting back with Sarah sooner than expected? If so, that would make Sandy and me very happy."

"Thanks, Riva. Time will tell."

"Sure," she said. "God forbid, you should sacrifice a single fantasy in life."

She's right, and it bothers me to hear it.

He grumbled, "Perhaps."

"Don't be coy with me, Allie. Remember, I'm married to your business manager. Face it, Cohen, you're not going to be there that much." Riva sensed that she'd made him feel like crap and changed the subject. "Are you sure you really love Carole? Maybe you're just overwhelmed by the enlarged world you're suddenly operating in."

"Well, we do have great sex."

"Is that it, Allie, great sex?"

"Riva, if you must know, the sex is amazingly the same as with Sarah, but you're still looking for an angle other than that a famous movie and singing star fell in love with li'l ol' Allie, formerly a poor teacher."

"That's strange about the sex part, and yes, it's true. Carole Herman falling for a high school teacher is straight out of fiction."

"Of course, it is. Hey, wouldn't you ball Peter Bates if you had the chance?"

"He's not one of my favorite male stars, but I'd probably ball him just to be in the same league as all those famous actresses who have."

"Exactly, and that's why I made love to Carole the first time, but I loved her by the second time and she me, and that's where it stands."

"Do you love Carole as much as Sarah?"

"No, I love Sarah far more and will forever. She'll always be my wife."

"I'm glad to hear that. So what is it then?"

He hesitated to speak for a few seconds but finally said, "I sense that the Lord has a plan for me."

Riva cracked up laughing as if it were the funniest thing she'd ever heard in her life. *I've always believed Allie to be the least religious close friend I have, and he's actually saying this to me.* "Are you serious, Allie? Are you telling me that God is directing you in some kind of master plan? Give me a break, please."

"Think about it, Riva. Only the Lord could connect me with the likes of Reagan and Carole and Sam Minkowitz and Peter Bates too. They all came out of nowhere to become my benevolent team, my incredible ways and means to make a difference."

"I guess you're right, Allie. Too much has come together to just be luck or coincidence. Life-changing opportunities have come your way and our way too. I'm just very sorry that you're causing Sarah so much hurt."

They left the restaurant; Riva again cracked up laughing so hard that she stooped over. Allie looked at her. "What?"

"This God-has-a-plan-for-you thing, knowing how religious you've been, this is really going to blow Sandy's mind." Allie and Riva laughed deeply and hurried back to the hospital.

Sarah was still only four centimeters, so Dr. Horowitz prepared her for a Cesarian.

"Allie, would you like to watch the delivery? Nurse, please get him a setup."

"Sorry, Doc," Allie firmly told the doctor. "Thanks but no thanks. I'll pass."

"Oh, come on now." Horowitz persisted. "It's a fantastic experience."

"Sorry, Doc, and I beg to differ because we did natural last time. And for twenty hours, I watched my wife almost die, defecate in the bed twice, and finally see a dead firstborn son lazily slop around in a bloody womb, and I especially don't want to experience a Cesarian birth. Thank you, but I prefer to act out the nervous father's role in the waiting room, only I won't be acting."

The next half hour passed as slowly as the Ice Age. Finally, Dr. Horowitz slapped open the doors. "Mr. Cohen, it's a boy, seven pounds, three ounces, a real toughie. Mazel tov."

Allie jerked Riva out of her chair and whirled her around like a Coney Island airplane ride and then shouted the same words his father Barney said at his birth. "Riva, I have a boy! Can you believe it? A son! Thanks, Doc, and thank you, Lord."

Hashem and I watched over Allie at the moment of birth and were thrilled for a man who'd known the loss of a newborn and the hurt that followed and lingered. Allie, also like his dad, cut the air with a jubilant punch that shook his long hair.

Riva and Allie darted over to the baby dormitory to see Ari and pressed their noses up against the glass. Cohen spotted the clear plastic carriage occupied by baby boy Cohen and watched a frumpy large nurse roughly tend to ten-minute-old Ari. She cleaned the crud out of his hair and ears and made him cry. Allie started to get angry with the nurse until Ari cutely wrinkled his lower lip similar to his mother when she stepped out of a bath and felt clean.

"Riva," he bragged, "look at that full head of dark hair. Lord Almighty, isn't he the most beautiful child in the whole dormitory? Ari, if I can help it, you're going to grow up and be the first Jewish president of the United States."

Allie prayed silently, *Dear God, I am so grateful for this twenty-inch-long, small miracle and impressive new successor to the Cohen family name.* He reverently opened a Philips *Daily Prayer Book* and humbly read aloud "Prayer for a Woman after Childbirth," page 361.

Riva stared openmouthed. "Now I'm really astounded by your new religiosity."

"Remember," he pointed out, "Sandy went to the Yeshiva Day School, and I went to public school and Hebrew school. It usually makes a big difference."

Cohen called both sets of grandparents. Each pair was equally thrilled by the safe birth and just as tepid for the name Ari—too much like an Israeli fighter pilot they both said.

Allie set forth to the recovery area; the temperature in the big room was below sixty degrees and caused a still unconscious Sarah to shiver in the corner. The attendant advised him, "Mr. Cohen, Mrs. Cohen is heavily sedated and also subject to periodic spasms."

"Do you think Mrs. Cohen is aware that she's borne me a son?"

The pretty blond nurse wriggled her nose. "Since Mrs. Cohen hasn't come to yet, there's no way to be sure."

Allie saw Sarah's lower lip quiver and wondered if she was aware of his presence. He held her hands, which seemed to ease the spasms, and spoke softly into her ear.

"My dear Sarah, you bore me an extraordinary little boy, and I love you very much and always will. I want you to know that I love you far more than Carole and that you will always be my wife. You and Ari are the most precious part of my life."

He suspected she might be cognizant but couldn't be certain, gently kissed Sarah on the lips, and wiped a tear from his right eye.

"Please understand, Sarah, that I believe that the Lord has a mission for me that will take me away from you and Ari for long periods. This mission can only be carried out with Carole, and I must follow God's will."

He gently kissed Sarah on the lips again and left the hospital with Riva. His feet barely touched the ground during the walk to the car.

"Thank you, Riva, for being there for Sarah and me at the greatest moment of our lives."

Riva steered across the roads Cohen had cruised for years. Although Sandy Springs was still a nice place to live, he felt surprised by the degree that he'd already detached.

Riva probed him as they pulled into the driveway. "Allie, are you missing Atlanta?"

Allie considered her question. "I miss my family and friends, but I don't think I'm missing Atlanta."

"I'm sorry to hear that."

He shrugged and asked Riva to please pop the trunk. Cohen got his bags, kissed Riva, and again thanked her for being there for him and Sarah. Allie watched Riva drive away, scanned the cul-de-sac, and breathed in the air heavily scented with honeysuckle, jasmine, and lavender.

There's no doubt about it. Few places on earth smell better than right here on this cul-de-sac in good old Sandy Springs.

Chapter 57

Allie toured the property to see how Sarah was maintaining the old homestead. True to form, she had ignored the grounds.

Uucch, I'm fighting my way through knee-high grass, spiderwebs are everywhere, and the creepy-crawlies are edging along the skin of my arms and face. I'll have Sandy hire a gardener for her.

He walked inside the house, muttering, "I'm surprised that the yard-work-loving Christians haven't burned a cross on the front lawn yet."

The house was rather unkempt too compared with the way his once immaculate wife used to maintain it, but Sarah had a good excuse. She was engrossed in Statistics II, and Allie remembered how difficult that course was back in graduate school, so he added a weekly cleaning service to the list.

Overall, he said, assessing, *it's still a comfortable little home, though it seems shabbier, the building materials cheaper, and the rooms smaller. The dampness of the lower level and the warmth of the upper level feel amplified, and even my once great stereo system sounds very inferior to Carole's state-of-the-art equipment.*

Cohen ritualistically rolled a joint and lit it. *With this, I celebrate the coming of Cohen the younger. How I've waited for this incomparable moment.*

Allie toked several times more and called Carole, who was sipping tequila and writing down lyrics for a new song. She picked up and was loudly greeted.

"It's a boy, seven pounds, three ounces—Ari Ben Cohen, my beautiful new son."

Carole tried hard to sound thrilled for him. "My god, Allie, a son. I'm so happy for you. Please tell me about Ari."

"He's so cute and has this big shock of black hair that makes him distinguishable from the hundred other babies in the dormitory."

Carole's heart ached. *I hate sharing Allie with Sarah and now Ari. I'm also worried that my biological clock is ticking down.*

She asked him, "How old is Sarah?"

"Thirty-two. Why?"

Carole did not like hearing that. *I'm thirty-seven. Better change the subject.*

And she asked the obvious. "You know, Allie, I like the name Ari. It sounds like an Israeli fighter pilot."

"Carole, you're not the first to say that."

She brought Allie up-to-date. "My album with Georgie Tyler is progressing very nicely, and I'm working with some fantastic musicians. Anyway, I was working on a new song before you called, so let me finish it before I lose the melody. I love you, Allie."

"'Love you too, babe. Bye."

The overload of angst that accompanied life with Allie made Carole blue. She sat down at her baby grand and plunked out a slow version of an old Hank Williams's tune, "Can't You See," later recorded by the Marshall Tucker Band.

"Ride me a southbound all the way to Georgia now till that train run out of track. Can't you see, oh can't you see what that woman, she been doin' to me." Carole changed *woman* to *man*. "What that man, he been doin' to me."

The phone rang again. "I sense it's Rose, the last person I want to speak to right now." She picked up the receiver.

"Carole, honey, it's your mother."

"Hi, Ma, how are you?"

"I'm fine, dear." Rose spoke hesitantly. "I was just wondering if you heard anything yet, you know."

Carole roiled her mother with "It's a boy, Mom, Ari Ben Cohen. His father says he's absolutely adorable too."

Rose, slow to react, thought, *Again, I'm sagging from my daughter's unsettled life. The challenges never stop.*

Carole, still wishing to finish her song and emotionally beat, wanted her mother to get to the point.

"What's on your mind, Mom?"

"Carole, honey, I don't want to sound interfering, but don't you think that maybe it would be better for everyone involved if Allie returned to his family? It really hasn't been that long yet and will just get harder later on. Frankly, it's also becoming a bit unseemly."

"Ma, are you telling me to stop loving Allie just because the situation is a bit messy?"

"That's all, a bit *messy*? I think you've been reading too many movie scripts. This is real life. Please, Carole, for me, I'm getting too old for all this nonsense."

"Ma, if you don't cut it out, I'm going to hang up on you."

Rose tried one more time. "Darling, you're a famous movie star and can have any man you want. Why can't you just say goodbye to him?"

"Ma, once and for all, we have this fantastic opportunity that we both have to see through. Allie and I can't punk out now. We'll hate ourselves for the rest of our lives if we do. So get off it, please."

"I can't, Carole, and *nu*, when all the traveling is over, then what? I'll tell you, he'll go home to his wife and little boy and leave you all alone, and then what?"

Carole tore at Rose's heart with "Maybe not. I just went off the pill."

Rose almost had a small heart attack; at best, she was dizzy. In moments such as this, Rose talked straight to the Lord.

"Please, God, tell her not to bring another child into the world."

Rose talked back at her daughter. "Carole, did you hear the Lord saying, 'Don't do it'?"

Rose's nagging bugged Carole, but because of the humor in it, she made a great effort to hold her temper but did have to make one thing very clear to her mother.

"Ma, will you please just let me and Allie do our damn tour, perhaps do a little good, maybe spread a little joy in the world? Now accept that, and please leave me alone because, if you don't, you're going to make me yell at you."

"You really love him, don't you?"

"Yes, I really do, and we're the perfect pair to make this trip the greatest experience of our lives. You know I'm not religious,

Ma, but I sense God has brought us together for a special purpose. I feel a sense of shared mission with Allie and am already a better woman for it."

"I wish I could bring myself to say 'mazel tov.'"

Rose, you are a good mother and mean well, but please take pride and pleasure in the Almighty's mission for Carole. She is the prophet's angel of beholding, a left arm of Adonai, and a blessed woman of courage and conviction.

Chapter 58

Cohen, still in deep slumber at 10:00 AM when the phone rang, stabbed at the receiver and was greeted by Sarah's cheery voice.

"Good morning, big daddy. Right now, I'm holding a short but handsome stranger. Guess what, the little munchkin has the farts. Listen."

Sarah put the receiver up against the infant's rear end. Ari didn't disappoint them; he ripped off a long and loud fart for a newborn.

"See what I mean?"

"Poor little guy." Cohen empathized. "He inherited his old man's stomach."

"He's beautiful, Allie, a perfect combination of both of us. He eats like a champ and hasn't cried once. I swear, every baby that they wheel down the hall is screaming its head off but not Ari. He's too busy checking the place out."

"How do you feel?"

"Other than the usual soreness, I'm all right."

"Did you hear me speak to you in the recovery room?"

"Yes, and what you said was very nice and sweet, and I appreciated hearing it, but I was too out of it to react. Come on, hurry and get dressed. The next feeding's in two hours."

"I'll be right over. Bye."

Ari consumed half his bottle by the time his slightly disheveled father arrived to feed him the rest. Allie stared at Ari and then lit the room with a radiant smile and a declaration of ultimate happiness.

"I have as fine a son, Sarah, as I could have wished the Lord to bless me with."

Sarah satirically introduced the two males. "Ari Ben Cohen, this is your father, née Allie. Take advantage of him in the next seven to ten days because, thereafter, you're not going to see him that much."

"Sarah, what are the benefits of a C-section versus the traditional birthing process?"

"Okay, C-section babies are quite serene because of their bypassing the dangerous fight through the birth canal. This spares them possible traumas that can occur during labor. Get ready, Allie. My busy, trusting son just downed his last drop of milk and is about to deliver a man-size burp."

Ari burped big, and Allie beamed with such joy that Sarah thought she spotted an opening in his defenses.

"Isn't it sad that you won't be around to witness Ari go through all his changes—you know cooing, walking, or holding a glass for the first time? You do understand, Allie, that you have traded family life for wealth and success."

"As I said to you last night, I'm not divorcing or abandoning you and Ari. You are my wife and will be for the rest of my life. I love you far more than Carole, plan to get back as often as I can, and intend to witness all the changes that Ari will be going through. Please take the word *co-living* at full face value."

He thought, *That statement of support should pacify Sarah, at least make things seem more hopeful.*

"I liked hearing that, Allie, but find it a bit hard to believe. So if you love me far more than her, what's really driving this thing with Carole?"

Cohen thought for a few seconds before answering. "The Lord has a mission for me, and Carole is my angel, and you are my rock that sustains me. I'm serious."

"You really are serious. I guess Carole is an angel from God. I mean, who can get you more attention for good than her?"

"Exactly. I just said this to Riva. Too many things have come together in the past month or two to just sum it up as simple coincidence—Carole, Reagan, Sam Minkowitz, Peter Bates, for example. I've been given the opportunity of a lifetime to do a lot of good and must see it through. I'm just so sorry that this mission comes at such great expense to you and Ari, but please have faith and trust in me."

Sarah, skeptical, asked, "Are you serious, Allie? The Lord has willed all this? When we first met, you were a card-carrying atheist who only started to believe in God after the stillborn birth of our first child. Since when did you get so religious?"

"It's not really being religious, Sarah. It's more a spiritual transformation. An opportunity to do good worldwide has availed itself. How can I turn my back on the Lord and all the good I might be able to do?"

"You sound sincere, Allie, and I do want to believe you. It's just your running around the world with a beautiful movie actress. It's not easy to buy into."

"I understand, Sarah, but Carole and I are an extremely effective partnership. Please remember too that I'm not making it any easier for her. Rose, Carole's mom, is all over her on this just as your mother would be."

"I get it, Allie, but admit that I'm having a hard time with you trying so hard to make her happy, the sex and love part especially. I don't know if I have the heart for all this."

"I understand, Sarah, and I wish I didn't have to put you and Ari through it, but I can't turn my back on the Lord, especially after He has given me this adorable son."

"Of all the people on the planet, Allie, why has God singled you out?"

He sighed heavily before revealing a story from his childhood.

"When I was a little boy, I overheard my grandfather telling my mom that he and I were descended from kings." Sarah's eyes lit up at the word *king*. "Supposedly, we were both the princely thirteenth grandsons of a royal line. My mom thought my grandpa might be showing signs of dementia, so I don't know if it's true, but it has always made me feel special and that I was predestined to do something important. That's at hand, Sarah. Think about it."

"I guess whatever your destiny is, Allie, you're about to find out."

Well said, Sarah.

"Exactly. Think. Reagan and the U.S. government are sending me virtually everywhere in the world that there is trouble. I'm not saying that I will solve all these problems, but I can at least add my own two cents."

"You're from a line of kings? It must be the Chazers."

They both laughed hard from her joke, more so when he told her it was true.

"Supposedly, Yahweh changed the Chazers into the Anatolian Jews, the lost tribe of Israel. King Echutz became King Avram Aron. That's my grandpa Aaron's Hebrew name and mine too. Maybe it's also Ari's."

Sorry, Allie, Ari's Hebrew name is Avram Baruch, after Aaron and Barney, and he is only a third grandchild; it is the will of Adonai.

Sarah laughed hysterically at Allie being a descendant of the Chazers for almost a minute. Finally, after a couple of coughs, her laughter subsided.

"For this Anatolian Jew story alone, Allie, I'm going to hang in there with you, but don't take fucking forever, you hear me?"

"I love you, Sarah, and I love this little boy. The Lord has given me the best wife whom I could ask for, but He has also given me a mission that comes at a great cost to the two people I love the most."

Sarah, with tears in her eyes, said, "You have made more references to God Almighty in the past ten minutes than during the entire eleven years that we've been together."

"I probably have." He switched into a Rod Serling *Twilight Zone* voice. "But then the Lord works in mysterious ways, doesn't He?"

Sarah laughed again, but she was tired and needed to close her eyes soon. The nurse came to return Ari to the baby dormitory for his nap too.

"Mom said that you have a meeting with Dad at noon. You better get moving," Sarah said.

Allie kissed Sarah and Ari. "I love you guys more than life itself. I'll be by tomorrow for the same feeding. Oy, what a cutie he is. I love you, Ari Ben Cohen."

Cohen drove to the corner of Peachtree and Piedmont Avenues. From a distance, he saw Harvey's big Buick parked in front of the Sit-In's entrance; and as usual, his father-in-law was busy poring over blueprints.

Cohen pulled up next to Kartzman's car. *Dad hasn't displayed any hard feelings yet.*

Harvey was thinking, *I am not going to let anything undermine my joy from my grandson Ari's birth or the grand opening of my megarestaurant, which is going to be a monster success.*

Hashem has blessed the Sit-In and Harvey's delicious delicatessen—which he produced with love, honor, and privilege—and touched a little Jewish soul in all who ate there. The customers would flock to the Sit-In from all over God's creation to delight in the richest and tastiest food in Atlanta.

Harvey, a man who never made scenes, curled a reserved smile in Allie's direction. He loved Allie but wasn't his biggest fan. Perhaps it was because they were very similar or maybe because Harvey was a workhorse and Allie a dreamer.

Allie felt he owed his father-in-law an apology.

"Dad, I'm sorry about all the disruption I've caused the family, but I have to see this mission through." Once said, the words sounded a bit empty, so he added, "It's the Lord's will, and He has linked me with Carole."

Kartzman's reply, a mild chastisement, sounded free of anger or disgust.

"Allie, I understand this fling with Carole and that a man's work is very important to him. I was away on business a great deal myself, but in forty years of marriage, I have never indulged in any extramarital affairs. Times have obviously changed though. People are now encouraged to do whatever fulfills them. Of course, she is a beautiful and talented woman too."

Allie smiled; Harvey typically ended his short lecture, for it was time to take care of business at hand.

"Okay, I've packaged your deli-diner-restaurant concept. And by next week, we'll have the Peachtree Corners meat-pickling and fish-smoking plant going full blast. We'll soon be challenging the New York and Chicago producers with better quality at a lower price because of scale and other efficiencies. I predict that the day we open for business, the Sit-In will blow away every small deli and middleman in town."

"Fabulous. Please describe the menu to me, Dad."

"It's six pages long and lists delectables from your local eggs and grits to bagels and lox to corned beef and prime steaks to the best damn hot dog, cheeseburger, knish, and smoked fish you ever ate and everything in between. We are the first true full-service restaurant in Atlanta."

"'Sounds delicious. How big is this place?"

"The Sit-In has 270 seats spread across three rooms and caters banquets and special events. Our key marketing factor is an in-house policy that any patron waiting more than twenty minutes for their food eats for free. The fast, casual-eating concept drives faster table turnover times."

"I like that, but it must be a huge challenge to the kitchen staff."

"Don't worry, we have a great team in the kitchen ready to go. The average plate delivery time is eleven minutes, and we expect to cut it to nine in a month. We also have the longest happy-hour bar in town and a dance floor to attract the free-spending younger set."

"I'm extremely grateful, Dad. Thanks for all your hard work in making my big dream come true."

Adonai has given Barney Cohen a pipeline to Harvey Kartzman's soul to collaborate in the development and management of the Sit-In, their temple of Jewish-style food. Hashem has blessed the Sit-In to expand into desirable locations wherever large clusters of Jews lived to enrich and nourish their souls and bellies.

"Well," viewed Kartzman, "I think Atlanta's finally ready to support something as ambitious as this. Luckily, that old furniture store proved to be an excellent location for such a space-intensive concept."

"What's the Sit-In's startup cost estimate?"

Kartzman grinned while giving Cohen the best news of all. "It cost us *nothing*, Allie. We made money and a lot of it too."

"Are you kidding me? This baby must cost five million, not counting the pickling and smoking plant, which is probably another couple of million."

"Sandy Forman had the wisdom to advertise in all the top industry trade journals and caught the eye of Sunshine Inns, an aggressive and well-financed hotel chain. Sunshine is on par with Marriott, Holiday Inn, and Ramada."

"Sarah and I have stayed at a couple of Sunshine Inns. They're a pretty good value."

"Well, it seems that Sunshine was searching for the right uptown location for three years. Common sense and economics dictated the construction of a joint multipurpose property. A condo and office tower will go up here too for an onsite population. Sunshine was glad to pay $7.5 million for our initial $5 million investment. The land alone would have cost Sunshine $3 million."

Cohen's brain reeled from the unanticipated Sunshine involvement. "Dad, what's the extent of this deal?"

"Sunshine is committed to building a minimum of three units a year until eventual major market penetration. Upon saturation of the top twenty urban areas with significant clusters of Jews or so, second- and third-tier cities will be considered with an aim to have fifty units by the year 2000."

The scale and scope of the expansion plan staggered Allie. "Do you think these sprawling low-density Sunbelt cities targeted in the plan are ready to support a Sit-In?"

Harvey shrugged to suggest, "Well, I guess we'll eventually learn the answer to that question. But for now, no one is putting more good food under one roof each day than us."

"What's the bottom line, Dad?"

"Our eventual take from the deal ranges from $51 million to $93 million. The spread is based on projected profitability curves. Allie, even if you never write another word again, you will still be a rich man."

"Those are serious numbers. What's the breakdown?"

"Your famous name earns you whichever is higher, $21.5 million base or a 50 percent share, which could hit $46.5 million. Poor Sandy and I will have to get by on a $12 million base or top of $23 million, even if there's a depression."

"I assume, Dad, that our biggest challenge is to find high-traffic and quality locations that can support our concept."

"Yes, but the key, in my opinion, is that the economy will keep growing. However, since I know how you feel about Reagan's blasting Mondale, I'll keep my mouth shut. Let me just say that Sandy and I are grateful for your new fame. Frankly, it's made us all rich."

"I'm amazed, Dad. We really lucked out."

"Allie," said Kartzman, rejecting that notion, "you were wise to become a teacher and writer. A smart businessman does not think like that. He applies a good concept and sufficient capital and times the market right. Luck helps, of course, but please give some credit to Sandy Forman because, man, he's a business genius."

Allie agreed that Forman had indeed struck gold and then asked Harvey what their great success meant to him.

Harvey replied, "For me, Allie, it's 'fuck you, money' to anyone who ever underestimated me, and there were plenty of them too. But mostly, I'm so proud to be in the position to leave serious money to my children and grandchildren. Oh yeah, the chamber of commerce headman called the other day to thank you for investing in the city of Atlanta. His name is Phillip Mason, and he sounded as if he'd like to draft you to be mayor."

Allie shuddered at the thought of becoming mayor of Atlanta. "No way a white man can run Atlanta anymore, Dad. Phillip Mason, though, is a good guy and was a great PTA president. I taught his two lovely daughters, who were very smart and nice young ladies."

Cohen thought of his long-deceased father and grew sentimental.

"Dad, I'd like to name the banquet room in honor of my father, Barney Cohen, and hang his portrait in it. It was Barney's dream for us to own the biggest deli and restaurant in New Jersey. His spirit can share our Atlanta version of it."

"Sure, Allie. I think your dad will be smiling down from heaven at you."

You're a fine man, Harvey Kartzman, because Barney Cohen already is.

"You know, Dad, it's too bad that you and Barney never met. You would have been fast friends, two fastidious food service pros."

It's true, Allie. I know of very few grandfathers in history that have matched up as well as Harvey and Barney. It's sad that they did not know each other in life and bounce baby Ari on their knees while schmoozing about the restaurant business. They will not meet for twenty-five more years, for Harvey will live until ninety. Bless his flavorful soul.

Allie's saccharine words made the austere Kartzman uncomfortable, and he typically curled his smile.

"Excuse me, Allie, I have to pick up Rebecca at her Buckhead beauty salon."

Chapter 59

Sandy Forman waited patiently in Global's office for his meeting with Sam Minkowitz. He thought how he'd promptly returned from all previous LA business trips, but this time, he planned to hang out with Rick Samuels for a couple of days.

Sam's cute blond secretary, Debbie, told Sandy to enter, and he walked into the spacious office filled with expensive art, tall potted plants, and modern white leather furniture set against pale lavender walls. Sam came out from behind his huge desk and greeted Sandy as if he were a relative.

Minkowitz discussed generalities—politics, the economy, the weather, Allie and Carole's latest plans, Ari Ben's bris, and so on.

He then blurted, "Rose is cooking her special pot roast tonight, and I insist that you spend the evening with us. Allie's almost like a son-in-law, so you're family too."

Sandy tensed up; he was dreaming of Libby's rump and not Rose's brisket.

"Sam, I'm sorry, but I already have a dinner engagement for tonight, but how about tomorrow night?"

"Sorry," explained Sam. "I have to fly to New York tomorrow for a stockholder's meeting. Don't worry, Sandy, we'll see you at the bris in a few days."

"Sure, I'm honored to hold Ari's legs."

Minkowitz smiled and then began a morality lesson by lavishly praising Cohen.

"You know, I love Allie just like a real son-in-law. I tell you, he's a genius, maybe a prophet—oh, excuse me, for his insurance company's sake, a sage."

Forman laughed hard until Sam asked, "Sandy, do you happen to know Rick Samuels?"

Out popped "Sort of." Sandy reconsidered. *I know better than to bullshit a powerful man like Sam. I'll come clean.* "Okay, Sam, it's Rick that I'm meeting tonight for dinner."

Sam's tone changed from talking abstractly to being very direct. "What do you know about Rick Samuels?"

"Rick and Allie have been friends since they're kids in Newark. Allie hung out with him for a few days before he met Carole."

"Do you know what Samuels does for a living?"

Sandy did, of course, but sensed that he should soften the description.

"He's a photographer, Sam, with a reputation for tasteful soft-core erotica."

Minkowitz became animated; sarcasm dripped from his lips.

"Not anymore, Sandy. Rick is now a pornographer, hard-core too. Unfortunately, Allie gets 15 percent of Rick's popular nude poster business through a dummy Bermuda-based corporation called RAL Productions. Since you're Cohen's business manager, that's no surprise to you, eh?"

"Sam, I'm also Allie's accountant, and you're discussing privileged information, but you've invested heavily in Allie's future and have a right to protect yourself. The bottom line on RAL is that it's been incredibly lucrative for no input at all."

"Lucrative, my ass," said Sam, scoffing at Sandy's claim of profitability. "A lousy quarter million a year is peanuts compared with the value of Global's new preferred stock offering. Taking into account projected revenues that Cohen's properties will yield alone, Global's new stock issue should double in two years and split. Are you getting this financial picture?"

"Sure, but, Sam, RAL occurred before the novel's publication. You know that."

"I don't care." Sam directed Sandy. "I just want every link to Allie erased. I'll instruct my studio financing section to show you how to hide it in our budget."

"Sam, I have a specialty in forensic accounting. I know all the ballets with the numbers."

"Okay, boychick, if you take care of this for me, I'll let you and Allie each buy $2 million worth of the preferred offering too. This stock issue has a first creditor payoff stipulation that will send the stock price straight up."

Sandy shook the hand of Sam, who gave him and Allie spot-on advice.

"You're being smart, Sandy. Holocaust writers can't own pornography businesses. We would have both suffered if that stink got out. Now I need another favor from you." Sandy nodded *what.* "Please keep Allie away from Rick Samuels."

"Sam, I'm not Allie's father and can't pick his friends. I only manage his business and finances."

"Let's see. Allie pays you a $65,000 base, plus 25 percent of all deals. You just made $12.5 million, which could double from your new restaurant chain that's based on Cohen's fame, am I right?"

Sandy tensed up. *Sam knows our entire financial structure.*

"Look, Sandy, we both know that Allie's a reckless genius. So if you don't want your Sit-In millions to go down the toilet, you'll clean up his act."

"A bit harsh, Sam, but I get the point."

Sam used his index finger to emphasize his point. "Look, don't forget that the press is busy building Allie up right now. They can just as easily tear him down. That's happened to much bigger people than Allie Cohen."

Minkowitz's knowing so much of his private business troubled Sandy. "Sam, I'd love to know how you obtained that much inside information."

Minkowitz smiled. "Let's just say that . . . I took an interest in you."

Chapter 60

Sandy got Sam's message. "I'll take care of everything. I assure you, Sam."

Minkowitz threw Forman another bonus for cooperating. "My own financial adviser says LA has 550,000 Jews and predicts that the Sit-In out here will be ultrasuccessful. If you grant me 25 percent of the gross profit, I'll pick up 100 percent of the cost of this investment."

"So you want to go in to the restaurant business, Sam?" Forman gently kibitzed.

"Between you and me, I've always wanted to be part of owning a great restaurant like the Sit-In and hanging out at my own table. Fuck Nate'n Al, the Fairfax, and Jerry's Deli—the overpriced pricks for mediocre stuff. Can you do this for me, Sandy?"

Sandy wasn't happy about Sam squeezing their profit margins but accommodated Minkowitz to keep him happy. "All right, Sam, you made us an offer we can't refuse."

Sam smiled appreciatively. "I believe that the day we open, we blow by everybody. Now go and have a good time at Rick's tonight, and say hello to the Lee sisters."

Minkowitz smiled wickedly. Forman shook his hand, said goodbye, and walked to his rented Ford.

Man, I feel like I just survived a lion's den.

He drove his rental past Global's front gates and out to the hills above Laurel Canyon Boulevard. The episode with Sam altered Sandy's perception of Rick as Allie's buddy from New Jersey to a problem that threatened their growing money machine.

Sandy parked next to Rick's new Rolls-Royce convertible, rang the bell, and was relieved when Samuels opened the door. *Thank god he looks like a regular Jersey guy.*

Rick invited Sandy in, who immediately glimpsed. *Man, there's nothing regular about the naked Lee sisters.*

"The girls," Rick explained, "are busy rehearsing a scene for our latest epic, *The Twin Courtesans of Emperor Ming.* Gorgeous, sexy women like Mamie and Libby and a $50,000 investment will yield up to $4 million in cassette purchases and rentals in the next month."

"Four million gross in one month, Rick, really?"

"Yeah, *Casting Couch Revolt* did over $5 million, and the sequel should double it. Sandy, please light up a joint and sit on the couch while the crew wraps the final scene."

Sandy puffed; Rick directed. "Sandy, you're watching Emperor Ming condemn his wayward son to a hideous death, coitus non-interruptus until expiration. The so-called victim is that nude Chinese guy with the big reddish dick."

Sandy watched the actor, Jimmy Yang, practice ghastly facial expressions. "Rick, this is an absolutely nuts scene you're shooting."

"Dig it, Sandy," Rick commented. "In seven hours of shooting scenes, Jimmy Yang here has qualified for the sexual Olympics by pumping eight fucking come shots. Think about that. Now the ninth money shot, synonymous with the nine lives of a cat, is to leave an insane smile on the dead man's face—"

"Eight fucking come shots for five hundred bucks," Jimmy interrupted Rick. "Now you want a ninth. You got to pay me more, Rick, at least a thousand. You take fucking advantage of me."

"Don't hold your dick, you fucking meathead." Rick coldly warned Yang. "Any extra money goes to my girls, my angels who have made me a rich man. Now get hard, pump that ninth money shot, or I'm not going to pay you at all, fuck face. Try to sue me too, you fucking illegal alien. You give me any more lip, and I'll turn you into immigration."

Rick walked away from Jimmy and muttered to Sandy while the makeup girl fluffed Yang with some success,

"The last scene didn't work at all. There was no chemistry whatsoever between the principals. Mamie and Libby did their best to keep Yang erect but kept losing their concentration. After working eight money shots out of him, they've mangled him with harsh mechanical strokes."

"My private parts," Sandy whispered to Rick, "almost hurt for poor Jimmy, who you may be acting a bit mean too."

"Maybe. Trouble is Libby is so bored she's nearly rubbed it raw as chopped meat. All right, she's finally got a decent stroke going. Mamie's helping her. He's starting to feel it. Okay, now he's getting a little worked up. We're getting closer. Camera, get ready. Yang's about to launch number nine. Wow, hell of a load for nine pumps. Okay, got it. Cut. Thank you, everybody, for all your hard work."

Oh my god. Sandy observed Jimmy. *He's lying there in near agony, and his dick looks like an inverted red carrot.*

"The fucking girls," Jimmy complained to Sandy, "pulled on my dong like it was a goddamned vacuum cleaner. Man, my dick hurts like hell."

"I don't know what to tell you, Jimmy," said Sandy, by now very stoned. "Maybe you should check with Blue Cross to see if they cover this type of injury."

The crew cracked up, and their loud laughter humiliated the vulnerable Yang, who took it out on Rick.

"Man, I have another hand job role tonight. Thanks to Libby, I lose work. My damn dick's too sore. Now I lose money, look unreliable. Rick, you should pay me more for nine money shots and an injury."

Rick threw five $100 bills on the floor and then laughed so hard at Yang's demand that he cried tears. Jimmy picked up the money while shouting at Rick,

"I'm never working for you again, Rick! Fuck you!"

Jimmy stormed out of the house slamming the front door. The sisters looked down at the floor.

Libby apologized. "I'm sorry, Rick, but Yang kept holding my head and shoving his fucking dick down my throat, and it got to me."

"Having to stroke him endlessly for the money shots, Rick," Mamie added, "made me hate him and his cock. I promise to be more professional."

"No big deal. The crap's in the can, and we begin filming the sequel tomorrow."

Rick hugged the sisters, kissed each, and promised;. "The guy lacks stamina, and his dong looks like a cross between an egg roll and a red noodle. As far as I'm concerned, he's finished in this town."

"Rick," Sandy insisted, "nine money shots in eight hours, and you say the kid lacks stamina, and he's finished in the business too. C'mon, give the kid a break."

"Sandy, you heard Libby. Yang's a dickhead. I'm the only guy in town whose ladies are partners, and we sell more tapes than anyone else. Duh, what's the message there? These beautiful and wonderful ladies hire the dicks whom they want to work with and who treat them with respect and kindness."

"Tomorrow," Rick happily informed the sisters, "we begin shooting *The Tenth Life of the Wayward Son*. We're going to begin and end with close-ups of the two of you in a threesome with Raymond 'Foot Long' Li. Now Ray, Sandy, is a true gentleman, treats my girls like gold, and is blessed with a giant magical cock that shoots come like a fire hose."

"Rick," Libby suggested, "I think I'll try anal with Ray tomorrow. I'm curious, and Ray is always so gentle and sensitive."

"Sure, sweetie." Rick bragged to Sandy, "My girls are already the greatest foursome in the history of the business. No group even comes close to the exquisite Greta and Reny and the magnificent Lee sisters, no one."

"It's true. My staff"—he pointed to himself—"sure doesn't look like that."

Rick laughed. "Girls, this is Sandy, Allie's agent."

"Sorry, Rick," Sandy corrected him. "I'm Allie's business manager."

"Excuse me." Rick laughed. "His business manager."

Libby wanted to know. "Why does a teacher need a business manager? It seems to me he'd be paying you more than twice what he'd be making."

Forman giggled. Rick asked, "Sandy, what do you want to do for the rest of the night?"

Sandy had a good idea but just said he didn't care and was glad to hang out if that was what Rick wanted. Rick thought about that.

"Sandy, do you mind waiting while I refilm a single scene from *Casting Couch Revolt II*? It'll only take about a half hour."

"I assure you, I'm quite content to be a spectator."

"Let me show you my appreciation, Sandy, by treating you to dinner at Orsino's, my favorite Italian restaurant. Tell me, what do you know about Greta and Reny?"

"Allie shared some of his adventures out here with me. Rick, I hate to change the subject, but I just came from a meeting with Sam Minkowitz, who's concerned that your business has radically moved in a new direction. Please bring me up-to-date."

"Okay, David and Greta are finished. She seems curiously relieved by the closure too. And why not? Greta made $350,000 from *Casting Couch Revolt* and will probably double that with the sequel. Preproduction demand for our videos is outrageous. I'm blessed with four superhot coproducers, who are recruiting their own stable of starlets to manage too. Man, Sandy, it's a fucking convergence that's raining money down on us."

"Rick, Sam's concerned about the poster. I quote him. 'Holocaust writers can't own pornography businesses. It's a stink no one needs.'"

Rick laughed at Sam's line and Sandy's impression.

"Don't worry, Sandy, I've already taken care of it. And at Ari's bris, I plan to present Sarah with a $250,000 gift. I put the poster scheme together in five days in a vain hope to entice Allie away from Malibu. It didn't stop him, and then when he came back with that big check from Sam, well, RAL seemed so damn puny. I just kept it a secret."

"But the money has come pouring in. Did that pay for your new Rolls?"

"Uh-huh, could have bought ten Rollses from what the three posters made me. Hey, don't worry about any links to Allie. Let me tell you, Sam is the last guy in Hollywood you want mad at you. Christ, not even the mob messes with Minkowitz. And who knows, maybe I'll need his help someday."

"Yes, he is good to have on your side. I sure wouldn't want to cross him."

"Sandy," Rick promised, "I swear that I'd never do anything to hurt Allie."

He poked fun at himself. "And to think I tried to steer him away from Carole. I guess nobody's going to ask me to write an advice column. For years, Cohen pushed me to photograph naked women. He told me I needed to get something like this out of my system and that it paid a hell of a lot better than sweating beer cans. Shit, I've already had such a bellyful of this business that I can vomit sometimes. Hey, I think I'm hungry. Let's go to Orsino's now and shoot later."

"That's fine with me, Rick." Sandy thought, *Despite Rick's making hundreds of thousands of dollars a month, he actually seems a bit miserable.*

"Man, Sandy," said Rick, pouring his heart out to Forman while driving to Orsino's. "I'm going to make so much money this year that I'll pay more in taxes than I made money my whole life before it, but for the right woman, I'd walk away in a minute. I'm dying to find a decent lady and thought it was going to be Mamie, but she became a porn star and has a new agenda, and it is not going to work out for us. I'm sorry too."

Sandy went "tsk, tsk" to suggest Rick was overstating his case.

Rick, insistent, said, "I'm serious. You won't believe some of the twisted things that have happened to me."

405

"Like what?" Sandy was dying to hear.

"Okay, last week, my brother and I were having lunch at Jerry's Deli in Studio City when this monster of a Mexican dude walked over to our table. This dickhead took out his twelve-inch burrito and laid it right on my pastrami sandwich."

Sandy laughed hard at that word picture. "Now my brother is very straight, and he went gaga, so I said to this schmuck, 'What the hell are you doing? Get your goddamned dong off my sandwich, you stupid asshole.'"

Sandy cracked up laughing. Rick continued. "Anyway, the dude came back with 'Man, I'm Big Dick Beniquez, been the stud in thirteen pornos. I'm eleven inches soft, thirteen and a half hard, so *you* got to have this *dick* in your next *flick*."

That convulsed Sandy, who held his sides. "So I told this Tijuana turkey, 'No way, man, and I don't want it on my sandwich either. Now get the hell away from me, or I'll stab your dick with my knife.' I swear, my brother Mel will not go out with me anymore."

Sandy wiped tears from his eyes. "Rick, that is truly outrageous. What about the spread of AIDS?"

"That's something I don't even want to think about. The industry is taking steps to deal with this plague, and I'll follow their lead. The problem is caused by porn's second rule of thumb— no condoms. So a testing system is being quickly developed."

They got up to leave the restaurant, and a *Penthouse* editor approached Rick with an offer for a fall photo spread showcasing his four fabulous queens of porn.

Rick thanked and told his colleague, "Here's my card. Call me at that number, and we'll schedule the shoot."

Sam's morality lesson and Rick's horror stories were not stopping Sandy from catching porn fever. The stirring increased with each flesh peddler's huge mansion that Rick pointed out on the way back to Laurel Canyon.

Rick and Sandy returned and found the crew hard at work, arranging the set. Lincoln Smith, the assistant director, instructed the girls in the fine art of fluffing or keeping a penis hard during retakes and dusted over the actor's blemishes.

Sandy watched the crew very intently. Lincoln told Sandy about a porn industry blessing just a year away.

"Have you heard that a pharmaceutical company has invented a little blue pill that will soon solve the problem of *wood*?"

"Look, Sandy." Rick felt him out. "I realize that you're married but figured that you might want to mix a little business with pleasure while out here—you know, grab a little nooky on the side. Forgive me, but I took the liberty of asking the girls to hang with us tonight. Please, if you're not into it, I'll gladly send them home after we finish the scene."

"On this night," the occasional reader for a conservative congregation assured Rick, "the charms of naked flesh are temporarily kosher, especially Libby."

Surprisingly and to his great delight, he wound up being mainly with Mamie and felt better inside for it.

The next morning, Forman offered to invest in *Casting Couch Revolt III*. Samuels, shocked, nixed that and called it *stupid greed*, the worst kind of all, and he learned it the hard way—Mamie.

Sandy persisted, but Rick had the last word. "First, Sam will kill you because you're too close to Allie. Second, it's not possible to jump in and out of the business without getting dirtied. Most of all, you should see the scum I have to deal with to get my product distributed. Goddammit, Sandy, they're the fucking mob! Sorry, an accountant from Atlanta ain't in the position to pull that off."

Allie and Riva both said Sandy was a very libidinous accountant, and hadn't Sam just told him that Holocaust writers can't be in the pornography business? Sandy's eyes pleaded for some secret involvement.

"Come on, Sandy, look at me. I'm headed straight for the toilet unless I can get out before it's too late. My plan is to have ten to twelve million bucks in a bank in Bermuda in two years and walk away."

Forman finally ended his flirtation. "Hey, Rick, why don't you fly back with me to Atlanta and stay with Riva and me."

"Thanks, Sandy, I think I will."

Rick barked at the fortyish actor, "Goddammit, will you get hard already? Or I'm going to fire your fucking ass!"

"Rick, he'll never get hard with you yelling at him like that."

"I guess you're right, Sandy. It's just that a flaccid penis costs money."

"I understand, Rick. The world and women have little use for a flaccid penis."

That's the way it is, guys. If it doesn't *stand*, it ain't *grand*. I think I should leave the humor to Allie.

Chapter 61

Cohen drove his son home from the hospital at fifteen miles an hour to not upset Ari's tender karma.

Sarah noticed and drilled him. "What a farce."

"What do you mean, money? I'm just driving carefully."

"I mean, you won't be caring this much a week from now. You know, I'm convinced that you would have made a great father."

"Hey, I'm not dead yet."

"Maybe I should hire a minion to say Kaddish for you."

Allie gave Sarah a look to cool it with the shots like the mourner's prayer.

"How many people," she asked him, "are invited to the bris?"

He was afraid to tell her and mumbled, "Two hundred confirmed. Up to three hundred may attend."

Sarah heard very well. "Allie, you're crazy, sixty to seventy tops. Our 2,700-square-foot house cannot accommodate any more."

"It's too late," he told her. "Most are confirmed and coming. Don't worry, the Sit-In's catering division is setting up gas grills, bars, and tables all over the property and with tents, TV monitors, and microphones, if necessary. The county loves the publicity and has waived all permits."

"This is so like you, Allie." She lit into him. "I remember wanting twenty guests at a hippie wedding at my aunt's Greenwich Village townhouse, but no, you had to have two hundred at a wedding factory in West Orange, which my parents are still paying for seven years later."

Cohen borrowed the punch line from an old French aviator joke. "When Pierre goes down, he goes down in flames."

Sarah, not amused, urged Allie to hurry because the baby was hungry. They arrived home; Allie set Ari up in his crib and showed his son the overhead mobile. Ari smiled at it until Cohen placed the bottle's nipple into his son's mouth. Five minutes later, Ari was satisfied, burped, and put down to nap.

Allie drove over to a garden center and bought a six-foot-high Japanese maple tree and a variety of shrubs and flowers. He returned home, took a spade in hand, and turned the red Georgia clay. Cohen nourished the soil with peat moss, mulch, and fertilizer to make the dirt loamy. Finally, Allie planted the maple to honor Ari's birth and added a circle of decorative flowers and shrubs, which I think was a very nice touch.

Sarah observed him while planting and gibed, "Perhaps you'll return home before your son is himself a six-foot maple."

When Allie pretended not to hear her, she informed him, "I need you to pick up the baby nurse who's waiting at a nearby bus station."

Cohen quickly taxied over to the corner of Roswell Road and Hammond Drive and spotted a black woman of exceptional girth. Aretha Griffin grunted as she pried her six-foot, three-hundred-pound frame into the compact Celica.

Aretha bears an amazing resemblance to Aunt Jemima, Cohen thought as he drove back to the house. *I swear, she beams a nonstop smile that reveals a shiny gold front tooth and makes her look like the ultimate mammy that's ever been born.*

Aretha instantly proved her worth by cooking up a mess of the best fried chicken and corn bread that Sarah and Allie had eaten since moving South. She shared her tortuous past with the Cohens while whipping together and serving a scrumptious macaroni and cheese.

"I'm the eldest of seventeen children of Alabama black belt sharecroppers and received my early training by helping Mom raise my brothers and sisters. Since leaving home, I've nursed 1,186 babies, 90 percent of them Jewish, and healed so many circumcisions that I once gave serious thought to becoming a mohel myself."

Aretha's huge belly belied her quickness and massive strength. When she complained to him that she'd had enough of nursing and was ready to become a nanny, he hired her on the spot and joked that Ari's tush was going to be the cleanest and driest in North Atlanta.

Cohen particularly loved the way Aretha carried Ari on her prodigious breasts, which supported him like a portable crib. Later that night, Allie was reading a newspaper at the kitchen table when Aretha walked by, with Ari suspended on her right breast. The munchkin's contented look inspired a wild idea.

"Aretha, did you ever see *Roots*?"

"Yes, sir, all twenty-six hours. Of course, I always had a young'un on my lap, but every time one of them ol' grandfathers held another Kinte baby up to the sky, the tears just poured right out of my eyes."

"They did, huh? Excellent. Hmm, did you notice the moon tonight?"

"No. Should I have, Mr. Cohen?"

"It's full, Aretha." Cohen nodded.

411

"So that's nice." She did not get it yet.

"You'll see. Please wrap Ari up in a blanket, and follow me outside to the backyard."

Aretha's look begged to know why. Cohen put up his hand up to signal *trust me*, so Aretha wrapped Ari up warmer than buttermilk biscuits right out of the oven and nestled him in her arms. She hurried after Allie, by now standing in a fenced-off space lit up like a streetlamp from the full moon and twinkling stars.

Although a beautiful spring evening, the protective Aretha still questioned Allie's judgment. "Mr. Cohen, don't you think Ari might be better off in his crib."

"You'll see, Aretha. It'll only take a few minutes." Cohen instructed her, "Since you're taller than me, please hold Ari up toward the full moon, which is directly overhead."

Aretha finally figured out what Allie was up to and squealed with laughter. "I'm glad you're a good sport, Aretha, and who gets it better than a black person about little Ari 'Kinte' Cohen having roots from Russia, Germany, Poland, Lithuania, Austria, New York, New Jersey and was born in the piney woods of north Georgia?"

Aretha laughed her head off when Cohen began humming the theme song from Alex Haley's family saga.

Ari smiled away. Aretha was cackling so hard that she could barely hold Ari up any longer and said in between giggles, "Mr. Cohen, you a crazy man."

Allie interrupted his humming to fill her in. "Look, I'm not Alex Haley, of course, but I'm a writer and a wandering Jew too."

Aretha got his point. "You mean, Mr. Cohen, how hard it is for minorities to make it in America. Look at me. I'm the ultimate

412

wandering nurse who has lived much of her life on a Greyhound bus going to my next job. I only have one sister left in Alabama. The whole family is dead, in jail, or moved on. I practically got no home to go back to."

"I understand, and now, Nanny Aretha, this is your home."

She beamed. "My little Ari, Aretha, will have to learn that because he's a Jew, he'll have to make his way in the world by being smarter than the next guy."

"Mr. Cohen, that's why I've liked working so much for Jewish people. Blacks and Jews got more soul than white Christians."

"We got more soul, Aretha, because we've had more suffering."

"Amen, Brother Cohen."

"Amen, Sister 'Retha." Cohen stopped humming and sang a little blues number.

"You got to lose to sing the blues. Yes, you got to lose to sing the blues.

And who done lose more than the blacks or the Jews."

Aretha cackled again, but her arms were tired. "Mr. Cohen, is it okay to put Ari down?"

Allie laughed and took Ari, who was smiling away at him, in his arms and said a few regretful words.

"I pray to the Lord Almighty that you'll always recognize and love the fatherly stranger popping in and out of your life. I love you, Ari, and I swear that I'll make it up to you anyway I can."

413

He handed Ari back to Aretha, who put him to bed, and he
sat down at his desk and ground out a poem, "The Fanatical Edge,"
in ten minutes.

Jewish parents don't just raise children;
Instead, they make their kids feel special,
Which makes them act smarter and cuter
And think they're the center of the damn universe.

They then selfishly dream and achieve
And forsake responsibility to all but themselves.

Thus is created the fanatical edge,
A powerful drive to surpass all the others
For the distant reward of self-actualization
On the narcissistic road to fame and success
And all that jazz and hurt that comes with the territory.

Chapter 62

Eddie yelled, "Hey, Lee!"

Lesotho Xeranga's nonnegotiable rule—never answer to the anglicized Lee.

"Sorry, man, don't know no *Lee*."

"Okay, man, whatever, let's call it a day and get us a cold brew."

"Now that's a brilliant idea, Eddie."

The lanky Xeranga and the thick-bodied White methodically put away their painting materials and walked to a nearby pub to down a beer or two before heading home.

Lesotho, a gifted artist and proud and secure in his blackness, was compared by many friends and associates to the late Malcolm X, his hero. He was born Richard Sampson and rejected the white slave name during his senior year at Morehouse University in Atlanta. After graduating, he dedicated a year to filling in the holes in his identity with a roots search.

Lesotho recalled as he walked with Eddie and related his process. "Two terrific breaks luckily preceded my pilgrimage to Senegal and helped locate my ancestral homeland, the Lesotho tribal area. Similar to the Kinte and Haley clan line, all the female Sampson family members passed down a peculiar okra recipe solely prepared by the Lesotho tribe."

The second clue, he discovered in the Savannah County Courthouse records. In 1758, a Chatham County plantation owner named Telford Sampson purchased the entire Ranga family from a British slaver that bought six hundred blacks at the mouth of the Bonny River in Senegal.

After four weeks with tribal elders responsible for maintaining the oral history, it was derived that Richard Sampson was, in fact, a member of the Ranga clan. It was there that Lesotho created Xeranga by taking X, the unknown factor and symbolic of the black Muslim's rejection of the slave past, and merging it with the clan name of Ranga.

"Let me be clear," Xeranga declared to the world. "I am problack, was born a Baptist, and am currently an atheist. I am not antianybody and certainly not a Muslim. I reject Jesse Jackson's demand for more welfare programs and hype Tony Brown's plan for blacks to buy most of their goods and services from black-owned businesses. I hate Reagan's insensitivity toward minorities but hate it more when blacks accuse me of sounding like a black Reagan.

"My main rap is economic and community improvement. Welfare is poverty, and the moment we blacks sell to one another more—and I don't mean *drugs*—we will become a wealthy minority, and white America will claim us as an asset. Socialism is not revolutionary. No, the real liberator is mucho coins in your pocket. Indeed, money can make your skin seem whiter.

"The white man and the corporations got all the money, and blacks ain't got shit. Blacks borrow from whitey at sky-high interest rates because the black dude's a high risk, so our capital costs more and gets less mileage. We then locked out of the market and lack the capital to pay the loan back, if we get it.

"Yes, sir, the two things keeping blacks down ain't segregated schools, because it shouldn't matter if a school is all black, or the lack of jobs 'cause those jobs don't pay for shit anyway. No, the real terrorists are the prime interest rate and the standard of living. No way that a poor black dude is a big white banker's favorite customer, so he's beaten right there.

They turn the brother down for the low-interest loan because they are put off by his condition. When you're living well, you look good, and just about everybody wants to lend you money and at the best rates too. But when you're poor and look it too, nobody will trust you with the down payment on a grape.

"That's the way it is, man. You give the blacks a long line of credit at low rates, and we're taking a bigger step than all the Great Society welfare programs put together. As I see it, the only people making money off welfare programs are white administrators. Man, they driving Volvos and Celicas for handing us a check and subway tokens."

Xeranga delivered his spiel to whoever would listen. His special talent was the ability to explain political economics in street talk to help even uneducated blacks grasp fairly high-level concepts.

Lately, Lesotho's been digging on Barbara Blumberg, a pretty blond-haired daughter of an orthodontist. Barbara, a respected journalist for the morning *Atlanta Journal-Constitution*, tried for a while to convert him to Judaism. Lesotho, though, couldn't imagine himself living in a Jewish world, but he was very tempted.

Barbara wanted to marry him and occasionally gave him money. He cared deeply for her but had no stomach for the hassles of interracial marriage. Lesotho also doubted that he'd ever measure up to Dr. Blumberg's expectations of a son-in-law.

His favorite lady was Tanya Nikki, a pretty dark-skinned woman of medium height and slight frame. Tanya, a widely known poetess, badly wanted Lesotho's baby and gave him money too. The trouble with Tanya was she had anger issues, and that kept him from moving in with her.

Xeranga was always short of money and, to pay the rent, found a Manpower Training Act job to paint six frames of major Afro-American historical events around a master theme of the black struggle for freedom and dignity. Eddie and Lesotho became close friends as they produced frame after frame. Antonio Willis occasionally showed up to check on the mural's progress but usually left quickly to escape Xeranga's barrage of put-downs.

Lesotho sympathized with Eddie's frustrating incapacity to express himself and admired White's Mandingoesque, brute strength and means to repulse violence, particularly unto Lesotho. A dude who worked as many sides of the street, and bedrooms, as he did was bound to antagonize someone sooner or later.

Eddie admired Lesotho's easy expressiveness; Xeranga appreciated White's good listening skills. Lesotho wrote streams of letters to newspapers and magazines; Eddie read them before he put them in the mail.

Partly out of friendship and maybe a little pity, Lesotho mentored Eddie to fill in the gaps in his education. During lunch breaks and after work, Lesotho rapped on, and Eddie listened to him like white on rice.

For the first time in his life, Eddie loved knowing facts, and his brain raced to absorb them as fast as Lesotho could spout them. It didn't really matter if Eddie was experiencing a delayed readiness factor or if Lesotho was a good teacher, which he was. What may have been most important was that Eddie's self-esteem was growing in leaps and bounds, and he felt a lot better about himself.

If asked, Farrah would tell you that, as a result, life was much improved at home too. Although she hadn't met Lesotho yet, she swore to everyone that the artist dude had sure made a world of difference in her man. Eddie hardly drank at all anymore, only a beer or two with Lesotho after work, so he was much better with the children.

Eddie emulated Lesotho in his dress too by wearing African garb and sporting a red, black, and green wool beret worn with bright, blousy dashikis. He let his hair grow in to a natural style and trimmed his beard closely. Old friends who ran into him always told him how good he looked.

"Maybe I'm nuts," Farrah said. "But I swear, the new clothes and beard make him look a lot smarter and gentler."

Lesotho and Eddie finished the mural in three months. Lesotho told Eddie their mural had been well received by the agency, which viewed it as a fine example of social art.

"Dig it, man. I think Diego Rivera," bragged Lesotho to Eddie, "the Mexican master himself, might have been proud to be associated with our people's work."

Six frames were set against the north side of an eight-story building, and each depicted a stirring moment in Afro-American history. In the first frame, Harriet Tubman was pictured leading slaves to freedom via the Underground Railroad. The second showed Frederick Douglass fighting the injustices of the slave and Reconstruction periods; the third showcased the Harlem Renaissance and the flowering of black arts in the 1920s.

The fourth frame bothered Lesotho, who did not believe in *turning the other cheek* and agreed with Malcolm X, whose belief was *by any means necessary*. Xeranga felt America's preference for King was an easy choice, but in the end, he respected Atlanta's civil rights hero by including a Montgomery-to-Memphis minimural.

The fifth frame, though, illustrated how Malcolm forced white people to confront and recognize their racial myths, and the sixth frame presented Lesotho's personal odyssey of how he found himself in Senegal.

While touching up Malcolm's teeth, Lesotho stepped back to see if he'd gotten Malcolm's mouth right.

"Eddie!" he yelled. "Will you look at the cat's teeth? I tell you, ol' Malcolm had the most expressive teeth. I swear, it's like the dude was going to bite whitey's ass with them."

Eddie laughed hard and also joked, "Well, Malcolm didn't exactly bite whitey's ass, but he sure was nipping at the man's heels. He he he."

Lesotho laughed and professed, "Eddie, I just know that I was Malcolm in another life. I can actually feel his spirit and energies within me."

Eddie gave Lesotho a look that he was crazy. "Shit, man, get too big, and they gonna shoot you down just like they did Malcolm."

"Maybe," pondered Lesotho. "But I've been touched by the man's ideals and got to finish his work."

"Bullshit," zinged Eddie. "You just touched, period."

Xeranga realized how he must have sounded and started to giggle. Soon both men were laughing so hard that they could barely stand up.

Lesotho put his arm around his buddy's shoulder and said, "C'mon, man, it's after five and motherfuckin' hot out. Why don't we go get us a couple of cold ones, huh?"

Eddie kicked back. "Malcolm breadth, now you making some sense."

Eddie finally found his mentor who would help him find the way.

Chapter 63

Several noted Jewish writers, Philip Roth in particular, have occasionally portrayed their ritual celebrations as gross displays of vulgar materialism. Allie Cohen, if asked, would claim that they just don't know how to have a good time.

Sarah and Allie's wedding captured the magical combination of a loving group of people, mountains of delicious food, a good dance band, and free-flowing alcohol and dope.

I hope to produce the same magic for Ari's peeling-off party, wished Cohen, minus the band and dope.

The reality of Jewish education for children in America is if you want your kids to speak Hebrew, live a Jewish life and likely marry another Jew - send them to the private Jewish day school.

This is costly, so if you're less wealthy and satisfied with your child learning to read Hebrew and receive enough knowledge of religion and culture to achieve bar or bat mitzvah, the Hebrew school experience suffices. Hebrew school graduates often drift from their faith until it's time to educate their children as Jews.

Allie, a Hebrew school graduate and a questioner by nature, embraced atheism during his freshman year of college. A brilliant Marxist history professor, Dr. Thomas Akins, introduced the term *religio* to an impressionable eighteen-year-old, and an atheist was born with the following lecture:

> Religio is an ignorant substitute for the universality of inner needs seeking understanding of the punishing forces of the cosmos, which humankind are powerless to control. The marginality of life caused primitive man to invent rain gods, sun gods, and others during periods of drought, deluge, or other dangers to their well-being.

Later, agricultural surpluses appeared, and a small farming class supported a division and specialization of labor. The base nature of the urban masses gathered required a code of daily behavior to follow.

Variable belief systems were provided by Zoroaster's monotheism, Moses's Ten Commandments, Christian dogma, Muhammad's Koran and sword, and Buddha's suffering and self-purification. Creative symbolism stirred mystical group participatory experiences, which in turn bonded the humanoid need to belong to a membership of diverse societies.

Adonai and I were very patient with Allie during his youthful questioning period.

In America, a Jewish male usually begins religious instruction at age six to nine. Hebrew school instruction mostly follows the regular school day several times a week. A practical child drained from the demands of state-required education may pay less attention to his sectarian training.

Allie's Hebrew school teachers in the 1950s tended to be severe or snobbish and expected much and received a little less. To maximize performance, they rebuked, chastised, shouted, and compared. As a result, many students—including Cohen—turned off, resisted, or rejected.

Success in Judaic studies necessitates a deep understanding of Hebrew culture, history, and traditions that are thousands of years old. To be welcomed into a membership of Talmudic scholars, one must deny self, defer gratification, and construct a reflective identity based on ageless knowledge and wisdom.

Success in America requires self-promotion, faith in modernism, acceptance of change, and a short memory. To be welcomed into a membership of secular consumers, an individual must cultivate a personal identity, seek instant gratification, and genuinely follow fads and trends.

Hebrew school was a five-year-long chore for Cohen. Rabbi Gurwitz was relieved to be rid of Allie, who shared his haftarah with another boy whom the rabbi was sad to graduate. The rabbi expected Cohen to make a few mistakes and the other thirteen-year-old to raise the spiritual level of the congregation.

Allie amazingly conducted his portion like a cantor, while the other young chap stumbled through his. Afterward, Allie thanked Gurwitz for his tutoring. The rabbi seemed confused but made peace with Allie on the day the tribe officially declared him to be a young mensch.

Allie, Gurwitz was confused because he was unaware of Hashem and I switching preparation levels so that the other young chap stumbled, and you, the prophet, sang your portion of the haftarah like a bird.

Mourner's Kaddish is a daily prayer that the firstborn male is expected to recite and perform for the deceased parent for eleven months. This exercise is conducted among a minion of at least ten men or considered invalid.

Several days after his dad died, Allie asked his grandma to please explain why he had to go to the shul for eleven months and what could happen if he got sick and missed a minion. Grandma Pearl set Allie's guilt in place with her understanding of the subject.

"Allie, it's like a stairway. And each day that you go to the synagogue, your daddy will take another step up the ladder to heaven."

"Then Daddy's going to heaven depends on daily minions and my staying healthy. So what happens if I get sick and can't get to the temple all the time to say Kaddish or if minions fail to form?"

Grandma Pearl, who was not gifted in handling the big questions of life, answered her anxious grandson, "I don't know, Allie."

The daily minion consisted of men ranging in age from forty to eighty. Sol Yellin, a kind tall man and neighbor, was the person most responsible for Barney Cohen's ascent to heaven.

Sol, whose father died of cancer, pulled Allie from countless sporting matches with his friends. He always quietly appeared and patiently waited on the sidelines until Allie excused himself. The two Stuyvesant villagers rode to the shul together, schmoozed with the other friendly mourners, read the nightly service, said the Mourner's Kaddish, and came home.

Allie evolved from the Akins era and atheism to evangelistic secularism, his new mission converting others to his own nonbelief. Allie's argument was so honed that, in less than an hour, he once persuaded a religious Catholic girl to forsake her faith.

The secularism lasted until the tragic death of his stillborn first son. After the beautiful limp baby boy lay dead in Allie's arms, after punching holes in a hospital door, and after stomping a Polaroid OneStep to pieces that was to record the blessed arrival, Allie pleaded to God, "If You do in fact exist, dear Lord, why did You take my infant son? Are You not a merciful God? Am I so arrogant to deserve this cruel fate? Was my heart spared for questioning Your existence?"

He searched but received no answers. Sarah and Allie accepted that they were simply victims of bad luck, three aspiration per every thousand births. Sarah, although not very religious herself, greatly believed in God and helped Allie heal.

Two years later, Allie Cohen was blessed with an exceptional infant son, and many people were coming from diverse places to pay tribute to the circumcision of Ari Ben.

Rebecca, Harvey, Janet, Max, Sandy, Riva, and the Sit-In Catering Department filled a dozen tables with Himalayan chopped liver molds, platters of rolled cold cuts, varieties of fish salads, and Jewish-style breads that provided a rich soft underbelly. Filets mignons, salmon steaks, and barbecued chicken breasts sizzled on gas grills while well-placed wet bars encouraged a normally light-drinking minority group to freely imbibe.

The hulking Aretha designated herself as Ari's shield. Allie and I noticed and figured that any infant about to have his penis trimmed back needn't have 210 coochie-cooers breathing in his face. Aretha, you go, girl.

Earth mother Mary Hayward, Allie's department chair at Buckhead High, was the first discouraged soul to be body-blocked by Aretha. Cohen overheard Mary mumbling to herself after being driven off, "Damn megaton brown bouncer won't let me near that darling little boy."

Aretha only permitted the immediate family to dote on Ari. Carla, dressed in a stunning yellow pantsuit, gently stroked Ari's little foot. Allie was touched by his sister's tenderness and told her so.

"Besides looking smashing Carla, I can't tell you how great it feels to have you and the rest of the family together for Ari's bris."

"I'm not so sure about that," Carla chided. "You seem to be missing one particular person, or is she just late?"

"I'm sorry to disappoint you, but this is a day for both tradition *and* conventionality."

"I wouldn't have cared. If you ask me, it would have been honest and liberating."

"Now don't you think that would have been rubbing Sarah's nose in it? And since Carole feels that way too, so can you."

"Okay, okay, I guess I'll just have to wait one more week, won't I?"

Their mother approached and marveled. "My newest grandson is so cute, Allie. I could eat him up like a cupcake. I'm only sorry that I won't be able to see him more often. If Atlanta wasn't far enough, now you have to go and live mainly in California."

"Ma, why don't you visit me in Malibu? You could get to know Carole's mother, Rose."

"I'm not ready to stay with you and Carole. Allie, as much as I love Ari, you think maybe you should have had a smaller bris. It looks a little disrespectful to Sarah. Forgive me. I didn't come here to tell you how to live your life."

Carla rolled her eyes while Allie hugged Janet, who asked, "By some chance, Allie, is this thing with Carole having maybe a little meltdown even?"

"Ma, please don't make Carole the villain, for you'd be surprised to learn that she sees the world a lot like you do. Her mother certainly does."

Carla, unable to resist herself, aggravated Janet. "I still think Carole should have come. I mean, everybody here knows what's going on, so why the big show?"

To that, Janet acidly addressed her. "Carla, that's plain irresponsible."

"Ma, you're hopelessly middle class. Christ, don't you think Daddy ever had an affair?"

426

Chapter 64

Carla really angered Janet with that line and put Allie in the middle again. He pleaded, "Carla, enough. Cool it, please." Luckily, Rabbi Silver has come over to coach him with his lines.

After a few instructions, the rabbi began the ceremony. The presence of a reporter from *People* magazine gave an unreal aura to a very physical ritual. Allie paid back Sam and Steve Hamall of Global Publicity by allowing one journalist to cover the bris for the pool of syndicates.

Allie's hands were soon sweaty while Sarah's legs swayed like palm trees in a strong wind. The punk reporter recited into a tape recorder while his cameraman recorded the affair and ceremony on videotape and also took stills.

"This is probably the most glamorous bris in Jewish history," claimed the punk. "Billy Diamond is standing behind Allie Cohen with his hands in his corduroy suit pockets. Other Hollywood notables such as Peter Bates, Daria Kelsey, and Sam Minkowitz are to Diamond's left. Obviously, Carole Herman opted not to come. Some other notables are smoking pot in the bushes along the back fence."

Allie looked at Rabbi Silver, who shushed the reporter and prompted Aretha to lay the naked infant on a small white changing table. Allie repeated the rabbi's words.

"I am here, ready to perform the affirmative precept to circumcise my son, even as the Creator, blessed be He, hath commanded us as it is written in the law. And he that is eight days old shall be circumcised among you males throughout the generations."

The mohel took the dazed infant and placed him on a blanket with a diaper on top. Ari's miniyarmulke was fastened to

427

his dark hair. Rabbi Silver spoke eloquently of the salvation of the throne of Elijah. All present were asked to respond in chorus.

"Oh, let us be satisfied with the goodness of Thy house, the holy temple."

Sarah looked at Allie, who smiled back at her and mouthed, *It is what it is.*

She laughed and Sandy Forman released Ari to Rabbi Silver, who placed the child on the knee of his godfather, Sarah's brother Jerry. The moment of truth had come for Ari as the rabbi positioned the knife.

Allie tensed and awaited the blow to his son's karma, a kid who rarely cried except to eat. Sarah was already looking the other way. Ari's first cries filled the room; Sarah's knees vibrated back and forth. When Ari's howling became a bloody shriek, Carla and Daria pitched in to hold Sarah up.

Rabbi Silver helped Cohen recite the blessing welcoming Ari into the covenant of Abraham. Aretha wrapped Ari up in the symbolic blue and white blanket and placed the whimpering child in his arms to hold.

Ari, though quivering, was amazingly serene for what he'd just been through. Ari's handsome face, the rabbi's further blessings, and the many loved ones in attendance produced in Cohen the first true religious stirrings of his life.

Rabbi Silver improvised on the closing speech. "We have gathered together today many famous people. This is particularly symbolic to myself, a conservative rabbi. At each bris, it is believed that this young male may be the Messiah."

Allie thought about Ari's possibly being the Messiah. *What kind of dues would my son have to pay to prove that was so?*

428

I know it is the father, of course, and the great question is the kind of dues he will pay, but this day belongs to the son.

Rabbi Silver continued his sermon. "Now I am for the Equal Rights Amendment, but Halakah, Jewish law, is the law. Still, I believe in the Messiah concept because if a Hollywood actor could make it to the White House"—

Rabbi Silver, having tickled everyone except Sam Minkowitz with that line, was first warming up—"and if Ari is not the Messiah, perhaps he will be the first Jewish president. But after Jimmy Carter, I doubt that there will be another president from Georgia for a hundred years, especially a Jew."

Rabbi Silver had the crowd eating out of his hand, except Sam, who did not like the Reagan *or* Carter crack.

"Reb," Billy Diamond kidded, "I can get you seven minutes on *The Tonight Show* with Carson. Tell me, do you do any Myron Cohen stories?"

"No, and no Henny Youngman jokes either, but I used to do a mean Natan Sharansky impression before they got him out of the Soviet prison and to Israel. I portray Jimmy Cagney with a Russian Jewish accent. 'Let me out. Let me out of here.'"

Cohen sensed that things were getting out of hand. Some of his guests had tears in their eyes; all were laughing hard. Aretha seized the moment by capturing Ari and, like a tank, blocking out baby lovers all the way back to his crib.

Allie toasted his son, Ari Ben Cohen, and challenged everybody to dent the huge stores of food and drink. He tried valiantly to talk to each person too.

Mary Hayward hugged him, hoisted a champagne glass, and toasted. "To the man who finally has everything he ever wanted—and more, I hope."

Her typically insightful words registered, but on this happy day, he let it pass. Mary volunteered next that the school hadn't been the same since he left.

"The students miss you so much. Can you speak at this year's graduation exercise?"

Jack Richards, Cohen's former principal, chimed in, "Yeah, can you?"

Allie thought it over while scooping up some chopped liver with a slice of pumpernickel bread and let them down gently while scooping up some more.

"I'd love to, but my schedule won't allow it. How about if I send a videotaped message? Is that okay?"

Jack and Mary said, "Sure, gladly. By the way, your book has been stolen six times from the school library."

That news amused Cohen, and he promised them that his publisher would donate thirty free copies to the school library. Sam coincidentally walked up to Allie, who introduced him to Jack and Mary.

Sam shook their hands and apologized. "I'm sorry, guys, for stealing your star teacher away from Buckhead High."

Sarah interrupted Sam to hand Allie a telegram with an official presidential seal fixed to the impressive envelope. She flashed a knowing smile and disappeared into the crowd.

Allie figured the sender to be Bell and wanted to strangle Ted for so visibly linking him to Reagan. Cohen forced a smile as he opened the envelope to show respect for the office and the kind gesture.

Congratulations to the Cohen family on this joyous occasion.

Sincerely,

Ronald Reagan

Allie graciously said, "On behalf of my family, I deeply appreciate President Reagan's telegram and congratulations. We are honored."

"Trust me, Allie," said Sam, "Ronnie's a great guy and a real sweetie."

"Sam," Cohen tactfully contested, "Reagan's deficits, forgetful memory, and foreign policy goofs will soon get this country in trouble. When that happens, his Teflon factor will erode very quickly."

"Allie," Minkowitz shot back with his defining truth, "Global's profits are up 158 percent since Carter left office. Better than that, we haven't paid a cent in taxes the past three years and are due a $3 million credit for next year. Need I say more?"

Cohen knew better than to say that Jews should vote their real interest, *fairness for all*. Sam voted his self-interest and let Allie know what should really matter in politics.

"Allie," Sam informed him, "the week after Yom Kippur, a premiere will take place somewhere in the world every hour over a thirty-six-hour period, the largest fund-raising concept ever attempted."

"But, Sam—" *Shit, he's talking right over me.*

"About thirty thousand people, Allie, will congregate in five hundred cinemas across the world to commemorate the movie of your book. This is a onetime star-filled showing that will place the film in the black before its general release."

"But, Sam—" *Damn, he's doing it again.*

"Grow up, Allie. That signifies points time for you the second the first regular ticket buyer plunks down their five bucks. Overall, I predict that your share of the box office receipts and cable TV options eventually will earn you $4 or $5 million."

"But, Sam—" *He won't listen.*

"Don't *but Sam* me. Just remember that Reagan's White House staff was instrumental in helping Global's marketing team put this huge structure together. You have no idea how many embassies and consulates were involved. Therefore, your lack of support for the Gipper is misguided, foolish even."

Allie held his tongue and just said, "Sam, you've seen Reagan at his best the past four years. I predict you will see him at his worst the next four years."

His prediction about Reagan's second term proved mostly true.

Daria butted in to whisper in Sam's ear; his eyes signaled serious trouble. Sam asked Allie if there was anywhere on his property they could talk alone. Sam and Allie walked to a hilly, empty corner of the property where Sam spoke in confidence to him.

"Allie, a little while ago, Daria and Billy stood here just to schmooze and get some fresh air. Daria thought she spotted someone and walked over into your neighbor's yard to get a closer look. Sure enough, it was Carole sitting in a cab a block away, sadly staring at your house."

Allie looked to see for himself, spotted Carole, and waved to her. Sam urged him to stop waving because it was amazing that she still hadn't been discovered.

"Allie, please don't bring attention to her and return to your guests. Peter, Daria, and I will take care of this."

"What's the plan, Sam?"

"We're going to register Carole in a downtown hotel under an assumed name and get you out of the house later under the guise of an emergency business meeting."

Allie listened and retreated to his house. Sarah came to him holding a bunch of checks.

"My god, did you ever make the right friends. Sam Minkowitz, a complete stranger, hands me a check for $25,000, Peter Bates, $10,000. Wow, he's even sexier in real life than on the screen. Daddy also gave us $20,000."

Rick Samuels saw his cue and handed Sarah his check for $250,000. Her eyes rolled like a Vegas slot machine's grand prize payout, and she hugged and thanked him.

"God bless you, Rick. You just provided Ari's college trust."

Carla pulled her brother aside. "You putz, you never once introduced me to Peter Bates. I thought I'd have an orgasm when he bumped into me by the chopped liver."

"There was a lot of action around the chopped liver today. I apologize about Peter, but I did see you talking a lot with Daria Kelsey."

"Christ," she raved. "Did you see that outfit from Giorgio's of Rodeo Drive that she was wearing? Do you have any idea what that cost?"

Cohen appeared clueless. "Of course, Allie Gandhi wouldn't. Only kidding. Guess what. *People* magazine interviewed me, and I only said good things about you, even Mommy."

Allie hugged Carla and saw over two hundred people having a terrific time until an awful ruckus poured out of Ari's room. Allie watched Aretha chase a terrified photographer and yell at him.

"Try that again, turkey, and I'm gonna wop you upside the head so hard your face gonna look like a big ol' corn fritter."

The fearful photographer hid behind Allie, who calmed Aretha. The nurse described what happened while huffing and puffing.

"Mr. Cohen, I told that turkey to take no pictures 'cause it might wake the baby. Sho' 'nuff, as soon as I turned my back, he popped that bulb, and Ari started screaming his little head off. Poor thing, now I got to walk him around a bit."

Aretha threatened the photographer with her massive index finger cutting the air like a Black & Decker drill.

"Turkey, if you do that again, I'm gonna make fatback out of you."

In this case, dear Aretha, for baby Ari's sake, that would be kosher.

Chapter 65

A few miles away, Sam entered the Northeast Expressway, I-85, and headed downtown. Carole, dressed in blue jeans and a blousy white silk shirt, withdrew into herself by looking aimlessly out the window.

Peter and Daria, visiting Atlanta for the first time, admired out loud the advancing skyline and lush green landscape from the back seat.

Minkowitz, worried, thanked God for the publicity void so far. Peter and Daria's running patter over the attractive Atlanta landscape aggravated Sam. He almost told them to "shut up back there with the fucking tree-cover-and-changing-skyline bullshit."

Okay, Sam. He calmed himself. *Get over it, take a deep breath, and communicate.*

"Carole, sweetheart," Sam quietly asked, "why did you take such a big risk today? You do realize that you could have ruined the bris."

"Sam, as you know, I've been cutting an album with Georgie Tyler, and he insisted I fly down to Atlanta to take advantage of some local musicians and sent a plane for me. I'm glad he did too because these musicians are all a joy to work with. Today, for example, I played with a Dixie-style horn section for two of the songs."

"'Sounds exciting, but you do realize that you risked ruining the bris for everyone."

"I understand, Sam, but Georgie's recording studio is in Doraville, a kind of blue-collar suburb only about five miles away from Allie's house."

"That was too convenient."

"Exactly, so when we took a break for a few hours, how could I pass up the chance to see how he lives, especially with the bris bringing together so many family members and dear friends?"

He thought; *I'm beginning to feel like Rose.*

He sighed deeply before describing plans for the evening. "I've arranged to get Allie out of the house tonight. He'll meet us in the Hilton Hotel that I rented you a suite in under the name of J. R. Jones. So what did you learn that was so important to risk a juicy headline?"

"I saw that Sarah's adorable and sweet, but I don't feel guilty because I sense we've been thrown together in a way."

"Sarah's a lovely woman, and Allie has a nice life with her, but I don't think it can compare with what you can offer him."

"You didn't mean to, Sam, but I think you helped me understand what's been nagging at me about Allie."

"What's that?"

"I'm his conduit or angel to help him achieve this great goal or mission, and I share it too. Unfortunately, starting a new family with me is probably not at all on Allie's radar."

"I'm not sure what you mean, Carole." He turned to look if Peter and Daria were listening; they weren't, so he continued. "Are you saying that all he needs from you is this mission, and once realized, he'll return home?"

"Maybe, whatever, he simply does not need me to replace this Atlanta part of his life. This is all the family he'll ever need, and he'll probably never leave them."

"So without a baby, the affair—excuse me, co-living will last a couple of years at most. Eventually, you'll get bored with a frozen relationship and throw him out."

Sam's prediction made Carole think about having even more frequent sex with Allie to get pregnant. Suddenly, she realized something. "You know, Sam, I'm hungry."

Peter and Daria heard Carole and spoke up. "Sam, we both ate only a little chopped liver at the bris, so we're hungry too. We vote for the Hilton's rooftop restaurant because people we know who regularly come to Atlanta on business have told us it's a must."

"Peter, its called Nikolai's Roof," said Sam, "obviously a Russian-themed gourmet restaurant, but I think that is a very bad idea. Let's instead order room service from Nikolai's and eat in my suite. Too many reporters are floating around, looking for an opportunity."

"Please, Sam," Daria and Peter protested. "No room service no matter how good."

Carole joined them, so Sam gave in. *I'm dealing with pampered people who hate limitations placed on them no matter how wise it may be to do so.*

They reached the massive blue-domed Hilton, where Sam took care of checking everyone in to their suites and contacted Nikolai's to make reservations. In his haste to escape the noise and confusion caused by dozens of guests checking out, he mistakenly gave his real name, along with reservations for five.

The Bobbin Show, Atlanta's biggest annual convention, was being held at the Georgia World Congress Center. Nikolai's, Atlanta's hottest restaurant with reservations needed weeks in advance, was booked solid.

The day before, the maître d' Terry Levy had read a review of *Dora* in *Newsweek* magazine, so he recognized Minkowitz's name. Levy bet the four who would join Sam would be Carole Herman and Allie Cohen, possibly Peter Bates and his girlfriend too.

437

Terry figured that a celebrity photographer would pay up to a thousand bucks to get near this new Hollywood-Atlanta rat pack. Nikolai's planned to fire Levy at the end of the week, so he decided to bolster his severance pay by penciling over the year-old reservations of Herb Baron of 3-B Textiles.

Levy cynically thanked Minkowitz and rang Art Tucker's phone. Tucker picked up the receiver and heard Terry's voice.

"All right, Terry, who is it, and how much do you want?"

Levy outraged Tucker. "The new Hollywood-Atlanta rat pack, so one thousand."

"Fuck, Terry, that's twice as much as I've ever paid before." He negotiated. "C'mon, I'll be lucky to get that much myself."

"Bullshit, Art." Levy scoffed. "You'll be able to sell this baby seven or eight times. Now if you're not interested, I'm sure Ed Waters is."

Fuck, Levy thought. *I have a reputation to protect and can't afford to let Waters scoop me, even if it means losing money on the deal.*

He gave in. "Okay, Terry, it's a deal, but don't forget to leave the keys to the side stairwell door as you did once before."

"I've already taken care of it, Art, and as a bonus, I'll throw in the use of my office a floor below to fax the photo. It locks too, so this is a sure thing."

"That's very helpful. Thank you."

"Be set up by 8:00 PM."

A half hour later, Herb Baron rang Nikolai's to reconfirm his reservations for that evening. His company, 3-B, had done very

438

little business at the show, and Baron needed to recoup some losses by wooing a large textile manufacturer that he'd coveted for years. Nikolai's, the hottest restaurant in the city, figured Herb should impress.

Levy picked up. Baron introduced himself. "Hello, Nikolai's Roof, Herb Baron of 3-B confirming tonight's reservations."

Terry's voice turned as cold as the icy, flavored vodka the restaurant was famous for. "I'm very sorry, Mr. Baron, but there must have been a miscommunication. It seems that your reservations are for tomorrow night. We look forward to seeing you then, sir."

"C'mon, those reservations were made a year ago and confirmed a month ago, and I'm reconfirming. The Bobbin Show is basically over today, and everyone big is out of here by tomorrow afternoon, and you know it. Hey, Nikolai, what the hell's going on here?"

"Mr. Baron." Levy's voice became as detached as a computer. "I will hang up if you don't lower your voice."

"Okay, I'll behave, I promise. Terry, please, there's two hundred bucks in this for you to make room for us."

"Mr. Baron." Terry employed his most condescending voice yet. "Even the most attractive of bribes cannot alter Nikolai's fair and firm reservations policy. Please, sir, the integrity of our reputation is at stake here."

Herb told him what he thought about the restaurant's reputation. "Fuck you, Nikolai."

Sam rented a limo for Allie to deliver him to the hotel by seven thirty. He walked across the atrium lobby and into one of the blue, neon-rimmed elevators that whisked him to the fifteenth floor.

Carole answered the door stark naked. He stepped in and closed the door, quickly undressed, and began kissing Carole's breasts and tonguing her nipples. She laughed lustily as they fell into bed and locked into a mission position.

Their lovemaking was as raw and wonderful as ever, and she exulted in her orgasm and then lit a joint while apologizing for her impulsive afternoon behavior.

"I'm sorry for possibly ruining Ari's bris. Thank god we've gotten away with it so far."

"It's cool, babe. There shouldn't be any problems. Let's finish the joint and take the elevator up to Nikolai's to meet Sam, Peter, and Daria."

Carole and Allie's giddiness telegraphed their being high.

Sam said, "You guys are irresponsible."

Peter and Daria commented, "You guys are selfish."

"I need to alter my consciousness quick," said Peter, taking charge. "Good, here comes a waiter." He ordered a round of double iced vodkas for everyone.

Lesotho and Eddie were celebrating too in the hotel's Sky-High Bar adjacent to Nikolai's. They completed their mural and treated themselves to a round of Chivas Regal. On their way out, they crossed paths with Peter and Daria headed for Nikolai's, and the cinema buff Xeranga asked for their autographs.

Allie and Carole arrived in front of Nikolai's entrance. Eddie recognized his old teacher.

Holy shit, that's Mr. Cohen. I'm not ready to talk to him yet. I'll turn my back toward him and pretend to be waiting for the elevator.

Cohen stared at White for a second. *Where have I seen this young man before?*

Sam called out to Allie and distracted him.

"Man," White whispered to himself, "that was close."

"Dude," Peter complimented Lesotho, "I love your dashiki. That's very cool."

Xeranga thanked him and then rapped for a few minutes about the expense of kente cloth, how he dug all their films, and how foxy Ms. Kelsey was. He walked over to Allie.

"Dr. Cohen, *The Lesson* is a must read, and I can't wait to see how they film that lampshade scene. That situation defined the word *gruesome* for me."

Levy informed the group their table was ready. Lesotho graciously excused himself; Cohen shook Xeranga's hand and thanked him. Upon being seated, flashes of the young man's face crept back into Allie's mind.

"You seemed distracted, Allie." Carole noticed. "Is anything wrong?"

"I swear that I've seen the big fellow somewhere before but can't remember where. Ah, forget it."

Terry Levy sat the group at a table that furnished a panoramic view of the dusky city right next to the stairwell. Outside, the city converted to its evening brilliance. Peter ordered a second round of iced vodkas while Sam stared at the exit suspiciously.

He felt a need to warn them. "People, I really don't like tables by stairwells. They're notorious setups for the paparazzi."

441

"Sam," begged Daria, "look how beautiful the view is. Now that's a gorgeous Georgia sunset, just like from *Gone with the Wind*."

"Sweetie, David Selznick shot that scene on a Hollywood back lot and sound stage."

"Okay, big deal. Sam, please don't be paranoid—for me."

Carole joined in. "Me too."

"I worry that I'm going to regret this, but okay, let's try to enjoy dinner."

Twenty feet away, Art Tucker loaded a high-speed, low-light film into his camera and adjusted the ASA. He crouched like a determined predator waiting to surprise his victims, who were blissfully consuming a delicious Ukrainian vegetable soup to be followed by tasty flaky meat piroshki.

The wine steward refilled their glasses with a mellow California Chardonnay. The sunset turned spectacular; a huge red sun hung over the skyline. The five friends shared a mutual joy and pleasure.

Carole joked with Allie that she was enjoying even Peter and Daria's company. Allie kept thinking, *All this and Ari too.*

Carole wondered if maybe she was rushing Allie too much and thought, *We do have the rest of our lives.*

Sam discussed projected grosses from *The Lesson* with Peter. Distributor demand was so great that they were striking 90/10 and 80/20 rental deals. The movie houses were left with making most of their money from refreshments.

Daria dreamed. *I think Peter is finally going to set a marriage date tonight.*

A photographer shattered their rapture by bursting in and hastily taking half a dozen pictures before they could react. Peter, the most scarred by these intrusions, leaped to tackle the cad but missed and tumbled into a loaded dessert cart.

Allie brushed off a fruit tart and chased after the SOB, who escaped down the stairwell and into Terry's office. Allie heard the door lock and was galled. He fruitlessly banged his fist against the door three times.

The posse gave up on their tormentor, who within minutes had sold the photo to a local TV station for $2,000. WALA's ratings strategy was to close on a positive note by exclusively airing a glitzy, happy news segment featuring celebrities. The next night, their affiliated stations across the country would air the photo.

"I'm so sorry for the intrusion," Levy, said, apologizing. "Please let Nikolai's Roof complement your dinners."

Cohen suspected collusion and charged Levy. "I think you're in cahoots with this fucking photographer. How come he was able to hide in your office? I'll bet he processed and faxed the photo from there, you evil fuck face."

"Allie," Sam urged, "back off. You have no proof. Let it go. My studio lawyers will handle this with the Hilton Corporate Office."

Autograph hounds lined up to worsen an already ruined meal. The four of them packed it in by retreating to their hotel rooms, Allie to Sandy Springs. Carole and Allie planned to meet up in LA in four days to pack for the Russia trip.

Sarah, meanwhile, felt happy for the first time since she began co-living with Carole. The big bris far exceeded her wildest expectations, and she actually had had a good time. She especially loved the $325,000 in checks she was planning to deposit the next day. She strolled into Ari's room to watch her first live child sleep.

Dear god, he's so adorable. I just know that he's going to be a great kid to raise and already have a nickname for him, Mookie. I'm beginning to believe Allie and his claim that our new reality has unlimited benefits.

She sat down on her bed and turned on the TV for the weather report and was a minute late. Her good mood was totally trashed when the newscaster read from the teleprompter,

"Atlanta, each day, increasingly becomes Hollywood South. Tonight Atlanta's own Allie Cohen accompanied movie star and songstress Carole Herman to Nikolai's Roof. Also having dinner with them were movie stars Peter Bates and Daria Kelsey and Global Pictures boss Sam Minkow—"

Sarah switched off the TV, took a Librax from a vial to soothe her stomach, and went down to the kitchen for some apple juice to wash it down. She calculated that about a quarter of a million Atlantans just watched her Allie romance a movie star in Atlanta on the day of his son's bris.

Sarah heard the limo depositing Allie at the side door and him fumbling with the key in the lock. Allie entered the kitchen and walked up to Sarah and tried to kiss her. She put up her hand to stop him.

"Where were you tonight? Tell me the truth."

"Let me guess. The photo has already been shown on TV."

"Yes, I just saw it. That was the end of my good mood from the bris."

"I understand how much that photo must have hurt you, and I'm sorry." A sense of guilt made him look away.

"And to think, Allie, I'd had hoped that this week might spark a healing, that this beautiful baby boy I've given you would

444

curb your selfishness. I was wrong. Chazer Cohen always has to have more."

"Sarah, I'm so sorry. I wish I could protect you from this media shit, but I don't know how. We were stalked tonight and set up for this."

Sarah put her hands on his cheeks. "Allie, I understand, and I also get it about the benefits. It would have taken us over four years of work to earn $325,000 between us."

She held up an envelope full of checks. "So go roam around the world with your angel, and get this mission thing out of you. I have to work through this in my own way. Spend the night here downstairs, and please leave in the morning to start your journey."

"Sarah, are you still planning to carry on my ethnic studies work?"

"Yes, Allie, and I'm starting to get used to this co-living thing too. I realize that my world has been expanded dramatically, and I plan to benefit in my own way. I'm trying, Allie, but you must accept that we, as a couple, are at risk."

"What do you mean?"

"It sounds to me like you're going to be roaming for three or four years. I can't promise you that that there won't be any consequences from being apart so much."

Allie hugged and kissed Sarah and then left the kitchen to sleep in the downstairs guest bedroom. Aretha slept on a cot in Ari's room that was next to Sarah in the master bedroom upstairs. Allie looked in on Ari one more time.

Aretha saw him. "Mr. Cohen, can you please give Ari his midnight feeding? I got to return an emergency call from my friend Tineja."

"Sure, Aretha, my pleasure."

She stuck her finger up under the Playtex feeder, drove out the air, handed Ari and the bottle to Allie, and sweetly said, "Now I'm going to leave you two men alone, but if you need me for anything, you just holler, and I'll come running. Okay, I gots to tell Tineja how to get rid of her baby's gas."

Allie plugged Ari's smile with the bottle's nipple, and he forcefully sucked half of it before requiring a couple of pats on the back to make him belch. Ari finished his feeding and, a second later, belched loudly and then had a bowel movement.

Ari's act was cute until he crapped right through his diaper and splattered Allie's pants too. Cohen placed his precious shit-covered son on the changing table, cleaned him up, and threw away the soiled Pamper. He then cleaned the crap from his jeans.

Ari immediately pissed into the air and showered Allie's arm with warm urine. Cohen cleaned this mess up too and looked Ari in the eye.

"Son, are you trying to tell me something I should know?"

Ari smiled at Allie and kicked his surprisingly strong legs in the air. Allie put his hands up against the tot's feet and encouraged Ari; "Okay, push hard with them."

Cohen's sturdy son managed to drive back his Dad's hand a bit. Allie choked up inside as he took an all-clean Ari in his arms. Cohen sat down in a Carolina rocker and cuddled his smiling baby boy. The feel of Ari's little hands clutching his shoulder caused tears of joy to roll down his cheeks.

For an instant, Allie wondered whose love he would miss more, Sarah's or Ari's. Allie spoke from the heart to his son.

"Ari, I love your mommy so much. She's a terrific mommy and very pretty and smart too. Now I want you to promise me that you'll be a good boy and a big help to your mommy."

Ari looked into Allie's eyes. *The kid's still smiling away at me. It's too bad that we have to have our first serious father-son talk.*

"Son," Allie told Ari, "I'll be leaving tomorrow. You see, I have to do very important work for the Lord, and it's going to keep me away a lot, but I promise to make it home as much as possible to be there for you."

Ari's smile weakened. "I'm sorry that I might miss a growth change or two."

Ari stopped smiling. "So please, little dude, promise me that you won't hold this against me someday. I love you so much and pray to the Lord that you'll love me just as much the next time you see me."

Ari whimpered and then softly cried. Allie patted and rocked him, but his crying grew louder. Allie sensed that this was not the cry of a child needing to be fed, belched, changed, or held. *No, this cry sounds emotional.*

Aretha ran into the room. "Mr. Cohen, what's wrong?" She took the infant into her arms to comfort him, but Ari continued to cry hard.

Aretha drew on her vast experience. "I can't tell if it's constipation or diarrhea. Whatever it is, he seems to be hurting, and I can't figure it out."

"Aretha," Allie reported, "Ari just belched twice, so it isn't gas. I also know it isn't constipation since he crapped all over me, nor was his stool loose enough to be diarrhea."

Aretha was mystified and declared, "Beats me. I'm stumped."

Allie paused before he gave his opinion. "Aretha, I think Ari is telling his old man that I have greatly disappointed him and really let him down big-time. He expects me to make this up to him too, and I will. 'You hear that, Ari? I promise you, son, that I will make this up to you and Mommy. I love you both and will never let you down if I can."

Ari stopped crying, smiled at his father, rolled on his side, and happily fell asleep.

Prophet, your father-son relationship has apparently bonded. Now begin your beholding.

Book 2

People, *Behold* the Prophet, Adonai's Einstein of Human Relations Research and His Teachings

My prophet does not walk on water, fly through the air, or hurl lightning and thunderbolts.

My prophet is the master teacher for showing the people how to come together and live in peace.

My blessings will cover all who embrace the prophet's message of love, friendship, and cooperation, and they will enjoy the fruits of prosperity and tranquility.

Darkness will fall on the people who fail to heed the prophet's light, and they will dwell in it until I, the Name that they dare not say, redeem them.

Chapter 66

What made me think that money and influence would eliminate the bullshit as usual part of life?

Cohen pondered that question as he sat on a chaise lounge by the pool staring out at the ocean, a smog alert and a smutty problem marring his beautiful seaside setting. The smog inflamed Allie's sinuses and caused a nasal drip that resulted in a cough. If that weren't bad enough, Sandy's porno flirtation was a total disaster waiting to happen.

Sandy Forman, making his first visit to Carole's Malibu property, got out of his rental car and scanned the property and vista for a few moments.

"Holy shit, now this is what I call a fucking beachfront paradise. My goodness, will you look at that gorgeous big house set in its own beautifully landscaped little canyon? *I'll bet this property is worth fifty million easy and might be the most expensive property in California, maybe the country. Not bad, Allie, from a Sandy Springs trilevel to California dreaming at its best."*

For the record, Carole paid twenty-five million for the only location on the coast inside the Pacific Coast Highway, where a three-sided private enclosure of low rocky hills came right up to the beach. David spent another five million on construction, decoration, and landscaping.

Sandy saw Allie sitting by the pool and sat down beside him.

"Allie, I've never experienced anything like this before in my life. I mean, this is the most perfect California setting and the worst smog I've ever seen out here. Talk about messing up heaven on earth."

Allie lobbied. "It's about time that Congress pass the new clean-air bill." He blew his nose twice.

Sandy, curious if their economic takeoff had changed them in any way yet, asked Allie, "You have become very rich, my friend, and in a relatively short period too. Are you any different yet?"

Allie thought for a few seconds before answering the question. "Sandy, money has given my words and deeds more credibility, but it's also made me a target of sorts." He asked Sandy the same question. "You've become pretty rich too, my friend. How has it changed you?"

Forman thought for a few seconds too. "Yes, I am much richer now, but I don't feel different at all yet."

"How come you don't, Sandy?" Allie asked, leading with a question to make his point.

Allie's using his Socratic teaching technique to lead me to a conclusion, thought Sandy. "Allie, please tell me what's on your mind and skip the damn questioning. This isn't Buckhead High, you know."

"I can't, Sandy. It's from being a social studies teacher for years, thinking on my feet, using the inquiring approach all the time. That's how I've come to work things out. So, Sandy, do you feel that you haven't changed that much because you still have to serve someone, namely, me?"

"All right, I guess so, yeah. Point please." Sandy smiled while employing the basketball time-out hand signal.

Allie smiled too at his gesture and then made his point. "And since you're not *famous* in your own right, Sandy"—he pointed at Forman with his index finger—"you don't have to serve as an *example* either, am I correct?"

"Well, I never thought of it in those terms, but I guess that's true." Forman was starting to grasp the tone and trend of the questions. "It's no secret that I have an independent streak just like you."

"Which might be realized by finding an even quicker, bigger, and easier score than the deals we're cooking, right?"

"Rick told you, didn't he?" He poured himself a glass of water from a pitcher.

"Both Rick *and* Sam did. Look, I understood the attraction to the porno business. I too flirted with the idea, but Sam is absolutely correct in demanding the business to be off-limits to us."

"I'm sorry, but it's just such a damn seductive way to make outrageous sums of money and literally overnight too."

"No apologies necessary. Just stay away from the porn business. Watch it all you want. Visit Rick's sets as often as you wish. Just don't invest in that market."

"All problems in life should be solved so easily, Allie."

"No more questions, I promise, and thank you too for all that you do for me, Sandy. You're the best at taking my dreams and ideas and turning them into physical and financial realities."

"Thank you, I appreciated hearing that."

They shook hands and slapped each other five, after which Sandy provided an update.

"Your sister, Carla, has called me twice to make sure that you're still bringing Carole to dinner. I told her that reservations were for 9:00 PM at Windows on the World. Carla and Joel will meet you at eight in the Eisenhower presidential suite, which I've reserved for you and Carole."

453

"Great, my sister is amazing, isn't she?"

"Yeah, even more high maintenance than you. Anyway, Ted Bell told me you're off to Moscow to meet with Mikhail Gorbachev, the new Soviet leader. The aim is to help thaw chilly relations a bit before nuclear arms reduction talks take place in Iceland. After that, you'll fly to South America for short tours of Chile, Argentina, and Brazil."

"Given Pinochet's current crackdown and state of siege," Allie cynically questioned, "how invisible am I expected to be?"

"Allie, Bell was quite clear on this point. Technically, the world shouldn't know that you even set foot in Chile. And if you behave yourself," Forman counseled, "the next stops are Egypt and Israel. My friend, there's a price to pay for everything in life, particularly when you represent the U.S. government abroad."

He surprised Sandy. "Hey, Carole and I are planning to go to this great little Argentine restaurant in Santa Monica tonight. How about joining us so you can finally meet her? She's in a rehearsal at the moment."

"I can't." Sandy smiled anxiously. "Uh, maybe another time, but thanks anyway."

"Oh." Allie played with him a bit. "That's too bad. How come?"

"I have a previous engagement," he said coyly.

"Really," probed Cohen, forcing the truth out of him. "And with whom, may I ask?"

Sandy cleared his throat and then hemmed and hawed for several seconds before coming clean. "Reny."

"Hey, Chazer." Allie laughed loudly and then advised, "Please make this your last indulgence because Riva is a great wife. What you're doing is certainly not kosher. Blame it on politicians, the press, and other lying creatures."

"I hear you loud and clear," said Sandy, a bit red-faced. "You know what, Allie, I'll cancel my date with Reny and join you and Carole for dinner after all."

"Wise move. I was just talking to Rick, who was busy shooting a scene from *Casting Couch Revolt IV*. Reny was doing a blow bang with three guys in the background, and they were taking turns coming in her mouth. That's the new porn requirement. Trust me, you're going to love this little Argentine restaurant."

I must say that Allie handled Sandy's porn flirtation very well. We all have to serve someone, but when you're *famous*, you also have to serve as an *example*. I like that proverb; it's very true, and I plan to use it as a quote some time myself.

Allie is famous, and yes, he also serves as an example, but at the end of the day, he serves Hashem, who has special rules and leniencies for the prophet.

Chapter 67

Carole intimated to Allie as they sat in the living room sipping tequila on the rocks and taking an occasional hit from a glass water bong.

"You know, Allie, David decorated this house without me, and I'm bothered that it reeks a little too much of him."

He clutched her hand. "I assure you, babe, that I am very content in what's probably the most beautiful home in LA, and frankly, David has fantastic taste."

He toked from the bong and poured another shot glass of tequila. Carole liked hearing that, smiled to show her appreciation, and then encouraged Allie to feel free to make some changes that fit his needs. She took a hit and shot of tequila too.

Cohen nudged her. "Sweetie, frankly, it's you who wants to remove remembrances of David and just need a good excuse to bring in a decorator and do a clean sweep. Frankly, I can't imagine what you'd want to get rid of. Everything's gorgeous and fits perfectly together in a beautiful art deco natural earth tone sort of way. I wouldn't touch a thing and don't know where you'd start."

She softly chuckled. "It's amazing how well you already understand me."

Allie and Carole spent an hour roaming the house, discussing possible renovation schemes that all made no sense to him given his lifetime history of middle-class furnishings. Regardless, the next day, Carole brought her decorator over to help identify what might stay or go.

Iris Pomeranz, a fast-talking decorator, saw a big commission to be earned and offered to rid the place of a lot more than Carole was ready to part with. Carole slept on it, decided to drop the project, and soon forgot about it.

"Babe," said Allie, expressing his feelings to her at dinner, "I just want to tell you how much I appreciate your making me a part of your life. Every day with you, sweetie, is a totally enriching experience."

Carole thanked Allie and then kidded and mugged at the same time about how it felt to be a big star who could now afford LA's expensive, good life of beautiful homes, fancy cars, and prized restaurant table places. She, an excellent mime, next pretended to smoke a big cigar and brazenly drop ashes on the floor.

They both laughed from her slapstick humor. "This is one star, Carole," Allie assured her, "who ain't lusting after the limelight so many others out here beg for. After the Art Tucker episode, my job is to keep my face out of the fucking newspapers and magazines as much as possible."

"I think that desire for privacy you described," Carole theorized, "is a big reason Los Angeles is basically a house culture. That's why the two of us regularly host dinner parties instead of going out to eat and drink all the time."

Their dinner party regulars included Global Books publisher Harland Cooper and his TV producer wife, Sylvia; screenwriter Bob Urban and his novelist spouse, Holly; Peter and Daria; and, of course, Rose and Sam. Bob and Allie cowrote the screenplays for *The Lesson* and *Déjà Vu Odyssey* and shared an enthusiasm for mountain-biking the nearby canyon trails or riding along the beach for miles.

Allie called Sarah nearly every day to catch up with Ari's latest development and, three or four times a month, flew in to spend two to three days with his family. Sarah and Allie regularly conferred on the advancement of the human relations research and joint projects that she was promoting and had overnight made her a major international education specialist and workshop facilitator.

457

Sarah bought a Polaroid and steadily faxed Allie pictures of Ari standing up in his crib smiling or his first time crawling on the floor or drinking from a cup. Sarah was making the co-living arrangement work, and Allie loved her more than ever for it.

Every time Allie left for Atlanta, Carole forced a goodbye smile. *I get it that to satisfy me in Malibu, he has to make things right in Atlanta. Still, I think I'm learning too well how to live with this arrangement.*

Sex with Sarah during the short fly-ins to spend time with her and Ari and advance the research was always an urgent catch-up. After a lovemaking session, Sarah asked him when and where she might join him during the world tour.

Allie pulled the itinerary out of his briefcase and scanned it for available dates.

"Money, these three days were set aside after visiting Argentina to be used for a quick flight back to the United States to take care of urgent business or take a short vacation to get ready for the tour of Brazil. I'll pull another day or two out for us to take some short trips. How about Patagonia? It's supposed to be beautiful."

"Buenos Aires, Patagonia, and Mar del Plata, their Atlantic seaside resort—that would be perfect for me. I'll work with Ted Bell to put an itinerary together for us."

Sarah, to fill the gaps when Allie was gone, took up with Lenny Meltzer, whom she always thought to be Allie's most attractive friend, and began meeting him one weekend a month in Washington. While jointly facilitating a workshop with S. K. Kapoor for 350 British teachers in London, two shared bottles of wine one night at dinner helped them cross over from colleagues to lovers, and they began meeting every other month in Bermuda for long weekends together.

Allie made it a daily practice to spend an hour in the recording studio with Carole and fell in love fooling around with an electric guitar, drums, a small tenor sax, and his trusty harmonica. In just a month of sessions, she taught him how to follow the metronome, read music a bit, and lay down tracks with her. His willingness to risk failure and humiliation in the recording studio influenced her.

"You know, Allie," she professed while sharing a joint and shots of Scotch with him after a studio session, "I've always wanted to dabble in acrylics, and I think it's time that I did. Maybe the two of us can jointly write a poem or song together too."

"That sounds good to me, babe."

During a late dinner the next evening, Carole asked Allie, "You seem to be adjusting to California life very well. Well, are there any negative aspects of life out here that stand out so far?"

He lamented. "People out here go to sleep way too early. East Coast people stay up much later. Our friends out here start leaving the dinner party at 9:00 PM so they can be home and asleep at ten. Then they're up at five or six, jogging or working out. The so-called healthy living can be terribly boring."

Cohen turned the question around to her. "So what negatives are you harboring, Carole?"

She laughed from it not being a big deal. "My sole irritant is that you occasionally leave the toilet seat up after urinating. I'm sure your mother and Sarah both got on your case about that."

Cohen, a bit red-faced, joked, "I've been taking vitamin E, and all the capsules accidentally fell into the toilet last week. Since then, I haven't been able to get the toilet seat to go down."

Before the coming of Viagra, vitamin E was believed helpful for sexual dysfunction.

Cohen carved out some personal space twice a week by meeting Rick for racquetball. Samuels usually flailed away at an array of low passing shots and received taunts from Allie for his efforts. One day after Allie beat him 21–7 and 21–5, Rick quit the game.

"Cohen, the truth is I hate fucking racquetball and your goddamn put-downs even more. I'm done with this stupid claustrophobic sport."

"You know what your problem is, Rick?" Allie asked with a smirk and then cracked up.

"No, but I have a feeling that you're going to tell me anyway, and what's so fucking funny that you're already laughing?"

Cohen kibitzed in between howls. "The only exercise you ever get is to hump a fuck queen or open the refrigerator door."

"Look, Allie, I'm really tired of all the fat jokes, and now you're into fuck queen jokes a lot too. Please stop it."

Allie playfully stuck a finger into Rick's soft abdomen and teased, "I'm not joking, Pillsbury Doughboy. You've also been bellying up to the bar a bit too much."

Rick had had enough and fought back. "Okay, so I'm a little overweight. Now if you'd like to play some golf for a thousand bucks a hole, let's go, and bring lots of cash too."

Rick suspected something. *Something is eating at Allie.*

He asked, "What's the matter, Allie? Why are you so fucking mean today?"

"Ah, I have to go on Johnny Carson's show tonight and hate being held back until the last seven minutes when 90 percent of the audience has already fallen asleep."

Rick kidded, "That's why they call it the 'old author plugging his book' spot."

Cohen mockingly spoofed Ed McMahon. "Annnnddd heeerrre'ss Alllllliiiieeeee."

"Stop bitching, Cohen. Just don't do it."

"It's not that easy, Rick. I've been putting it off all week but finally caved in when even Peter Bates scolded me for not doing my part to promote the book and movie. Hey, are you going to watch your old buddy plug his new book tonight on national TV?"

"Nah, I'll probably be asleep by then. Besides, who the fuck reads anymore?"

Chapter 68

Allie waited in the famous green room with July Tam, a stacked starlet, and Bill Burson, a worn comic who smoked a joint to prop up his third comeback. July, a curvaceous brunette, wore a sheer, semi-see-through blouse and a tiny miniskirt. Allie observed her staring in the mirror, studying how to best enter the stage and optimize jiggling breasts.

"Ms. Tam," Cohen joked with July, "trust me, you are going to inspire a giant animalistic chorus of howls and whistles from every oversexed jackal from Iowa, Kansas, Missouri, or wherever."

She smiled gratefully at Allie, who thought, *How the fuck am I going to push a Holocaust novel after her voluptuous tits and ass?*

Allie shared a feeling with Bill. "Since there's only the three of us, Bill, I think Johnny may do a Carnac the Magnificent–type sketch. What do you think?"

"I doubt it, Allie, because the producer told me of some big surprise guest at the end. Hey, do you want a toke?"

"Thanks, Bill, but I prefer to be clearheaded before fifteen million viewers. You're on soon, man. Good luck to you."

"Thanks, Allie."

Bill offered July a toke before pushing through the curtain. July's ultralungs blew the sizable roach off in single toke, smiled, and then asked Allie if she looked all right.

"Honey," he reassured her, "this crowd has come all the way from Omaha and Sioux City just to see you walk to your seat."

She liked hearing that and smiled cutely but still considered going further. "Are you sure, Allie? Perhaps I should open two more buttons, maybe raise my skirt a little bit more."

July opened two more buttons, and her cleavage immediately challenged a last brave button, and then she hiked her skirt about an inch.

"I think, July," Allie hinted, "you may have crossed the line because I can see halfway to Honolulu and the NBC censor from here."

July laughed heartily; her adjustments naturally proved to be a smash hit with the mostly midwestern audience.

The producer summoned Allie much earlier than Cohen expected, and he experienced difficulty finding his way through the curtains and had time to think. *It's strange that Carson is devoting twice as much time to the author than the huge tits. Maybe Bill was right about a big surprise at the end. Hmm, I wonder what or who is going to follow me.*

The producer conspired with Carole to surprise Allie by showing up in the last segment. The premise was for her to sing a pair of songs and hype his book and upcoming movie and the world tour for President Reagan because Sam lacked confidence in Cohen to effectively promote his own product.

Allie found his way through the curtain and received a little more applause than a consumer advocate but probably less than what Ralph Nader might get. He customarily shook hands with Johnny, Ed McMahon, orchestra leader Doc Severinsen, and Bill Burson.

July Tam gave Allie a gyrating hug, and she faced the camera and bragged, "Allie's an old friend."

Cohen looked at the camera and then the audience while clarifying, "For the record, we just met in the green room."

Carson introduced Cohen to the audience by talking to him. "Allie, you've really burst onto the scene. Your novel, *The Lesson*, is a best seller, and with all the other things you're now into, well, the money must really be rolling in."

Carson seemed friendly enough, but Cohen was uncomfortable with Johnny summarizing his so-called sudden rise to fame and wealth, more so when Johnny rolled his fingers like he was counting a pile of money, and the crowd laughed harder. Allie hoped to discuss his book but humbly tolerated a short diversion.

Carson harped. "It seems, Allie, that every time I pick up a trade paper, Global is announcing another project with you. I understand that the movie's a guaranteed hit and that there's a whole chain of restaurants opening. Well, with today's grosses, if that's not big bucks, then I'm not wearing a Johnny Carson suit."

Carson's frank joke about his men's clothing line made the audience roar with laughter, and the gifted clown milked the line for every last chortle. Cohen risked Carson's displeasure by topping the host with a zapper.

"From those polyester threads, Johnny, you'd never know it."

The audience roared even louder, the crack stunning Carson, but the audience was rocking with heavy laughter. *The audience likes me*, Cohen thought. *And if you're a hit with the audience, Johnny will probably let me get away with that put-down of a line.*

Carson did and typically came back with "Hey, these threads aren't so cheap. You won't believe what I make on each one."

Carson rolled his fingers in a money-counting way again to keep the audience laughing, a classic case of one-upmanship. That was why his salary was $18 million a year, and he had a line of suits named after him.

Man. Allie sighed. *I'm not on the show to do seven minutes of one-liners and shtick. I'm on camera to promote a Holocaust novel and a political goodwill tour, and time is running out.*

Allie imagined Holocaust survivor Seymour Umansky, *The Lesson*'s main character, teaming with Bill Burson to play the Carson show.

"We just flew in from Auschwitz, and are our arms tired?"

"Oy vey, did you see the Nazi's gas bill?"

"Guard, take our wives instead, please!"

"Concentration camp food is so bad."

The audience yelled back, "How bad is it?"

"It's so bad that we all ask to go out for Chinese."

Allie faded back to reality. Carson was still fixated on the same topic.

"Allie, if the movie is as big as the book, you certainly won't have to teach school again. That is what you did before your novel became a best seller, isn't it?"

Frustrated, Allie stoically worked the novel's theme into his response. After about six seconds of plot and character description, Carson received a signal from his producer to interrupt Cohen.

"Allie, I'm sorry to cut you off like this, but I'm sure that most of our listeners are aware of your being romantically linked with movie star Carole Herman."

That was the cue for Carole to appear from behind the curtains, a schmaltzy scene that viewing audiences loved. The crowd shrieked in the same way they did for showbiz giants such as Bob Hope, Lucille Ball, or George Burns when they did it. The legends of the entertainment world would stroll in unannounced, lending an impromptu air to a tired format. Carole, like all great acts, could get away with overtly plugging her product and be loved for it too.

Allie expected *The Tonight Show* to indulge in light chitchat rather than heavy intellectual discourse. Tonight, though, was a new low for the Carson show for, in seven minutes, Cohen said maybe nineteen words about the book and tour.

Carole sang six minutes of material from her new album and finished any further discussion. She had a fine voice as usual, but Allie stewed in his gut from the Carson show's misplaced priorities.

Carole finished singing, and Allie walked over to put his right arm around her waist. She lovingly kissed him on the cheek and put her left arm around his waist, and both stared into the camera.

Carole tried to speak over the audience's sustained applause. "This week, Allie and I will be flying to Moscow for—"

The show ran overtime, the director cut her off, and the red light dimmed. Allie looked at the monitor; the Ty-D-Bol Man praised sweet-smelling toilets.

"Holy shit, now we know which message rules the TV medium."

466

Rebecca and Harvey Kartzman and Janet Kamensky watched Allie's interview and Carole's performance and were unable to fall asleep for hours. Sarah watched with Lenny Meltzer at his place, and both sensed Allie's frustration and felt sorry for him.

During the ride home from the studio, Allie continued to boil inside from the network's interruption and impulsively suggested they move up their departure. "Babe, I can't wait to get out of LA for a while, so why not move our New York flight up a day? After the fucking Carson show disaster, the Ukraine is starting to look pretty damn good to me."

The reference to *A Day in Hollywood / A Night in the Ukraine*, a modestly successful Broadway musical from 1979 to 1980, has become a running joke for Allie, Mike Schwartz, Carole, and other friends.

Chapter 69

Carole and Allie flew to New York and were installed in the Waldorf Astoria's Eisenhower presidential suite. She initiated lovemaking, and afterward, both napped for a few hours before dressing for dinner. Carole put on her makeup in the palatial bathroom and spoke to Allie while applying lipstick.

"I'm excited to finally meet your sister, Carla."

Allie responded as Carole placed her lipstick on the pink Italian marble basin and picked up an eyeliner pencil.

"Carla and I are close now, though there were times when there were strains between us. I'm sure the excitement factor for Carla is ten times higher than for you, and tonight should become her peak life experience."

"What was it before?" She put the eyeliner down and looked at him.

"A few years ago, Steve McQueen and Rock Hudson accidentally spilled wine on her in a small Greenwich Village restaurant. The best part for Carla was when they both politely tried to wipe it off."

"Ha ha! I think I am going to like your sister. You know, he he, I always found it amazing how McQueen and Hudson"—more laughter from her—"two very different men I assure you, were such good friends. What's Carla like?"

Carole asked while fitting her long black silk dress over her head. "Is she anything like you?"

"You won't believe how different we are," Allie answered with a broad grin. "My mother has spent her life trying to figure out how Carla wound up in our family."

"Why?" She put on her shoes.

"Carla's a walking specimen of contradictions. For example, she's the nicest clothes-and-jewelry freak in the whole world."

Carole fastened a turquoise necklace around her neck and wore four rings, a rare blue diamond, a perfect huge ruby, a sparkling deep green emerald, and an exquisite sapphire all in a variety of beautiful settings.

"And you, Allie, could give two shits about clothes and jewelry."

"Exactly, Carole. I'm probably more like my parents though, to be fair to Carla, I can be excessive in my own way, and this has traditionally been the main source of tension between us."

Carla Kamensky, downstairs in the lobby, sat on an uncomfortable gray sofa alongside Joel, her nervous but normally calm husband. She fidgeted with her diamond earrings and adjusted the belt of her exotic black culottes with matching mesh top. Her continual tugs reminded Joel to pull down the vest of his three-piece white suit and to pull up his white socks sagging toward white Gucci loafers.

"Mrs. Kamensky," Adonai could have told Carla, "you and Joel are easily the most attractive and best dressed couple in the whole Waldorf lobby. Trust your Creator."

"Sorry, Lord, and thank you," she would have told the Almighty. "But I'm having trouble believing that tonight."

"Joel," she complained, "what's keeping them?"

"Nothing, honey, your screaming at me to hurry made us a half hour early."

"I was afraid of traffic."

"That's a rationalization." He scoffed. "You were afraid of missing this dinner with your favorite singer and movie star."

"It's true. I'm dying inside. Let's go home. I don't want to make a fool of myself."

"Relax, I bet Carole will love you. After all, she hooked up with your brother, so she has to be a down-to-earth person. Christ, I hope he knew enough not to wear jeans. Even our sons ask him why he always wears jeans."

"I tell you, Joel, the world is nuts." She sighed. "Carole Herman dropped that gorgeous hunk David Conte for my little brother."

"I figure she must have fallen in love with his brain. Even I finally accept his being an extremely smart fellow. Seriously, look how goddamned rich he's become after all those years of voluntary poverty as a teacher." He tugged at his vest.

"Joel, I could handle his being so smart when we were growing up." She reminisced. "It was that noble streak in him that almost drove me nuts. It's funny. Now that he's become everything I ever wanted in a brother, I almost miss the old Allie." She crossed her legs.

"You do?" said Joel incredulously. "Not me, there was always a subtle tension that we had so much more, and he made me feel like a bourgeois pig for it too."

"Ha ha ha! I know what you mean, but now the shoe is on the other foot, and I don't like it. Shit, where are they? Uh-oh, I think I recall his business manager telling us to meet them in their suite. Please give them a ring to find out."

Joel got up to use the hotel phone to call Allie and returned a minute later. "We *were* supposed to meet them in their suite, but they're ready and will be down very soon."

"Christ, I see them exiting the elevator. They're walking toward us. Oh dear."

Allie held Carole's hand while introducing her. Carole warmly kissed Carla's cheek and then Joel's. "Carla, I had no idea how beautiful you are. And, Joel, you're a handsome dude."

They loved hearing that, relaxed, and smiled radiantly. Allie also wore a three-piece white suit with white Gucci loafers and teased Joel,

"Hey, man, with these three-piece white suits and Gucci loafers, let's flag an uptown cab and work the Apollo Theater tonight. What do you say?" Allie's icebreaker of a joke worked nicely.

Carla noticed something. *I think I'm more stylishly dressed than one of the world's most glamorous women. Her rings are so incredibly tasteful and must cost hundreds of thousands of dollars. In comparison, I feel like I'm wearing four tropical fruits on my fingers. Funny, if I didn't know better, in some ways, I'd swear that I'm out with Sarah and Allie.*

Carla's heart skipped a beat when Carole said that Allie had told her so much about his beloved sister. Allie took charge by hailing a cab to take them downtown to the World Trade Center and Windows on the World, New York's showcase restaurant. A half hour later, the foursome was seated near a huge window that revealed a billion lights a thousand feet below.

Their first bottle of wine arrived, and Allie called for a toast. "To *family* and *friendship* and *love*, the three pillars of life."

"That was a perfect toast," Joel seconded.

471

At that moment, a UPI reporter snapped a picture that was printed in over five hundred newspapers. The next day, teeth were grinding away in Atlanta and Westfield, New Jersey. Carla obtained a negative from the source and had it blown up, printed, framed, and exhibited on her living room wall.

Carla bombarded Carole with questions concerning Hollywood, the tour, the scripts she was considering, her new album coming out, and so on. Each time, Carole politely smiled, gave a short answer, and then changed the subject back to picking Carla's brain about her and Allie's childhood.

Cohen refilled everyone's wineglass, and after a couple of more sips, Allie expected Carla to become nostalgic. She was right on schedule.

"We were divided, Carole, by our parents. Allie was considered the good child, so naturally, I resented him at times. This tension continued well into adulthood, but now we accept each other completely. Indeed, I feel that we've never been closer."

Carole asked Carla a personal question. "What was your dad like, and what do you remember most of him?"

"My dad spoiled me rotten. He was not a big gambler but loved the track and played in a weekly poker game with a group of deli owners and furriers. He was also an elegant man who dressed very sharply. Women were crazy about him."

That word picture, Carole thought, *differs a bit from Allie's description of his dad as a successful small businessman and devoted husband and father who had trouble satisfying a demanding daughter.*

"Our mother, in comparison," Carla began a less romantic description of Janet, "was the practical one. After our father died, she always appealed to Allie's good nature and turned him against me to help her."

Hmm. Carole contrasted. *Allie said that Carla's unrealistic demands forced him to side with his mother for the family welfare.*

"Carla," Allie provocatively stated, "it's always been my impression that you would have preferred that Mommy die instead of Daddy."

Carla choked a bit on that statement, paused, took a sip of wine, and then dragged on her last Marlboro cigarette.

She declared, "I'm quitting smoking tomorrow. This is a disgusting habit, and advertising made me think it was glamorous."

She did quit but finally admitted, "I can't quite bring myself to say that I agree, Allie, but Daddy did have more style and was surely a hell of a lot more fun."

"And he made a hell of a lot more money too. Daddy could provide most of what you wanted. Mommy couldn't come close to that. This conflict carried over into our adult lives, but we've overcome it because we've succeeded in obtaining most of what we both want, so all is resolved."

Joel usually stayed out of Carla and Allie's outpourings but, for a change, decided to offer his own view.

"Carole, since you've hooked up with my wife's crazy brother, please let a less biased member of the family express himself."

"Sure, go right ahead, Joel."

"My wife is a fantastically vital woman who is a thrill to go through life with, but—"

"But what?" Carla interrupted. "Up until that *but* part, you were doing great."

473

Joel grinned. Carole and Allie laughed. "My wife lives in an elegant cocoon and is not fully aware of what I go through in the real world to provide her with the unreal world she prefers. Frankly, Allie is more like Carla than he thinks."

Cohen squinted. "What?"

Joel smiled and then made his case. "Allie has never worked a seven-to-eleven day doing hard work with his hands, yet big bucks were supposed to come to him despite working to three thirty and going home to read *Newsweek*. He lives in his own liberal cocoon."

"Excuse me." Allie challenged that simplistic description of him. "You're not taking into account homework that had to be checked; tests graded; new curriculum, lessons, and exams designed and constructed; letters to be written; and phone calls to be made and much, much more."

Joel again smiled and continued. "Carla has always wanted to be rich and might have done it all by herself in the business world, but she quit and instead married me and raised our kids. Conversely, Allie spurned wealth and was going to make the world perfect or at least better."

"Yeah, remember that." Allie sighed.

"So what the hell have you changed, Allie?" Joel put to him. "You're one thousand feet above the ground and can see fifty miles in every direction. Name one thing that's better out there."

"That's pretty heavy, Joel."

"Damn right, it is. Hey, remember when you were against the war in Vietnam? Well, look at what those cruel Marxist fuckers did to Saigon, Laos, and Cambodia despite Jane Fonda telling you that those Marxist maniacs were liberal Democrats. Are you still so proud of your relentless protesting?"

"Joel, the luxury of hindsight doesn't make what we did wrong." Cohen reasoned with him. "It was still a stupid war to blow the national treasury on and forever defer the Great Society and a chance to end poverty."

"Great Society and end poverty, my ass. The government pissed away a lot of your hard-earned cash and still does, right?"

"Well, I guess some of it is pissed away in protecting tobacco companies, Reagan tax cuts for billionaires, and stupid Pentagon weapons programs."

All laughed, even Republican Joel who was not through with Allie. "Christ, Allie, you spent four years at a one of the best business schools in New York City majoring in the liberal arts. Fuck, liberal arts!"

"You're assuming options, Joel," Cohen reminded him, "that *I* didn't have."

"Bull, look out that window." He pointed west. "Over there is Newark. You spent three years there teaching while the greatest bull market in history raged. You could have made a fortune in the stock market instead or worked for a Wall Street bond house. The bond market is even bigger than stocks, but no, you toiled for ghetto kids who are probably in jail by now."

"You're wrong, Joel. The time spent in Newark was a great education, and if I hadn't taught, I'd have been drafted and possibly killed in 'Nam. Hey, that ghetto kid crack crossed the line."

"Okay, I'll give you that. But admit it, Allie, you were conned. Look around you. Newark is in ruins, and the country is being ripped off by the rich like never before. Face it, you can't save shit."

"Sorry, Joel, I prefer optimism over total surrender of hope."

"Give me a break. The system used your services dirt cheap. Reagan will tell you himself. You have to look out for number one."

The frankness of the conversation amazed Carole. Carla noticed. "Does your family ever behave this way?"

"Never, Carla, and I'm not sure why either."

"This one is almost as wild as the time when Allie was twenty-two and got everyone in my dinner party stoned on pot. My cousin Teddy started to get rushes from the pot and thought he was having heart palpitations. His wife, Mandy, started crying about anti-Semitism she experienced as a child growing up in Staten Island."

Carole laughed. "Carla, your family is something else. Mine gets along okay, though my sister and I live in such different worlds that it tends to make us strangers and a bit formal. As the older one and in show business too, I guess it's up to me to try harder to close the gap between us. If you ask me, your family may try too hard."

Joel started in on Allie again. "Look down on the Lower East Side over there." He pointed east. "Is it better or worse since Allie Cohen taught there?"

"Possibly better, Joel, maybe worse, but who really knows?"

"You see, Allie, it's up to people to help themselves. Just because you care doesn't mean that junkies and bums plan to change their ways, and I sure as hell ain't paying more taxes so they can get high and screw in the afternoon. I'll bet you don't really like people that much, especially the poor."

"Maybe, Joel, but I haven't fully sold out yet."

476

"Too bad, I was just about to declare you a mensch who'd finally grown up. I think Reagan has been one of the best presidents in my lifetime. God, did I hate Jimmy Carter and that stupid grin of his."

"Joel, you'd really love Reagan," Allie teased, "if he let you print money to cover your deficits just like him and the U.S. government."

Everyone laughed, including Joel. "Besides, there's more to life than just pocketbook issues. For example, Carla, I'll bet you were excited by Geraldine Ferraro's place on the ticket."

Carla did not share her brother's enthusiasm. "I voted for Gary Hart and his new ideas in the primaries, brother, but I voted for Reagan in the general election because I couldn't stand mush-breath Mondale that much."

Allie brushed it off after Carla toasted him. "Allie, it's my opinion that you already deserve minor saint status. The question left is, will you leave the planet as a major saint? I'm beginning to believe that you have a fighting chance."

"Allie," Carole joshed, "we're all going to have to work very hard for your sainthood."

Allie stopped laughing and made it clear. "A selfless type like Mother Teresa, who fed the starving masses of Calcutta—she's a saint. At best, I'm a slum alley saint whose depraved past will be lucky to make it past the pearly gates."

"I used to think," Joel kidded, "that maybe you ate a little too much acid during the late sixties and that you possibly fried your brain. I'm starting to believe that you have a kind of *fine madness*. Now whether that qualifies you for sainthood, I don't know."

"Joel," Carole corrected, "I think you mean the *fanatical edge* rather than fine madness."

"The fanatical edge, yeah, I like that."

Carla called for another toast. "I vote for slum alley saint. 'Sure sounds like a lot more fun to me."

Who votes for *prophet*?

Angel's note: Fifteen years later, on September 11, 2001, Windows on the World—the planet's highest-grossing restaurant at $60 million a year—was destroyed by al-Qaeda and Osama bin Laden in the hijacked airliner attacks on the World Trade Center's twin towers. Harvey Kartzman frequently called the restaurant the greatest of its time.

Chapter 70

George Feifer, the famed Sovietologist, accused the USSR of suffering from a *lack of tolerance in its political affairs* and *honesty in its assessment of its problems.* Allie's great-grandfather Anatoly Kamenev said the same thing in fewer and less elegant words: "Never trust the Russians."

Anatoly was Grandma Pearl Cohen's father; she was five years old when the family was deported from Russia. Barney told Allie the story during a delivery to the Stuyvesant fish and dairy store when he was also five years old.

"Your great-grandfather Anatoly ran a successful caviar company in Minsk, Belarus. He got greedy one day and put on his jars phony labels with the czar's official endorsement. 'Service to the family Romanov' or something like that."

"No kidding, Dad?" Allie was fascinated. "Did Great-Grandpa Anatoly get away with it?"

"No, he didn't, and my grandpa never got within five hundred miles of the czar either. His deportation started—he told me the story when I was a little boy about your age too—when he turned down a galoot's request for a pay raise, and the no-goodnik snitched to the authorities that Anatoly substituted regular roe for the highest grade. That's how he talked. He liked to use words like *galoot* or *no-goodnik* a lot and make people laugh."

Allie laughed. "What happened, Dad?" He had never heard this family story before.

"The Russians deported the family to America, and Anatoly was lucky this happened before the Communists took over. Lenin might have done a lot worse to your great-grandfather. Stalin, forget it."

"Dad, how did Grandma Pearl's family wind up in Newark?" Allie was glued to his dad's every word.

"The Kamenev family landed on Orchard Street in the Lower East Side. Supposedly, the Hebrew Immigrant Aid Society helped them move to Newark, where Anatoly opened up a dairy store featuring smoked fishes, creamy salads, and a variety of pickles like this one and did okay."

"How did Grandpa Alvin and Grandma meet?"

"Your mother," said Barney, "told me yesterday that you're always asking her questions about the family. Anyway, one day your grandpa Alvin, who was a good-looking guy, met your grandma Pearl in the park. Six months later, she brought him home to meet her parents, and they got married."

Barney did not tell Allie the rest of the story because Janet forbade it. He instead began discussing the New York Yankees' chances of winning the World Series.

"Hey, this is Joe DiMaggio's last year, and this new rookie Mickey Mantle is supposed to be his replacement in center field. I know that you have their baseball cards, so what do you think, Allie?"

What Allie did not hear was what Anatoly really told Alvin: "You lousy shegetz, get the hell out of my house, and go get lost. For generations, our family has suffered pogroms, beatings, and worse for just being Jewish."

Shegetz means "male gentile"; *shiksa* is the female equivalent.

"Please, Mr. Kamenev."

"I'll be frank, Alvin," warned Anatoly. "I'm not ready to give my beautiful daughter to the goyim, and there'd be one less

Jew in the world. Sorry for putting it that way, but that's how I feel."

Alvin returned a week later to beg Anatoly for Pearl's hand and promised to her father. "Mr. Kamenev, I want to convert to Judaism and raise our children Jewish. I love Pearl that much. Please, sir."

"I'm impressed, Alvin," admitted Anatoly, who had one more test. "So you love my beautiful daughter that much to win her hand. Okay, how about one more proof of love for my darling Pearl?"

"Sure, whatever you say, Mr. Kamenev."

"Are you circumcised?" Anatoly smiled knowingly while staring hard at Alvin, whose breath began slowing and his knees swaying.

"No, Mr. Kamenev, I'm not." Alvin looked down at his feet.

"Alvin," declared Anatoly in a raised but even voice, "an uncircumcised man will not enter my daughter. However, I know a mohel who can do this for you. Officially joining the tribe will earn you my beautiful Pearl. That kind of sacrifice shows me a lot about what kind of man you are. So, Alvin, what's it going to be?"

Alvin shuddered at the thought of trimming back his private part at age twenty-four but decided he loved Pearl enough to do it. "Yes, Mr. Kamenev." Alvin promised before the Lord, "I will become a Jew."

It was hard to say how Jewish Alvin became. Barney's stories of his difficult childhood shaped Janet's perception of her father-in-law as a hard Protestant type to the day he died. Regardless, Alvin did produce two fine sons, Barney and David, two years apart.

Barney earned a night school degree and married Janet, his depression bride. They built a good life by following the prescribed five-year plan for couples starting out with nothing—having children five years apart, buying a house five years later—but that was all they had in common with the Soviet Union during the twin emergencies of the 1930s and 1940s.

The Russian people endured awful suffering during Stalin's purges and show trials; millions of citizens disappeared. Tens of millions more died during the 1941–1945 Nazi invasion and the Soviet fight for survival.

Allie flashed a memory on his Russian roots as security agents of Moscow's Sheremetyevo Airport searched his luggage for contraband, which was anything the Soviet government said it was. *You commie bastards,* he mused, *won't find any phony caviar in my suitcase, but I sure hope you miss those joints stashed in Carole's sanitary napkin holder.*

Cohen put one over on the Russians and was soon signing the desk pad of the drab and musty Europa Hotel. Carole put her arm through his, and the bellhop led them to their suite, a large but depressingly drab and airless place. The bellhop held out his hand, so Allie dropped 2.00 rubles, valued politically at 1.62 per dollar, into the Cossack's palm.

"Doesn't Marxist dogma," Cohen wondered out loud to Carole, "proclaim tipping to be a capitalist crime? I guess this dude needs a winter semester at a Siberian reeducation camp."

Carole cracked up and then fell into Allie's arms, and they kissed hungrily. Seconds later, they tried out their Soviet-made bed for lovemaking—it worked well enough.

The American delegation's itinerary listed a visit to a statue honoring the fortieth anniversary and the twenty million dead of the Great Patriotic War, a.k.a. World War II. Later that evening, Carole and Allie were to be feted at a banquet with the newly installed and ambitious Soviet leader, Mikhail Gorbachev. *You can bet, when my tough questions start flying, I intend to have a good last laugh at the Russian's expense, and ol' Anatoly's going to be smiling from the grave.*

Carole's great-grandparents were also from Russia—Smolensk, a small city in the western part. Eighty-five years before, the czar's secret police instigated a pogrom against the Jews of that town. The Hermansky family got away a few days before the town's Christians massacred half the Jewish community. After the massacre, the Christians returned to their serfdom, poverty, ignorance, and vodka but felt better from killing a few hundred Jews.

The Hermansky family, like so many others at the turn of the century, settled in the Ocean Hill section of Brooklyn. Eight decades later, their internationally famous granddaughter returned to entertain their oppressors.

"Man, Allie," Carole commented, "this room sure is gloomy."

"And bugged too, babe," he whispered into her ear. "And I don't mean *roaches* either."

"Allie, are you saying that we better watch what we say to each other?"

"Yes, sweetie, that is, unless you like show trials with zero Nielsen ratings."

Carole bent over with laughter and sat down on a lumpy green sofa and related how, fifteen years before, she'd met Bob Hope at a Palm Springs party.

"I remember asking Bob right after he'd returned from making a TV special in the Soviet Union how his trip had gone. He typically wisecracked. 'Great. We came back.'"

Allie laughed and then asked Carole if she wanted to get high. "You bet. That's the only way I'm going to get through a memorial to twenty million dead people. Christ, I can see that Russia's not an especially up place to visit."

"In all fairness, babe, we are on a peace mission. Therefore, paying tribute to Hitler's slaughtering twenty million Russians is appropriate."

"I don't know, Allie, maybe you're right. Tell me, are those tough-looking guys hanging around the lobby in their ill-fitting suits and raincoats KGB men?"

He confirmed her suspicion. "This is the hotel for foreigners, so they are probably all KGB agents keeping an eye on us and any other visitors staying here."

"What should I do if a KGB man stops and questions me?"

After finishing the joint and feeling nicely stoned, Cohen borrowed a line from Mothers of Invention band leader Frank Zappa.

"Tell him that you're a *dental floss farmer from Montana studying collective agriculture.* That will keep them busy for a while trying to figure that out."

Boris, their friendly aide and interpreter, drove his anesthetized charges over to Red Square and let them out in front of the perpetually lit flame several feet from the Kremlin's foreboding walls, where a small party of politburo members, military leaders, and state historians were already in attendance. The ceremony was mercifully short and sweet, and afterward, Carole surprised everyone by commemorating the solemn occasion with a ceremonial song. Her hosts smiled and enthusiastically clapped their hands in appreciation.

"What song," Cohen questioned, "are you planning to sing, babe?"

"I want to bring truth to the Russians in a sweet manner, so I am going to sing Eric Andersen's famous profreedom folk song 'Thirsty Boots.'"

"Great choice, babe, I love that old folk melody but have to warn you that this may be pushing the envelope."

"Exactly, and that is why we're here, Allie, for this is what we've dreamed about, our being bold and brave."

She's right. Let me think fast. He nervously snapped his finger. "Okay, Boris, please tell everyone that Carole wishes to sing a glorious antifascist melody."

Carole's heavenly voice and the hopeful 1960s folk song touched old feelings in Allie, and he thought back to when he was in college. *Man, she's singing it just like I heard Andersen do it at the Village Gate.*

"So take off your thirsty boots,

and stay for a while.

Your feet are hot and weary from a dusty mile.

And maybe I can make you laugh.

And maybe I can try just looking for the evening and the morning in your eyes."

Allie anxiously scanned the Russians' deeply appreciative faces while Carole sang the second stanza, which called for the Russian people to rise against the Communist system and force its collapse. *Thank the lord for only warm, happy applause. 'Got to salute her instincts. Carole called for the Gulag to crumble, and the Soviets thought she was putting down the Nazis.*

Allie kissed Carole on the cheek. "I'll bet, Carole," Cohen predicted, "Reagan falls out of his seat laughing when he hears this story. Sweetie, if only your beautiful singing voice could melt these monsters' Iron Curtain hearts, now that would be a real miracle."

The miracle would happen on November 9, 1989, with the tearing down of the Berlin Wall. Perhaps Allie and Carole's efforts hastened its collapse with their one small hammer at the reinforced concrete's soft spot, the people's hunger for freedom.

Chapter 71

Cohen shook Boris's hand. "Thank you, Boris, for all that you do for us."

"You are very welcome, Ms. Herman, Dr. Cohen." Boris instructed, "Your next stop is a banquet hosted by our new Soviet leader, Mikhail Gorbachev."

"Allie," begged Carole, "please brief me about this guy Gorbachev and the Soviet Union in general."

"Okay, Carole, the USSR is collapsing under the weight of overextension and unsustainable deficits. They have a rigid, sclerotic system that, with the digital electronic revolution, can't steal secrets fast enough to keep up, so they're falling dangerously behind America and the West technologically and heading toward weakness and possible surrender."

"Walter Cronkite came to one of my New York dinner parties, a lovely man." She recollected. "Anyway, he was arguing some point with Bill Buckley, and I heard Walter say that the Russian economy is only a quarter the size of ours, yet they somehow manage to match us militarily and globally."

"Exactly, the vigorous Gorbachev has been elevated into the position of first secretary to save Soviet Communism from collapsing. Gorbachev's plan is *glasnost*, encouraging constructive criticism to solve problems, and *perestroika*, economic restructuring."

"What does that mean in plain English, Cohen?"

"That means," he said, "inputs of capitalism and common sense to stimulate economic growth, and capitalism and honest assessment to save Communism, a sign that the Soviets are scared of losing the Cold War. Gorbachev may be a last gasp to save a failing Communist system."

"That's kind of scary. So this guy is *the man*."

"Yeah, Carole, he the man."

Carole and Allie both laughed, and she professed, "I love how much we laugh. We're almost always laughing, and you keep saying more funny things all the time. May our laughter last forever."

"I agree, let us keep on laughing constantly and forever. But seriously, babe, look at Gorbachev. Doesn't he remind you of an American corporate CEO in his prime? About fifty-five, well fit, and ultraconfident of his ability to produce results. Andrei Gromyko, the Soviet's number two man, probably summed him up best. The man has a nice smile and iron teeth."

"That's a good line, Allie. God, can you imagine if I had brought David? He'd probably want to make a monster movie, *The Man with the Iron Teeth*." She chopped her lips up and down to imitate a man with iron teeth biting.

Allie noticed that Carole was staring at Gorbachev's birthmark on his forehead and signaled her with his eyes to stop.

"I wonder if David," she whispered in his ear, "would have been stupid enough to ask Gorby about his birthmark, like if it was the sign of the Antichrist."

Carole pretended to be playing charades and began acting out clues for the Antichrist.

"The really big question—please stop making me laugh, babe, and let me finish—is how soon Soviet troops will be leaving Afghanistan in total defeat. Although 110,000 soldiers are still tearing up the country in a losing effort, their withdrawal is inevitable, and it's getting closer by the day."

The Soviets pulled out of Afghanistan a year after Allie's statement. Carole remembered President Carter on TV prohibiting U.S. Olympic athletes from competing in the 1980 Moscow Olympics over the Soviet invasion of Afghanistan. The Russians reciprocated by pulling their teams from the 1984 Los Angeles games.

"Babe," Cohen predicted, "the age of Communism may be coming to an end. Gorby or his successor will likely be the last Soviet leader. The real challenge to America might be managing the Russians' collapse and transformation."

"Do you think Reagan or whoever follows, probably Bush, will be up to that challenge?"

George H. W. Bush's deft management of the Soviet transformation and Gulf War I was the crowning achievement of his single term in office. Bill Clinton helped Boris Yeltsin gain power and complete the transformation into a democratic republic that's been reversed by Vladimir Putin and his thugocracy.

"We better be up to the challenges—for our kids' sake. Hey, let me look into the eyes of old Spothead to gauge his heart and soul. Soviet leaders are believed to be forbidden to display either."

Cohen continued to examine Gorbachev for signs of being monstrous enough to start a nuclear war. *Is Gorby sincere in his statements to make the world safer for children? If not, what's the cost of a nuclear-winter-proof Pamper for Ari?*

The first secretary delivered a short but pleasant welcoming speech to the visiting Americans and called on the United States to join the USSR in a great common goal. "Please halt the militarization of space, and drastically reduce atomic stockpiles."

Similar to Anatoly a century ago, Allie whispered to Carole, "Can the Russians be trusted? Reagan demands trust and verification for any arms control deal to happen. Now I'm no arms

489

expert, sweetie, but I'm sure of this. Nuclear weapons are cheaper than conventional weapons and keep the larger Soviet ground forces in check. Until Russian nuclear and conventional forces are reduced, the Western democracies remain wedded to atomic and neutron bombs."

Gorbachev snapped Allie from his analysis by inviting the Americans to ask questions. L. Ridley Dimple of the U.S. Embassy went first. "What grave concern drives the Soviets to mass defense forces far beyond perceived security needs? For example, a half million men and fifty-two thousand tanks massed at the Fulda Gap on the Czech border with southeast West Germany."

"The Soviet Union," Gorbachev explained, "is surrounded by hostile collective security groups who threaten our existence with more than two million troops, thirteen thousand tanks, twelve thousand war planes, and twenty thousand nuclear weapons." He then propagandized. "This question reflects the whimpering lies of warmongering Pentagon brass."

Carole bravely stepped to the microphone and pleaded with the first secretary. "I am concerned about the continued repression of Soviet Jewry. Is it not time for these practices to end?"

"All Soviet citizens are treated equally under our glorious constitution." Gorbachev deflected her question but smiled warmly at her, flashing his iron teeth.

Frank Johnson, a U.S. Embassy official and Ridley Dimple's superior, inquired, "Why do you think so many Americans feel that they cannot trust the Soviets?"

"The synthetic U.S. democracy," said Gorbachev, resorting to Marxist dogma, "is manipulated into a constant state of crisis and agitation by the military industrial complex and bourgeois press." Gorbachev confidently smiled.

"Oh?" said Johnson, scratching his head, a PhD in Russian studies from Duke.

These exchanges, Allie debated, *show that the Russians are experts at playing tit for tat. I don't want to waste my one chance in life to have a heart-to-heart with a Soviet leader. I know, I'll request to toast my host.*

Permission was granted for Cohen to step forward and personally meet Gorbachev, who was standing behind a handsome teak podium imported from Finland. A steward wearing a starched white linen jacket poured clear, iced vodka into crystal shot glasses and nodded.

The odd couple, Gorby and Cohen, downed their drinks. Both men heartily exhaled the fire from their bellies with muted but cheerful *ahhs* and smiled.

"Mr. Premiere," Allie stated, "it is with great enthusiasm that I return to the land of my great-grandfather Anatoly Kamenev's origins. It is also my pleasure and privilege to meet the esteemed leader of the gracious Soviet government."

Gorby expected Cohen to return to his seat and brushed him off with a nice smile. But Cohen did not go and proceeded. "In seventy years, the progressive Soviet society has produced many fantastic scientific achievements and surely has much to be proud of."

Gorby may have been smiling, but his body language signaled to Cohen to sit down and shut up. Allie felt the heavy vibes and got to the point.

"I am sad to say that both of our great nations are caught up in a tragic ideological rivalry that threatens all human existence. Because we dare not clash with each other, we fortify savage strongmen and proxy armies willing to further our geopolitical ends. As a result, millions of people are harmed in the cross fire between competing politico-economic systems, and much love and joy is robbed from the world."

I'm aware, Allie thought, *that I'm taking advantage of my host and would never have a chance to harangue Reagan like this, but my point is democratic capitalism works far better than Soviet Communism, so let them call me an ingrate.*

"Tell me, Mr. Premiere, which piece of distant real estate may seem so vital to spark a nuclear exchange? Will the price be worth the lives of perhaps two billion people?"

Gorbachev's stare signaled that he agreed and that enough was enough. Cohen was just getting there.

"If the two superpowers cannot be friends, we must try harder to coexist in peace and freedom. May I please present my five-point peace plan?"

Gorbachev's face suggested that an ambush was taking place but tolerantly nodded yes. Cohen took two Xerox copies from his pocket, handed Gorbachev one, and read from his own copy.

1. Let us both tear down all walls keeping our peoples apart.

2. Let us drastically shrink our armies into true defense forces.

3. Let us destroy all nuclear weapon systems.

4. Let us expand trade and cultural exchanges.

5. Let us go forward together in to a shared future of peace, freedom, and prosperity.

Gorbachev, galled, tried to shut Cohen up and diminish his peace plan as a stunt by aggressively toasting to peace.

"Dr. Cohen," Boris advised, "you appear to be lecturing your gracious host."

Allie looked at Carole; her eyes silently screamed at him to shut up, so he finished. "So may my infant son, Ari Ben Cohen, someday share an educational exchange with a grandson of yours eighteen years hence and in a peaceful and happy USSR and USA?"

Gorbachev looked relieved and instructed his guest to click glasses and down another ounce of grain alcohol. Gorby smiled cordially. Cohen extended his hand, and Gorbachev vigorously shook it and smiled.

Mir and *cil* are the Russian equivalent of *peace* and *strength*. Gorbachev impressed Cohen as being *mir*-ish. Allie cannot foresee twenty-first-century echoes of a new cold war starting with *cil*-ish Putin and the Russian mischief making in Georgia, Ukraine, Estonia, and Syria.

For the rest of the evening, Americans and Russians downed vodka like it was water. They also ate a sumptuous dinner, danced to Russian and American patriotic and popular songs, and hugged a lot. A large white cake decorated with national political icons—the stars and stripes and the hammer and sickle—was served for dessert.

Carole thought it to be a good time to take over the microphone and sing a song. Her eyes were full of love as she paraphrased a Beatles standard, "Give Peace a Chance."

"All we are asking is to *stop the arms race*."

The representatives of both countries joined hands in singing the line six times, each time louder and more hopeful.

Gorbachev showed why he was the new Soviet leader when he asked Carole to substitute a line. "Ms. Herman, please let us now sing 'all we are asking is to *ban weapons in space.*"

"Carole," Allie quietly counseled, "Reagan is building *Star Wars* and a space station that supposedly can shoot missiles down from orbit. The president's supercharging the space race is an economic trump card in Iceland to get Gorbachev to agree to a round of arms reductions. You should know that singing this line six times may not be in the president's or America's interest, but this is your call."

She sang it. "All we are asking is to *ban weapons in space.*"

The group repeated that line six times, each time more sweetly. Carole's beautiful voice and words enhanced a spirit of mutual trust, and many people had lumps in their throats.

But not right-winger L. Ridley Dimple, who approached Allie and Carole and declared Cohen a mushy-headed liberal and Carole Herman an erratic and sentimental woman. "As I see it, you've both allowed yourselves to be badly used by the first secretary to undercut the United States' negotiating position in Iceland. Your tour should definitely end here."

The conservative but amiable and pragmatic Frank Johnson, Dimple's boss, intervened. "Allie and Carole, I am touched by your efforts in behalf of peace and understanding and apologize to you for my assistant's rudeness."

"But, Chief Johnson—"

"Dimple," ordered Frank, shutting L. Ridley up, "you will take no action or file any report. Please apologize to Ms. Herman and Dr. Cohen right now."

Dimple hunched up and managed to say, "I'm sorry."

Frank appeared unsatisfied but let it go while adding, "You are further advised that I was sufficiently moved by Dr. Cohen's five-point plan for peace to nominate Allie for the Nobel Peace Prize."

This is the first time in my life, a stunned Cohen thought, *that my name and Nobel Peace Prize were used in the same sentence.*

He thanked Frank profusely. "Mr. Johnson, thank you very much for your support and nomination. I am honored, sir."

Frank and Allie hugged. Carole and Allie returned to their hotel room that night feeling fulfilled and celebrated by making love. They purposely groaned and grunted loudly to embarrass the KGB operative listening in.

The Kremlin scheduled three major concerts for Carole, who was a very big star in the USSR too—in Moscow, Kiev, and Leningrad—but not with Cohen, who the Soviets claimed was *prone to lecturing.*

Allie was ordered to stay in Moscow, where the KGB could keep an eye on him. That was all right with Allie because he used the time to visit with and encourage a dozen Jewish families wishing to immigrate to Israel or who were being harassed for practicing their Judaism.

"I promise," Cohen told each family, "that the American media will spotlight your situations to keep pressure on the Soviet government to ease restrictions."

The KGB was kept very busy taping all of Allie Cohen's declarations of solidarity with their dissidents and refuseniks.

Chapter 72

The CIA also taped Cohen's interactions with Soviet Jews and gave a copy to Frank Johnson, who transcribed and attached them to his nominating letter. Carole returned from Leningrad, and Boris reported to her that the Soviets were ready to declare Cohen persona non grata and kick him out of the country.

"Boris," pleaded Carole, "you must intercede on Allie's behalf and stop any official complaint to the U.S. State Department. They may not let him continue with the tour."

Boris did by appealing to Frank Johnson, and from Moscow, Herman and Cohen flew directly to Washington to meet with Ted Bell and plan their South American excursion. Bell brought Herman and Cohen up to speed.

"The president loved that antifascist melody, guys, and after a good laugh said your charade didn't undercut his position at all. In fact, he feels that you softened Gorbachev up a bit for him. Dr. Cohen," Ted warned Allie, "you are very lucky that Frank Johnson is Ridley Dimple's superior. If it were the other way around, this would probably be our last meeting, and I'd be giving you survey feedback forms."

Allie smiled gratefully and chortled a bit but had to know from Bell. "Ted, how did you learn of this pretense?"

Ted carefully followed national security guidelines. "I'm going to write a response on a sheet of paper."

It read, "Boris is on our payroll and sold out years ago to the CIA. Boris's deal is to defect someday and retire to a villa in the south of France that we bought for him to grow roses in his old age. Yes, he managed the idioms in Carole's song and your lecture to Gorby."

Bell burned the sheet up in an empty wastepaper basket and informed Allie, "Dr. Cohen, while your behavior in Russia was tolerable, we still expect you to follow protocol and keep a low profile in Chile."

Cohen challenged. "Why is it okay to undermine a *totalitarian* regime and not an *authoritarian* one?"

"Good question, but American policy," Bell patiently elucidated, "is to apply quiet pressure on the general's junta. The State Department's strategy is to slowly terminate Pinochet's rule and regime and assist him and them into exile in Spain with our policy of constructive engagement."

"I acknowledge being forewarned, Bell, but the United States is practicing a double standard. Constructive engagement ignores the thousands of political prisoners rotting in concentration camps in the northern Atacama Desert, the driest place on the earth. Also, America's policy of promoting slow, organic change rarely works."

"The CIA," countered Bell, "is formulating an evolutionary middle-of-the-road movement to force free elections and engineer the Chilean military in accepting the result. Please don't forget that the Chilean Communist Party is one of the largest and best organized in the entire hemisphere."

"Bell, I think the CIA is exaggerating the Communist threat to Chile, particularly the size and power of the party."

"Whatever, Dr. Cohen, this evolution will likely not happen fast enough for you or the frustrated Chilean people. Rest assured that Pinochet is an embarrassment to the United States, and we are working for his removal."

Cohen rolled his eyes; Bell pretended not to see him.

"This is officially classified material I'm passing on to you," Ted warned. "Therefore, failure to maintain confidentiality will result in you being in violation of espionage laws and subject to possible government prosecution."

Ted tried to sound less harsh. "Dr. Cohen, Chile is a pretty country, and Santiago is a very nice city. If you like, I can arrange for you to go trout fishing in the beautiful Lake District in the mountainous south."

"Trout fishing, Bell." Allie raised an eyebrow. "Man, are you serious?"

Bell brushed that aside. "Carole, Allie, have a safe and pleasant journey."

"Allie will be a very good boy, I assure you," Carole promised Ted. "And thank you, Ted, for all that you are doing for us."

Carole hugged Ted warmly and kissed him sweetly on his cheek. Cohen thought he saw Bell dream as Ted's eyes followed Carole's shapely body out of the room. *I can put up with Allie Cohen and his antics for a little more of that kissy and huggy stuff from Carole Herman.*

In three days, Carole and Allie were to fly from LA to Santiago on LAN Airlines, Chile's flag carrier. Carole flew home to Malibu to pack, open the mail, and get ready. Cohen stopped in Atlanta for two days with Sarah and Ari, who were thrilled to see him, and the family made every moment count.

"Your stopovers, Allie," Sarah teased him, "are the ultimate wham-bam-thank-you-ma'am situation."

"We're joined at the hip, Sarah. I know I'm not around much as we'd like, but when I'm with you, our communication and lovemaking is greater than ever, and I love you more than ever for believing in me. I can't do the Lord's work without your blessing."

Sarah kissed Allie passionately, and they fell on to the bed and made love for the second time in six hours. Afterward, Allie fed Ari, gave him a bath, and tested his leg strength as usual. Allie held Ari in his arms for an hour and sang old Motown hits to him, his favorite being the Tymes' "So Much in Love."

My hope as a dervish dad, Allie prayed, *during these periodic times with Ari is that, by the time I leave, Ari is clutching my face, putting his little arms around me, smiling at me, showing me he loves his daddy. Ari's love and Sarah's belief in me are my core strengths. Without that, I'm worthless to Carole.*

Invariably, when Allie returned to Carole after an Atlanta stopover and he saw concern in her eyes, he'd reassure her, "Carole, by my being a good man to my wife and son, I am able to be a better man to you."

That line never failed Allie, for Carole always threw her arms around him when he said it. Clothes usually dropped to the ground, and she'd jump on him, but this time, she started pulling down his jeans and drawers.

"Come here, lie down on the bed. I missed you and want to give you some good head."

Allie obediently followed Carole's every command. *Co-living sure has its benefits.*

Yes, it does, Allie. It's good to be the prophet.

Chapter 73

For the first time in Allie's life he was flying first class regularly and really liking it too. Cohen compared it with economy.

The stewardesses wait on you for your every need or want. In comparison, the airlines ought to rename economy class to refugee class because that's how the airlines are starting to treat economy-class passengers.

Carole's celebrity status necessitated their seats being curtained off from the rest of the section for the ten-hour, 5,600-mile flight from LA to Santiago, Chile. Herman and Cohen took advantage of their privacy privilege by frequently fondling each other to break up the trip's monotony.

"Allie, what are you reading?"

"This book features the top ten Chilean poets and their most famous poems."

He showed her the cover page. "They're the rock stars of their country, and I hope to meet with some of the more prominent ones like Jaime Magosin, whose poem I'm reading right now. Hey, how are you coming along with that article I gave you to read?"

Allie referred to Seymour Hersh's 1983 *Atlantic* magazine accounting of how Nixon and Kissinger toppled the democratically elected Salvador Allende and installed the Pinochet dictatorship.

"It's very interesting and informative, Allie, but there are so many gaps in my knowledge of U.S. history and foreign affairs that sometimes I wonder if I'm getting everything."

"Great, Carole, the whole plane's asleep. Look, Sarah's good friend is Elena Sarasohn, whose family during the Allende upheaval immigrated to America, where they've spent the past twelve years of the Pinochet dictatorship."

"I'll bet they miss home."

"They sure do. Anyway, her elder sister Natalie is a professor of Hispanic studies at Harvard and just raised $75,000 from rich Boston liberals for Chilean church relief agencies. The money is being distributed to Chilean regional archdioceses to set up food and clothing banks for the poor."

"That's wonderful."

"Yes, and twenty-five thousand of it is mine. That's the price for obtaining a meeting with the radical priest of Valparaiso's angry Hill Parish slum."

She disapproved. "I think you're fishing for *trouble* instead of trout. Christ, you really do encourage yourself, don't you?"

"Look, I can't sing folk songs," he argued. "I have to follow my conscience and my instincts and take direct action."

"Okay, do what you want?" remarked Carole, annoyed. "But if you get caught being too outrageous, our last official place to visit will be LA."

"Yeah," Cohen quipped, "the cocaine Ukraine."

His one-liner made her laugh and ease up on him.

"The Sarasohns sound interesting." She coaxed. "Allie, please, tell me more."

"Okay, Dr. Julio Sarasohn once headed the University of Chile's College of Law and his wife Francia's family owned the largest import-export firm in Vina del Mar, Valparaiso, the country's main port city. In 1962, Julio—a respected legal scholar and human rights activist—was nominated for a Nobel Prize."

"A Noble Peace Prize, very impressive. You know, that's something I'd like to help you win, Allie, a Nobel Peace Prize."

Yes, Carole, a Nobel Peace Prize is a best first step in the beholding of the prophet, and that is precisely why Adonai and I teamed you with Allie.

"Thank you very much, Carole," said Allie appreciatively. "But to get nominated, we'll have to be busy undermining a lot of dictators and other bad guys."

Both laughed until Allie described the domestic situation that forced the Sarasohns to flee to America. "In 1968, babe, there was a worldwide student rebellion and strike, Chile included. Julio's prelaw freshmen demanded a financial grant to set up a free street law center in La Victoria, a poor south-side Santiago barrio."

"Allie, I like kids who want to get involved."

"Yes, Carole, so do I, but the kids can't run the school. Julio's students liked hearing him applaud their idealism. Unfortunately, they attacked him when he turned them down."

"How come, Allie? It could have been a good learning experience for the students."

"Julio told them they were too inexperienced and unqualified to help the poor, and I agree with him. The poor deserve well-trained and able lawyers to satisfy their legal needs too, not college freshmen who may be well-meaning but don't know squat yet."

"Now that you put it like that, Allie, I agree with you too, but I'll bet the students sure didn't like that."

"You're right, Carole, and they brandished Julio an establishment symbol of elitism and took him hostage in his own office with Salvador Allende, egging them on to further his own political goals."

"That Salvador Allende, he sure was a real instigator." Carole was putting the many pieces of the Chilean political puzzle together.

"Yep, and when Julio learned of Allende's actions, he quickly accepted a long-standing offer from Emory University in Atlanta to teach constitutional law."

He asked the stewardess for a bottle of water. Carole showed how much she'd learned from the Hersh magazine article.

"And after Allende got into power, Allie, the CIA helped him commit suicide and placed Pinochet in power. After the coup, they must have felt at risk."

"Exactly, my good student," he answered proudly. "And I'm very happy that Julio, Francia, and David, an Emory University senior, are visiting Mrs. Sarasohn's mother in Vina. They've invited us to join them for lunch the day after tomorrow."

Casually dropping an invitation on Carole like that made her a bit anxious, but she instead told Allie, "I'm very excited by the opportunity to meet a Chilean family."

"Well," Allie admitted, "they're not exactly your average Chilean family."

"Allie," Carole wondered, "why do you care so much about Chile?"

"I care because the United States trampled on 160 years of Chilean social democracy. America was losing in Vietnam, and after Castro and Cuba, the United States was not going to tolerate another Communist regime taking hold in the Western Hemisphere. General Pinochet took over and quickly restored stability, the economy improved a bit, and more conservative Chileans believed he was doing a good job under the circumstances."

"I assume, Allie, that the guy has outlived his welcome in office though."

"He sure has, Carole. Essentially, I'm coming to Chile to learn the answers to two questions. First, was Allende a Marxist-Leninist as Nixon, Kissinger, and the CIA claimed? Second, were his policies a grave enough threat to justify a U.S. overthrow and installation of a military dictatorship?"

"Man, Allie, you have your work cut out for you."

"Carole, I hate what Pinochet has done to his people and this land, but I'm going to stop thinking about the damage to calm down."

Carole tried to take Allie's mind off Pinochet by joking with him. "So, Allie, what type of fishing gear did you pack for Chile?"

Her good-natured tease succeeded in making him laugh and loosen up a bit, but he didn't lighten up.

"You heard Bell, Carole. The United States will throw its weight behind any group proposing an Argentine political model for Chile. Since a nonviolent centrist movement must form to replace Pinochet, I need to come up with a nonviolent plan to jump-start this process."

"What plan?" asked Carole, shocked by his intentions. "Are you crazy?"

"I don't have a plan yet, but knowing me, I'll come up with something soon enough."

I'm not sure what aggravates me more, his aim or his confidence, she thought. *What the hell, let me nap.*

Night lifted, and a brilliant sunshine roused Carole in time to perk up with a light breakfast snack before landing and deplaning. Jim Magruder, a high-level U.S. Embassy official, met them as they stepped down the gangplank.

The beefy blond ex-college professor waltzed them through immigration with pre-filled-out visas; Special Guest was stamped on Carole's and Tourist on Allie's. They left Santiago Airport and were stunned by a billboard message: "Peace and prosperity through <u>order</u>—General Pinochet, president of Chile."

Magruder had observed dozens of foreign guests react in the same shocked or threatened manner and habitually recited the United States' position on the vexing sign.

"Our government considers the message to be unnecessarily provocative and have repeatedly asked General Pinochet to remove it."

Magruder, a straightforward fellow, unofficially remarked, "I guess you can see how much control we have over the obstinate bastard. Historically, great distance and national pride are two main reasons for the United States having little influence over Chilean domestic affairs."

Is Jim setting us up or the odd man out? Cohen contemplated. *A decent and honest guy in the State Department? His frank and perhaps intemperate comment makes me wonder. Man, I'm already caught up in tempestuous Chilean political currents.*

Magruder, in perfect Spanish, instructed the cabdriver to go to the Carrera Hotel, a turn-of-the-century marble masterpiece that no one could afford to build today. The cabdriver tried to schmooze with Cohen, and he conversed in a halting Spanglish. The cabdriver bragged; Magruder translated for him.

"I used to be a research scientist in Antarctica. I was part of a team that studied the age of plankton frozen in the ice."

"His driving a taxi should shed light," Magruder commented, "on the fact that over a hundred thousand Chilean professionals out of eleven million people are spread across the United States, a huge loss of talent, creativity, and skills—a classic brain drain."

The ride into central Santiago from the airport appeared nondescript until fairly close to downtown. Cohen reacted to a street name.

"The taxi just turned onto Boulevard de Bernardo O'Higgins, the George Washington of Chile. I remember reading all about him in my Latin American history class."

Magruder registered Herman and Cohen into the majestic Carrera, located on Constitution Plaza less than five hundred yards from Pinochet's palace. *No government*, Cohen thought, *expects an opponent to operate from right across the damn street.*

The Carrera's management gave Carole the VIP treatment and mostly ignored Allie. Cohen informed the entourage that Carole and he badly needed to nap. Magruder and the army of servants left, and both enjoyed several hours of buffered sleep.

While you sleep, prophet, I will brief you on current Chilean politics and the Manuel Rodriguez party in particular. You are entering a dangerous den, and to succeed, you must be armed with more powerful and wiser ideological arguments than the leaders of the revolutionary front.

Chapter 74

Allie and Carole awoke and acclimatized by making love in the late afternoon. After dressing for the evening function, Allie led Carole over to their suite's big picture window and briefed her by pointing across Constitution Plaza to the presidential palace.

"This is how we will help each other succeed in Chile. For eleven years, Pinochet has played the Soviet Union threat card while liberating the treasury of 190 million bucks to Swiss and Paraguayan banks."

"Well, Allie, the poor guy has to survive on what he can scrape together. If he suddenly has to leave, he'll need some traveling and pin money."

He enjoyed her sarcasm, gave her a kiss, and then pointed out, "Carole, never forget that the brutes you're entertaining use torture and murder to muzzle the press. They also ban all gatherings, carry out secret arrests, and detain suspects indefinitely in a random and indiscriminate manner."

"Is that all?"

"No, babe, they also maintain order by tapping phones, opening mail, and pulling out *tongues* with *pliers*."

His last three words sent a shiver down her spine, and the marvelous comedienne pretended to have no tongue while trying to talk. Allie laughed and then continued his analysis. "Change has to come from within and hopefully without bloodshed. In a nutshell, the longer El Caudillo maintains his grip on power, the more he squanders his ability to transfer it peacefully."

"Is there any time left?"

"Although the explosion has plainly begun, I estimate there's still time to prevent another full-scale civil war like in El

Salvador and Nicaragua. The key is to create a moral offensive to unite the masses into an unstoppable democratic wave."

"How do we do that?" Carole, ever the performer, mimed for a few seconds by acting out *baffled* and *overwhelmed.*

"Please stop making funny faces. Ha ha! Okay, thank you. My challenge, Carole, is to bring the divergent factions within the opposition together to foster widespread alienation and disaffection inside the military."

"That's all?" she joked and then asked, "And my challenge is?"

"Your role is to keep the state terrorists entranced with your dazzling talent, beauty, and charm. My job is to sell the revolutionary front on my plan to melt the military's support for the government."

"And to what ultimate end, Allie, is this all for?"

"To help a society of eleven million people avoid civil war and usher in freedom and democracy, the first steps toward prosperity. I realize that the odds are very long, but we might pull off a miracle if we play our cards right."

My instincts, Carole thought, *tell me to give Allie a chance, but I also dread what the sadists might do to him if they catch him in a politically naughty act.*

Instead, she told him, "I'd prefer you at my side, Allie, even though I know you must act as a tourist, but it's a lot easier to cross a snake pit together than alone, right?"

He knew better than to try to top that line; instead, he casually remarked, "You know, Bell and Magruder did me a favor by assigning me tourist status only."

"I don't understand."

"If I was accompanying you around, babe, I'd probably wind up cursing Pinochet and his thugs out, maybe even try to punch one in the mouth just for general principles. My hostility can be put to much better use than calling the bastards names and getting kicked out of the fucking country."

Carole hugged him. "David would have killed to go trout fishing in the Lake District. You've come to save the country. You are a very exciting man, Allie Cohen."

Cohen gave Herman a warm big kiss. "Try to have a great time at the banquet tonight."

"What are you going to do, Allie?"

"Carlos Martello is coming to pick me up in a few minutes. His wife, Dulce, is making me a home-cooked meal."

Carole, amazed, said; "We landed and took a nap, and now a total stranger is cooking fresh string beans for Allie." Both laughed, and she marveled. "Laughter is our greatest glue, and sex is right up there too."

"Yes, they are. Okay, Carole, blink if you get it. Carlos heads Catholic University's School of Dentistry and graduated from Emory University in Atlanta. That's where he met Dulce, and like a fairy tale, Emory's only two Chilean-born students at the time fell in love, married, and returned to their homeland to settle down and start a career."

Carole blinked again, felt like a fool, and started to laugh. Allie laughed too and then specified, "Elena arranged the dinner with the Martellos so that I could be briefed by people she trusted. Given the lack of parking on Constitution Plaza, Carlos has directed me to wait out in front of the hotel for a quick pickup."

Allie looked at his watch. "I've got five minutes to get downstairs, babe."

Allie kissed Carole goodbye and assured her he'd be back by the 1:00 AM curfew. Cohen took the elevator to the lobby and walked down the hotel steps.

Constitution Plaza teemed with people cutting across it on their way to the downtown hot spots. Within a minute, a small black Subaru sedan drove up, and a pleasant Italian Chilean man of medium height and build got out. The brown-haired gentleman, perhaps forty to forty-five, walked over to shake Cohen's hand and introduce himself.

"Dr. Cohen, I am Dr. Carlos Martello, and it is a pleasure to meet you."

"Likewise, Dr. Martello, although please call me Allie."

Carlos smiled. "Allie, please call me Carlos too. Let's get in the car as we have about a half hour's drive."

Martello talked a lot about the tight economic situation while leaving the central business district and heading east toward the snowcapped Andes Mountains. Carlos drove through residential areas consisting of small to average-sized ranch houses and apartments.

Allie asked him what Chile's per capita income (PCI) was. "Allie, I estimate that maybe 80 percent of the population lives on less than $2,500 a year. That's a 1980 census statistic, so it might be a bit higher by now."

Allie used the statistic differently. "Comparatively speaking, Haiti has a $300 per capita income, for example. I believe that your PCI reflects a fairly well-developed society. Of course, I can make such judgments since I don't have to live on fifty bucks a week or less."

Martello chuckled while parking along a tree-lined curb right in front of his sturdy compact ranch house set in an upper-middle-class residential neighborhood.

"Carlos," Cohen commented, "I admire the solid building materials used to construct your homes."

"Allie, our construction code demands that all structures be as earthquake-proof as possible. The walls are made of foot-thick concrete and four-by-eight-inch wood beams. The parquet floors are of polished oak, and we still plaster instead of using Sheetrock."

"Compare that with the materials used by American developers—matchstick two-by-fours, Celotex insulation, and plasterboard interior walls. Average U.S. homes, in my opinion, are put together with spit and glue compared with yours."

Dulce Martello—an attractive, easygoing, earth-mother type—came out of her kitchen to meet Allie and saw his Semitic nose.

"Please, Dr. Cohen, forgive me. I shouldn't have roasted a pork loin for dinner."

"Dulce, don't worry," he assured her. "I'm not kosher and enjoy pork now and then. Please call me Allie too."

Carlos poured Allie a glass of the best inexpensive red wine that he ever drank. Dulce self-consciously placed before Allie a plate of sliced roast pork loin, seasoned rice, ironically string beans marinated in red wine, and a delicious fresh tomato salad.

"Dulce, this feast of fresh vegetables," Allie praised, "has saved my stomach from the ravages of airline food. For that, you are truly a modern-day heroine."

511

The modest Dulce laughed happily and sat down at the dinner table to partake in the lively and friendly conversation. Albeit a respected technician and researcher in her own right, Dulce—similar to most Chilean women—normally deferred to her husband, but a visit from an important American writer made this evening different, and she expected to speak her mind freely.

The Martellos and Cohen shared their six-thousand-mile-long Georgian-Chilean connection by swapping experiences dealing with rednecks and good ol' boys. Dulce left the table to prepare dessert and returned with three slices of freshly baked cherry pie, a pot of robust coffee, and a small pitcher filled with steamed cream.

Carlos sensed that Allie was ready to discuss Chile's political situation. "This morning and this afternoon, Allie, the government detained thousands of young men living in the shantytowns of La Victoria and Raul Silva Henriquez. The official figure they give out is 690, yet everybody knows that it's at least four times higher."

"Carlos, that's an instant extraction of over 2,500 to 3,000 young men and should devastate any community. My guess is it produces instant radicalization."

"Exactly. The sweeps," Martello sarcastically described, "are an instrument to prevent leftist violence, but the more they raid the slums"—he spoke in a disgust-filled voice—"the more the slums seethe with angry guerilla activity. Naturally, the Communists, whom they fear so much, just sit back and hatch their chickens."

"Dulce," Allie asked, "which political party would the people, if given a truly free election, probably elect?"

"That's easy." Dulce reflexively answered, "The Socialists."

"I'm not so sure, my dear," Carlos vigorously disagreed. "But then I've been a lifelong Christian Democrat, the American equivalent being a moderate Democrat like Jimmy Carter or, to show my age, Henry 'Scoop' Jackson of Washington State."

Allie nodded that he understood, and Dulce agreed with Carlos, who continued and despaired. "What Chile needs now is for another Christian Democrat like Eduardo Frei to step forward. He was the one Chilean politician who embodied the qualities of Argentina's Raúl Alfonsín, who has just led his country from military dictatorship to democracy and freedom."

Carlos dramatized his country's plight by faking a cry for help. "Eduardo, where are you when we really need you?" He next faked a death rattle. "They took a poll the other day." He faked two chokes. "And they discovered that the best known public figure in the country is a vapid TV talk show host similar to your Johnny Carson."

Cohen faked three big long chokes at Carson's mention.

Carlos laughed hard and continued. "We are being gradually depoliticized as democracy has been dead now for so long that there's no one person who can actually lead the nation."

"And so," Allie delicately asked, "the two of you have become used to living without your freedom?"

Carlos scratched his head while Dulce wiped a tear away from her eye. It was a tough subject for them to deal with, though Carlos tried. "I do what I can to help in my own quiet way yet admit that I am no boat-rocker. I have a family and a career I love, so I cannot afford to take great risks. It's not that I've become more conservative, no. I think I now may fear the Socialists coming to power more than Pinochet remaining in it."

513

"Why, Carlos?" Allie wondered. "Because the Socialists are more likely to institute democracy than Pinochet? It's too risky to place your faith in a tenuous status quo."

"Allie, I acknowledge your point but think it a bit naive. I have a friend who knows the radical priest of Valparaiso, whom you're going to meet—the soul of the revolution, or so they claim. This so-called lover of Jesus uses the words *a type of democracy*."

"That sounds like the Sandinistas in Nicaragua, Carlos."

"Exactly, so may God forbid the priest and his gang from making it because if they do, once again, they'll be cursing us for owning our own home and car."

"You're right, Carlos. You have worked hard and should not have to apologize for living well. You know, the middle class makes it almost in spite of the rich and dreads being dragged down to the level of the poor."

Dulce lamented. "Allie, the worst thing about the Socialists is that the CIA will soon make the food disappear from the shelves of all the stores. And yet even though I know the worst will come, in my heart, I am a Socialist. Am I crazy or what?"

"My darling Dulce," Carlos told his wife, "you have too much heart for your own good, my beautiful sweetheart." Dulce lovingly blushed.

"Was Allende," Cohen asked the Martellos, "really a Communist?"

"Allende," Carlos stated, "was a democratic Socialist, and that's it. His mistake was not being a Marxist but rather being a weak and stupid man."

"What do you mean by that description?" Cohen doubted it could be that simple.

514

Carlos grew animated. "That damn fool simply didn't wait long enough to win the trust of Chile's large middle class. If he had, a true center-left coalition might have eventually formed and supported some of his policies."

Allie nodded. Carlos specified, "*Some*, not all, mind you. He only had 34 percent of the vote in a three-man race, but the jerk caved in too soon to leftist pressures to nationalize U.S. copper holdings. He also invited Fidel Castro to visit his first month in power, and the Beard stayed for five weeks—five weeks."

"I am sure, Carlos, that the Beard's long presence drove the local CIA crazy."

"Yes, think about that. Was Allende truly stupid or what?"

He asked the Martellos if they'd supported Allende. Carlos and Dulce remembered the Allende era as an idealistic period and, as youth, got swept up in the exciting prospects for social change. Over the next three years, however, U.S. imperialism taught them many hard and sad lessons.

"The only time I disliked Allende," shared Dulce, "was when he used Julio Sarasohn as a scapegoat to get the students behind him. I do not blame Allende for bringing Pinochet to power as so many do. He was a doctor, a patriot, and a caring and compassionate man, Dr. Salvador Allende."

"Dulce, Carlos, I'm interested to know what you think the future holds for y'all."

Dulce worried. "I'm concerned that America will become a fallback society for Chileans and siphon off the best and brightest of our children and cause a brain drain."

Carlos maintained that the gravest threat was political in nature. "Allie, it would not cost the right wing that much of their wealth and property to throw the poor a few crumbs and make

515

their lives more bearable. Once upon a time, a progressive impulse existed, and there was a tradition of establishing programs to relieve misery. Today they eliminate it with Israeli submachine guns and American tanks."

Allie suspected that Carlos had not completed his thought, and he rambled off on a tangent.

"And the left wing, I would guess, suffers from incurable stupidity."

Carlos's eyes lit up. "That's very perceptive of you as I'm always amazed by how Marxist assholes condemn bourgeois materialism, and then when they get into power, they live well, and nobody else is allowed to."

"And I imagine," Cohen tendered, "that you do not feel enslaved by Pinochet at this very moment, though you guys do seem pretty free to me."

"No," Carlos firmly answered. "Chile is an authoritarian society and not a totalitarian one. I am much freer under Pinochet than I would be under Cuba's Castro or Daniel Ortega of Nicaragua."

"I think that's true."

"I also have no illusions about the opposition as the majority of the front's members are far to the left of Allende. A hard-core 10 percent are Communists, another 25 percent are far left Socialists of varying degrees, the rest are beguiled liberals and moderates being led by their noses to their own funeral."

"Why is that so, Carlos, if I may ask?"

"I'll give you an example. The last time the Sarasohns were in Chile, they brought their son along with them to dinner. All through the meal, David raved on and on about how Chile was being manipulated by American capitalist imperialism and needed Socialism to solve its problems. After dinner, I asked him if he planned to return to Chile after graduating from college."

"He goes to Emory University too, right?"

"Yes, he does and said he is considering returning, so I asked him if he might become a dentist since our people's teeth are a national disgrace. He told me, 'No, there's no money in it because Chileans don't bother to take care of their teeth.' He went on to say that when Chile has Socialism, dental care will then improve. But right now, he needs more than $75 a week and plans to get an MBA from the Harvard Business School or London School of Economics."

"Carlos," pleaded Dulce, "David is a beautiful kid who's just going through a stage."

"I know, Dulce. Anyway, Allie, Pinochet will be president until 1989 because the opposition grossly underestimates his ability to keep the middle class more scared of the left than the army. I would not be surprised if someone did manage to kill him and pretty soon too. What will happen then, only God knows."

Allie looked at his watch and saw that the hour was late. The Martellos had work tomorrow, and Carlos had barely enough time to get Cohen back to the Carrera and him home before the 1:00 AM curfew.

"Thank you, Carlos and Dulce, for being such charming and gracious hosts and for the thorough briefing."

Allie kissed Dulce on her cheek and left the house to get into Carlos's Subaru.

"Ironically," Carlos shared, "this inexpensive Japanese import is how Pinochet manages to keep the middle class in his pocket."

Aware that Chile was an immigrant nation like America, Cohen—curious about Carlos's origins—asked when and why his family came to Chile.

Carlos recalled. "My father was both poor and unemployed around the time Mussolini allied himself with Hitler and coincidentally read an Italian-language *Reader's Digest* article about Chile. The reprint from the *Christian Science Monitor* praised the South American country as a land of opportunity and freedom, so my dad and his pregnant new bride borrowed money from her parents and departed for Chile the very next week. Over the years, so many other men followed suit that the village, less than fifty miles from the Swiss border, stands half-empty today."

"That's amazing. What did your dad do for a living?"

"My dad built up a thriving fruit and vegetable distributorship. He bought an old Ford pickup to truck in fresh produce from the small farms encircling Santiago and sold it to the capital's better hotels and restaurants, including the Carrera. My old man did very nicely until the Allende years, when his business went under during the economic collapse. Two weeks later, he was dead."

"I'm sorry to hear that. Your dad really achieved the Chilean immigrant dream."

"Yes, he did, but still, you can't believe," Carlos described, "the extent that Allende stoked the fires of class warfare. Imagine less well-off friends attending your father's funeral and afterward cursing your family for being fortunate enough to own their home. I am sure that you have never heard of such a thing occurring in the United States. Thankfully, Julio obtained the Emory scholarship for me, and I gladly accepted just to get the hell away from the resentment that was everywhere at the time."

"Carlos, why did you return to Chile upon graduating from Emory? If you had stayed in Atlanta, you'd probably be raking in

$150 thousand a year, which translates into driving a Mercedes and living in a big house in Dunwoody or East Cobb with a pool and hot tub, not to mention the gold chains dangling from your neck."

Carlos laughed richly and then spoke from his heart. "Allie, for me, the quality of life is higher here. And despite the oppression, in my heart and soul, I will always be a Chilean. America is, without a doubt, a great country and a wonderful place to live in. Still, Chile is my home, and it is the same with Dulce too."

They approached the central business district, and Allie observed merchants scurrying to close up their stalls a half hour before curfew.

"Carlos, it seems strange for a Latin culture to be running home at 12:30 AM."

"True, it's very unnatural, and there is a darker side to this too—what has happened to a growing number of drunks and hearing-impaired people. Envision a man"—Carlos lowered his voice—"having a few too many drinks at a restaurant or party and is so out of it that he fails to hear the soldier shouting at him to stop. The poor drunk or hard-of-hearing person also appears to be ignoring orders to stop."

"So they don't."

"Yes, Allie, they continue on driving. And after a third shout to stop, the soldier suspects that the driver may be a terrorist and blasts away. It is rumored that as many as two dozen innocent people may have died this way."

"Carlos, no one knows about this in the States."

"Well, did you hear this? The driver who tried to take out the junta last night came within a few feet of succeeding. The shaken junta reacted by stepping up security precautions for the presidential palace and barricaded all streets within three blocks of Constitution Plaza."

"So my hotel is in the middle of an armed camp under attack?"

"Yes, and that is also why I will not be able to get anywhere near the Carrera Hotel and must let you out three blocks away, and you will have to walk the rest. I'm sorry for the imposition and urge you to please be careful of the soldiers patrolling the streets."

Carlos shook Allie's hand. "I hope that someday we will get together again, either in Atlanta or in Santiago."

"I hope so too," Allie told Carlos, "because I'd like for you and Dulce to meet Sarah, my wife, whom I am meeting in Argentina next week."

Allie watched Carlos drive away, a man who had become a trusted friend in a single evening.

Chapter 75

Allie stepped lively on the three uneventful blocks to the hotel and, once inside, went straight to his suite. *It's empty. Carole's banquet must have gone overtime. My mind's racing like a pinwheel, so why not walk the two flights to the hotel's rooftop bar to check out the place? I could use a drink to chill out.*

Allie entered the bar with a long rectangular pool and a spectacular view of Santiago. *This bar's really impressive*, he thought, *but also nearly empty because curfew is only a few minutes away.*

Cohen sat down on a stool and ordered a Chivas Regal on the rocks with a splash of soda. The bartender put the drink and the bill down in front of him.

"Holy cow, this is about twice the U.S. price," he told the bartender, who explained in perfect English that a luxury import tax had gone into effect that morning.

Cohen wondered if the bartender belonged to the security forces to keep an eye on foreigners and other types. *I think I'm starting to get a little paranoid.*

The bartender, a handsome tall guy, appreciated Cohen's good-natured reaction and quelled any suspicion by pouring the bottle's last two ounces into Allie's glass for free. Cohen nursed the drink and evaluated his first day in Chile.

It's clear that things are falling right into place— His mental audit ceased when a stunning girl and what appeared to be her date entered the bar. Allie's eyes followed the short dark-haired beauty as she and her escort walked around the long rectangular pool to stools far in the rear.

He listened. *The tall thin man speaks with a clipped Spanish Australian accent that's practically unintelligible. The*

521

woman's fractured vowels suggest a UK origin, but there is something in their body language that tells me that the man is a lot more sexually interested in the woman than she is in him.

The bartender informed Cohen and the two new patrons that curfew had started, so he had to close down the bar. Cohen paid his bill, generously tipped the bartender, and took another look at the beautiful stranger. *Oh shit, she's staring right back at me. Man, she's so gorgeous that she nearly cracked my cool.*

He maintained his self-possession, but an image of the beautiful stranger's face danced in his head all the way back to the suite. *I have to get a handle on this because fucking around on Carole again in such a short time is seriously risky.*

Carole unlocked the door, entered, and appeared exhausted and emotionally drained. He flashed a smile and gave her a needed hug.

"You know, Allie," Carole reported while he helped her out of her sand-colored evening gown, "I actually managed to have a halfway decent time tonight. The generals and ministers were all so charming and gracious that, after a while, you almost forget that they're responsible for God knows how many murders and massacres."

"My view, Carole, is that the junta is nearly tame compared with the Russian Communist leaders who murdered maybe ten million people, or Mao in China who killed an estimated eighty million."

Carole, fully naked, undressed Allie and then pressed up against him.

"I love your brain. Intelligence is incredibly sexy, and your dick is pretty good too."

Both laughed loudly and then engaged in some foreplay; soon they were making hot love. A few images of the stranger flashed in Allie's mind but quickly passed.

Carole and Allie experienced very different evenings; he spent an hour relating the Martello briefing, she her assorted attentions and flatteries from high Chilean government officials. They both suddenly crashed and fell asleep.

Carole, ever the trouper, dragged herself out of bed at 7:00 AM to dutifully attend a brunch in her honor at the U.S. Embassy. Allie, the tourist, luxuriated between the sheets until 9:00 AM and then enjoyed a hotel breakfast of fresh fruits, hard-boiled eggs with small rolls and butter, and a sampling of local cheeses and coffee before taking a cab over to the Central Bus Station to go to Valparaiso and Viña del Mar, adjacent coastal cities.

Uh-oh, I'm already running a half hour late for my appointment with David Sarasohn at the Place Vengara at noon.

At the Santiago bus terminal, Cohen was accosted by swarms of aggressive young men competing for the right to lead him to the ticket seller's window; their pathetic motivation was the faint hope of receiving a Chilean quarter tip, about a U.S. nickel. Cohen learned that the beggars' second act was escorting him less than twenty feet to his bus seat to earn another tip.

How sad, thought Cohen. *These poor, desperate men are masking their begging by pretending to be useful and are really a nuisance.*

The bus pulled out of the station with only four passengers. An example of "pretending to be useful" was the *conductor*, who aided the bus driver by walking the aisle to collect four lousy tickets. Every ten minutes, he got up to offer warm cans of soft drinks to tuned-out passengers, who totally ignored him. Unless he had thirstier customers on the return trip, the chances were that he'd earn no money today.

The ride took two hours to cover eighty miles of sparsely populated land. Allie was the last passenger to get off the bus at

Place Vengara. Curly-haired blond David Sarasohn was waiting and introduced himself.

They shook hands, and David led Allie through the bustling central plaza to his grandmother's apartment. Lithe, handsome, and the same height as Cohen, David connected the dots to how Allie knew his sisters.

"David, your parents and I met at Elena's home in Roswell last year. Now you guys are welcoming me to Chile and Vina."

The Sarasohn family was glad to see him again and appreciated hearing that he liked their country very much. Francia introduced Ida, their loyal Indian Chilean house woman of thirty years.

"Allie, Ida is our genius cook with vegetables and an unofficial member of the Sarasohn family."

Ida served Allie a tangy tomato soup, tiny tender lima beans in a special succotash sauce, and a delicate burrito filled with a mildly spicy spinach stuffing.

She is *a genius cook with vegetables.* He took another bite of the exquisite burrito. *I can taste why they treat her as part of the family.*

Cohen waited ten minutes to discuss politics. Julio shared his opinion of Pinochet.

"Our president is a poor sequel of Francisco Franco, the late Spanish dictator."

"Somebody, sooner or later," David boldly declared, "is going to kill that guy."

The elegant Francia disdained politics.

"I'm glad that at least we all still eat well. Pity us if it we didn't. What do you think, Allie,'" she asked him, "about Chilean fruits and vegetables? I'll bet you find them fresher and better than America's, don't you?"

"Yes, and I imagine that's because they are being trucked in daily from farms around the city instead of weeks on trucks or trains from California or Texas. This seems to be a big part of the nice quality of life in Chile that I learned last night at the Martellos, and thank you for having them brief me. They're terrific."

"You're a gringo, Allie," said Grandma, who supposedly spoke limited English, "because you speak such limited Spanish."

Allie, familiar with the term, did not know how to respond and just politely smiled at her.

For dessert, the Sarasohns treated him to a ten-mile-long cab ride up the coast to Reñaca and back and left Grandma at home.

Julio cleared it up. "Vena and Reñaca are twin vacation resorts. Reñaca is sedate and residential. Vina—larger, older, and glitzier—has a casino, the only place in the country that is never under curfew restrictions. Some things in life," he joked, "are very important, of course."

"Allie," Francia proudly stated, "this is our new beachfront hotel, where all the rich Jews are having their kids bar mitzvahed." She then spoke in a whisper. "Across the street, wealthy Arabs— mostly Lebanese and Syrians—own that attractive swim club."

David seems strangely remote, Cohen thought, *like his mother's beloved area isn't the real Chile but rather the oppressor's exclusive reserve.*

David seemed to read Allie's mind and suddenly told Francia, "Mama, its three thirty. Allie and I have an important appointment to keep with one of Natalie's contacts up on the hill."

"Okay, David," said Francia, disguising her anxiety. "You go and give Allie a nice tour of Valparaiso, especially those quaint little houses on the hill. Julio and I will walk back to the apartment from here and take a nap. Allie, I hope that you enjoy your tour."

Francia, bless her heart. Allie shook his head. *I'm sure she's aware of what David is talking about but acts like a mother typically ignoring unpleasant situations her family might be involved in.*

The Sarasohns walked across the street toward the Arab swim club, turned north, and waved goodbye.

Allie joked with David. "Your mom and dad are beating it out of there as if they were fleeing PLO terrorists in bathing suits."

David laughed and guided Allie. "We need to move around as inconspicuously as possible, so let's take a bus over to Valparaiso and get off at the piedmont of the Hill Parish, where the working class and the poor live."

The ride lasted five minutes, and they stepped off and looked up at the Hill Parish slum stretching high into the clouds.

David prepared him. "Allie, here, gainful employment is as rare as hunger is prevalent."

Thus began their ascent into one of the three angriest sequestered areas in the country.

"Allie, although Santiago's La Victoria and Raul Henriquez's shantytowns have been the scene of more demonstrations and arrests," young Sarasohn warned, "the soul of the revolution really springs from the bowels of the hill. Because of that, Allie, keep an eye out for sudden landings by helicopter gunships or government troop movements."

"David, about your depiction of terrible poverty and widespread hunger, I have seen far worse conditions in rural Mexico. This level of development makes me doubt that Chile's circumstances justify a bloody revolution."

David challenged him. "But, Allie, the priest feeds three hundred starving kids every morning. Without that breakfast, many would die."

"I don't deny that many are hungry, David, but there is no shortage of food in Chile. The poor simply can't afford to buy it. Subsidies could take care of that, of course, but Pinochet's economists limit their use to curb deficits and inflation to please the middle class. Also, look at the homes. They are decent row houses, and here and there, you see a car. The level of social disorganization also appears less than comparable poor neighborhoods in the United States."

By the time they reached the top of the hill, the seaside humidity had caused both to perspire heavily. David wiped his brow and suggested, "Allie, I'd like you to meet two of my dearest friends before visiting the priest, Jaime and Juana Magosin."

Allie's eyes lit up as if he'd hit the jackpot. "Jaime Magosin, he's one of your most famous poets. I read a poem of his on the flight down here."

"Yes, he is and makes so much money from his popular poems that Juana works in a beauty parlor to support them. In Chile, we love our poets the way Americans worship rock stars but let most of them live in poverty."

Chapter 76

Allie felt his first revolutionary tingles since the late 1960s and early 1970s as he followed David down the stone steps leading to the Magosins' bohemian digs. David knocked on the door, and a pretty freckle-faced woman of about thirty-five opened and kissed David on his cheek.

The friendly redheaded Juana hugged David and Allie and invited them into her kitchen, which was plastered with posters of Jaime's poetry readings. A minute later, Jaime—a large bearded, slovenly man—gladly halted his writing to meet with Allie.

David, Jaime, Juana, and Allie drank wine and talked mostly of America as the Magosins had visited New York and California the year before for Jaime to give poetry readings. Jaime generously read two of his revered poems for Cohen and then described his string bean poetry project idea—give readings from the southern tip to the northern border to turn people, particularly children, onto poetry.

The Magosins then escorted Allie and David over to the church for his meeting with the radical priest. "The favela," warned Jaime, "is so tense that not even the police enter it anymore, only the army and usually with helicopter gunships made in the USA."

"I'm not sure," Allie whispered to David, "if that warning and everybody on the street treating Jaime like an underground hero makes me feel more safe or less."

The group entered a shabby gray stucco Catholic church, a mere two blocks from the Magosins' apartment.

"Watch what you say," Jaime warned Allie as he closed the front door. "The priest can be curt with liberals and has no use for your sympathy, only your money."

Allie warmly smiled. "Well, Jaime, I've already given the priest enough of my money to expect him to be very polite."

They all laughed carefully, after which David and Allie followed Jaime and Juana down the corridor as they made their way through the tired old mission and finally entered a small room full of serious bearded young men sitting around a heavy wooden table.

Allie felt very thick paranoia, a sense he remebered from his SDS days. *Who the hell is this wiry, tough little guy who got up and looks like an electrician or labor leader? Man, no one is talking while this tight-lipped man leads us down a corridor and now into a cell-like room that, I swear, is lit by a single exposed bulb hanging from a brown cord. Man, is this fucking proletarian or what?*

David introduced Allie to the tight-lipped man. "Fr. Mario Alvarado, this is Dr. Allie Cohen."

David led Allie to an old black vinyl couch and served as his interpreter. The priest, dressed in a baggy green work outfit, warmly hugged Jaime and Juana, respectfully shook David's hand, and politely nodded to Cohen.

I'm detecting a bit of an attitude of the priest's suffering yet another tourist of the revolution, Cohen noted. *I expect the left to view me as a sympathetic figure and receive me in friendship and trust. From Father Alvarado, I pick up mixed vibrations, feel he originally underestimated me and now views me more seriously.*

Cohen spoke first and stated his case. "Father, I have traveled almost six thousand miles to meet an opposition leader, and my hope is to help shape a successful nonviolent centrist movement and admit to concerns over the movement's current direction."

"What direction is that?" asked Jaime.

"Father Alvarado, Jaime, Juana, I understand how thirteen years of dictatorship can foster extreme attitudes. That's why I'm worried that the Nicaraguan Sandinista model is the preference of the revolutionary front and not Alfonsín's Argentine democratic model."

Jaime nodded blankly, so Cohen continued. "I worry that if or when the Manuel Rodriguez group takes power, it would not make the same mistakes as Cuba and Nicaragua. If that is so, I pledge to do whatever I can to avoid another Allende-type tragedy."

"Chile has a long history of Socialism," Alvarado argued. "Allende's being a weak and stupid man's the real tragedy, not Socialism."

"Father," Cohen articulated, "your opinion of Allende seems to be the consensus, but you're living in the shadow of the bulwark of capitalism, the United States. Please consider that if Allende hadn't caved in to leftist pressure and nationalized the copper companies, he might still be president today."

"So what you're saying," questioned Jaime, "is that Chile must be a slave to capital. Please, we are not the fifty-first state."

Alvarado smiled wickedly. "Dr. Cohen, Chile is a long way from Washington DC. If the United States doesn't like our brand of Socialism, I say tough shit."

I must cut through their machismo with facts and reach out to them . . . or fail miserably.

"A map of the world, Father, will show that Chile is half the distance of Vietnam. The United States is also acting like a great power again. An aircraft carrier group is closer than you think. Please, I urge you not to copy the Cuban or Sandinista model. Unless you move to pluralistic democracy, you may be doomed to poverty and civil war."

Alvarado and the Magosins still stared blankly.

"Please," he persuaded. "I have no argument with your values. I too am nearly always in disagreement with Reagan administration policies. Please see me as a friend who has come to tell you what kind of world my country can or will live with. Forgive me, but I must speak the truth as I see it."

The priest excitedly jumped up, methodically walked two steps back and forth in front of his seat, and finally answered after thinking on his feet and sitting down, "So you're saying that it's Alfonsín's Argentine model or nothing, correct?"

Allie nodded and added, "It's right next door too. A high Reagan administration official told me that the United States will engineer Pinochet out of power and into exile in Spain when a credible centrist opposition fills the current void."

The reference to Ted "Still in the Pits" Bell as a "high administration official" would provide Carole with a rich laugh when Cohen shared it with her later that evening.

"Argentina," Jaime insisted, "is richer and in a better position to make capitalism and democracy work than us. Chile is poorer and needs Socialism to help all the jobless and starving people."

"Yes," Allie agreed. "Argentina is a little richer now, but with your good school system and fast-developing agricultural export industries, I predict Chile will surpass its neighbor in a decade and, in twenty years, be close to a first-world-nation status."

Allie's prediction about Chile's agricultural export industries—fruit, cut flowers, winter vegetables, and wine— fueling an economic takeoff into near first-world-nation status in two decades would prove mostly true.

"That is a pipe dream." Jaime challenged. "But if it were to happen, Socialism would get us there just the same."

"Maybe so, Jaime, but what's most important about Argentina is they *have* freedom, and you *don't.* Alfonsín's model will win you freedom too. Just as important is holding on to your freedom."

The priest, in a grim and humorless voice, argued back.

"Chile is not Argentina. We can and will make Socialism work here. How many times do I have to say it? If Washington doesn't like it, tough shit."

"At least until the United States overthrows you, and we've done that more than 220 times in Latin America over the course of a century. Furthermore, your own army is very professional and quite capable of hunting you all down like dogs and killing you. Look, the United States can live with a lot of Socialism as long as you set up a multiparty democracy and don't mess with the private sector too much."

The priest started to argue back, but Allie managed to complete his thought. "The key to helping the poor is not to drive your middle and upper classes out of the country along with their money. If you practice class warfare, you will fail the poor and leave them worse off than ever."

Alvarado, a hard-nosed man of few words, seemed deaf to Cohen's warnings.

"We will help the poor just by winning."

"And when we win," bragged Jaime, "for a change, we will do what's good for the people and not just the goddamned American banks."

I'm caught between two competing ideological visions. I'm pushing individual freedom, and they want to replace the present tyranny of the right with their own tyranny of the left. It's tiresome to debate dogmatists, but I'm worried that if they actually manage to win and start seizing private wealth, they will drive out good people like Carlos and Dulce Martello and beggar the nation.

Cohen spent the next ninety minutes going back and forth with Alvarado and Jaime. The raging argument turned out to be exciting, emotionally draining, disillusioning, and ultimately fruitless.

Allie asked for a short time out to privately consult with David in the hall.

"I have failed, David, to change a single position, and no matter how hard I press these spiritual and temporal leaders, they doggedly cling to their Socialist beliefs. Alvarado disappoints and frustrates me more than Magosin."

"I urge you, Allie, not to judge a man who pays the dues Alvarado does, a man often called the male Mother Teresa of Chile. This good shepherd tends to his flock by serving over five hundred hot meals a day and directing a dozen different community programs. One outreach program is run by Juana Magosin, who provides assertiveness training to help battered wives of overmacho Chilean men."

"How can Alvarado love Jesus," Allie wondered to David, "yet stray all the way to the altar of Marx? I sense that the key to reaching Alvarado may be helping him face up to any alienation from the Catholic faith. I have to reach this priest to unite and support an unstoppable political front."

They went back into the room, and Allie questioned the priest.

"Father Alvarado, please pardon me for asking, but I beg to know if you—a Catholic priest, a man of God—are truly a committed Marxist."

The priest answered *si* as if it was a fact known by all. Cohen viewed Alvarado as a believer in liberation theology, the new Latin mix of Catholicism and Marxism. Young priests, in the name of social justice, promote Marxist ideals to break up the old elites and reactionary economic cliques.

"Father, how can a Catholic priest," Cohen asked, "be a Marxist? Communism is a godless religion."

Alvarado shrugged and simplistically lectured.

"The United States owns Chile's copper companies and the biggest banks and doesn't give a shit about the people, only their damned profits."

Alvarado has succumbed to quick fixes, and it was up to Allie to get through to him.

"Father, you know that if the front wins and declares itself an enemy of capital, the United States will resurrect the Monroe Doctrine or the Rio Pact to overthrow you. All the money you free up to help the Chilean poor will be wasted on military defense, living standards will plunge, and the middle class will leave."

Alvarado appeared undaunted, so Allie tried harder.

"With *la revolución* under siege, repressive measures like press restrictions will need to be implemented. You will wind up bartering your copper for second-rate Russian military equipment and fourth-rate material goods. You will cling to power by tenaciously keeping a restive people under control, and eventually, the Chilean KGB wins, and love, joy, hope, and faith lose."

Cohen noticed Alvarado staring at him as if he were out of line. "So I beg you, Father—for Christ's sake, you, a Catholic priest—is that the so-called Christian utopia that your heart cries out for?"

Alvarado's sarcastic smirk dissolved. Allie had wiped it off his face, and an indignant scowl stretched across his lower lip and downward. Still, he said nothing, his silence hinting that he would not be so stupid.

Cohen finally pierced Alvarado's armor with "Father, would you please describe your relationship with Jesus for me?"

The blood ran out of Alvarado's face. The priest, though, was a tough customer and defiantly rebounded.

"No, why should I, and who the fuck do you think you are, the Vatican inquisitor?"

Cohen pretended to laugh good-naturedly but repeated the question. Alvarado, after staring blankly at him for several seconds, got up again to think on his feet. The priest eventually spoke in a monotone while pacing back and forth and then sitting down as usual.

"I serve the poor in the name and the spirit of Jesus. As I see it, capitalism has failed my people. Too few are too rich, while too many have nothing to eat. Since Socialism more fairly distributes the wealth—look at western and northern Europe, for example—it is the more Christian of the two systems. Marxism is essentially Christian charity without God or formal religion."

Cohen started to talk; Alvarado put up his hand to signal that he wasn't finished.

"Chile is a 90 percent Catholic nation and blessed with a tough people who will fight to defend their God and church. No one is going to take our Christ away, certainly not Moscow, which

535

is even farther away than the United States. I am also convinced that my Christian utopia is a better model for Chile than your dog-eat-dog capitalism and stupid materialism. America has to be dumb not to replace Pinochet with my vision for Chile."

Alvarado was pleased with his definition, though Allie felt he knew better.

The priest's beautiful political architecture is a dead end, more likely to subvert Chile than lead to his Christian utopia. Alvarado's lips are tightening, a sign that I should ask a final question and leave.

"Father Alvarado, what's wrong with just being a Christian Democrat and raising taxes on the rich?"

Alvarado readily had the last word. "Even welfare capitalism permits too much poverty and suffering. Only Socialism can bleed enough money out of the private sector to help the poor."

The priest confidently shook Cohen's hand, his way of saying goodbye, and excused himself to be interviewed by a reporter from the *Christian Science Monitor*. Allie expressed his profound gratitude and thanked him.

"I am so inspired by the dialogue," Jaime announced, "that I must run straight home to write a poem glorifying the exchange."

David and Allie walked Juana to her assertiveness training session and then took a ten-minute cab ride to Vina. Allie paid the fare and invited David to discuss Alvarado and the exchanges over a couple of beers.

"Okay, Allie, I'm eager to hear your perceptions. I'll take you to the most popular café in Place Vengara."

It was nearly 8:00 PM when the waiter sat the two of them at a small table and brought two bottles of good domestic beer. The sidewalk was filled with heavy traffic of young people on the make. This made great cover for a charged conversation taking place under the noses of the ubiquitous security police.

"I think Chile is on the brink of a Spanish-style civil war." David worried. "I've been working with my dad to develop an escape plan that will relocate the family business in Atlanta just in case. My mom's brother is currently managing the company down here, but currency controls and bribes to port officials and high government officials are bleeding us dry."

Allie suddenly thought out a centrist political strategy and bounced it off David. "Pinochet's supposedly impregnable military is a thin line to power. Military dictatorships exist by the support of the army, and an example is the shah of Iran's military melting away from love and flowers showered on them by Ayatollah Khomeini's followers."

"Allie," responded David incredulously, "you can't be serious about asking us to love motherfuckers who have tortured and killed us. Hand flowers to bastards, and tell them they are good Chileans?"

"Sort of. Look, adults won't risk urging soldiers to defect, so why not have teachers guide little kids to write and hand-deliver messages to the army? For example, a child goes up to a soldier with a note.

It reads, 'You are really a good man. Wouldn't you rather protect me in a free and democratic Chile? You have nothing to lose and can keep your cheap mortgages and car notes and gain your own freedom too.'

After the soldier reads the note," Allie added, "the kid hands the soldier a flower and blesses him—a *flower child's revolution*. There's your political slogan and banner."

"Allie, that's sweet, but I resent appealing to men who sold out their land and people for middle-class status and comforts."

"Look, David, the soldiers face the same four life alternatives all poor Chileans do—earn very little money by being a cabdriver, be part of a restaurant wait scrum and earn less, sell silly things in the street and earn practically nothing, or immigrate. Soldiers are trying to survive in tough times too, and the army is a sure ticket out of poverty."

Allie pressed David, who was not convinced.

"Please see the soldiers as men and not as labels in uniforms. The soldiers are probably rationalizing that they are able to put a roof over their kids' heads, food on the table for them to eat, and drive them to school. Their government and church are telling them that they are brave, patriotic heroes."

"Allie, I have a hard time with your leap of faith."

"David, please arrange another meeting with the priest tomorrow for the same time. I am returning to Vina with Carole to have lunch with the Sarasohn family."

Cohen joked, "For that, your grandma will stop calling me a gringo."

David didn't laugh and stonily told Allie, "Your price for freedom is way too high. Man, Allie, thousands have disappeared, and you want us to reward these cocksuckers? Shit, I want to purge the fucking army and stick their asses in jail."

"David, the opposition must first bloodlessly obtain power and reinstitutionalize democracy."

Cohen patiently encouraged him. "Freedom through nonviolence furnishes the moral capital needed to depoliticize the military. The army's will bows before civilian authority similar to

538

forcing the top down on a jack-in-the-box, and the soldiers go back to their barracks."

"Allie, I acknowledge the merit in your take-the-high-moral-ground strategy, but I doubt that Alvarado will go for it. Christ, the priest might even laugh in my face when I tell him to give the soldiers fucking flowers."

A beautiful slim blonde strolled by their table. Both of their eyes followed her sexy body swaying down the sidewalk and caused Cohen to wonder.

"Hey, David, are the chicks here easy?"

David smiled coolly. "Chilean chicks go all the way on the second date. Last year, my friend and I must have laid half the city two dates at a time."

He held up two fingers, and both laughed loudly. Two soldiers walked by as David declared, "I think the easiest and fastest way is to keep trying to kill Pinochet. Sooner or later, someone's going to get lucky. Though militarily strong, his rule is a house of cards and will collapse with his death."

The soldiers apparently heard nothing and kept walking.

David, Allie thought, *is like a younger brother as nearly everything out of his mouth sounds like me at the same age when I was ranting out against Lyndon Johnson and his Vietnam War. I really think that David can play a key political role in his nation's future, perhaps even be a future president of Chile.*

I told you, Allie, that you would be living a political thriller in Chile and have no time for writing one.

Chapter 77

"It's getting late, David, and the last bus to Santiago is leaving soon. I thank you for arranging the meeting with Alvarado and a memorable day overall."

Allie entered the bus, took a seat near the front, and waved to David as the bus pulled out of the Vengara Station on its express run to Santiago, two hours away.

Uh-oh, I should have used the bus terminal's men's room because I normally pass quantities of beer like water through a garden hose.

Sure enough, twenty minutes out of Vina, Allie had to piss so bad that he could hardly hold it in much longer. He looked to the back of the bus—no toilet—and then looked out the window and saw that they were careening through a barren countryside. Allie hesitated to ask the driver to stop and let him piss on the side of the road.

Christ, I'm in a fucking dictatorship on top of everything.

The thirty or so other passengers had no clue of the tight he was in. Cohen, a minute from wetting himself, informed the driver in fractured Spanish, "Por favor, señor, es necesario este voy el baño in la calle," which he hoped meant "It's necessary that I go to the bathroom in the road."

It didn't matter as the sight of Cohen's shaking and crossed legs accurately conveyed the nature of his physical desperation. The young conductor, with a sweep of his hand though, rationally gestured that there were many people aboard and that he couldn't just stop the bus. Cohen's leaky eyes signaled that his sphincter muscle was seconds from giving out and repeated his request to stop the bus in even lamer Spanish.

The conductor conferred with the driver, who quickly pulled over to the side of the road. Cohen stepped down from the bus and viewed a treeless and shrub-free land, only skinny dispersed cacti here and there.

The only thing to pee behind was an odd foot-wide cigarette billboard that concealed nothing, and he stood mortified by his reservoir, taking an interminable three minutes to drain. He slithered back to his seat thoroughly humiliated though very grateful to the passengers for acting as if nothing happened.

It was almost midnight when he returned to the Carrera. The desk attendant told him that Carole wasn't back from a concert performance for the government, so he took the elevator up to their suite. He was still revving too much to rest and revisited the dead rooftop bar for a drink.

He stepped fast up the last flight and strode through the doors. Incredibly, the only two patrons were again the mystery woman and her escort quietly sitting on high barstools nursing beers. Allie unobtrusively sat a stool away and ordered a beer too.

Less than a minute passed when he heard Madame X defiantly tell her friend, "Well, if my boyfriend doesn't like my making it with another guy, he can go fuck himself. Now don't get me wrong, I've been living with him for seven months and have been faithful the whole time. Still, if I get an itch to sleep with someone and he doesn't like it, well, he can go stick it in one of his damn cows. Oh, I forgot to tell you that he's the rodeo champ of Australia."

Man, that is the lead-in of a lifetime, Allie thought. *Let me break in by asking the strangers where they're from.*

He asked, and the petite beauty answered, "I'm really Welsh, though I've been living in Sydney for nine years. Let's see, you're a Yank, aren't you?"

"Yep, Allie Cohen from Atlanta, Georgia, uh, I mean Los Angeles. Well, I'm originally from New Jersey and New York. Eh, forget it. Hey, what's your name?"

"Victoria Stewart," she said in a sparkling tone. "Gee, it's wonderful to finally meet someone who speaks English as his mother tongue."

She introduced her escort, Jose, a pleasant tall Chilean-born fellow who'd lived in Sydney the past twelve years and now called himself Josie and who said the obvious.

"I've come home to visit my family, met Victoria on the plane, and invited her to stay with me at my parents'."

My guess, Cohen thought, *is Victoria took Josie up on his offer but has not become his lover.*

He asked Victoria what brought her to Chile and Santiago.

"I'm here on business," she said matter-of-factly.

"What kind, Victoria, if you don't mind my asking?"

"No, I don't mind. I give facials and body massages in a Sydney beauty parlor and am purchasing a shipment of hair care products to bring back home." He nodded; she added strangely, "I just bought a $150,000 town house condo and am closing on seventy-five acres in Queensland, on which I plan to build a sprawling ranch house with a swimming pool and tennis courts."

She sounds to me, Allie thought, *like she's bragging. I'm also curious to know how a salon operative can afford such expensive properties. You don't earn that kind of money giving happy endings in a massage parlor.*

Cohen questioned Victoria, and she said, "I'm good at handling money, mate."

542

The remaining half hour before curfew was spent sharing individual perceptions of Chile. Joblessness drove Josie to Australia shortly after the Allende removal.

"I don't recognize my old country anymore," he sadly related, "and am unlikely to ever move back. I'm an auto insurance adjuster and doing pretty well in Australia now, much better than if I was still living here, like my parents."

"Despite the political situation, guys," Allie expressed, "I'm fairly comfortable in Chile."

"I think," Victoria said, "that Pinochet and the threatening circumstances make the place feel all the more exciting."

Given Cohen's intrigues that flirted with grave reprisals, he nodded in agreement.

"Victoria," Josie urged, "if we're to beat the curfew home, we'd better leave now."

"Is it okay, mate," Victoria asked Allie, "for me and Josie to pick you up for dinner at eight tomorrow night?"

"I gratefully accept and look forward to it. Thank you for asking me."

Victoria hugged him, Josie and he shook hands, and they left. Allie ordered another beer and sipped it until a big, beefy red-faced oilman from Odessa, Texas, tried to start a conversation about a dry hole he just drilled in the northern Atacama Desert. Cohen smiled, finished his beer, said he was suddenly very tired, and politely excused himself.

He thought only of Ari on his way back to the room and wondered if his kid was eating solid food yet. Allie stifled any sense of loss when he encountered a bored and slightly drunk

Carole fumbling with her room key and quickly helped her into the room and out of her evening clothes.

"I'm getting really sick and tired, Allie, of attending banquets without you, and I really miss you during discussions with the junta leaders. This tourist designation was a big mistake because I can use your knowledge when they ask me questions about this U.S. policy or that one."

"You live and you learn, sweetie."

"True, and since I hate disappointing the people of Concepción, I will go, but it will be the last one during this leg of the tour."

After a quickie, they both fell right to sleep; and during the flight to Vina in the morning, Carole tipped him off that the CIA was following his every movement and also taping conversations whenever possible.

"Who's your source?" he asked anxiously.

"Magruder," she whispered in his ear. "He's working with the CIA who is tailing and protecting you."

"I'm not aware of any device on me"—he felt his pockets and collar and then checked his shoes—"or seen anyone following me, yet they're tracking my every move. That's wild."

The helicopter landed on the front lawn of the elegant casino located along the ocean's edge. A police car ferried Carole and Allie over to the Sarasohns' exclusive apartment house high on a hill overlooking the Place Vengara. Two hulking security police escorted the couple through a small crowd of tenants, who hatefully glared at the security officers.

It's ironic, thought Cohen, *that it might be safer for Carole and me to go it alone than to be protected by the security police.*

The first words out of Grandma Sarasohn's mouth after meeting Carole were "I apologize, Allie, for calling you a gringo."

She spoke in perfect English too.

Although Carole charmed her hosts, Allie sensed something was bugging his lover. Ida's refilling of Carole's glass with good red Malbec wasn't washing away whatever was bothering her.

Francia noticed that Allie was quieter than yesterday and teased, "Allie, you should feel freer to talk today as my mother has forgiven your Spanglish."

The telephone rang while Ida served a dessert of fresh cherries in a delicate crepe. David looked at Allie as he got up to answer it. He talked for about five minutes and said *si* a lot. Carole became withdrawn and stared at Cohen as if she were expecting trouble.

Julio picked up on tensions forming and tried to lighten things up with a Reagan and Gorbachev joke that Allie urged him to tell. Before he could complete the first sentence, David returned.

"Please forgive me, Dad, but that's a very long joke, and we don't have the time. Allie, we have a short walk, and it's a bit cool outside, so let me give you one of my sweaters."

Carole's eyes flashed that she needed information. Allie looked at her and said, "I just have to meet someone important for a drink. Don't worry, I'll be gone maybe an hour at most."

"Allie," Carole risked saying, sounding indignant, "I really need to know who this person is."

While putting on the sweater, he again told her, "It's cool. Don't worry, babe."

His evasion disturbed her. "Allie, we're in a strange country, and I have a right to know who you're meeting. Your evasiveness is making me nervous, and that's not fair of you."

Julio hoped to cool tempers by cracking a one-liner. "I'll bet he's meeting someone who'll become a character in a novel he'll write someday."

Everyone at the table laughed except Carole. Allie also laughed and then told her the truth.

"Look, I've come up with a nonviolent plan to overthrow the dictatorship just like I promised you I would. So I'm off to try to talk the radical priest into using it. Since you, more than anyone else, knows what this moment means to me, I'll expect you to understand and wish me luck, okay?"

She buried her face in her hands to show him that, as much as she wanted to bless this action, it wasn't that easy.

"I understand, Allie, but I'm also scared shit. There are two pressing matters you're forcing me to reveal in front of the Sarasohns."

Carole dropped the first of two bombshells. "Allie, I sincerely hope that the priest buys your plan, I really do. Still, I found out yesterday that I'm pregnant."

"You're pregnant!" He rejoiced. "That's fantastic. Why didn't you tell me?"

"God." Carole threw up her hands. "You can be so maddening. I was planning to tell you right after dessert, but suddenly, you're splitting to save Chile. Christ, I'm having the baby of a man who squeezes in undermining a foreign government between the coffee and the after-dinner mints."

Carole, the comedienne, cracked Allie and the Sarasohns up; her second revelation, though, was not nearly as funny.

"Bell cabled me that you'd made arrangements for Sarah to meet you in Argentina in a couple of days." Her eyes looked down at the table.

"Bell and Forman are doing a good job of keeping Sarah and me connected from everywhere so far."

"Frankly, I'm not crazy about this meet-up, but I can handle it." She looked directly at him. "All right, I know you have to start *la revolución*, so I'm sorry for kind of blasting your head. *Vaya con Dios.*"

Carole's memorable words—may you go with the grace of God—thrilled the Sarasohns and so warmed Allie and David's hearts that Cohen passionately kissed Carole on the lips.

"Thank you, babe, for being so understanding."

They left for what Allie hoped would be a meeting that sparked democracy. It was twilight and breezy as both walked across the busy plaza. Carole's pregnancy and Sarah's Argentine rendezvous made Allie's head swim while getting his rap together to sell Alvarado on the plan.

"I must warn you, Allie, not to expect the priest to go for it. Remember too that you're an outsider, so your concept will be viewed as an import."

"Tell me, David." Cohen questioned, "If freedom through nonviolence is an import, how indigenous is the Marxist-Leninist doctrine?"

David's smile said *he got it* as they walked into the exclusive shopping center on the main floor of a huge apartment complex. The priest was already waiting in a hole-in-the-wall bar on the Place Vengara side of the mall.

"David," Cohen said, "Alvarado's alone and drinking pretty hard for a priest and so early in the day too."

The priest, he learned again, was not one to extend a hand and appeared to be very troubled. Allie exchanged pleasantries and, when none were returned, got right down to business. Cohen watched Alvarado; his face expressed disbelief and impatience.

The priest seemed not to care at all that Cohen's presentation placed his life in jeopardy. Allie put the specter of grisly torture out of his mind and appealed to Alvarado with all the power of his heart and mind that he could humanly muster.

Allie finished and waited with bated breath for the priest's answer. What he heard, he didn't like. With each word, his hope for a bloodless democratic revolution fractured a little bit more.

Alvarado made it very clear. "Dr. Cohen, I will not indulge a military that acts as an occupying force over a phony threat." He banged a fist on the table. "Our first act in power will be to shrink them by half and transform the fuckers into a little technically advanced defense force."

David and Allie nodded, and Alvarado finished his plan for the military.

"The navy and air force are okay as they are. The army, though, will be reduced to the point that it can never enslave the people again."

"Firing thousands of soldiers," Cohen warned, "will dramatically increase the jobless rate that's already over 40 percent."

"That doesn't matter." Alvarado brought his argument to a conclusion. "The threat to the Chilean nation is not Bolivia or Argentina but its own fucking army. The money is better needed to help the poor and improve the schools. Screw the military."

Although Alvarado's comprehensive view implored Cohen not to argue the point, he was not to be denied.

He pushed the priest. "Please tell me how the hell you plan to force the army's collapse if not by my little-child-shall-lead-the-way plan."

"Our winning will force the army's collapse." That sounded arrogant to Cohen.

"You are not in the position to take on the army. They are impregnable, yet you act as if they were a Maginot Line to be walked around."

"I have heard your plan and believe that it cannot work."

Alvarado stubbornly concluded, "The security forces are capable of killing the teachers who instruct the children. The *arpilleras*, in my opinion, are the lone Gandhi-type concept that has a decent chance to succeed. Here, take this one as a souvenir for your superstar girlfriend."

Allie examined the square-foot-wide handmade needlepoint carpet and form of social art. Each was crafted by a mother whose son was detained by the army and then mysteriously disappeared—in Spanish, desaparecidos.

"Father, I respect the *arpilleras'* branding value, but I beg you to give my children's crusade a chance to work."

"It's impossible, Dr. Cohen. The Chilean Army is fully capable of harming little kids too."

"I seriously doubt that, Father."

Alvarado produced a list of names of whole communities of young men that had disappeared and another list of sites believed to be their mass graves. The priest tried to prove that the regime was much more draconian than widely perceived, and he depressed Allie with a ten-minute-long litany of known horrors and atrocities. After listening to Alvarado's overkill of torture and murder, Cohen so ached for the Chilean people that he gave up and withdrew his plan.

"I will discuss your idea with my comrades," Alvarado promised. "But I am sure they will reject it. I'm the most moderate one of all, and that's only because I'm a priest. If it wasn't for me, a hell of a lot more blood would already have been spilled."

Alvarado knew that his promise would make Allie feel better and waited until the priest saw it in Cohen's face. Allie perked up as Alvarado set him up.

"Now that I've listened to your plan, I'd like you to hear one of mine. I hope that you will at least return the favor."

"Yes, Father, that is fair."

"Good, now listen well. We know you are staying at the Carrera. We heard the junta is sleeping at the palace tonight, and it is very vulnerable to a bomb-laden car. The biggest obstacle preventing us from pulling it off is an inability to penetrate the tight security and maze of roadblocks."

The little hairs on the nape of Cohen's neck began to rise as the priest continued.

"With your cover of fame and respectability, you can help us get the limo into the plaza area. Then after we drop you off at the hotel, our martyr will smash through the front gates and blast

550

into Pinochet's apartment. So, my friend, if you really want to help Chile, help us kill Pinochet tonight."

Cohen, whose only plan for the evening was to get into Victoria's pants without Carole finding out, realized the priest was asking him to be an accomplice to the mass murder of a foreign government. If Carole had heard Alvarado's request, she'd have had a heart attack.

Alvarado noticed that Allie was wavering and stepped up his sales pressure by playing to what he thought was Cohen's vanity.

"I sense that what drives you, Dr. Cohen, is to wind up in the history books. Your humble claim to just make a difference conceals a hidden wish to have a road or school named after you."

The priest ignored Cohen's acting offended and continued. "So, if you help us, I will have you declared another Bernard O'Higgins. Our first public works project will be to build La Boulevard de Allie Cohen, or do you prefer a park or university? Look, time is running out, so shit or get off the pot."

Alvarado's asking me to kill and his Monty Hall and Let's Make a Deal *attitude is fucking outrageous and disturbing.*

Cohen concluded, "Sorry, Father, I'd have to be out of my fucking mind to do something that stupid."

"You're wrong. We worked it out and have it down to a science."

Allie saw that Alvarado was pumped and pushing hard. Cohen recalled Carole's tip of the CIA's reporting his actions to Magruder at the U.S. Embassy and urged caution.

"I'm sure that this conversation is being recorded, Father. I'm being tailed and my conversations taped. Unless you desist, you risk endangering your life too."

"Fuck 'em! They wouldn't dare come after me. They know better."

Alvarado's arrogance, Allie figured, made further discussion pointless.

"Father, I'm truly sorry that we cannot do business, but perhaps someday we will meet again. *Vaya con Dios.*" Alvarado got up to shake his hand.

"I am sorry too, but I want you to know that I respect you, Dr. Cohen, and think you're a good man. Now since I can't talk you into wiping out the junta, maybe I can hit you up for another donation. *Si?*"

Allie laughed and put his arm around Alvarado's shoulder. "Father, I appreciate the compliment and pledge $200,000."

Tears formed in Alvarado's eyes. "Bless you, Dr. Allie Cohen, for your great generosity. Two hundred thousand will help me buy in such bulk that I can feed two thousand of my people really good food every day for a year."

"Indeed, I will donate two hundred thousand a year for as long as you have the need to feed hungry Chileans. The Lord has given you a gift for this job, and it has become your shield. This money should help keep you protected from the junta."

Alvarado was genuinely touched by Allie's offer of protection.

"For your blessing and good heart, Dr. Allie Cohen, I will nominate you for the Nobel Peace Prize. I promise that the letter goes out as soon as the money comes in."

The promise brought tears to Cohen's eyes too, and he gave Alvarado his business card.

"Here, call my friend Sandy Forman at this number, and he will have the money in your account ASAP." He hugged the priest. "Take care, Father."

Allie and David left the bar and, while walking back to the apartment, calculated that the front would fail in their car-bombing attempt that evening. Allie told David that the junta was planning to stay overnight in Concepción.

"And with security so tight," David declared, "the odds against the suicide driver making it inside the cordon were staggering at best."

The sound of Allie's voice coming through the front door lit Carole's face up like a lantern. He went straight to Carole and romantically kissed her on the lips for several seconds and then hugged her.

With a heroic aura bathing him, he thanked Mr. and Mrs. Sarasohn and family for providing him the rare insider's involvement in an actual revolution. Allie approached each family member, even Grandma, and either hugged, kissed, or shook their hands.

Eventually, Allie reached Julio and David and put his arms around father and son. Cohen said to Sarasohn the elder, "Julio, how does it feel to be the father of a future president of Chile? I know that you are very proud of this fine young man. Now please tell me that Reagan and Gorbachev joke."

Cohen's prediction affected Julio, who after laughing hugged his son and nearly wept from pride, although David would not become president of Chile. He would head a software group that developed the agricultural software that computerized

Brazilian and South American farmers' operations, resulting in dramatically increased crop yields.

The software and new fertilizers transformed two vast regions into agricultural powerhouses, first the Mato Grosso in the southwest and later the Cerrado northeast of it. Brazil equaled the United States as the world's largest food producer in 2010 and daily exported to America over half of its citrus products.

David became a billionaire Socialist and helped advance democracy by investing much of his fortune in innovative schools for poor children and financing over ten thousand college scholarships for students in need. He suffered a fatal heart attack at age fifty-seven while skateboarding with his grandson Seth down the long Hill Parish incline.

Chapter 78

Carole's security agents arrived, so they warmly bid their new Chilean friends farewell, drove to the casino with Magruder, boarded the helicopter, and flew to Santiago to drop Allie off. From there, Jim accompanied Carole on a flight to Concepción for a short performance and banquet.

Cohen was chauffeured to the Carrera for a change of clothes; quickly showered and put on a blue oxford shirt, gray slacks, and a blue sport jacket; and waited for Victoria and Josie in the lobby. He only had to wait a moment when Victoria, clad in a low-cut, formfitting black knit dress, sexily glided up the steps leading to the mezzanine. Josie, dressed in a gray suit with yellow shirt, followed her.

Allie stood up to greet them, shook Josie's hand, and politely kissed Victoria on the cheek. Josie tendered an evening destination for their consideration.

"My parents suggest Los Adobes de Argomedo and describe the place as a traditional, folkloric restaurant and nightclub and very lively too."

That sounded fine to Allie and Victoria, and the cab ride across downtown took ten only minutes. They were quickly seated at a table in the cavernous and half-empty restaurant, and in seconds, six waiters surrounded them to take drink and food orders.

This sad gang of six, thought Cohen, *makes me wonder if a local priest is also helping feed their children.*

Los Adobes's shellfish appetizers were tough and flavorless, but the hearty red wine soon loosened inhibitions. Allie rationalized that he liked Josie and felt mixed emotions about moving on Victoria.

But she's so fucking hot, and tonight's my last shot.

Luckily, Bonita, an old Chilean high school girlfriend of Josie, recognized him. Bonita and Josie started talking, she asked him to dance, he smiled happily, and they disappeared for the next hour. Allie took notice of their prolonged absence and asked Victoria if she was doing a thing with Josie.

"By a *thing*, I think you mean," she cutely answered, "am I sleeping with him?"

Allie smiled sheepishly and nodded yes. She looked him dead in the eye.

"Eight days ago, I met the bloke on the plane and accepted his offer to stay with him at his parents'. For eight straight mornings now, Josie's crawled into my bed and put his hands all over me. And for eight straight mornings, I've pushed him away. I guess he's just not my type."

Allie translated her remark. *She fancies me instead.*

And he impulsively asked, "Victoria, please sleep with me tonight."

She flashed a smile that said *yes* but then addressed the obvious. "Josie may not like being brushed off so easy, unless he's out back in the alley giving his old schoolmate a poke or two. You know what I mean?" She elbowed him, and he laughed.

"Fuck it, Victoria, let's dance." Allie pulled Victoria down onto the dance floor.

"Allie," she warned him, "I've never learned to cha-cha-cha."

"Okay, follow me. You go back three steps and then forward three steps. You move to the side like this. Hey, you're picking it like a natural."

556

Two minutes passed. "You know, we're a pretty nimble dance team," he joked. "Maybe we should turn professional and call ourselves Barbara and Nate or something like that."

Six dances later, they were both dripping wet with sweat and retired to their table. "Josie is nowhere in sight. Victoria, please tell him that you'll be leaving with me."

Victoria responded by giving Allie a wet kiss, pressed her hot body against him, and fondled his dick under the table.

"Please, Victoria." He cautioned, "If you don't stop now, I'm going to come in my pants like a teenage boy."

"Ha ha ha! I love it. Okay, look, while I tell Josie that I won't be home tonight, you go fetch a cab, all right, mate?"

Five minutes passed before she joined him in the cab, and they fondled each other all the way to the hotel. The desk clerks looked at them with disapproving eyes as they passed by and into the elevator. They both began removing clothes as soon as Allie opened the door, and Victoria was faster.

Allie sat down on the bed right next to Victoria, already naked. *Man, she looks even better with her clothes off than on.*

Victoria pulled a joint from her purse, lit it, toked hard, and passed it to Allie. "This pot is Aussie, homegrown from my property in Queensland."

Two tokes later, Allie blessed the herb. "I pronounce Queensland's finest Awesome Victoria Homegrown."

Victoria stroked his cock to make him really hard and then got on top and stayed there until they enjoyed a powerful orgasm.

"I've become an old-school Australian woman about sex, Allie."

She laughed heartily and then illuminated him. "We get our men off twice, so they tend to come back home or stay put. They know a good thing when they feel it."

"I strongly agree with the custom and psychology, Victoria, and recommend it to all couples."

Both of them laughed. "Now." She purred. "I'm gonna suck your hard dick and prove it to you."

"I never doubted your word, ha, oooh, ahh, wow, what you can do with your tongue. Ooohh, you're magical, baby."

Victoria got Allie off and, a few minutes later, drew a bath for the two to relax in. The front's car-bombing scheme suddenly popped into Cohen's brain, and a cold dread came over him. Allie sat up abruptly; Victoria sensed something was bothering him.

"What's the matter? Did I do something wrong, Allie?"

"No, not at all, sweetie, but please come here."

He walked her over to the big window, spoke in a soft voice to her, and revealed, "I think there's going to be a possible assassination attempt against the junta tonight. I'm kind of indirectly involved but not complicit in any way. I don't know if that makes any sense, but all hell may break loose at any minute."

Victoria, more impressed than scared, repaid Allie's trust with an electrifying revelation of her own.

"You asked me about my owning such expensive properties. Well, let me start by telling you how cocaine has spread like wildfire across Australia. My exclusive salon introduced nose candy to our rich patrons, and they immediately became ultraloyal customers, and a few became our partners. In three years, we've moved nine shipments out of Chile totaling 1,530 kilos or about

3,060 pounds. We also bring stuff in from Indonesia and Burma or Myanmar as they now call themselves."

"'Makes sense. You have to hide the cash by buying houses and cars or whatever."

"Exactly, I'm known down under as the Cocaine Queen and have earned more than three million tax-free in less than five years. That's why I'm in Chile. It's my turn to be the mule. Luckily, my load this time is only 190 kilos."

Allie was curious about how she got the cocaine out. "My syndicate smuggles it out in custom-made beauty packets that we designed for this job and sell the packets through a chain of two dozen hair and nail salons in Sydney, Melbourne, Brisbane, and Surfers Paradise. Let's pray that it works one more time."

"How did you wind up in Australia, Victoria?"

"I married at seventeen to escape my tyrannical Welsh father." She winced. "My dad was a navy man and the worst control freak you ever met. We were stationed in Malta for years, so to get away from him and Malta, I married a handsome local brute and ran off to Australia." She winced again. "After two kids and ten years, I couldn't fake love anymore and left him a year ago."

"I understand." Allie nodded. "Life forces us to make tough decisions."

"I'm counting on this last big score to secure me for the rest of my life. If I get caught, though, I'll jump the surety bond of $100,000 the organization has set up for me to flee to South Africa." She looked nervously to Cohen.

"Do you want to become a marginal outlaw," he asked her, "living on the fringes of the waning British Commonwealth?"

"Allie, you just made me nervous as hell by putting it like that."

"Good, your kids need you too much to be risking their stability on an unneeded coke deal. If you get caught, they could declare you an unfit mother and place your kids in foster homes, maybe even put them up for adoption too."

She wavered for a moment, so he stepped up the pressure on her. "Please, for me, don't do it. Hey, you don't need the fucking money that badly, so why the hell can't you quit when you're ahead?"

Victoria trembled and reached out for him to hold her. While he comforted her, a speeding black limousine raced across Constitution Plaza. Victoria and Allie got up fast and stared disbelievingly at a 4,500-pound ramrod going at least seventy.

"Shit," Cohen cursed. "I bet it's loaded with at least 300 pounds of dynamite."

Three army jeeps firing machine-gun rounds followed in hot pursuit after the limo until the vehicle smashed through a protective gate and raced up the long presidential palace alleyway. The army jeeps, having failed to stop the vehicle, reversed gear to get out of there as fast as they could.

Allie reacted by grabbing Victoria. "Let's take cover under the bed."

And they did in the nick of time too, for the powerful blast hurled debris for hundreds of yards in all directions and cracked one of his windows. Cohen switched on the TV and translated a news flash from the government broadcast station.

"The latest assassination attempt against the administration has failed. The palace was empty because President Pinochet

560

and the government were staying in Concepción tonight. The perpetrators will soon be rounded up and punished."

Hey, he thought. *I better get the hell out of Chile fast. The safest place to hang out is probably the American Embassy, but it's the middle of the night, so I need to lie low until morning at least.*

The incredible excitement and Victoria's sexuality combined to produce a near-sleepless evening. By 6:00 AM, Allie was so satiated from sex and hyper about leaving Chile that he called the desk to arrange a cab for his Aussie sex machine. Victoria slowly put on her clothes, wrote down addresses where she might meet up again with him someday, and left Allie with a soulful long goodbye kiss.

As luck would have it, Carole stepped out of the elevator. Because of the terrorist attack, her security guard was recalled from Concepción, so she impulsively hitched a ride in the hope of surprising Allie in bed and the two of them making love for hours. As she turned the corner, Victoria left the suite with a smug smile on her face.

So this is my reward for running home to make love for hours—catch Allie take a two-to-one lead in sex with others. Should I make this a big issue or just reserve a freebie for myself in the future? Whatever, but I'm sure as hell going to wipe that smile off that woman's face. That's for damn sure.

"Look, honey, I can see that you and Allie had a good time tonight, but please don't advertise it with your obscene smile."

"Oh my god," Victoria raved. "Don't tell me you're Allie's girlfriend who's here singing for the junta? Jesus Christ, Carole Herman, the movie star. Hey, you're big down under too, sweetie."

Carole said sarcastically, "That's nice, honey."

561

"Listen, sweetie," Victoria teased. "I'm genuinely flattered, but don't you worry, I won't be asking you for an autograph. You see, Carole, I already know how you sign your name, cha-cha-cha."

Carole considered slugging the shit out of her but ruled it out for all the right reasons, especially in a foreign country, a dictatorship no less. She let it go and entered the suite.

Let me focus instead on the real culprit—Allie, my lover and partner.

Carole avoided making a scene by dead-bolting the door and acting horny toward the sexually spent Cohen.

"Come on, Mr. Tourist Man, let's fuck for hours. We've hardly had any time together in Chile. That's because you've been catching a lot more than *trout*, Mr. Tourist Man, haven't you?"

"Carole, I'm exhausted and not in the mood for mind games, so please remove your hand from my penis. Look, babe, I'm glad you're home safe, and it's great to see you. I heard the exchange with Victoria, so yes, a second meaningless thing fell into my lap. You now have an entitlement and feel free to use it, but if you don't mind, I must sleep. 'Night.'"

My god, he's out cold just like that. Carole pressed her hands up against her face. *His indifference worries the shit out of me.* She pondered, *Are we approaching the "too much water over the dam" stage?*

For the first time, her mother's words rang in her ears. "You and Allie are on a fast track to nowhere." She recalled Sam's words: "A frozen relationship with Allie will drive you to leave him."

But I'm pregnant and want this baby, and in all fairness to Allie, I've left him alone with too much free time as a tourist. I've learned a lesson from this. He needs a real partner and to be at my side. I need him by me to take advantage of his genius and will get Ted Bell to stop isolating him from me.

So far, the tour has been challenging, but it's also promising to be one of the most vital experiences of my life. Allie's crime is cheap and empty sex on the run with a ravishing creature. The girl is gone, and I'm still here, pregnant and moving on to Argentina with my one-man university to hang with. God, I really want this baby.

No one said it would be easy, girl. There is always some bad with a ton of good, so go to sleep and get some rest too.

They awoke at noon, and Carole still wanted to make love.

"Please forgive me, Carole, for being selfish and insensitive. I love you, babe, you know that. I'm just still too drained."

"I can live with that."

Sure you can, Carole. By the way, Victoria succeeded in her smuggling effort and got out of the trade. She took up with Louie, a five-foot-two-inch Maltese bodybuilder, who got it up six times a day and made her very happy indeed.

They retired comfortably on her Queensland property and raised sheepdogs and Awesome Aussie Homegrown for ten years until Louie had a heart attack and died while having sex for the seventh time that day. Victoria would live until ninety-two and outlast seven husbands, though Louie was the great love of her life.

Chapter 79

Allie and Carole stealthily fled the hotel at 1:00 PM and took a cab over to the U.S. Embassy to seek protection.

Magruder, waiting for them, speculated. "You know, Allie, I sense that you've learned a real hard lesson about the Latin left, eh?"

"I sure did, Jim. I'm impressed with their idealism, but I'm really disillusioned by their methods and stubborn blindness to geopolitical realities."

"I agree. Anyway, this is a file listing the times and places, Cohen, where you stopped to piss the past three days, including behind the odd foot-wide sign along the road."

Allie cracked up laughing. "An agent was riding on the bus with you and was going to come to your assistance in case the driver didn't stop the bus. Luckily, he did."

Cohen quickly thumbed through it, laughed at its extensiveness, and kidded back, "Has the CIA done a stool sample yet?" Magruder and Carole laughed tears.

"Allie," Jim admitted, "I've always had a fondness for well-meaning, wise guys like you, so listen well. We're concerned that the junta might try to pin this on you instead of Alvarado. Someone has to pay, and Pinochet and company fear looking weak. They might also lose public support if they go after him because his feeding programs keep him alive and virtually untouchable."

Magruder changed gears. "Allie, speaking from my heart, I must congratulate you on the excellent judgment you displayed in Vina yesterday. You truly are a man of peace, and I have the tape recordings to prove it."

Allie shook Jim's hand; Carole hugged him. Magruder smiled and continued.

"In my opinion, this so-called priest whom you pledged two hundred thousand big ones to forever betrayed your trust."

"How, Jim?"

"Jaime and Juana Magosin"—Allie's eyes widened— "dressed up as you and Carole to enter the security zone."

Cohen gasped; Magruder choked up a bit. "The soldiers figured out they were carrying out a suicide bomber mission after Jaime stopped in front of the Carerra, nobody got out then sped up and raced at seventy miles per hour toward the presidential palace."

Cohen felt sick inside; Jim wiped a tear from his eye. "The army chased after them in jeeps, shouting from loudspeakers that the palace was empty, but the Magosins must have figured that they were being tricked. The army finally tried to shoot their tires out but it was in vain."

Jim looked up at Allie. "They fucking killed themselves for nothing."

"Jim, how do you know it was them?"

"Jaime and Juana jointly published an epic poem, essentially a political suicide and martyrdom note, to explain their reasons and titled it 'Jaime and Juana's Last Will and Testament for Chilean Freedom.' They also found his driver's license. Is that enough evidence for you?"

"I never would have thought them capable of doing something like this. Shit, I drank wine with them the other day. They discussed a new poetry program called String Bean Poetry Road, in which he reads his poems from one end of Chile to the other. David Sarasohn is going to take their deaths very hard."

Jim revealed classified information. "The junta has been shaken by the left's new strategy of martyrdom missions that create heroes for the opposition to rally behind."

Carole stiffened up. "Jim, that makes me very anxious. Both of us were possibly exposed as terrorists."

"Not quite, Carole, though the security forces, Allie, are employing torture in wholesale fashion. Given their typical ruthlessness in leaving no stone unturned, you are potentially in very grave danger."

Carole gasped. "Now I'm terrified." She playfully punched Allie in the arm for getting them in trouble.

Allie laughed off her little shot and reasoned, "Jim, even if they tear out the damn tongues of every poor bastard in the Hill Parish, all they're going to discover is that I wasn't involved."

"That's not the point," advised Magruder. "Eventually, they're going to tear out your tongue to get more goods on Alvarado and his Manuel Rodriguez group. Therefore, I've got to get your ass out of Chile as soon as possible."

"How?"

"I'm going to send you to Buenos Aires disguised as an embassy courier. A seat is already booked on an Eastern Air Lines flight that's due to leave in an hour, so we don't have any time to waste. Carole, don't worry, I have a whole bag of tricks to dig into for you if necessary."

"I sure hope so, Jim." She had calmed to edgy.

"You know, Jim, I'm going to give Alvarado the money to help Chile's poor until they are a first-world nation. For what it's worth to the Nobel people, he pledged to me his nomination."

Jim gave his opinion while dragging long and hard on a cigarette. "I think he forfeited your gift and earned your contempt, but it's your money. Regarding U.S. policy, we wouldn't have minded if he'd succeeded. If Pinochet and his forces kill Alvarado, a beloved Catholic priest, he'll be martyred in a second, and a bloodier revolution than El Salvador's will start."

"We're all lucky," declared Cohen, "that such an outcome hasn't already happened. The key is organizing an unstoppable nonviolent centrist movement that shames the soldiers into putting down their guns, right?"

"Yes, Allie, but it will not be fast enough to satisfy you or me. Anyway, the embassy will work with the hotel in packing up and forwarding your clothes and other property. Now let's get going."

"Thank you, Jim, for all you're doing for us."

"My pleasure. Hey, Ted Bell cabled me. Allie, you're to meet Mrs. Cohen in the Argentine Airways terminal. She'll stay in the Hotel Elevage just off the Avenida de Florida, the fashionable walking street."

"Is the Elevage a big place or a boutique hotel?"

"It's a cute clean boutique hotel, and Tony—the owner—is an old friend of mine, so he'll take good care of you. For security reasons, you and Carole, who'll fly in tomorrow morning, will stay in the more fortresslike Sheraton. After a tour of the capital and country, you'll be the guests of President Alfonsín, whom I think is a great guy."

Magruder, driving even faster than he talked, made Cohen's heart race. About a mile or so from the airport, Jim touched Allie's heart.

"Allie, the best part of working in the foreign service and the agency in the past twenty years is the friends I've made. Coincidentally, my closest buddy in life—and the godfather of my children—is Frank Johnson, a swell guy I'm sure you remember meeting in Moscow."

"Yes, Frank Johnson—God bless him—really kept Ridley Dimple off my back and nominated me for the Nobel Peace Prize too, a hell of a guy."

"Dimple drives Frank nuts,."

Magruder dragged off his cigarette. "Allie," said Jim in an emotional voice. "I'm sorry for assigning special agents to track your every movement in Chile, but I'm proud of those transcripts and how they captured your efforts at peacemaking. I swear that the passages in the church and bar with Alvarado are God's words in action and good old American common sense. Your appeal to the priest to pursue nonviolent change agents warrants my Nobel support too."

Jim held his own nominating letter up and waved it in the air.

"Allie, I adore your 'a flower child shall lead the way' plan and think it could work, but the front probably rejected it because they're too full of hatred for Pinochet and his gang. As soon as I get back to the embassy, I plan to mail this to a certain Norwegian assemblyman who, I know, is on the nominating committee. And, pal, I surely hope the plan and the transcripts are the tipping point in your favor."

Magruder's lavish praise made Cohen blush and kid Jim. "I forgive you, Jim, for your undercover transgressions." Then he laughed. "Can you imagine a radical priest and a CIA agent both nominating me from the same country? What are the odds against something like that happening?"

Magruder laughed hard. Cohen stopped laughing when Jim told him his courier alias, J. Tinsley Ellis.

"Come on, Jim, you got to be kidding me." The absurdity wasn't lost on Magruder, who smiled and briefed Cohen on a diplomat's customs procedures. Afterward, Allie praised Magruder that he was restoring Cohen's faith in the government again.

Magruder smiled happily at that line while parking in front of the airport entrance.

The first thing Jim did when he got out of the car was hire a cab to take Carole right back to the Carrera. Carole initially balked until Jim convinced her that her presence endangered Allie and him.

She saw the light, passionately kissed Allie goodbye, and left in an agitated state.

Once Carole's cab was out of sight, Magruder led Cohen through the diplomatic channels section of the Chilean Immigration Authority. Jim behaved as if he was performing a routine task and joked around with some of the officers.

The act worked perfectly until a newly appointed security chief questioned Jim's presence. Cohen's heart pounded while Magruder massaged the situation as a matter of official business of the United States.

The security chief challenged Jim and barked, "I don't believe you. The assistant chargé d'affaires doesn't have time to bother with menial tasks like this. Now tell me the truth. Why are you really here?"

The smooth Magruder didn't miss a beat in devising a shrewd cover.

"Please try to understand that this guy's the not-too-bright son of an extremely rich sponsor of President Reagan's new presidential library he's going to build in Simi Valley just north of LA. The secretary of state himself wrote a personal memo directing me to help the lame from screwing up. Hey, have you ever seen a duller face on a State Department employee?"

Magruder scrunched Cohen's face with his hand to make him look stupid.

"Also, look how slovenly he's dressed to fly to Argentina on official business. My god, jeans and a Members Only jacket. Now do you understand why I'm here?"

Jim continued to scrunch Cohen's face until the Chilean condescendingly grinned, making Allie suppress laughter and anger. Jim's laying it on thick worked beautifully; they breezed through immigration, but a minute later, the airport announced that mechanical trouble delayed the Eastern plane for three hours.

Cohen tensed up, but Magruder quickly found him another seat on an Iberia Airlines 747 flight due to leave in ten minutes. He handheld Allie out to the plane and seat, and that made his day.

"Congratulations, Allie, on beating the junta. Man, you are something else. You've given me some great stories to tell Frank and the boys the next time we all get together."

Jim rejoiced a minute too soon; the pilot approached him. "I'm sorry to say that leftists have phoned in yet another bomb threat."

"Shit," he complained to Cohen. "They are relentless in their efforts to undermine the economy by disrupting basic services like transportation systems."

The Iberia pilot announced to the passengers, "The flight has been delayed. All passengers are to immediately vacate the craft."

"Jim," said Allie, sounding fearful and paranoid, "I just imagined Pinochet himself sticking a hot poker up my ass to make me talk."

Magruder giggled loudly and then calmed Cohen down. "Allie, the platoons of security men running around here are looking for a bomb, not you."

Cohen remained a nervous wreck until cleared for takeoff. The cold sweats stopped when the plane left the ground. The tightness in Allie's chest disappeared upon the airliner's clearing the Andes range into Argentine airspace. With the fading away of the last snowcapped peak in the distance, he beamed a satisfied wide grin.

By the time Allie landed in Buenos Aires and easily cleared customs, he was smiling uncontrollably and had a bop in his step. Cohen naturally got his luggage first and walked out of baggage with a shit-eating grin on his face and a hip hop in his step.

Chile, for Allie, was a great political thriller that earned him two Nobel nominations, a total of three major and four minor supporters to date. It is rumored that consensus for a nominee usually forms after the fourth or fifth major endorsement.

Adonai is very impressed by your overtures for peace in both Russia and Chile. Keep up the good work, prophet. People are taking notice.

Chapter 80

Allie strutted around the huge Argentine Airlines terminal building to rendezvous with Sarah and quickly spotted her fending off the advances of tangoing Argentine males. She raised her right foot to threaten the more persistent peacock with a kick in the shins if he didn't cool it.

A single glance was all he needed to see why the Argentines were hitting on Sarah. *My wife looks hot.*

He hugged and held her tightly. "Sarah, us meeting up five thousand miles from Atlanta is the most romantic and exciting thing we ever did. I swear, I've never been happier to see you, babe."

"This is exciting, Allie, a five-thousand-mile hookup." They both laughed.

"Sarah, my darling redhead, I love your new semipunk hairstyle, and this denim outfit you're wearing is really cool."

Allie brought tears to her eyes with his greeting. They kissed openmouthed, and Sarah could feel Allie burning as hot as ever for her and suggested, "Let's put our lust on hold, pal, and hail a cab to take us to the Elevage."

They got into a taxi, and Allie immediately asked Sarah, "I know you have lots of pictures of Ari to show me. Please let me see them."

She pulled out a dozen Polaroids from her travel bag and provided a detailed account for each. He stared intensely at every one to assess his infant son's growth and development.

"Ari's more adorable than ever, and his personality seems to be emerging. There are so many things, Sarah, that I can't wait to do with him."

Allie's being more interested in Ari's changes than telling Sarah his Chilean adventures first thing impressed her.

After her umpteenth motherly brag, she thought, *I'll check his eyes for signs of glaze. Wow, none, total focus. I'm impressed.*

"Okay, Allie, I'm ready to hear about your political adventures in Pinochet Land."

Allie happily shared his tales of risk and chicanery with David Sarasohn, Alvarado, and Pinochet and his flower children's revolution.

"I'm proud of you, Allie, maybe in awe too at the chances you took for Chilean freedom. I have a reading workshop focusing on multicultural resources at Elena's school two weeks from now, so we should have a lot to talk about."

"Your being behind me, Sarah, enables this peace mission. You keep me connected with Ari and you. That makes me love and appreciate you more than ever."

"I have come to understand, even love, my part in this mission, Allie, but that doesn't mean it's easy. I just hope that you hurry and get your peace offensives out of you and then come home for us to grow old together."

The taxi edged its way through the heavy downtown traffic and onto Maipú Street, a short distance from the famous Plaza de San Martin. Sarah, taking in the sights and liking Buenos Aires and glad that things were going well, reminded herself,

Make no demands, set no expectations, and just enjoy yourself.

The first bloom off the rose came while registering Sarah into the Hotel Elevage.

Allie needlessly told the desk clerk, "I'll be paying for Mrs. Cohen's room with my American Express card."

The laconic tall Dutchman drolly replied, "Well since your Amex card says that you're Mr. Cohen, that isn't so unusual now, is it?"

Allie thought the clerk to be a bit out of line but bungled his effort at damage control.

"You don't understand. I'm staying at the Sheraton."

"Well, then I wish you luck on your reconciliation."

The presumptuous clerk bruised Sarah's good mood. Allie drew back, took a deep breath, and then directed the bellhop to carry the luggage to their room. Cohen remained mum until he tipped the young man and then tried to erase the disappointed look on Sarah's face with a one-liner. "They say that an Argentine is an Italian who speaks Spanish and acts like an Englishman."

The one-liner worked, and she managed a short laugh. Allie resorted to the one magic elixir that never failed them; he made love to her. Great sex always put a smile on Sarah's face, and afterward, she beamed from within.

She delighted. "My god, Allie, that's the first time during oral sex that you ever got me off. I think that alone may have been worth the long flight."

Allie laughed loudly and switched on the TV set.

Allie, Sarah thought, *normally irritates me when he puts on the TV news right after good sex. I prefer to savor my orgasms. This time, I think I welcome any distraction from the sentimentality welling up in me.*

Sarah, fluent in Spanish, got up from the bed to pee and was stopped cold by a breaking news report about the recent assassination attempt against the Chilean government.

"The Chilean authorities," Sarah translated, "suspect possible involvement of a visiting American activist who is believed to have fled to Argentina." She sat back down on the bed. "That's you, isn't it?"

Her eyes were full of wonderment and fixed on him.

"Yes, two of David Sarasohn's friends, Jaime and Juana Magosin, dressed as Carole and I entered the plaza area to carry out their suicide car bombing. Jim Magruder at the U.S. Embassy knows all this, and so do Pinochet's security forces, which, I imagine, fear that looking penetrable will inspire more bombing efforts."

"That's spooky, Cohen."

"If you think that was spooky, you should have seen those army jeeps chasing that limo packed with dynamite. Man, the army was firing machine guns at the car's tires like in a damn war movie."

Allie looked down; Sarah noticed sadness. "Allie, what's wrong?"

"A couple of days ago, David Sarasohn and I were drinking wine with Jaime and Juana Magosin. They were happy, normal people and telling us many exciting future plans. The day after, they wrote a suicide poem to explain their martyrdom mission to take out the junta. I'm bewildered by their actions, Sarah, because I believe in living for a cause, and prefer not to die for it."

"What's going to happen? Will death squads come after you?"

"I doubt it."

"That's a relief." They both grinned. "You know, Allie, I've never shared my bath before with a real revolutionary on the run. 'Care to join me?"

"Yes, that'd be nice."

They bathed, dressed, and took a cab to register Allie into the Sheraton. During the ride, Sarah expressed a yen to sample some good Argentine beef, so they left the Sheraton and crossed the eight lanes of Avenue Antardita Argentina to eat at La Chacra, a homey and popular steak and pit barbecue restaurant.

While waiting to be seated, Allie pointed out to Sarah a valued aspect of Argentine life.

"Watch this short bull of a gaucho chef hack apart sizzling slabs of beef and pork and methodically turn over rows of those plump, little sausage links. Argentina is similar to America, The sweetness of life is often celebrated in the abundance of relatively cheap good food."

"Not cheap enough, Allie, for the malnourished 40 percent of the population who can't afford to buy enough of it. I read that statistic on the flight down here."

Their attentive tall waiter brought platters full of tender, charcoal-broiled meats; crisp salad vegetables; hand-cut, fried potatoes; and oversized glasses of rich red wine and cold golden beer. The owner showed his appreciation with a complementary appetizer of grilled blood sausage.

Allie messed with Sarah. "I bet ol' grandpa Alvin is smiling down from heaven at my eating one of the most unkosher foods."

La Chacra's relaxed atmosphere provided a pleasant setting for the Cohens to discuss how terribly complicated their lives had become. Sarah related her daily demands of maintaining a household, raising a child, meeting doctoral requirements, advancing the human relations treatment, and trying to have some semblance of a social life.

She neglected to mention that she had maid service and a live-in nanny and was flying next week to England to speak at S. K. Kapoor's symposium. The Cohens did not go near the subject of Sarah and Kapoor's discreet Scottish getaway after the conference.

"Sarah," Allie said, busy munching away, "these are the best damn short ribs of beef I've ever eaten."

Allie,.with one breath, whined over not witnessing Ari's graduation to solid food, then bubbled over with enthusiasm at the prospect of visiting Patagonia with Sarah.

"I'm sorry, Sarah, for not having as much time to spend with you as we'd like."

"That's okay, Allie." She smiled at him. "I'm glad for the time we have together."

"I appreciate that, thank you. Now let me suggest dessert elsewhere. Let's take a cab up to the Quintana Avenue in the heart of the Recoleta district."

During the cab ride, he showed her how Buenos Aires had elements of New York, London, Paris, and Madrid in its construction and was mainly peopled by Italians, Spanish, Germans, Irish, Russians, and Jews. Buenos Aires residents struggled daily to maintain personal dignity in the face of economic difficulty. It was hard to figure how the restaurants stayed so full when the per capita income was so low.

Allie and Sarah settled into a dessert place called L'Azucar. That worked nicely, and he next suggested they walk up to the place's second-floor disco to dance some calories off and have a good time. It all came together beautifully, and they capped the night off by taxiing back to the Elevage to sip liqueurs in the hotel café before retiring to Sarah's room for the evening.

The next morning, Allie served as Sarah's tour guide.

"Any tour of Buenos Aires, Sarah, starts with La Boca, the mouth of the Rio de la Plata, which is as wide as an inland sea. Historically, La Boca was an undesirable area because of flooding and yellow fever fluxes, but waves of poor immigrants gravitated to the district, the last of which was so heavily Italian that they stamped their identity on it."

"I love the Caminito, Allie. The grillwork on the houses on this special street is to die for."

The Cohens left the Caminito and walked up the slightly seedy Necochea Street. Edginess began replacing Sarah's air of delight because the place was getting increasingly tougher looking. By the time they reached the next corner, Brandsen Street, Sarah's curiosity of La Boca waned.

"Allie, I think I'm ready to move on to your next stop, the San Telmo area, I believe. But first, I need to snack and go to the bathroom."

Cohen scoured the four corners for a suitable pit stop. "We have our choice of the three cantinas on this corner." He selected the cleanest-looking Italian-style café.

"Sarah, this place is the best available. Please promise not to overreact to what threatens to be fairly primitive conditions."

They entered the bar and sat down at a worn old table. "Sarah, look at those four thick-bodied guys consuming yards of pasta in a tomato sauce."

The four men spooled and devoured pasta for ten minutes before one finally stopped eating long enough to take their order. In the meantime, Allie sat back and admired the cantina's proletarian charm.

"I wonder if these guys eating pasta are labor officials or fences for the local Mafia. You know, Sarah, this place is kind of quaint."

"Allie," said Sarah, looking through a different prism, "this place is a second-world dive. Quaint it ain't, pal. My two concerns are what I can eat without suffering an attack from my colitis that's behaving nicely and how I can relieve myself without catching a communicable disease to bring home as a souvenir."

Sarah ordered toast and coffee and carefully urinated into a relatively benign French-style squat, a hole in the ground set between two tracks for placement of feet.

In comparison, Carole found Necochea Street enchanting and boldly entered a private courtyard to closely observe how the people lived. The entire cluster of households saw her and instantly lined up for autographs. Carole graciously endured a half-hour-long siege by hundreds of La Bocans hungering for her to sign their pathetic scraps of paper.

My romantic notion that I could move freely about without being recognized has been smashed by this horde. Carol lamented.

Carole and Allie ironically took refuge in the same cantina he ate at with Sarah the day before. The men inside didn't ignore Cohen for a second or remember him. The owner acted so honored to welcome a famous movie star that he put his arms around Carole's waist, picked her up, and placed her on the long wooden bar.

She'd gotten his message to sing a little song, and in the gutsy manner of great saloon singers, Carole belted out "Don't Cry for Me Argentina."

One of the guys eating pasta accompanied her on the upright old piano. A huge crowd gathered outside the cantina and applauded the moment as magical as in the movies.

Allie found it curious that Carole could be an even bigger star in Argentina than America; crowds mobbed them wherever they went. In contrast, people reacted to Sarah and Allie as just another American middle-class couple. Global was readying his novel's rollout in Latin American markets, so Cohen was still mostly an unknown in Argentina.

At first, the adoring crowds were exciting; but after two days of jostling from strangers, a creeping sense of danger formed. Buenos Aires so hysterically reached out to Carole that Allie was forced to rent a stretch limo and a team of bodyguards for protection.

The worst incident occurred while enjoying a warm sun and snacking on the outdoor patio of the Café de la Paix across the Plaza Francia in Recoleta. Surrounding diners in droves recognized Carole and rushed in to share her space.

Allie felt a mass contagion surging toward them with the intensity of shock troops assaulting enemy positions.

"Carole, let's get the hell out of here before they fucking trample us to death."

Allie grabbed Carole's hand and retreated to safety in the limo, which left the waves of crazed autograph seekers in the dust and sped back to the Sheraton.

Inside the living room on wheels, Cohen bitched. "Dammit, Carole, your stinking fans wouldn't let me eat a fucking grilled cheese sandwich and drink a lousy beer."

"It's a shame." She shrugged and philosophized. "Celebrity and anonymity both come in extremes."

Allie experimented the next day by returning with Sarah to the Café de la Paix. The Cohens sat at the same table and were served by the same waiter, who did not remember him. The lone person to approach Allie and Sarah was a blind panhandler, thus allowing Cohen the pleasure to consume a hamburger, french fries, and two beers in total obscurity and comfort.

With Sarah, I'm a regular tourist who can walk anywhere, anytime to my heart's delight. With Carole, I can expect to be smothered by a swarming blob of humanity seeking a silly scribble of a name on paper. Where's the happy medium? I'm John Doe with Sarah and overrun by Carole's lemmings. How do I balance this?

You merged two different worlds. You probably can't and should not lose sleep over things that you have no control over, prophet. What is more important, Allie, is that Carole's celebrity status will attract at least half of the world to behold you, the basis for your exaltation and awe.

Chapter 81

Sarah and Allie greatly enjoyed their day in Mar del Plata, an Atlantic coast beach city, and a quick two-day helicopter tour of Patagonia.

"This trip has gone so well, Sarah, that I figure that you can meet up with me anywhere in the world."

"I agree, Allie, and look forward to other breaks in the itinerary."

The next day, Ted Bell contacted Allie with a problem he'd dreaded.

"Allie, President Alfonsín needs you and Carole to tour Argentina with him for the next three days. His hope is to brighten his countrymen's drab existence and his own image by showcasing two American celebrities in major cities and scenic backdrops. I think we should help him out, don't you think?"

"Oh no, Ted, I really want to help but have to cut Sarah's last day of the visit. Let me get with the concierge to help me rent a car."

"I appreciate this, Allie." Ted assured Allie, "And I promise to work with Sarah. I'll call her right after you and explain everything and then promise invitations to other places—at this point, Israel for sure."

Sarah said very little for most of the ride to the airport, and her silence prompted Allie to ask, "Sarah, is something bothering you, babe?"

"Everything is jake, Allie," Sarah confirmed. Her mother Rebecca was noted for using the word *jake* like that, so they both laughed.

Allie worried, *I'm a bit nervous that she's going to drill me with a moral or message. She often fakes reluctance to talk about it, only to later sting my ears with a heartfelt phrase or two.*

"Look, Allie," she told him. "I love you more than ever. You're my husband, the father of my child, and the only man I care to make a life with. I will do my best to preserve our union and love, but as I've said before, I can't guarantee this status forever."

Allie reacted exactly as she'd hoped; he cried. His ability to openly show his emotions was one of the things Sarah loved most about him. His tears usually turned her on sexually too, and she felt like making love right there at the gate, but with a plane to catch and an infant son to return home to, Sarah just kissed Allie goodbye.

She disappeared into the Pan Am Clipper; he then watched Sarah's plane taxi away and take off.

Thank you, Lord, that our bond remains strong because I'm asking so much of my wife and admit that it's way beyond unfair to her.

Allie headed over to the Sheraton to pick Carole up for a meeting with President Alfonsín, who looked like a regular guy and everyone's nice uncle, but the poor gentleman inherited staggering national problems that had defied solutions for decades. Cohen asked President Alfonsín what his two main goals were.

"That's easy, Dr. Cohen—improving the faltering economy and keeping the army in its place. I wish it was that simple, though, because the public's clamoring for prosecution of the army officers responsible for the nine thousand desaparecidos and moving aggressively against them could spark another right-wing takeover."

It's easy to see, Cohen thought, *that Alfonsín's appeal is his ordinary appearance. He's like a man who wears an expensive tuxedo over worn old underwear.*

"In terms of the economy, Dr. Cohen and Ms. Herman," the president lectured a bit, "despite decreasing personal income, the Argentines spend and borrow to maintain a standard of living they can't afford and don't earn. My nation, the ninth richest in the world in 1927, is now seventeenth and sinking fast. Economists predict that we will drop to twenty-seventh by 2000 and anywhere from thirty-seventh to forty-seventh by 2020."

The International Monetary Fund listed Argentina as fifty-fifth in 2015; President Alfonsín was overoptimistic. Argentina is descending into ever deeper and entrenched poverty much faster than the economists predicted. Cohen asked President Alfonsín how it happened.

"Our downward spiral, Allie and Carole, began accelerating when, in 1970, the junta made the mistake of following Milton Friedman's advice to deindustrialize and compete in world markets by only doing what we do best—grow and export agricultural commodities. Fifteen years later, we've given up stopping the economic contraction and are hard-pressed to just slow it down." They never have.

"It's the University of Chicago School of Economics philosophy, President Alfonsín," explained Allie. "They preach that free market crap that expects you to write off whole industries. A huge chunk of your job base was deleted and gone forever instead of modernized."

"Yes, Dr. Cohen, and that made us overreliant on our commodities that are vulnerable to the boom-bust cycle. When prices are high for our commodities, times aren't so bad. When world prices are low, we have recession or worse."

584

"What do you see, President Alfonsín," asked Carole, "as your gravest challenge?"

"The outcry for a Nuremberg-type tribunal to square accounts for the Dirty War of the 1970s when the army drowned thousands of suspected leftists by dropping them from helicopters in to the deep, wide Rio de la Plata. Rumors abound of possible mutinies by middle-level officers who argue that they simply followed orders and deserve leniency."

"And you have to balance the officers having the blood of nine thousand people on their hands," Allie reasoned, "with the mothers demanding immediate prosecution of them?"

"Yes, the mothers of the desaparecidos protest daily on the Plaza de Mayo that all killers be convicted and jailed."

Alfonsín rubbed his brow; his pain showed from it. "The mothers have morality and right on their side and pressure me and the government to take tougher action, and I really wish I could for their sake."

Carole marveled. "By the Lord's grace, you have so far succeeded in this delicate balancing act."

"Yes, but I am worried, Ms. Herman, that one of these days my luck will run out."

President Alfonsín looked down at his shoes. The more he droned on about Argentina's seemingly insoluble problems, the more Allie worried about his country's future and people.

"President Alfonsín, if the Argentines—with their exceptional agricultural bounty, pride, and dignity—collapse into a failed promise, what are Argentina's and Chile's fate and Latin America's in general?"

"Dr. Cohen, two starkly different futures await Argentina, Chile, and Latin America. The first is the dream of sustained economic growth and social progress. The other is the horror of rampant crime, drugs, and Communists stoking the fires of class warfare. I pray to God that it be the former, but only time will tell."

Alfonsín's chief aide entered. "Excuse me, Mr. President, you have an emergency meeting on the deficit with the Council of Ministers."

The president turned to Carole and Allie. "My new friends, this has been my most pleasant time in office. Godspeed."

He hugged and kissed Carole and shook Allie's hand with both of his.

The next day, Carole and Allie flew to Brazil's inland capital, Brasília, to honor the new democratic government of Pres. Tancredo Neves, whose inauguration was to take place that very evening. Sadly, the seventy-five-year-old Neves had to be hospitalized just hours before being sworn into office. The president-elect, over the next three weeks, endured seven emergency operations.

With the inauguration on hold, the Brazilian government moved Herman and Cohen to Rio de Janeiro and provided a luxurious suite in the Caesar Park Hotel across from Ipanema Beach. The penthouse vistas provided clear views of the ocean to the east and a densely populated favela to the west that crawled up a small mountain and crowded the comfortable Ipanema residential community below. Allie showed Carole this stark dichotomy and briefed her.

"Surging crime is turning Rio from a playground into a battlefield. Once upon a time, the poor had faith in the system and blamed themselves for their lowly condition, but twenty years of military rule and economic mismanagement changed the poor's perception of who was at fault. The slum dwellers no longer stay

586

put but daily come down from their favelas to steal from the richer beachgoers."

"That's a plague on all the people, Allie."

"I know, and this plague mugging the Carioca, a growth industry, is destroying Rio's image of a beautiful and carefree tourist mecca. Rio's crooks, Carole, thrust as many as eighteen thefts a day on their countrymen. They rob entire busloads of people, the mass production of theft by taking."

"Tsk, tsk, the thieves are very busy indeed, Allie. I gather that crime does pay."

Carole and Allie wanted to go to the beach, so the hotel management assigned two armed guards to protect them. Cohen debated if real freedom could survive in a state where Beretta-packing hulks sealed off every tourist's beach blanket, and he asked Guillermo, the taller of the two bruisers, about it.

"We're just going to the beach, yet we're preparing for a war."

"Well, it is a kind of war, Mr. Cohen." The slim muscular black man described, "Jesus, tourists have been held up less than five feet from the hotel entrance, others while stopped for the red light over there."

He pointed to the hotel entrance and then to the nearby intersection.

"Criminal groups penetrate security companies and rob entire luxury apartment buildings floor by floor, unit by unit. Remember to never take jewelry, money, or credit cards to the beach, even with us around."

"Oh," Cohen said and then asked the guard, "Do you like living in Rio?"

The Carioca flashed an honest big grin. "Sure, Rio is a fabulous city, the beaches are beautiful, and the nightlife is exciting."

"The landscape," Allie added, "is physically gorgeous and dotted with dazzling architecture too, but crime, Guillermo, and the grime of poverty are taking a big toll on the place."

Tancredo Neves's final words shortly before dying were "I didn't deserve this fate." And he didn't, but the fragile democracy held firm. VP José Sarney assumed office and carried out Neves's mandate. But as Neves lay near death, Carole and Allie endured a boring stretch of cool, cloudy days and nude mulatto floor shows at night. Ambitious excursions were quickly organized to fill their days of waiting with tours that took them into three very different pockets of the huge country.

They produced two concerts at the Manaus Opera House deep in the Amazon that infused an array of indigenous musical groups and their sounds of Amazonia. Carole sang and played with these tribal musicians, and she brought Allie onstage to wail his harmonica with an unusual wind instrument group. Cohen also joined a thirty-man percussion group and played a type of bongo drum.

Boat and helicopter tours of the area captured the grandeur and scale of the huge river basin and sheer size of Amazonia, the lungs of the earth. Cohen and Herman saw firsthand the destruction caused by large-scale mining companies and wholesale rain forest clearance for the world's fastest growing agribusiness sector.

The second concert was held on the beach in beautiful and romantic Salvador, located on Brazil's impoverished northeastern coast. Carole shared the stage with popular local jazz and acoustic guitar musicians and a hundred-person chorus that backed her on most of their region's most famous melodies.

Allie and his harmonica again joined in, this time a twelve-man smooth jazz band with a fabulous horn section, while Carole sang scat over their beats. Cohen and Herman were discovering Brazil's galaxy of talented musical cultures and falling in love with their harmonious sounds.

The last outpost was in Porto Alegre's main square down in the heavily German southeastern tip of the country. Carole performed with traditional Brazilian, Portuguese, and German musical groups; the two of them even did a chicken dance in the traditional German-style and laughed so hard that they had trouble completing it.

After this final concert, Carole gushed to Allie. "The tour is turning out to be everything I'd hope it would be. I think the incredible musical influences I'm being exposed to are the most exciting part for me."

"I feel you are peaking as a singer and musician and love watching you grow artistically like this, tone-deaf me too."

The month on the road and seven frustrating inaugural postponements caught up with Allie and Carole. Their opportunity to opt out and go home happened when Cohen cracked a tooth eating a baby duck egg at La Pomme d'Or, an excellent Copacabana Italian restaurant famous for its fettuccine Alfredo. They used his split molar as a cover for packing their bags and heading home to LA.

Home to LA, huh? Cohen meditated on that notion somewhere in the air between Rio and Malibu.

My home is where my heart is, and that's with two extraordinary and beautiful women. One angel lives in Atlanta, the other in LA, and my heart and home is with both.

Yes, Allie, they are your left and right arms from Hashem, who is pleased that co-living is working out reasonably well so far.

Chapter 82

Lesotho and Eddie stood back to admire a mural they'd just completed on the wall of a black-owned insurance company. The three great religions—Christianity, Judaism, and Islam—were featured in the top right corner panel.

"Eddie, I don't get it why Malcolm has been pushed out of the civil rights narrative and shunted aside. Malcolm's fury was the force behind King's nonviolent application."

Lesotho once more worked an image of Malcolm X into an adjacent frame that was supposed to focus exclusively on Martin Luther King. Eddie surprised Lesotho with a sharp insight.

"You're forgetting that Martin King won a Nobel Peace Prize, man, and Malcolm X's anger fueled urban riots. That's a pretty big difference right there."

"Yeah, you're right, but I wish Malcolm—a true prophet, if there ever was one—was more appreciated. Anyway, I'm doing what I can to earn his reward."

"Earn his reward, eh? Last month, you were thinking of converting to Judaism. Who was rewarding you then, Sammy Davis Jr.?"

Lesotho bent over laughing. "That was good, Eddie." He got serious. "Barbara's a terrific woman, and she really wants to marry me. I like her a lot but not enough to change my whole life for her."

"Why do you have to convert?" Eddie waited for an answer.

"Her parents don't want her to marry outside her faith like her elder brother did. They claim that they've kind of lost a son to the Christians and fear it happening to their daughter too."

"That's bullshit, man. The Jews are racist," claimed Eddie, "and use their religion not to marry blacks."

Lesotho and Eddie put away their materials and crossed Techwood Drive and entered Bennie's Tavern, a nearby beer and sandwich joint. The bartender brought them two Buds, and they took a couple of swigs.

"I disagree with you, Eddie." Lesotho sipped his beer and continued making his case. "The Jews have been victims like blacks, and I think it has made them less racist than regular white people. Look how many rabbis walked with King, a Jewish man started the NAACP, and almost every major city has a black-Jewish coalition."

"Listen, man, my aunt Blanche cleaned Mrs. Feldstein's house for years. They always treated her real nice to her face, but behind her back, they referred to her as *the schvartze*." He emphasized *schvartze* with a bent index finger of each hand. "Those are my aunt's own words."

Lesotho was ready to drop the subject when he noticed two very pretty black women enter the bar. Eddie saw them too and then remembered them.

"Holy shit, Sharon and Andrea Johnson, I went to school with the sisters. I don't think they recognize me. Maybe I should be glad. Neither of them would go out with me and always told me that they respected Farrah too much to date me and that bullshit. Inside, I knew my very black looks turned them off, and man, it hurt bad because they're both so fucking pretty and sexy. Damn, they even had better bodies than my Farrah, who's still superfine."

Xeranga eyed Sharon, the slightly older, prettier, and smarter of the two. Eddie didn't tell Lesotho that Sharon was one of Cohen's favorite students. She'd just turned twenty-four and was trying to make it as a dancer long after the optimum time to start

591

had passed. In her favor were beauty, strikingly long legs, and a terrible fear of failure.

Lesotho strategized. *Man, this chick is so damn hot. 'Got to make a move.* "Hi, I'm Lesotho Xeranga."

"You look familiar," said Sharon, who'd watched him paint frame after frame for weeks.

He refreshed her memory. "I'm the dude that's been painting the black history mural across the street."

"Oh yeah, that's right. By the way, it's excellent, especially the tribute to Malcolm X."

His eyes lit up like full moons. "Thank you very much." His full moons focused on her.

"You're welcome." She smiled sweetly. "It's funny, I barely knew who Malcolm was until a former teacher put on a black history assembly that celebrated his contribution to the civil rights movement too."

"That's very cool. Who was that teacher? Jesus, I wish I'd had him."

"Mr. Cohen was the first white man I ever heard say Malcolm was just as great a black leader as Martin King and that Malcolm, in fact, helped make Martin possible."

"Mr. Cohen was right. What's your name:" He thought, *Man, will you look at those big oval eyes and tight body. Christ, she's an ebony wet dream.*

"'Sharon Johnson, didn't matter though." she recalled. "It got him into trouble with the dumb-ass principal who thought Malcolm was too controversial and that only King should have been honored. I thought that was the weirdest scene I ever saw, a white man arguing with a black man that Malcolm X was as great a force for racial change as Martin King."

"No shit, Sharon? Tell me, what else did Mr. Cohen teach you about Malcolm?"

"That Malcolm spoke the harsh truths that finally made white people face up to the lies about justice for black people." She looked at him with her big oval eyes wide open.

I think I'm falling in love with Sharon Johnson. Xeranga felt his heart expanding and reminded himself, *Okay, act well-mannered, and let me introduce Eddie.*

"Sharon, you just made my day with that quote about Malcolm. Most of the ladies I know hardly remember him. Their Atlanta schools only taught them about King. Hey, let me introduce my friend, Eddie White."

The Johnson sisters hadn't recognized him and were floored. After the shock wore off, Sharon apologized.

"I'm sorry, Eddie, because Farrah and I were close friends in high school, and you and I go back to the eighth grade. How is Farrah?"

He quickly summarized for Sharon the poverty of their marriage and careers before making a joke.

"But then I wasn't voted most likely to succeed in life neither, was I? And since you were the valedictorian, I guess life's been a whole lot sweeter for you, well, has it?"

One look at her blank face told him something was wrong. "You know, I once heard Mr. Cohen and you talk about Spelman College in class. Let's see, you should have graduated by now."

"No, Eddie, I didn't."

She confessed, "I made the bad mistake of hooking up with a flashy cosmetologist who snowed me about us owning a chain of makeup schools and getting rich. Within a year, he went bankrupt, split Atlanta, and left me broke and in debt. Without a college degree, all I've gotten is some department store makeup jobs and a temp position in NationsBank's mortgage division that I hate."

You didn't tell them, Andrea thought, *how you also borrowed money from me to pay for an abortion.*

"And you, Andrea." Eddie was curious. "What's going on with you?"

"Nothing much, Eddie," Andrea admitted. "Just a crummy secretarial job in the same office. I'm really ready to meet a nice guy and get married and have kids."

Lesotho was beginning to put some pieces of Eddie's life together.

"Hey, Eddie, how come you didn't say hello to Allie Cohen that time we met him at the Hilton bar?"

The Johnson sisters, both eyewitnesses to Eddie's checkered past, clammed up and looked away.

"Man, I just didn't dig the dude at all in high school, but Antonio Willis helped me put it all behind me, and it's cool now."

"Cohen sounds like he was a great teacher, and to tell you the truth, I'm sorry that I never had him myself."

"This isn't any of my business, Eddie," said Sharon, hoping to set him free from his past. "But by any chance, are you still upset with Mr. Cohen over that, uh, you know, incident?"

Eddie glared at Sharon. "You're right, it's not any of your business."

The hint of steel in his voice made her uncomfortable. "I'm sorry I brought it up, Eddie. I won't do that again."

I'm dying to find out, Lesotho thought, *what happened between Eddie and Cohen. I also wonder if the incident is the cause of Eddie's occasional flashes of anti-Semitism.*

"What happened, Eddie?" Lesotho looked him in the eye. "Please level with me."

"Lesotho, you're out of line." White stared defiantly into the eyes of Xeranga, who did not blink or relent. Eddie stroked his beard several times before appealing, "If you're my good friend, man, you'll just drop it."

Lesotho desisted but did not let it go. During the next few weeks, he saw more and more of Sharon Johnson and less and less of Barbara Blumberg and Tanya Nikki. Lesotho quietly sought out the truth about Eddie from Sharon, and by the time Barbara and Tanya had faded from his life, he'd learned the full story and planned an intervention.

Over lunch one day at Bennie's, Lesotho told Eddie that he knew about his high school football exploits.

"How come you never told me you were a star fullback? Sharon told me that you once scored five touchdowns in a game against Washington High."

"Well, you know, Lesotho."

"No, I don't, Eddie. Why didn't you tell me?"

"Look, Lesotho, it was a long time ago, and it don't matter no more. What can I say?"

"I know what happened, Eddie. You can't progress in life until you come to grips with the incident. In all fairness, I want to hear your side of the story too."

A volatile large black fist smashed the tabletop with intimidating force. The tavern patrons heard the powerful thud and stared at Eddie.

"Goddamn it!" he shouted. "Why she'd have to tell you? Who brought it up?"

"Me, I made her tell me because I love you, man. You're my bro, and I'm going to make you really deal with it if it's the last thing I do. This is the one thing holding you back from being more in life."

Lesotho calmed his buddy by paying the check, placed his arm around Eddie's shoulder, and led him outside.

Eddie pulled away from Lesotho, turned his back to him, and leaned against an old Jeep Cherokee. Tears streamed out of his eyes, and he cried like a baby.

"Man." Xeranga consoled his tormented friend. "You have needed to get this out of your system for a long time."

Six forgettable years of stored-up pain and disappointment was unleashed through White's heavy sobbing—a dashed dream that wrought bitter tears.

"Dammit, Lesotho, I could have been somebody, maybe even a football star. Christ, I could have had women like Sharon hanging from each arm."

"Farrah's a beautiful lady, Eddie, and you got nice kids too. All you need is a good job that you can be proud of."

"I don't know, seems like we been together forever, and it just never gets better. I mean, how am I gonna get a good job? Christ, I'm gonna pay for one lousy mistake for the rest of my fucking life. Cohen runs around the world with a movie star, and I ain't got bus fare to get home."

"Hey, c'mon, don't get so down. You know I'm always glad to lend you bread when you need it."

Eddie started to regain his composure. Lesotho sensed it. *This is the right time to get to the bottom of the story.*

He asked the hard question. "Why heroin, Eddie? Smack is such bad shit."

"Please understand," Eddie begged Lesotho, "that I never did heroin or dealt it or anything else. I was always too much into sports to do heavy drugs, only some pot. My problems began when I did some dumb things and got Cohen and a few other teachers down on me."

"Like what?"

"It all started with Richard Lewis, a big-time drug dealer who once killed a guy over money and ruled the damn school. Things came to a head when Farrah got pregnant and wanted to get an abortion. She asked me for the money, which I had only one way of getting. Lewis lent me the cash, but the price was I hold some product for him until he's ready to move it."

"Yeah, man, that was your first mistake."

"Well, Lesotho, the next day, Lewis told me that the cops were after him, and he expected me to hold some stash until things cooled down, a dozen packs of smack."

"That was your second mistake." Xeranga shook his head back and forth.

"The trouble started the following day when Danny Hall approached me to buy three of the packs. I was fucked-up by Farrah's considering an abortion and wasn't thinking straight. I passed the heroin to Danny, Cohen stepped into the hall and caught me, and Meacham, the principal, busted me."

"Mistake number three. Wow, you really struck out." Xeranga bobbled his head up and down twice.

"There's more." Eddie, out of shame, looked away from Lesotho. "Lewis heard about the bust and, thinking that I might tell the cops about him, threatened to cut Farrah with a knife. Farrah got cold feet over the abortion and used some of that money to bail me out. Danny Hall helped with the rest, and Arvida arrived five months later."

"Arvida is a blessing and not a fourth mistake." He smiled at Eddie.

"Well, the worst fucking mistake of all was when I showed up at the school a couple of days after the incident intending to punch Cohen and ol' bantam rooster Meacham out."

Lesotho laughed at the bantam rooster reference, but Eddie didn't.

"Like a fucking idiot, I was stopped at the entrance and, again, bear-hugged to the ground by fat fuck Marcus Miller, the goddamned black refrigerator."

"Yes, that was your worst mistake. You were fucking out of control."

"I know, Lesotho. Anyway, they provided Cohen with police protection, and shitheads Miller and Meacham testified in court that I was incorrigible. I was banned from all Atlanta high schools except Vo-Tech night school, arrested, and paroled before I ever spent a day in jail. From that day on, I blamed Cohen for my miserable life and vowed to get even someday until Antonio kind of chilled me out."

"Well, Eddie, we got to do something fast to help you get it totally behind you and move on with your life. The mural is done, and there are no more to paint. That means your job will be terminated in two days because Reagan just abolished CETA, the Comprehensive Employment and Training Act, which paid for our program."

Lesotho worried. *Shit, what the fuck can I do for him? I know that he can't return to lugging garbage no more. His assets, strength, and loyalty are not exactly in great demand in this computer age that's taking off. I know.*

"Hey, Eddie," asked Lesotho. "You ever hear of a group called BUSHAC?"

"No, what the hell is bashcan?" Eddie showed interest.

"Not bashcan, it's BUSHAC—Blacks United to Save or Help Advance Careers."

He described the organization's role. "BUSHAC is a black support group that provides services like placing drug addicts in treatment centers, reaching out to hookers and crooks to change their ways, and advising and assisting ghetto kids in trouble."

"You know, Lesotho, I think I could get into that."

"Good because BUSHAC also helps smart black kids get into college and young college graduates into good jobs. Whatever is needed to improve black people's lives, BUSHAC tries to provide."

"You think they need any help?" Eddie wanted to believe they did.

"BUSHAC's director Mack Thomas is a good friend of mine and heard that he needs an office assistant to do mostly low-level tasks. Mack is the best around at obtaining foundation grant money, so the job should be secure for a while."

"That's good to hear."

"Remember, I'm getting you an interview, Eddie, that's all. Mack could pick someone else, you understand?"

"No problem."

The interview opportunity offered a chance to a man who had no hope at all. Lesotho went back inside Bennie's to call Mack, and ten minutes later, he emerged sporting a grin.

"I got you the interview scheduled for this Thursday afternoon around two thirty."

"Thank you, Lesotho. Hey, what do you call this job?"

"General assistant. Now I know that doesn't sound like much, and the pay ain't that great either, but remember that if you get it, you'll be in a position to move up to something better later on. BUSHAC is a fast-growing organization."

"Thank you, Lesotho, for going out on a limb for me."

"It's cool, Eddie," assured Xeranga. "Just keep on being the good dude that you are, and things will work out. Trust me, you'll see."

On Saturday night, Eddie and Farrah went to the Rib Shack on Campbellton Road and feasted on ribs, beer, and peach cobbler topped with vanilla ice cream. After dinner, the Whites took a long drive and sang along with the radio all the way home. They felt great and quickly undressed to get into bed.

Eddie proved unusually tender in his lovemaking and helped Farrah achieve her first orgasm in weeks, and she squealed in delight from a second. Afterward, she soulfully reflected aloud while smoking a cigarette.

"I don't know why, Eddie, but I feel real good about this interview. Not only do I think you're going to get this job but I also sense that it's the one that's going to turn the corner for us. What do you think?"

"I sure hope so, Farrah," said Eddie in a sad low voice, "because I just about OD'd on disappointment."

"You can't let it get to you, my man. You just got to keep on pushing ahead."

Farrah's encouraging words brought forth another flood of tears; the rest of the stored-up pain poured out of him. Farrah held her man tightly and rocked him.

"You got to get all the hurt out, Eddie."

Her comfort influenced him to apologize for past bad behavior.

"You've been a great wife, Farrah, and I been such a shit husband that I'm lucky you stayed with me. Please forgive me for the times I got out of control and hit you. Frankly, I don't deserve you, Farrah, and it would have served me right if you left me long ago."

Eddie started to cry again, if not quite as hard. Farrah continued to rock and soothe her man until he was calm.

When his self-control returned, Farrah assured him, "Things are going to get better, Eddie. You'll see."

"I sure hope so, baby," Eddie prayed, "because it's probably the last fucking chance in life I'll ever have."

Listen to Farrah, Eddie, and have faith in yourself. That's the only way for things to get better for you and your family.

Chapter 83

In contrast, life opportunities for Allie and Carole, relaxing in Malibu, were limitless and fantastic. They prepared for a three-week-long jaunt across Egypt and Israel and were on the phone daily with Ted Bell at the White House; concerts had to be produced, security and transportation arranged, a million details to attend to.

Allie flew to Atlanta for three days to spend some time with Sarah and Ari and visit his dentist for a crown.

I pray that when Ari sees me, he'll recognize his dad and reach out his little arms to be held. That will be the key sign that my effort to be a part of his infancy is producing a loving father-and-son bond.

The cab dropped him off, and he entered the kitchen of Sarah's new condo across the road from the Dunwoody Country Club and near the Orchard Park commercial junction. She was feeding Ari pureed plums, which had dribbled down his face and bib.

Allie appeared; Ari looked at him, and his face lit up like a baby sun. Plum dribbled out of his mouth from his shouting, "Dada, dada, dada!"

Ari pushed up in his feeding seat and reached out his little arms. Allie picked him up, held him in his arms, and kissed his messy cheek over and over. Ari put his arms around his dad's neck and then touched Allie's face all over and played with his beard and nose. Ari laughed happily, a tear rolled down Cohen's cheek, and he thanked the Lord.

"My son loves me as much as I'd hoped." Tears formed in both of his eyes. "I must be making this co-living thing work."

"You're a lucky guy, Cohen," said Sarah, crying tears of happiness too. "He really loves his daddy. You're enough of a presence in his life to matter. God bless."

Allie pulled Sarah into a group hug with Ari, who kept laughing, gurgling, and making happy baby sounds. Cohen kissed Sarah sweetly on the lips and thanked her.

"You are the rock of my life and an angel from heaven that sustains my mission. I love you more than ever, money."

"You've tried hard to be a father to Ari, and it's worked." Sarah dried more tears in her eyes with a tissue. "Although I wish you had more time for us, hopefully, the time thing will even out more in the weeks and months ahead."

"Sarah, I'm just thrilled how we're managing to build a family bond through all this. I suspect the White House is going to move us around a lot for the next year or two because we're becoming very useful to them."

Allie spent the next few hours playing, holding, and singing to Ari, and then he put him down to nap and brought Sarah up-to-date on plans.

"Our next stops are Egypt and Israel. I know that Ted Bell is arranging for you and Ari to meet me in Tel Aviv for a couple of days. We'll introduce Ari to all your family who lives there."

"I'm going to mark that on my calendar, Allie, and begin making plans."

Ari woke, and he and Allie rolled tiny Hot Wheels cars across the kitchen floor when, suddenly, the cracked tooth fell apart, and air rushed against the exposed nerve.

"Sarah, I'm experiencing a sharp, recurring stabbing in my lower left jaw, and I can hardly talk. Sorry, but I can't wait until tomorrow to take care of it."

Sarah got Dr. Kalish on the phone, scheduled an emergency appointment, and put the phone down. "Are you able to drive yourself?"

"Trust me, money," he assured her. "No problem."

Allie headed over to Irving Kalish's office. He was happy to see Cohen, exchanged a few pleasantries, and displayed that he was current on media gossip about Allie's tour with Carole. Finally, Irving took a look at Cohen's demolished molar and injected enough Novocain to turn the left side of his cheek into what felt like a slab of liver.

The more Irving packed Allie's mouth with gauze to limit saliva flow, the more questions he seemed to ask. "Allie, did I hurt you?"

"Naht tchoo muccchh."

Irving picked away at the dissolved tooth. "Sarah was in last week and told me about some of your Chilean adventures. You're lucky they didn't throw you in jail or even kill you. So where are you and Carole off to next?"

"Eesjwypt and Ischwreel."

Kalish stopped stabbing away with his torturous pick.

"No kidding, I just returned from Israel last week. Will you do me a favor, Allie?" Irving removed the gauze.

"That depends on what you have in mind, Irving."

"Yigal and Shulie Mayer, who live in Haifa, are very close friends of mine. Shulie gave me a daily Hebrew lesson, and I fell in love with the Hebrew word for anteater, *ochel nemolima*. My saying it over and over became a running joke between us."

"*Ochel nemolima*, it rolls off the tongue nicely."

Kalish removed some saliva with his suction and provided a little more information.

"The other night, after eating at Petite Auberge in Toco Hills, my wife, Betty, and I were browsing in an art gallery. Lo and behold, I found an incredibly ugly oil painting of an anteater and impulsively bought it with the intention of mailing it to the Mayers."

"So you want me to deliver it?"

Cohen made sure his tongue was still there. A trickle of saliva dripped from his paralyzed mouth down to the chin.

"I'll make you a deal, Allie, partly because I think you guys will also love the Mayers." Irving cleaned up the saliva trail. "If you schlep this painting to Haifa to hand it to the Mayers, the crown is half-price."

"Deal, Irving. What's the Mayers' address?"

"It's right off the Carmel, and the Mayers will love you for this. Yigal Mayer is a friend of Schlomo Pincus who commands an Israeli jet fighter group. Schlomo took me for a spin in a Lavi trainer jet the year before. Maybe Yigal can arrange a ride for you too."

"That is the perfect incentive for me to drag that ugly painting." Irving appeared a bit hurt. "Sorry about that, Irving, but you have to admit that it is a really ugly painting."

"Okay, it is an incredibly ugly painting, but I think your rewards will be well worth it. Trust me on this, Allie."

"Well," Allie said, "I'm good friends with Schlomo Pincus too. Dave Golden, whom you bought this practice from, introduced Sarah and me to Schlomo and his wife, Yael."

Allie flew back to Malibu with the painting and showed it to Carole, who laughed. "That is the ugliest fucking painting I've ever seen. Dr. Kalish, though, has given us a good reason to visit and see Haifa."

Sam volunteered to drive Carole and Allie to the airport. Cohen showed Minkowitz the painting before packing and securing it between two garment bags. Sam told Allie what he thought the painting was worth.

"I wouldn't be caught dead schlepping that painting for free bridgework."

"Sam," Carole stated, "enough with the critique and dental values. Please drive."

Sam laughed and got behind the wheel to head to the airport. Upon entering the expressway, he described a problem to Allie about *Déjà Vu Odyssey*, which was scheduled to start filming soon.

"An Atlanta black-advancement group called BUSHAC, Allie, has accused the project's concept of being a black Tarzan movie. The group and its leader, Mack Thomas, are threatening Global with an injunction to kill the idea. The protests are forcing the banks to withhold development capital and publisher Harland Cooper to put the project on ice."

"Sam, may I ask, who the fuck is Mack Thomas and BUSHAC? I lived in Atlanta for eleven years and never heard of *him* or *them* once, so why are you bothering to listen to them now?"

"Allie, we have to, and if the outcry doesn't end soon, Global may have to shelve the venture entirely."

Sam waited for Allie's hurt feelings and outrage to surface and then planned to tender a compromise, his usual carrot and stick. *Ah, he's finally done venting, time to deal.*

"Allie, this BUSHAC group believes that a white writer may bias the portrayal of the true black experience. Their stated position is the immediate cessation of all protests upon your being replaced by a major black writer."

"Sam," Allie argued back, "a less biased white writer cannot be found on the face of the earth. Give me a break. Didn't I develop the world's leading international education and prejudice reduction treatment?"

Carole saw that Allie was mad enough to be tongue-tied and intervened.

"Sam, that's like saying you have to be black to sing the blues, and just because BUSHAC says it doesn't make it right or true."

The ever-practical Minkowitz argued from a business point of view.

"Look, Allie's contract calls for a *bovie*, which means the movie must first succeed before the book comes out. Demonstrations are box office poison, so if the movie fails, so will his book. My first responsibility is always stockholders' before artists' feelings. As you can see, I have no alternative but to replace you with a fine black writer."

Cohen punched the dashboard. Minkowitz moved to step two of his plan. He started as an agent and had forty years of dealing with artistic egos and knew when it was time to dangle the carrot.

"Look, Allie, Bob Urban is okay with this, so you can relax too. Both of you will still be paid and receive your customary percentage. I'll also make you both assistant directors or producers or whatever to get your names on the credits."

Sam saw that Allie was still angry and laid it on.

"Boychick, I assure you that we have a black writer whom you'll be proud of being associated with. Bob has already approved the guy, so you know he must be all right."

"Who is he?" Allie was really curious.

"Harry Jackson. Plus, he loves your novel and greatly respects you as a writer. Harry plans to just give it a once-over and will virtually leave your work intact. Think of it as a charade in which everyone wins."

"All right, Sam, if it has to be anyone, it might as well be Harry Jackson, but it still sucks."

Here I go and give a modestly talented little putz a break, and overpay him a ton as a favor to Carole, and now he's acting like a big shot. For crying out loud, Allie, have a few bombs, and you'll be back in Atlanta counting pine trees.

Sam's Rolls stopped in front of the United Airlines terminal, and Allie got in the last word on the subject.

"You're right, Sam, it's better to be profitable than scrupulous."

Sam's blood pressure rose. Carole appealed for fairness.

"Sam, your advice, though well-meaning, was still very crass. Frankly, Allie handed over his work with only a mild stink.

609

It could have resulted in a lawsuit that he'd probably win, and you know it too."

"Maybe you're right, Carole."

"Thanks for taking us to the airport. 'Love you." Carole kissed Sam on the cheek.

"For what it's worth, Carole, I do respect Allie's right to be pissed off and will make it up to him, I promise you. Please, you two, have a happy and safe trip."

Sam is really a mensch in his own way.

Chapter 84

Two thousand four hundred miles away in a south-side Atlanta office building, BUSHAC director Mack Thomas stared out his office window in silence and reflected on his Global Pictures victory.

Man, Sam Minkowitz, maybe the most powerful man in the history of Hollywood, caved in just like that.

He snapped his finger. *Normally, I'd be running around high-fiving the entire staff, but it doesn't matter one bit because I'm so fucking sick inside that I could puke.*

Mack continued to stare out the window, trying to sort it all out. *My victory came at Allie Cohen's expense, but I got a much bigger problem than taking his script away and giving it to Harry Jackson.*

A terrible man has threatened Mack's family with violence and harm. Five years of work in taking BUSHAC from fantasy to a nationally recognized organization that made Sam Minkowitz cave in didn't matter. Mack again played back the gripping voice mail that put fear in his mind and heart.

"You remember me, you yuppie black motherfucker? You know, the guy you stole five years from for ripping off a whore for fifty bucks? Well, I sure as hell didn't forget! Listen good, motherfucker, your wife and kids are dead fucking meat."

The ambitious Thomas looked back on his moving to Atlanta in 1974 right out of University of Georgia Law School and landing a job as an assistant prosecutor with the Fulton County district attorney's (DA) office. Mack made his reputation with the first case assigned to him, the prosecution and conviction of Lemuel "Scoop" Harrison, an armed robber.

The judge, Mack recalled, sentenced an unrepentant Harrison to ten years without parole for robbing and pistol-whipping a massage parlor hooker. At the time, Mack felt the maximum sentence was too harsh by half but no longer.

Motherfucker should be locked away for five more years, but time served before sentencing, time off for good behavior in prison, and a fucking poor excuse for a parole board halved it.

Mack's desk phone rang three times before he picked it up. It was Amanda, his secretary, and he breathed a sigh of relief.

"Mr. Thomas, a Mr. Ed White is waiting to be interviewed for the newly created position of general assistant."

"Yes, Amanda, send Mr. White in." Mack calculated. *This new position should probably include an added dimension of bodyguard. I hate the loss of privacy, but the safety of my family is paramount.*

Eddie White trembled while turning the polished brass knob, humbly entered Mack's spacious office, and walked toward his desk. White wore a well-tailored brown suit, a pale yellow shirt, and a brown and yellow tie. He stood tall and proud and tried to look Mack in the eye while talking.

His lack of self-esteem, though, soon had him looking down at his feet.

"Mr. White," Mack directed, "the interview process has started, so please permit me thirty seconds for silent evaluation."

Well, he's no genius but does seem to have basic street smarts. He is a veritable hulk, though, and looks like he could Kung Fu a fucking neighborhood. This White fellow may be just what I'm looking for. Thank you, Lesotho.

612

Thomas asked White a single question. "Mr. White, are you skilled in martial arts?"

"Mr. Thomas," asked Eddie, puzzled, "why do I need to know karate to work a Xerox machine? Do you need me to kung fu it if it gets jammed?"

It suddenly sounded crazy to Mack too, who laughed hard.

"Eddie, please call me Mack, and that was a good comeback line too. I like people with a sense of humor around me."

"Okay, Mack, and thank you."

"The reason for the martial arts question is that a threat has been made against my wife and two little girls. The Thomas family needs protection, so it was my hope today to find a tough, smart guy who could both help in the office and work security for my family."

"Mr. Thomas—"

"Mack, Eddie, call me Mack."

"Okay, Mack, yes, I know some martial arts and have always been good with my hands, maybe too good at times."

"Fine, I'm offering twenty-five thousand to start, plus full benefits. The job is yours, if you want it."

Eddie flashed the brightest smile of his life. "I'm ready to start right now, Mack."

"I like hearing that, Eddie, but you go home and celebrate with your wife and kids tonight, report to this office at 9:00 AM tomorrow, and welcome to the growing BUSHAC organization and family."

Mack came out from behind his desk to shake Eddie's hand and tell him his duties.

"I'm enrolling you in a bodyguard training program at the Wackenhut Agency, and for the time being, I'll use a private security firm until you're ready to assume the role. You'll also help Amanda in the office reproducing print materials."

"I'm very excited by this opportunity."

"Eddie, let me show you how important this new job is."

Mack pointed to a large family portrait hanging on the wall overlooking his desk.

"This beautiful woman is my brilliant wife, Charlene, and those are my two adorable little girls, Jessie and Kyra."

"You have a beautiful family, Mack, and your daughters are adorable. Where do y'all live in Atlanta?"

"We live in Hembry Heights." Mack rubbed his chin with his fingers.

"I've heard that's Atlanta's most exclusive all-black subdevelopment. Hank Aaron supposedly lives there and a lot of wealthy business people do to."

Mack smiled. "Charlene has built a very successful financial planning company by investing a lot of our affluent neighbors' money, especially the professional athletes."

"Mack, I'm ready to go."

"Okay, your mission is to become the Thomas family's shadow and keep them out of harm's way. Scoop Harrison is to be viewed as a terrorist and dealt with accordingly. Your wife, Farrah,

614

and children will have to learn to live with this constant danger in your new line of work."

"Mack, I promise that I'm going to make you feel smart that you hired me."

"I'm glad, Eddie. Hey, I see that Lesotho's really hot for Sharon." Mack put his arm around Eddie's shoulder to escort him out of the office.

"Man, I thought Xeranga was too cool to get stuck like that. You know what I mean?"

"Yes."

"Sharon sure is wonderful, though, very beautiful too. Don't you think so?"

"Yes, we went to school together."

"Well, I can see that you're a man of few words. All right, I'll see you tomorrow at nine, and have a good evening."

Mack walked back to his office thinking, *Why am I cursing so much today? I almost never curse. This is how crazy Scoop has made me.*

Eddie White practically danced out of Mack's office and could not wait to get home to tell Farrah. For the first time since high school, he finally felt like he had a future.

I feel so good and proud I think I'm gonna cry.

Now that you finally have a life, Eddie, treat your wife and children better.

Chapter 85

On the flight from New York to Cairo, Allie penned a historical and messianic poem to be read to an Israeli audience at the Yad Vashem Holocaust Memorial in Jerusalem. He wrote nearly the whole time in the air and did not finish the undertaking until almost ready to land in Egypt.

He titled the poem "If Hitler Had Been a Friend of the Jews" and handed it to Carole, who'd been eager to read it for hours. The title stunned her.

"Are you serious, Allie? This title is straight out of the mind of Mel Brooks."

"Carole, I'm serious. Please get past it."

"Okay." She began reading.

The Nazis made the world a zoo,
But imagine if Adolf Hitler
Had been a friend of the Jew
And not an enemy oh so bitter.

Envision Hitler valuing Jewish citizenry
And creating a humane national Socialism,
Rebuilding Germany's shattered economy
Out of the ashes of World War I militarism.

Fantasize Hitler supporting a homeland
For all European Jews seeking Zion,
Fair rewards for loving the Fatherland,
Instead, Auschwitz, Dachau, terror, and dying.

If Hitler had acted like America's FDR,
Soothing the fears of his troubled nation,
Alsace-Lorraine, the Ruhr, and the Saar
Left in peace with no emasculation.

A responsible Germany, Beethoven's land,
Civilized, progressive, technologically advanced,
Committed to goodness, this Reich and Deutschland,
And not mass extermination in Ukraine and Poland.

It should have been in the Allies' interest
To return from Versailles all that was taken,
Welcome back, rearm, do what was best,
And forget the blame when all were mistaken.

Stalin's hordes might have been halted
By a Berlin, strong, vital, and prosperous,
Europe's balance of power kept, not altered,
By a Reich believing in freedom and justice.

Another strong hand to ease British decline,
A world of peace, cooperation, and order,
Alliances stretching from the Potomac to the Rhine,
Collectively securing all democracies' borders.

"The Messiah tarries; an Antichrist we await,"
Claim the Revelation and fundamentalist sages,
For was not Hitler the devil incarnate;
Did he not rise from politics, the sea that rages?

Why was mankind deaf to their screams?
Why was he blind to the gas and crematoria?
Fruitless are lists of what might have been;
The six million dead are to them a memorial.

The monster Hitler, 86 percent extermination,
Thank god he failed with his Final Solution,
A war against the Jews and Europe's nations,
Vigilance now to Hamas, Sunni, and Shiite revolution.

Today terrorists and assassins freely roam about,
Single out Jews among a planeload in Lebanon,
Receive training in Syria and comfort in Moscow,

Drive truck bombs, take hostages nudged by Iran.

And so the world becomes a more volatile place;
A nuclear holocaust threatens the human race;
The killing goes on; dear Lord, make it cease.
The world awaits a savior, His prince of peace.

We beseech thee, Messiah, oh make thyself known;
The seeds of destruction have already been sown,
And hurry, sweet prince, before it's too late;
Armageddon is before us; please spare us the fate.

"Allie, this poem is great, but I don't think you needed to include the cry-for-the-Messiah part near the end."

"In the face of Armageddon, Carole, there must always be hope. That's why people cry out for a messianic figure."

"What are the criteria, Allie, for deeming one a messiah, and how would we recognize a first coming, if God miraculously decreed one?"

"Good question, babe, because I'm not really sure and will have to locate an Old Testament Bible."

"Allie, what is our main aim in Egypt? Give me some background information and what we might possibly accomplish here."

"Egypt, Carole, combines one of the world's oldest civilizations, fastest-growing populations, and worst structural poverty. Annual *real* per capita income stagnated at $300 for a population doubling every twenty years. Cairo was built to hold eight hundred thousand. It's almost 1986, and twelve million are crammed in there. Its unworkable infrastructure is crumbling six times faster than New York City's and without a Wall Street financial district to pay for the repairs."

"Oh my god, the fucking place is falling apart."

"And it's falling down too. People wait decades for an apartment while many spend lifetimes camping out on roofs. Several times a month, another overburdened apartment building collapses from supporting an unsustainable weight."

"Oy vey." She sympathized. "The Egyptian people are so poor."

"Yes, they are. Meanwhile, I respect Egyptian president Hosni Mubarak for keeping Anwar Sadat's peace with Israel. The Camp David agreement engineered by President Carter left Egypt isolated diplomatically. The Arab nations shunned Sadat and denied him his prize of glory. Sadat stood accused of selling out the Palestinian cause, and some of his army officers that belonged to the Muslim Brotherhood killed him for it."

"Sadat paid the ultimate price for making peace." Carole saluted Sadat by smiling up at the sky with laughing eyes.

"Yes," said Allie, admiring her radiance. "Mubarak has skillfully moved Egypt back into the fold of leading moderate Arab nations. Without Egypt, Arabs cannot successfully make war against Israel. Mubarak, though, kept his treaty with Israel as a cold peace to mollify the Saudis and Saddam Hussein."

"So he's become part of the problem instead of the solution?"

"Yes, and his crony government is corrupt and gets richer, while the poor struggle to survive. Fifteen years after Sadat kicked the Russians out, twenty billion in U.S. aid has barely dented Egypt's teeming social problems. An explosive situation is building, the people's expectations are rising, and their patience is wearing thinner."

"So, Allie, we're visiting a time bomb that's ticking?"

619

"That's a good way to put it, and the main ticking bomb is the fundamentalist Muslim Brotherhood whose sworn goal is the creation of an Islamic republic. Mubarak calls them the Beards. They call Mubarak *Pharaoh*, which aggravates tensions among Egypt's lower and working classes."

"What do you think the total cost to fix Egypt would be to lift everyone out of poverty?"

"At least a trillion dollars of investment," Allie estimated, "is needed to make a real difference in Egypt, but a quarter to a half of it would probably be stolen by the government and elites and easily squandered."

"So, Allie, how can we help when the problems are so overwhelming?"

"Babe, when in doubt of how to help a country like Egypt, give concerts."

"I get it. Thank god we're landing soon because my back is starting to hurt."

"My back is okay. It's my butt that's getting sore from sitting so long. Anyway, Bell has planned three huge events, and Mubarak's fourteen security forces will keep a lid on things to keep us safe. The United States has rewarded him with F-16 fighter planes, helicopter gunships, and Abrams tanks to do the job."

The government honored the Herman-Cohen peace mission's first night in Cairo by throwing a lavish affair. Carole and Allie mingled with the Egyptian establishment and spoke with a number of important writers, artists, and film people. They both found the Egyptian people to be polite, kind, and very hospitable.

After a round of official speeches lasting a half hour, President Mubarak welcomed Carole to the stage and personally introduced her; Allie escorted her.

"The Egyptian government and people welcome America's greatest female singer. This is something that President Reagan and I absolutely agree on."

Many connected people in the audience laughed quietly.

"Allie," she whispered into his ear, "what's the laughter about?"

"Mubarak drew the laugh," Cohen whispered back, "from well-publicized recent disagreements with the Reagan administration over his refusal to ease repressive measures against the Beards. America worries that the rough tactics of his fourteen security agencies are aggravating tensions that will explode into a revolution."

After the laughter subsided, Carole took over the stage and, backed by select musicians from the Egyptian Symphony Orchestra, superbly covered an hour-long survey of easy-listening pop music, soft ballads, and a medley of top Broadway show tunes. The audience generously applauded her performance, with the kind of songs she began her career singing, and many new fans threw flowers.

Mubarak, his government, and their wives formed a line for Carole to shake each of their hands. They all wanted to hug her or tell her how much they appreciated her performance or for coming to Egypt to help. Mubarak showed his appreciation by providing his Imperial yacht for a three-day boat trip down the Nile. Sani Hassan, his chief aide, acted as tour guide and host.

The dreary sight of unending, grinding poverty along the riverbanks so depressed Allie that he urged Sani to shorten the trip to two days. "Sani, please, we don't need to go that far down the Nile. The Pyramids and sphinx are plenty, thank you."

Upon returning to their Cairo Hilton VIP suite, he and Carole concluded that Egypt's problems were intractable until

Mubarak and the Beards agreed to share political and economic power and attack their structural poverty.

"So, sweetie, let's rock those mummies' bandages off and get our asses to Israel ASAP."

That night, Carole shook the base of Cheops with good, old-fashioned rock 'n' roll and thirty state-of-the-art speakers. For the first hour, she sang an eclectic set that ranged from the Grateful Dead's "Friend of the Devil" to Jimi Hendrix's "Purple Haze." Allie marveled from behind the stage.

Jimi, I think you're smiling down from heaven, man. Jerry, I think you too should love Carole's treatment of your song. Dudes, y'all should both be very happy indeed.

While the second set covered a range of great U.S. female rock singers, Cohen went over the plans with the road crew for the following night's concert at the University of Alexandria. Carole's remarkable range, power, and energy mesmerized twenty thousand young Egyptians dancing in the desert, and Cohen cheered her on from backstage.

During a short break, he told her, "Babe, this is your greatest performance ever. After tonight, you're the best female *rocker* in the business too."

Martin Vincent, a Jamaican American roadie, rolled Allie a spliff that had a quarter ounce of pot he called Blue Mountain Dream, a premium Rasta variety. Cohen lit up backstage during "Purple Haze," kicked back, and grooved on Carole's interpretation.

Allie was unaware that he was photographed with the outrageously large joint in his hand and a loopy grin on his face. The Frenchman who took the photo faxed it to Claude Gold, his *Paris Match* editor.

I influenced Claude to pay the photographer but put the picture in his drawer to kill the photo and let Claude think about what to do.

I'm determined to interview Allie Cohen, and if anyone can score one, it's Tina Debres, my top freelancer. If I publish this picture and cause Cohen trouble, forget about him ever sitting down with Tina and Paris Match *to talk. My killing the story saves the rest of the tour for Cohen, so he owes me big for this. Visas might have been hard to obtain after the photo went worldwide.*

That's very good, Claude. You have it all figured out.

The crowd demanded an encore, and all lit candles and shouted their love for Carole. She finally appeared, but her voice was mildly strained from singing "Purple Haze" and covering so many different female artists in the second set, so she promised a single soft melody that would send the crowd home peacefully— Crosby, Stills & Nash's "Teach Your Children." Carole's raspiness added a soulful quality that fit the moment perfectly.

The crowd was brought down gently and headed for their train, bus, car, or motorbike; no donkey carts for these young people.

While waiting for the crowd to leave, Cohen peered through binoculars at the Pyramid of Giza and stared for several moments at the pharaoh's first massive public works project for his Hebrew slaves. Egypt's greatest treasures, Allie realized as a brisk wind blew out of Sinai and chilled him, were all monuments to death.

The future isn't bright for a people who peaked three thousand years ago. Today's pharaohs erect no landmarks to life or death, and the only thing they build is their cash deposits in Swiss, Qatari, and Panamanian bank accounts.

Two days later, after finishing the Alexandria concert, Carole and Allie dressed for a farewell dinner with the Mubaraks.

Attired in black tux and feeling spiffy, Cohen researched messianic guidelines for Carole by rummaging through his luggage in search of the Illustrated Jerusalem Bible, a wedding gift from Sarah's grandfather.

Allie pushed back the pages to the table of contents when he suddenly heard gunfire. Staccato blasts from machine guns were coming closer and closer and caused him to drop the Bible to the floor, but he picked it right up and kissed it.

The deafening bursts terrified Carole, and she ran to Allie for protection. "What's going on? I'm scared."

Cohen threw his arms around her and summoned courage. "I wish I knew."

A dozen ear-blasting rounds then destroyed the lock and blew the door open. He and Carole stared directly at three muscular Arab men brandishing automatic weapons.

"What do you think they want with us?" Carole fearfully whispered to him. "Do you think they'll kill us?"

"I think they're going to take us hostage. If they were going to kill us, I figure we'd be dead already."

The tallest and apparent cell leader barked at Cohen, "Please listen."

"I firmly believe," Allie answered, "in following the orders of any man wearing a ski mask and pointing an assault rifle at me. Sure, by all means, speak."

He made the intruders and even Carole laugh a little.

"Look, we mean you no harm. We have come in peace and ask only for a few hours of your time. Our imam requests a private conversation with the two of you."

Allie looked at the tall man, who described his intent as peaceful, and then pointed to the half dozen dead army guards splattered across the hallway. "That is peaceful?"

"The Pharaoh's flunkies resisted our efforts to approach you. Please, we must go now and hurry."

"Okay." He held Carole's hand while following the trio down the back stairwell secured by two dozen heavily armed Muslim Brotherhood fighters who lived in the area. Very little communication took place during the half-hour ride through crowded back streets.

Cohen, familiar with the historical development of the Muslim Brotherhood, quietly briefed Carole.

"Babe, members generally rise from the lower classes, become imbued with the ideals of the Islamic resurgence, and form Communist-type cells to subvert shaky Arab governments."

"How does the government deal with them, my man?"

"Mubarak bans them, drives them underground, and keeps up the pressure. He allows the brotherhood to run candidates in national elections and lets their followers vote for them. Unfortunately, Mubarak simply rigs the elections and permits a handful of the most moderate candidates to take their seats."

"How long has this been going on?"

"The movement was established in Egypt in 1928 by Ḥasan al-Bannā' and currently wages covert war in six Arab nations. The Egyptian seer at the moment is Abu Sallah, a blind preacher whom Mubarak recently drove underground because of his growing popularity."

The sedan parked in the courtyard of a small religious school in crowded south Cairo, where they were led into a square fully carpeted room, walls and ceiling included, to await the imam.

While waiting for their host, Carole asked Allie, "Yo, Cohen, what should I expect from this imam dude?"

Cohen did not mince words. "You are the vestige of everything they are trying to rid their society of, a whorish drunken doper mocking traditional Muslim roles for women."

"I can see, Allie, that I'm going to be a big hit with him. Tell me, what are the roles he'd prefer me to act out?"

"To be dumb, barefoot, pregnant and bow to him."

"Well, I guess one out of four ain't bad, huh, Cohen?" She rubbed her tummy.

That made Allie want to kiss her belly and put his ear to it but wasn't sure if he heard a heartbeat yet. *It's funny*, he thought. *I recall being able to hear Ari's by this time.*

Mustafa Mohammed, Abu Sallah's personal secretary, stopped their bantering to introduce Mubarak's major political threat, who entered the room wearing a loose-fitting white robe. His faithful servant Mustafa carefully sat Abu down, took his place by him, and served as his interpreter.

Sallah sat cross-legged as Mustafa presented him.

"Abu Sallah is the Mahdi who will unite the Arab masses against their governments and establish Islamic republics across the Arab world."

The short, squat Abu Sallah spoke. "I have heard a great deal of your strutting around the world in the name of peace and have asked to meet you. Many of my young people, including my two teenage children, were at the desert concert and say you are genuinely good Americans."

Carole and Allie jointly responded to the imam, "We appreciate your kind compliments and warm hospitality."

They were served tea, figs, dates, and cookies by two women with covered faces and slits for eyes to see.

"My wish," Sallah expressed, "is to engage you in a meaningful dialogue since we have different visions about what path will lead to a lasting regional peace. How may we close our gap that now divides us?"

Cohen spoke for him and Carole, "We are honored to discuss this matter with you. Please proceed."

"I'd like you to carry a message to President Reagan and other world leaders. It is an offer to form better policies for this region. Allah has spoken to me. 'When the Pharaoh has been driven from the land and the people accept the Koran in good faith, the Arab nation will rise in greatness under the banner of an Islamic society.'"

Cohen signaled to Mustafa to please interject. "Sallah is preaching a seventh-century vision that was also former president Gamal Abdel Nasser's old 'greater Arab nation' plan. Sallah has the Koran but no army like Nasser, and the colonel died a failure."

"Nasser," Sallah volleyed back, "did not ask for or receive Allah's blessing, and that was the difference."

Allie let that pass; Sallah continued. "We ask that the West suspend all aid to the Pharaoh and help the brotherhood govern Egypt, and we will guarantee Israel's right to exist. Jerusalem, though, must stay divided."

"Two things," responded Cohen. "First, the United States will not see that as a bargain. America already has this deal with

Mubarak, who has a track record. Second, Israel will not divide Jerusalem for the Palestinians. This is a no-go, maybe an inch of land close to the Green Line for a symbolic Al-Quds capital."

"I understand." Sallah's head bobbled three times. "And let me be clear. The Zionists' terms are acceptable as long as Muslims possess the Temple Mount. Muslims must have access to the Dome of the Rock from where Muhammad ascended to heaven. A total jihad might be necessary if the Zionists deny the Islamic peoples free passage to the third holiest shrine of Islam."

"Please, Sallah." Cohen logically countered, "All previous wars with the Israelis have been equally disastrous for the Arabs. Why should the next one succeed when the Jews are more powerful than ever and the Arab nations are fighting among themselves?"

The imam put his finger to his chin and rubbed his eyebrow; he was hearing Allie, so Cohen had to know one important thing.

"Imam, please, why is the brotherhood in extreme conflict with the West? Trade with the United States brings miraculous technologies, medical advances, and beneficial educational, agricultural, and environmental practices."

"The problem with the miraculous technologies," Sallah specified, "is the sordid values that usually come with the new inventions."

He directed his attention to Carole. "Your country spreads its moral pollution, and we are resolved to stop it from contaminating our holy Islamic society."

Allie deflected Sallah's attention from Carole. "Imam, all life is a trade-off. With advanced Western technology often comes elements of the more liberal culture that produced it. The benefits of the technology, however, should outweigh any measure of moral decline, and we in the West call this progress."

Carole, though appreciative, was not to be denied expressing her view. "Imam," said Carole, hoping for a breakthrough, "what is wrong with women expressing their humanity just like men?"

"Did the laws of Abraham and Moses state that women should live like whores?" Sallah chilled Carole. "You roam the world openly with a married man and have even bared your breasts in a film. A number of my young followers have studied in California and told me of your ways."

Blood drained from Carole's eyes. Sallah reminded her of Old Testament figures learned at her grandmother's side. She intuitively joked to ease the tension.

"Imam, you sound a little bit like my mother, Rose. She says some of the same things you just said."

Sallah laughed. "I am a forgiving man. I ask you again to please bring my message to President Reagan."

An aide summoned Mustafa Mohammed. The translator listened and then announced, "The Pharaoh has discovered your absence and ordered the army into action against us. A tank column has been spotted heading this way, so we must quickly evacuate. Allie and Carole, the same driver will safely deposit you within distance of your despotic rescuers."

"It is your American weapons," Abu Sallah declared, "that the Pharaoh uses to sap the lives of our brothers."

"Yes, and before Sadat allied Egypt with the West," Cohen reasoned with him, "it was godless Russian weapons that sapped your brave brothers' lives. Is not the one true answer for all the peoples of the Middle East peace, love, and cooperation?"

"Perhaps," said Sallah, as self-convinced as Alvarado. "But this cannot occur until the imperialists withdraw and a pure Islamic state allowed to flower. I am sorry, but I must go and apologize for a rude departure. I thank you and urge that you educate the imperialists of Allah's just vision for the Arab world."

The last words of a twice-disheartened Cohen echoed Sallah's.

"I am grateful for this encouraging meeting, Imam, but I fear that neither of our visions for the region is likely to flower, and that is the real tragedy of the Middle East. May Yahweh and Allah bless both of us and our peoples. It has been my great pleasure and privilege, Imam."

Cohen turned to the interpreter and gave him his business card and pointed to Sandy's name on it.

"Mustafa, please call Mr. Forman and ask him to transfer $200,000 into the brotherhood's food banks, and work with him to get around the U.S. sanctions against the brotherhood. This is purely a humanitarian act. The Lord in heaven wants no child, Muslim, or Jewish to go hungry, and I have seen too many malnourished Egyptian children."

Mustafa smiled appreciatively, shook Cohen's hand vigorously, and thanked him.

Cohen had affected Sallah, who while fleeing in a camouflaged jeep shared his surprising perceptions of Allie with Mustafa.

"I detected the special quality of painful wisdom in the messenger Cohen's voice and heart. He is no ordinary Jew, for he reached out to my heart and head and touched them deeply. It deeply saddened me when he said that neither of our visions flowering is the real Middle East tragedy."

"Frankly, Imam, he touched my heart too with his gift of $200,000 for our food banks so that no Muslim child will go hungry. So I understand what you are telling me. He is a very special man."

"I really heard his great, shattering truth, Mustafa, and it has changed the way I see the world and our situation. Allah must be speaking to us through Cohen. I think we should recommend him to that, uh, uh—please, what is that name of the imperialist peace prize organization with the pretentious title?"

"The Nobel Peace Prize Committee. A certain Norwegian politician specializes in these matters. I will call him tonight on the phone to tell him that you want to nominate Cohen, and I will fax the letter and transcripts to him tomorrow."

Abu Sallah is the fourth major nominator and most unexpected by far. It was I, Gabriel, who spoke to Sallah and not through Allah or Adonai, but I am most flattered that Sallah believed so. This is why Hashem calls me His *gentle vise of a persuader.*

A mile away, Allie and Carole emerged from a crowded alleyway and met up with a commando unit. The Egyptian government apologized and promptly complied with their request to fly to Israel immediately. They were transported by a military cargo plane to Lod Airport in Israel that very evening.

Somewhere over the Negev Desert, Allie showed Carole the messiah's qualifications and presented them with a joke.

"I don't think the job is an affirmative action position, though any Puerto Rican Jew, except Geraldo Rivera, may apply."

Carole, who knew Geraldo, laughed tears. "What grief or dues to be paid awaits the person daring to claim the messiah title?"

She imagined. She shuddered and then asked, "Can the messiah be female? How about me, for example? Aren't I a messenger of peace?"

"You're right and an ideal messenger of peace too," he explained. "But Halakah and the Orthodox say no. It says here that he must be an anointed king who is descended from Yishai, also known as Jesse, or his son David."

"So, Allie, what will he do?"

"This person, who is not at all to be equated with the Lord, will bring the dispersed of the Israelites and Jews together in the land of Israel. The messiah will establish a uniform, monotheistic Jewish religion in Israel, Orthodox I presume, and will institute an era of everlasting tranquility and justice after a period of cataclysm and upheaval, which we refer to as Armageddon."

"So all the Jews," Carole summed up, "must live in Israel and practice the same Orthodox faith. Man, Allie, that sure isn't going to happen anytime soon. You know, after reading your poem, I thought you were nominating yourself. Please tell me that I'm wrong, please." She put her hands together.

"Nah, I don't think I'm religious enough. I can still read Hebrew okay but can barely speak a word of it. I'm a cohen, though, so I might be related to King David."

You left out thirteenth grandchild to go with cohen.

"So it could be you?" Carole stared at Allie while waiting for his answer.

"Possibly, Carole, but I doubt it. A secular Jew like me just doesn't fit the traditional messianic formula. The Lord would have to shortcut the process for a nontraditional messiah to appear. I just like to go around telling people how we can have eternal peace without the cataclysm-and-selective-survival crap."

"The biggest problem as I see it," Carole stated, "is that Jews are taught to thwart the appearance of a false messiah. Allie, think how hard they would try to thwart you."

Allie felt a cold dread. "I don't want to go there, Carole."

You will, prophet, when the Master of the universe thinks you are ready.

Chapter 86

Herman and Cohen landed at Lod Airport, were whisked through VIP customs, and driven to Jerusalem by their Israeli security team. Carole again mulled over the messiah's stipulations.

"Allie, I'm trying to figure out how anyone will know if a real messiah claim is true."

Allie thought that over for a few seconds. "For me, as a start, I'd need a special report from Dan Rather, followed up by Ted Koppel and Walter Cronkite grilling the dude for ninety minutes in prime time. So what would it take for you to think the dude is legit?"

"I don't know, Allie, maybe walk on water or fly like a bird, perhaps hurl thunderbolts that demand respect or submission, whatever."

"No, Carole, the people are to behold, exalt, and follow in awe."

Allie facially expressed *awe* for her. "I'm not sure where that came from."

Don't worry about it, Allie, although I am concerned over this popular expectation of *superhuman actions* and none for a *superintelligent being* like you, prophet.

Herman and Cohen dubbed their secret service contingent the Iron Matzoth for how seriously they took their job. The team consisted of four well-chiseled agents led by stone-faced Menachem Harel, who checked them into the Jerusalem Hilton.

"Menachem," Cohen questioned, "why are we staying at the Hilton and not the King David Hotel, which supposedly has a lot more ambience?"

Harel slowly answered, "For security reasons that we prefer not to go into, we consider the Hilton an easier place to protect you."

"Could it be Menachem," teased Allie, "that your former prime minister, Menachem Begin, blew up the place in 1946 and killed 250 British officers and soldiers?"

Allie referred to a July 22, 1946, Irgun Zvai Leumi terrorist attack that became a major force in the British withdrawal from Palestine. By evacuating, the English "let the chips fall where they may" in the fight between the Zionists and Arabs for control of Israel's coastal plan and west Jerusalem.

Carole gave Allie a look that said he was pushing Menachem—who stonily ignored him—too far. Upon installment, Cohen agreed with Harel. "Our suite is very plush and quite convenient to the banquet room, only a flight below. I understand that a reception in our honor is scheduled for tomorrow afternoon."

"Yes, that is so," affirmed Harel. "Now we will let you two get some sleep."

He told a little of himself. "I used to be an El Al pilot for five years, so I know very well the effects on the body of a ten-hour, fifty-five-hundred-mile flight from America."

They went right to sleep and did not awake until noon the next day, just in time for their banquet. Carole and Allie were bathed in the universality of Jewish warmth by their Israeli hosts, who loved to mingle with famous Jewish American stars. The two celebrities patiently signed autographs and took snapshots with dozens of admirers.

The coleaders of Israel's national unity government, Likud's Yitzhak Shamir and Labor's Shimon Peres, were meeting with English Prime Minister Thatcher in London and with President Reagan in Washington, respectively. Arieh Rudin, Peres's right-hand man, subbed for his prime minister as chief speaker and introduced Carole, who needed none. The hall went wild with applause, whistles, and a few foot stomps.

"It is also my great pleasure tonight to introduce Dr. Allie Cohen, an important Jewish American writer who has shown all of us our ultimate moral responsibility as Jews."

Rudin's introduction received about three seconds of polite rhythmic patting of hands together.

Arieh refreshed the audience's memory of Cohen's accomplishments by sharing his own reactions to his book. Rudin finished his description, looked straight ahead at Cohen, and pointed toward him with his right hand.

"Dr. Cohen"—he paused to heighten the moment—"I am privileged to be the first person in the world, even before Ms. Herman"—he pointed toward Carole—"or even your wife or mother, to announce a true mitzvah. Ladies and gentlemen, I just received a very exciting phone call from Stockholm, Sweden, and learned that Dr. Allie Cohen is this year's Nobel Peace Prize recipient. Mazel tov, Dr. Cohen, congratulations!"

Rudin shocked Cohen, who was glad to be sitting down. The full force of the most cherished award that a peacenik can receive humbled him before Hashem. Shouts of praise reverberated from an audience cognizant of a historic moment, the acclaim deeply affecting Allie and causing him to weep openly.

Carole threw her arms around Allie and held him tightly. She kissed him over and over and crowed, "Allie, I can't put into words how proud I am of you."

Tears of joy rolled down her cheeks. "My god, I'm crying from happiness for you. I look back at that moment in my house when we first met. I knew instantly that you were special, and now the rest of the world does too."

Choked with emotion and with a bowed head and tears streaming down his cheeks, Cohen got up from the chair.

"Thank you, Carole. I'd never have won the prize without the chance to work for peace that you and the tour have given me. You are my special partner, my angel of peace and goodwill." He hugged and kissed her.

Rudin called out to him, "Dr. Cohen, here, take the microphone from me." Allie ambled over to the bald middle-aged official, who kissed him on both cheeks.

Rudin whispered into his ear before surrendering the microphone, "The Norwegian assemblyman told me that no recipient in the history of the prize ever had such diverse nominees as Chilean Marxist Mario Alvarado and his CIA antagonist, Egyptian Islamist Abu Sallah, and a U.S. State Department official in Moscow who nominated you, claiming you brought earthly action to his best Christian ideals. By the way, Israeli Intelligence told me that you are the first Jew that Abu Sallah ever talked to in his life. You must have really impressed him to nominate you for the Nobel Prize, truly amazing."

For the first time since the tour kicked off, the world completely focused on Allie; the beholding had begun. The newest member of a most exclusive club spoke in a slow, deliberate voice.

"I am overwhelmed by the consideration that I have done more to wage aggressive peace than five and a half billion peers. My award is proof that a person's efforts in behalf of peace do not necessarily go unnoticed. This too is why I believe that the wrong person was honored today."

A buzz went through the audience. "I am a lucky man to have a partner who shares the same vision, risks similar dangers, and sings the same message of peace. Ms. Carole Herman is an indefatigable fighter for freedom, and without her, I would not be standing before you today."

Carole gazed at Allie with loving but watery eyes as he continued. "This honor really belongs to an angel of mercy and compassion, a selfless talent without limits, and the brilliant and beautiful lady who is my partner in peace. I also want to recognize my wonderful wife, Sarah, who is the anchor and rock that supports my peace missions." Allie beckoned Carole to come and share the limelight with him.

"This is your moment, Allie." She resisted. "And you alone should receive the glory."

"Carole, please, babe, come here."

She relented and joined him at the lectern, and he spoke to the audience with his arm around her waist. Adonai selected Allie's words to simplify his message of peace to the people.

"I ask, why do we sometimes resort to evil and justify it as doing good? Humans often shortcut good with evil acts by claiming they are restoring or maintaining order or fostering economic stability and prosperity or protecting the nation.

The ends supposedly justify the means, or do they? No, our means must justify our ends too. We must only do good so as to banish evil from our world forever.

When we all do what's good and right, then and only then will we have true peace on earth for all mankind."

Cohen's brief, clear, simple words were taped by the Israeli media and fed by satellite to American counterparts and around the globe. He excused himself from the stage to call Atlanta and tell Sarah before she heard it from the media.

Sarah picked up in Atlanta. "Allie, I've already heard. Tom Brokaw of *NBC Nightly News* just interviewed me, though I do appreciate you calling me personally."

"How's Ari?"

"Ari"—she laughed—"was watching TV with me and saw your face on the screen. I swear, he pointed at the TV and yelled out over and over, 'Dada, dada, dada!' It's too bad that you couldn't see the smile on his face and watch him point as he stared at the TV."

"I miss you guys so much."

"I'm so proud of you, Allie. You deserved this prize too."

"Without your love, trust, and support, Sarah, I never would have received it."

"Allie, I now understand how important your mission is, and I love you, and I am a hundred percent behind you. I just regret not being there to share this fabulous moment with you personally."

"I assure you, money, that you'll share the Stockholm award ceremony with me and Ari too. Sandy Forman is renting a plane to fly you and Ari, my mother, the Kartzmans, Carla and Joel, Jerry and Laurie, and whoever the hell else wants to come to Stockholm." He said goodbye and returned to the banquet room.

Carole spoke to the audience.

"My new friends in Israel, Allie has written a special poem that I think perfectly commemorates this moment."

The crowd chanted, "Please read it. Please read it."

This audience, I feel in my bones, is as likely a group to appreciate the poem as any, so I will begin.

They were appreciative, for many cried from the might-have-beens. The audience loved the poem and gave Allie another standing ovation. Cohen ended one of the greatest moments of his life by handing the microphone to Carole.

She closed the ceremony with a bluesy "Hava Nagila" and a heartfelt "HaTikvah." The Hilton was deluged with congratulatory telegrams and phone calls from all over the world. Carole bought a scrapbook and filled it with many news articles and telegrams.

The media scrambled for interviews until Allie passed the word that none would be given until the Stockholm reception. President Reagan, actually Ted Bell, and so many Georgia and California politicians called that he unhooked the phone.

Rick Samuels and Mike Schwartz sent a humorous singing telegram. An elderly messenger stood in the hallway belting out, "Mazel tov. Mazel tov." Carole and Allie fell out laughing from the absurd sight.

All night and the next day, the hotel lay under siege as congratulations of all types poured in. The print and TV media haunted the Hilton with their aggressive methods to capture an exclusive interview.

Allie finally appeared in the hotel ballroom and read a paragraph-long statement.

"I thank the Nobel committee; Carole Herman; my wife, Sarah, and family; and President Reagan for the support that enabled me to work for peace.

I ask for a little time to set an agenda to advance peace in the year ahead. I look forward to spending time touring Israel with Carole and having a combination of reception-celebration and family reunion in Stockholm. That is my prepared statement. Now I'll take a few questions."

"Dr. Cohen," Schmuel Joel, a *Jerusalem Post* stringer, asked, "what do you have to say about a few carpers who've had the chutzpah to claim that you don't really deserve the prestigious award?"

"Schmuel, I don't expect everyone to agree on my selection."

"So you don't think the Nobel people were really desperate to find someone who did anything relatively significant in a nondescript year with forty-three conflicts raging?"

"I hope not, and frankly, Mr. Joel, my initiatives incurred serious risks, including a short hostage situation, which I am not at liberty to discuss."

"Dr. Cohen," asked Judy Rubin, a pretty female reporter from *Haaretz*, "what might be the first global issue or problem that you want to address?"

"Less developed countries (LDCs) that are all too often militarized and murderous enterprises, which I call MMEs. A vision of sorts will be expressed in my acceptance speech in Stockholm. I thank everyone for their interest and attention and conclude this press conference."

Cohen's new global status so worried Israeli security officials that they ratcheted up their already tight protection. The Shin Bet informed their American charges that the agency worried about an assassin passing himself off as a reporter. Menachem smiled cutely as he issued a directive.

"We have banned the press from approaching both of you for the rest of the tour. I have a feeling that you will not mind this regulation at all." Harel giggled, a truly rare sight.

Carole and Allie savored the triumph with a candlelit dinner out on the terrace of their luxury suite, which overlooked the beautiful well-lit city and star-filled heavens. Carole held his hand and asked, "Why don't I have a need to get high in Zion?"

"You're not bored." He stroked her fingers. "In the United States, you're an active consumer. In Israel, you're an activist."

"I think it's more than that. I feel a tremendous warmth and spirit that's not quite the same as in America."

They made love twice that evening and slept with smiles on their faces. During breakfast, Cohen read a *USA Today* interview with his mother, who described where and how she first heard the news.

"I was listening to the ten o'clock news that always asks, 'Do you know where your children are?' When I heard that Israel honored my son with a banquet for receiving the Nobel Prize, I went straight to the kitchen table and cried from joy. For a Jewish mother to have her son win the Nobel Prize and be honored by Israel is the ultimate bragging right. I'm so thrilled with pride that I'm bursting."

"Carole, I love my mother's comments. The paper also has a report of Sarah's comments to Tom Brokaw, which are equally touching."

"Believe me, I know that my husband touring with Carole Herman is controversial, but this mission has provided him with many opportunities to advance peace. He'd never have won this most-important-of-all recognitions without President Reagan letting Carole Herman utilize his knowledge and skill set. I'm so proud of Allie that I've been crying tears of joy on and off the whole day."

"Mrs. Cohen," Brokaw inquired, "what moment felt most special to you today?"

"For me"—she thought for a second—"it was when our son Ari recognized his father on TV and yelled 'dada' over and over. My son, still in a high chair, already gets it that his father is a person *of* the world and *for* the world, and with a role model like Allie, maybe Ari will win the Nobel someday too."

Sarah, sweetie, you publicly thanking President Reagan and Carole was brilliant. Money, you've become a very good politician, and I particularly like your choice of the words "utilize his knowledge and skill set."

I must say that was very good PR, Sarah, Allie's angel of the hearth and home.

Chapter 87

Tall dark Schlomo Pincus, age thirty-eight, kissed his wife, Yael, and his three sons goodbye to wait outside in front of his house. It was a cool Sunday morning, and he thought as he walked down the steps leading from his spacious Mediterranean apartment,

Allie is coming. It's been two years since we last met.

Pincus reminisced. *It was a good time for Allie and Sarah. He'd just completed his doctoral dissertation and impressed me with his knowledge of computerized statistical analysis and procedures and the social science research and methodologies supporting his prejudice reduction treatment. Sarah was pregnant and expecting. This time, he returns with a Nobel Prize and a movie star mistress who's also expecting. That's my Allie.*

Cohen prepped her. "Carole, Schlomo's office is just down the hall from the famous Chagall windows in the Hadassah Hospital. His genius at building control data systems and computerizing Israel's medical and hospital programs brought him to the Pentagon for a year to study radiation poisoning. He then did six months at the RAND Corporation in San Diego brainstorming innovative military applications for the neutron bomb."

"Allie, what the hell's a neutron bomb?"

"The Carter administration conceived of a huge radiation blast without fireball that microwaves and sickens people to death without destroying the real estate. Until this bomb, we were stupidly destroying western Europe with A-bombs to save it from Communism. Carter feared mass manufacturing of this weapon would make it too easy to use and canceled the project. Reagan's revival of the neutron bomb brings further pressure on Gorbachev to reduce arms."

"So," Carole asked, "Schlomo is both a doctor and a soldier?"

"Yes, in addition to his demanding career, Pincus serves eight to ten weeks a year in the army reserves and is subject to do so through age fifty-five. Think about that."

Schlomo expected that Allie would probably beg him to take him up in a trainer. *I must think of an appropriate cover.*

Two government sedans stopped in front of Schlomo's home. Cohen got out of the first and hugged his friend on the ground that had been an Arab-occupied territory seventeen years before. The two cars headed straight for the old city and the Wailing Wall. Schlomo sat in the back seat with Carole and spoke to Cohen, seated in the front right seat.

"Allie, so much has happened to you since our last time together. I remember our visit to the wall. You prayed for a son, and now you have a fine son from what I hear. Mazel tov."

"Yes, thank you, Schlomo." Allie looked down and then said, "But Ari is our second try." He bit his lip.

Pincus looked down. "I didn't know." He bit his lip. "I should have known better. I am sorry, Allie."

Carole patted Schlomo on the shoulder for Allie, who asked, "Tell me, how is Yael?"

"Fine, pregnant again. This baby will be number four. The Israeli women make it a patriotic duty to match the Arab women birth for birth. It is a battle of the wombs, and the Holy Land will be won by who has the highest fertility rate."

"How come Yael or your sons did not join us?"

645

"Yael felt very close to Sarah and is uncomfortable with your arrangement with Carole. I have no such problem. My sons are busy all day with athletic contests, academic projects, and a friend's birthday party tonight. Yael is really a homebody and will happily drive them to their matches and party."

"Schlomo," Allie asked in code, "have you been able to take care of that certain matter?"

What matter? thought Carole.

"Not completely, Allie, I am still seeking an angle to get you inside the basement."

What basement? Carole wondered.

Pincus snapped his fingers. "I got it. You're almost a clone of a guy I know. Give me a day or two to put it together."

"Sure, Schlomo, I'm very grateful for what you're trying to do for me."

Schlomo noticed that Carole seemed annoyed from being left out of their secret. He did not want to get Carole mad at him, so he told her of his past promise to Allie.

Carole listened and voiced her concern. "Schlomo, all I want to know is, can something happen up there?"

"Carole, this is Israel. Anything can happen at any time. We are going to the wall and a seafood restaurant and theoretically can ride over a bomb or get blown to bits by Arab terrorists detonating themselves for seventy-two virgins. They say that danger is a *fact* of life in Israel. I prefer to say danger is a *way* of life."

"Please describe the plane you'll be flying in," asked Carole, who surprisingly knew a little bit about jet fighter planes.

"It's Israel's Lavi jet fighter, which is based on a French Mirage frame, powered by U.S. General Electric engines, and outfitted with dual controls and armaments."

"I've heard rumors," Allie added, "of Israel's discontinuing production because of a cost structure that's unaffordable."

"Allie, please don't change the subject. I heard the word *armaments*. Schlomo, why armaments if it's only a trainer?"

"Because, Carole, the Syrians have attacked trainers before too."

"Forget it, Allie, you're not setting foot in that plane."

"I fully intend to fly, Carole, regardless of what you say or do."

Allie tried to change the subject. "Schlomo, you don't have to answer this if you don't want to, but did you ever have to kill anyone?"

This time, Cohen succeeded in changing the subject because Pincus amazed even him with his openness.

"I have to differentiate between shooting down six Syrian and Egyptian MiGs, which mainly appeared as blips on my radar screen, and a terrorist attack I lived through when I visited my cousin in Qiryat Shemona."

Carole begged to know. "What happened, if you don't mind sharing it with us?"

"Sure. A small band of PLO terrorists snuck across the border and raided my cousin's kibbutz located in the Golan. They quickly killed three settlers and wounded five others. I managed to grab a rifle in time to shoot two of the Arabs in the eyes and blow part of their brains away. I admit to never being able to wipe that scene totally from my brain."

The sedan parked a block away from the historic gate leading to ancient east Jerusalem. Menachem and company directed their three charges through a tour of the crowded Arab market and then down a hill leading to the sacred Wailing Wall. Pincus stood back to let the pilgrims pray at Judaism's holiest site.

"Ms. Herman," directed Menachem, "you will be segregated according to Orthodox strictures into the area reserved for females."

Cohen edged up to the wall and saw an elderly Orthodox rabbi examining his clothing as if it was too stylish. The old man sounded like he was chanting prayers of redemption for Cohen's soul, which Allie found vexing.

Forget about it, man. I'm before the wall with my note in hand to stick in a crack and desperately want to experience a religious feeling. If there's a pipeline to the Lord, this wall is the surest place to send Adonai a message or voice mail. Twenty years of challenging the Almighty's existence ended with Ari's birth, and my many recent blessings have convinced me that I am worthy of the Lord's love and charity.

Cohen closed his eyes and prayed, *Dear Lord, the world is a troubled place today, but lately, life has been very good to me. I especially thank You for my son, Ari Ben Cohen, and pray that he will grow up in a more peaceful world. You have promised to send a messiah to show us a better way. When will he finally arrive, and who will he be?*

Cohen had folded two prewritten notes and stuffed them in a crack in the wall. The first was the Passover prayer, Ani Ma'amin. "I believe in the coming of the Messiah, and though he tarry, yet will I believe."

The second note thanked the Lord for a small blessing. "May Ari Ben Cohen enjoy a long, safe, and happy life, so please bless Ari and You, oh Lord."

Schlomo treated Carole and Allie to a dinner of St. Peter's fish at a Downtown Jerusalem restaurant and insisted they try the eggplant salad appetizer and smear the tangy tahini sauce on it. They quickly consumed the eggplant salad, and the waiter brought out three fish plates.

"Be careful, babe," Allie warned Carole. "This flat fish is dangerously bony."

"I refuse to eat a bite of it," Carole joked, "until Schlomo proves he can perform a Heimlich maneuver."

"This Red Sea delicacy," Schlomo eulogized, "is fast becoming an endangered species."

Cohen looked at Schlomo to make sure his eyes were not deceiving him. "Are these fish a lot smaller than last time?"

Schlomo nodded and warned, "And more polluted too."

Carole threw a one-liner. "Oy vey, the Promised Land of milk and honey."

"Let me tell you, Carole, God's promise to Eden costs 50 percent more than last year and is down from 432 percent the year before. With three boys and a fourth child on the way, the milk is enough. Forget the honey."

Allie tried to comprehend an inflation rate that high. "So Israel can't produce what it consumes, and the military burden forces you to do without."

"Yes, oddly, we do without to create jobs. You Americans consume to create jobs. The Israeli government keeps raising taxes to cut consumption and to make up deficits. Then we are encouraged to save and invest but lack any real incentive to do so."

"It sounds, Schlomo, like the economy is in bad shape."

"Yes, but we have had good times in the past and will so again. I believe that with our brainpower, thirty or forty years from now, Israel will be the richest country in the region. We are laying the groundwork for adopting cutting-edge military technologies to transformative civilian uses through analog and digital applications."

Schlomo's prediction proved very true. Israel today is known as a *start-up nation* and a global leader in developing high technology products and applications.

"I once heard my uncle Micha share a hope." Cohen recalled the quote. "Someday Israelis will not have to choose between their homeland and America. American prosperity will come to Israel."

"We should be so lucky, Allie," kidded Schlomo. "Anyway, expect a call in the next twenty-four hours and don't romanticize flying in a Lavi. An Israeli air patrol was attacked the week before by five Syrian MiGs in a dogfight."

"Yes, but you guys shot all five MiGs down without a single bullet in a fusillade."

"Yes, we did. My neighbor's son alone got two of them."

Carole pressed the issue of possibly being attacked. "Schlomo, is there a remote chance of another Syrian engagement?"

Schlomo's answer did not allay her fears. "Very slim chance, but yes, it is possible, though very unlikely."

Carole gave Schlomo a go-to-hell look but felt bad about it and asked, "Can you at least guarantee Allie's safety?"

Schlomo threw up his hands in frustration. "This is Israel, Carole. The only thing that anyone can guarantee is that prices will go up."

She laughed. "Schlomo, I don't like hearing that, but I'll back off on this, but please be very careful with Allie up there, you hear me?"

Forget Schlomo, Carole. I'm not going to let anything happen to Allie up there.

Chapter 88

Cohen's phone rang at five forty-five the next morning. He groggily picked up, and a voice instructed, "Be ready to go in a half hour. Menachem and his team are napping in their cars, so be on time."

At 6:15 AM, Allie snuck out of the Hilton's side door and into a waiting Volkswagen Beetle.

"Schlomo, I am wiped out that you still have this car. What, it must be nineteen years old by my reckoning."

"Yes, but it is still worth $16,000. Given the cost of raising four kids, I will have it for another nineteen years."

Schlomo drove out of Jerusalem and onto a military highway that hugged the inner perimeter of the West Bank. They drove northward for the next twenty minutes, and a mile or so past Tiberias and Lake Kinneret, the Sea of Galilee, the Beetle turned westward and passed over a hilly green land that had been a marsh twenty years before.

Halfway between Tiberias and Haifa, Schlomo turned left onto an unmarked road.

"Allie, we're driving toward a small mountain and around the mostly Polish Kibbutz Gvat, located in the green Jezreel Valley, where Jesus grew up. This is where the Basement One is located."

Alert guards with Uzi submachine guns pointed Schlomo through a well-secured field leading up to a huge hill. Pincus circled around the base of the mountain and past the kibbutz's groves of neatly tended citrus and almond trees.

"That's it, Allie." Pincus pointed toward the mountain.

Allie's jaw dropped at the sight of an impervious steel curtain flush in the heart of a tremendous mound. He'd read of the basement in *Newsweek* magazine but now stood before it in person.

"Praise be the Lord, Schlomo, and all His might."

Pincus explained the need for such deterrence capability.

"Israel can never afford to have its planes destroyed on the ground, so we have to park our fighter planes underground. There's another one like this in the Negev, Basement Two. Hey, watch this."

The monumental steel door opened to let an F-18 taxi down a short runway. Allie evaluated the Jewishness of the enterprise.

"The damn elevator door seems as large as Macy's basement. Judaism's arsenal smites you with a lot more than a jawbone."

Cohen said to Pincus while being outfitted for flight, "Schlomo, I've read reports that five or six dozen atomic devices are stored in the basement. Under what conditions might Israel use nuclear weapons?"

"Allie, I believe that many contingency plans will precede Armageddon. One possibility is a squadron of our fastest jets will head straight for the Arab's biggest oil fields. A dozen F-18s each armed with two A-bombs will irradiate the oil fields for ten to seventy-five years and nullify the Middle East's importance."

"What will Israel demand?" His helmet was in place.

"Israel's blackmail price will probably demand the right to exist, annexation of Eretz Israel, and most importantly sincere absorption of all Palestinians in refugee camps into Arab nations."

"And the second plan is?"

653

"Mossad agents will sneak small but very powerful atomic devices like neutron bombs into Mecca and Medina, same demands."

"That would spark the holy war to end all holy wars."

When the flight personnel strapped Cohen in, it sunk into his head that he risked armed combat but manned up by remembering that Irving Kalish risked armed combat too.

"Allie, let me quickly lead you through a crash course in how to work the controls, rocket systems, and computerized howitzers. Technically, you should be able and independent because if not, we won't return."

Cohen asked the unthinkable. "Schlomo, let's suppose we were attacked and you get killed. Could I use what you're teaching me right now, plus radio the basement for instructions to guide this baby in? Is it possible for me to be led through steps?"

"Possibly, but you will probably crash and die."

"Wow, you sure don't waste any words."

Schlomo laughed before reasoning with Allie. "Look, the Lavi is no Piper Cub or glider. It's so sophisticated it can defeat you."

"Okay, now that we've established that, Schlomo . . ."

He thought, *I'll be damned if I tell him that the engine's roar slightly nauseates me or that the pinning acceleration hurts my nuts.*

Schlomo followed the northern coast, veering inland, and just before the Lebanese border, he directed Cohen's attention.

"Over there's a PLO stronghold that the IAF recently executed defensive strikes against and took out."

Typical military lingo, Cohen thought. "Schlomo, how is a strike *defensive?*"

"When you employ disruptive tactics, Allie, to deter or defer aggression. Preemptive strategies prevent the foe from achieving massive offensive readiness."

"That sounds like aggression pure and simple to me, Schlomo."

"It isn't, Allie. The police action utilizes defensive strategies only, such as strafing, bombing, random targeting, and depopulation."

Cohen said incredulously, "Those are defensive?"

"Yes," insisted Pincus, "because we strike to deter prescheduled future aggression. Our aim is Palestinian demilitarization."

Allie sincerely asked, "When will that goal be achieved, my friend?"

"When they," Schlomo neatly summed it up, "stop fighting us and peacefully negotiate a mutually agreeable governing arrangement."

"And that could be, Schlomo, when Yessir 'Yourafārt is the last poor bastard left fighting."

"If those are their terms, then yes. Ha ha ha! Yāsir 'Arafāt is the last one left."

Nearly two decades later, on November 11, 2004, Yāsir 'Arafāt died. A decade and a half have passed since his death, and peace between the two peoples is no closer. The Palestinians have divided into bitter Fatah and Hamas factions, and the Israelis do not sufficiently trust their West Bank and Gaza neighbors to make a real peace and keep it.

They were flying over the Golan Heights near Syria. "Schlomo, I want you to know that I am not judging you. It's the madness of militarism. It puzzles me."

"It's okay, Allie, the Jews chose to live in a tough neighborhood. It is that simple."

Schlomo had an afterthought as the jet followed the eastern border from north to south.

"Allie, if you dislike militarism, why did you want to fly in a jet fighter plane?"

"A superfast jet, Schlomo, is like the ultimate amusement park ride. I overlooked the rocket-missiles-and-howitzers part."

The world at thirty thousand feet seemed safe and calm, so Schlomo stretched the plane a bit and went into an air circus act that nearly turned Cohen green.

"Ha ha ha! Are you still with me, Allie?"

"I'm with you all the way, Schlomo." The softer U.S. Jew refused to concede that he couldn't take it.

"Okay, Allie, once more around the rim. It'll only take fifteen minutes. An IAF takes off and meets the enemy in two minutes. That's how small Israel is. The neck of the country was once only ten and a half miles wide and could be bisected by an Arab tank column in thirty minutes. After the Six-Day War, the neck was extended to forty miles."

The Lavi cruised just south of Syria like a carefree bird when suddenly two Syrian MiG-29s, the fastest Soviet jet, roared out of a cloudless blue sky and stalked the trainer. Fear gnawed at Allie as Schlomo tried to shake the MiGs hugging their rear; cotton mouth and a headache followed. The wild swerves and two errant air-to-air missiles made him wish he were wearing one of Ari's diapers.

Pincus dipped, rolled, dived, and climbed. Schlomo, after rolling and diving twice more, plunged ahead at 950 miles per house across the northern Jordanian desert and circled back toward the Golan. Caught up in a fight for his life, Cohen yearned for Irving Kalish's 500 mph aerial waltz.

Anteater Breath enjoys Six Flags over Israel, and I get a near Mach 2 dogfight.

"I am very sorry, Allie. It's my fault. I drew attention to us with my little circus act. We've been receiving some positive signals from the Syrians lately."

An air-to-air missile whooshed by them. "Well, that's certainly not one."

"You know, Allie, this has happened only twice in our history."

"And what were the outcomes each time?" Cohen's focus was laserlike.

"The two trainers were destroyed so not very good odds. Don't worry, Allie, I'm going to get us out of this. Trouble is the extra weight—you, the armaments. After 900 miles per hour, every pound counts."

"Man, Schlomo, want to talk about Jewish guilt trips, eh?"

"Ha ha! Hang on, Allie. Now we go on the attack."

Cohen spotted tracer bullets above him and then heard another missile whoosh over and around.

Pincus is living up to his reputation as an ace pilot. The Syrians have thrown most everything in their arsenal at us, and we're still here.

Schlomo violently pulled the Lavi out of a dive, thrust the engine to climb, and looped the loop behind the MiGs. While Cohen checked himself for a hernia, the hunters became the hunted.

"Allie, now we have the Syrians on the run."

Schlomo fired a U.S.-made Tomahawk missile that blew the lead MiG out of the sky.

"Let's finish off the other Syrian," Schlomo declared, "and go home."

He relentlessly tracked the surviving Syrian and had him dead in his sights. Cohen saw his chance to extinguish a threat and begged Schlomo to take the shot.

"Nobel Peace Prize winners," Schlomo argued, "should not kill."

"Very few men," Cohen claimed, "merit the right to kill with no questions asked. This will be the only time in my life when the action taken is justified. Fuck it too. The Syrian was damn well trying to kill me, so this is technically self-defense."

"Okay, your neo–Middle Eastern eye-for-an-eye logic makes some sense to me, but you must act quickly. We are only twenty seconds from the Syrian border, and their air patrols are probably starting to scramble already. Allie, line up the MiG in the little square in the radar scope, and push down the joystick's button to activate the missile systems. That's all there is to it. Good luck."

Cohen took the mechanism in hand, lined the MiG up in the four unconnected right angles, fired, and scored a direct hit.

"Poor Syrian bastard," he sadly declared as the enemy plane exploded into flames. "Forgive me for taking your life, but this was a justified defensive action. If the Syrian had won, I'd not live to receive my peace prize."

"Allie," Schlomo warned, "I am duty bound to file an accurate combat report and must alert you to the infamous basement grapevine. Our flight conversation was monitored by radio, and the aggressive action was verified and recorded."

Arieh Rudin was busy studying a confidential currency evaluation when an aide handed him a memo describing the IAF's most recent aerial confrontation. With Peres in Rome and Shamir in Bonn, West Germany, Rudin angrily tapped a pencil while deciding what to do about the matter.

"Ephraim, tell the air force to bury all proof of this dogfight in their most secret files. Next, deny that the incident ever occurred. We can be sure that the Syrians will go along, preferring to hide still one more embarrassment."

"Is that all, Arieh?"

"No, it seems that we must protect this adventurer Cohen from himself and a legion of Arab assassins. If news of this ever gets out, Cohen will become a target of the Arab's international terrorist network."

Ephraim raised an eyebrow while Arieh summed it up.

"A Nobel Peace Prize–winning American Jew in an Israeli warplane shooting down a Syrian MiG also presents President Reagan *and* the Norwegians with a grave set of circumstances too, not just us."

Back at the basement, a forlorn Pincus wearily filled out many lengthy forms.

"Here, Allie, take the keys. You have better things to do than watch me fill out forms for three more hours. By the way, I am very sorry."

"Sorry for what, Schlomo? It wasn't your fault. You couldn't have known that the MiGs would attack us."

"'Doesn't matter. I involved you in our conflict, and now you are endangered."

"Look, Schlomo, today I did something important, not just plant a tree in Israel to honor a dead relative."

He smiled. "I risked an important life today. Our war, Allie, has spilled over into your existence, and that should not have happened."

"My life, Schlomo, is not any more important than yours or anybody else's."

"Okay, it's more like an accident of geography. Israel needs American Jews' financial aid and political support, Allie, so we can handle the military part ourselves."

"Schlomo, thank you for my real bar mitzvah today. When will I see you next?"

"Two years from now, I will spend time in Silicon Valley studying the industry's latest technologies and software. I will write you before I come. Allie, it is time to go. Your lovely girlfriend is waiting for you."

Three months later, Schlomo showed relatives from New York the Arab marketplace in east Jerusalem. A terrorist placed a bomb in a vegetable stall located on the main walkway, the Via Dolorosa, that exploded and killed three people and injured nine others.

Schlomo Pincus—husband, father of four young children, medical doctor, computer specialist, air force pilot, and unsung Jewish hero—was dead at thirty-eight. Cause of death: an accident of geography.

Chapter 89

The ride from the basement in Gvat to Haifa took a half hour. Cohen crossed the Carmel and spotted Carole waiting in an outdoor café.

Oh shit, she looks really angry.

He also spotted the Shin Bet protector Menachem Harel, who apparently was on his case too. Menachem resolutely strode toward the Beetle as he parked it.

Damn, Menachem looks even angrier than Carole, and his team's nickname for him is Ol' Stone Face.

Harel waited for Cohen to turn the engine off before expressing his disgust and disappointment. "Dr. Cohen, your rash behavior jeopardizes our ability to protect you. If you pull one more stunt like today, I will see that the government immediately suspends your visa and expels you. Then I will personally buckle your seat belt. Is that clear, Dr. Cohen?"

"Yes, Menachem, you made that quite clear, and I am extremely sorry too."

"Very well, I trust that you are a gentleman."

Allie glanced at Carole, who gave him the silent treatment until they returned to their suite. The second he closed the door, she let him have it. First was a punch in the chest with a roundhouse right and then a barrage of curses.

"You goddamned selfish bastard, all you ever think about is your fucking self. Man, I still can't believe how you almost got yourself killed."

"How did you find out? Did Schlomo tell you? Shit, he warned me about the basement's grapevine right before I left him."

"No, Ephraim from Rudin's office told me." She dramatically threw her hands up in the air. "I hope you're sorry that you got Schlomo grounded for six months."

"I am, Carole, and promise you that I won't do anything like this again. To be honest, once was sufficient, I assure you."

"This thing you have about living out all your fantasies before age forty, Allie, is neurotic, maybe sick." She expressed frustration by grabbing her hair with her hands.

"I know, Carole, but I can't help it. I can't take for granted that I'll live past forty until I actually do. That's what drives this crazy need."

"Do you have any idea how I'd feel if you died up there?"

You're laying guilt on me in your mother's scolding voice, he thought but instead said to her, "I understand, babe, and I'm sorry for scaring you."

"Okay, forget about it. Life is too short. Frankly, I'm suddenly feeling very sexy. C'mon, let's make love." They did and, because of the arguing, more urgently than usual.

An hour later, they were still lying in bed, fondling each other, when Allie suddenly remembered something. "Carole, I almost forgot. *Ochel nemolima.*"

"Allie, what the hell are you talking about?"

"You know, the stupid anteater picture, where the hell is it?"

"It's over there on the chair in the corner. Allie, I was enjoying the fondling. Can't we do it a little longer?"

"No, babe, we have to deliver the painting now. There's no other time to do this."

They dressed in a flash and were out of the room in a minute. Amazingly, Menachem and the Iron Matzoth were nowhere to be found, so Carole and Allie stole away from the hotel by quietly turning off on Tchernichovsky Street and onto Shomron. Cohen followed the directions carefully but could not find the street.

"Carole, we've been looking for the damn street for ten minutes. Please read Irving's directions again to me."

"Okay, it says to make a right on Hanassi Street and follow that past the Nof Hotel. Continue on the route, and pass the Rothschild House. All right, we did that. We turned onto Moria Street and reached Tsafririm, just off Lotus Street behind the Ohel Shem Synagogue. According to these instructions, we should be here."

"Babe," he guessed, "I think we've found the street but not the house because I can't find any numbers on them."

A middle-aged Canadian woman from Winnipeg came home from shopping, saw them parked in the middle of the street, and offered to help the anteater find its new home.

"It's the pastel blue house across the street, about twenty feet away."

Allie took charge. "I feel like a schmuck, Carole, but must honor my promise to Irving. You stay here until I'm sure that somebody is home to receive the painting."

He schlepped the garish painting to the front door of the handsome town house building.

How about that? A late model BMW is in the driveway. With Israel's sky-high import taxes, the Mayers must be part of the Israeli upper class.

The door opened and a drop-dead gorgeous blonde, perhaps the most beautiful woman in all Israel, stood before him. Allie thought, *I sure don't feel like a schmuck anymore.*

Later that evening, he would learn that Shulie Eban, Ms. Israel of 1970, finished second in the 1971 Miss Universe contest held in Miami Beach. Fifteen years later, she was Mrs. Yigal Mayer, wife of one of the country's richest men and a devoted mother of twin ten-year-old sons.

She flashed her sabra smile. "My guess is that you are an American and probably speak very little Hebrew, so yes, what can I do for you?"

"My name is Allie Cohen, and I am performing a favor for our friend in common Dr. Irving Kalish." He held up the painting.

Shulie made the *ochel nemolima* connection. "I can't believe what I'm seeing." And she repeated herself until he hoped she would finally say something else like *hello.*

Carole watched Shulie from the car. "Christ, she's so beautiful. I can see her big blue eyes from here."

"Please, Allie, welcome to our home. Crazy Irving, you are so kind to schlep this ugly picture all the way from Atlanta for him. Please, let me make you some tea, and forgive my messy house as we are moving."

"Please, Shulie, I'll be right back. My companion is waiting in the car."

Shulie, meanwhile, prepared a colorful table of sweet tea, tasty little cakes, and a bowl of Jaffa oranges. Cohen returned with Carole.

"Shulie, this is my partner, Carole Herman."

Shulie peered at Carole. Cohen watched various reactions surface and swirl across the sabra's face—first, vague familiarity; then fantastic surprise; and ultimately sheer ecstasy from meeting her favorite movie star.

"I'm stunned." She placed her hands against her cheeks. "The most famous Jewish star in the whole world is standing in my doorway. Please come in, shalom."

Carole scanned the spaces and furnishings. "Shulie, this is an exquisite townhome and reminds me of some beautiful Nob Hill town houses in San Francisco."

"Thank you. We were very comfortable here but will move into a new home in a month. Please eat something."

Shulie passed the cookie tray to Carole. "Here, take one. It's from the best bakery in Israel. At least I think so."

Carole took a cookie. Shulie raved, "Vey iz mir, I see every one of your films. Oy god, did I cry from your last one—you know, the one you fall in love with the older man, and he dies right before you marry. Did you ever deserve the Oscar for that, but no, they go and give it to Shirley MacLaine. Things like that must be fixed, no?"

A Haifa matron blabbing on about Hollywood bullshit, thought Carole. *'Sounds so bizarre it's funny.*

Shulie recalled a recent column in the *Jerusalem Post* that listed the names of many famous Jewish American celebrities, including the Cohen-Herman relationship.

"Let's see, you must be Allie Cohen, the famous author of *The Lesson,* no?"

Cohen nodded yes and smiled. "My god, I can't wait to tell my sister Hilda. She was at the government banquet and has not stopped bragging about how she met Carole and her brilliant writer boyfriend who'd just won the Nobel Peace Prize. Nu, does this not top her, having the two of you right here in my kitchen?"

"I would think so, Shulie," said Carole; Allie nodded too.

A sheepish grin appeared on Shulie's face. "You two are lovers, right?"

Allie made it clear. "Yes, but we are much more than just lovers. Carole is a best friend and a great partner. We are an outstanding team, and this tour has already exceeded our wildest expectations."

I like hearing that, thought Carole. *And for once, he didn't add that Sarah was his other best friend and great partner.*

"Excuse me," Shulie begged. "I didn't mean to sound judgmental."

They both nodded and shrugged that they understood.

"I must tell you, Carole, that you're even more beautiful in person than on-screen."

"Shulie," said Carole, blushing, "I am plain compared with you. God should have blessed me with your face and figure. Add in your warmth, honesty, and humor, well, you could have easily been a big movie star."

"I'm very flattered, Carole."

"I'm serious, Shulie. Weren't there any film producers back then in Israel?"

"There were a few." Shulie blushed.

Carole was surprised. "Then are they that dumb not to have cast you in pictures?"

"Right after I was named Ms. Israel," Shulie said and recalled, "a couple of the producers asked me to take a screen test. When they all seemed more interested in testing my body on the couch than giving me a good part, I said, 'The hell with pictures.'"

"I can't believe it's the same way here too. I swear, movie producers are the same everywhere because I had my own share of experiences when I broke into film."

"Carole, I have no regrets. I soon married Yigal, gave birth to two fine sons, and have been very happy. Allie, your book is a best seller in Israel too. All my friends have read it, including me and my husband."

"Thank you, Shulie."

"I became very upset from that chapter with all the horrors."

She shared, "You see, my mother's beauty helped her survive Dachau. The Nazi pigs made her sleep with the Gestapo. You must remember that scene from the movie *Exodus* where the British turn back Paul Newman's boat just before its ready to dock." They again nodded yes. "And remember that scene where Sophia Loren and all the others wade ashore to the beach and change their clothes?" They gave a final nod. "My mother was on that boat. May she rest in peace. She died of cancer three years ago. You wouldn't believe how much my mother looked like a blond Sophia Loren when she was young. I will show you the boat tomorrow, which is now a memorial museum located across from the Quiet Beach."

Adonai and I guided that boat and looked over them. Shulie's mother was indeed beautiful. Sophia Loren did a fine job portraying her character.

Chapter 90

While Shulie excused herself to use the bathroom, Allie conferred with Carole.

"You know, babe, I expected the *ochel nemolima* drop-off to be an in-and-out visit. Shulie's insisting on providing a grand tour of Haifa and that we stay for dinner and overnight with them. What do you think?"

"Why not stay over? It should be interesting to spend a night in an Israeli home."

Shulie returned from the toilet and insisted, "Please, Allie and Carole, I will be insulted if you do not have dinner and spend the night with us. We Israelis like to make our new friends feel like family."

"Shulie," they both said, not wanting to hurt her feelings, "we figure twenty-four hours away from the Iron Matzoth is a tonic."

"Good," said Shulie with an illuminating smile. "A potful of cholent is cooking on the stove, more than enough for our dinner and plenty left over for the Sabbath too."

Carole asked Shulie, "What's a chun?"

"It's spelled c-h-o-l-e-n-t and pronounced *chouln.* Anyway, it's a slow-cooked stew full of potatoes, beans, and kishke—you know, stuffed derma to thicken and flavor the gravy. I guess you'd call it a kosher goulash."

Kishke, stuffed derma in English, is a Jewish delicacy. Frankly, one is better off not knowing the ingredients that give kishke its unique flavor and texture—and your heart doctor fits.

669

Shulie called Yigal at his office. "Yigal, please bring home an extra bottle of wine."

Cohen asked, "What does Yigal do for a living?"

"He's in the import-export business," she answered, her modesty preventing her from mentioning that Yigal headed one of the largest trading companies in the country.

Shulie gave a short family history. "Yigal's father, Nathan, a true Zionist, migrated to Haifa from Poland in 1932 when our city was still a predominantly Arab village."

It was a very short history because Shulie did not include rumors that the elder Mayer quickly established a thriving business running contraband—guns to the Jews, gin and Scotch to the British, and hashish to the Arabs. A half century later, similar rumors circulated about Nathan's son.

Shulie did share how Yigal was one of the many heroes of the 1967 Six-Day War.

"Yigal commanded a tank division that seized control of a key Sinai pass and blew up nine Egyptian tanks to clear out the southern portion of a strategic land bridge. Two years later, he married me."

After a delicious Israeli dinner, Shulie served dessert. Yigal ate a mini–crumb cake and then wanted to know from Allie if Reagan would risk World War III to save Israel.

"Yigal," Allie answered, "all remaining liberal democracies must be saved, not just Israel. I suspect that Reagan's belief in Armageddon would be an influence of sorts. You know, I think I'll have a crumb cake too."

Cohen's slightly vague reply prompted Yigal to try to pin him down.

"Then you are saying, Allie, that Reagan would risk it, right?" Yigal finished his crumb cake and licked a finger.

"Yes, Reagan's probably the best friend Israel's had in the White House to date and likely committed to your survival. These little crumb cakes are so perfect, Shulie, that you're right about your bakery being the best in Israel. The bakery products in Jerusalem Hilton aren't half as good as these."

Cohen finished his crumb cake and licked a finger.

Yigal envisioned. "Allie, would the United States stop an American Jewish force of, let's say, a quarter to a half million men from fighting to save Israel from a jihad?"

Allie sipped some good white wine before answering. "To be frank, Yigal, I doubt that number and think it'd be more like twenty-five thousand, maybe fifty thousand tops, but it doesn't matter because there aren't enough available boats and planes to transport them six thousand miles. The United States would probably land the Sixth Fleet and later send the rapid deployment force. At least that's our stated policy." He sipped some more wine.

Carole stunned them all with "You know, guys, I feel so comfortable here that I think I'd like to build a house to give the child I'm carrying dual citizenship."

Allie acted amazed to hear her say that. Shulie and Yigal cheered their new friends with shouts of mazel tov and then got the same idea.

"Shulie and I," Yigal proposed, "are building a new home out on Abba Khoushy Street, not far from Haifa University and the Druze Village. It's our pleasure to show you guys the one-acre plot next to the lot that we own."

"The view of the Mediterranean is fantastic," raved Shulie. "What do you have to lose by taking a look?"

671

"My uncle is a master builder and can construct your house in a few months." Yigal made the undertaking sound like a snap.

The two couples got into Mayer's BMW and drove out to the site. A full moon lit up the property and outlined the horizon in all directions, from Lebanon to the north and inland to the Galilee to breathtaking vistas of Haifa far below and the sea to the west.

"Special construction features," described Yigal, "include a foundation of steel beams and reinforced concrete that doubles as a bombproof bunker. The exterior walls are a foot thick and adorned with a granite skin capable of withstanding the explosive force of a mortar shell."

"Are there any less fortresslike features?" Cohen kidded.

"Yes. Ha ha! There are three spacious bedrooms, two outdoor decks, solar panels, skylights, and radiant coils lain into poured concrete."

Carole and Allie revisited the lot the following day in the brilliant sunlight. "Allie, the views by day are even more spectacular."

"Haifa," Cohen cautioned, "is known as a city of views, and other than the Carmel café corridor and Druze villages for falafels and shopping, there isn't much more to it."

"I understand, Allie, but that's easily one of the most magnificent views I've ever seen anywhere, including California."

"My uncle Yossi Navon," Yigal again promised, "told me last night that he can have this house ready to move into six months from today."

The next morning at breakfast, Shulie heard someone knock on the front door. She opened it and discovered Menachem and his detail.

"Menachem," Cohen teased from the dining table, "what happened? We looked all over Haifa and couldn't find you."

Menachem typically did not break a smile. "You didn't have to. We've been out of sight tailing you ever since you left the hotel. The tight security seemed to be making you antagonistic, so we gave you some artificial breathing room."

"Thank you, Menachem. It worked."

"I am here," Menachem informed, "to keep you on your itinerary. Dr. Cohen, Ms. Herman, I believe you have some commitments to fulfill—a concert here, an appearance there. Perhaps it is best to first satisfy our obligations and then return to Haifa and relax with the Mayers, nu?"

Allie always deferred to Carole in these situations. "Very well, Menachem." She guided him. "What's the first stop on our itinerary?"

"Edward Gropper, the U.S. ambassador to Israel, has scheduled two banquets to be televised live to America. Israel hopes that you will communicate to the American Jewish community the great respect and affection the two governments have for each other and how Israel is the only ally the United States can count on in the region."

"Tell Ambassador Gropper that one televised banquet is enough. I'm having too much fun here in Israel and don't want to get bored or overworked. Otherwise, it sounds fine, so where to next?"

"We are returning to Jerusalem, where you will sing a few psalms at Yad Vashem. Dr. Cohen will read his poem again too. After that, there will be visits to a kibbutz resort in the Golan, a defensive settlement in Judea and Samaria also known as the West Bank, and some quick public relations stops in Beersheba and Elat."

673

"Is that it?" Cohen cocked an eye.

"No, from Elat, you will fly to Tel Aviv for Gropper's concert to be broadcast live to ten U.S. cities. Large fund-raisers have been synchronized with the United Jewish Appeal so President Reagan will follow your performance with a closed-circuit address and express his commitment to Israel's survival to hundreds of American Jewish community leaders. You will be accompanied by the Israel Philharmonic Orchestra and soloists."

"Very nice, Menachem, but I hope that's it."

"Sorry, Ms. Herman, the last concert is in Haifa next Friday afternoon for Israel's college and trade students. Then you are free to relax and enjoy Israel."

"How long will we be on the road touring?"

Menachem told her, "Six, seven days at most."

"You will not work them on Shabbat, yes?" Shulie asked.

"No," answered Menachem in a comforting voice. "They will have completed their schedule by then."

"Good, I will have a cholent cooking on the stove. I expect the two of them for dinner next Friday night, or I will be insulted."

Shulie waved a finger under Menachem's nose. "You promise now?"

"Mrs. Mayer," said Menachem in a straightforward and sincere voice, "a lion tamer would not dare incur your wrath. With God as my witness, I promise to have them back in time for Shabbat."

"Good. Until the Shabbas meal, Carole and Allie. Go now and discover the Israel of yesterday, today, and tomorrow.

You know, *yesterday* we saw Jerusalem. *Today* we're in Haifa. *Tomorrow* it's Tel Aviv. Ha ha! Get it?"

They did, and both laughed with her, especially Allie.

Shulie kissed her new friends goodbye. "I can't wait for Friday night to hear your impressions of our land. Shalom."

Chapter 91

Mack and Charlene Thomas celebrated Eddie and Farrah White's realizing personal milestones—his graduation from the Wackenhut Body Guard Training Program and Farrah's landing a secretarial position in the mayor's office. Mack considered their joint achievements as one of BUSHAC's greatest accomplishments to date.

Charlene and Mack honored the Whites' officially joining the middle class with a night out in Buckhead, a nice dinner at the Peachtree Café, and dancing afterward at the Acapulco Bar to cool Latin jazz.

Mack talked *Atlanta Journal-Constitution* columnist Jerry Barnes into writing a human interest column on Eddie and Farrah, two people who'd struggled mightily until BUSHAC helped them pull themselves up by their bootstraps.

Barnes interviewed Farrah first, and his leading question was "How has Eddie's job changed him since his promotion?"

"Jerry, he loves his new job as Mack's chief of security and general assistant. Every day he comes home excited about something new and interesting happening and regularly works ten- to twelve-hour days."

"Mrs. White, please tell me some of his more important job functions."

"The most important and grueling task, Jerry, is coordinating the Thomases' home and office security systems as the slightest margin of error might prove fatal to Charlene and the girls, so all possibilities have to be considered. After each threat, a few have been false alarms, the system has to be reprogrammed. Please be careful how you word these security descriptions."

"Sure, Mrs. White, are there any other benefits or blessings since Eddie's promotion?"

"Oh yes, although the job consumes Eddie, when he's at home, he makes a strong effort to help me around the house or the kids with their homework. He's learned to spend quality time with Arvida and Dennis, and his change in attitude and personality is remarkable."

"What's the major downside, if you don't mind my asking?"

"Well, I got to admit that, while the increase in pay has been a blessing, it's too bad the risk factor is so great."

"You know, Eddie," said Farrah after dinner in the night of the column's publication, "the danger you face wasn't really driven home to me until Mack got you a concealed weapons permit. Suddenly, when you started wearing that holster with a gun in it, well, it hit me like a ton of bricks, and I pray to the Lord, Eddie, that you never have to use that fucking thing."

"Me too, Farrah." He sighed. "And yesterday I got a twelve-gauge shotgun for backup and more firepower. I keep it loaded in the trunk of my car just in case, but it's in a locked box, of course."

"I pray that the shotgun stays that way, but I'm feeling in my bones that something is going to happen soon. So, my man, you be real careful, you hear? I love you, Eddie."

"I love you too, Farrah. You're the best thing that ever happened to me."

Eddie shuddered as he got into bed to go to sleep. *Oh shit, when Farrah gets that feeling-in-her-bones thing, it always happens, like, the next fucking day.*

The next evening, Eddie completed his final check of the Thomas property by cruising in his black Mustang up and down

677

the cul-de-sac, looking for signs of Harrison. It was half past nine, and as usual, he had not found a thing.

Eddie laughed to himself. *That's the first time in your life, Farrah, that you've ever been wrong about one of your feelings.* "Oh fuck, no, you ain't. Ah shit," he cursed after spotting his walking nightmare. *There's Scoop slipping through the clump of trees behind Mack's house. He's making his move tonight. Farrah, you are too fucking incredible.*

White pretended not to see anything, knocked on the front door, and impatiently waited for someone to open it, hopefully Mack. Finally, Charlene unlocked the door and was frantic.

"Eddie, Mack received a call from a person claiming to represent his mother who was sick in a Tampa hospital. He checked that out, and a spokesman confirmed that an Alvira Thomas was placed in a private room that morning."

"Shit, Scoop somehow tapped into your phone line to snow Mack out of the house."

"I think you're right. Mack demanded to speak to his mother, but the spokesperson said she was in intensive care and that the doctors forbade all calls. Mack tried to contact you but couldn't and flew down to Tampa to investigate. Scoop's trick to get Mack out of the house obviously worked, didn't it?"

He nodded that she was right. "How could we be so dumb, Eddie? Mack's probably stuck in the Tampa Airport and unable to get a flight out until 5:00 AM. Scoop's making his move tonight, isn't he?"

Eddie knew he had to take charge and coolly rolled his eyes to signal that Scoop was already hiding nearby.

"Help set the trap," he whispered to Charlene. "Walk with me to my car, and say the lines we rehearsed for this situation."

Charlene did as instructed by lingering next to the driver's window, talking loudly, enunciating clearly, and directing each word to the clump of trees.

"So, let's see, you're leaving now and won't be back until 9:00 AM, right?"

Eddie vigorously nodded up and down and loudly said, "Yes, ma'am."

"So with Mack in Tampa, it's just the three of us here tonight. Eddie, what do I do if something happens?"

"You immediately call the cops, Charlene, and then me at home, and we'll both get here as fast as we can. What can I tell you? That's the best I can do. Sorry, I got to get home to my family. Christ, I haven't seen my kids since the day before and miss them badly."

Charlene stood in the driveway smiling while he backed out, waved goodbye to her, drove away, and turned the corner. That activated the plan. Charlene walked deliberately into the house, roused her daughters from sleep, and led them to the large front door closet to temporarily hide from the harm that stalked them.

Eddie turned the corner and parked his car in the adjacent cul-de-sac. He took the pistol from the glove compartment and put it in his holster as usual. The plan was to cut through the property of the house facing the Thomases' backyard and, from there, silently make his way through a dense strand of pine trees and azalea bushes to remain unseen. White made his way through the pine strand but tripped on a tree stump hidden by the azaleas and hit the ground hard. He quickly got up, circled around to Harrison's position, and figured out what to do next.

I got to sneak up behind Scoop and grab him. If I fail, Charlene and the girls might be kidnapped for ransom or killed in revenge. Ah fuck, there's Scoop sprinting across the backyard right now.

679

Eddie tensed up. *Shit, he's gonna get in the house before me.*

Scoop stopped in front of the two-story house, took out a gun, and wrapped it in a bandanna. He knocked out the panes around the knob of the French doors, unlocked the door, and entered the house.

Charlene should have heard the tinkling of broken glass, Eddie thought, *shoved open the front door, and run hand in hand with her daughters as fast as they can and get as far away from the house as possible. While Scoop searches the house for them, she's supposed to outrun him to a neighbor's home and take refuge or, better yet, flag down a police cruiser.*

Charlene begged to the Lord, *Please, God, don't let Scoop hurt my little girls.*

"Please, girls, we need to run even faster. Come on, step it up and stay with Mommy."

Eddie remained hidden in the woods until he saw Scoop's flashlight beam snake in and out of rooms and closets. White then raced across the lawn, followed Harrison's path through the French doors, and reached down into his holster for his gun.

"Oh shit! Where's my fucking gun?"

He searched his holster. *Damn, it's unsnapped. Shit, it must have bounced out when I hit the ground hard. There's no fucking time to look for it or get the shotgun out of the trunk. Maybe I can find a butcher knife in the kitchen. If not, my hands will have to do.*

Eddie tiptoed out of the bedroom and down the hall leading to the juncture of the kitchen and foyer that faced the front door. The flashlight beam cut the dark and knifed toward him. The beam stopped a few feet from his shoes and then danced out the front door and down the front steps.

Scoop knows that Charlene and the girls are on the run in the neighborhood, and I'll bet he's already after them.

He looked out the big front window and up the street. *Uh-oh, they've only made it to the corner and are exposed under the streetlight.*

Eddie ran after Scoop, who was overtaking Charlene and the girls. Scoop heard White pounding the ground behind him, whirled, and saw Eddie coming at him like a middle linebacker on steroids. Harrison fired his gun at Eddie and missed.

Charlene and the girls watched Eddie plunge forward and hurl his body like a cannonball at Scoop, who fired again.

"Eddie, watch out!" yelled Charlene.

He took a slight nick in the shoulder, but it didn't stop him from putting a hit on Harrison that would have knocked most men out. Harrison, though, was a real tough big guy and quickly got up, staggered a bit, and then found his gun and aimed it at White.

"I got to admit, man," Scoop stated. "You are one brave nigger. You're also one dumb fucking nigger too. Lord, I don't know why you so willin' to die for Mack 'White Man' Thomas, but you gonna die, motherfucker, right now too."

Harrison fired a bullet that tore through the far left side of Eddie's waist because he quickly moved to the right like a soccer goalie to avoid it. The shot luckily missed all organs as it passed through the soft flesh. A trickle of blood soaked through White's shirt, so he used whatever quickness he had left to grab Harrison's wrist and point the gun away from him.

Charlene watched, horrified by the struggle to the death ensuing, as White and Harrison wrestled back and forth across the lawn for possession of the gun.

Please, God, don't let Scoop kill Eddie. He'll kill us next.

Two wild shots penetrated the evening sky and sailed off into the night. Charlene screamed "help" at the top of her lungs over and over from the end of the block. The front lights flicked on in one neighbor's house after another, and a few of the braver neighbors came out to investigate. An old woman ran back into her house to call the police; her ninety-year-old husband followed suit to get his shotgun.

The neighbors watched in horror at the battle to the death taking place on a front lawn.

Harrison, almost twice Eddie's age, started to tire. White was close to gaining the upper hand for control of the gun. *I got the fucking barrel of the gun pointed toward his neck, but I can't quite get my damned finger on the trigger.*

He lost the advantage. Scoop tapped his remaining strength to force the gun into White's mouth.

I ain't got much left myself and am losing a lot of blood.

Eddie drew on every last resource to finally win control of the trigger and gun.

Scoop's got nothing left to stop me. Motherfucker seems to be looking up at someone behind me.

Eddie pulled the trigger and fired two bullets into Scoop's chest and then one in the back. Harrison bounced up and down with each bullet, a death rattle gurgling from his throat, and he died facedown in a pool of blood deep enough to drown in. Eddie wiped Scoop's spit from his face, stood up, and saw the ninety-year-old neighbor with his trusty shotgun who had been standing over him.

"I would have finished him off if you hadn't. He gave up when he saw me getting ready to shoot, but you bravely risked your life and deserved to take him out. You know, Mister, I took out more Krauts in Italy during World War II than people living on this block, so I can still bring it."

Eddie smiled, wobbled a bit from loss of blood, and nearly fainted. The elderly gentleman, Mr. Alonzo Evans, held Eddie up and steadied him. The crowd of onlookers rushed to aid White and rejoice at his survival, for he'd heroically risked his life to save Mack's family.

No one was more grateful than Mack Thomas, who showed appreciation by immediately promoting Eddie to director of job training programs with a bump in pay to $42,500.

Mack also got columnist Jerry Barnes to again interview Atlanta's newest hero for an exclusive front-page story for the *Atlanta Journal-Constitution*. Barnes started the interview with Mack, who bragged about how brave his buddy was. The long article featured Eddie and his family with seven color photos of them. It was a heady time for White, who loved the attention from numerous major media organizations, and he handled it well.

Eddie left the hospital after a week to finish his convalescence at home, and each day Charlene brought him fresh fruits and a pot of herbal tea to speed his recovery. Farrah White loved sharing an anecdotal moment with Jerry Barnes.

"When my big hero began to feel better, Arvida needed help with her homework one afternoon and paid him a visit. My firstborn nestled up in her daddy's lap and listened to him explain how to work out fractions."

She imitated his deep voice. "Let's see, honey, three-fifths and four-tenths. Okay, we double both the numerator and the denominator just like this, and then we add the two top numbers. Now get this, ten-tenths equal one whole. You see how that's done, honey?"

"Uh-huh, could you work a few more for me, Daddy, so that I can be sure that I learned it real good?"

Dennis jumped on the bed to join them. "Daddy, show me how it's done too."

"Sure, Denny, my little dude, be glad to."

"Jerry, I watched that beautiful scene of my children nestled in their daddy's lap from the hallway. The strong, brave black man teaching his children fractions made me cry tears of happiness. My husband rarely drinks anymore and only socially and moderately. He works hard and lavishes love and affection on his children."

Jerry smiled; Farrah reflected. "Lord, Jerry, it's taken a long time, but I feel we're finally a normal middle-class family, and I pray to God that we stay that way."

Farrah worked hard that day and got into bed to go to sleep. Eddie, starting to get his strength back, offered to massage her neck.

"I know, Farrah, that you probably typed an awful lot of letters as usual, so let me loosen that knot I always feel in there after a long day of typing."

"Oooh, Eddie, feels so good. Thank you, honey."

"I promise you, babe, someday you won't have to work anymore."

"I don't mind working, Eddie. Actually, I love my job, more so when you visit me in one of your new suits. You always look so handsome in them."

"With your city hall salary and my new job, I think we're ready to put a down payment on that nice little house in Home Park we looked at a few weeks ago. What do you say?"

"I say that's fantastic, Eddie."

Farrah fondled him while proudly stating how far they'd come.

"It's hard for me to believe that we're actually in a position to take on a mortgage." She put her hand down his shorts and made him hard.

"I'd love to have sex, Farrah, but my pain is still too bad."

"It's okay, Eddie. Let me get you off tonight, my big brown hero."

She started to jerk him off but suddenly quivered.

Eddie worried. "Farrah, babe, is anything wrong?"

"Every now and then, I get this feeling that I'm going to wake up in the morning and discover that we're back where we started. You know, Eddie, middle-class life is everything it's cracked up to be. Life is so good now it's almost unreal."

He held Farrah in his arms and vowed, "Honey, we've made it this far, and I aim for us to do even better in the future. This I promise you, Farrah. From here on out, someone else is going to pay their dues."

"'Sounds good, my man. Now you relax, Eddie, and let me give you a nice, sweet orgasm on your back."

Farrah covered her palms with baby oil and used both hands to sensually jerk Eddie's large, thick penis up and down.

I told you, Eddie, to listen to Farrah and have faith. I'll shut up now and let Farrah take you over the rainbow.

Chapter 92

Young people from across the country came to Haifa for Carole's final concert, a gift from the Israeli government to its youth. She performed for three hours and engaged in a lovefest with eleven thousand college and trade school students.

Carole's world music education progressed deliciously; her band consisted of Tel Aviv's top rock group fused with three major symphony members on piano, violin, and cello. Three diverse singing groups and genres—klezmer, Moroccan jazz, and Yemeni Israeli hip-hop—collaborated with her onstage and produced musical magic.

This is my greatest reward to Carole for being Allie's beholding angel—an exposure to and infusion of fantastic strains of diverse sounds that will forever enrich her music, voice, and soul. Carole's life will be long and extraordinarily rich, and she will make great music until she leaves this planet at age eighty-eight.

Allie too was enjoying his exposure to the enthralling new sounds and sat backstage mesmerized by the best expression of Jewish music and sounds that he'd ever heard. Jews from all over the world were making beautiful and innovative music together.

I'd join them with my harmonica, but I'm experiencing my second spiritual moment.

Allie was tested when the roadies passed around a burning pipe full of blond Lebanese hashish, and it reached him. He held the pipe in hand and stared at the superpremium hashish burning away in the bowl for a couple of seconds and then passed it to the next guy.

"Nah." he declined. *My consciousness is already altered. This moment is too special to risk dulling.*

The students clamored for more, but a setting sun, national religious law, and Menachem and the Shin Bet prevailed. An hour later, Carole and Allie were seated before steaming bowls of chicken soup and cholent at the Mayer dinner table. After a great meal, the four of them enjoyed a dessert of sweet melons and tea while schmoozing on the back terrace.

Cohen sipped a creamy golden cognac and held it up to the light to study it.

"How come the expensive French cognac I buy in Atlanta sets my throat on fire and this Israeli cognac goes down as smooth as honey? Why isn't this stuff in my liquor store in Atlanta, or do you have to make aliyah to Israel to drink it?"

Yigal and Carole were a bit antsy and decided to cruise around the city with the car's top down, listening to music. The two Mayer boys left to visit friends who lived across the street from the Quiet Beach. Shulie and Allie felt mellow and were content to sit on the terrace and schmooze.

Allie sat back in a comfortable deck chair and nursed another cognac while sensual classical music drifted from the stereo. The night was warm and clear with a full moon, and stars were beginning to dot the sky.

The ambience is very relaxing for a house in the process of moving, thought Shulie. *So why is Allie tapping his foot?*

"Allie," she asked him, "you remind me of a four-cylinder engine that still races despite the driver putting it in neutral. Aren't you ever completely calm?"

"You think I'm anxious, but I'm not at all. I'm just thinking how I miss my wife, Sarah, and son, Ari."

"If you don't mind my asking, how is this two-woman arrangement working? I must say that Carole and Sarah are more magnanimous than I think I could be." She laughed.

"It's working better than I'd hoped for, even dreamed. We'll see what happens, though, when Carole gives birth. Two families and U.S. law should force an outcome."

Shulie giggled. Allie continued. "For the time being, Sarah is my anchor and rock, and Carole is the angel of my mission. They are my right and left arms and gifts from heaven above."

"You miss your son very much, don't you?"

"Yes, Ari's changes are coming so fast at this stage, and I don't want to miss any of them. Sarah's been great about faxing me pictures of him almost daily, also putting him on the phone. Wow, do I love hearing dada, dada, dada, but it's not the same as being there. I'll see him in a few days and walk around for hours, holding and playing with him."

"You are a blessed man to have two such fantastic women in your life." She noticed it again. *Uh-oh, he's tapping his foot again.*

She asked, "Allie, maybe you should have gone with Yigal and Carole."

"Why? I'm enjoying hanging out with you. Look, let me be frank with you." He changed the subject to the lot. "Although you and Yigal are the best, Haifa is a city of spectacular views. The lot that Carole wants to build on is like an Eden, and we love you, guys, but I wonder if there's enough here for me to buy into. Frankly, I think I'm more of a Tel Aviv–Jerusalem axis guy."

"That's because you Americans are so driven for more of everything. You like Tel Aviv because of the manic energy and Jerusalem because it is spiritually overwhelming."

"Whatever, Shulie, this I declare. Before I leave this planet, I will live here for a year to really experience Israel."

"I'm sure you will, Allie, because after what you did at the basement, you are more of a son of Israel than you admit. I am very proud of you."

"How did you find out?" He was nervous that it was the basement grapevine.

"Yigal's partner is a reservist in the basement's computer operations and heard it through the grapevine."

"I wonder who will do me in first," he humorously worried out loud. "The Arabs or the damn basement grapevine?"

"You joke around, Allie, and make fun of your important action."

"Shulie, let's be real. I'm not a true warrior like Yigal. Advanced technology made it easy as a kid's video game. Frankly, because I have good eyesight, I can imagine shooting to kill as a sniper but not knifing someone. I'm a lover and not a killer."

Shulie laughed, got up to get him another cognac, and returned from the kitchen. Cohen got up from his chair to take the drink from her hand and sensed that she was standing dangerously close to him.

Shulie stared into his eyes. "You are an attractive man of heroic dimensions. I think if I had grown up in America, I could have easily loved and married you too. Geography is funny like that."

Shulie gently touched Allie's cheek and then tenderly kissed him on the lips. Allie embraced Shulie and held her tightly in his arms. They both realized what was happening and drew back for a few seconds.

Allie held Shulie's hand and stared into her eyes. Their powerful chemistry overruled normal caution, and they began making exquisite love on the living room carpet.

A few miles away, Yigal and Carole descended the steps leading to Bahá'í World Shrine, a holy place entered only in bare feet. Yigal taught Carole that the Bahá'í faith originated in Persia in 1880—Iran before 1930—and stressed the unity of God and the need to adapt basic truths of all religions to modern circumstances.

Infidelity, for example, thought Carole. *I can almost hear Yigal's hot Mediterranean heart beating.*

They removed their shoes, and Yigal offered his shoulder to Carole to remove her sandals. He wrestled with his lust for her. *She's so beautiful and sexy I can hardly keep my hands off her body.*

She accepted his assistance with concern. *I'm not comfortable with the way his hand is wrapped around my ass.*

Yigal stood face-to-face with Carole and complimented her. "You are even more beautiful and erotic than in your movies."

She smiled while thinking, *Holy shit, his hands are all over me in a very public garden. Now he has one hand on my waist, the other on my shoulder. The left hand just slid down to my butt and is squeezing my left cheek. His other hand is feeling on my right breast.*

She smiled at Yigal, took his hand from her butt, held his right hand, and pulled him to walk with her. Carole's shirtwaist hung sexily on her ripened body early in pregnancy, causing the ever-confident sabra to perspire like a pubescent boy.

I rate the tour of the golden domed shrine as one of my highlights in Haifa, but containing his frisky hands is not one of them. I've heard a number of American women visiting Israel complain about Israeli men's aggressive sexual attitudes and figure that Israeli women must spoil them because of the men's constant risk of war and possible death. She considered.

Yigal and Carole departed the shrine and felt the pulse of the Carmel's nightlife starting up while rambling by cafés full of young people discussing life, arguing politics, or perhaps just digging on music.

Maybe some of them are even listening to mine, she thought.

Yigal selected a cute little café to watch the crowds of people and ordered two cognacs.

Carole thought, *I wonder what Allie and Mrs. Israeli Wet Dream were up to. Frankly, I can't blame him for lusting after her, but that doesn't give him my permission to take a three-to-one lead in fucking around.*

Yigal startled her by putting his hand under the table and on her knee. He sipped his cognac while slowly moving his hand up her dress until it rested high on the inner thigh.

Holy shit, he just pushed his luck by sticking his hand between my legs and stroking me with his middle finger.

She removed his hand and gave him a mild look to act more gentlemanly. Carole smiled at Yigal to soothe his high-powered Israeli male ego and reasoned with him.

"Yigal"—she placed her palm on his cheek—"the media stalks me, I'm pregnant with Allie's baby, and there's simply no way that I can have sex openly with every Tom, Dick, or Yigal who comes along."

He laughed at himself. "I heard that phrase used a few times when I was in the United States but with Harry, of course."

"Look, Yigal, you're a very dashing and attractive man, but you're married to Shulie, so let's respect our positions."

Yigal laughed again. "I get the message. Let's finish our drinks and continue this cruise with the warm feel of cognac in our bellies."

"Where are we going, Mr. Hot-Blooded Mediterranean Man?"

He self-consciously laughed hard. "We just went down Ben Gurion Street and are making a left onto Derecho Yafo and heading north up the coast highway and out to the Quiet Beach."

He put an eight-track tape in the deck, and an upbeat number from her most recent greatest hits album blared into the convertible's breeze. His next move, lighting up a joint, shocked her.

"Yigal, I didn't think anybody in Israel smoked pot at all."

"I guessed that the two of you probably smoked pot, hadn't done it since you're here, and figured you might like to get high. Frankly, I've only smoked a dozen or so times and mostly when in the States. Well, do you want to take a hit?"

Carole toked hesitantly. "My visit to Israel has been one great natural high. This kef stuff from Morocco, though, is a very powerful shake. Two hits are enough."

She put the joint out. "I like the feel of this pot but not being a bit out of control in a land where anything can happen and usually does."

"Come on, Carole, it's a hot night, and the sea breezes feel good. Let's walk along the water's edge."

She consented by nodding but prepared for a seduction-in-the-sand attempt. Carole loved the feeling of the warm Mediterranean waves rippling through her toes as they strolled barefoot along the water's edge.

Amazing, Yigal's behaving like a perfect gentleman.

"Carole, I think we're getting too far away from the car. Uh-oh."

About a hundred meters up the beach, he saw three heavily armed men covering a raft with sand to obscure it. His military instincts surfaced, and he grabbed her by the hand. "Come, let's run as fast as possible to take cover."

He pulled her toward the night shadows cast by the Rambon Hospital; his plan for her was to hide in the car while he battled the terrorists. Mayer, a reserve office of an Urdu—a small fully equipped military force of eleven thousand soldiers with combined air, tank, and infantry components—put Carole down on the floor of the Mercedes's back seat and put up the top.

"Please be silent, Carole," Yigal quietly instructed. "And just lie here without saying a word. I will be back for you as soon as possible."

"Yigal, I beg you, please drive away and leave this beach now."

Yigal ignored Carole's pleas to leave and instead opened the glove compartment, took out two pearl-handled revolvers, and speedily loaded them.

"Yigal," Carole again begged him, "let someone else fight the killers."

"Carole, we Israelis are not trained to *let someone else do it.* The terrorists are sneaking across the beach to commandeer a bus and murder innocent civilians, women and children too. If no bus, they will randomly kill as many people as possible until our forces stop them."

Carole looked out the car's side window and watched Mayer position himself to defend her and Israel. Yigal counted on the element of surprise by hiding behind a pillar, ready to take aim at Arafat's mujahideen. He waited until the attackers had crept up to only a few yards of him, and then he stepped out from behind the column, blasting away, six bullets blazing from each of his twin pistols.

Yigal stopped firing; two terrorists lay dead, and the lone survivor helplessly held a jammed Kalashnikov with one hand and tried to stop the blood gushing from two serious thigh wounds with the other. Mayer picked up one of the dead men's assault rifles and fired at the head of the teenage warrior.

The shot blew his nose off, and it skipped along the sand toward where Carole was hiding. She heard the awful scream and snuck a look to see if Yigal was still alive. If not, she planned to run for it rather than stay and await certain death.

The skipping nose splattered against Carole's ankle and stuck to it. She screamed uncontrollably while shaking off the bloody slab of flesh and cartilage. Yigal shot the faceless but still alive terrorist through the heart and then turned to help Carole deal with the exposure to the most hideous sight of her life. He tried hard to calm her and help her into the car.

"Carole, please calm down and listen. We must go now."

Menachem and the Shin Bet bodyguards atypically arrived after all the action had taken place and begged forgiveness. Menachem hugged Carole to calm her.

"I'm sorry that we lost sight of you, guys, because of a rare car accident. Thank god you were with Yigal, one of Israel's greatest warriors, which you saw firsthand tonight. Yigal and Carole," Menachem sympathetically told them, "please, both of you, go home and leave the cleanup details to us. We're sorry that you had to endure this horror. The memory of this incident will be left only to us, and we'll report that we killed the terrorists to keep it secret."

A state of shock descended over Carole, who couldn't utter a sound during the ride back to Yigal's house. Anguish and revulsion overwhelmed her as she tried to sort things out.

Yigal was poised to die and leave Shulie a widow. He also drew me into his conflict and could have left my children motherless.

Yes, Carole, but are you not both Jews and menaced by the same monsters?

Carole's psyche was plagued by the region's frequency of violence.

In two weeks, Allie and I have witnessed the deaths of eleven Arabs. What murderous creatures might yet seek revenge for their slain buddies? How wise is it to build a home in a city where ground-to-air missiles are openly deployed? Christ, we're passing a bunch of missile sites right now.

The Shin Bet promised Carole that the world would never hear of the terror and blood of the Quiet Beach attack.

May God, Carole prayed, *bury all word of the killings into a very deep grave of silence forevermore.*

Up on the Carmel, Allie playfully patted Shulie's lovely bare ass. Suddenly, she had enough fruit of the flesh and quickly arose from the bed she shared with her husband.

Cohen philosophized as she gathered her clothes strewn about the floor in the heat of passion. *"Ochel nemolima,* it all started with the ugly anteater picture."

"God and Irving really rewarded you for schlepping it," she jested and, after thinking about it for a second or two, warmly added, "I guess I did too."

Cohen was still feeling coltish and got an idea to do it again. He pushed up against her, but she coolly pulled away.

"Shulie, did I do something wrong? If so, I'm sorry."

"No, it has nothing to do with you . . ." Shulie did not finish the sentence and anxiously peered out the window facing the harbor.

"How come the Central Railroad Station's floodlights are turned off?" She speculated. "I think there may be trouble down at the Quiet Beach."

Shulie martially pulled up her panties and threw a dress over her head and naked chest. Cohen scurried around for his clothes.

"Hurry," she commanded in an authoritarian voice. "Dress faster, damn you. I pray that my boys are okay."

Allie finished dressing and asked, "What's happened?"

"I think that there may have been a terrorist attack at the Quiet Beach. Guy and Amit, my sons," she added, "are visiting friends nearby, and I'm frightened for their safety."

Shulie removed two Uzi submachine guns from a broom closet. "Allie, have you ever used one of these?"

"No," Cohen looked at her as if she were out of her mind. "As a teacher, I never had a class that bad."

Her scowl demanded he cut out the jokes. "No, Shulie, I don't know how to load it but believe I can shoot it."

She jammed an ammo clip into the Uzi like a marine. "Here, it is ready. All you have to do is aim."

Shulie showed Allie how to unlock the release and pull the trigger and marched out of the house with the Uzi strapped to her back like a soldier going off to war. Cohen walked behind her, holding the alien hardware and practicing how to shoot. She stared back at Allie to see how far behind he was.

Cohen interpreted her stare. *That sure is a condescending expression of scorn, if I ever saw one.*

Shulie threw her car keys at him with disgust. "Here, drive. Be useful some way."

Cohen started the car and backed out of the driveway. Shulie compared being under attack with Yigal versus Allie.

Peaceniks are pretty good lovers, but when your life is on the line, they're like a lox. Shulie regretted her behavior; Allie was a plaything, a child-man from a safe place temporarily residing in a more hostile environment.

Cohen drove Yigal's BMW up the street, turned right, and saw Shulie's boys running toward them. They got in, and he steered onto Moria Street.

Shulie, though grateful for Guy and Amit's safety, urged him to drive faster.

"Please hurry. We must find Yigal and Carole."

697

Yigal and Carole honked at them while crossing central Carmel, and both pulled over to the curb along Bikurim Street near the Maccabi Pool. Yigal and Shulie embraced while Allie held Carole, who was still distraught, and comforted her by stroking her neck and cheek. She cried and, in between sobs, told him of the terrible scene.

"I no longer want to build our fortress-home on the hill." She decided while he wiped a tear from her eye. "You're free to pursue it, Allie, that is, if you still want to."

"Not me, babe. I'm more of a Tel Aviv–Jerusalem kind of guy."

Frankly, Allie, so am I.

Chapter 93

Carole finally laughed a little. "Allie, promise me you're going to book us on the first flight out of Israel to almost anywhere."

Back at the Mayer house, Shulie recommended a destination.

"Allie, please call Yigal's cousin who's an El Al reservations agent because flights are limited in the small Israeli market. My favorite for some R & R is Nice, always a relaxing place for a short vacation."

Cohen contacted Yigal's cousin, who called back with good news.

"Fortunately, El Al has a flight to Nice leaving tomorrow afternoon. I can arrange for a limo to pick you guys up at the Nice Airport and drive you to your hotel."

Yigal drove Carole and Allie to the Dan Hotel to spend the night for some quiet time together and took them to the airport in the morning. He sensed during the ride to Lod that the shock of the Quiet Beach attack was still hanging over everybody.

My new friends are experiencing difficulty trying to find the right words to convey their feelings, and I have seen so much war that I have become numb to such feelings.

They reached the terminal, and Yigal put his arms around Carole. "You'll see, my friend, time does heal all wounds."

She smiled. "Thank you, Yigal, for saving my life and for your friendship." Carole warmly hugged Yigal, who also hugged Allie.

"My friends, please promise me that you will both keep working for more peace in the world, especially for Israel."

The Mayers had worn Carole out. "Allie, I need a nap and must skip the nosh and drink with your uncle Micha Ben Naor."

Carole napped in the VIP lounge on a sofa while Uncle Micha and Allie met in the airport lobby bar, hugged, and sat down. The bartender served glasses of iced aquavit, a clear Norwegian liquor.

"To Allie, I salute your winning the Nobel Peace Prize."

Micha toasted him, and then the two kicked back for a few hours with a plate of hummus, pita, and pickles and a bottle of aquavit on ice. Micha—fifty-five years old, tall, and distinguished looking—wore a stylish brown leather jacket, which he'd recently bought in San Francisco.

"Sarah told me that you were an architect." Allie asked Micha, "What have you built that I might have seen?"

"In the 1950s, I built much of the Israeli housing supply. I always hoped for us to be a rich nation, so from the start, I tried to construct first-world housing with Mediterranean accents. I was criticized a lot for not building cheaper housing. My answer to them was always 'You want cheaper housing? You build it, and you live in it.' That always shut them right up."

"I saw some of the apartments you designed. You infused Bauhaus, art deco, and other modernistic influences."

"You have a good eye. In the tighter 1960s and 1970s, I made my money building housing projects in Nigeria and the Ivory Coast. The 1980s are tough here, but I'm doing fairly well as part of a team designing a new airport for Tel Aviv and Jerusalem to share. It's named after Ben-Gurion, and I'm part of a team that selects and places art pieces throughout the facility."

"That's very exciting. How is your family?"

"Everyone's doing well. My lone misery is that my recently married son, Yitzhak, is flirting with taking a higher-paying job with an electronics firm in Chicago. Hey, I saw you on a talk show. You were saying how busy you were."

Cohen silently translated that remark. *He didn't find a minute to visit with relatives who love him and will not be here forever, only one uncle a few hours before leaving. Shame.*

Micha asked a bunch of questions about Sarah and Ari, Allie's amazing relationship with Carole Herman, his impressions of Israel, and how the tour went.

"To be honest," Micha admitted, "while I admire your novel as a literary work, I suspect Global's powerhouse marketing division is the major force that made it a must-read book worldwide."

Allie smiled and told Micha that Sarah and Ari were scheduled to visit him and the relatives in Tel Aviv next week.

"She's bringing our son, Ari, to meet his Israeli family. I originally planned to meet up with them, but unfortunately, because of some scary incidents that I'm not at liberty to divulge, the Israeli and American governments think it's best for Carole and me to depart Zion now."

"I look forward to their coming, Allie, and will begin to organize their visits with all the family members."

"Uncle Micha, last week, I saw a photo display in the Israel Museum that described where the 250 men who, in 1947, took Jerusalem from 10,000 Jordanian soldiers are in life thirty-eight years later. There was a picture of you that included a short bio. Uncle Micha, you have played an important role in Israel's birth and development."

All Cohen could get out of Uncle Micha was "Allie, such exploits are a fact of life and accepted by every Israeli. The Jews made their mark in the West, and they made their stand in Israel."

Micha spoke passionately of his struggle to keep his son, whom he adored, from emigrating.

"Allie this generation of sabras lacks the idealism of their Socialist fathers. They are like your Republicans who are driven only by a larger take-home pay."

"A lack of idealism, Micha, may be a worse threat to Israel than the Arabs."

"You're right, this negativism, Allie, will undermine us from within. Oh, by the way, I have a friend whose younger brother serves in the basement and heard how you became a true son of Israel."

"Uncle Micha, thank you, but I shudder at the absurdity of a wide-open secret."

"I am very proud of you, Allie. You defended your people. Trust me, you are still a peaceful man and deserve your prize."

"Dear lord, hundreds of people must know by now. Uncle Micha, this is not a secret. It's a well-known fact. It might as well be in the encyclopedia already."

"Ha ha! Don't worry, Allie." He laughed more. "The Arabs will never know of it. Israel will keep the peace and keep your secret too. That is one of the more peculiar aspects of Israel— secrets that everybody knows and keeps."

"I know better than to ask what other open secrets are kept by Israelis."

"Allie, it is amazing how far you've come in such a short time. Sometimes you remind me of a weird secular rabbi teaching people how to come together."

Cohen nodded that he understood. They both took a last long drink, for the time had grown late.

"You must forgive me. We're due to board soon, and I promised Carole I'd wake her up from her nap, and I have to get over to the lounge. I am a very lucky man, Uncle Micha, to have two such extraordinary women in my life."

Uncle Micha kibitzed. "Allie, you're as lucky as a big dog with two dicks."

"Uncle Micha, you have a way with words."

They both laughed hard. Allie paid the bill and promised to definitely visit the whole family on his next trip. They shook hands and hugged.

Micha left Allie with "Shalom to the sole Nobel Prize winner I will probably ever be related to, if only through marriage."

Allie realized, while walking to the lounge, that he was suddenly making a lot of promises that he was expected to keep. Two hours later, Carole ordered coffee as their plane flew from Tel Aviv to Nice. They were off to the Riviera to rest and play for a few days before moving on to Stockholm to receive the prize.

Allie briefed Carole. "Sandy booked us into the Carlton Hotel, a stately beachfront palace to prepare me for the rigors of being a recipient. From Stockholm, I'm next scheduled to fly to Atlanta to be honored by the city's white and black establishment with a reception."

Carole observed Allie tapping his finger against the armrest. She thought, *I swear he's churning inside from something, maybe the struggle between Arab and Jew or another conflict or injustice elsewhere.*

She said to him, "Allie, you know what your damn problem is?"

Allie borrowed a line from Rick Samuels. "No, Carole, but I imagine that you're going to tell me anyway."

"Radicals like you are always minding the whole world's business instead of your own."

"I'm sorry I asked." He wrote out a telegram to send later to Sandy Forman in Atlanta. "Apologize to Harvey Kartzman for missing the Sit-In's first anniversary party. Purchase at least six fabulous toys for Ari's upcoming first birthday. Start with tricycle, wagon, and fire truck."

Carole viewed her Israel experience. "You know, Allie, I don't recall meeting a single Israeli who played head games or bothered with formalities. Friendships bond amazingly fast too."

"When you live on the edge, Carole, there's no time for fools, pretenses, or snobbery."

Their Carlton Hotel suite had its own small pool and a personal concierge. Allie and Carole spent three days sleeping, staying up late, and eating in small bistros and cafés.

They took long walks on the beach and a day trip to Grasse to explore the town's perfume factories and because Picasso once lived there. The pretty scenery, good weather, and fine food readied them for Stockholm.

The prophet will receive the Nobel Peace Prize, and the world will formally behold him for the first time in Stockholm. He will speak the Lord's defining truths of the human condition. The great question is, will the world hear him and listen?

Chapter 94

"I must be setting a Guinness World Record for Jewish mother pride today."

Janet Kamensky, Allie's mother, joked with her daughter Carla and son-in-law Joel, "Brooklyn's been my eastern limit, and now I'm sitting in a big hall in Stockholm. Who could have imagined?"

An introductory speaker's droning on caused Janet to drift. *I used to think he was a chronic dreamer. His sister just thought he was lazy, but by receiving this award, Allie has showed everyone that he knew what he was doing.*

Carla Kamensky sat next to her mother. "Joel, I'm astounded that my little brother has won the Nobel Peace Prize. He sure left slum alley saint way behind and just qualified for minor saint status."

Joel expanded on Carla. "I think Allie has already passed that and is closing in on major saint status."

She flashed back to when Allie was a freshman in college. The family was eating dinner one night, and to make conversation, Carla asked Allie, "So have you given any thought to career plans lately?"

Allie thought it coincidental. "Yes. In fact, yesterday I decided to switch from business administration to social science and become a social studies teacher."

"How the hell," she said, which she later regretted, "could you be so stupid?"

"Stupid? We're Jews, Carla. We're supposed to value education. Wow, you'd think I'd get a pat on the back for seeking a profession that I can help young people prepare for life to achieve their dreams."

"Teaching is a dead-end job, Allie. You'll barely make twelve thousand bucks a year and drive a Chevy your whole life."

"Which to a JAP is hell on earth, I'm sure."

"You're a kid, Allie. Listen to me. Go into business, or you'll starve to death."

Janet shushed her. "Carla, it's Allie's life, and what's wrong with being a good teacher? And if he marries another teacher, they'll do just fine."

"Carla, please understand that I was tailor-made to be a social studies teacher. It's in my DNA."

Allie looked into his sister's eyes to see if he got through to her. "I see you're unmoved by that. Ehh, what does it matter? You don't get it, but you can bet I'm never marrying a JAP like you."

He called me a JAP once too much, Carla recalled. *Still, I shouldn't have picked up a heavy stainless steel butter knife and hurled it past his left ear.*

The knife smashed through the kitchen window behind Allie and fell two stories to the ground. He rose from his chair with a fury in his eyes. Carla knew she'd crossed a line and saw that Allie's nineteen-year-long record of never striking her was at end.

Allie strode toward Carla with such outrage and determination that she wheeled out of her chair and backpedaled as fast as she could. Carla, however, wasn't fast enough, for Allie delivered a hard right to the small of her back.

"Goddamn it, Carla!" he yelled. "You could have taken my eye out! Don't you ever do something like that again!"

706

I crossed the line. He was right, admitted Carla, whose shouted threats to leave home were heard throughout the apartment house, so the neighbors never bothered to ask why she moved out. The following year, Carla met Joel, and her hypermaterialism was off to the races.

Today, though, Carla sat in Sweden watching her brother, the former social studies teacher, about to give his Nobel acceptance speech.

I am so proud of him that I could cry. She wiped a tear from her left eye.

The prophet stands behind a teak podium and faces the audience. The Creator has empowered Allie with an *ultimate teachable moment* and monitors his train of thought.

Cohen smiled first before addressing his distinguished audience.

"I intend to speak directly to this remarkable assembly and the world beyond it. My aim is to identify all the misinformed, misguided, evil, or negative forces in the world that are all on the wrong side of peace, goodness, and morality."

Cohen was interrupted by strong applause and a standing ovation from both sides of the moral spectrum. *This applause*, Allie thought, *means half the audience has no clue of who I am or what I'm going to say. Man, are they ever in for a learning experience.*

He quieted them down. "I'll begin by mildly punching a few holes in French existentialism and Scandinavian and Swiss neutrality. Fifteen years ago, I fancied being an existentialist in the mold of Jean-Paul Sartre, who rejected his Nobel Prize, claiming the award compromised his East-West clarity.

I respect Sartre's decision but disagree with his view. In fact, I am no longer an existentialist because Western power, principles, and freedom now shape my moral clarity these days."

707

Over half the audience stood and applauded.

Those who are sitting, Allie thought, *are sensing my direction.*

"Furthermore," stated Cohen, "I have no intention of rejecting my prize, indeed deeply value the award, and respect the important role it plays in promoting peace in the world. Let me say that I am very grateful to the Nobel Foundation but am still processing in my mind how I will best serve the cause of peace this next year."

There was a thirty-second-long applause. French officials politely patted. He continued.

"In reality, there is no *existentialism* or *neutrality*. Both are a state of mind. French existentialism was a luxury of NATO, for when Charles de Gaulle pulled them out because he didn't believe America would use nuclear missiles to save France from Communism, they were still protected by the collective security arrangement and American might."

The faces of the French stiffened up.

"Neutrality is studied detachment from the forces that really protect you and selfishly reaps the benefits of collective security without contributing to the burden. The U.S. reactive stance supports the free ride of neutral nations and allows French existentialists the freedom to write popular left-wing tracts that would be banned in Moscow. One cannot intellectually or morally stand on two sides of the fence."

Swedish and Swiss faces stiffened and joined the annoyed French. "Today I stand before you—ironically in a highly cultivated neutral nation—and proclaim my opposition to despotic creatures of all types. It is a depressing fact that only the aggressive power of the United States and its allies contain the hegemonistic Soviets and the machinations of countless petty tyrants acting

708

in concert. This aggressive Marxist network freely maims and subverts for a phony faith that has failed to deliver on its promises wherever it's been employed."

The representatives of Western countries stood and applauded. The seated dictatorships appeared angry, disgusted, or stewed in stunned silence. The Russians and other Soviet puppets joined the French, Swedes, and Swiss in making up a legion of stiff faces.

"Soviet clients all have one thing in common—categorization of people according to handy political tools. Whether the construction is Marxist dogma or a little red or green book, the result is usually an inhuman social order."

With that last salvo, the Russians and Soviet puppet leaders and the Chinese and Libyan delegations, from the references to Mao's Little Red Book and Gaddhafi's Green Book, all walked out on Allie in protest. The next day, major newspapers were full of Soviet quotes that Allie had abused the Nobel setting by slandering the Russians and their friends with calumny and lies. Gaddhafi called him a capitalist stooge of the Western imperialist forces.

Yahweh is disgusted with their errant ideologies and utter corruption that blind them to the needs of their people or to listen, behold, and exalt the prophet.

Cohen continued his relentless finger-pointing.

"I invite the monsters of the earth to change their stripes and become good guys too. I'll first point my roving finger at the cruelty and immorality of the so-called third world, countries often described by economists as less developed countries or LDCs. I have said before that many LDCs are highly developed *militaristic* and *murderous enterprises* or what I prefer to call *MMEs*."

Cohen let the joke sink in; a slow low giggle grew into a loud laugh and reverberated around the huge hall. The monsters' faces showed how they hated being the butt of his scalding humor.

"My menu of third-world tyrants lists Communist maximum leaders, Islamic fascists, Latin torturers, Asian strongmen, and African megalomaniacs. Their callous governments are synonymous with blatant corruption and random mass murder and daily make the lives of over three billion people miserable."

Prophet, you called them all out in a beautifully broad and clear manner.

Cohen viewed the faces of the MMEs. Representatives from bloody dictatorships on all continents felt ambushed; some stood up in protest and booed him. All the MMEs, as a show of solidarity for their common and collective evil, walked out.

"The MMEs faceless victims," Cohen shouted directly at the dictatorships as they left the hall, "include peasant farmers and city folk, seekers of truth and justice, and purveyors of peace and freedom!"

Sadly, the prophet exceeded the limits of truth the dictators can handle at one time, and they fled. I fear that up to half the earth is displaying that they have light-years to go before being worthy of redemption.

"The bloody refugee-ridden twentieth century," Cohen claimed, "has suffered a never-ending battle for the hearts and minds of the peoples of the earth. Standard operating procedures for dictatorships are to grab their societies by the groin so that the people's hearts and minds blindly follow. Truth, perception, and reality, therefore, differ from Madison Avenue to Moscow, Jerusalem to Mecca, and the Holy See to Havana.

Contrary to Christian dogma, the meek are not inheriting the earth. The weak, sick, docile, unarmed, and hungry are being plundered, trampled, or caught up in destructive power struggles and cross fires."

The remaining audience applauded. Sarah smiled proudly at her husband and told Ari, "Your father son is brilliantly and starkly defining good and evil and human reality."

Carole worried. "Allie, is saying such harsh truths that he might be stoking the hatred of bad guys, who might come after him and me."

Janet Kamensky beamed. "My son is shaming the world to behave itself. Give 'em hell, Allie. I'm so proud of you I'm going to burst."

Carla beamed. "My little brother is making the ultimate call-a-spade-a-spade speech. Good for him."

The White House and the State Department gritted their teeth from Allie's hot-button rhetoric. They basically agreed with him but, for diplomatic reasons, dared not say so. So many offended representatives had walked out that the auditorium was barely half-full.

Cohen continued to hammer away. "The world appears hopelessly corrupt, hateful, and dangerous. Perhaps a handful of exceptional leaders exist, and historically, there seems to be fewer great men and women than ever."

The audience gasped at his description. The Nobel Foundation leaders' nervous eyes begged Cohen to calm the rhetoric and stop using their platform to smear half the earth. They were provided no relief.

"And yet the world hungers for extraordinary souls to step forth and lead us out of the moral wilderness. Unfortunately, for the many brave men or women who do step up, the assassin's bullet may be forthcoming."

Much of the audience held its breath.

"Four of my political heroes—John Kennedy, Malcolm X, Martin Luther King, and Robert Kennedy—a quartet of 1960s lights in the darkness, were all murdered. Each loss was a hammer at mankind's hope that a better world can be forged through the expression of truth, compassion, and social justice."

Respectful applause lasted a few seconds. "Still, I have not lost all hope and, in fact, remain a believer that world peace may someday be attained, that good men and women may yet prevail, that all will renounce war and terror."

The half-full audience applauded. "My dream for world peace requires a great leader, or a messiah if the Lord so wills it, to shame our species out of its current political ignorance and ideological and military madness. Goodness, mercy, kindness, decency, and charity must fill our collective souls instead."

A loud enthusiastic applause lasted ten seconds. "If not, we may all perish from the earth and our souls rot in a damnable hell. A nagging fear is that human beings have strayed too far down the path of nuclear insanity to be rescued."

A large collective sigh came from people scattered across the great hall, so he wrapped it up on a positive note.

"I challenge humanity to face up to the fate of the earth and soon. So may the Lord bless the *children* to lead the way to peace and freedom and all good and rightful people follow His commandments to receive His blessings."

Allie looked up at the audience to signal that he was done. They stood and applauded his controversial speech for a full minute.

They finished clapping, and he called out to Sarah and Ari to please come and share the stage with him. Ari was now eleven months old and already said many words and walked easily. He was also starting his me-do-it stage and followed Sarah onto the platform and jumped into his dad's arms. Allie picked Ari up and kissed his cheek.

Ari threw his little arms around Allie as if he never wanted to let his father go. Cohen proudly held up his adorable son while Ari kept saying "daddy," and the surrounding crowd applauded the display of love between father and son.

Sarah moved in for a family group hug. Carole watched from the side and felt left out of his core life and wiped a tear from her eye but not for long as Allie called out to her.

"Carole, please share this moment with us, for you were so much a part of making this celebration happen."

She gave in. Sarah brought Carole into the group hug, and she happily joined. Sarah wiped a tear from Carole's eye and then her own.

Carole began to cry openly when Sarah whispered into her ear, "Thank you, Carole, for all you have done to help Allie have this chance to change the world. He calls you his angel sent from the Lord to realize his mission. As crazy as it sounds, Carole, you and I have become a team."

Carole's eyes lit up like two headlights. "We are a team, Sarah."

Carole bawled and hugged Sarah. "I know Allie calls us his left and right hands of God. It's crazy, isn't it?"

Both women laughed and hugged. The Cohens held Carole's arm up; all three had tears in their eyes, except Ari, who was smiling from all the attention.

Allie encouraged the crowd. "Let's give a big hand to Ms. Carole Herman, one of America's greatest advocates for peace. Half of this award belongs to her, so please recognize a true heroine and angel of mercy and compassion."

Chapter 95

The next day, the front page of Rupert Murdoch's *New York Post* focused exclusively on Nobel winner Cohen and company. The headline, spread across the top half of the page screamed in big black bold ink: NOBEL PRIZE WINNER ALLIE COHEN WITH WIFE, SON, AND *PREGNANT ACTRESS LOVER*.

Yes, those last three words were in italics. The bottom half of the page was covered by a picture featuring Cohen sharing the podium with Sarah, Ari, and Carole, his *pregnant actress lover.*

The Russian ambassador to Sweden was pictured on page two of the *New York Times* and was quoted, saying, "Cohen's a decadent reactionary with a long history of criminal instigations against Socialism and the glorious Soviet motherland."

The Libyan government declared in a press release, "Cohen is a stooge of the Zionist imperialists that occupy Jerusalem and oppress the Palestinian peoples." Gaddhafi apparently liked the word *stooge.*

Fidel Castro and the Cuban government labeled Allie "a lackey for American imperialist and colonialist forces."

Plainly, it was a speech that Allie loved giving, and he purposely made it short enough to be broadcast or printed in full. Many Western governments, including the United States, viewed the address as extremely inflammatory for a peace advocate and distanced themselves from the message's angry citations. The great powers and half of the earth distanced themselves from the truth.

The White House—Bell, of course—released a statement. "Although the Reagan administration applauds Dr. Cohen's passion and principles, the speech overall was not helpful and should not be confused with U.S. policy in any manner."

Cohen was reminded by the media of his Jerusalem promise to grant a mass interview after the reception. He kept his word and fielded questions from dozens of reporters, dignitaries, fans, and even a few relatives. Allie made for interesting and colorful copy and was generally rewarded with favorable articles, editorials, and columns.

Allie, old boy, he self-advised, *enjoy the good press you're receiving now, man, because it probably won't last much longer.*

Carole took advantage of Cohen's press conference to seek out his mother and sister. Carla's feet almost left the ground when Carole came over to hug her and say hello.

"It's so good to see you again, Carla. Our slum alley saint sure has moved up a notch or two, hasn't he?"

Carla laughed and agreed. "Allie's leapfrogged mere minor saint status. Joel thinks Allie is nearing major-league sainthood."

"I promise, Carla." Carole put her arms around her. "The next time Allie and I fly through New York, we'll do dinner again at Windows on the World. That place brings out an interesting side of you and your brother."

Carla laughed loudly. "I insist, Carla, that you and Joel visit us soon in California and spend some time with us in Malibu."

Carla smiled wildly, and her heart rate quickened; she'd seen pictures of Carole's house in *Architectural Digest*. Carole hugged Carla and moved on to Cohen's mother, who was another story. Her challenge was to crack Janet's standoffish veneer, as hard as ever.

"Mrs. Kamensky, I sincerely respect your feelings concerning my relationship with your son, Allie. I also believe that sufficient time has passed for you to finally accept us as a couple.

715

Please, nothing would make me happier than to be able to call you Mom."

Carole, admitted Janet to herself, *said all the right things and certainly seems very friendly and down-to-earth, but I can't disregard my values or ignore the fact that she's an Oscar-winning actress.*

"I'm sorry, Carole, but I don't quite see it like that and had a hard time watching you share the stage with Sarah and Ari. I'm amazed at how gracious Sarah was to you. I couldn't do that. She really loves my son, and I'm sure you do too, Carole, but it's just not kosher in my book."

"Mrs. Kamensky, I understand how messy this situation is, but what Allie and I have accomplished, today for example, is proof that we're a real couple too."

"It is true that you have been marvelous for my son's career," acknowledged Janet, "and his winning this award too. I hear what you're saying, and I understand that you're pregnant, so I'll be fair. When this child is born, I will accept you as a couple and urge you to call me Mother and Janet. That's the best I can do, Carole, and that was hard for me."

Carole hugged Janet. "Thank you very much, Mrs. Kamensky. I appreciated this opportunity to get to know you."

Janet smiled politely before excusing herself. "There's a break in the question and answer, and I want to give my son a big hug and a kiss."

I'd hoped for more, thought Carole, *but am glad for the small opening. I think my real distress is straight ahead, a handsome face from the recent past who'd apparently overheard my exchange with Allie's mother.*

716

David Conte stood before Carole, trying hard not to gloat; his family unconditionally loved her, and he wanted her back more than anything else in life.

"Shit." she cursed. *There's a small army of journalists milling about in search of a juicy story. I better get back to our suite to play it safe.*

David pursued Carole and pleaded his case by yelling through the hallway and then through her locked door. After a minute or so of shocking the floor's other guests, Carole opened the door to let him in.

"Are you crazy?" she curtly asked him.

David was resplendent in his formal wear and oozed humility in answering, "All I want, Carole, is you."

"Ha!" ridiculed Carole. "You're a little late for that, aren't you? For Chrissake, I'm nearly two months pregnant with Allie's child."

"I don't care." He stared at her. "I want you back with or without his child."

"That's pathetic." She looked away in disgust. "And besides, what makes you think I'd ever want to take you back?"

"Because I love you, and my family loves you, and you know that. So I come with no strings attached and know that I can make you happy because I already have. And if you give me another chance, I bet I can do it better than ever."

"David, you've delivered your lines perfectly and even managed to sound sincere, but it's all in vain. I have zero trust in you, so move on with your life."

"I swear to god," he begged, "I'll never cheat on you again as long as I live. Please give me a break and one more chance to make it up to you."

"Look, I never once loved you half as much as I do Allie. And unless you're prepared to cut off half of your dick, don't come anywhere near me. So please leave me alone, and find yourself another Greta, whose calling in life, I hear, was obviously to become a big porn star."

"That big-dick crack was mean, Carole, and yes, Greta has become a big porn star. That was mean too. Since being nice and even begging has failed me, let me try intimidation. I'm giving you one more chance, Carole, to take me back or else."

"Or else what, David? Have you lost your mind?" He was exhausting her.

"You and Cohen are on this big love-and-peace trip, and I'm going to take you down. Then you're going to take me back on my terms." He looked hateful.

"What are you going to do besides make a fucking fool of yourself?" His tone had unnerved her a bit.

"Never you mind." Conte angrily pointed his finger at her. "Just remember that one way or another, sooner or later, I'm going to get you back."

He slammed the door shut and left. That was the end of David in her life for good. Sam Minkowitz preferred it that way.

Chapter 96

The Pan Am charter jet that Sandy Forman rented to ferry relatives and friends to Stockholm and back turned into a wild and crazy cocktail party in the sky. Passengers and reporters consumed pitchers of margaritas and cases of beer and wine. Three stewards served meals and snacks from rolling carts, and light jazz music purred from the plane's sound system.

Allie wasn't partying with his entourage of forty-five; instead, he was holding an important business meeting in a closed-off section in the back of the plane. An inner circle of privileged confidants listened to him describe new short- and long-term plans that sounded so out of character that they wondered if maybe his nose was a little out of joint.

"Prize or no prize," he stated, "now that I've given my scathingly truthful speech, what's going to happen or change for the better? Nothing because I'm just as impotent to affect world events as when I was a teacher. The one difference was that they now print what I say in the paper. Big deal, I'm still powerless because I lack the one thing that really makes a difference—money."

"What are you talking about?" countered Minkowitz. "You're already a rich man, and I know because I'm currently remilking"—everyone laughed hard—"excuse me, repromoting your book back to the best-seller list and anticipate gross receipts from the movie re-release of around thirty-five million. Your take from the new round of book and movie cuts should be an extra four million easy. You probably made ten million this past year and are projected to double or triple that next year."

"Yesterday that was enough, Sam. Today it isn't. I'm talking hundreds of millions tomorrow and billions in a few years. Now that's power."

"I'm not so sure about that, Allie," declared Harland Cooper. "Frankly, I find it curious to hear a supposed selfless-type talk of amassing a huge personal fortune and must question whether having a billion or more would make any difference at all."

"Harland, allow me to be indelicately frank. Money is influence and the vehicle to change things around. You know the old expression: 'Money talks and bullshit walks.'"

"All right, I assume you want to build a fortune for philanthropic benefits. There's a provision you're not considering. Money has a corrupting influence. The actual gathering of real wealth exacts a compromise from its holder."

"I acknowledge that's a problem and plan to utilize the most advanced technology for the greatest efficiencies possible."

"Allie, you're not getting it. Don't you think that raising consciousness levels by speaking out and organizing is a more worthwhile and dignified means of affecting change? How does growing a pile of money compare? I don't see it."

"Harland, you've argued your point very well, but I'm the recipient and the one spending a year making countless speeches or writing articles. There's nothing to add to my Nobel spiel except maybe repeat myself or get even more strident and personal."

"Try harder, Allie. I have faith in your creativity and power of self-expression to keep coming up with fresh material to inspire hope and faith. The world has given you a one-year-long platform for peace. Please use it."

"Harland, I defy you to recall an angrier Nobel acceptance speech. Has any human ever defined good and evil more sharply than I did or identified monsters of every political stripe as curtly?"

"Granted, you did that splendidly, but a year goes by very fast. Trust me on this."

"Harland, can I really go around the world for a year angrily denouncing every bad guy and regime at the top of my lungs? What will change from calling them bad names, and how many may come after me for that?"

"Today's monsters *do* have a long reach. I grant you that."

"So after my year of giving speeches, writing Op-Ed articles, marching, or whatever, who's out of power? How will the world be better?" Cohen took a sip of water.

"Probably nobody, and nothing will change, Allie," argued Rick. "But you still have to use this bully pulpit to the fullest because it's part of receiving the prize. Sorry to say it but I feel that you're at risk of degrading your award by frankly wasting it."

"My friend, Nobel has been awarding peace prizes for eight decades, and there are currently forty-three wars or conflicts raging. War is a growth industry."

Sandy Forman questioned Allie's business vision. "Allie, money is hardly a civilizing agent, and Sam actually underestimated your projected grosses. That gives me forensic bookkeeping concerns, Sam."

They all laughed, including Sam. Forman smiled that he was kidding and then smartly questioned Allie.

"Why isn't our current well-planned and orderly wealth accumulation rate sufficient? Remember, Allie, the bigger and faster you grow, the sooner your problems happen, and the larger they quickly become."

Harland agreed. "Well said, Sandy."

"Yes, Sandy," Allie agreed too. "But it's money that ultimately moves society. Look, I'm sorry that my new pursuits will force me to be a low-visibility recipient. I have a yearlong reign like a Ms. America or *Playboy* playmate. After that, I'm assigned to a slightly less exclusive club than the Baseball Hall of Fame." The playmate and Hall of Fame references put a smile on everyone's mouth.

"My calculus," Cohen put forth, "is to not waste twelve months scolding people to make nice. I hope to make a quick few billion and start injecting money into economies, school systems, communities, wherever I think I can do some good."

Carole sat there listening and thinking, *I'm not happy with this sudden lust for wealth. Allie is sounding a lot like David after he'd made his first million bucks and believed that real power would only come with his first hundred million and fucking mogul status.*

She imitated David. *"Then I can really operate." My gut feeling is it's time to go home and back to acting and singing. I miss my kids, bed, bathroom, and mother and in that order. Allie can go back to writing or manufacture money or whatever his latest gig is now.*

Carole asked Cohen point-blank, "You really think you're the messiah, Allie, don't you? Please be honest with everyone." She'd put him on the spot.

"That's absolute nonsense," Cohen indignantly responded.

"Don't brush me off. Everything points to it—the long poem, your Nobel speech, your own words. You're trying to save mankind."

"Give me a break, please."

"Come on, you're the Nobel Peace Prize winner. Change the world through direct action. Why become a money-making hermit so, years later, you could fix up a slum? And didn't you learn anything from your visit to Egypt? You'd need trillions to pull off what you have in mind, and you're never going to get close to that."

"You need trillions in Egypt," he argued, "because the elites are stealing most of it instead of money going directly to the people who really need it."

"It doesn't matter, Allie. When you try to be the savior, the world will block you at every angle and destroy you in the end."

"Hey, I'm not trying to be the messiah, Carole. Fate has happened to cast me in a role where I can do a little more for people than the next guy. The usual interested parties are leftist groups who only have OPM, other people's money, to spend."

"Give me a break please."

He took a breath to calm himself and collect his thoughts.

"My goal, Carole, is to acquire enormous economic power to counter evil and eliminate as much misery as I can afford. Now if I can make a small dent in the world's problems, maybe eliminate a disease and some hunger and misery, then what's so wrong with that? Jimmy Carter's doing a very similar thing, except he's successfully focusing on a couple of diseases and peace."

She worried. "You're going to spread yourself thin for all the wrong reasons and ultimately disappoint everyone who depends on you. You might even make a lot of money and not accomplish anything meaningful."

"Carole," begged Sam, "I'm fascinated by how Allie plans to generate all this new wealth. Hey, are you thinking of going into the oil business, Allie?"

Everyone laughed, after which Cohen handed out Xerox copies of a blueprint that included four general goals, including the energy business too.

Goal 1 – Produce a large number of commercial literary, movie, and TV properties

Goal 2 – Invest on a large scale in global real estate, currencies, commodities, equities

Goal 3 – Obtain key information sources needed to gain market advantage/leverage

Goal 4 – Reorient the earth's economic calculus into a matrix that works harder at helping poor people meet basic needs and perhaps enjoy some modest wants

"Allie, please." Sam jokingly put his hands over his ears. "I've heard enough activist talk today to last me a lifetime. Boychick, tell me, I'm dying to hear your ideas for blockbuster movie grosses."

"Sure, Sam. When I visited Russia, I overheard in the Europa Hotel elevator two obstetricians attending a world gynecological conference in Moscow. An American doctor convinced a German that not a single roadblock existed to prevent a man from giving birth."

Sam was stunned, Carole shocked, Harland disbelieving. "How can that be?"

"Easy, a test-tube baby is planted in the male's abdomen in an amniotic sack resembling a woman's. Theoretically, there isn't any reason it shouldn't work. We can spin off a franchise of films using the mad-scientist format."

"Boychick, you got my ear. Please describe."

"Okay, Sam, imagine *the boy*, the product of two huge parents who becomes a super football, basketball, and baseball player and can either terrorize or save society. The tension is the temptations toward wealth, fame, and power that distract him from becoming a super public defender."

"Not bad. I see the possibilities."

"Exactly, the franchise begins with *The Girl*, same concept but female, and then *The Dog: General K-9*, a superlarge and intelligent German shepherd that leads a pack of Westminster Kennel–type superdogs that attract the family audience and dog-loving public in particular."

"Let me mull that over." Sam closed his eyes and then opened them and spoke. *"The Dogs, Return of the Dogs, Day of the Dogs*, and *End of the Dogs*, wow, that franchise might cost a hundred and fifty million and gross two billion."

"Allie," said a visibly unhappy Harland Cooper, "why do you want to crank out schlock? Global is renowned for that already, and I prefer you using your talent to give the company prestige properties. Granted, your B-film concepts are a cut above. But in my humble opinion, talents like you should be barred from grinding out crap, even for a straight 12 percent of the gross."

"That's kind of you to say, Harland, but over-reductionist."

"Okay, your point is acknowledged, but aren't you the least bit concerned about signing your name to drivel?"

"I've already thought of that and come up with a pseudonym, Enigma Productions, a division of AlCoCorp."

Carole looked back in time. *I once believed that life was eating the top half of ten melons and throwing the bottoms away. Allie came along and showed me a richer world than the material one I was caught up in. His new business plans seem shallow and improbable to me, and I think he's setting himself up to fail.*

Carole, Adonai gave the world an opportunity to behold the prophet, and half will probably ignore or disregard him. Frankly, people love money as much as life itself. And if Allie becomes super-rich for good, the people may more likely exalt him and his money than he and his words.

I hate to say it, Carole, but great wealth may more likely inspire awe than great words, especially in the age of television. In the year 2016, a man named Donald Trump will prove this truth by revealing how moronic, shallow, confused, or hateful the white American masses can be.

Chapter 97

Cohen spent the rest of the flight cutting deals with Minkowitz and Cooper. Carole read out of boredom, especially when Allie was in the curtained-off area reserved for Sarah and Ari and the Kartzmans.

The plane first landed in Newark to drop off the Kamensky family and then hopped down to DC to drop Allie off for a meeting with Lenny Meltzer and a secret mission. The next leg hopscotched to Atlanta to deposit Sarah, Ari, and the Kartzmans; Sandy Forman continued on to LA with Sam, Harland, and Carole to close deals.

Allie paid a surprise visit to Lenny in the hope of tracking down an old friend of Meltzer's and learned that Jay Dean, a former CIA operative, now ran a sailing and salvaging operation out on Maryland's eastern shore. After a nice night out in a DC sushi bar with Lenny, Cohen borrowed his car and drove four and a half hours to the inlet and marina where Dean anchored his forty-two-foot sailboat. Allie found Jay busy cleaning his sloop, which also served as his home and office.

Curly-haired blond Jay Dean was as tall as Allie and twice as wide and could break much bigger men in half. In 1962, the CIA drafted the ex-Indiana farm boy out of the army intelligence corps; JFK was sending his first fifteen thousand advisers to Vietnam. Langley assigned Dean to the American Embassy in Phnom Penh, Cambodia, to work with the State Department.

Jay, an old hell-raiser, spent most of his decade in Cambodia playing tennis with embassy and agency staffers. He often played while the Communists lobbed mortar shells into the city, and he liked to kid, "Sometimes I wasn't sure if the sphere coming at me was a tennis ball or a Khmer Rouge hand grenade."

Allie knew Jay from previous visits to Washington with Sarah. They'd had dinner several times with Lenny's wives and

727

Jay's girlfriends, and Dean always had an entertaining agency story ready to spin.

Jay saw Cohen approach his boat. "Allie, I'm glad to see you, man. Let me give you a free sailing lesson out on beautiful Chesapeake Bay."

"That would be my great pleasure, Jay."

The two men caught up on life while sailing the afternoon away, and that evening, Cohen treated Dean to a crab dinner at a nearby seafood house, where they devoured a half dozen each and teamed up to drain two pitchers of creamy dark Schlitz on draft.

Jay once again had Allie spellbound, this time with tales of the seven years he'd spent in Tehran during the shah's reign and at the height of Iran's oil boom too. By midnight, both were half-drunk, walked back to the boat for a nightcap, and sat on the deck nursing Heinekens, enjoying the warm winds blowing off the bay.

"Allie," the conservative Jay teased, "you are the most distinguished guest to sleep in my humble boat, even if you are a liberal."

"Right." Cohen kidded back, "This so-called humble boat is a $100,000 ocean-worthy craft capable of circumventing the globe."

"Don't be so impressed. I'm experiencing serious cash flow problems."

"Tell me about it, Jay."

"In 1982, after twenty years with the agency, Allie, my career stalled, and I qualified for early retirement. I figured that if I didn't start living out my fantasy of starting a sailing and salvage service, I'd never do it." Jay drained his beer and cracked open another.

"Nice dream, man."

"Unfortunately, the dream isn't turning out like I'd hoped. The business is losing money, and my pension isn't covering the difference. My savings are nearly exhausted, and my last option is to borrow money from my ex-wife."

Jay tightened a sail rigging. Cohen felt the moment right to make Jay an offer he couldn't refuse.

"Jay?" Dean nodded that he was listening. "I want to buy your boat as a tax shelter and recapitalize the sailing service with sufficient operating funds."

"Man!" yelled Jay, jumping at the offer. "I got to show you the eyeball-sailing straits of the Abaco Islands in northern Bahamas. Hey, let's snorkel off the Abacos' fabulous coral reefs around Great Guana Cay for a week."

Let me carefully phrase my words, Cohen thought, *so that my offer won't sound like it might lead Jay straight to prison.*

"Jay, how would you like to make really obscene amounts of money?"

Dean's eyes opened wide. The words *obscene amounts* got his blessed heart beating really fast. Cohen presented his plan, and each word further brightened Jay's smile.

"So, Allie, let me get you right. You want to be able to digitally transmit cash by a secret satellite channel into numbered accounts in banks in Switzerland and the Bahamas."

"Yes, so we can escape all tax and regulatory restraints."

"Man, are you ever singing my tune. So you want me to recruit fast-track dudes on the inside capable of pirating worldwide commodity prices before they hit the markets?"

Dean was singing Cohen's tune now. "Yep, insiders on the CIA's Economic Projection Council, dudes who can clandestinely feed our lair of computers with market prices hours before the brokers receive them."

"How obscene is my cut of the scam before I commit?"

"You get 10 percent of the gross and pay your team from that, but if you need more, no problem. Your job is to maintain the connection that keeps us two steps ahead of the speculators. Your commissions from our play should yield tens of millions of dollars. You're the sheriff who keeps everybody from getting sloppy or greedy. Are you up to the challenge of policing this operation?"

Jay shook hands with Allie. "Your timing is perfect, Cohen. I might have killed myself before asking my ex-wife for money. Bitch took it all from me in the first place."

"Glad to be able to help you realize your dream, man."

"All right, Allie, let's get to work. As I see it, the key to this operation is bribing the agency official who works with AT&T and the other phone companies. I estimate that one to three million bucks a month is needed to assure unrecorded reservation of satellite transmission space so that each transaction technically does not exist and is allowed then to go unrecorded and untaxed."

"Whatever you need, Jay, you have it. Remember, this information can earn us billions in just a few years."

"True, Allie, but there's always a bottom line in life. Are you willing to gamble that much cash with the possible risk that our insiders could take the money and turn us in to the authorities?"

"That's your job, man—keep the insiders straight. I understand that you may have to rip a dude's nose off to keep his mouth shut. My legal defense is Robin Hood. I'm making a shitload of money to give it away to the poor and needy, and I really am."

"I like your thinking, Cohen." Both agreed with a firm handshake. "It's risky as shit to rely on three insiders, Allie, but necessary to make all that fucking money."

At breakfast the next morning, Allie and Jay worked out plans to buy Lenny's Georgetown restaurant and use it as their front.

"Jay, I envision our first step is purchasing the adjoining warehouse for conversion into your secret communications center. The contiguous spaces will be connected through a hidden door and tunnel running between Le Canard's business office and the windowless electronics hub."

"'Sounds good. I like that."

"Meltzer designs and constructs your covert sanctum, including a redundant unit in my girlfriend Carole's Malibu home. Sandy Forman pays for all this. Jay, you keep the infrastructure running, and my cousin Ira will manage Le Canard and access to our master control and command center."

"Allie, how will we physically manage all the cash?"

"Sandy Forman will handle the accounting ballets with the books, set up the dummy corporations, scrub the money, and hide everything in AlCoCorp's growing structure. I'll have my father-in-law integrate the running of Le Canard into the Sit-In chain."

"Allie, we have to buy some fast cars, boats, and planes and have them readily available. Man, I'm talking Porsche 928s, cigarette boats that can do ninety in choppy water, and fortified Learjets."

"You're getting carried away, Jay. A fast car and a cigarette boat are cool, but nix the Blue Thunder helicopters and armored private jets. We've *moled* our way into the CIA to help poor people. We're not at war with the agency."

"I got it, Allie."

"Jay, forgive me, man, but I have a flight to catch."

They shook hands on their quest to amass great personal fortunes—Allie for altruism, Dean for liberation from work.

Cohen drove over to Lenny Meltzer's office to personally apologize for gross improprieties and presumptuousness. *Meltzer has no knowledge of my involving him in felony-level acts and certainly hasn't given me permission to include him.*

Allie arrived at Lenny's office building and conceived a plan as he rode the elevator to the seventh floor. Normally, when he stopped by Lenny's office, Meltzer was conducting an important meeting or other business, so he just waited. This time, he intended to stick his head inside Lenny's door to get his attention.

The eight architects in the room saw Allie and gasped.

An obese young woman blabbed to the group, "Holy shit, it's him—you know, the Nobel Peace Prize guy who's disappeared and gone into hiding in Malibu of all places. The biggest problem there is outrageous housing prices."

Lenny glared at Allie. "Thanks, Cohen, and now that my staff's concentration is wrecked, what the hell was so important that you had to interrupt my meeting like that?"

"Lenny, I urgently need a ride to the airport and have life-changing news for you."

Life-changing news, huh? Lenny tried to process that. "Allie, why do those three words scare the shit out of me? Could it be, Allie, that radical acts are at work here?"

"Maybe, Lenny."

His half admission made Meltzer very nervous. Lenny drove and listened while Allie described the projects with Jay Dean. Cohen's long and outrageous explanation was occasionally punctuated by a progression of Lenny's reactions.

"My god, Allie, how could you?"

"Cohen, you have the most incredible fucking nerve!"

"Oh shit, Cohen, we're all going to fucking jail for sure!"

"Allie, how much fucking money did you say I'd make?"

He closed the deal with "Lenny, you're into Le Canard for a half million, and it hasn't shown a profit yet. I'll assume your debt and free up a lot of cash for you."

"How did you know that? I don't recall telling you."

"Let's just say, Lenny, that I took an interest in you."

He laughed. "Fuck it. Thanks to Carole, I can finally afford to live in my townhome that I designed and built for myself. Now thanks to you, I can enjoy my paid-off restaurant across the street too. That is about as good as it gets. Hey, are there any other strings or fringe benefits attached to this offer that I should know about?"

"None, and for immediately designing and constructing my business command centers and for each year you manage to keep this scam secret, I'll annually increase your cut of my gross by 1 percent. I'm projecting three years at most and hope that we can get away with it for that long."

"Architecturally, I've always wanted to tackle a project like you have in mind. The technology part alone is fascinating, and I have some cool ideas how we can make the system faster, more efficient, a lot smaller, quieter, and cheaper too."

"Lenny, I figure that from the design-and-build contracts and the cut of the gross, by the time Reagan retires to his ranch, you should be out of debt and worth $40 to $60 million."

Lenny's smile radiated *done deal* as he deposited Allie at the terminal's baggage check-in desk. Cohen waved goodbye to him and headed toward his gate. As his plane soared into the night sky, Allie felt great satisfaction from what he'd accomplished because he knew the right people and had adequate capital.

We'll see, Allie. The jury, Adonai and I, will let you act on your new intentions for a while but not indefinitely. We will calibrate your impact and redirect you if we feel you have deviated too far off the track.

The problem for Hashem and I is that you are the Einstein of human relations and are now committed to making a vast fortune for good. Time will soon tell us if we are letting you wander down a wrong path.

Chapter 98

John Whalen, a prominent white attorney and advocate for moving the Grant Park Zoo to Stone Mountain Park, welcomed Mack Thomas to the Commerce Club's bar. John shook Mack's hand.

"How's the family, Mack? Bartender, two Scotch on the rocks with a splash of soda please."

"My family is fine, thank you, but you didn't invite me to the Commerce Club to talk about our families. You want to persuade me to foolishly move a community anchor of a zoo to a place where it isn't needed."

"Mack"—Whalen sipped his whiskey—"what data do you have to support your proposal to upgrade the zoo and park as a magnet for redevelopment?"

"John, Grant Park and the zoo is surrounded by classic craftsman homes, which are back in style. Granted, many are run-down, but I believe that we can spark a Grant Park renaissance by improving the zoo and the park. Stone Mountain has enough attractions."

"Stone Mountain, Mack, has the room for a great zoo and a big lake for the animals too."

"So what? Each year I see more and more Tech, Emory, Southeastern State, and Atlanta U. graduates stay in Atlanta and redevelop those houses. They don't want to live in the suburbs like their parents. These young people, a lot are gay, have regenerated Virginia-Highland into a pedestrian village and a popular destination area."

"My daughter," Whelan admitted, "is gay and just bought a house in Virginia-Highland for those same reasons. Now you have my interest, Mack."

"John, all the realtors in the area tell me that these young urban pioneers have set their eyes on Grant Park next, and there is already surprising activity. These people are naturals for zoo improvement plans, renovating houses, starting local businesses like restaurants, volunteering in the schools, you name it.

"Realtors are good data-driven sources. All right, Mack, you sold me. I'll put Stone Mountain to rest because you sound like you have an exciting vision for Grant Park. Hey, Mack, why don't you run for a seat on the city council? That district could use your leadership."

"If you'll be my campaign finance manager, John, and help me raise a hundred thousand to start." Frequent tennis buddies Whalen and Thomas shook hands on it, downed their drinks, and took a cab over to the Civic Center.

"Mack, what do you think about the city of Atlanta honoring Allie Cohen's winning the Nobel Prize?"

"What awes me the most, John, about this event is that it started out as Cohen's ethnic studies festival for teachers until he bailed out on it. Now we're honoring Cohen today with the treatment that the business community denied King."

On this day, 4,600 people were coming to honor Allie Cohen and his contribution to international education and world peace. Eddie White tested himself by attending and met up with Mack and John as they entered the auditorium. Once inside, Eddie saw Lesotho and Sharon down in the first row and decided to sit with them instead.

Outside in the lobby, a dozen different ethnic groups were either performing native dances or serving favorite delicacies. Phillip Mason, the handsome middle-aged president of the Atlanta Chamber of Commerce, halted the festivities to begin introducing the speakers.

Allie sat onstage with Sarah and S. K. Kapoor, whom Phillip Mason introduced to open and address the first—and last—Atlanta International Summer Symposium.

Kapoor began speaking. "I would like to deliver a short and hopefully humorous description of my perceptions of the U.S. ethnic mosaic during two months of traveling about the United States this summer and an overview of my joint prejudice reduction projects with Dr. and Mrs. Cohen."

Kapoor's excellent multimedia presentation lasted for forty minutes and was well received by the audience, which enthusiastically applauded.

Phillip Mason presented Cohen next.

"It is my great honor to introduce to you one of Atlanta's most distinguished citizens. In a very short time, Dr. Allie Cohen has gone from being perhaps the best teacher in the Atlanta Public Schools to an accomplished novelist right up there with Margaret Mitchell and also become the second Atlantan to receive the Nobel Prize for Peace."

The audience applauded warmly. "Dr. Cohen's accomplishments range from selling millions of books worldwide to owning the hottest restaurant in the city and soon the country to acting as a public and private emissary to resolve conflict globally."

Mason was interrupted by a longer applause. "Rest assured that Atlanta is proud to share Dr. Cohen's great wisdom with the rest of America and the world. Ladies and gentlemen, it is my profound honor to present one of the most brilliant men of our times, our own Dr. Allie Cohen."

Cohen stood, shook Mason's hand, graciously smiled, and waved to the hometown crowd that greeted him with sustained clapping. His hawklike eyes scanned the audience for familiar faces while waiting for the applause to end. Mack Thomas took notice of the friendly cheering from more militant younger blacks, especially Lesotho Xeranga.

Hashem has again empowered the prophet with another *ultimate teachable moment* for the people of Metro Atlanta. The clapping subsided, and Allie politely recognized all VIPs in attendance and captured the audience with a joke about Mason's origins.

Cohen satirized, "Our chamber chief comes from a long line of city boosters. In fact, all the Masons possess an extra gene. It's called the jobs relocation gene."

The gag summoned a nice laugh that heightened the good feelings enveloping the crowd. Inside the Civic Center, a hall built on the site of a former slum called Buttermilk Bottom, love and buttermilk constituted what Cohen was about to serve up in what became known as his Atlanta caveat.

"Almost a decade and a half ago, I moved to Atlanta and discovered a cultural milieu that was more than I expected but a little less than I needed. Right from the beginning, though, I sensed the dynamic of change and promise, and both came as Atlanta is fast becoming one of the world's next great international cities."

Atlantans were proud of their city, and they applauded loudly. Cohen shushed them by speaking.

"I, like more than three million other Metro Atlantans, have come to love this city, and Atlanta is where I come home to."

The audience interrupted Allie to cheer a transformed son of the New South.

Cohen proceeded with more image-building words for adopted city number 1. "Atlanta now lies in the mainstream of American life and culture. Atlanta and the South today are plugged into the global electronic and commercial grid, and our urbane culture includes a fusion of Southern graciousness, Atlantic culture, heartland values, Pacific fads, and European, African, Latin, and Asian influences. Atlanta is a city without limits and has formed into a rich and vital human mosaic."

Cohen was again interrupted by enthusiastic hoots of approval. Chamber of commerce members sounded the most supportive.

Lesotho Xeranga, in contrast, was unhappy and complained to Eddie, "I'm close to writing this honky off as hopeless unless his tone changes rapidly."

It did. "I am sad to report that, despite the fact that Atlanta is basically thriving, there exists a host of difficult problems. Atlantans delight so in their fair city that they may overlook the underside of life, this condition being a national trait, prone to all who have great stakes in their city's business arena, especially real estate. My aim today is to analyze Atlanta as one example of this American dilemma."

Cohen's direction made Phillip Mason and John Whelan uncomfortable. Mack Thomas liked where Cohen was going, and Lesotho suddenly hung on every syllable.

"There is still a lingering habit left over from the days of segregation for Atlanta to divide along racial lines. This schism will remain unchallenged until direct immigration expands dramatically and other large ethnic groups organize and demand a place at the table of accommodation."

"I hope," Sharon Johnson told Lesotho and Eddie, "they're listening to his predictions, for they ignore him at their risk."

"I predict that Hispanics will soon become that third big group to demand their place at the table. Asians will soon follow Latin footsteps in dissolving the century-old black-white dichotomy."

"I'm impressed," Lesotho told Sharon, "with Cohen's understanding of demographic trends and their effect on traditional power structures."

"White ethnics and Asians traditionally follow white Anglos to the suburbs to leave urban black poverty behind. Middle- and upper-class blacks seeking better housing and schools often follow suit. Atlanta's central business district is the primary area where the predominantly biracial population interacts daily."

A short loud applause came from a small chamber of commerce group. Cohen smiled benevolently at them as if they were odd children.

"The Midtown, Buckhead, and Perimeter corridor markets, in comparison, are mostly white interactive zones. Their commercial real estate occupancy rates and rents subsequently are higher than downtown's rates."

Cohen looked at the audience, held his notes in hand, and smiled at all to stretch his dramatic pause and build the power of his next two sentences.

"The whiter the commercial and residential real estate zone, the higher the real estate values. In contrast, the blacker the real estate zone, commercial or residential, the lower the real estate values. Blacks are 30 percent of the metro population, yet total black real estate valuation of the metrowide black communities can be tucked away in a small corner of the predominantly white Buckhead."

Lesotho couldn't contain himself and yelled out, "That is the best description of modern-day racism ever told!"

Sharon joined him and followed with a perfect summary. "Dig it. The whiter the zone, the richer they are. The blacker the zone, the poorer we are. Whites, by shunning us, confer wealth on them and poverty on us."

"Ms. Johnson," Cohen complimented, "that was a typically excellent analysis. You get an A+." Sharon's smile lit up the packed theater. "The purest equality that blacks or people of color have in Metro Atlanta, Ms. Johnson, is when they have the income to buy their way into the mostly white zones like edge city. Think Sandy Springs, Dunwoody, Roswell, and Alpharetta, but please, I'm getting ahead of myself here."

He warmly smiled at Sharon Johnson and then focused back on the audience.

"Downtown is, for the time being, the largest commercial real estate market in the Southeastern United States. The value of steel and glass fortresses and superblocks is roughly $100 to $200 billion. Let us be frank. Enhanced perceptions of crime erode property values."

A few major downtown property owners coughed.

"The fortresses of downtown are connected by pedestrian sky bridges. Visitors can walk across the central core without touching down on the sidewalk and see few black people while carrying out their business. The whiteness factor, safety perceptions of white people toward people of color in this internal space, is the driver of the downtown economy and high real estate values."

The section full of young blacks applauded. The office tower and wholesale mart owners frowned, and a major property owner was heard choking.

"I predict that because of heightened perceptions of downtime crime, false if police statistics are to be believed, the whiter Buckhead, Midtown, and Perimeter commercial real estate markets will grow faster. In one to three decades, they will all equal or surpass the central business district, with the northern Perimeter arc exceeding all local and southeastern U.S. markets by 2010."

741

Thundering standing applause was heard from suburban commercial interests. Cohen's predictions based on real estate trends were fully realized.

"We hope, of course, for downtown, the city of Atlanta, and the suburban ring to all prosper. A strong, fast-growing economy is the adhesive that holds us together."

Cohen's prediction inspired Sharon, who whispered to Lesotho, "I think we should obtain real estate licenses and focus on Midtown, Buckhead, and the Perimeter corridor area."

His eyes lit up at the idea of being the first black real estate firm to serve those markets.

Cohen continued with his address. "It's up to all of us to make downtown, Atlanta, and the suburbs better. But that takes trust, cooperation, and a shared vision called *regionalism*, which to some is a dirty word. This hope requires diverse peoples to come and work together and interact in harmony for the sake of public progress."

Broad loud applause shook the hall from progressives inside and outside the Perimeter.

"There will be a price to pay down the road unless white Atlantans stop moving ever farther away to hunker down in exclusive exurban enclaves. The growing number of cloisters filled with like-minded people will skew our politics."

That line drew even louder applause from the same people.

"Suburban sprawl," preached Cohen, "worsens maldistribution of Atlanta's economic glue and is the root cause of most social problems. Atlanta's south side, save for a few pockets of black and white affluence, is virtually a cheap labor colony for the expanding and predominantly white north side."

Lesotho led his whole section of young blacks in applauding that line.

"Unfortunately, sprawl prevents low-income blacks from reaching the jobs increasingly located in the outer-ring counties, where the land is cheaper for corporations to build warehousing space, for example. Low taxes make public transportation minimal at best with expansion thwarted by status quo advocates who distrust the government, with some extremists even hating any form or mention of it."

The same group of young blacks applauded even louder. Conservative white suburban leaders frowned or rubbed their chin with their hand.

"Blacks who aren't comfortable living the edge city life and need affordable housing will recongregate in the core center out of need to survive."

Lesotho and Sharon stood up to second Cohen's claim, and many other educated young blacks joined them. John Whelan and Phillip Mason expressed their concern by rubbing their chins and cheeks with their hands.

Mack Thomas noticed. "I sense that the political equation in Atlanta is changing, and Cohen is an agent of sorts."

Cohen hammered away. "Welfare barely blunts the hard edge of unemployment or underemployment, while the welfare taxes that the suburban middle class so vehemently opposes are actually transfer payments to the poor to stay out of the tidy lives of white people in Cobb, Gwinnett, north Fulton, north DeKalb, and increasingly Cherokee, Forsyth, Henry, and Fayette Counties."

Half the audience, assumably from Atlanta, applauded. The other half, assumably from the suburban safe zones, did not.

"Atlanta and America are pigmentocratic. Lighter skin color is assigned more favorable status and better jobs. Darker-skinned people are often less favored and funneled into work no one else wants to do except new immigrants."

Eddie White stood up to cheer Cohen's claim. Allie recognized Eddie, smiled, and gave him the thumbs-up. White smiled back, stuck his thumb in the air, and sat down.

I'm really over my Cohen thing. He was actually glad to see me.

Allie's already sharp rhetoric grew hotter as he verbally pointed a finger at the angry white guys in the audience.

"I recall how angry white guys used to be proud rednecks until that word and image became bad for business and real estate values. Now they proudly call themselves conservatives, constitutionalists, and libertarians."

The white liberals in the audience laughed loudly, and all thought he'd stolen that line from them.

"Many Atlantans sow discord when they make malevolent comments like 'Why won't they work?' or 'They just sit around having babies and collecting checks' or 'The I-285 Perimeter is the ring around the Congo, and MARTA stands for Moving Africans Rapidly through Atlanta.'"

He made the blacks in the audience laugh at those old racist put-downs and the whites very uncomfortable.

"That cynical mentality and lingering evidence of racism needs to be expunged."

He treaded on racial thin ice. "The truth is that white people won't pay for the social remedies needed to expel the social pathologies created by their racist legacy, and the right-wingers

744

fight welfare payments tooth and nail that sustain, contain, and isolate poor blacks from them."

Lesotho, Sharon, and Eddie stood up to applause. Virtually every other young black person did too, and some white liberals joined them.

"President Reagan has assured white middle-class Americans that it is a Christian act to disinvest in our minorities. Conservative Christian whites proclaim they help wean blacks off their dependency on the government. They are friends of the poor by making them poorer."

Cohen's harsh rhetoric angered some whites to boo. "Reagan deserves better."

One older white man heckled, "You owe him your godforsaken Nobel Prize."

Phillip Mason was livid. *Cohen's called a lot of people names and rehashed a lot of old shit better left unsaid. Stoking Xeranga's rallying cries and angering conservative whites is a big step backward for the city's image.*

Allie kept pounding away. "Our homicide rate shocks the nation but not the average Atlantan. We claim to want higher salaries for our police and then demand that our underpaid centurions crush frustration with firepower."

James Epworth, CEO of Atlanta's third largest bank, was aggravated by Allie's harsh rhetoric. *If I had a gun, I'd shoot that damned demagogic Jew bastard right on the spot.*

Cohen's next words cooled Epworth's anger momentarily. "All Atlantans should never forget that this city's prosperity is stimulated by the collective intelligence of its audacious and concerned commercial sector."

Epworth ached for Cohen's positive streak to continue. Allie's pause made the banker paranoid. *I know that Cohen's setting us up to drive home still another bitter impression of us.*

He was right. "The white corporate elite sits precariously perched on the backs of a sullen large underclass that has little regard for central city real estate values or the well-being of the community at large. Survival and pleasure are the underclass's preoccupations and pursuit."

Lesotho, Mack, and the rest of the audience were transfixed by harsh truths rarely heard from privileged white men. Cohen expressed black feelings more intensely than they were comfortable hearing. He was determined to make whites and blacks honestly face up to their social realities and pathologies and finally deal with them.

"What can we do for or about our sizable underclass, the product of the defects in free market capitalism, slavery, the Middle Passage, segregation, lingering racism, and disastrous social welfare experiments?"

That question sucked the air out of the audience and hall, and silence ruled.

"A stigma of worthlessness has been stamped on a segment less equipped to compete to the degree that the group has, for the most part, given up. Stand forewarned. We can't go on ignoring the alienated hordes of forgotten America."

The air did not return to the hall and audience until after the next statement. "I urge you to consider my perspectives and not easily dismiss them as simply another do-gooder's lament. With all of us pulling together, we can achieve an improved quality of life for all Americans." A few people applauded.

"I present a remedy by sharing details of National Defense Metropolitanization Act (NDMA), designed to merge the

746

central city and suburbs into a unified tax district. The result of consolidation is equalization of municipal service costs across the designated metropolitan district or region.

I conclude my speech with a quote from Leviticus 19:33–34. 'If a stranger sojourn with thee in your land, ye shall not vex him. But the stranger that dwelleth with you shall be unto you as one born among you, and thou shalt love him as thyself; for ye were strangers in the land of Egypt.'"

Half of the audience roared their approval and support with a standing ovation. The much less enthusiastic element responded with polite clapping of hands, sitting on hands, or silent stares.

The full text of Cohen's speech was printed in the *Atlanta Journal-Constitution*. The editorial staff denounced the speech as *needlessly negative* and *grossly overstated*.

Local conservative columnist Jerry Barnes labeled Cohen the "Malibu Beach Bolshevik who seeks to transform America into the United States of Doonesbury."

In comparison, the national press treated Cohen's speech as an important message. The *NY Times* Op-Ed page debated that "Cohen forced Atlanta and the nation to come to grips with its race-based myths."

"Cohen presented," the *Washington Post* printed, "a frank portrayal of forgotten Americans trapped in central city slums and how that shapes lives and real estate values."

Lesotho was the first to congratulate Allie, who was mobbed by well-wishers, doubters, and determined reactionaries.

Mack Thomas shook Cohen's hand and said, "I apologize, Dr. Cohen, for the whole Harry Jackson episode."

"Don't worry about it, Mack, I've gotten over it. Frankly, Harry added some nice touches that helped the book and movie do very well."

Allie saw Eddie, called him over, shook his hand, and gave him a little hug.

"It's good to see you, Eddie, and you look great. 'Seems to me you have really turned your life around and moved forward. I'm so very proud of you, and seeing your success is the best reward a teacher can have. Please say hello to Farrah for me, and all the best to both of you."

Cohen was so nice to Eddie that he held back tears of joy. All was forgiven; the past was dead and buried.

Mack Thomas asked Allie, "Dr. Cohen, are you thinking of entering politics?" A reporter stuck a mic in front of Cohen's mouth in case he answered yes.

Cohen emphatically stated, "No, and I have no intentions of ever running for office, but I will gladly endorse Mack Thomas for public office and imagine that he might have an eye on a city council spot."

Mack quickly got puffed up from the flattery until Charlene reminded him, "You are going to need more than John Whalen and $100,000 to win this Old Fourth Ward thing." That let some air out of his balloon.

Cohen spent an hour patiently explaining NDMA details to supporters or welfare foes and told one very bigoted man Dick Gregory's old joke.

"If welfare was called foreign aid, no one would care."

Your Atlanta caveat speech today, Allie, showed how all politics is local. The red state south is a product of separate white and black bloc-voting patterns that perpetuate maintenance of white supremacy. But as the poet said, "The times they are a-changing."

Chapter 99

Sarah drove Allie home by taking a long slow ride up Peachtree Street, one of their many Atlanta pleasures.

"I congratulate you, Allie, for having the guts to remark on matters most people ignore or are ignorant of but know is the truth when they hear it. I just question why you felt the need to make it so stern."

Cohen employed a Yiddish phrase to describe his concern over officially becoming a member of the establishment.

"I can't be a *shanda?*"

"What's a *shanda?*"

"You know, Sarah, a suck-up or sycophant, right-wing Jews who, for money, tell powerful Christians what they want to hear instead of what they should know. It's hard, Sarah, to be a gadfly and a pillar of society at the same time, and I have a reputation to protect."

Sarah laughed hard while her new Mercedes 450 SL sports car glided through Buckhead on the way to the Sit-In. A mile north, Harvey Kartzman, her father, was busy reviewing the Sit-In's meal and bar tabs for the past week and glanced at the leading industry trade journal that sat on top of a pile of mail.

What do you know? Restaurant *magazine lists the Sit-In as the top grossing restaurant in Atlanta and seventh in the United States and rising fast. Excellent.*

He refilled the cheesecake station. *I'm sixty-seven though.* Harvey looked at the big picture. *The pace is grinding me down, but who else is there to manage the business?. Sandy Forman is consumed with expanding corporate affairs and my son-in-law with saving humanity from itself and now making a big underground fortune to help the poor. My son, Jerry, is a happy jock who loves his sports rep job so much that he turns me down no matter how much money I offer him.*

"Harvey," a customer asked, "is Allie around?"

Kartzman, amused, curled a smile. *People think Allie's in the office writing tomorrow's menu. He hasn't even been here yet, but I have to admit that he's made me a very wealthy man. The Sit-In's gross shot up 30 percent after the Nobel Prize. Patrons suddenly lined up like they'd get nominated too for eating a pastrami sandwich. Only sure thing was the pickle that came with the sandwich.*

Allie, Sarah, and Ari walked into the Sit-In and almost bowled Harvey over. He reminded himself not to ask Allie if he was back with Sarah full time yet.

They are an extremely handsome family. Then he admired his grandson. *Ari inherited the best of both of them.*

"Holy cow, Allie, I was just thinking about you." Harvey hugged and kissed his grandson and then his daughter.

"I hope it was all good things, Dad." He hugged Harvey. "It's great to see you."

"Elliot, the accountant, told me today how much money you made me this year. The big surprise to me, Allie, is not that the deli is doing great. What's made me the happiest is that word has gotten around that our lobster, dry-aged steaks, and veal and pasta dishes are just as good for less money than the fancy white tablecloth joints. Our average plate check is now $2 per higher than we originally projected."

"You're amazing, Dad."

"Next week, Allie, we're adding ribs, smoked brisket, and homemade sausage—beef, veal, and lamb—to grab some of the barbecue market, frankfurters and brats we've been making from the start. I'd like to include pork ribs and sausage too but can't figure out how to add it to what's primarily a kosher-style Jewish deli menu."

"Can you imagine? Upscale dining, deli, and que too. The restaurant is everything my dad and I dreamed of and more. I noticed you set up a big cheesecake station too. I like that."

"Try a slice of this black cherry cheesecake. I came up with this recipe myself. Here, taste it. Ari and Sarah, have some too."

"Dad, it's delicious. This is the best cheesecake I've ever eaten. Harvey, you've earned a good long rest. Please hire someone to help you with this place, and then take a nice long trip to Hawaii or Israel with Mom."

"Mother will really love that."

"When you get back, Lenny Meltzer will help you with the Sit-In expansion and construction program, also tweaking the Sit-In concept, whatever. We just added his Le Canard restaurant in Georgetown to our new restaurant construction, design, and management group. It's a good location to switch over to a Sit-In concept."

Harvey smiled appreciatively but had some bad news.

"Sunshine Inn's parent company lost a takeover battle to AmerCorp, a Philadelphia-based holding company. None of these new guys are Jewish like Sunshine, who was an absolute pleasure to work with."

"Dad, do you expect any fallout on the Sit-In from the buyout?"

"Sunshine, in my opinion, was more committed to quality control and market penetration than short-term high profits.

AmerCorp's larger and could do more for us but has several divisions that are deteriorating and might drain capital away from the Sit-In."

"So what's AmerCorp's plan for us?"

"Over the next ten years, AmerCorp will exercise Sunshine's plan to open a Sit-In in every Sunbelt city over a quarter of a million stretching from Washington DC to Houston to LA, San Francisco, and Seattle. Our new line of flash-frozen prepared meals just won freezer space in two major supermarket chains, and demand is growing so fast that we've expanded our production facility in Peachtree Corners. We're moving our bakery division from the Sit-in to out there too because of a growing heat and fire risk that's been building up in the restaurant."

"I think AmerCorp is useful for the time being, Dad. I have a plan to take them over but when the time is right."

"Allie, it's often cheaper to move sooner rather than later."

"I sense that our opportunity is only a few months away. Dad, thanks again for making the Sit-In a great success."

"Don't mention it. I'll see you tomorrow at Ari's first birthday party. Can you believe it? Ari is a year old already. I don't think a grandfather ever enjoyed a grandson more than I do him. Thank you, Allie."

It's nice to see Harvey a little emotional for a change.

Allie hugged Harvey again. "Dad, please pack up a tongue sandwich for me, pastrami for Sarah, and a hot dog for Ari. Add some sides and a couple of slices of that cheesecake for us to go, also throw in a half dozen bagels and a quarter pound of lox. I need to visit my new corporate office for the first time too. Sandy told me that the AlCoCorp headquarters takes up the top floors of an office building across from the Lenox Plaza shopping mall."

"Sandy's in here nearly every day to eat and talk a little business with me."

Sarah drove through the heavily trafficked Buckhead-Lenox corridor and pulled into the building's parking lot. They took the elevator up to Sandy's plush tenth-floor office; he had two conversations going at once and terminated them when he saw Allie and Sarah.

"So this is where I send my telegrams. Man, it's amazing how many employees are needed to support my gigs."

"This is nothing. We'll be taking over two more floors next month. Our staff will double by the end of the year, so I'm now looking into buying this building."

"Hey, I'm pretty good for the economy, aren't I?"

"You're very good. Three hundred and ten employees already depend on AlCoCorp for their income."

The three old friends tried to discuss their lives the way they had before becoming rich. That soon failed as Forman's phone rarely stopped ringing long enough to have a decent conversation. After the eighth interruption, Allie threw in the towel and listed a series of instructions instead.

"Sandy, please merge Lenny Meltzer's design and construction firm with AlCoCorp's restaurant management division to build all-new Sit-Ins. Please hire more staff to help Harvey tweak restaurant chain quality and help him with the Buckhead Sit-In management."

"I will take care of Harvey's matter ASAP. I've already supported Lenny and Jay by integrating and covering the new rogue component. That's done, but I worry that this new structure may not hold up for three years. We're going to have to be very lucky indeed."

"We never have any time to schmooze anymore," Allie grumbled. "We've become incredibly rich but also created a growing structure that's consuming us."

"Well, you're invisibly operating out of California, and Washington, like a clandestine gnome, is surely not helping to close the gap." They both laughed. "Allie," whispered Forman, "since Ari's here, I'll bring his presents to the birthday party tomorrow myself." Allie hugged Sandy to show him gratitude.

Sarah told Allie during the seven-mile ride to Dunwoody, "I completely understand your reasons for making a huge fortune. It spares you from having to sell anyone on a good idea anymore."

"My finally being able to act on good ideas my self, Sarah, is the best part of our success."

Sarah waited until they arrived home to ask, "Allie, you could function more out of Atlanta if you built one of those hubs here too."

"Babe, I already have one redundant unit. I'll try to visit a little more frequently and stay a little longer each time. I think it unwise to promise more right now."

I'm glad that Sarah didn't push me or get aggravated.

Allie changed the subject. "Where's Aretha? It seems that she's always taking care of personal business when I'm in town."

Sarah giggled. *He's finally picking up on my purposely giving Aretha days off so we can both have more time with Ari.*

Allie got down on the floor to wrestle with Ari, now a beautifully filled-out little boy cutely laced with dimples and double-folds.

Ari's such a little person now. Wrestling on the floor with him is the best.

Harvey and Rebecca dropped in with a feast of the new smoked brisket and barbecue lines from the Sit-In and the best potato salad and coleslaw in Atlanta. They all munched and talked, with most of the conversation focusing on Ari's growth.

"Allie," Rebecca lovingly bragged, "look at how early Ari walks, talks, and turns the pages of picture books. He's as good a little boy too as he is cute."

After cake and coffee, the grandparents left, and Sarah and Allie bathed Ari. Cohen crooned every hit song from the 1950s and 1960s that he could remember the words to, about five. Ari's favorite was still the Tymes' "So Much in Love." The kid was a good audience and smiled and laughed until Allie did a Perry Como imitation that put Ari right to sleep. Sarah chanced on the scene.

"Watching you croon Ari to sleep was great theater. Hey, why don't we get high and sit in my new hot tub?" She sexily whispered, "Or should we sit in the hot tub and get high?"

"The latter choice appeals to me more, Sarah."

She switched on her new expensive stereo system and filled the spa room with the creamy sounds of a Windham Hill album. Sarah's naked body intimately pressed against him, and she initiated foreplay. After climaxing, Sarah smoked her customary victory cigarette the way Red Auerbach smoked his victory cigar after each Celtics win.

Allie fired up a joint that put Sarah to sleep during the TV news but helped give him an idea for a TV cop show. He puffed and jotted it down before falling out too.

He gave the concept to Sarah at breakfast. "Money, you own the rights to this new TV show exclusively. Please contact NBC programming chief Milton Seltzer. The show's called *APD, Atlanta Police Department*. The novelty is a black Jewish police chief based loosely on Charleston's Reuben Greenberg."

"Why not put the show in both of our names?"

"For a number of reasons. I'm creating a nice big income stream that's solely yours. If something crazy happens to me and my money gets tied up for years by the government, your income will support you and Ari in your accustomed lifestyles. I plan to funnel other properties your way as ideas come to me."

Sarah reflected. *In past years, Allie had a thousand great ideas that went nowhere because of lack of money or connections. Now he has all the factors of success working for him, an alchemy that stamps solid gold on everything he touches. Our getting back together as a normal family should be as sure as* APD *becoming a hit.*

Sarah and Allie dressed Ari for his birthday in a sharp olive green suit that zipped up the front. Rebecca's favorite pastime was buying Ari cute little outfits so her grandson could be "dressed to the nines," one of her favorite expressions. Ari typically looked so adorable that they celebrated with another family group hug.

"I have to say, Allie," Sarah complimented, "that you're handling yourself very well on the rounds of talk shows. I'm surprised that you haven't lived out the fantasy of acting yet, even a bit part in a movie or TV show."

Cohen scoffed. "Sarah, I couldn't act my way out of a nativity scene."

Sarah laughed hysterically. "Come on. Ha ha! You can draw on your teaching experience. You know, you acted out a lot to keep your lessons interesting. Teaching is probably your persona base to draw off."

"Maybe, but the reason I've never acted is why I became a teacher. I have the middle-class curse of purpose and service to society. Good acting requires me to become the purpose and serve only myself."

Sarah reacted with a quote from Victor Hugo. "To dare is a form of wisdom."

She let it go. He gave an acting experience a second thought.

Chapter 100

Two dozen babies aged six months to two years cried, babbled, or drooled. Ari, the happiest child in the room, poised to blow out his candle and snuffed it with one short breath. Allie typically beamed proudly.

"The kid," joked Sarah, "has a good set of lungs."

Allie kissed and hugged his precious son and then excused himself to take a call from Jay Dean. "Allie, I tracked you down to tell you we're plugged into the CIA's EconProj."

"That's fantastic news, Jay. Our mission begins today."

"We have some trouble though." Jay instructed, "We need a million in cash by eight tomorrow morning to bribe the key Ma Bell operative. Sandy's assistant will bring by the cash, and you will deliver it to me by flying to Washington on a private jet out of Peachtree DeKalb Airport. You'll land at Baltimore-Washington Airport and be met by a DC limo service that will take you straight to my boat."

"I'll have to leave my son's first birthday party early and hope my wife, Sarah, won't get on my case for it. Hopefully, my gift overload will smooth over any hurt feelings."

Ari tore into Allie's gifts—a red and white tricycle, a little red Radio Flyer wagon, a monster-sized fire truck, a stand-up punching bag with Richard Nixon's face on it, and a ministereo home entertainment system. Ari loved his gifts, jumped into his dad's arms, and kissed him on his nose.

Ari made Allie's day by almost saying his first sentence. "'Love you, Daddy." Ari's profession of love produced Allie's third religious stirring.

Hashem blessed his efforts to be there for his son. Sarah shared Allie's very special moment by blessing the short business trip.

Two thousand miles away, Carole wrapped her wet hair in a towel and took a good look at herself in a full-length mirror.

My god, the doctor is going to get on me for a slight weight gain so soon, though I'm only 103 pounds, so big fucking deal.

She stared at her hair. *Shit, split ends, need to visit my stylist. Uh-oh, my legs have swollen a bit. Better cut down on salt some more.*

Male voices coming from the living room distracted Carole from her self-loathing.

Is that Martin returning from a Lakers game with Myron? It is them, and wow, Myron looks terrific. He looks really fit for the first time in his life, and the salt-and-pepper hair has softened his once angular face.

Martin kissed his dad good night and went to his room to watch *Dune*, a science fiction movie. Carole was left alone with Myron.

"Did I ever tell you, Carole," he confided in her, "that Martin and Caryn are easily the best of my four kids? God, I love them so much."

"What's the matter, Myron? You're not so crazy about Estrella and the twins anymore?"

"It's worse than that." He lamented. "I married the wrong woman and had the wrong kids with her."

"I don't understand what you're trying to tell me. I mean, I'm glad that you love Martin and Caryn so much but kind of sorry to hear how dysfunctional you and Estrella as a family have become, particularly for the twins' sake."

Uh-oh, Carole thought. *Myron's walking around the room as if he were following a director's cue to hit his marks. I sense he wants to tell me something important.*

"Carole, I made a terrible mistake when I married Estrella and compounded it by having the twins with her. I really fucked up my life. You were the best thing that ever happened to me, and I treated you badly."

Carole appreciatively smiled at hearing that and what followed.

"You'd make me the happiest man if you could find it in your heart to take me back someday. I was young and stupid, your career zoomed, and mine didn't. I was frankly lost and never really figured it out until yesterday. I guess you call that breakthrough, don't you?"

"Myron, Myron," Carole related, "I'm pregnant with a man I've half-taken away from his wife and little boy. Now you're asking me to take you away from your wife, whom you have two babies with." She held up two fingers. "And what am I to do with Allie's baby inside of me?"

"I'm content to wait a decade if necessary. You look fabulous and seem to have a greater balance in your life. I swear, you're glowing again for the first time in years."

"Thank you, I liked hearing that. Your compliments scored you a few brownie points. Still, you're a fair lover, an indifferent father, and a C bankable actor, and those are your good points."

"Okay, I admit I was a bum to you and a failure as a father, but I'm getting my act together and want to make up for all the years I wasn't there. Now be honest with me. Can Allie ever replace me as a father to our kids?"

Carole looked away. "I'm right, Carole, aren't I? You know too that I won't be running around the world trying to save it."

"Look, Myron, I'm impressed by how repentant you are and that you also want to become a better father, and I promise to keep that in mind. But I have some things to deal with me before I could ever think about settling down with you again."

"That's fair enough. I'll take my chances."

"Understand that I love Allie more than you. Nobody has ever stretched me like him, and there's more for us to get into, but your desire to shape up as a dad gives you some credibility again. That's the best that I can do, Myron."

"That's fine. At least I feel that I have a chance. I can deal with that and vow that I will become everything you ever expected of me and not just for the sake of Martin and Caryn."

"Well, you can start with giving up gambling for good. Also, cut back on the vapid sports scene in general."

"I promise to only take Martin and Caryn to Dodger games like any other father. Since we're communicating so well, what caused David's downfall?"

"Rose walked in on him balling Greta Person, and he went Hollywood even worse than you did."

Carole looked Myron in the eye to see if her answer got through to him—it did.

"I'm not surprised, Carole, so what about Allie? Is his problem trying to save the world?"

"Nah." Carole shrugged. "I'm not hundred percent sure we're best friends anymore. When that goes, you're kind of just lovers."

It was your shared sense of mission, Carole, that drove you to become partners and lovers with Allie. Conversely, as your sense of mission diminishes, so does your partnership.

An hour later, Sam removed medium-rare T-bone steaks from the patio gas grill while Rose tossed salad and split open two steaming hot baked potatoes. A silver gray Mercedes convertible glided up the long driveway and parked behind the Rolls.

Rose nearly knocked over the salad bowl when she saw who it was. "Myron, it's so good to see you again, and you look terrific."

Myron Silver took off his frosted aviator sunglasses and kissed his former mother-in-law, whom he still felt close to.

"Nu, Myron, are you hungry? Please, Sam can throw another steak on the grill. You look so thin. Let me make you something."

"Ma," begged Myron, "please don't bother. I just need a few minutes of your time. On second thought, a beer would be fine, Ma."

"A beer isn't food, Myron. Here's some salad. I made the Thousand Island dressing myself. It's good, isn't it?"

Myron ate a forkful of salad with dressing applied. "It's delicious. You're still the best Brooklyn cook ever, Ma. I'll never forget your own version of Ebinger's famous blackout cake. You look fantastic too."

"Thank you, Myron. Your last picture was a hit. Sam says you're going to be nominated for an Oscar for Best Supporting Actor."

Minkowitz handed Myron a bottle of imported beer. "Sorry, I know your contract permits you to drink a certain Western beer only. I just drink Beck's."

"You have to promise," Myron kidded, "not to tell the brewmaster who pays me a half million bucks a year to endorse his watery beer."

After laughing, Sam turned serious. "I read this morning how your film is one of the top hits of the summer and has grossed fifty-three million in twenty-eight days. With those numbers in the trades, you shouldn't have to sell beer anymore."

"That's nice of you to say, Sam, but I don't have any points and only got a lousy two hundred grand up front. Gil Wildstein, my new agent, says I better follow it up with another hit, or I'll be squeezing the Charmin."

They all laughed. Myron had Rose's interest. "So what can we do for you?"

He described his conversation with Carole and confused them more by the minute. By the time he was finished explaining his need to rejoin his former family, Rose was perplexed, and Sam was scratching his head.

"Myron." She sighed. "Since Allie is in the middle of this picture, all I can tell you is let's wait and see. In the meantime, since I think it would be best for Martin and Caryn, I'll nudge things along in my own way. That's all I can do without my daughter hating me."

"You're a good friend, Ma, and you're a lucky man, Sam."

Sam walked Myron to his car and felt in his bones an opportunity had presented itself—hedge his bet on Allie by enhancing Myron's stature in Carole's eyes. If or when Allie returned to his family or Carole finally kicked him out, Myron would be positioned to step right in.

Sam dealt. "Myron, I'm offering three films at two million per with three points per film. So are we good to go?"

"Normally, I'd scream for five points," negotiated Myron. "But you're the guy who gave me my first big break and the only one willing to give me another. I love you, Sam, and gratefully accept."

"One thing, Myron, this is a secret between you and me and to be kept from Rose and Carole. Neither is to ever know about this deal. I will have my lawyers work out the details and explain it to you."

They shook on it. Sam returned to the kitchen and witnessed Rose praying.

"Dear God, thank you for this visit from Myron. But, Lord, one thing, please don't drag it out for ten years like a soap opera."

We promise, Rose.

Chapter 101

A week later, Carole and Allie were eating breakfast and reading the *Los Angeles Times*. He scanned the sports section; she read the front pages and found an Op-Ed that she'd expected for some time.

"Allie, I'm reading an editorial that criticizes you for being the least active and most disappointing Nobel recipient in decades. I'll read these last two paragraphs to you. 'Instead of using his position to counter evil, Cohen has virtually disappeared from view. The African famine is worsening, South Africa's apartheid system is throwing the country into chaos, and Soviet Jews are suffering oppression and being refused immigration to Israel.

And that's just to name three problems. So where's Cohen, and why is he hiding out in Malibu of all places? Can the Nobel people just take it back from him and give it to someone who will actually speak out against tyranny and try to work for peace?'"

Carole sarcastically suggested, "Allie, I advise you to issue a press release that you've become a subterranean financier in Malibu to escape taxes to help the poor and wretched a few years from now."

"That's not fair, Carole," he protested. "If you only knew what I was trying to accomplish, you wouldn't put down my aims like that."

"And if the world only knew what you were up to," she suggested, "they might just think you're a schmuck."

Cohen pursed his lips to maintain patience and stifle anger and then decided that this was the perfect time to invite Carole into his operations center and educate her about what he was embarking on. He briefed her as they walked down the corridor leading to his center.

"Brickell & Groot, the world's largest contractor and who developed the bulk of the Saudi infrastructure, worked with Lenny and me to transform a small corner of your house into my one-man corporate complex."

The scale of his office stunned her. She thought, *I sure didn't have this in mind when I encouraged him to feel comfortable to make some changes too.*

"Dig it, Carole. I installed two of Cray's most advanced microprocessors to compute and keep track of all transactions. The Bloomberg custom-designed terminal and software provides a global info feed of worldwide commodity and stock prices. A large generator provides power to the computers and cools the processors and other machines."

"My god, Allie, this is right out of science fiction. The ultimate home office of the future is here."

"From Hewlett-Packard, I got two satellite transmitters and earth receiving stations capable of performing more than five hundred bank and market transactions a minute."

"Wow, Allie, these sophisticated computers and buzzing terminals are fascinating. There are so many bells and whistles going. The only thing missing is a slot machine."

He laughed. "I have my own kind of slot machine, sweetie, except the house—namely, me—always wins. Watch me now."

She stood behind him for the next eleven minutes watching him follow prompts with keystrokes.

Holy shit, he just made $103,000.

He depressed a few more keys, reacted to several cryptic messages, punched in a couple of more commands and— bingo—$87,000 cleared in a minute.

The dollar amounts boggled her mind. "Allie, how does it all work?"

"I'm grateful you're finally interested enough to ask, babe. One computer automatically sells off currencies declining in value and buys currencies rising in value and at a rate of up to four transactions a minute. The algorithm alone for driving this nonstop currency trader cost three million to write."

"So this machine of sorts is making money every second of the day and at an astonishingly fast speed."

"Exactly, my original twenty-three million of capital will swell to thirty-four million in the next six days of nonstop trading. I expect to clear a billion in 364 days, a second billion 257 days later, a third billion 180 days after that, and so on. This is more than a money tree, Carole. It's a fucking exponential money plantation."

"Allie, I'm trying to understand the systems and margins at work here. Please explain."

"Okay, sweetie, the second system trades commodities, clears the differences, and instantly reinvests the profit and original investment in market goods increasing in price somewhere else in the world. Let me demonstrate for you. I'm trading Egyptian cotton futures for Sri Lankan tea and expect to make at least a $406,000 profit. It will take me a half hour to set up and execute the trade."

I didn't tell her that CIA weather satellites informed me hours before the world business community learned that hail was damaging the cotton crop or that a spy in a multinational corporation in Colombo tipped me off that a Sri Lankan bumper crop will hit the market tomorrow while blights are ravaging Chinese tea harvests.

Carole stood behind Allie while he speedily placed half of his currency holdings into fast-rising German marks and Japanese yen.

"A week from now, babe," he explained, "my yield will double when the White House leaks news of a record trade imbalance with both countries. The Baker Plan, to further devalue the dollar, will earn me at least an extra 30 percent bonus."

"The three-year plan you've quoted me, Allie, has altered my previous view. It's dawning on me that you actually are an invisible financial force to be reckoned with. I just hope that you have time too to do a lot of good along the way."

"The problem, Carole, is you respect and admire my social science knowledge more than my business intelligence. I was a very entrepreneurial teacher and now have a chance to develop my business side too."

"That's crazy. Like my mother says, smart is smart."

"Sorry, babe, did my social science knowledge stop Alvarado from the suicide bombing mission against Pinochet?"

She nodded no. "Did it stop Abu Sallah from killing six Egyptian soldiers to talk to us?"

"No, of course not, and please stop reminding me of all those horrors?"

"Okay, but if I had a hundred million to give Alvarado to feed a hundred thousand poor parishioners a year for the rest of his life, might he call off his car bombings?"

"I see what you mean."

She sounded unconvincing, so Cohen piled on.

"Carole, if I had a billion bucks to give Abu Sallah to make the lives of his followers easier by creating thousands of jobs and affordable housing units, do you think I could modify his behavior to Israel?"

"Probably yes too, but I sense he and Mustafa would use a lot of it for weapons to fight Mubarak and the army."

"Did our efforts change a single note of theirs, Carole?"

"Maybe a little bit, but yes, really serious money is high impact. You're right, Allie, I'm wrong, and I'm getting it, and I promise to be more supportive and give you the time to prove it."

Carole, get in line with Adonai and me. We too are limiting his time to prove it.

She kissed Allie and then stared over his shoulder at a message instructing him to temporarily refrain from further stock acquisitions.

"I'm ignoring it, Carole, and am buying every available share of AmerCorp, whose stock price is dropping faster than its profitability level deserves. My buying spree should trigger a stampede for AmerCorp and make it a hot stock of the day on Wall Street."

I'm not going to tell her about insider information I have that AmerCorp's directors, flush with windfall capital, are greedily accelerating the Sit-In's expansion rate by 25 percent. That's exactly what I hoped they do.

"Watch me, babe, begin a hostile takeover of AmerCorp. Over the next few weeks, I will repeatedly drive up AmerCorp's stock to inflated levels and then divest portions in phased selling binges that send the stock plummeting to new lows. The frenzied buying and selling yesterday caught the eye of the Securities and Exchange Commission, and it suspended trading for a few hours.

"The SEC just green-lighted me, so I'm manipulating the market price where I left off two days ago. My aim is to constantly pick up bigger and bigger blocks of shares at lower and lower prices to engineer AmerCorp into a fairly undervalued company. When I'm the dominant stockholder, I'll swoop in and snap it right up."

Carole sat for hours each day watching him facilitate wildly profitable transactions and relentlessly building his humanitarian pool of money. Her usual stance was to put her hand to her mouth in amazement at the scale and scope he was already operating at.

"Allie, what are you punching in at the moment?"

"The U.S. tourist invasion of England is driving the pound up and the dollar down. I just bought £4 million for $6 million and expect an increase in the pound of 10 percent and a $390,000 profit."

"I have to admit it, Allie, I'm very impressed. This is all typically brilliant, but I just wonder about the ethics of it. You claim to be making money to help save the poor from capitalist or Communist exploitation, but you just parlayed a fortune off peasant tea farmers and poor Egyptian cotton pickers, so what separates you from the rest of the financial piranha out there?"

Since Allie had yet to perform a significant benevolent deed, he changed the subject and pointed to a mainframe computer.

"Carole, every novel and movie script ever written has been input into this IBM mainframe. The ultraexpensive software package requires just eleven inputs of basic information—or *threads*—to synthesize a fairly polished new literary property and then prints it out at forty pages a minute too."

Allie handed Carole a mix of the old James M. Cain novel *The Postman Always Rings Twice* and the Oscar-winning film *Double Indemnity* with 1980s language and settings. Carole thumbed through it while Cohen tried to sell her on playing the lead.

"The scariest factor, sweetie, is that the product is halfway decent. It now only takes me a week to rewrite former hits into good new scripts. This blended double remake is tentatively called *Temperatures Rising.* 'Sounds hot, doesn't it?

He watched Carole, a seasoned actress, quickly peruse the script and conclude that the story was chock-full of very erotic scenes. Her lips tightened.

"You've also switched the ending. The guy gets away with the money and tags the girl with the crime."

"Carole, I swear, this part will easily be one of the best roles you've had in years."

She finished reading and, without looking up, told him, "While I'm glad that you've finally produced a work for me, the many nude sex scenes are disturbing as hell."

"I think the timing is right for a role and film like this, babe."

"Doesn't it bother you, Allie"—she looked at him directly with an unhappy face—"to show off your woman like that?"

"I'm sorry." He apologized but also urged her, "Please understand, Carole, that for the movie to work, it has to be really hot, the sexual tension palpitating."

He looked into her face. *Carole's enthusiasm for the project, I see, is cool at best.*

She summed it up. "So you, my man, are asking me to be nude or topless on screen twice and simulate intercourse and oral sex once. Oh, sorry, I forgot about all the heavy petting in between too."

"Carole, it's about generating heat on the big screen. If you can generate enough heat, you can leave more clothes on and get away with less petting and maybe even a sex scene or two."

"That's a cockamamy answer, Allie, but I am attracted to the role. I just fear that Rose will have a conniption."

"We'll bar your mother from the sets."

"That's a lame answer too. Okay, Cohen, before agreeing, I need to know who you have in mind for the male lead."

Shit, the moment of truth is here.

Cohen stammered and coughed before summoning his courage.

"I have in mind someone who's extremely handsome, has wavy dark hair and a slightly wicked on-screen image, and should fire up the cinematic sexual chemistry."

"Come on, spit the name out already. Hey, what about Myron? He was my husband, so the sex scenes would have unusual authenticity."

"Myron is a comfortable choice, but I feel the part requires someone more believable as a dirty rat."

"Okay, I can accept that. So who do you have in mind?"

Allie nearly swallowed his tongue trying to say the name. "Peter . . . Bates."

Carole spoke in tongues until her dumbfoundedness lifted and angrily told him, "Peter is simply too much of a pig to let his hands all over me like that, end of story."

"Babe, the screen will sizzle and break box office records."

That's exactly, she thought, *what David would say.*

"One's heart must be in a script like this. With Peter, I feel I'm over and beyond the call of duty to my craft. Anyway, when did you plan to begin shooting, sometime next year?"

"No, we need to start next week."

"Next week? What about my waistline changing in the next month or two?"

"No problem, I fed that into the computer, and it diagrammed correct camera angles for the director."

I'm torn between two poles, Carole thought. *This movie has "monster hit" written all over it. The problem is my lover is an active genius who, day in and day out, does the damndest things and has just shamelessly exploited me.*

"Carole, the printer just finished spitting out a copy for you to read and get into the role." He handed it to her.

Lord, I love Allie, but I'm wondering how much more of his daring I can take. He's stretching me wildly but also wearing me down fast.

Chapter 102

However, he's never boring. Temperatures Rising *will get Rose's one-woman censorship board off my back, and I've never looked better. There's barely a baby bump yet, and I'm not going to improve with age, so why not now?*

Carole, ever fascinated by Allie's computers and operation, loved to hang in his hub; the wealth accumulation process never failed to boggle her mind.

He explained to her his major challenge.

"The process, babe, is a lot more complicated than you think. I understand you're impressed by what appears to be enormous profits from riding the crests of rising markets. However, you have to subtract 20 percent in varying cuts to secret partners and occasional unavoidable tax bites or brokers' commissions that I can't sidestep. There are general operating expenses as well."

"So what does that come to, my man?"

"If you follow the money, Carole, you'll find that I ultimately wind up with about 70 percent of all I earn. I hope to be one of the ten greatest holders of cash on the planet in three years but suspect it's hard to keep score at that level."

"The neighbors are complaining about the generator's noise. They won't wait three years."

"I'll call Lenny and Brickell & Groot about installing a sound deflector that directs the noise out to sea. Luckily, because we're in our own little canyon, no one can see or hear the hub from the road. Since it's only the people up in the hills above us and east of here who are complaining, this should work. Anyway, I'd like you to switch obstetricians."

"Why?" He shook her with his request. "What's wrong with Dr. Simon Green?"

"I don't trust him, and I have my reasons." He executed a big trade.

"Simon delivered both of my kids, Allie, and I'm very comfortable with him. What kind of reasons do you have because I consider Simon a friend too?"

"First, he's too damn relaxed and practically oozes California mellowness. Second, he blinds me with his $5,000 caps."

She laughed at his impression of Green. "You're crazy. Simon's a nice guy and caring doctor, and besides, a mellow atmosphere helps produce a tranquil baby."

He didn't argue with her; instead, he printed out a vita.

"This is the résumé of Dr. Lester Granet. I searched for the smartest ex–New York and Jewish doctor living in Los Angeles by feeding all metro baby doctor names and backgrounds into my computer. Granet was at the top of the list."

"Sorry," Carole insisted. "I'm staying with Simon, and please don't push it. Jesus, suddenly, you're living or dying by your computers."

"Please don't put down my computers, Carole. They earned me $900 a minute yesterday or $1.3 million per twenty-four hours."

Cohen's tone sounded arrogant to Carole, and another tension developed between them the next morning. She awoke, took a shower, and dressed to go out for breakfast with Allie. Carole made some coffee and heard the sound of a sports car racing up the driveway. She looked out the window and saw Allie parking a glitzy convertible she'd never seen before then ran down the front steps and greeted him with a bunch of questions in the driveway.

"When did you buy that?"

Allie became defensive. "I got it this morning about an hour ago. I've been breaking it in on the 405."

"What the hell is it, Cohen? You must be the only one in LA with one."

"It's a Bitter," he informed her. "And yes, I am the first one in LA with it."

He thought, *She's suddenly calling me by my last name a lot. How come? When Sarah does it, it's usually affectionately.*

"A Bitter? I never heard of it." She sounded a bit of a sourpuss while saying it.

He continued to defend his purchase. "It's a new German car, babe, and they will only produce 150 this year, so they are automatic collectibles. The salesman told me that its value should double in five years and triple in ten."

"How much did it cost?"

He looked at her as if she was out of line.

"Fifty-two thousand. Why and what does it matter?"

"Frankly, I'm not that impressed with the car's looks and think it's overpriced. Fifty-two thousand for this car, don't you think that's a bit much?"

"No, it's actually a very good investment, Carole, and rides like a dream. Hey, I earned the damned money for it in fifty-two minutes of work."

"What was wrong with your Toyota Supra?" She stared at him.

"It was getting mushy." He stared back at her.

"Your head's mushy."

Cohen took note. *She's now putting me down fairly regularly. This is not a good sign.*

He checked his temper and defended his purchase. "I can afford it, Carole, so fuck it, okay?"

Carole, standing with hands on hips, said, "You're falling into the old Hollywood trap of people thinking that you're a star by what you drive."

Allie put his hands on his hips to imitate her stance and chill her out; she laughed.

"Carole, do you really think that I give two shits if people think I'm a star or not? Give me a break. The Bitter is like a BMW convertible body with a Corvette engine. Would you like to take it for a ride?"

"No. Look, I used to love the fact that you drove a Toyota even though you could afford ten Rolls-Royces."

"Dammit." He lost his temper. "You've got a Porsche 928, and you're giving me shit about the Bitter!"

"Please don't yell. I'm sorry, but you're so different now from the Allie I first met." She put her hands over her ears.

"Hey, I'm human and have a right to change like everybody else." He stared at her.

"Yes, you do, but I really liked the old Allie. And frankly, I'm having problems with your new persona. What surprise is next? Let me guess. You'd like to try *acting*?"

"Not quite, but I do plan to write myself a part into *Temperatures Rising*. Sarah thought it was time that I act at least once in my life."

"Sarah said that, eh? Okay, so what role do you have in mind?"

"I'm a local teacher," described Cohen, "who eats at the diner regularly where you waitress. I'm crazy about you, but you're hot for Bates, so you just serve me my meal, take my tips, and never give me a second look. That will be my first and last acting job."

"Hmm, doesn't that scene occur right before the major sex scene with Peter?"

"Yes, Carole, I intend to be on the set so I can be there to help protect you." He put his hand to his mouth. *Oh shit*, he thought. *She's going to have a fucking field day with that answer.*

"Protect me?" She threw her hands up in the air. "You disrobe me on screen and have me grunt before millions of viewers, and now you want to protect me. Protect me from whom, Peter Bates, whom you're giving full license to my body?"

"I refuse to fight with you, Carole, and I don't think that my actions of late are either radical or out of character."

Let me retreat to my bunker to make beaucoup money, for I'm not going to make empty promises to change or insincere apologies for a later failure to do so. I know I'll make amends instead by performing multiple good deeds. I did inflict Peter Bates and an uncomfortably sexy role on her, so let me create a more middle-of-the-road project for her.

He input the eleven data threads into the screenplay software, and five minutes later, *A Majority of One* popped out, a sweet little film that originally starred Rosalind Russell and was one of Carole's favorite movies.

I know. I'll pair her with Japanese film star Toshiro Mifune in this nice, sweet dramedy. While I'm at it, let me create a balm for Sam too. I know he's shopping around for the perfect film to launch Myron's comeback.

Allie synthesized and printed out *Lost Weekend in Los Angeles* (*LWLA*), a thinly disguised Philip Marlowe–type detective and murder mystery set in LA's sex-for-hire industry.

LWLA contained just the right balance of lurid sex, violence, and suspense to propel Myron back on the sacred list of ten most bankable actors. Cohen's reworking of the *LWLA* script took only two hours, less time than he spent with Sam making changes that Minkowitz demanded.

That evening, at the weekly dinner, this time over Chinese food, Allie presented his two new concepts to Sam, Rose, and Carole, who were crazy about the projects. They devoured a very diverse and delicious pupu platter. Cohen felt good cheer from his quasi in-laws and knew it was time to break the news of *Temperatures Rising.* Rose and Sam listened while tearing away at their spareribs.

Allie's revelation shredded any positive feeling that Rose still had left for him. Cohen looked in Rose's eyes and swore that he saw daggers in her pupils.

He used to look adorable to me when I first met him. Rose simmered. *Now he doesn't even look cute anymore.*

Sam, the businessman, was a lot more interested. "Allie, a film can be hot without showing a lot of skin and sex."

"Sam," he urged, "it's an altered remake and must go as far as an R rating permits. I would even accept an NC-17 if necessary." Rose and Carole's jaws dropped.

"Allie, I smell box office smash."

Cohen watched Sam check out Rose's face, and what he saw told him to tone it down a lot.

"Allie, I push for a rough PG-13."

"What does that rating allow, Sam?"

"Well, not too much skin and a lot of off-camera heavy breathing."

Sam looked at Rose again—she had warning eyes.

"Nah, that won't work, Sam. To really click, we got to have some skin and body contact with a lot of on-camera heavy breathing."

The across-the-table bartering session bothered Carole and infuriated Rose, who voiced her displeasure.

"I can't believe that the two most important men in Carole's life are sitting right there and sexually exploiting her."

Sam and Allie let Rose vent her disgust and scheduled shooting to start the following week. The last great tests of co-living were coming.

Chapter 103

Carole got into the role but silently protested, *I know he's figured out by now that I'm not giving him any head until the film is done.*

On the day of the big sex scene, the director Hal Wilson closed the set to all except the most basic cast and crew members. Wilson, a profane but personable and humorous man, went over the script with Jed Kolko, his second assistant director.

"Jed, the scene calls for Peter and Carole to finally consummate the growing attraction between the handsome drifter and the unsatisfied wife. The repulsive old husband stands in the wife's way of having the drifter and diner all to herself. Hot illicit sex erupts in the diner's kitchen, where Peter forcibly undresses Carole and makes violent love to her on the countertop."

"I got it, Hal. I'll go show my assistant where to chalk the marks you want on the floor."

Allie drove his Bitter to the studio and up to Global's regular security guard, Georgia-born Enos "Fishhook" Shoob, who stood ready to wave a fellow Georgian through the gates. Enos, an avid fisherman, earned his nickname from applying the bait, cutting his fingers, and sporting big white bandages.

"Good to see you again, Allie." Enos teased, "Don't worry, ol' buddy, the Nobel people aren't here looking for you. Ha ha! Soundstage H is the third set on your left. Have a nice day."

"Thanks, Fishhook. I see you got a new bandage there. Be careful, and please give the missus my best."

Allie parked in front of the soundstage, entered, and was sent to the makeup room for preparation. He emerged a half hour later and sat down on a lunch counter stool a few feet from Hal.

782

"Allie, why are you here today?" Hal's face expressed surprise. "You aren't included in the filming today. Your scene and lines are scheduled for tomorrow. You could have stayed home and saved yourself a schlep down here."

"There's no way, Hal, that I can write a nude scene for my woman and not be there for her on the set."

Hal curiously looked at Allie as if he could use some consciousness raising.

"Big shit, my wife's an actress, and I twice directed her in sex scenes, once with Peter Bates too. Allie, please understand that Peter is going to put his hands all over Carole today and that she is going to act like she loves and craves it. This is a big part of film life today, and that's what the scene calls for."

"I understand, Hal, though I do admit to being a little uncomfortable."

Allie sat in a director's chair next to Wilson and stared straight ahead. The sudden sight of Peter's large member clued Cohen to Carole's reluctance to shoot a steamy sex scene with him.

If I am suddenly feeling lurid, what's it doing to her?

Cohen saw Bates put on a robe and walk toward his dressing room. He asked Hal if anything was wrong.

"Peter," Hal divulged, "has a boner and is trying to relax it."

Allie was not sure if Peter could, and he certainly did not want to hear what Hal said next.

"And with a fucking schlong like that, I'm telling you he's the real Johnny Wadd of Hollywood, not John Holmes. My guess is that he's had over six hundred women in just the past ten years alone, and I've probably directed about fifty of them."

Allie did not laugh and stared stonily ahead.

Hal directed Carole. "Darlene, I've dressed you in this ugly yellow chenille bathrobe to quietly dice vegetables for the diner and then have it easily fall off."

He turned to Bates. "Peter—excuse me, Mort, you enter the kitchen wearing your worn designer jeans and ripped new wave T-shirt. Follow your cues, and stare oozing lust at the sad, frustrated housewife, whose eyes drip sex and whose bikini panties are hot and wet for your manhood."

The crew laughed; Allie did not. Peter did it in one take, but Hal wasn't satisfied and asked him to act more aggressively. The thought of a second take annoyed Allie, still slightly freaked at watching Peter's hands all over Carole and her resultant enthusiasm.

"Okay, people, let's try this instead. An aroused Mort can't restrain himself and ravishes Darlene, who at first resists him by brandishing a butcher knife. Mort wraps a dish towel around his forearm and knocks the knife out of her hands. Okay, you two, let's see what we can do with this scene. We're close but not quite there yet."

Carole leaned against the sink.

"Okay, roll film. Darlene, you try to fight Mort off, but he opens your robe, revealing your naked breasts, and then Mort kisses your nipples."

Peter and Carole, Cohen uncomfortably thought, *don't seem to be acting. Does she really have to surrender her body to Bates so completely like that?*

Allie's face tightened as Hal directed Peter. "Mort, arouse her nipples with your tongue."

784

The cameraman moved in for a close-up to catch Carole's nipples extend; Peter sucked on her right one.

"Okay, Mort, remove Darlene's robe, leaving her in brief panties only. Good, now pick Darlene up and carry her over to the kitchen table. Yeah. Now shove your hand down her panties and simulate penetration."

Allie's face screwed up watching Peter stroke Carole's pubic hair and her move her hips erotically like he actually was fingering her and making her really hot and wet.

"Mort," Hal forcefully whispered, "drop those damn jeans and drawers, and get on Carole to fake intercourse. The audience, of course, has to think you guys are fucking like there's no tomorrow."

Cohen's face froze when Peter placed his nine-inch soft penis on Carole's belly just above the pubic hair line, perhaps an inch or two from penetration.

Hal micromanaged. "Okay, Mort, now for about ten to twenty seconds, I want you to move in a soft-core gyrating manner until I yell 'cut.' Darlene, pretend to receive him as if it were the best damn dick you've ever had in your life."

Peter and Carole laughed; Allie's face resembled marble. Hal and Allie watched Peter's penis grow harder from the up and down rubbing. After only about ten seconds, the director yelled *cut* before penetration occurred.

"Peter and Carole, two true professionals, both of you, extremely well done, and thank you very much."

Peter got down from the table with a foot-long erection that sucked the air out of the set. Allie rubbed his face with his hands and pondered the formerly unimaginable.

Has she and Peter become attracted to each other during filming because he's been putting his mitts all over her and she's enjoying it like those are mine? Is she punishing me by being so free in Peter's arms and hands?

Hal read Cohen's face and put an arm around his shoulder. "Don't take this personally. Carole and Peter did their jobs perfectly. The scene called for expression of sexual tension and satisfaction, and they delivered like pros. This movie is working. Hey, maybe you'll win an Oscar for Best Screenplay."

Cohen imagined his acceptance speech. *I want to thank my IBM mainframe for helping me thread together and polish a hybrid script in two hours and twenty minutes.*

Carole and Allie both acted like civil adults and never discussed the scene, but their relationship was never the same after that. Perhaps it was guilt on his part or her teaching him a lesson out of anger or disgust; it simply became a place they did not go.

As Allie suspected, twenty years later, in her best-selling memoir, Carole confessed to a short romance with Bates.

"During the filming of *Temperatures Rising*, Peter and I got turned on by all the simulated sex we were having on the set and did it every day for two weeks. He claimed to have fallen in love with me and proposed marriage. After the sex scene, he asked me to elope and run off to Tahiti or Australia with him.

"I was greatly flattered and actually considered it for a day or two. The sex with him was so good that Peter's attentions lifted me out of a funk that Allie had created. Although I developed affection for Bates during the filming, I gently declined his offer. I simply didn't love him enough but did come to really like him as a man and respect him as an artist. Over time, we have become very dear friends, and I would love to act with him again."

Carole, who also revealed her two-day fling with Georgie Tyler, rushed into shooting *A Majority of One* the day after finishing *Temperatures Rising*. The remake was completed in six weeks and well under budget, Hollywood's favorite kind of film, especially Sam's.

Allie pissed Carole off by taking a week to sail the Abaco Islands with Jay Dean and Allie's new accomplice Seth Lightman. Seth, a former student, was the son of a legendary Atlanta venture capitalist and one of very few students to become good friends with Allie. Cohen hired him to take some of the growing financial load off Sandy Forman and focus on revising stock and commodities trading algorithms and laundering profits.

Seth hacked into DARPA, the Pentagon's high technology research department, to obtain basic Internet protocols, the ground floor of cyberspace. Seth and Allie, at the forefront of venture capitalism for Internet development, moved audaciously into funding the development of desk top hardware and software.

Seth also learned from DARPA about the black Internet made up of untraceable servers that routed messages invisibly. Lightman created secret back channels for executing deals and moving money offshore to recently acquired private banks in the Caymans, the Bahamas, and Panama without leaving digital fingerprints of any kind.

Adonai and I understand it's a capitalist world and that Allie is trying to earn the people's exaltation to set the stage for awe. It's the prophet's growing number of tawdry financial practices and personal behavior that are causing us ever deeper concern.

Chapter 104

My friend Sophia Loren, thought Carole after production wrapped up, *confined herself to bed the last month of pregnancy to help ensure a safe birth, and it worked. Hopefully, it'll work for me too because I really want this baby. This could very well be my last pregnancy, and I want a third child.*

Allie kept a log of his Abacos sailing adventure and videotaped important discussions because it was a lot easier than taking notes.

Carole rested in bed while Jay and I and Seth and his beautiful girlfriend Lacy, who shunned clothes, sailed the northern Bahamian straits for a week. During breakfast on the second day out, I lit a joint and passed it around for inspiration.

While the crew toked and Seth recorded, Allie described a vision. "Yo, guys, I got this idea for an epic movie that guarantees at least two sequels. What do you think, over the next week, we flesh out and jot down all three plot treatments?"

"Allie," Seth reminded Cohen, "we're on vacation doing eyeball sailing, toking, and snorkeling, man. I'll get into this if we can limit work to two hours a day after breakfast and leave the rest for fun."

All agreed, and Allie jump-started the brainstorming session. "Dig it. *The Unbinding* describes how society falls apart with the story modeled on us. Four thirtyish urban dwellers innocently take a sailing trip, and a catastrophic nuclear war starts. Fortunately, they have a well-stocked, ocean-worthy craft and make a getaway to South America."

"Allie," claimed Jay, "you need a sexy element."

"Okay, Captain Jay, please imagine."

"How about a beautiful, sexy blond female friend who keeps coming out of her clothes sells off all our property to buy provisions and guns and links up with us on Grand Turk Island? Man, I always wanted to sail around there guys. That's why I'm writing it into the script. Ha ha! Anyway, we come across other similar groups with more hot women, redheads and brunettes also coming out of their clothes. This resistance forming fights their way down the Atlantic coast to Tierra del Fuego to start the world over again. You like?"

All three of them gave him the thumbs-up. "Yahoo, I tell you guys I was made for the goddamn movie business."

Allie praised Jay. "Yes, you were, Jay, and that's a perfect springboard for a sequel too."

Seth stood up to think; Jay recorded. "Okay, how about *The Unyielding* for the franchise? Tierra del Fuego becomes irradiated too, and we and other survivors battle atomic and other horrors across the heart of South America before fighting our way across the Pacific Ocean to safety in New Zealand or Australia."

"Seth," Lacy stated, "that's a very broad landscape to act out a script. Two remote continents to stage battles and stuff could be very expensive."

"Don't worry about it, sweetheart," Seth assured with a cool smile. "A guy I know pirated the latest special effects software from George Lucas and sold me a copy. With this package, we can create a big-movie feel for low-budget costs and never leave the soundstage. Imagine crossing *National Geographic* scenes of South America's physical wonders with battle scenes, the Pacific and Australia too."

Lacy stood up and put on microbikini jean shorts and a tight, ripped tank top.

"Sweetheart," Seth, puzzled, questioned, "you've been naked for three days. Why get dressed now, though the Who's song 'I Can See for Miles' comes to mind?"

Allie began recording Lacy, who cutely told Seth to shut up.

"I'm sorry, but I can't think without clothes on, and I have a terrific idea for the next sequel. Okay, the third one is *The Bequeathal.* The world begins to return to normal, and we slug our way back across the Pacific to regain Hawaii and onto mainland United States to help establish a new America. The emphasis should be on the regaining of Hawaii and rebuilding America part. Enough with the slugging-across-continents shit."

"Now I know, sweetheart," Seth complimented, "why you put all those clothes on, excellent finishing. Anyway, the three budgets should range between twenty million and forty million per film. Let's shoot sequentially, so we'll need only nine months to produce all three instead of three years. We can cut costs by another third if we shoot it on Paul Johnson's soundstage down in Wellington, New Zealand. I volunteer to produce it, if that's okay with everyone here."

Allie envisioned. "Seth, I like the idea of a sequential shooting plan. If we release the films four months apart, we could gross $1 to $1.5 billion in a year and a half. That translates into staying in the top five VCR rentals position for sixty or more straight weeks, which would be a film industry record."

Jay toasted. "Friends, we went on vacation and came back with a solid gold corporation. Yahoo!" They all joined in Jay's rebel yell.

In the final month of her most challenging pregnancy, Carole sat in bed alone and grew increasingly depressed.

Allie's not there for me anymore. The fucking Bahamas trip and his new trilogy project and now weekly visits to Atlanta are killing what's left of our relationship. The last Atlanta visit, he stayed five days. And when home, he rarely leaves his hub to hang with me in the bedroom. I've got a week to go, and I can't count on him anymore.

Allie felt Carole's alienation deepening. *Why is she so down on me? I'm just being myself, staying involved and productive. It's not neglect because I'm respecting her space and rest.*

Carole expected him to hold her hand during this whole scary time.

In contrast, Allie thought, *I need to step up my transactional pace to make up for lost time consumed by childbirth and rearing.*

Allie's last-minute transaction binge, in turn thought Carole, *is so incredibly selfish.*

I'm just being practical, thought Allie, *because unanticipated windfalls fell into my lap in a huge way.*

The gold rush has financially troubled Jeffrey Picker, the rock 'n' roll recycling king, who called on Cohen to bankroll his latest undertaking. For a change, Picker had a fresh idea; actually, his friend choreographer Earl Richards did and described it to Allie.

"Allie, we've observed rising patriotism in Reagan's America forming and developed the perfect act. Jeffrey and I recruited four sexy nineteen-year-old girls to form a singing group, American Beauties, a.k.a. AB. This nubile foursome includes a black bombshell of a lead singer and a buxom blond Jew who can ironically sing just like Carole Herman."

"'Sounds very interesting. What are the other two like?"

"The hottest," claimed Earl, "is a svelte dark Latina girl who can sing and dance her way into a man's heart. The coolest one is a pretty slim Asian with a cute figure and an outrageous deep bass voice. All four are beautiful and erotic and can sing like angels in the shower."

"I'm shaping an easy listening sound for them," Jeffrey added, "while Earl has whipped up a lavish stage show for presence, spectacle, and very soon Las Vegas."

AB took the country by storm, grossing forty-nine million in their first year and doubling that total the next. In a year, AB were fixtures of radio, TV, and Vegas and had a musical film franchise in the works.

Jeffrey finally scored a big recycling success with Tiger Bay, "TB," an English heavy metal rock band who'd recently been dropped by their record label. Cohen's bucks fired up the star-making machinery for the cheeky boys from Brighton, and within three months, the thirty-five-year-old heavy metal rogues once more filled up giant arenas with zonked-out suburban twelve-year-olds.

Allie funneled all his AB and TB profits into Sarah and Ari's growing private trusts because, when the EconProj scheme collapsed, he expected the government to come after him and put a tax lien on his assets.

Sandwiched between AB and TB was a mitzvah opportunity to do some good, a well-meaning deal but with a cruel and pathetic outcome. Cedric Miller, a wealthy South African entrepreneur and a friend of Cape Town's Jewish mayor—Sarah's uncle Saul on Harvey's side—called on Allie for an investment. Cedric—who owned vacation resorts in relatively prosperous South Africa, Botswana, and Namibia—presented his plan.

"Allie, I want to build a gambling resort in Ciskei, a newly created autonomous tribal homeland, two hours' drive from Johannesburg, South Africa's largest city and richest market. With $6 per capita income and 80 percent jobless rate and no mineral or agriculture assets either, the poor people of Ciskei really need your blessing and help."

"Holy shit, Cedric, they must be far and away the poorest people on earth."

"They are, and for that, I and the national government guarantee you a 100 percent return on your investment in five years and paid in gold too if so desired. Other assets are my political connections, and it has minimal capital and labor costs."

"Cedric, you want more than just money from me. Frankly, you're enlisting me to support the Afrikaner government that's oppressing the blacks you want to help."

"Allie, financial inputs from an eminent man like you will stamp moral certification on the project. Please be the first spark to get Ciskei going. Once accomplished, the international business community will follow suit."

"Cedric," Cohen reasoned with him, "you're making it sound like I can help a lot of poor people, make a fortune, and not risk a thing. You know damn well that Ciskei is an apartheid sham condemned by South Africa's black population and the global community. The UN just recently passed a disinvestment resolution, and not a single nation has recognized Ciskei to date. In fact, abolition and dissolution of this state is expected and soon."

"Fuck the UN resolution." Cedric calmed himself. "Allie, these are desperately poor people in need of your wealth you claim so ready to give, according to your foundation's mission statement. They need food, housing, medical care, and education, the most basic needs of human existence. Please make their wretched lives a little easier."

"Cedric, I get how poor they are, but you know it's not as simple as just writing a check. Ciskei is desperately poor because the national government herded them up, declared them an autonomous tribe—whatever that is—and marched them to the most worthless and desolate part of the country. Now you come to me to subsidize a racist policy that created this pathetic pseudostate. Sorry, the damned national government should pay for the problem they so readily created."

"The national government intended to, but the growing cost of the security threat posed by the African National Congress is forcing them to redirect resources, so please, Allie, a little constructive engagement, eh?"

"Cedric, constructive engagement on behalf of a destitute pseudostate risks pariah status for me. A global wave of condemnation will pour down on me, which I don't need. A failure to act, however, only renders me a fucking hypocrite. Sorry about putting it like that."

"You know, Allie," said Cedric as he stood up to leave. "You just turned your back on the poorest fucking people in the world. I think you'll always find a reason not to help. In fact, Cohen, you're full of shit."

"Cedric, please say hello to Uncle Saul for me the next time you see him, and don't let the fucking door hit you on the way out."

Cohen faced a no-win situation and had to do something. *I know I'll alleviate slum conditions in Tel Aviv and Jerusalem, a benevolent deed sure to bug no one.*

His massive cash infusion worsened Israel's fickle inflation rate; the vast neighborhood reclamation plans so overwhelmed the tiny nation's planners that they pleaded with him to do less.

Uncle Micha sent a telegram. "Allie, please forget building thirty thousand units. Do three hundred units."

Rudin pleaded to him in a handwritten letter for moderation. "Dr. Cohen, please reduce the scale and scope of helpfulness."

794

The Georgetown hub messaged Allie to sell off slumping oil stocks and buy soybeans and pork belly futures. OPEC was overproducing, and China's appetite for soy and meat was booming. Cohen did and gave the $430,000 profit to Rudin to pass on to his favorite Israeli charity, food banks.

Carole—by now three weeks late and terribly uncomfortable and extremely worried—sat, waited, and stewed. She saw Allie—when he was home—at some meals and when they went to sleep. She hardly ever entered the hub anymore to see what he was up to. Their conversation was tense and sporadic and their body language ice-cold.

Cohen, in his hub, felt pressure. *I have to do something good, especially after the Cedric Miller Ciskei disaster and Israeli housing fiasco. I know. I'll start a nonprofit alternative energy corporation called the People's Exploration, Distribution, and Conservation Organization (PEDCO). My aim is to weaken the market dominance of the seven sister oil companies starting with Exxon and Texaco.*

Yahweh and I strongly support Allie's energy initiative as a fine use for the great fortune he's accumulating. Hopefully, more poor people will have access to inexpensive oil and gas resources to protect them from the cold of winter and the fierce heat of summer.

Cohen's resolve to build his nonprofit was speedily tested when a significant volume of natural gas and sweet crude was struck at Gates, Wyoming, within the month. The oil industry companies held out fistfuls of money to buy him out of their business.

"Y'all can go to hell," he told them in his best southern accent.

He plunged ahead for maybe a week when he learned that AmerCorp lost $57 million the past twelve months and expected a similar amount of red ink for the next twelve.

Investors know that AmerCorp's old rust belt industries are being kept afloat by cash infusions from their rising service companies like the Sit-In. Man, I want to own my restaurants outright more than I want to build an energy company.

The seven sister oil companies valued Cohen's new gas and oil holdings at over $1 billion and offered a $200 million premium for PEDCO to get Cohen out of their industry. A $1.2 billion check from the American Petroleum Institute was more than enough for Cohen to gain control of AmerCorp and own his restaurants outright again.

In a chesslike move, Allie paid $608 million to buy the board of directors two million shares and a dominant ownership block. AmerCorp's directors gladly took his money, resigned their positions, and left very rich and happy men.

Cohen was the new owner of America's 474th largest corporation; it controlled the fate of seventeen thousand employees in forty-one states and thirteen countries.

Thirty percent were no longer needed, so Allie liquidated three money-losing old divisions, which earned him a $112 million tax credit. These big moves, he estimated, resulted in his net worth doubling to almost $2 billion in assets.

Cohen's first move was to hire a big headhunting firm to oversee the massive job placement program. A financial news reporter asked him if it was worth $46 million to find workers positions within the AlCoAmerCorp business empire or award them very generous early retirement buyouts.

"It was worth every penny because no one called me a capitalist pig. I tried to be fair to everyone involved, and I think I achieved it."

Yes, but you are not doing enough for the poor, and the patience of Hashem and I is nearly gone.

Chapter 105

Carole still sat, five weeks late, and called Dr. Green, who assured her that if nothing happened in the next day or two, he'd induce labor. She kept asking herself why she was still carrying. Could it even keep them together anymore? Allie was transfixed in his hub, making money, and had spent less than forty-eight hours with her over the past thirty-five days, and she hated him for it.

Water gushed out of her. *Thank god my water has broken.*

She walked, actually waddled over, to Allie's hub to tell him. *Shit, he's watching a porno flick that one of his satellite dishes must have picked up. 'Looks and sounds like it's from Thailand. Christ, my baby's practically fallen out of me. We have to hurry.*

"Allie!" she yelled. "My water's broken, and you have to drive me to the hospital!"

He didn't hear her, so she walked a few steps closer to get a better look and caught him masturbating. That did it; she lost it and took her shoe off and threw it at him.

Good, she thought. *The fucking moccasin bounced off his hard head.*

"Fuck!" he yelled as he stood up and looked at her. "Damn, that hurt like hell. Why'd you do that?"

She ignored him and huffily urged, "Allie, my water has broken, and we have to go to the hospital now."

Allie quickly rose to help her out of the house and into the car and said he was sorry for being too into himself. He burned rubber out of the driveway, roared through the streets to the hospital, and stopped the Bitter in front of the entrance.

797

"Oh shit." He cursed as he got out of the Bitter and saw it belching blue smoke from its dual exhausts. Allie left the car running to get a wheelchair sitting empty a few feet away. Cohen sat Carole down in it, and he pushed her into the emergency room to start the admission process and then ran back out to park the car.

He watched in horror as flames shot out of the Bitter's engine, and the car was about to explode any second.

Dammit, I'm witnessing the most beautiful car I've ever owned blow up and burn right in front of me. I worry that the child Carole is carrying may be in trouble, and this could be an omen.

I transformed myself in to an elderly Jewish man who happened to walk out of the hospital and view the burning car.

"Ah," I said to Allie. "It's Tisha B'Av, the most calamitous day in Jewish history. A burning car is not a good sign."

Allie looked at me very sadly and affirmed, "I agree, sir, and am preparing for the absolute worst."

A fire engine pulled into the hospital entrance to control the fire. Allie remembered Carole, ran to the obstetrics section, and saw a solemn-looking Dr. Green.

"Doc," Allie anxiously asked Simon, "is everything okay with Carole and the baby?"

Green looked down while updating Cohen on the situation. "I'm preparing Carole for an immediate C-section. The baby's in terrible trouble and may already be dead. The fetus may have become strangled in its umbilical cord."

Cohen's heart sank, and he tried to fathom the Lord taking a second son from him at birth. *Why, benevolent One? Is this punishment for some past misdeed or just another act of nature again?*

No, Allie. Adonai and I believe that your mission with the angel Carole is over. It is time for Carole to return to her Hollywood life and Malibu world and, prophet, you to your family and get back on track for direct action only. Hashem foresaw that the prophet should not be bound with child out of wedlock, for if the time of exaltation and awe come, he must be as worthy of redemption as the people.

After ten of the longest minutes of his life, Allie felt a hand tap his shoulder from behind, and he turned to look Green in the eye.

"Doc, I've seen that dejected look before. The baby didn't make it, did it?"

"No, Allie. I prayed for a miracle, but God didn't answer me. Carole thankfully is fine and doing well."

I will not curse the Lord, thought Cohen, *and will even thank Yahweh for one small favor. Simon is not saying, "You guys are young. You'll try again. You'll see."*

Green watched Allie walk toward an exit door and asked him where he was going.

"To punch that fucking door, Doc. It's a tradition, and if I still had a Polaroid OneStep, I'd smash that next."

Allie lived up to his tradition by punching the broom closet door twice. He broke his hand with the second shot and collapsed to the floor and cried. Green helped Allie up, put his arm around his shoulder, and admitted him to a private room. Simon assisted the attending doctor in treating Cohen's hand and administered a sedative that induced sleep.

The next morning, Sarah Cohen opened the refrigerator. *Uh-oh, the only thing to eat is eggs, and who knows how fresh these four are?*

Aretha was in Alabama taking care of a sick sister and her young family, so Sarah was making breakfast for a change.

Since it looked like rain outside, she turned on the news for a weather report. CBS's Maria Shriver told of still another Beirut bombing while Sarah dropped a pat of butter into a skillet. Shriver's next news item wrenched Sarah's attention away from the cracking of eggs toward the crack-up of two celebrities' lives.

"I have sad news to report out of Malibu this morning. The expectant child of movie actress Carole Herman and novelist mogul Allie Cohen died in its mother's womb. Ms. Herman is recovering nicely and will begin work on a new movie next month. However, rumors circulating around Hollywood have it that the singer and the remote Nobel Prize winner will soon separate.

"In South Africa today—"

Sarah switched off the TV set and the stove and slumped down in the kitchen booth. She buried her face in her arms and felt Allie's grief. A few seconds passed before she looked up and saw Ari sitting down next to her.

"Are you okay, Mommy?"

"Yes, Mookie, but you won't be going to nursery school this morning."

"Why, Mommy?"

"Because, Mookie"—Sarah kissed his cheek and explained while getting up to pack—"we're flying to California today to visit your father. We'll have our breakfast in the airport. The plane will feed us too."

"Mommy, I can't wait to see Daddy. I really miss him."

"Me too, Ari, me too."

800

Chapter 106

Allie came to, opened his eyes, and discovered Sarah and Ari standing before him. *Am I dreaming? Nah, it really is my wonderful wife and son. Thank you, Lord.*

He held up his cast, displayed it like a badge of adversity, and explained to them, "Dr. Green thinks I punish myself for absolution from blame. Who knows? Both of you, please come here."

They did their family group hug, and Allie kissed Ari on each cheek and then held him in his arms. Sarah stroked his hair while feeling his pain; it was her pain too. Sarah's heart also broke for Carole, for she knew that terrible sorrow all too well.

"Sarah, did the Lord punish me again?"

"It's not your fault, Allie. We learned that the hard way, and we just learned it again."

Ari, now twenty months old, had grown from an infant into a little boy. He'd slimmed down a bit and showed his dad how fast he could run by doing short sprints across the hospital room.

"Sarah, I'm amazed by how Ari is already placing the noun before the verb and direct object and speaking in relatively complete sentences."

"I predict that Ari will be reading before he's three. Our son is brilliant, Allie. Some might say he's precocious even, but I prefer to view him as a normal child with acute giftedness in up to three areas—language, music, and athleticism."

Carole's nurse just happened to walk by and see that Allie was up, and she headed straight to her patient's room to tell her.

Carole had been up much of the night, thinking over her future with Allie and decided that she still loved him. If he'd stop the saving-the-world gig and returned to writing and business, she'd let things be. *I can live with the LA-Atlanta triangle,* she reasoned, *and have an itch to take another trip for Reagan before he leaves office, preferably to a warm, pretty, and safe place like Australia and New Zealand.*

Carole—hoping that they might marry in middle age after Ari went off to college, own homes in several countries, and spend specific seasons of the year in each—impulsively got out of bed and wheeled herself over to Allie's room to present her plan. She rolled up to the open door and saw Allie, Sarah, and Ari in a group hug.

Oh dear, look at Ari hug his daddy so tightly. He obviously needs his father for more than a couple of days a week.

At that moment, Ari put his arms around Allie's neck and said, "I love you, Daddy. I miss you so much. Can't you come home with us?"

Carole openly cried. *Ari needs his daddy full time. My plan is selfish and wrong, and it's time to say goodbye.* She put her wheelchair in reverse and scooted back to her room. After a long cry, she composed a tender goodbye letter.

Dear Allie,

Our beings can never fully be one, and we must separate for our own good or risk destroying our special love and time together.

Allie, I will never forget you. You fulfilled me more in our short time together than any other man in my life.

Take care, my love. Stay in touch. Maybe we can do a joint project sometime in the future. If I can ever help in any way, please feel free to call on me.

Love always,
Carole

Carole gave the note to her nurse. "Please deliver it to Dr. Cohen. Thank you."

The nurse handed the sealed envelope to Allie, smiled, and left the room. Cohen opened the envelope and read the enclosed note. Sarah watched Allie closely as he comprehended it. He handed the note to Sarah and buried his head in his arms while she read it. Sarah finished and looked up when she was done.

"Is this what you want, Allie?"

"Yes, Sarah. Carole and I shared a great partnership, but the mission with her is over. You are the only angel in my life now, and it's time to come home to you and Ari, that is, money, if you'll have me. I love you, money, and want to be with you and only you from here on out."

Sarah called for group family hug. "Welcome home, Allie. It's good to have you back, right, Ari?"

"Right, Mommy. Daddy, you and I can play baseball. I can hit now. Grandpa taught me yesterday. I lined it off his head, and he fell down."

"Ari, oh, how I would have loved to see you blast a Wiffle ball off Grandpa's hard head." They all laughed. "Son, I plan to cut down a broomstick and teach you stickball. Ari, if you can hit a pink bouncer with a broomstick at two, you'll be able to hit with anything after that."

Allie touched Sarah's face. "You've dealt with a lot these past three years, babe, and you're still prettier than the day I met you."

Sarah smiled appreciatively. "I admit to being a hell of a lot smarter for sure. While we all have lived very large lives these past few years, there's a hole in my heart that can only be filled by going home with my husband and son."

Allie called for another group hug. Sarah asked, "Does Atlanta still feel like home to you, Allie?"

"Yes, to a point, though I sense we should give New York a try for a while. I need to get the Big Apple out of my system. Just as I was getting a foothold there, I had to leave. And since then, I've always wanted to live in the city for more than two months."

"I think New York is a great idea, Allie. I too never got the chance to live in Manhattan as an adult and would like to experience that."

"What would you prefer, Sarah, a Fifth Avenue penthouse overlooking Central Park or an Upper East Side brownstone?"

"That's easy, Allie. After loving Atlanta's being so green, the Central Park penthouse is a no-brainer."

If asked, Cohen would plead guilty to a past history of abrupt departures and was about to meet with the man whom he depended on most for tidying up virtually every one of his loose ends in LA. Sam Minkowitz arrived first and directed a waiter to move the table and chairs out to the pool. It was a typically sunny day in LA, and Sam wanted to enjoy some rays on his face.

Cohen arrived ten minutes later. "Sorry, Sam, I ran into traffic jam."

Sam hated to waste ten minutes and got right down to business. "So, Allie, how long do I have to wait before AlCoAmerCorp takes over Global?"

I have to show Sam that I truly appreciate all that he's done for me and only want peace and friendship with him.

Allie smiled before asking Sam how he was.

"I'd be a lot better off, Allie, if you'd tell me that I won't have to fend off a wasteful takeover attempt. Global is noticing a familiar pattern of stock purchases and sell-offs. We're becoming undervalued, and you're now our largest stockholder. Well, imagine that."

"Doesn't my investment in your company, Sam, show confidence in present management to make substantial profits?"

"Come on, Allie, cut the bullshit. Your independent production companies have more projects in the works than Global. Sandy, you, Seth, and now Jay, Lacy, and Mike Schwartz create, produce, and finance your own properties. That reduces our role to basically a releasing agency and distributorship. The probable next step is to grab the whole package and cut us out entirely."

Cohen aimed to show Minkowitz his due respect.

"Sam, you were a life changer for me, and I want to pay you back for all that you did. Yes, I do plan to take over Global, but I want to give you a $50 million bonus for letting me do so without a stupid fight. You've been that good to me, and I love you."

Sam smiled and then teared up. "You've become a mensch, Allie." He wiped tears from both eyes. "You've learned everything I taught you, and I love you for it."

"Sam, you've been like a father to me and want you to run Global independently for as long as you desire or remain healthy.

Thank the Lord. May we continue to engage in numerous fun projects and interesting good works."

Sam hugged Allie. "I love the deal. It relieves me of all stockholder pressures, my biggest pain in the ass. Now I can finally just make pictures again, beautiful."

"I'm glad that you're happy, Sam."

"Fifty million too, Allie, real fuck-you money. You have learned the art of the deal so well that it is my pleasure to help you finish up all your projects in good fashion."

"Thank you very much, Sam."

Sam referred to one last sore point between them. "You know, Allie, you're returning to your family, and Carole is alone. I always doubted that you would break your tie with your Atlanta family."

"Please understand, Sam. I'm thrilled for these years with Carole. She was one of my two best friends, my better half when I was with her, and she made a better man out of me. I will always love her for that."

"Well said, Allie."

"And I treasured these years with you and Rose. You guys have been family to me, and I also love y'all for it."

"Thank you, Allie. What do you think Carole should do?"

"I hope she gets back with Myron. You gave him a three-picture deal at $2 million per and three points to help that along, and I think it will work." Cohen winked at Minkowitz.

Sam's mouth opened wide. "How'd you learn that? Carole doesn't even know it."

"Let's just say that . . . I took an interest in you, Sam."

Minkowitz cracked up laughing. "Her getting back with Myron would be good for Carole's kids, Sam. He can also give her stability, after his divorce, of course."

"I got to give you credit, Allie. You're trying to make amends as best as you can, and you've done a good job. Now you move to New York and heal your family. We'll be okay out here. This new conglomerate should have such awesome market power that I'll be real surprised if the Antitrust Division approves it."

The merger will be approved, Sam, but it will not bring new market advantages, only unpleasant challenges and many of them. The prophet's corporate reckoning is coming but not quite yet.

Chapter 107

During Cohen's ten years of living in Atlanta, he recalled hearing many ex–New Yorkers sing the same old siren song.

"I love New York but could never return there, at least not right now. My career has advanced more rapidly in Atlanta than expected, and I'm living much too comfortably to go from four rooms back to two rooms. But if I somehow became incredibly rich, I would then consider moving back because it takes a lot more money to live well in New York than it does in Atlanta."

Cohen said that too, and now he was doing New York on his terms and not the dreadnought of a city that previously sank him. Billy Diamond vacated Carole's penthouse to make movies in Europe for a few years, so the Cohen family leased the four-bedroom, three-bath penthouse that came with a four-hundred-and-fifty-square-foot terrace and a clear view of the park. Central Park, right across Fifth Avenue, became Ari's playground.

Aretha's sister and family relocated to Jacksonville, Florida, so she followed them and retired near the beach. Allie expressed his gratitude by paying off her mortgage so she could live comfortably for the rest of her life. Ari cried when he said goodbye to the warm, kind woman who'd been such a big part of his childhood. Allie had to pull him away from Aretha; his little arms did not want to let go of her.

The Cohen family enjoyed waves of visiting family and friends who helped them discover the city's best restaurants. With Billy Diamond in Europe filming, Allie and Sarah joined the comedian's tableful of friends who met regularly at Elaine's.

New York Post journalists began reporting New York's newest celebrities' every appearance; coverage soon graduated to stalking. *Post* reporters' audacity caused Cohen to lose his cool twice, and it would have been more, but the resultant bad publicity was usually a worse outcome.

The new AlCoGlobalCorp multinational conglomerate consolidated eighteen divisions with total staff numbering thirty-seven-hundred employees in a forty-story office tower bordering Park Avenue and Fifty-Second Street. Allie reigned over the entire top of a pleasure palace that included a boccie court and pool table.

Stanley Joffre and Marvin Wilensky, Global's division chief operations officers, occupied the thirty-eighth floor. Sandy Forman headed all AlCoAmerCorp enterprises and was sandwiched between Cohen and Joffre and Wilensky to act as Allie's main gatekeeper.

At first, Allie loved to peer out his floor-to-ceiling window from his prized perch high above the city; but within a few months, all joy disappeared from his corporate kingdom, and he and Sandy turned to each other for help with a growing storm.

"Allie," Sandy reminded him, "I told you on the way home from Sweden that accelerated growth accelerated problems. A backlog of almost three dozen projects is squeezing the three hundred high-priced employees I hired just last month.

"I'm sorry, Sandy. The ideas came so fast, and you have to act, or they're lost."

"Okay, I'll give you that, but the one thing we didn't see coming was this sudden decline in box office receipts that's caused a severe profit slump. Wall Street is punishing us with lowered stock values and issuing financial reports that investor confidence is eroding. This giant eruption of legal claims from the two assholes two floors below undermines our ability to solve any of our problems."

Allie poured two Scotch on the rocks for them. He sighed. "Sandy, I loved building this incredible empire, but our past informal management style is a distant memory. Crisis management has become our daily grind, and it's fucking awful, man."

"I know, Allie. We built AlCoGlobalCorp into the greatest money-making machine in history. We own the best damn restaurant chain in the country and made some really great movies, TV shows, and music. Now it's simply a giant pain in the ass to run."

They looked at each other's miserable faces in a floor-length mirror and chose to laugh instead of cry.

"Sorry, man." Sandy summed it up. "I wish I could tell you that I have short- and long-term fixes, Allie, but I don't."

They downed their Scotches and went to a nearby steakhouse for dinner and more Scotch. Sandy and Allie sat at the bar and watched a financial news report on the TV. A Wall Street reporter who never owned or built a successful company wisecracked in prime time. "AlCoGlobalCorp is suddenly a Misfortune 500 company."

If that wasn't bad enough, the reporter's twenty-three-year-old female sidekick rubbed it in with "Does Alco tell Global? The company's left and right hands are at each other's throats. No company in that shape can boldly or nimbly respond to today's demanding marketplace realities."

Sandy and Allie again looked at each other and thought; *Man, we are in big fucking trouble.*

Cohen remembered something. "Harland Cooper was right about money getting in the way of doing good. Looking back, I guess I should have kept speaking out instead of making money."

Hashem and I are pleased that you understand, Allie, that your time in business is ending, even if you were the richest man in the world. But you aren't and won't be, so feel proud that you and Sandy have been fabulously successful and have accumulated the necessary resources for the challenges ahead.

Corporate dissension intensified while Sandy sparred with Joffre and Wilensky to ease the growing pressure on Allie. Tempers invariably flared at meetings, so expensive hordes of lawyers soon communicated for them. Allie appealed to Sam for help in dealing with his two Global division nemeses.

"I wish I could help you, Allie, but I have no control whatsoever over them. Joffre and Wilensky are major stockholders, their combined shares exceed mine, and they often block me from acting too. Their fathers and I started out as agents together and formed our own agency—Minkowitz, Joffre, and Wilensky. We did well, it grew into GMEI, and the rest is showbiz history."

"You started as an agent, Sam?"

"Allie, most suits started as agents. Anyway, I loved Wilensky and Joffre seniors like brothers. I was blessed to have them as partners and friends. Both were very smart and true gentlemen. Arguably, the two nicest guys in Hollywood both amazingly raised the most arrogant and mean little sons of bitches that make you want to punch their fucking faces in. Go and figure because I fucking can't."

"You almost never curse or get angry like that, Sam. I don't think I ever heard you say the word *fuck* before. You command such authority and respect that you don't need to enhance what you say by cursing."

"Thank you, Allie. I know, and that should tell you even more about them."

"How's Carole doing?"

"She's back with Myron. The children are very happy about it too. I think Carole finally has true stability for the first time in her life."

"I'm very glad to hear that, Sam. In fact, it made my day. Please give them my love, and all the best to you and Rose."

Jay Dean called the next morning with jarring but not unexpected news.

"Allie, I had to permanently close down the inside-the-CIA scam. One contact is a dying alcoholic. The other ran off to Brazil, which has no extradition treaty with the United States. The three insiders colluded against you to rip us off for almost $200 million."

Cohen felt a knot tighten in his stomach. "Jay, we've evaded taxes on a massive scale. That means we're powerless to move against them and leaves me no choice but to absorb the loss and grin and bear it."

Cohen hung up the phone and assessed his current net worth. Although net holdings were still about $1.5 billion, AlCoGlobalCorp's financial arteries were hardening fast and asset values eroding. Allie thought of *Pogo* and the old Walt Kelly cartoon strip's famous line about who the enemy often is.

"We have met the enemy, and he is us."

Sandy and Allie prudently called in an outside management team for a secret audit and survival impact study. Ninety days later, IMI & Associates completed their evaluation.

"AlCoGlobalCorp is a relatively solid, if temporarily unhealthy, company. Strengths are sizable assets, enormous economic reach, and exceptional diversification. Although the conglomerate is in absolutely no danger of going under and is practically unsinkable, AlCoGlobalCorp will probably experience five to ten years of limited growth because of an insanely hostile and divided group of executive officers."

Chapter 108

Forman and Cohen agreed with the report; Sandy then advised, "We know that we cannot endure a decade of frustration and aggravation. Let's ask IMI what we should do."

The three IMI consultants conferred for ninety seconds and recommended a simple plan.

"If you can't hack it, take the money and run, for Dr. Cohen about $1.3 billion, Mr. Forman around $565 million. And, gentlemen, please complete your sell-offs soon before stock values further decline."

Forman and Cohen started selling off small blocks of stock to liquidate their holdings over a nine-month period so as not to destabilize the company.

"I'm worried," Allie complained to Sandy, "about possible depression overtaking me. New York is also starting to bother me. The regulars at Elaine's suddenly seem like a garish tribe of obsessive-compulsive egotists."

Sarah, Ari, and Allie began escaping the city's pressures by spending weekends at a rented Fire Island beach house. The quiet off-season walks along the ocean's edge with Sarah and Ari helped him cultivate an inner peace of sorts. Gradually, the short getaways evolved into minivacations. As the weeks turned into months, Cohen stopped coming in on Monday and then Tuesday. Sandy loyally covered for him and increasingly served as stand-in CEO.

With the coming of spring, Allie showed up on Wednesdays only, a ten-to-four stretch that was at best bearable. Corporate ballbusters Joffre and Wilensky chafed over Cohen's laxity and pushed for his removal. The two vultures taped Allie's pleas for cooperation and understanding as evidence of unfitness, but Sandy and his high-powered team of lawyers managed to fend them off.

Allie received a $3 million offer from the Andersen Press to write his autobiography, but the project had to be shelved. He plainly lacked the serenity needed to sort his life out, for his perspective was dim and priorities confused. The river of desperation finally overwhelmed Cohen, and he retreated into literature to seek answers.

Let me reexamine T. S. Eliot in a hope that the poet might yield some insights and relieve my drowning sensation. I imagine an English professor quoting to a freshman literature course one of these days, 'Mistah Cohen, he dead, a penny for the old guy.

Allie read and reread *The Hollow Men* and discovered that he was indeed a stuffed man and had a headpiece filled with straw. Four lines from *The Love Song of J. Alfred Prufrock* held out some clues.

I am no prophet—and here's no great matter;

I have seen the moment of my greatness flicker,

And I have seen the eternal Footman hold my coat, and snicker,

And in short, I was afraid.

Cohen was not really afraid, though, for he feared no man. At times, however, he did fear the Lord but when he usually needed Him. The eternal Footman did take two sons from Cohen at birth. Cohen had sworn to the Redeemer at the Wailing Wall that he would obey the Almighty's ways and receive the love of Adonai into his heart. In truth, he rejected traditional Judaism and always made excuses.

"Am I rudely defying the Lord?" he questioned. "Or do I defer completely to Yahweh and practice a Judaic lifestyle as my answer? If so, why am I unable to cross that threshold and embrace religion?"

Plagued with doubt, Cohen sensed he first needed answers about reality more than faith and met with Dr. Ruben Engel, a psychoanalyst.

Engle's first question was "Allie, do you ever feel a need to cheat on your wife?"

"Not really, Doc, but I have, despite our sex life being very satisfying. I'm a Chazer. I had to have more even though I already had the best, but what to do you do, Doc, when beautiful, sexy women literally fall into your arms or penis?"

"Ha ha! Cute. Do you have any trouble communicating?"

"No, Doc, I tell her anything and everything."

"And it's obvious that you still love her very much?"

"Yes, Sarah is a blessing, and Ari is a fantastic little boy. I guess that I am a very lucky man in that respect."

"Then you just feel empty?" The doctor nodded sympathetically.

"Yes, that's right."

Cohen met with Engel twice a week for a month and began what became their last session by delving into Allie's feelings about living in New York.

"In my heart and soul, Doc, New York is a home of sorts, and I'm one of the lucky few to deal with the city on my own terms. But lately, New York's been bugging me. Do you think I should move?"

"Allie," Engel revealed, "your problem is not one of geography. Your malaise is a spiritual crisis caused by dissatisfaction with your values."

"So you're saying, Doc, that New York is not my problem?"

"No, in fact, if you moved to Jerusalem tomorrow, it wouldn't change a thing. The answer to your problem lies within you, and to be really honest with you, I can't help you anymore either."

"Gee, Doc," Cohen quipped, "I must be really fucked up if you're that willing to give up two hundred bucks an hour."

Engel did not laugh. "I'll pretend I didn't hear that remark. Seriously, Allie, as far as I can tell, you're not suffering from any acute emotional or mental problem. Christ, you're not even anxiety ridden. In fact, everyone in New York should be as relaxed as you are."

"Then what the hell's wrong with me, Doc?"

"Allie, this may sound a little strange coming from the epitome of a so-called secular humanist, but I think you'd be better off seeking the counsel of a rabbi."

"Why, what for, Doc?"

"I believe you are seeking God, Allie, yet you view faith as a sign of personal weakness rather than a source of strength and divine inspiration."

"Then you're telling me, Doc, that unless I become religious, I'm probably doomed to feeling empty and miserable."

"Yes, I'm afraid so, Allie."

"But I'm not religious, Doc. In fact, I'm irreverent."

"Yes." Engel shook his finger at Cohen to drive home his point. "That's the crux of your problem and, pardon the symbolism, your cross to bear."

He jabbed his finger forward with each word. "Mr. Iconoclast, you're irreverent and need to become religious."

Dr. Engel rocked Allie with the heaviest revelation of his life. Shaken, Cohen spent the next two hours wandering through Central Park, seeking truth and the way.

Lord, must I integrate Orthodox Judaism into a lean lifestyle to feel spiritually whole? Did I not place enough shekels into the collection plate for an exemption?

No, Allie, you won't receive any exemption because you did not do enough good deeds when you had the chance.

Central Park was devoid of answers, so he wearily returned to the office to ponder his fate. In his quest for meaning, he searched the late afternoon sky for a righteous disclosure. On the wings of hope and a prayer, a little light was shed.

I acknowledge that I've lived a life of indulgence and taking and merely talked a lot about wonderful humanitarian acts of charity. The worst example was PEDCO, which I sold to buy AmerCorp. Another was my not always doing right by the people who loved me. Am I a sham? A real shit? I mean, well, I swear that I do.

Cohen looked out his large window and saw an ethereal cloudlike form rumble across Times Square. He stood in awe at the swirling gray mass of light and darkness that swerved over Rockefeller Center and headed straight toward the slender and illuminated AlCoGlobalCorp Tower.

The formless, swarming mass stopped short of Allie's window, and he beheld a force greater than anything he'd ever seen before. The force pierced the sky with short bursts of blue, white, and yellow lightning bolts, followed by a rolling thunder that shook Manhattan's east side like an earthquake in the air.

817

Am I experiencing a nervous breakdown, Cohen wondered, *or hallucinating from an acid flashback?*

The omnipotent whipping shroud enveloped Cohen's tower and shook it. Allie's legs jellied, and he was made to feel a pitiable wretch. Cohen sat down and closed his eyes. "I humbly obey and exalt, oh awesome force."

A Sinaiesque sermon on Cohen's mount pummeled his soul. A supernal ray of light streamed a harsh candor that flushed him of false pride, immorality, and immaturity. Allie vowed to the force, which now appeared as a swirling shroud of energy and light, "I will swear off swinish behaviors and yearn to be reborn." Allie listened with eyes shut and in total devotion. "I am ready to die or be transformed."

The all-knowing Voice, Hashem, commanded unto Cohen, "Repent, arrogant one, and take upon yourself the ways of the Lord, and be blessed with sanctification. Depart from your wicked and materialistic ways, and if you follow, wisdom may be imparted."

"I'm sorry, Lord, and I promise to do better."

"Fill your mind with truth, Allie, your heart with justice, your soul with honor and commitment. Contentment will be yours, I promise."

"The Lord is speaking to me, showing me the way, preparing me for a greater purpose."

"Surely, you know that the Almighty's consent demands your obedience to My commandments, to the prayerful observance of My book, to the study of My Torah and Talmud. If you keep faith, Allie, I will lead you out of the valley of darkness and into the light of day."

Allie bowed his head. "I realize that more is yet demanded of me and that I will hear my life revealed to me."

"Allie, you were not content to be a fine teacher or a gifted writer of words. No, not fame or riches satisfied your boundless greed and lust. You were the counsel of great men and afforded a worldly impact, but you chose to strive for the damnable goal of ill-gotten riches and power."

Allie humbly nodded and put his hands over his face. He felt shame and begged to be forgiven and saved.

"Live righteously and hallow yourself by worshipping the Creator, and the meaning of life shall be no more mysterious than the way of Adonai. Consecrate your tabernacle, make the hearth holy, and respect the Sabbath Day."

"I stand before You, Yahweh, on the threshold of transformation."

"You are redeemed and forgiven by Me, but I suffer no fools. A relapse on your part will test My trust."

"I understand, eternal One, and promise to be worthy of Your trust."

"The time of exaltation will not be fulfilled by half of the planet, yet the time of awe will soon be upon us. I doubt, Allie, that the woeful people will shape up and bestow the claim of prophecy upon you, but we shall see about that. The Redeemer, in the meantime, instructs you to go forth and be holy and seek My blessing."

Allie awoke to a headache and the darkness of night descending on the Midtown Manhattan skyline.

He rose slowly from his chair and pledged, "I shall go into the world and live according to the gospel as delivered unto me by the holy One, blessed be He."

Cohen quietly walked through the outer office to the elevator.

819

Sally Woods, his secretary, commented, "This strange storm, Mr. Cohen, is finally subsiding. I never saw weather like this before, all wild lightning and crazy thunder with no rain, a lot of sound and fury signifying nothing."

Wrong Sally, it was terribly significant.

Sally noticed Allie's ashen color. "Mr. Cohen, is everything okay?"

He nodded and answered, "I'm fine, Sally."

"Would you like me to call Mrs. Cohen and tell her that you are on your way home?"

"Yes, that would be very thoughtful of you, Sally. And while you're at it, please call Mr. Forman too."

"Sure, what's the message?"

"Tell him to buy the Peachtree Plaza Hotel in Downtown Atlanta and sell this building. I will join him in negotiations with Mr. Portman on financial terms."

"Mr. Cohen, are you serious?" Sally, stunned by his request, looked ashen in color too.

"Yes, Sally, I'm very serious. My family and I are moving to Atlanta, and we don't have any place to stay. The hotel looks like a welcoming big mezuzah."

Allie took out a handkerchief, covered his head, and forever left the AlCoGlobalCorp Tower and its accordant lifestyle behind him.

"Lord, I finally get it that a person does not have to be a nebbish to be religious."

- Mezuzah – religious object fastened to a door with a holy message on a parchment stuffed inside.

- Nebbish – bloodless, nerd, follower

Book III

"Those who are holy shall praise *Thee* every day."

Third Benediction—Holiness

Chapter 109

Five years have passed since Adonai and I teamed Allie Cohen with Carole Herman to realize the prophet's beholding. Allie no longer split time with his family and Atlanta, for he has returned home to be holy and a loving husband and father.

The Creator's plan for Cohen, beheld by the world as a man of peace, is to lead the people down the pathway to mutual respect, cooperation, and prosperity—the genesis of the prophet's exalting. If humankind manages to get it right—Yahweh and I are nearly convinced that about half the earth is a basket of deplorables and won't—there will be a global manifestation of awe from witnessing the prophet's genius and light.

Hashem's Einstein of human relations teachings said a prayer for a safe landing as the Cohen family's private jet set down at Peachtree DeKalb Airport, where a limo met and ferried them downtown.

I am returning to Atlanta to establish an honest relationship with my Lord and finally tame my Chazer appetites. This may be easier to accomplish in a city where people talk more softly, dress more conservatively, and have shorter emotional ranges. I will await a message from the Almighty for direction and purpose. An inner proximal compass will direct me toward salvation and contentment.

The limo pulled off the South Freeway and onto International Boulevard and cruised up the hill to the Peachtree Summit. The management and half of the workers of the world's tallest hotel waited at the entrance to greet their new boss and famous occupants.

Sarah and Allie looked into the eyes of every staff member, asked for and repeated their names to memorize it, and then asked each person what their job was, all the time smiling at their hired help. The mostly black staff appreciated the Cohen family's manner

825

and interest and began working hard to please them with many assorted attentions and favors.

"Man, the Cohen family," a young male desk clerk joked, "just turned this cold, stiff tower into the world's tallest family inn."

Allie raised his salary to incentivize the staff to be humorous, for laughter generated warmth, comfort, and happiness. The friendly staff became a surrogate family for the Cohen child, who was overwhelmed by the hotel's vastness.

Ari marveled as he entered the atrium for the first time. "Dad, this place is really big. Cool, there's a lake in the lobby, and I love that outside elevator. That's even cooler."

"Ari, I will buy you boats for us to sail on Lake Lobby." Father and son laughed. "I imagine that this elevator just became your newest toy, eh?"

They slapped each other five. Ari's face lit up as he clutched Allie's and Sarah's hands while the outside elevator whisked them up sixty-seven floors to the Sun Dial level. The Cohen family then took a second private elevator two floors up to their unusual new residence. The oversized front doors opened to a 3,450-square-foot bilevel luxury suite located 700 feet above the ground.

"Allie," Sarah wondered, "although I love these cylindrical white-on-white walls and floor-to-ceiling windows, I need to know, money, how long do you plan for us to live in the clouds like this?"

She rolled her left fingers at the words *long* and *clouds* and made him laugh.

"I'm not sure, Sarah." He mulled that over. "I guess it'll take six or eight months to either build or renovate a home. At the moment, though, there's something a lot more important on my mind."

Cohen looked northward, his eyes following Peachtree Street as the boulevard snaked through the heavily forested city that spread out to the horizon. Midtown and Buckhead office and condo towers lorded above the vast green sea of slender pines and broad oaks.

"What's that, Allie?" Sarah put her arms around his waist and hugged him.

"Like what I'm going to do with myself, money." He played with his lower lip. "It's weird waiting for a signal or whatever from the Lord."

In Washington DC, Ted Bell of Theodore Bell & Associates Inc.—a hot new Democratic direct mail, lobbying, and research group—took a call from one of Gary Hart's associates.

"Mr. Bell," complained Dena Ferst, Hart's publicity director, "your last newsletter included an article that spread unsavory allegations about Donna Rice and implied that Senator Hart was a womanizer. That is very unfair, and the senator demands a retraction."

"Look, Dena." Ted swiveled in his black leather chair and then offered, "I'll give you three paragraphs of space to combat the truth, which you prefer to call rumors."

Dena said hesitantly, "Thanks, Ted, I guess."

"You got my fax number?"

"Yes, but I'll hand-deliver the news release myself when I'm done. I have another damage control stop on K Street just around the corner from you."

Bell put the receiver down and looked over his plush office decorated with contemporary furnishings and two dozen potted plants, which he religiously watered.

827

It's amazing how far I've come in a year, he thought as he circulated around the office, meticulously watering or misting his beloved plants. *It was a lot of hard work computerizing Washington's largest direct mail list of political activists and contributors, but it'll be worth over $500,000 this year for bothering.*

He drained the collection bowl of an overwatered African violet. Ted looked back at the past year. *Stealing the secret Republican National Committee election plan book from Chip and trading it for the assistant chairmanship of the 1988 Democratic Party Platform Committee was my life changer. The timing was perfect. Many liberal lobbying groups were pressuring legislators to support NDMA. Voila, my direct mail list targeted moderate and suburban Democrats who we've been urging to stay in the party and give metropolitanization a chance to work.*

The Democratic National Committee (DNC) is desperate because Reagan has twice captured over 60 percent of the white ethnic vote, a former core party mainstay that Bush is likely to hold on to also. However, I'm using two of Cohen's ideas to show the DNC how to win back the white ethnic swing vote that's very badly needed to recapture the White House.

Bell's research learned that NDMA for many white ethnics translated as not being able to run anymore from the blacks moving into their neighborhoods.

My staff just developed a campaign message to white ethnics that in unity there is strength and that appreciation of diversity is a core link in that unity. Conservatives made our job, though, a little harder by labeling National Consortium of Ethnic Culture Centers (NCECC) as patronizing.

These two hot-button issues are keeping many white ethnics from returning to the Democratic camp, so I'm telling them this: NCECC is a lynchpin in the preservation of your own rich ethnic cultures. Americans must come together and once again believe in each other if they want a better future for their children.

Ted emptied some water from a rubber plant collector. *Allie Cohen is the best teacher I ever had, and now I'm making serious money from his ideas too. I owe him most for helping me find myself and settle my problem with my father.* For the record, Leo Bellinsky was considered by midcentury California government leaders to be the greatest political fixer in California history.

Leo was the ultimate extrovert and could tell stories about Nixon, Reagan, or Pat Brown and have the room rocking with laughter for hours. Everybody loved him, and I miss him so much. I'm quieter like my mother, but I know that my dad is really proud of my following in his political footsteps.

For that, Bell planned to pay Cohen back by persuading the president to make Allie the U.S. ambassador to the United Nations.

Reagan has granted me fifteen minutes tomorrow to make my case for Cohen, and I plan to call in all my father's chits. Reagan owes Leo big.

Allie, meanwhile, was praying to Adonai in his personal tabernacle 650 feet above the ground. Every morning his alarm clock rang fifteen minutes before the sun rose over Stone Mountain. He then showered and dressed, put on his phylacteries and tallit, and walked down a flight of stairs leading to the Sun Dial Restaurant, where he'd sectioned off a corner for his combination prayer center and office.

Allie prayed twice daily; Jews call it *davening.* The morning session started with the sun rising, the evening session with the sun setting; each was an hour-long rotation around the city. Every afternoon, he took two hours of tallit and tefillin lessons and the study of Torah and Talmud from his personal tutor Rabbi Joseph Lischkoph.

Tallit is a prayer shawl that wraps the shoulders, upper body, and arms; tefillin are phylacteries, which are leather straps that are wrapped around the left arm and a small leather box placed on one's upper forehead.

The gaps in my Hebrew education are filling in nicely. Cohen smiled. *And I am happier than ever. Thank you, Name.*

Halfway through his morning service, an upsetting rush of great money-making deals and humanistic ideas interrupted his davening.

I'm stifling two surefire movie and restaurant concepts. Man, this struggle is like a smack addict's fight to stay clean.

Cohen started to pray again, but another idea popped from his brain.

Oh crap, another notion, but at least it's something funny for a change—organize NARC, the National Association of Reformed Chazers.

That is a cute idea, Allie, but for reasons previously stated, please leave it at that.

After completing his morning service, breakfast was brought to him by Bea, a sweet slim elderly black woman who wore her hair in a bun. Bea waited on Allie like a loving grandmother and always hummed to the background music he played.

"Good morning, Bea. I'm glad that you like my choice of Jewish religious music."

Bea usually just nodded and smiled, but this morning, she really surprised him.

"My lesbian granddaughter and I just joined a tiny Reconstructionist congregation over on Briarcliff Road that has a fabulous choir. They've cut a tape that I play at home all the time, and it sounds just like this too. Excuse me, the oatmeal looks a little too thick today, so let me mix in some milk."

As usual, she shoved aside his three newspapers to make room for two poached eggs on buttered wheat toast, a very small cup of oatmeal that she added two teaspoons of milk to, a small glass of freshly squeezed orange juice, and a pot of Colombian coffee.

"Thank you Bea."

She smiled motherly at Allie and returned to the restaurant. Cohen spent the rest of the morning writing and typing memoirs in his domed revolving office. Allie was already up to the part where he makes it with Carole by telling her the prisoners' number gags and the rest of his shtick.

I think laughter and sex is what bound us most. Allie looked back on his time with Carole. *And we sure had a lot of each. I'm glad for her that she's going to let Myron move back in after his divorce, but I'm even happier for Martin and Caryn.*

The noonday hours were passed with a short nap, after which Rabbi Lischkoph arrived at one thirty to tutor Cohen on Torah and Talmud. Phil Brodsky, a friend in common, introduced Lischkoph to Cohen thirteen years before when they worked on a bicentennial human relations project. Allie needed to tape an interview with an Orthodox rabbi, and Phil recommended the youthful and lively Lischkoph, who did a great job of explaining Judaism to the mostly black Atlantan fifth-grade students.

Allie, when he returned to Atlanta, asked Joe to please coach him to get up to speed in Hebrew, Torah, and Talmud. Lischkoph poured himself into Cohen's education because he liked Allie and had always wanted to become friends with him. Allie liked Joe too, but his past pot smoking made him uncomfortable hanging out with a rabbi, and he once questioned Joe on young U.S. Jews' considerable drug use.

"Allie," replied Joe, "using drugs amounts to idolatry, a replacement for belief in Almighty God Himself."

"So young Jews are doing something *wrong*, Joe, not simply doing it first?"

"No, G. K. Chesterton said that when a people cease to believe in Hashem, they do not believe in nothing. They believe in anything. Drugs, Allie, are similar to believing in anything."

"That's a good line, Rabbi, but I have to challenge the *believing in anything* part."

"Hey, didn't Bob Dylan warn about believing in false prophets or that we all have to serve someone?"

Joe's remark about *serving someone* lingered in Cohen's brain for a decade and finally drove him to seek Lischkoph's help in lighting Allie up spiritually.

The light, though, had dimmed in Joe, whose every attempt to make friends with young congregants was stifled because of their getting high. Lischkoph, isolated and depressed, began using drugs to break out of the box he'd been trapped in. At first, he got high with *a* congregant, who introduced another member who brought in a couple of more. Soon it was dozens.

The drastic step worked; it became cool to get high with the rabbi. His congregation membership soared; people joked that the synagogue's new name was B'nai Drugs.

While Allie davened in the brilliant sunlight cutting the plane of the curved windows, Lischkoph carefully laid out four hefty lines of exceptionally pure cocaine. The rabbi jokingly sang, "Happy birthday to you. Happy birthday to you. Happy birthday, dear Allie. Happy birthday to you."

Cohen put down his prayer book and stared in disbelief at the lines of cocaine and then at Lischkoph for serving them.

"Joe," he demanded, "what the hell are you doing?"

"I hoped, Allie," said Lischkoph sincerely, "that we might mark a milestone in your life with a very special treat."

"Joe, it's not my birthday today, and I don't get high anymore." He put down his prayer book and frowned.

"Come on, Allie, you won't believe how pure this nose candy is."

"I told you, Joe, that I do not want to get high, especially with my rabbi. What part of that do you not get?"

"What's my being a rabbi got to do with it? I'm just proposing a simple social toast, that's all."

"Joe, someone has to be the parent," Allie scolded. "The rabbi should be the shepherd tending to the needs of his flock, so if the sheep gets lost, the shepherd can show them the way. By the way, whatever happened to the ritual of just drinking a glass of wine?"

"That's pretty heavy, Allie. Let me write that down."

"Joe," Allie asked sadly, "why the hell did you become a rabbi if you must resort to using and selling drugs to succeed at it? Didn't you tell me ten years ago that drug use was idolatry and amounted to people believing in anything?"

"Allie, getting high with you is like getting high with Dylan."

Cohen scoffed at that with a look that drove Lischkoph to admit that he'd won a contest. That wiped Cohen out.

"So in twenty-five words or less, on a box top of kosher cornflakes, I presume, you wrote why you wanted to be a rabbi."

"No, and I didn't mail it to Battle Creek, Michigan, with a quarter either. My synagogue held a raffle, and the prize was a four-year rabbinical scholarship to Hebrew University in Jerusalem, and I won."

"So you had to accept it?"

"Yes, it's funny. I had just enrolled in Brandeis and was on my way to becoming a social worker or a lawyer. My grandfather, a third-generation rabbi, and everyone else kept telling me that I had to be nuts not to take it."

"So you caved in, Joe, rather than follow your intuition and heart?"

"Actually, Allie, it was the smartest thing I ever did. Oh man, I loved those years in Jerusalem. They were the best four years of my life and always will be because I met my wife there. My problem began when I returned home to Great Neck, Long Island, one of the so-called five towns, and became assistant rabbi of a large conservative synagogue. I was twenty-six years old, and no one wanted to hang with me, no one."

"So you started tooting up with the cokeheads and stopped trying to reach them the right way, guiding them to be holy."

"Be honest. I couldn't reach them for the same reason I couldn't reach you ten years ago. Now I have the youngest, hippest, and happiest synagogue in Atlanta."

"Good for you, Joe. In the past, I might have been your most devout follower. But now instead of being into myself, I'm getting high on the Lord, Torah, and Talmud."

"My sins are not so great, Allie. For the most part, they're the same as yours, and you've surely been blessed."

834

That line earned Lischkoph some serious scorn. *Joe hasn't got a clue of the demons that swim in my soul.*

Allie tried again. "Joe, the reb can't drop ludes and lead the way. If the reb can get stoned, sleep with other women, and easily divorce his wife, all the rules blur and become meaningless."

Lischkoph's eyes beckoned that maybe they should talk less and toot more.

"Joe, your behavior is doubly idolatrous—loving coke and getting high with a celebrity. Please stop before I lose all respect for you. Uucch, I'm even allergic to that crap you want to give me. I think you need to leave and go pray to Hashem for forgiveness."

Cohen pointed the way to the door. Lischkoph's eyes leaked shame and tears as he gathered up his religious tools. Allie began praying for his restoration.

"I thank the Almighty for the strength to resist your temptation. I also beg Adonai to help you, once again, live according to His commandments. If you'll excuse me, I must seek out a new tutor."

Three weeks later, Rabbi Joe Lischkoph was arrested in the Downtown Atlanta bus station. The mule from Miami, who supposedly had three ounces of pure coke, turned out to be an undercover narcotics agent and handcuffed Joe in front of his little boy. Congregation Beth Coke fired Joe the next day. Lischkoph was sentenced to three years at Alto, a minimum-security prison located in the north Georgia mountains. Joe agreed to serve as prison chaplain, so the judge shortened his time by a year.

Cohen passed Yahweh's test and proved worthy; holy status was very close. Ill-fated Joe failed his; his two great tests to remain a rabbi were to seek redemption and to search for rebirth.

Chapter 110

Whenever someone asked Allie to explain his aversion to joining a synagogue, he would tell the same joke.

"A Jew, shipwrecked on a South Seas island for three years, is finally reached by a team of rescuers. He proudly shows them around and points out his comfortable home, orchards, pastures, irrigation systems, and many other constructions. 'At the end of the island are two small buildings,' he says, pointing them out. 'Those are the synagogues.'

"'Two of them?' he's asked. 'But you're alone here.'

"'Well,' he says, 'this is the one I pray in, and the other I wouldn't go in even if they paid me.'

I have belonged to three congregations and won't join another synagogue even if they pay me. Cohen chuckled to himself. *Life is good. Between seeking holiness in my own sanctuary and supervising the construction of our Paces Ferry Road property with fabulous water features and the most advanced electronics, security systems, and protective landscaping, life is keeping me nice and busy.*

Sarah groaned to him. "Allie, I've lived for six months in a cylinder and eighth of a mile above the ground."

Then Ari and Sarah, in a duet manner, told Cohen, "We're sick and tired of living in a hotel."

Allie threw up his hands. "I'm sorry, but Neil Franco, the architect, told me this morning that the move-in date has to be pushed back a month because the security systems and a lot of the landscaping are taking longer than expected to acquire and install. What do you want me to do?"

They did not bolt, but all things considered, the Buckhead utopia was progressing nicely. The compound included a shallow, 1.5-acre walkable lake stocked with fish, a pedal boat, and a kayak. A catchment lay adjacent to an intimate sand beach set against manicured grounds with a heated pool and a two-bedroom carriage house for guests.

After school one day, Allie and Ari checked to see if the catchment and beach were operational yet. Ari's face lit up at first sight of the property and could hardly wait to bring friends over to use it with him.

Allie eased Sarah's frustration from the construction delay by planning a month-long trip to France. He also made arrangements to move out of Six Flags over Portman and leave Ari with the Kartzmans while they took a second honeymoon.

"Cohen," Sarah whined the next night at dinnertime, "I must get out of this hotel tonight, or I'm going to go nuts. I'm so damn sick and tired of room service too. It all tastes the same to me already. Come on, how about some New York pizza tonight?"

"There won't be enough time, Sarah, to get back to my conventicle before the sun goes down. I apologize for not being able to join you but urge you and Ari to pig out on pizza without me."

"Sorry, Allie, apology not accepted." She insisted, "We need to do something as a family tonight. God will surely forgive you if you're late for a single evening service and instead have a little fun with your family."

Sarah's twice emphasizing the word *family* forced Allie to reconsider. *I'm torn between my rational brain and faithful heart.*

He conceded. *I'm worried that my Orthodox ways are preventing us from going out as much, and that my new religiosity is smothering my wife and son.*

"Okay, Sarah." He flapped his arms with palms out. "Let's all do pizza."

They headed over to Franco's Pizza on the corner of Piedmont and Cheshire Bridge, were seated quickly, and ordered three small pies.

Sarah noticed something. *Allie selected three vegetables—onions, mushrooms, and eggplant—for his toppings and left off his usual Italian sausage. He really is becoming kosher.*

Sarah, to fill the time while waiting for their pies to arrive, showed Allie and Ari etchings that she'd done that afternoon.

"Guys, I took them off gravestones from the Marshall family burial plot tucked away in a clump of trees near the corner of Briarcliff Road and Clairmont Avenue. Your father, Ari, accidentally stumbled on it in 1973 while searching in the woods behind our apartment complex to plant great pot seeds."

Ari cracked up laughing; Allie laughed hard too but thought, *Even though I've stopped using, I'm still uncomfortable with Sarah casually sharing that tidbit with Ari. How will I handle it if or when Ari, at age twelve to fourteen or so, starts smoking pot with his friends or experimenting with hallucinogens or some other drug?*

Sarah sentimentally described her drawings of headstones that dated back to the 1840s. Allie tried hard to listen. *Uh-oh, I'm distracted by an incredible idea for a movie, and I can't suppress this one like I have all the others. I'm sorry, babe, but your etchings are simply no match for* Son of Hitler.

The plot's set in 2030, when an Israeli federation extends from the Sinai to southern Lebanon and from the Golan to the southern Jordanian port of Aqaba. On Tisha B'Av, an Arab jihad aided by Iran and Russia suddenly smashes the Zionists on all fronts, and eight million Jews reel from the onslaught but manage to hold out for a month.

Collapse is imminent until an eighty-five year-old former German Air Force officer steps forward to shame the West. Alex Hellring reveals that his actual name is Hitler and that he was the world's first test-tube baby.

Adolf Hitler was sterile, so the sperm belonged to his brother Alois, and the egg was Eva Braun's. A special team of Nazi medical scientists working in Vienna, Austria, figured out how to fuse the egg and sperm and nurture the zygote into a fetus and ultimately a healthy baby boy.

The child grows inside an artificial amniotic sac and is born a week before his parents commit suicide in their bunker as the Soviets roar into Berlin. Infant Alex is snuck out of Austria by escaping Nazi officers led by Josef Mengele, who places Alex in a Jewish orphanage in Buenos Aires to disguise his origin. The infant is adopted by the Hellrings, a happy, warm Jewish locksmith family that gives Alex love and every advantage in life.

The Hellring family business declines along with the Argentine economy, so Alex decides to move to Germany as a young man, makes the military his career, and becomes a respected NATO officer. When the onslaught against Israel begins, Alex steps forth and chastises the Western democracies.

"There is already far too much Jewish blood on German hands, and the son of Hitler will not allow a second Holocaust to occur. I demand to lead a one-hundred-thousand-man NATO army to save the Israelis and call on the U.S. Air Force and airlines to fly us."

The Zionists are petrified "Is this Hitler for real? Is he the good man he claims to be, or is he coming to finish his infamous father's crime?"

"Allie, are you listening to me?" His fade-out annoyed Sarah.

"I'm sorry, babe." He sighed and thought, *Another great idea that wouldn't be holy to act on anymore.*

Allie quietly drove down Peachtree Street to return to their hotel suite and decided Ari was ready for basic religious instruction.

"Son, please join me in the evening service tonight. I think you're ready to start davening with me."

"Sure, Dad, I've been waiting months for you to ask me."

When they arrived home, Ari went to get his prayer book; and while searching, he switched on the TV. Bill Moyers and Dan Rather were discussing the merits of NDMA.

Ari remembered. *I think my dad is the author of those initials.*

Ari ran out of his room to tell Allie, "Dad, hurry, you have to watch this on TV with me. Bill Moyers and Dan Rather are talking about NDMA."

Cohen followed his son into the bedroom to listen to the centrist Moyers shed light on the puzzling congressional action to a mostly resentful American people. "One may ask why Morris Winters, a man from a Kentucky mountain hamlet of two thousand people, is trying to ram NDMA through the Congress. Popular rumor has it that Congressman Winters is punishing President Reagan for failing to deliver on the New Right's conservative social agenda.

"Frankly, I find that difficult to believe as Reagan has pushed hard for the implementation of school prayer and antiabortion legislation. Proof of that is Atty. Gen. Ed Meese asking the Supreme Court to overturn the 1973 *Roe v. Wade* decision that originally legalized abortion.

"In my opinion, the truth is that Morris Winters has outlasted five presidents and will still chair the powerful House Committee on Ways and Means long after Reagan has retired to his California ranch. Winters's constituency, made up of people in hollows or very small mining towns, will be untouched by NDMA and could not care less.

"I suspect the real reason Morris Winters is calling in forty years of political IOUs is that he believes that Allie Cohen's idea is good for America, period. However, the red herring that Reagan failed fundamentalist America will play a lot better in the conservative Baptist hamlets of Appalachia that he represents, which I guess is smart politics because 70 percent of all Americans who do live in cities will benefit from NDMA, an idea whose time has come. The odd coupling of Allie Cohen and Morris Winters is why I love this country so much. We will surely be the world's last great hope when the congressman no longer has to mask his historic action with a phony political payback story.

"This is Bill Moyers wishing all a good evening, and good night, Dan."

"Good night, Bill, and thank you. This is Dan Rather signing off."

Allie switched off the TV, hugged Ari, and kissed his cheek. The proud little boy sensed it from his father's loving hug and kiss. *I think an important moment has come about, and my daddy is responsible for making it happen.*

"My lifelong hope, Ari," Cohen shared with his son, "of bringing Americans closer together, making the system work more efficiently and effectively for everybody, and building more beautiful cities with greater conceptual reach is at hand. Thank you, Lord."

Yahweh and I are glad that you are back on track, Allie. Indeed, Adonai is again smiling down at you from a perch over Atlanta, where the Redeemer will keep a lid on local passions from boiling over. Hashem wants you to succeed, Allie, for Atlanta's sake and the world's and against all odds.

Chapter 111

On the negative side, realized Cohen, *NDMA has sparked a huge reactionary backlash. Gun and ammo sales are at record levels, and domestic factories can't meet the demand. The bill passing on a shabby pretense and not on its merits helped fuel this backlash, and many people, including me, are scared that the mood could turn violent.*

Local resistance, Allie assessed, was strongest in ultraconservative Cobb County in Metro Atlanta's northwest quadrant, the national headquarters of the fiercely anti-Communist John Birch Society, which was headed by their late extremist congressman. Cobb rednecks in pickup trucks were stating their displeasure with NDMA by emptying out gun stores and displaying their rifles in their trucks' back window rack. Their clear aim—to visibly intimidate drivers next to and behind them to resist NDMA—was trouble just waiting to happen.

Two miles away, Rev. William Walker parked his Cadillac Sedan deVille in front of the BUSHAC Job Training Center (BJTC) on Irwin Street. Walker looked at the converted red brick structure, a former Atlanta middle school.

This center, praised Walker, *is a symbol of hope to two hundred teenage dropouts trying to make it in the predominantly white-collar Atlanta job market. God bless Mack Thomas, Eddie White, and BJTC for making a real difference in the lives of our most troubled inner city youth.*

The kindly seventy-year-old Walker—a nationally respected civil rights champion who, as a divinity student, marched alongside Martin Luther King during the desegregation movement—carried a mantle of dignity capable of scolding the city into behaving better.

His ability to sit down with the white business community earned him a reputation as a *moderate*—a white code word for *reasonable man.*

The reverend, a close friend of Mayor Mack Thomas, called on the BUSHAC coordinator and Atlanta Youth Development Center (AYDC) director Eddie White.

"Eddie," complimented Walker, "you are providing an extremely important service to our black and poor youth."

"Thank you, Reverend," White said humbly. "I am honored by you, sir, a respected community leader. Praise from you is very special."

"And let me tell you something else, Eddie. A lot of other people are noticing the fine work you're doing too."

"Sir, those are such beautiful words that you're going to make me cry," said Eddie appreciatively and then, like a politician, asked, "Now what can I do for you, Reverend?"

"One of my parishioners," Walker pleaded the teen's case, "is a sixteen-year-old boy who's trying to get off hard drugs. Hayward Smith, a recent dropout, needs immediate entry into a halfway house where he's pee-tested and gets help from a counseling center, as well as entry into a job skills training program and night school. That's what's needed to turn Hayward from a serious underachiever into a productive citizen."

"I understand."

"Eddie, I realize that Reagan's relentless budget cuts might make it tough to get Hayward all the help he needs to get clean and healthy."

"Hayward," White assured Reverend Walker, "will get his chance to turn his life around. I will personally see to it, and that's a promise to you and his mother."

"Thank you, Eddie. You know, I used to teach Sunday school to Hayward when he was just a little boy." The minister choked up. "He's really a nice young man. 'Guess he just took up with a fast crowd at Washington High. Thanks to you, though, I think we can save this boy from a life in jail or worse."

Eddie nodded that he understood, and the reverend exited, saying, "You're a good man, Eddie. Well, I'll be going now. You take care."

Shortly after Walker drove off, Celia Wilson, Eddie's secretary and Farrah's sister, buzzed his office.

"Mr. White, Mayor Thomas has scheduled an emergency meeting, and he expects you at the city hall in twenty minutes."

White steered his new black Nissan Maxima sedan out of the parking lot and headed toward downtown. He parked in his reserved spot in the municipal lot and entered through the great brass doors. Although he'd marched up the two flights of steps dozens of times, his chest still puffed up a bit with each visit.

Eddie smiled and waved to Farrah and then entered the wood-paneled mayor's quarters. Mack, Lesotho, and Roger Wilcox—the city council president—were engaged in what appeared to be an important policy-making session. Lesotho was the first to notice Eddie arrive and uncomfortably looked away and then down at his shoes.

The sight of my best friend avoiding my gaze ain't good, thought Eddie, no stranger to bad news.

"So, Mack, what's the word?" The *word* destroyed Eddie's pleasant day.

845

"I'm sorry, Eddie, you didn't get the grant. Son of a bitch Reagan is cutting back again. That bastard wipes out people's programs left and right and gives them more interest on the national debt instead."

"I'm more interested," expressed Eddie, "in how the cutbacks affect *me*."

Mack looked at Roger, who simplified it. "Eddie, your job training center might have to be shut down if the business community is unable to increase its subsidy."

He lamented. "Man, just to kill programs that needy people depend on is a damn crime. Reagan's ideology makes no sense. To offer hope to the hopeless and recycle losers into winners has to be cheaper in the long run than throwing everyone into the prison system."

"Eddie," Roger reminded him, "you're preaching to the choir."

"Mack," begged Eddie, "can't those cocksuckers understand that the center's a bargain? If Reagan believes so much in the system as he claims, then why is he pushing so many out of it? Man, I just promised Reverend Walker that we were going to help a young man named Hayward Smith."

Mack shrugged. "Eddie, that's what Republican politics is becoming. Conservatives view shrinking government as a mission, and killing off a liberal program is a victory."

"Man, that's politics-as-usual bullshit." Eddie argued back, "People's lives are at stake, and the business community needs to know that too."

"Atlanta's power structure," defended Thomas, "probably digs into its pocket as often as any other big city in the country."

"Yeah," White stated. "Well, if that's so, why can't they dig one mo' time?"

"Eddie," Thomas urged, "don't give up hope. The establishment might just surprise you."

Lesotho cynically wisecracked. "Eddie, nationally, teenage black unemployment is only 46 percent right now. Locally, they tell you Atlanta's a job mecca for blacks because minority youth unemployment is way down to 43 percent. Shit, we're practically enjoying a boom, but then we're in the magical Sun Belt, where all the money and action is, right?"

Wilcox, a corporate lawyer for Coca-Cola before becoming the city council president, chuckled before promising help.

"Eddie, don't panic yet. Maybe we can pull some money from somewhere else in the budget."

"Eddie, we'll hustle like hell for you," stated Mack. "But we can't vow to keep the center open at any cost. You need to understand how tight the budget already is. Atlanta's got all the problems of a northern city. We're just prettier and have a better climate."

"I have connections in the music industry," volunteered Xeranga. "How about a series of benefit rock concerts? Acts like Earth, Wind & Fire and Stevie Wonder could keep the center open for six months to a year."

"The city fathers dislike benefit concerts," advised Roger. "They feel that the notion demeans Atlanta by giving it a hand-to-mouth image."

"Roger, I don't give a shit about what the fucking city fathers think. If the motherfuckers are so worried about the city's image, let them cough up the damn money themselves."

White turned to Wilcox to reason with him. "Roger, have you any idea how many kids we got jobs for or how many we've gotten off drugs? The AYDC's doing the best job of solving the two biggest inner city youth problems that Atlanta's got."

"AYDC still has six months of operating revenues left," Wilcox assured White. "So things aren't as gloomy as you're making them out to be."

"Relax, man," urged Mack. "A lot can happen in six months. You, more than most people, should know that."

Lesotho planned. "If the center is actually forced to shut down, you'll help me and Lucius North run Mack's reelection campaign. Atlanta will be at least 70 percent black by then. We'll surely win in a landslide unless whitey steals the city back from us."

Well, Lesotho, I wouldn't quite put NDMA in those terms.

Chapter 112

The passage of the Voting Rights Act of 1965 based
on *one man, one vote* resulted in the election of more than two
thousand black public officials across the South. Their nagging
reality was that conservative white legislators could adjust the city/
country boundaries and cause dozens of black mayors to disappear
overnight.

"Stop acting paranoid," Wilcox told Xeranga. "There's
no way that NDMA will fly. It's just Washington bullshit, a lot of
sound and fury signifying nothing."

Eddie and Lesotho did not agree with Roger and gave him
that skeptical look common to black people when asked to place
their faith in white institutions and assurances. A few seconds later,
Lucius North, Roger's assistant, walked into the office with the
early edition of the evening newspaper.

"Have you guys seen this?" North asked, pointing to a bold
Atlanta Journal-Constitution headline.

All four responded in chorus, "No."

North threw the newspaper down on Mack's desk. Mack,
Lesotho, Roger, and Eddie stared at the incredible headline that
threatened the privileged world each had worked so hard to attain:
SENATE TO VOTE ON NDMA TODAY.

Right below that earthshaking message in smaller bold
print were similar career-changing words. "Measure likely to pass
House and become law in ninety days."

A mutual "holy shit" transcended the room; a choruslike
"I don't fucking believe it" followed seconds later. "What a
motherfucker" finally prompted a statement from Mack.

"Well, I guess that I just became the ex-mayor."

Lesotho put one and one together. "And I'm the ex-media-spokesman."

Roger had a good idea who might be replacing him as the city council president.

"Mack, I think you just got my job. But instead of dealing with white people from Morningside and Buckhead, you'll be getting shit from Sandy Springs, Decatur, and Jonesboro instead."

Eddie opened up to his buddies about his insecurities.

"I'm the most vulnerable one here. I'm carrying big banknotes on my house, the Maxima, and Farrah's Toyota Celica. Arvida is being fitted for braces, and Dennis is attending an expensive private school in Sandy Springs for children with attention deficit disorders. All that I own or have going in life I owe to Mack, whose world just caved in too. Man, I could be left out in the cold just like that." He snapped his finger.

Wilcox tried to ease White's concern by reminding him that there was still a chance that the bill might not pass Congress.

Eddie differed by pointing to the headline. "You're wrong, Roger. I think that's going to be my pink slip."

"In the new order of things," Mack argued, "the power structure that's likely to emerge will still need to serve black citizens who make up 30 percent of the metro population and mostly live in a few clumps. Black people with governing skills like Lesotho and Eddie will be just as valuable as ever, maybe more so."

White turned to Wilcox, who nodded, and then to Lesotho, who didn't believe it.

"You don't see it, Mack. You and Roger got law degrees, light skin, and white-sounding names. You two are A-OK superniggers according to whitey, but can you imagine some white mayor named Alton Andrews III having a spokesman named Lesotho Xeranga? Or Eddie, with his very black looks, being ol' Alton's community relations specialist or whatever? Forget it, ain't gonna happen."

"Christ, Lesotho, how many whites," Roger pointed out, "do you think will be lining up to manage the Perry Homes housing project?" He formed zero with his fingers. "None, that's how many."

Mack sided with Roger. "Give me a break, Lesotho. Most whites that I've known are happiest when they never see a black person. The north side and the suburbs are proof of that. I mean, look at the distance that they've put between us. Frankly, I think they'll be glad to let us administer the hood."

"You guys are forgetting," said Lesotho, feeling he knew better, "whitey will demand administrative and management degrees. Whites will swear that they are experts at everything, even have PhDs in niggerology. There's your Perry Homes manager."

He pointed his finger at Roger and Mack who cracked up, Eddie chuckled, and Lesotho warned them, "Man, start saying goodbye to ten years of picking our own players from our own playground."

Roger laughed again at Lesotho's wisecrack and then found some of his own black humor in the dark news of NDMA.

"And to think that Mack was just honored as one of the ten best mayors in America. He may be the ex-mayor before the article is even in print."

Thomas pondered out loud, "Do you think it's possible for me to attract a large enough suburban vote to possibly win?"

His friend's facial expressions told him, "What, are you fucking nuts?" Mack frowned.

"Do the math." Roger identified the obvious. "Whites are 70 percent of the population, and up to 70 percent of them vote in crucial elections. Blacks, in comparison, are 30 percent, and a good turnout for the community is 50 to 60 percent."

"I need to know," White said, "the name of the motherfucker responsible for mucking up my life with this shit."

Lesotho recalled the incident but chanced the truth. "Allie Cohen."

"I should have known." Eddie laughed. "Cohen taught it to me in sociology at Bankhead High. Jesus, my class wrote it and sent it to the White House. It's funny. I didn't believe for one minute that NDMA was possible back then, but now I may be screwed by it. Fucking incredible."

Eddie and Lesotho looked at each other, shook their head before laughing, and cursed Allie Cohen.

"Motherfucking Cohen pulled the rug out from under us. Fucking unbelievable."

"Gentlemen," Mack Thomas scolded them, "a little decorum please. You know this is the mayor's office."

Lesotho and Eddie both said, "Screw decorum."

Lesotho added, "Decorum is whitey's genteel way of getting us to act like Velveeta and talk like loan officers."

Mack appealed to Roger for help. Wilcox couldn't resist kidding him. "Mack, maybe you should run for mayor with a paper bag over your head to disguise being black."

Lucius North laughed at his boss's joke and then followed him out of the office and back over to the city council's chamber.

Farrah watched a visibly distraught Eddie blow by her desk and worried that something bad was happening and called out to him. "Eddie, what's wrong?"

Eddie turned back toward her and bellowed, "Our old teacher screwed up my life again." He grimaced, pivoted, and left.

Mack had watched the exchange and filled in the gaps for the bewildered Farrah. By the time Mack finished, she recognized the explosiveness of the situation.

"Mayor Thomas, may I please take the rest of the day off to quickly defuse this?"

The mayor granted Farrah's request. "Don't worry, everything will work out. You'll see."

Farrah tracked Eddie down at home and, to her great relief, found him sitting on a kitchen stool, calmly staring into space.

Elated and thankful to God, she intuitively suggested, "Honey, how about if we go to Nino's on Cheshire Bridge Road and feast on some veal marsala, pasta, and red wine?" Farrah held her breath, though she needn't.

"Sure, babe." He smiled. "I like the idea." He laughed again. "I mean, we should go before the money's gone and we're back in the ghetto eating chitterlings again." They both laughed so hard at his joke that soulful tears formed in their eyes.

Later that evening, after sharing a great meal and making love, Eddie asked Farrah if she thought he was insecure.

"That's a question, Eddie, that I've been waiting years for you to ask me. Yeah, I do. I really think you got a lot more going for you than you give yourself credit for."

"You really mean that, Farrah, don't you?"

"Uh-huh, I'm telling you that you've made a name for yourself and can stop worrying so much already."

"Maybe, but all the people who owe me favors are black, and there ain't no white people really aware of all the good I'm doing."

"But your supporters are important black people who *know* important white people and *speak* to them regularly."

Eddie kissed her breast. Farrah, though, was too tired to encourage him. She rested his head on his chest and told her husband, "Baby, good is good, white or black, and I think we're going to be okay no matter what happens."

"Oh yeah, Farrah, what do you know that I don't?"

"I guess this is a good moment to finally tell you, my man. For the past five years, I've been socking away over three hundred a month for a rainy day. So in case the worst happens, we got almost twenty-five thousand bucks to open that rib shack you always dreamed of."

"No shit?"

"That's right, Eddie, and you also badly underestimate your connections. Yeah, maybe we might have to tighten our belt a bit for a while, but I'm not worried anymore for us. We're okay."

"Farrah, I hate to disappoint you. But these days, twenty-five thousand will hardly buy you a damn barbecue pit."

"True, but we can sell the house, also quit our jobs and empty our pension funds. I figure that's almost sixty thousand. Some bank somewhere is going to match that with an SBA minority entrepreneurship loan."

"I guess so. Maybe we should get something that's really our own. A rib shack would be nice. I ain't ever had anything I could call my own, and as long as I stay in politics, I can't take anything for granted either."

Why must I keep reminding you, Eddie, to have faith and keep it? Trust yourself and Farrah's belief in you because if you aren't careful, this is going to be your downfall.

Chapter 113

Allie completed davening and remembered his to-do list.

I have things to do all over Buckhead today—drop Ari off at school, meet with my architect Neil Franco at the house to finish the interior and set up a move-in date, and lunch with Harvey at the Sit-In to catch up on business.

He drove and thought back in time. *Seth Lightman went to Cates as a child and once told me that the school maintained a 10 percent Jewish quota. My guess is it's up to 20 percent now.*

Cohen pulled up to Cates's entrance, a fine private school that was distinguished for its strong K-12 foreign language instruction. Allie gave Ari a kiss on the cheek as usual, but Ari just sat there and did not get out of the car. Allie, surprised, asked his son if everything was okay.

A startling question emerged from Ari's young lips and clouted Cohen's ears.

"Dad, what's a nigger lover?"

He blew my mind with that. Allie calmly asked, "Ari, please explain its usage."

"The two biggest boys in the class," Ari anxiously accounted, "called me that because they said my father is ruining Atlanta by helping the niggers take over. Those are their words, Dad. It's the NDMA thing, isn't it?"

"Ari," Allie explained, "you're a very smart little boy to figure that out by yourself. Your classmates, though, are not smart because they got it all wrong. Black Atlantans are being asked to give up a lot of their hard-earned power that was won with a great deal of sacrifice and hardship."

"Sorry to disappoint you, Dad," answered Ari in a tone that warned more mind-blowing news was forthcoming. "I had a lot of unexpected help."

"From whom, who helped you? What do you mean, son?"

"Right after those boys spoke so nastily to me, I went straight to Mr. Hamby, my teacher, and expected him to make sure that they never said that to me again. I was shocked when he said that the boys were probably right to do so. I started to protest, Dad, but Mr. Hamby said he'd moved his family to East Cobb so his kids wouldn't have to go to school with niggers—"

"Ari," Allie interrupted, "did your teacher actually use the *n* word to you?"

"Uh-huh, he said that, with NDMA, he'd have to put his kids in Cates and pay over $5,000 a year for each because the academy makes teachers pay at least half the tuition rate. I started to protest again, but he told me to forget it. He was not going to report the incident to the headmaster and believed the boys had a right to say it to me."

"Ari, you did everything right, and I'm very proud of you. I will take care of this, son. I promise you that."

"Dad, I want to leave Cates. Mom thinks I'd be better off by going to either one of the nearby public schools or maybe the Hebrew Academy."

Man, Allie thought. *I'm ready to breathe fire.*

Dad recommended to son, "The reason I put you in this school was for fluency in multiple foreign languages unlike monolingual me who's mostly forgotten three languages. Ari, let's finish out this year at Cates and consider the Hebrew Academy for next year. Hebrew day schools are best for learning to speak Hebrew, which I'm only starting to gain fluency in."

He parked his car, took Ari's hand, and headed toward the main office. Allie threw open the front door and blew in like the north wind.

"Please, ma'am, I need to speak to the headmaster immediately to present him with a seven-figure gift."

The school secretary observed Cohen's smoldering rage and worried about it but smiled gleefully at the words *seven -figure gift*.

"Sure, Dr. Cohen, I'm buzzing Headmaster Ashley Campbell right this second for you to present him with it."

Campbell, a southern WASP who always wore a bow tie, politely received the visibly steamed Cohen and pretended to be pleased with Allie's unscheduled visit.

"Why, Dr. Cohen, you surprise me. Apparently, sir, you are of a mind to express yourself, so please feel free to do so."

"Mr. Campbell," said Cohen, making the headmaster a conditional offer, "I'm in an unusually altruistic mood today and would like to donate a million dollars to you and your headmaster's personal discretionary school fund. However, Mr. Campbell, there is a single nonnegotiable stipulation."

Campbell held his hands together joyfully; his eyes lit up.

"For five years now, I've wanted to double the number of books in the school library, and now I finally have the funds to fill all those empty shelves. Bless you, Dr. Cohen, for your generosity, so what is this lone condition?"

"You fire Wayne Hamby today for using the *n* word to Ari, or I cancel my pledge and withdraw my son from Cates."

Campbell thought for a few seconds before answering. *Let me think this over. Although I like Wayne Hamby and think him to be a fine teacher, I respect a million dollars in cash a lot more, and doubling the library's offerings will allow me to raise tuition—and my salary—at least 10 percent. For that, I will ignore my aversion to pushy Yids barging into my office and making outrageous demands.*

"Well, Mr. Campbell," said Allie, visibly tired of waiting.

"I assure you, Dr. Cohen, that Hamby will be cleaning out his desk by the end of the day. We can't tolerate our teachers using that nasty *n* word in front of students."

"Thank you, Mr. Campbell. Ari's grandfather, Harvey Kartzman, will deliver the check later this afternoon."

Campbell tried hard not to sound patronizing. "You know that my wife and I go to the Sit-In a lot, and Mr. Kartzman always takes very good care of Mrs. Campbell and me with great advice on what to order." He put his hands together again. "I swear, that man is a restaurant genius."

"That's nice, Mr. Campbell." He turned away. *Having won my war*, thought Cohen, *I'll exit more graciously than I entered.*

From there, last-minute lighting fixture and home electronics installations and paint pattern plans were worked out with Franco, and then Allie drove to the Sit-In to fill in his father-in-law on the Cates caper.

Harvey cheered. "I am very grateful for the opportunity to stick it to a bigot."

"Dad," Allie related, "I want to take Sarah on a tour of France for most of June."

Grandpa immediately volunteered, "Rebecca and I look forward to taking care of Ari, anything to make my daughter

859

happy, you know that. By the way, what places will you be visiting?"

"I'd like for us to spend a week each in Paris, Cannes, Saint-Tropez, Monaco, and back to Paris and home."

"Those destinations sound like a perfect itinerary. I think I'm jealous, Allie. The only time I was in France was with General Simpson's Ninth Army sweeping across the country, cleaning out Krauts."

Harvey Kartzman was a decorated WWII veteran, one of the 640,000 Jewish men who served out of a total of 1.8 million U.S. adult male Jews at the time. In each French town that the Ninth Army seized, Kartzman took over the city hall for administration and communication and the church as a mess hall for feeding the troops and townsfolk if necessary. His feeding challenges, upon leaving the army in 1945, proved to be a great education and training ground for the restaurant business and being the future Sit-In maven.

Harvey suddenly recalled something. "Oh, I just remembered that the governor stopped in the night before to talk and eat and asked to meet with you right away."

"Do you think ol' Tillman wants to talk about NDMA?"

"Is the pope celibate?"

Allie cracked up laughing; his father-in-law almost never told jokes. "Dad, I think you mean *Catholic*, but your line is a lot better than mine. Anyway, NDMA is a damn good reason to get lost in France for a month. Please invite Governor Hebert over for lunch in my office."

"'Will do. Sarah told me that you're going to do the whole seder this year. If you want, maybe we should hold it here. We'll be

860

closed all week because you're building a separate kosher kitchen and dining space for ultra-Orthodox customers."

Allie nodded that it was a good idea. "Fine, the lunch rush is starting, so let me go and check on the kitchen. I'll send the governor in as soon as he comes."

Tillman Hebert, Georgia's businesslike tall chief executive, arrived sooner than expected. Kartzman escorted the governor, a religious Southern Baptist and teetotaler, to Allie's office.

"Governor," Harvey recommended, "we'll be serving a delicious braised brisket with crispy golden brown potato pancakes and a pickled beet garnish. May I suggest a Dr. Brown's cream-flavored soda to wash the dinner down?"

"Certainly, Mr. Kartzman. I always enjoy whatever you suggest."

Harvey again smiled and then let the governor in and catch sight of Allie wrapped in his beautiful tallit. Cohen's prayerful state made the governor respectful and a bit uneasy.

"I am honored, Governor," Cohen told Hebert, "by your presence, sir, but suspect that you have a lot more on your mind than brisket."

The pained smile on Tillman's face set Allie up with clever one-liners.

"Governor, has Kennesaw passed a law requiring a tank in every home? Or have black militants in Atlanta received money from Gaddhafi to build an atomic bomb?"

"Those are funny lines, Dr. Cohen, but I apologize for not being able to laugh. Sad truth's that Cobb County is arming itself to the teeth, and black activists in Atlanta are planning big demonstrations to shut this or that down. Frankly, I'm nervous as hell. NDMA may be the greatest threat to civil order in Georgia since Sherman's march to the sea."

While Hebert rambled on how it would "take the patience of Job and the healing power of Jesus Almighty to make NDMA work in Atlanta," Kartzman stealthily wheeled in a rolling cart and cut thin slices of masterfully browned brisket. Hebert smiled at Harvey and then turned toward Allie to proudly declare his sacred love for the good, hardworking people of the great state of Georgia.

"I'm ready, dammit," ol' Tillman stated, "to trade places with the devil to keep the lid on things. Klan membership is skyrocketing down in Clayton and Fayette Counties, and Cobb and Gwinnett are circling their wagons."

Hebert fessed up. "I think I prematurely endorsed Mack Thomas and should have waited for later in the race."

"Governor, I declared my support for Mack Thomas's candidacy at the same time as you did and have provided stronger financial backing as well."

"I'd breathe a lot easier," Hebert said, "if a majority of Metro Atlantans felt the same way as we do. Fact is that they don't."

Cohen shrugged to convey "There's nothing that we can do about that, Governor, except teach them to change their minds."

"There are a slew of candidates," the former Savannah native said deploringly, "promising to pull things together, Allie, but there isn't one trusted by both races."

Hebert labeled the current field of candidates the "not up to the job" group.

He looked Allie in the eye. "Dr. Cohen, you staying on the sidelines has created a political void that only you can fill. The truth is I didn't come here just for the brisket today. I'm here to ask you to run. Before you turn me down, I think you'll find out that you're a natural politician."

Cohen swallowed hard. "I'm sorry, Governor, but I have no interest in seeking public office. Frankly, I am temperamentally unsuited for it."

Allie then tried to gently terminate further discussion with a joke.

"Governor, let me illustrate what a bad mistake my being mayor would be. Two Jews are in front of a firing squad. The first man, a Yankee Jew, shouts 'Long live the Jews!' The second man, an Atlanta Jew, says, 'Shhh, don't make trouble.'

The governor broke a smile.

"My point is I'm a Yankee Jew who migrated to Atlanta, so the Christians can't say, 'Ah, what the hell, at least he's a southerner, or he was born here.'"

Hebert refused to accept Cohen's analogy. "Now what the hell is an Atlanta Jew? For Chrissake, more New York Jews have moved to Atlanta in the past fifteen years than in the previous hundred."

"Yes, but one of those previous New York Jews was Leo Frank, hanged in Atlanta in 1915, the only Jew ever lynched in the United States."

Tillman pulled at his collar. "Let's be fair, Dr. Cohen. Leo Frank was lynched over seventy years ago. Things have changed. Christ, Atlanta is one of the most wide-open cities in the country. Proof of that is Mack Thomas's being here only fifteen years, and he's the mayor. One of our U.S. senators and a congressman came from Pennsylvania twenty years ago. Atlanta's had a Jewish mayor before, and you're here only ten years and in line to be the next Jewish mayor."

Allie's look pleaded that the former Jewish mayor was minimally Jewish and a native and that he, Cohen, was not running plain and simple. Tillman took issue.

"Jesus, once again, you're not being fair. Look, I admit that you're not really one of us, if you know what I mean. You understand that it's nothing personal now. I'm just being honest and realistic."

"No hard feelings, Governor, I understand perfectly."

"Still, Dr. Cohen, these are unusual times, and weird times often call for unconventional candidates. After all, you did write this thing and cause all this trouble, so you should know better than anyone else how to get us out of it."

"Well, I hate to disappoint you, Governor. Just because I authored it doesn't mean I necessarily know how to better activate and implement it. The simple truth, Governor, is that I already did my job."

Hebert cocked his head back. "What job is that?" His brow crinkled.

"I showed the people how to more equitably distribute municipal services. Whoever wins can just follow the plan."

Hebert tried the most powerful Jewish strategy—guilt. "So you're turning me and your fellow Atlantans down, Allie? You're willing to let some political midget play side against side, possibly tear us apart?"

"Governor Hebert, you're not a Jewish mother. Sorry, guilt doesn't work for you. Seriously, I'm afraid my candidacy will result in unnecessary grief for my family, namely, becoming the target of extremists."

Since Hebert had failed with guilt, he tried shame. "This city's been pretty good to you, Cohen. You ought to pay Atlanta back for the opportunities it afforded you."

Allie looked at the governor with his head cocked. "Are you trying to tell me that I owe it to this city to run?" His brow crinkled.

"Yes, I am, Allie, and it's time to pay back your note."

Sarcastically, he replied, "You mean, Governor, like it's my *dues* or something?"

"Okay, if you want to put it like that, yes."

"Sorry, Governor, the price is way too high. My former cost of living in bland Atlanta for ten years was a body with a limited soul. This time around, I don't want to become a body without a body."

"Come on, Allie, you are overstating the danger factor. I beg you, Allie, please reconsider. Atlanta needs you."

"Governor, what you're asking of me is like you running for mayor of New York City. Still, I'm flattered, and thank you, but you'll have to find another candidate."

To his credit, an unhappy Hebert left graciously, after which Harvey popped in to get the lowdown.

"The governor's got the savoir faire of a mobile home salesman. You were right to turn him down. Sarah and Ari need you too much."

"Atlanta doesn't need me, Dad. The people are too damn fearful and hateful to know that they need one another."

So true, prophet, so true and so sad at the same time.

Chapter 114

The amazed stares from the thirty family members and close friends in attendance, Cohen felt, *tell me I'm proficiently conducting the Passover seder with the appropriate solemnity.*

An important part of the ceremony is the youngest child asking and answering the four questions signifying why this night is different from all others.

The happy daddy beamed. *My son, Ari, a first-year Hebrew student, skillfully sanctified the seder by saying them perfectly.*

No one was more astonished than Sandy Forman in how expertly Allie facilitated a service that ideally combined the talents of a rabbi, a cantor, and maybe even a Talmudist.

"Tonight we join together," said Cohen, stating the reasons for partaking in the seder, "to pay homage to our forefathers and to strengthen the bonds of community, for no Hebrew may truly thrive in a world wholly unto himself."

Allie's mother was so moved by her son's spirituality that tears welled up in her eyes. *I'm afraid that I'm going to cry and ruin the beautiful seder for everyone.*

Janet got up from the table to sob alone. Allie followed his mother into the nearby kitchen and hugged her. Janet forced an unnatural smile in a vain attempt to disguise her grave concern.

Allie saw and asked, "Mom, what's the matter?"

"All right." Janet unburdened herself. "It was your birthday last month. How did you feel about turning forty?"

He tried to change the subject. "When I turn forty-one, I'll tell you how it felt turning forty. I don't know what else to say."

Janet would not laugh at his weak attempt to protect her from a thinly veiled truth. "Promise me, Allie, that you won't let them talk you into running for mayor. This so-called groundswell developing that only you can unite Atlanta is bullshit."

Cohen brushed a tear from his mother's cheek. "I assure you, Mom, that I have absolutely no intention of letting *them* talk me into anything."

Janet managed a chuckle before a second round of tears started flowing.

"I sense," Allie correctly guessed, "that this set of tears has to do with Carla and Joel, doesn't it?"

"Yes, I'm sorry to say that their high-living ways and the decline in his market drained his business. They owe the Feds $295,000. The IRS will seize their house in ninety days unless they can come up with the money. Max and I bailed them out twice before, but this debt is way beyond our ability to help. There's no one else, Allie."

Allie granted them the sum. "We'll find a good job for Joel in the business, possibly open a New Jersey Sit-In for him to manage. You know, Mom, I just paid the IRS $250 million to settle up from my gnome-of-Malibu days."

"My god, I can't believe how rich you are."

Allie expressed his concern. "Mom, I'm worried that the huge fortune may spoil Ari and the future Cohens. I'd like you to work with Sarah, Sandy, and the lawyers to set up a trust that provides within defined limits fine college educations, limited career startup capital, comfortable homes, and incentives to pursue artistic or political involvements. That's probably more than enough, don't you think?"

"Yes, Allie, and it's my pleasure to help."

It was time to finish the seder, so Allie urged all to return to the table.

Ari reminded his father, "Dad, the wine ritual is left to perform. Can I say it?"

Allie nodded yes and smiled. While Ari performed the prayer like a little mensch, Allie refilled everyone's glasses with the syrupy kosher wine. Soon many cheeks were flushed from the effect of the alcohol.

My family and friends are a buffer from the power structure's stepping up the pressure on me to run. A liberal white man with steel in his voice is being called forth to convince the blacks that he alone can be trusted to do right by them. That same steely voice also has to satisfy the conservative whites that only he can control the blacks.

Allie possessed that voice but wasn't saying very much at the moment.

Riva Forman, amused by the rainbow phoenix sewn onto Allie's floor-length tallit, teased, "I don't think you're living up to your promise not to make any political statements."

"The phoenix," Allie responded, "is an icon to remind the extremists that it isn't necessary to first burn the city down to rebuild it. An inner force the other day commanded me to get out of my car at Tenth and Peachtree and pay a black hippie artist to embroider the robe. The crimson-colored bird spread across the back of my prayer shawl symbolizes a rebirth out of the ashes of destruction."

Riva pressed him on that. "That sure sounds like campaigning to me."

Allie made it clear. "Riva, I'm merely spreading the Lord's Word in a personalized manner."

Sarah, across the table, worried. *I fear that my husband has started receiving signs from God to lead the people. Unfortunately, on the south side of town, black teacher friends of mine are telling me they're aggravated from hearing harsh threats that, unless they better discipline their children, the whites will do it for them. Somewhere in that configuration lies a social tragedy waiting to happen, and I aim to prevent that tragedy from including my husband.*

However, two days later, Sarah wrote into her diary, "Life with Allie is always so full and rich, his belated fortieth birthday party last night, for example. Every human whom Allie has cared about in his four decades—except for Carole, who's filming a movie in Italy—was flown in for the special occasion. One good thing about owning a big hotel is being able to put up 437 people at your place; a bad thing was a two-month streak of huge conventions that prevented an empty block big enough to hold it until now."

Rick Samuels videotaped the party, and Mike Schwartz, working with Sam Minkowitz and Peter Bates, presented a multimedia presentation of Allie's life. Sarah and Ari's gift was the fastest and most powerful laptop computer produced to date, and at the evening's conclusion, the gallery of close friends sang "Happy Birthday," causing Allie to weep openly.

Afterward, the Cohens glowed from the lovefest of a banquet and happily soaked in their suite's marble hot tub. Sarah watched Allie compose a poem on his new laptop. *I wonder if he's receiving a message from the Lord.* A minute later, he was done and gave it to her to read.

If we want to avoid violence,

We have the answers within us.

If we are to escape hatred and ugliness,

The ways and means are all around us.

Whether we are successful or not

Depends on how hard we try.

"Your poem is beautiful and inspiring, but I don't want you to get too deep or reflective on what has been a splendidly upbeat evening."

It is a beautiful and inspiring poem. It is also an antidote for the growing hate and resistance.

She made Allie laugh by kissing the tiny beanie bobby-pinned to his hair and then laughed a little herself before asking, "How're you doing, Cohen?"

Cohen broke his wife up. "I'm sitting here with hot water shooting up my butt, so I figure that this is probably as close to a kosher baptism as it gets."

Sarah loved soaking in the big tub and recalled their teacher-salary days when they lusted for one.

"The reason I always wanted a big tub was to fuck away safely and not wind up in the hospital."

They made love in their tub for the next half hour.

"I want to impregnate you again," Allie told Sarah, "and give Ari a brother or sister and also get you to kick the damn Marlboros for nine months and maybe for good."

She surprised him with the best possible news. "You already did, money. I've been pregnant for over a month, have already stopped smoking, and was waiting for the right time to tell you. Allie, can I smoke one more joint, please?"

"Sure, Sarah, that's fair and reasonable. And, money, you really made my day with that fantastic news."

"I've got to know"—she looked him in the eyes—"how you could smoke for over twenty years and suddenly give it up just like that."

"I simply promised Yahweh," he explained, "not to indulge in mind-altering substances anymore and placed my faith in Him to give me the strength to stay clean."

"Well, thank you, Lord, because this'll be my first pregnancy that you won't be surrounding my face with clouds of pot smoke. *Kein ayin hara*, knock on wood, it's a miracle that Ari is so smart and normal." A memory flashed in Sarah's brain, and she began laughing very hard.

Allie asked her, "What's so funny, money?"

"Do you remember the time you taught the legal concept 'habeas corpus' and the whole class missed it on the midterm exam?"

"Yeah." He laughed. "And I grabbed the biggest and darkest-skinned kid in the class right out of his seat and then told the class that Ervin was visiting his aunt in a small Mississippi town who sent him to the pharmacy to pick up her medicine. A potbellied sheriff mistakenly suspected Ervin for another guy who'd been accused of raping a white woman, pulled a gun on Ervin, handcuffed him, and threw him in jail."

She remembered. "Yes, you then pushed Ervin into a closet, even though he was claustrophobic, and started banging on the door. At that moment, you asked the class, 'Now how do we get Ervin out of jail?'"

Allie managed to stop laughing long enough to deliver the punch line.

"Carl Smalls yelled out, 'Writ of habeas corpus, plus Edward Bennett Williams and the whole damn ACLU defending him, the ghost of Robert E. Lee testifying as a character witness, while the shroud of Jesus appears on Ervin's right arm just as he swears on the Bible to the Lord that he didn't do it.'"

"Cohen, you were some kind of teacher. Ha ha! Don't you ever miss it?"

"Yeah, for about five minutes, but the reality of its limitations set in, and the feeling goes away. Every once in a while, I get a grand feeling that the world is my classroom. But then within a short time, I get humbled in a strange way."

She thought, *His acting on lordly signals never ceases to amaze me.*

"Please, Allie, I'm dying to know if you've received any divine nudges lately."

Cohen self-consciously smiled for a second or two. "I assure you, mon, that you'll be the first to know if the Almighty beckons me."

"Allie," Sarah sweetly reminded, "it's incredible that you were once such a hardheaded atheist."

"Sooner or later, Sarah, every wise man gets the message."

Yes, Allie, but I believe that you overdid the irreverent and iconoclast acts.

Chapter 115

The drab Perry Homes housing project in northwest Atlanta, since torn down and replaced with a mixed income neighborhood, may be viewed two ways.

First, the architect's vision is Perry Homes is a sprawling urban village that furnishes eleven hundred units of decent mass housing for predominantly poor and black people.

The second view is grim: Perry Homes is an isolated warren peopled with welfare recipients trapped in a distressing cycle of poverty and violence.

Eddie White, who had lived in Perry Homes and left it far behind, bought into the grim view. He entered the project cut off from the city's mainstream by a four-lane truck route, a railroad, and another similar colony across a gulch. Eddie knew firsthand that perhaps half the tenants graduated from high school, maybe a handful from college. Most of them, unfortunately, never left, and too many of them preyed on each other.

Eddie parked his Maxima in front of his alma mater, carefully locked the car, and bumped open the swinging faded red doors of the Atlanta Vocational Technical Institute, a.k.a. Vo-Tech. Dozens of Krylon-sourced eat-mes and fuck-yous had been spray-painted on the yucky green walls by early arriving vandals.

I used to do it too to Bankhead High before they kicked me out.

He reminisced. *I'm struck by how offensive the practice now seems to me. Dig it. I'm returning to Vo-Tech as a distinguished alumnus working for the mayor. Man, you can't come from any more humble circumstances than me. In fact, I was subhumble.*

He laughed to himself.

Mr. Eric Hargrove, Vo-Tech's hulking principal, stood before the restless assembly and bodily communicated "trouble unto thee who does not shut up and sit still real soon." The stern Hargrove—a former Vietnam vet, a woodshop teacher, and a part-time NFL referee—nonverbally quelled the young audience and began introducing Eddie White.

After describing White's many accomplishments, Hargrove handed the podium to Eddie, who began speaking in a soft, well-modulated voice.

"Mr. Hargrove, teachers, and students, I promise to make this short and sweet. All I ask is that you listen real hard to what I say today because it's important. You see, the politicians in Washington passed a law called NDMA or National Defense Metropolitanization Act. Learn what those big words mean because they are going to change the way you live.

"This new rule says that the city of Atlanta and the suburbs are soon going to be one big city. White people and black people all got to live as one and wherever they want to. Regional mass transit will tie us all together, and that's the way it ought to be.

"But there's one big problem. There's a lot more white people than blacks, 70 percent to 30 percent. Mayor Thomas has been a good mayor, but the next one is likely to be white. We have to see that we get our 30 percent of the jobs and political and financial power that should come with NDMA.

"The man's telling us that if we give up the city hall, we'll all be better off than these past fifteen years that we've controlled the mayor's office and made most of our gains. Now how they figure that we're gaining by giving up so much beats me, but that's a long story I'll leave for your teachers to explain and discuss with you.

"The mayor thinks he deserves the people's backing, and he does. The mayor wants to stay in office, and he should. I believe that Mayor Thomas is a strong leader and more than capable enough to govern the white folk too.

The problem is that the white people don't seem to have the same faith in him. Some openly say it's because he's black. Now I don't mean all the white people, just some of the meaner ones.

"Frankly, no matter what happens, black people must stick together to assure our 30 percent. So I'm asking each one of you to fill this form out with your name, address, and telephone number. This way, we can get in touch with you when or if we need to get the word out to everyone. Now I want to see two long lines of people to make sure that the blacks are well organized, okay?"

The two lines promptly formed and soon stretched up the aisles and out into the hallway. White had repeated this call to arms more than twenty times in the last three weeks and succeeded once more in enlisting droves of student volunteers. The Thomas political machine was solidly lining up its core network—black Atlanta University complex, the inner-city high schools, black church networks, white liberals, and gays.

Eddie left Vo-Tech a hero and headed directly to the mayor's office for a planning session over lunch. To his surprise, he found Mack and Lesotho drinking champagne and acting unbearably smug.

"What you guys sitting around drinking wine for, in the morning no less?"

Lesotho gibed him. "You hear that, Mack? Dude calls Dom Pérignon wine. Dude's got no class. Hey, don't you know what happened?"

"No, shithead, I don't, so please start telling me already." White stared at Xeranga.

Lesotho handed the morning *Atlanta Journal-Constitution* to Eddie and said, "Here, read it."

The *AJC* headline turned a glare into a million-dollar smile. Cohen again endorses Thomas for metro mayor.

The subset's bold print showed Cohen's support was firm. "Mack Thomas is the best prepared candidate for metro mayor and possesses strong crossover legitimacy."

Lesotho and Eddie agreed that Mack now had a real chance to get into the runoff. They passed the champagne bottle back and forth and high-fived one another.

Roger assessed all strongholds, their core being the city of Atlanta, North Clayton, South Fulton, South DeKalb, and small pockets in Henry, Gwinnett, and North Fulton. Times sure were changing when four black men could dream of governing the five core counties and five outer counties.

"We have to rework our campaign strategy," Mack guided, "to better penetrate opposition strongholds and generate mass appeal and interest."

Lucius North offered to work the phones to raise a hundred grand to open storefront operations in target areas. Roger Wilcox directed Lucius to focus on opening storefronts now; they had more money than time at the moment.

Less than a mile away, Allie taught Ari the Lord's lone condition for His gift of the Torah to the Israelites.

"Son, when Israel stood to receive the Torah, the holy One, blessed be He, said to them, 'I am giving you My Torah. Bring Me good guarantors who will guard it, and I shall give it to you.'

"'Our fathers,' they said, 'are our guarantor.'

"The holy One, blessed be He, said to them, 'Your fathers are unacceptable to Me, yet bring Me good guarantors, and I will give it to you.'

"'Master of the universe,' they said to Him, 'our prophets are our guarantor.'

"'Your prophets are unacceptable, yet bring Me good guarantors, and I will give it to you.'

"'Behold,' they said, 'our children are our guarantors.'

"'Ah yes, the *children* are certainly good guarantors. For their sake, I will give the Torah to you, amen.'"

Ari expressed how he enjoyed the story called "And It Will Be an Inheritance unto You and Your Children" and then requested from his father, "Dad, I need a favor. Do you promise not to get mad?"

Ari's prefacing his appeal made Allie wonder, and he typically answered, "Son, that depends on what you're going to ask me."

"Yeah, I figured you'd say that. Okay, here goes. Dad, I invited my friends over tomorrow for a water polo match."

Allie stifled his disappointment and calmly reminded, "Ari, tomorrow is Shabbat."

"Dad," reasoned Ari, "I'm the captain of the team, and the coach asked me if we could practice in the hotel pool over the weekend to prepare for our league championship against Waldorf Prep on Monday."

"I assume, of course, that you're the only kosher preppy on the team."

"So what else is new, Dad? The coach just made me captain because I'm the fastest swimmer and leading scorer too."

Ari was pleased that he didn't sound insolent or a braggart. "This place is my home of sorts, isn't it?"

"Ari, the Plaza is a hotel. Our real home will be ready in less than a month."

"Dad," Ari differed, "I haven't lived in the new house yet, so it's not my home until I do. I kind of grew up in this place, Dad. I played with my Hot Wheels in the restaurant and sailed boats and rode my tricycle in the lobby. All the workers have looked after me like I was a little brother, and I'm going to miss them. Now with you and Mom running off to France and leaving me alone with Grandpa and Grandma, well, I need my friends over now and then to practice in the pool and have some fun."

"Ari, Mom and I are taking a second honeymoon. Your grandparents will move in here. They love you, Ari. This is quality time for you to spend with them. You know they won't be around forever."

"I understand, Dad, no Sabbath matches again too. Hey, will you watch me play?"

"Sure. By the way, how many kids are coming?"

"Uh, seventy." Ari smiled. *I can imagine what my dad is thinking.*

"Seventy? Ari, who plays water polo with thirty-five on a side in a pool? Someone could get killed."

Ari giggled. "Well, you know, you own this place, so everybody wanted to come. Some parents volunteered to chaperone, and a few teachers heard that there was a pool party. Well, I admit it grew too big."

"You think maybe we should close off the pool and Sun Dial areas to entertain everybody after the practice?"

Ari's answer was right out of the saying "The child is the father of the man." "Dad, Uncle Sandy says that you have to stop closing off whole sections of the hotel whenever you want because you make a lot of conventioneers mad that way. Have you forgotten that we have over five hundred dentists staying here this weekend? Uncle Sandy says Sun Dial profits are way down."

Allie laughed from his son sounding like a little businessman.

"Don't worry, Ari, I'm selling the hotel back to Mr. Portman, who was very nice to work with me for us to live here. Now I plan to raise the capital needed to start a new cable TV channel."

"Wow, that's great, Dad. What kind? Is it a hot new movie channel, all sport programming, or rock music maybe?"

"Nope, it's the first Jewish network, and I plan to call it Judah Vision."

Allie expected his son to be excited. "Are you kidding me, Dad?"

Ari's disappointment surprised Allie, so he enthusiastically described the concept to his doubtful son.

"Ari, we're going to broadcast behind the Iron Curtain to reach and refresh Soviet Jewry and then to northeast Asia to convert millions of Japanese, South Koreans, and Taiwanese to Judaism. Isn't that an exciting vision, son?"

Ari's enthusiasm for Judah Vision matched his feelings regarding his daddy's running for mayor.

"Dad, what are you trying to be, a Jewish Billy Graham?"

Allie couldn't believe his young son's words. "Did you hear that from your mother?"

"Yeah, Mom also said that Jews shouldn't go around converting others. Supposedly, our religion forbids it because it's not easy to become a Jew."

The Lord is mixed on proselytizing Allie; He likes the idea of many more Jews, but pseudo-Jews are potentially a lot more trouble than mere lapsed ones, like you used to be. And yes, it is hard to become a Jew as it should be.

Allie's and Ari's mutual looks communicated that maybe it was best to end this discussion. Ari politely smiled, kissed his daddy, and caught an elevator to the pool level. Allie searched his Bible for any references to Jewish law, tradition, and culture that discouraged the practice.

I can't find any references, but to be safe, I'll pull the proselytizing component to avoid a needless fight. Judah Vision will serve as a Jewish educational service broadcast like PBS and focus entirely on being informative, entertaining, and enlightening.

Cohen looked at his watch. *It's time to begin packing for France, a vacation that can't come at a better time. Man, I am so ready to get out of town. Hey, let me turn off my phone so I don't get interrupted over and over.*

At Cohen's corporate headquarters ten miles up Peachtree Street, Sandy Forman gobbled a tuna fish salad on a seeded kaiser roll and washed it down with a Coke. He'd just returned from the Sit-In to pick up lunch and finally had a chance to read the morning newspaper. Sandy scanned Bob Askew's popular *AJC* "Along Peachtree" gossip column and discovered an alarming news leak.

"Rumor has it that Allie Cohen and his wife, Sarah, will tour France during the month of June. Wise move, Allie, and if you are as smart as I think you are, you'll stay there until Wednesday, November 8."

I have to warn the Cohens that their secret getaway is now common knowledge. I hope that the wire services fail to pick up on the leak so the French media won't know. Shit, why doesn't he pick up?

Sandy put the phone down and then picked it up to call Riva and complain, "Riva, how come I can never reach the Cohens when I need to?"

"You know them. They're going on a second honeymoon, so maybe they're already screwing as usual and don't want to be interrupted." That made sense to Sandy.

One Atlanta group that didn't mind Allie leaving town was the Jewish community. Cohen's wrenching NDMA threatened to disturb the Jews' comfortable niche and force them into a decisive swing-vote situation. The Jews' liberal traditions were being tested because of the coming election's possibly restoring the white majority to political dominance over the blacks.

In Atlanta, marching is a powerful black social and political tool, and some Jewish leaders and rabbis marched with blacks during the civil rights demonstrations.

"According to an *Atlanta Jewish Times* poll," Cohen read, "many of Atlanta's Jews want to forced-march me out of Atlanta pronto."

The day after Cohen left for France, the leaders of the Jewish community met at the Federation Building and debated whether to support a white or black candidate. The no-win issue of endorsing Mack Thomas and possibly antagonizing conservative whites was hotly debated.

Insurance magnate Ben Epstein counseled, "Endorsing Thomas could be very divisive. I say we wait and see what develops."

The downtown power structure of mostly rich white Christian businessmen enlisted Jewish real estate developer Martin Schonfeld to start the clamoring for Cohen who owned $225 million worth of prime central business district property.

Industrialist Joseph Berger responded to Schonfeld's pitch by discouraging it. "I once met Cohen at a Holocaust education committee meeting, and frankly, he didn't impress me as being all that stable. Also, if you check the record, he gave a crummy $25 a year to the federation. I don't care if he was a poor teacher back then. He could have given more than that."

Michael Simon, a prominent surgeon, motioned to draft a resolution. "I say that we endorse Mack Thomas because he at least has his feet on the ground."

Restaurant chain owner Henry Golden cautioned, "Simon, in case you haven't noticed, those feet on the ground happen to be black."

Simon overreacted. "You know, Henry, a Jew bigot is the worst type."

Henry returned the favor. "Well, at least, Michael, I'm not a goddamned liberal schmuck like you." And so it went, self-interest or morality?

Shortly before landing at Orly Airport, an Air France stewardess told the Cohens, "Dr. and Mrs. Cohen, a small army of journalists is waiting in the concourse to interview you. What would you like Air France to do about this?"

Sarah whispered to the stewardess, "It's our second honeymoon. I can't let those pushy bastards ruin our trip. Please, is

882

it okay if the crew lets all passengers disembark first and the airline brings a vehicle alongside the emergency exit for us to escape the press? We'll cover whatever it costs the airline."

The stewardess assured them, "It isn't every day that Air France has a former Nobel Peace Prize winner fly with us. The airline wants your trip to France to be as pleasurable as possible and have a plan for this."

"You know, Allie," Sarah reminded her husband, "this madness wouldn't be dogging us if you hadn't sold the jet."

"I'm sorry, but it was far too blatant a symbol of my wayward corporate past."

The Air France captain escorted them to a waiting limo that took them to a VIP customs office and then straight to their hotel. Upon settling into their room, the Cohens celebrated their successful end run around the French media by making love.

One reporter whom Sarah underestimated was Tina Debres, a beautiful freelancer for *Paris Match*, which commissioned her to track the Cohens from start to finish. The slinky dark Socialist and Claude, her editor, had a hunch that Cohen would change his mind about running while vacationing on the Riviera.

I am determined to obtain an exclusive interview by putting my assets to good use.

While Debres and her colleagues milled about the hotel lobby, up on the seventh floor, the Cohens were climaxing. Spent and smug, they lay in each other's arms for a few golden minutes until Allie suddenly shouted out, "I've got it!"

"Allie, I do not appreciate your enthusiasm puncturing my afterglow. Okay, Cohen, you got what, dammit?"

"I just thought of a way to avoid the media."

"Oh yeah?" That always got her interest. "How?"

Allie described his plan to Sarah, and she bent over laughing. "That's hysterically funny, Allie. Okay, let's do it."

"The stores are closing for sundown, babe, so let's dress quickly, hail a cab right outside the hotel, and make our way to Montmartre."

In this case, Allie, you're fortunate that Hashem has a sense of humor too.

Chapter 116

The Cohens got out of their cab in Montmartre; Allie spotted a news kiosk to buy an *International Herald Tribune* (*IHT*) and read the main news story to Sarah.

"Money, the Supreme Court, in a narrow and strongly contested 5–4 decision, affirmed the constitutionality of NDMA. States are forbidden to annul, subvert, or undermine federally specified guidelines. With all legal hurdles cleared, the Democratic Leadership Council intends to implement NDMA nationally after the election."

"So your high school sociology class's term paper project that was dumped into a congressman's filing cabinet until Reagan supposedly roused him will become the law of the land. I tell you, it is insane how politics works."

"The Republicans, though, are threatening to block it any way they can. If NDMA passes, George H. W. Bush promises to repeal it the day he takes office. If repeal fails, he'll refuse to enforce it. If regional populations want to metropolitanize voluntarily, that's up to them and their state legislatures."

With great fanfare, the Democrats selected Atlanta to host their 1988 convention, Dan Daniels being a prime mover behind this. The local media czar, eager for his cable channel to gain video parity with the three major networks and Fox, paid ten million for the most favorable floor positions inside the Omni and Georgia World Congress Center.

In 1986, Rick Samuels sold his porn business for thirty million cash. Rick took twelve million to get out and gave the rest to the Lee sisters and Greta and Reny, four and a half million each to get out too if they wanted to. The lawyers asked him why he gave the ladies a majority share.

"Sam Minkowitz and Carole Herman were Allie Cohen's life changers. These beautiful, wonderful women were mine. They gave their bodies, their reputations, and maybe their souls to make me a very rich man. I love these ladies for their trust and faith in me and am as proud as a man can be that the four queens of porn are the first females to become financially secure from the business. With the rise of gonzo and cheap tape, they're going to be the last four."

Rick began producing nature documentaries to cleanse his soul and crossed paths with Dan Daniels, a naturalist and sportsman, in Yosemite National Park. They shared similar interests and quickly became buddies, so Daniels hired Rick as a camera positioning expert for the convention.

Daniels's critics put nothing past him, and one night at dinner, Dan confided to Rick after killing a bottle of wine.

"Some media critics and Wall Street investment groups have accused me of occasionally manufacturing news stories to boost ratings and company stock prices. I swear to God it isn't true, Rick, but because it's not worth the effort to constantly refute it, I've stopped bothering, and it's morphed into a mystique."

One such Daniels WDDT-TV caused controversy occurred the day the Cohens left for Europe, when anchorman Ned Bryan led with a local bombshell of a story.

"An unnamed source in the Fulton County attorney's office has leaked that Atlanta mayor Mack Thomas allegedly received illegal campaign contributions from the convicted pornographer Jake Teal. Supposedly, eighty-five $1,000 donations were made through dummy corporations owned by Teal and under various assumed names also. The money was laundered through popular banking havens known for washing illegal cash.

"The source suggests too that a possible impropriety may exist because the then city council president Thomas defended

Teal against 1979 racketeering charges. Once again, Atlanta mayor Mack Thomas . . ."

And once again, bile rampaged through Mack Thomas's bloodstream like Peachtree Creek after a severe rainstorm that flooded Woodward Way.

"I'm afraid that my little girls will hear this garbage about me spewed all over the airwaves."

Thomas turned off the TV set and sulked until Charlene asked him who he believed was behind the attack. "I'm not sure," he answered. "But I guess that Republican prosecutors are fishing for big-name black Democrats."

The devoted Charlene held Mack's hand. "Assess the political damage for me, my darling Mack."

After a couple of seconds of analysis, Mack supposed, "Well, my love, I sure don't look like Mr. Clean anymore, now do I?"

The elderly owner of the Hebrew religious article store located in Paris's old Jewish quarters near Pigalle and Montmartre recognized the Cohens as American Jews.

"I am Yossi Melniker and speak eight languages, so nu, what can I do for you?"

Allie leaned over the counter to whisper his unusual request. Yossi's raised eyebrows expressed disapproval.

"I am sorry, Mr. Cohen, but such a thing is not right. It could even be blasphemous."

"Please, Mr. Melniker, it could mean a mitzvah for my wife."

"I'm sorry, but what you ask of me is just not kosher. It's irreligious at best."

Cohen practiced questionable ethics.

"I apologize if I offended you, Mr. Melniker. Please forgive me and let me make it up to you by doubling my offer."

Apparently, the new higher price nullified Yossi's ethics.

"I will do this for your wife."

He pointed a finger at Cohen to emphasize his point and walked away whispering to himself, "Meshugga Americans."

Yossi began outfitting them and speedily adjusted their garments while bellyaching three times in five minutes. "If I don't finish before sundown, the kashruth authorities may revoke my certification. Without that, no real rabbi will come near me." The grateful Cohens thanked Melniker and took a cab back to their hotel.

At that moment in Atlanta, Lesotho Xeranga held a press conference in the city hall atrium and read a specially prepared report that addressed the prosecutor's charges.

"Mayor Mack Thomas thoroughly refutes all Justice Department allegations suggesting unsavory dealings between Thomas campaign staff members and convicted pornographer Jake Teal. The mayor accuses the Justice Department of rank political headhunting through the brandishing of lies, distortions, hearsay evidence, and innuendos.

"Mack Thomas, a staunch foe of pornography, has led a continuous war against sleaze, and his closing down of three of Jake Teal's masturbation-for-hire parlors during his present administration is a matter of public record. I also present a related *AJC* editorial of the same day taking Mack Thomas to task for not defending Jake Teal. Quote, 'Even a pornographer deserves his day in court.'

888

"A final note, the mayor has hired the law firm of Barclay, Havermann, Elston, and Spilner to protect his good name. We have been instructed by legal counsel to take no questions from the media.

"This has been a full disclosure and should satisfy all public concerns regarding these false charges of impropriety. The press conference is now over, and I thank the members of the media for coming."

Coreen Mathews, a reporter for a moderate black local newspaper, had covered the city hall beat for five years and knew all administration figures on a first-name basis. The daughter of one of the most famous Negro Republicans in the United States was close to Eddie and spotted him leaning up against a plaza wall. The tall, pleasant, and attractive veteran journalist asked White, "What do you think of the Teal affair?"

Eddie said exactly what was on his mind, "They hung Teal around Mack's neck to dirty him up. Now no matter how hard he tries to clear his good name, people will always remember the smell of this garbage."

"Who do you think," Coreen asked, "these white conspirators prefer to see as the first metro mayor?"

"Some might say that they prefer Cohen," perceived Eddie. "But I don't think they want Cohen that much either because he's Jewish. You know, they want one of their own, a real right-winger."

"Can I print that too, Eddie?"

"Be my guest, Coreen."

Eddie said goodbye to Coreen and drove to an emergency meeting at Mack's spacious Hembry Heights home. Mack, Lesotho, Roger, and Eddie munched on ribs, barbecued chicken, and french fries while debating if any political damage was suffered.

Roger felt they were weathering the storm pretty well.

"I don't know, Roger," said Mack, expressing deep concern. "Fishing expeditions make me nervous as hell. You never can tell what the grand jury might yet dig up."

"I disagree, Mack." Lesotho saw it like Roger. "I think we bluffed 'em pretty good. Now all we got to do is stonewall it for a month or two, and we should make it."

The use of certain words confused Eddie. *I assume my pals are innocent and will defend their honor with my fists if necessary.*

"Lesotho," he probed, "what do you mean by *we bluffed 'em*? And please explain this *stonewalling* shit too while you're at it."

Lesotho looked at Mack, who looked at Roger, who looked away. Finally, Lesotho told Mack that he'd made a major error by including Eddie in the meeting, so he should be the one to fill him in.

Mack looked Eddie in the eye and then looked away and gave the thankless task to Roger, who also could not look Eddie in the eye while cluing him about Teal.

"It's true, Eddie. We took the money. We needed it for the campaign. Look, Cohen was a major downtown property holder. The business establishment, especially the developers, must have figured that Cohen had a stronger stake in protecting their investments. They held their donations back, very little came in, and Teal was offering serious money, so we swallowed hard."

White's world was crumbling; his idols were showing feet of clay. *I can't believe that my guys did this, and I'm guilty by fucking association. Worse, without them, I'm nothing, but I got to know what kind of fucking deal they made with that white trash.*

Eddie asked, and Roger briefed him. "We promised to stop busting his escort services and to also look the other way when his strippers fondled conventioneers to buy them overpriced drinks. With me heading the Public Safety Oversight Committee and Civilian Review Board and with Chief Lane being Mack's cousin, well, I think you can see how we have Teal and the public in our pocket."

Eddie's stomach ached, and his head hurt. He looked at Lesotho. *What's different about the dude? Hmm, his hair's much shorter, and he's wearing a three-piece suit too. Dude kind of reminds me of a corrupt lawyer now. Man, I can remember when he channeled Malcolm and he and his dashikis scared the fucking shit out of city hall.*

Eddie turned to Mack. "I hate to say this, Mack, but I got to know how such a smart man like you could wind up in such a stupid goddamned mess."

Shit, thought the mayor. *I resent having to justify my actions to a semiliterate street hustler, but for the sake of peace and group unity, I'll do so anyway.*

"All right, Eddie," he responded. "With Cohen's backing, the money should have flowed in, but it didn't. It only flowed from Cohen and the governor. While that was a lot of money, they were our only major contributors, and it wasn't enough. Teal's money was the equalizer."

He finished a rib and put it down on his plate.

"It seemed pretty clear," Roger added, "that the moneymen wanted a white man, and the black community had not been stirred up enough yet to dig deep into their pockets. A numbered bank account in Zurich, Switzerland, was secretly credited on the first day of each month via a certain Panamanian bank noted for safely laundering money."

Wilcox shoved a couple of french fries in his mouth.

"Roger," White insisted on knowing, "what amount of money was worth taking a stupid risk like this?"

Eddie demolished a chicken wing.

Wilcox did not appreciate his tone or language but spelled it out while picking up a rib and chewing the meat off the bone.

"Teal nets three million a year while serving time, so he doesn't mind paying a third for insurance. His eighty-five thousand a month kept us in the game."

Roger made the enterprise sound easy.

"We had a Miami bank lined up to represent a slew of rich out-of-state contributors hoping to get a license to enter the growing Atlanta banking market."

Eddie hated what he was hearing and then helped himself to another chicken wing and a handful of French fries.

"The trouble is it wasn't that easy. Murphy's Law happened. A spy planted in our midst dug up the dirt on us. Chief Lane just sent a *plumber* over to the campaign office to plug the damn leaks."

"Do you guys really believe that you can control a massive cover-up?" reasoned Eddie. "The Nixon administration sure couldn't."

"Man, don't be so damn naive." Mack stared at Eddie as if he should know better. "There are no laws compelling whitey to finance the campaigns of ambitious black people seeking elective office."

"Come on, Mack, Cohen's endorsed you twice. He wouldn't have done that if he was going to let you go down the toilet."

"Man." His confidence in Cohen astonished Lesotho. "You, of all people, putting your faith in Allie Cohen like that is remarkable, maybe fucking crazy."

"Maybe it's about time we all did."

Eddie was surprised that he said that and even more so that he meant it.

"Look, guys, it's got to be better than getting down in the gutter with fucking white trash like Jake Teal."

Roger waited for Eddie to shut up so he could lay out their new strategy.

"As I see it, Cohen or Teal are not the issues here. Our great challenge is to first make the race and place in the runoff."

Thomas fatalistically summed it up. "I suspect that we'll all face a day of judgment someday and can deal with that, but what I'll never be able to deal with is having the fucking door closed in my face just because I'm black. That's not right, so we all have to hang in there and flush out that goddamned spy and then stonewall it to the bitter end."

Mack, you are foolishly ignoring the law of unanticipated consequences.

Chapter 117

Allie and Sarah, disguised as a Hasidic rabbi and his rebbetzin, stepped lively across the swank lobby of the Ritz-Carlton Hotel and into a waiting elevator. Just as they hoped and schemed, the small army of bored reporters, camped in the lobby to cover the Cohens' whereabouts, completely ignored them.

A few seconds after their elevator door closed, one journalist thought it odd that ultra-Orthodox Jews were staying at the most expensive and fashionable hotel in Paris. Tina Debres laughed out loud when she figured out it had been the Cohens disguised as Hasidim. He fooled her today, but now she had an inkling of how his mind worked.

The English-speaking young hotel desk clerk overheard the Cohens discussing their next day's schedule while rushing through the lobby to buy their disguises and auctioned the info to the journalistic horde. Tina topped the previous high bid of four hundred francs.

"I'll give five hundred francs to tell me the Cohens' next destination."

"Sorry, Tina." The polite Parisian male of Tunisian descent told her the figure in his head. "I want a thousand francs. *Paris Match* has a lot more money than me."

Debres balked. "That is common thievery. Fuck you."
The North African is letting me rant and curse. Now he points his Tunisian nose in the direction of the mob of reporters congregated near the elevators. Okay, he's got me.

Tina peeled out five hundred more francs and, ready to spit nails, warned the clerk, "You better not send me off on a wild-goose chase, or I'll be back to kick your damn Arab ass right here in front of all the reporters in the lobby."

"Believe me, I take you at your word, Tina. Now please be nice. The Cohens are supposed to visit the Centre Pompidou tomorrow after breakfast."

Museums, like talking in the library, Tina thought, *do not usually lend themselves to meaningful one-one-one conversations, but it is a lead, and I am glad to escape the hell of the lobby scrum.*

Allie Cohen, from his hotel room, called Rick Samuels in Atlanta.

"Rick, I'd like you to head up my new Judah Vision cable channel, all Jewish educational programming."

"I'm flattered, Allie, but I can't wrap my head around the concept of a Jewish TV network. Remember, I wasn't even bar mitzvahed because my brother died the day before. Are you sure that you really want to do something like this?"

"Don't worry about the religious theme and content," Allie assured Rick. "I've got writers, producers, and even rabbis for that job. What I need is a guy who really knows how to run a television network. Plus, I'll top by one hundred thousand bucks whatever Daniels and WDDT is paying you."

A hundred thousand, huh? mulled Rick. "Do I have any time to think it over?"

"Yes, Rick, forty-eight hours."

"Okay, Allie, I'll speak to you in two days."

Two very hectic days of touring the City of Light passed, and Allie called Rick to get his answer. "So what's the word, good buddy?"

"I don't know, man. I don't think so." Rick's response took Allie by surprise. "I'm sorry, Allie, I really am."

"If it's a matter of money, Rick, I can up it."

"No," said Samuels. "Money's irrelevant. I simply can't leave Daniels right now. It just wouldn't be right."

"There are limits to loyalty," Cohen countered.

"Look, Allie, WDDT has experienced a terrible tragedy, and it simply isn't the right time to leave, and please let it go at that."

Allie pressed Rick for a full disclosure; Samuels asked him, "Haven't you been reading the *International Herald Tribune*?"

"No, Sarah's banned me from reading the *IHT*. She refuses to let me spoil her trip, so she keeps me running from one great museum, park, or neighborhood to another."

"Allie, keep this a secret. WDDT's news department planted Teddy Hicks, our ace investigative reporter, inside Mack Thomas's campaign headquarters. Hicks needed only five days to trace the Teal connection and discovered other irregularities too, but then a horrific thing happened."

"Like what, Rick?"

"Someone must have discovered what Hicks was up to and offed him."

Cohen reeled from the news and then wasn't sure if he heard right.

"Rick, what did you mean by *offed* him?"

"What, are you fucking thick? He's *dead*. Someone killed Teddy."

"Rick, you're shitting me. Wow, that's really awful."

"Tell me, Allie. I'm the one who had to tell his poor wife."

"Are there any leads?"

"The police report," according to Samuels, "claims that a wino found the body in Underground Atlanta. Teddy's wallet had three hundred in it, so the police have ruled out robbery. One detective thinks it was a professional job because Teddy was a very big man and skilled in karate too."

"Are there any leads?"

"Daniels suspects city hall's complicity but hasn't any proof. One doesn't have to be a genius to imagine why Mack Thomas and company might have wanted Hicks out of the way. Remember too that the mayor controls the police force and his cousin Richard Lane is the chief."

Cohen's head was spinning as he said goodbye to Rick and hung up the phone. Allie went straight to the hotel kiosk to buy an *IHT*. While paying for it, a *Le Soir* reporter recognized Allie and barraged him with questions regarding the Hicks case. Cohen smiled and just uttered, "No comment. Au revoir."

The first week of the Cohens' vacation flew by. The French were very kind and helpful to the Americans, and they were having a terrific time. *I love Paris so much*, Sarah thought, *that I'd like to buy a condo. I'll take up painting. Allie will write, anything to keep him out of Atlanta until November 8. I really like this Châtelet area with its open and dynamic walking space.*

Sarah worked her way through the many satellite galleries. Allie asked her what pieces she had selected.

"I picked out two dozen varied originals and prints for our Buckhead home and gifts for family and friends. What about you?"

"I indulged myself with three attractive sculptures for the gardens and a large raised black leather mask of two lovers for over our bed."

Sarah smiled and kissed Allie and then looked him in the eye.

"For once in my life, I'd love to do something that really rich people do."

She pointed to one of the new town houses being erected around Châtelet Square.

"I want to buy that powder blue one, love that color. Imagine walking outside and having all this to explore. Look, I'm not saying move here, just own a home like this to bring us back to Paris now and then plus it could be a good investment too."

"I agree that the row of town houses and the area overall is very attractive." Allie pointed to a nearby outdoor café. "Let's sit down at this little bistro and discuss it over a cup of coffee and apple pie. I don't know why, but I suddenly have a yen for it."

Tina Debres sat at a table two rows away and listened to the Cohens converse.

"So will you let me buy it, Allie?"

"Are you going to manage it too?" he asked, grounding her into the realities of second-home ownership. "You know, work with realty companies to do repairs or renovations when necessary, pay taxes, maybe rent out too? Frankly, I'm not equipped right now to manage multiple properties, but be my guest if it will make you happy."

"So we can add it to my personal estate that you set up for me, right?"

"Yes, Sarah. In fact, the *APD* cop show and AB and TB royalties could cover the cost and upkeep of a couple of homes. We may never spend a night in this place, but it's only money, babe, so do it. In fact, call Sandy to take care of it for you."

"Thank you, Allie, for indulging me. I love you for it, money, but on second thought, I'm just going to roll over it in my mind for a while."

I'll give Allie the impression that I appreciate his satisfying my wish. She prayed, *The truth is that we have two weeks on the Riviera before us, and I beg God to show us the one blessed spot with the incomparable quality of life that even Allie will be drawn to escape the pressures building up in Atlanta.*

Allie prayed to Yahweh too; indeed, a near-constant devotional rushed from him.

Please, Lord, forgive me for being slack with daily services and keeping kosher, but Sarah's been such a wonderful wife, Almighty, that she really deserves a great vacation. Please cut me some slack, Master of the universe.

Sarah and Allie shared a slice of French apple pie.

"Sarah, I think I actually am changing for the better."

"What do you mean *for the better*, Allie, and how exactly?"

"For example, I like France and its people and have fondly thought of them as maybe one of the most civilized nations in the world. Now I see the French as the most civilized Chazer nation, for they combine maximum satisfaction of self and appetites with minimal inhibition or restraint from God, religion, or guilt."

"I never thought of them that way before, but maybe you're right."

"Let me explain the Chazer thing I feel about the French. You know how I love their food and the cute outdoor cafés to consume it. Well, the cafés and their smells are now so ubiquitous to me that, at times, it causes me pangs of nausea. As a twenty-year-old, I also loved and saluted Paris's relaxed sexual attitudes. Twenty years later, though, sexual stimuli so saturate the city that prurience is nearly mainstream. I sense I'm making real progress in taming my Chazer traits, and France is a true test."

Sarah minored in art as a college student. "Allie, I've always wanted to experience the Moulin Rouge, but I'm sorry if that feels like another test to you."

"No, it's okay, money. I always appreciated Toulouse-Lautrec's artwork too, so let's dress up for *le revue exotique*."

He snapped his fingers and made her laugh by shaking his butt cancan-style. They dressed and hailed a cab for Place Pigalle. The driver cut across Saint-Lazare and darted up the Boulevard de Clichy.

Cohen asked the cabbie to please detour through the Jewish quarters.

"We're leaving Paris tomorrow, and I'd like a last look of the old ghetto."

The tired urine-stained neighborhood had huddled down for nightfall by the time the Cohens reached it. Pigalle's being around the corner bothered Allie.

"Sarah, I can't stand how closely Pigalle's sex plague has crept up to the Jews' poor commune. Dear Adonai, it is right around the corner."

You can't fight it, Allie. Twenty years from now, the Jews' poor commune and Joe Goldenberg's famous deli will be torn

900

down and replaced by a huge mixed-use real estate project that may temporarily beat back the sex plague one lousy block.

The taxi deposited them right in front of the historic Moulin Rouge, where Allie and Sarah anxiously sought refuge in the lobby of the still grand nightclub and were quickly seated up front.

"Give me a break," Cohen commented. "First act is a fat middle-aged torch singer wearing lame gold pants. Man, I'll be grateful to her if she keeps her clothes on."

"She has a pretty good voice, Allie, so what if her pants are a little snug?" Sarah giggled causing Allie to laugh too.

"Ah, she's left the stage still fully clothed. Yes. Uh-oh, here come three grinning Argentine bola dancers who resemble the Marx brothers dressed as gauchos."

"Allie, the running commentary is not necessary, though you are funny as hell."

"Sarah, I can't take these guys blasting their big brown marbles in rapid-fire on the wooden stage. They're giving me such a fucking headache that I thank the Lord I'm unarmed at the moment."

She laughed tears. After the show, he reviewed his experience.

"Somehow, money, I endured three naked Peruvian jugglers, four nude Swedish seal trainers, and even a topless Italian sword swallower. The Moulin Rouge spares no expense in scouring the world for the best naked talent on earth."

"For me . . ." He made her laugh with a funny face. "Stop it, Allie. The revue was a lifetime dream come true."

"The old saying, Sarah, that Jewish men will do nearly anything for their wives is really true."

She laughed hard again; her beauty amazed him. *I swear, she's more beautiful than the day she appeared at my door in Manhattan.*

He tried to be fair in rating the show. "Okay, I guess I got my money's worth. The costumes were lavish—"

Pigalle after dark stopped Cohen in midsentence. Fear forced Sarah to grab his arm.

"Allie, this human sewer is making me nervous. Please find a cab to get us out here as fast as possible."

"I feel the same way you do, Sarah, but none are to be found. I suggest that we walk a block or two from the nightclub as Moulin's regulars are lined up and stepping into one waiting taxi after another."

She took his arm, and they walked briskly.

"With the passing of each live, hard sex show or XXX movie or dirty bookstore, babe, my sense of human worth slides to the amount of francs in my pocket."

Finally a taxi appeared. *I'll throw my body in front of it to force the driver to halt.*

Allie opened the door and said, "Monsieur, I'll offer you double fare if you take us to Place Vendôme."

The bushed-looking driver followed the transportation code, set the meter running, and the Cohens got in.

"Were our fears real or imagined, Sarah?"

Their uneasiness, however, diminished with each kilometer of distance they put between them and Pigalle.

The next day, Allie rented a shiny black Porsche 928 to buzz down the autoroute to the Riviera. Somewhere south of Beaune, a metallic black blur cruised at 115 miles per hour in the direction of the walled ancient city of Avignon.

Sarah felt a hunger pang. "Allie, I can't wait to get to Avignon already. I'm craving lunch and can picture us munching away in an old town café."

She looked at her watch and then the road. *Everything seems to be blurring by.*

"Allie," she asked, "how fast are you going?"

"Oh, I'm going about 190, babe."

"One ninety, are you crazy?"

"Sarah, that's 190 kph, not mph."

"Okay, well, how fast is that in mph?"

"Around 110, mon."

Sarah's jaw dropped. "Must I threaten to leap from this speeding vehicle if you don't dramatically slow down?"

"Money," he pleaded with her, "I rented this speed machine so the European leadfoots can't make nervous wrecks of us. One literally has to drive 115 in France to stay alive as guys are whizzing by at 140, even 150 mph."

"You're full of shit, Allie, but you're having a lot of fun, aren't you, money?"

Cohen flashed a happy grin and changed the subject.

"We're crossing Valence, the mythical line that supposedly divides the federated industrial North from the Latin and Mediterranean South."

"You mean like the Mason-Dixon Line in America?"

"Yes, exactly and with similar North and South divisions too."

After a marvelous lunch in Avignon's old town, they drove straight to Toulon, a small port city thirty miles east of Marseille. Allie cruised up a steep hill lined with small vendors on both sides of the street—the stalls manned by poor and angry-looking North African Arabs.

The Cohens emerged from the hilly market area, and La Tour Blanche, one of the most beautiful hotels in all France, majestically appeared before them. The hotel set perched on the summit that overlooked the town and harbor below. The Cohens settled into an exquisite and spacious guest room, savored their spectacular view of the Mediterranean, and then made glorious love for the next hour.

The beautiful South of France can have that kind of effect on you.

Chapter 118

The Cohens savored a great meal in La Tour Blanche's restaurant—awarded two stars by *Michelin Guide*—and enjoyed a splendid night's rest. Breakfast was served out on the terrace; a deep turquoise sea blew soft breezes that frizzed Sarah's hair. The Cohens consumed fluffy croissants, Sur la Mer preserves, and perfectly brewed coffee.

Sarah, in between bites, wrote a dozen postcards to family members and friends. Allie, in contrast, read a worrisome news article in the morning *IHT.*

With each sensuous breeze felt, postcard completed, puff of cigarette inhaled, and sip of coffee ingested, Sarah edged ever closer to nirvana.

Suspicions of the Thomas administration raised by a discomfiting news article, in contrast, had Allie worrying about a dark cloud over Atlanta.

Sarah put down her postcard for a second to see if Allie was as happy as she was.

My god, he seems depressed. She was amazed and wondered, *How can a man appear so troubled in paradise? Ahh, yes, it's the newspaper, of course.*

"Allie, please stop reading the paper," she insisted. "Here are a couple of postcards to write. It'll get your mind off whatever."

Allie implored Sarah, "Please read this article."

She hesitantly glanced at the bold headline and two and half column report. HICKS MURDER CASE SUSPECT TO TAKE POLYGRAPH TEST TODAY.

The description of an alleged cover-up, a.k.a. Thomasgate, imperiled her gemütlichkeit, and she got right to the point.

"Is Hicks's murder why Rick turned down your Judah Vision offer?" Allie nodded yes. Sarah next asked, "Do you think the Thomas regime is capable of murder to hold on to political power?"

Allie threw up his hands. "I doubt it, Sarah, but you can't rule out the possibility. My guess is some very stupid unexpected thing took place, and a bad mistake happened."

"I have to know, Allie. Has Thomasgate changed your mind about running?"

"I've said that I'd stay out of it as long as viable alternatives existed," answered Allie in a deliberate voice. "But now with this investigation, I'm not so sure anymore because I twice endorsed Mack Thomas."

Allie's moving so close to running provoked Sarah.

"I can't take being a political wife, Allie. I happily married a teacher and adjusted to your becoming a writer. Looking back, I've no regrets. But looking ahead, I can't bear the scrutiny that comes with a political career."

He heard me, but is he listening?

Sarah worried. *I'm afraid that Allie is getting that "only I can save Atlanta" outlook.* She prayed to the Lord for her sake, *Please, God, shush. Don't send my husband any more signals.*

Allie got up to pay their room bill and pack the Porsche. The Cohens checked out of La Tour Blanche and headed eastward on the coast road and toward Saint-Tropez. "For the next five days, Sarah, we will be house guests of Gerard Mandel, France's best-selling novelist, a man who writes on many of the same themes that I do."

"I've read two of his books, Allie, and liked them both. He intensely explores the French Jewish experience and you the Jewish American world. You're both fascinated by the madness of race too."

That pleased Tina Debres, who trailed the Cohens. The Thomasgate revelations had made her more determined than ever to interview Cohen, and she sensed that the right time to approach Allie was very close.

In an empty corner of the Atlanta City Hall cafeteria, Public Safety Commissioner Richard Lane and Mayor Mack Thomas met to discuss the Hicks affair. The Atlanta media glare forced them to move their weekly meeting from Paschal's, Atlanta's historic black-owned restaurant, to the city hall canteen, a drab snack space with vending machines only.

"You can relax, Mack," said Lane as they sat down with two cups of coffee. "Judo Cummings just passed his polygraph test."

A two-ton safe was lifted from Mack's uptight chest. He looked around to make sure that they were alone.

"Richard, how'd you pull it off?"

"I coached Cummings to take deep breaths to constantly rid the body of anxiety. This form of meditation," Lane described, "relaxes the brain, which reduces the stress factor to a normal level. The needle hardly moved."

"Richard, I just took a deep breath to relieve some of my own stress. Man, if we ever manage to put this mess behind us without going to jail, I'm going to become religious. By the way, how did we ever get into this fix?"

"Murphy's Law and awful luck," philosophized Lane. "I mean, who'd expect Hicks to attack Judo as if he were Bruce Lee? When Hicks went into his ninja act, Cummings was forced to apply the outlawed choke hold."

"That damn choke hold is always trouble, cost the city $170,000 last year in legal and court costs."

"Yeah, but all Judo did was use the police lock to exploit pressure points, but that damned crazy reporter struggled so hard that he aspirated. Judo just wanted to contain the dude, not kill him."

"Cummings then panicked and dumped the body in Underground Atlanta, right?"

"You got it, Mack, but thank god that he passed the polygraph with flying colors. All the hearing can turn up now is two main dead ends for the prosecution."

"Richard, how many people do you estimate know what happened?"

"Let's see, Mack. There's me, you, Lesotho, and Roger Wilcox. What about that guy who works for you? What's his name again?"

"You mean Eddie White."

Richard nodded. "Yeah, where's he at?"

"Don't worry, Eddie's okay. Richard, do you think we're doing the right thing?"

"What, and take your chances with Lucas Sanderson, Fulton County DA?"

"I guess not, Richard, huh?"

"Mack, Sanderson would have Judo halfway to the electric chair already. After that, he'd nail us all as accessories."

"Damn, Richard, I used to take pride in being an honest man."

"Uh-huh, but then you got involved in politics, Mack, a business where damage control becomes a way of life."

"You're right. Anyway, thanks for everything, coz. You're a terrific friend and a great police commissioner too."

"Ahh, don't mention it, Mack. You know what they say, 'Blood is thicker than water.'"

Race too has a bonding capacity through thick and thin. The cloud hanging over the city's black administration loomed as a fulmination against the Afro-American community and its leaders.

The day before, thirty black clergymen led by Rev. William Walker circulated a petition calling on Lucas Sanderson to conclude his investigation by stating in a news release, "Serious charges have been levied that cannot be substantiated. Groundless but detrimental accusations abound. Unless solid evidence is immediately forthcoming, the Black Ministers Association urges the Fulton County district attorney to cease and desist. Failure to do so may yet result in a class action suit demanding that an injunction be served to stop a witch hunt."

The day after the secret Lane-Thomas meeting, reporter Coreen Mathews interviewed petition organizer William Walker. The Mathews-family-owned weekly, the *Atlanta Crier*, printed the transcript as their lead story.

MATHEWS: Do you believe that there is a cover-up at city hall?

WALKER: No, I do not. I suspect the manufacturing of a premeditated attack on the Thomas administration, the aim being to defame the most powerful black challenger and discredit the black's rightful claim for sharing power and economic resources under the new NDMA arrangement.

MATHEWS: Then how do you explain the death of Teddy Hicks?

WALKER: We believe the investigators should first find out who Hicks worked for and what his motives were. My hunch is that Dan Daniels is behind all this and should be investigated. I'm very sorry about Hicks's tragic death and pray for his family.

MATHEWS: Therefore, in your opinion, Hicks found no incriminating evidence, and all Thomas administration officials are innocent.

WALKER: Until any damning evidence is forthcoming, yes.

MATHEWS: What about the alleged illegal campaign contributions from pornographer Jake Teal and his gang?

WALKER: What about them? Where's the evidence?

MATHEWS: According to Lucas Sanderson, Hicks's killer allegedly shredded the evidence that Hicks probably had on him at the time and disposed of it. Is it not possible that a cover-up does, in fact, exist?

WALKER: Doubtful, and since no evidence exists, Sanderson should terminate his investigation. If there's any finger-pointing to be done, it should be leveled at the black community for not financially supporting Mayor Thomas. This deficit helped allow a perception of impropriety to occur.

MATHEWS: Are fund-raising efforts improving?

WALKER: Yes, the Black Ministers Association has started a campaign to seek pledges from members of our respective congregations. Black businesses are being called on to dig deeper than they ever have before. The initiative gains strength with each new attack by a white interest group.

MATHEWS: Reverend Walker, the *Crier* thanks you for taking the time to share your wisdom with us.

WALKER: You're welcome, but let me again say that unless these attacks cease, the ministers will consider the boycott. The white downtown power structure stands forewarned. Please heed our call to decency.

Chapter 119

The Cohens arrived at Gerard Mandel's country beach home in Saint-Tropez in the middle of the afternoon. The smooth, handsome bachelor novelist just happened to be outside checking for mail and greeted his American guests.

"Allie, Sarah, welcome to my home. Please relax after your long ride, and forgive me, for I have a few more pages to write for an article I'm doing for a French literary journal."

"No problem, Gerard," Allie assured him. "Please go finish your piece, and I look forward to reading it when you are done."

"Thank you. Your room is the first one down the hallway on the left, and over there is the kitchen and the fridge. Help yourself to anything. The beach is a few hundred feet beyond that privacy wall of cypress trees, so just go and enjoy."

He pointed to a long strand of the tall, narrow trees.

"Allie, I'm a bit tired from the drive from Toulon and need to nap for an hour or two. I'll go lie down."

"Babe, I'm still revving from the drive and will check out Tahiti Beach."

A minute later, Allie emerged from the dry scrubland dotted with wild roses and into a crowd of half-naked women.

Mandel's being able to write seven solid hours a day in one of the great T&A capitals of the world astonishes me. I gather that the nudity simply becomes part of the Saint-Tropez landscape.

Cohen was quite the sight strolling along the beach in his aviator sunglasses, Atlanta Braves baseball cap, and blue thongs flip-flopping in the little waves. He held an aluminum chair in his right hand while his left squeezed a Bible. After about five minutes of searching for a few spare feet of unoccupied sand, an opening in the jiggly sprawl of beachgoers appeared, and he sat down in his chair.

Everywhere I look, there are bare tits, men compacted into tiny skintight briefs, or little uncircumcised boys, some with hideously bent penises, scurrying around. The display, he thought, *is swinish, and it cloys in my throat and stomach.*

Cohen's face stiffened from the sight of naked grandmothers feeding crackers or grapes to their naked grandchildren and judged that it distracted from the beautiful setting of mountains behind him, the sea ahead, and the bay full of world-class yachts drifting offshore.

He laughed at the notion that his former self would have said, *Oh yeah, right on, all this and nudity too, far fucking out.*

A European rock star playing sand soccer accidentally kicked a hard shot off Cohen's head. Allie intuitively sensed that it was time to pray, which would help screen out the decadence all around him.

Let me randomly select a chapter. Okay, I'll read Isaiah chapter 56 from my Illustrated Jerusalem Bible.

The passage's content, though, he quickly realized, made him wonder if his choice was coincidental or intended to be another message from above.

The passage read, "Thus saith the Lord, keep ye judgment and do justice: for my salvation is near to come, and my righteousness to be revealed. Blessed is the man that doeth this . . . that keepeth the Sabbath from polluting it, and keepeth his hand from doing any evil."

Cohen trembled and sweated. *It's Shabbat. Blessed be He may view my presence on fleshpot beach as a pollution of His day.*

The Lord surely understands that I've come to Tahiti Beach only to please my giving and devoted wife, Sarah.

Cohen's confidence in Yahweh's benevolence eroded. *Uh-oh, a gorgeous girl, perhaps twenty-five, with perfect tits is walking straight toward me wearing a G-string and sunglasses. Lord, are you testing my resolve?*

Tina, as planned, was putting her assets to best use. Allie's breathing slowed and heartbeat quickened as the trim knockout crept closer. Cohen glanced at the sky or the sand below as the comely woman put down her trusty Nikon and tape recorder and introduced herself.

"*Docteur* Cohen, my name is Tina Debres, and I desire to interview you. I am a freelancer for *Paris Match*, and all you have to do is say yes, and you will be next week's cover story and featured article, *mais oui?*"

Cohen tried to answer, but he saw Tina's magnificent nipples suddenly extend a quarter inch right before his eyes and had to look away.

Tina watched his reaction. *Ah, Cohen's looking up at the sky or down at the sand to avoid my nudity. I think it's making him anxious, so let me put on my T-shirt and jean shorts and flash him a warm big smile to set him at ease.*

Allie smiled back at Tina, who reinforced him as she dressed.

"I've gotten the message, Allie. The price for this interview is professionalism and respect for boundaries."

"Tina," asked Allie, "please state your reasons for interviewing me."

"Okay, you are a very rich and famous man, a successful novelist, a former Nobel Peace recipient, and a former partner of Carole Herman, whom I'm a very big fan of."

She finished dressing and took a picture of him.

"All in all, those are the same pat reasons that I always turn down *People* magazine. Come on, *Paris Match* can do better."

"You are right, no celebrity babble, I promise. All right, you have changed the way your countrymen will be governed, and your city is coming unglued and urges you to run for metro mayor, yet you resist. You have also wrestled your way into the position of a privileged few who can change the destiny of the world by what you say or do."

"A bit overstated, Tina," said Cohen, nodding three times. "But overall, not bad. The resistance to NDMA is mistaken. Areas are encouraged to incorporate into new cities if they wish. For example, because of growth along the northern perimeter arc, a new city of Sandy Springs or Dunwoody would be formidable new economic gateways to the Atlanta metro region."

"So, Allie, you're saying that critics are overstating the centralization factor?"

"Yes, Tina, the law simply demands equalization in provision of basic services and costs. Water, power, education, health, roads, and transportation service costs are to be spread as equally as possible across the metro region."

"So it's all about equal municipal costs to all, not centralized control?"

"Yes and no. There is a measure of centralization in Atlanta City Hall to coordinate and manage, but cities and counties are free to share, experiment, or cooperate in services provision in the most commonsense manner. The cost to taxpayers is always to be fair and smart and the search for savings and reductions relentless."

"So it could even result in lowering taxes for the rich too?"

"And they might for the wealthy people in the higher taxation areas of Buckhead and North Fulton and North DeKalb County, but ultimate executive authority resting in Atlanta City Hall, a mostly black city with a possible Jewish mayor, is at the heart of a dated controversy."

"I am Jewish also, a child of Holocaust survivors. I changed my name because people named Dubrovsky don't go so far in France."

"Interesting. Where did you learn to speak such good English?"

"I spent a year at Berkeley on a Fulbright scholarship. Hey, I'm supposed to be the interviewer and ask the questions."

They both good-naturedly laughed, and Tina, in the course of an hour, asked a dozen intelligent questions that drew Allie out with subjects like his beliefs in God, politics, and love. Cohen, in an expansive mood, agreed that it was time to start becoming more involved in NDMA implementation and rated presidents from Kennedy to Reagan.

Eventually, Debres got around to Thomasgate.

"Allie, do you think there is a cover-up going on or not?"

"Tina, why should Europeans give two shits about Thomasgate?" He laughed at the scandal's name.

"You're wrong," Tina told him. "First, it's a damn good story. You have the history of racial conflict, political power plays, and big money up for grabs all set against the backdrop of the Gothic South."

Allie laughed at that description too. "Tina, I'd hardly call Atlanta *Gothic*."

"But that's part of it too. Many French see Atlanta as a future U.S. apex. Sure, Atlanta's not there yet, but I predict that Atlanta will be one of the preferred U.S. cities in thirty or forty years."

"Tina, have you ever visited Atlanta?"

"No, Allie, but I have friends and associates who are trade officials, real estate investors, media executives, people whose business is to know which cities are on the way up or down. It's their perception that Atlanta is doing a better job of cooperatively solving the usual American problems of race and poverty."

She smiled and then startled him. "Allie will help realize Atlanta's rosy future by ultimately running and getting the job done."

Her endorsement unnerved him a bit. "I'm not so sure if I should thank you, Tina, for that ringing vote of confidence."

"You know, Allie, many Europeans are fascinated by the crosscurrents of a rich and liberal ex-Yankee being promoted as the compromise choice between feuding white racists and angry militant blacks. That's why you had to dress up as a Hasidic rabbi the other day to escape the press."

"You were able to see through my disguise?"

"Well, not right away, Allie. It must have taken me . . . thirty or forty seconds to figure it out, just in time for you to make it to the elevator. Why are elevators always waiting for you? The door always closes after you get in too."

Debres's cute wit made Cohen laugh, and he gave her a playful hug. Sarah finished napping and joined them.

She smiled at Tina, introduced herself, and told Debres, "Tina, you are very beautiful."

Sarah then teased Allie, "I can *see* that you sure didn't miss me that much." And she rolled her eyes.

Debres politely laughed. "Sarah, please join the interview. Permit me to take some pictures of you and Allie from different angles. Allie, put your arm around Sarah, good. Now both of you stick your sunglasses in your hair to look less American, yes, good too. Europeans love that. I know, it's crazy, but the French eat it up and the Italians too." Tina put her camera down.

"Sarah, can I interview you alone later this evening, perhaps over drinks after dinner? I'd love to hear how you're handling the political pressures being placed on Allie, the woman's point of view and all that."

"Tina," said Sarah in her usual straightforward way, "there's really not that much to say. I don't want Allie to run and don't think I'm equipped to be a politician's wife."

"Great, I love it. I can't wait to talk to you. Later on, I insist that you both be my guests at Dado's birthday party, you know, the Dutch rock star. Everybody's going."

"Tina," Allie inquired, "will they be doing drugs there?"

"Of course, everything—hash, pills, coke, you name it."

"I'm sorry, but we'll have to take a rain check."

Allie peripherally saw Sarah hide her disappointment and was glad she said nothing.

"Allie, I was sure you got high." Tina, exasperated, said, "I mean, I once saw in my editor Claude's desk a picture of you smoking a giant joint at an African concert, the Egyptian pyramids I think? Claude killed the story, so you owe *Paris Match* big-time. That picture could have ended your tour."

"I didn't know that. Please thank Claude for me. Anyway, I get high on the Lord now. However, do you happen to know of a nice little restaurant that serves bouillabaisse?"

"Sure, Les Moustarden; I'll pick you up at eight and remember to dress casually like jeans, shorts even, because it's hot tonight."

Sarah removed her bikini top; Tina applauded. Allie smiled and questioned, "How does it feel, babe?"

"Actually, I've never felt freer. Saint-Tropez is absolutely one of the greatest places I've ever visited."

"Why'd you do it, money?"

"Why not, Doc? I'm the free spirit in the family. You're the conservative one. Why, does it bother you?"

Cohen thought about that for a few seconds before answering his wife.

"No, Sarah, but going topless is hardly an unconventional act here. Frankly, one sets a trend by keeping their shirt on."

Chapter 120

Tina drove into Saint-Tropez, talking and smoking a cigarette with her left hand, steering with the right, and almost wiping out a half dozen tourists as she barreled down the narrow village road to the marina. The Parisian backed right into a tiny parking space on her first try.

"You know, Tina," said Sarah, unable to restrain her admiration for another ballsy Jewish chick. "I really like you."

"Well, now that we all like one another," kidded Debres, displaying a cool wit, "let's go eat and talk."

Les Moustarden, an adorable bistro, sat high and diagonally over an elegant junction. A golden orange sun set slowly over the jetty and bathed the tawny brick brasserie that divided a cozy beach from the rock-lined bay.

For starters, the Cohens and Debres downed a good cold Mouton Cadet. For the next hour, Allie patiently listened to the two women discuss the life of a political wife.

Tina gained Sarah's trust so completely that she commented on subjects that she might balk at even with close friends.

Allie thought he heard Sarah say that she could handle his running after all.

"If it comes down to an absolute must situation," he blurted out, "Tina, where a real idiot or monster threatens to get elected, I'd have to consider running to keep the city from tearing itself apart."

He heard wrong. After that public declaration, Sarah bolted from the table, stormed out the door, and ran wildly toward the village beach. Allie, stunned, finally acted as Sarah headed toward the rock seawall that held back the harbor. Nightfall was descending, and waves at high tide washed the giant boulders forming at the wall.

Allie looked back at Tina and yelled to her, "Please excise this embarrassing scene from the interview!"

"Of course, what do you think I am, a whore? Now run fast after her. Sarah could kill herself on the rocks, and the bouillabaisse just left the kitchen."

Allie's last words as he left Les Moustardens and began closing the gap were "I have a feeling that, when this night is over, I will still not have eaten a bouillabaisse. *Man, I'm running as fast as I can and don't think I'm going to catch her before she charges over those fucking rocks. This damn embankment must be a quarter mile long and slippery as all hell.*

"Money!" Allie screamed at Sarah. "Please stop this crazy running before something terrible happens!"

The crashing of the waves and a moonless dark night amplified her stubborn silence. The breakwater was made slicker by each wave that the choppy surf washed over. With the heart of a mountain goat, Cohen managed to cut the distance between them by leaping from stone to stone. Finally, with one last thrust, Allie caught up with Sarah and threw his arms around her. It took all his might to hold his hysterical wife in his arms.

"Promise me you'll stop running, Sarah, please."

Sarah sobbed heavily and spewed out curse after curse but eventually submitted. When Allie released her, she sought one more satisfaction and punched him in the chest as hard as she could.

"You bastard, Allie!" she screamed. "You don't give a shit about Ari and me!"

"Please understand," Allie begged, "that the people of Atlanta deserve better than elected officials who kill to hold on to power."

"I don't give a flying fuck about the people," argued Sarah. "The people get the candidate they deserve."

"Usually, okay."

"Isn't President Alzheimer's re-election absolute proof of that?"

To that, Allie pleaded, "This is no ordinary mayor's race, Sarah, and frankly that was a little unkind."

Sarah yelled back at him, "That's precisely why I'm so unyielding! I want you alive and all to myself because I don't know what I would do if I ever lost you again. And since when have you become Reagan's defender?"

They both laughed, and Sarah hugged Allie as if she never wanted to let go.

Allie urged her to grasp, "NDMA, Sarah, is urban Play-Doh in the hands of a master builder. We're on the threshold of formulating a world-class city."

That left Sarah visibly unimpressed.

"Save the crappy campaign speeches for the dumbass rednecks and blacks. They'll both be humping to be the first to shoot the little Jew mayor when their crummy lives don't change a bit."

The depth of Sarah's anger and her rank cynicism disturbed Allie, and he did not know how to ease her concerns. His frustration deepened when Debres caught up to them and took Sarah's side.

"She's right, Allie. The asshole will plead insanity and be out of jail in seven years, and your little boy will be without a daddy."

Allie was emotionally overmatched; Sarah held her ground. "You see, Allie."

Tina supplied devastating new information.

"Allie, the inside word is that the Thomas regime will get away with it. The alleged killer, Judo Cummings, just passed a polygraph test that cleared him of both murdering Hicks and shredding the Teal evidence. The local prosecutor has already freed Cummings and dropped the charges against him."

Cohen, shocked by the revelations, asked how she knew.

"My editor, Claude, just called to tell me. The black community in Atlanta is charging WDDT with undermining Mayor Thomas, and a black ministers' boycott has started. News reports out of Atlanta claim that racial tensions are the worst they've been in twenty years."

"There's your first set of losers," identified Sarah, "four hundred thousand pissed-off metro blacks, and remember, it only takes one bullet to make me a widow."

Debres had the last word. "Claude also told me how mean rednecks once came down from Marietta to lynch a Jewish industrialist named Leo Frank. Claude, who is Jewish himself, said that it was the only lynching of an American Jew in U.S. history. He also said an odd monument to fried chicken stands there today."

Tina's dredging up of the seventy-year-old Leo Frank case, which he'd used to back off Governor Hebert, drove Cohen crazy.

"Please stop with the big chicken sign. I can't take any more of your ganging up on me, and since I haven't filed and am still on vacation, I want to have some fun. Now will you two please stop hocking me, or do I have to find some other company to have a good time with?"

They all laughed and held one another. The humor relieved Sarah of her dread, and she suggested that the three of them go dancing.

"You guys," Tina reminded them, "are missing out on something really special, Dado's birthday party."

"Tina, the drug use, I can't," Allie reminded her.

"Dado," she promised, "will put away the drugs if you come."

"Tina, I am hesitant to expect strangers to do that for me."

"Allie, Dado will do it for me. We are lovers."

Cohen appeared still unsure. Debres said the magic words, "I just don't want you guys to miss out on Dado jamming with a couple of the Stones."

Allie wasn't sure he heard right. "Tina, did you say *the Stones*?"

"Yes, Mick and Keith, also Eric Clapton and Jimmy Cliff. They're all jamming. I heard Paul McCartney might drop by too."

"Well, all right!" shouted Cohen. "Let's boogie on down."

Gerard joined them at Dado's for a remarkable night, and for the rest of the Cohens' visit, they all partied, discussed literature, wrote, or talked of love. Saint-Tropez with Gerard was a blowout, which was what made Cannes—their next stop—a nice change of pace.

The stately Concorde Hotel stands in the heart of La Croisette, the oceanfront boulevard of beautiful floral arrangements

924

and exclusive shops. Tina accompanied them to Cannes but passed after seeing the Concorde Hotel.

"Sorry, guys, Cannes is a bit sedate for my taste. I'm going to split back to Paris to file my story. You guys are my favorite interview subjects of all time. I love you, guys. Let's stay in touch please. Au revoir."

Sarah loved the laid-back Cannes.

"Allie, relax. I'm retiring my bathing suit top for the rest of the week, so get used to horny French guys looking at my tits."

They both laughed hard; Cohen stopped. "There's the first horny French guy to walk by and stare at your tits, Sarah."

She laughed while Allie stared the guy off. The Cohens spent warm, relaxing days on the beach soaking up the sun and surf and enjoyed memorable nights at L'Algonquin, a cute little grill across the street from the Carlton. Marcel, the prematurely white-haired owner who resembled a youthful Buffalo Bill, virtually adopted the Americans.

"Allie, Sarah, I will show you my Cannes, a social milieu few tourists ever see."

Marcel was good to his word, and he and Allie became buddies at that moment. "Allie, the kashruth rabbi in Cannes is a close friend of mine. He is a part-time butcher too and will work with me to kosher all your meals for the rest of your stay."

Their wonderful week flew by, and Allie showed his gratitude to Marcel for all he'd done for them.

"Please, Marcel, permit me to show my appreciation for this hidden world of Cannes you have shown us by buying for you and your lovely wife, Louise, airline tickets to come to Atlanta and visit Sarah and me."

Their last destination before returning to Paris was Monaco, which became a key memory. During the short ride, Allie challenged the Porsche through mountain turns and made Sarah a bit dizzy, so he hung a quick right into Cap Ferrat to stop the car and let her rest for a while. Sarah took an immediate liking to Cap Ferrat, a small elite residential paradise.

"Look, Sarah." Allie pointed. "Across the street is actor Gene Hackman standing in front of the village market, holding a sack of food he just bought and schmoozing with some woman. How come we can't make in Atlanta a nice crusty baguette like the one sticking out of his sack?"

"Because the French don't put preservatives in their bread and buy it fresh daily. Did you notice? Hackman's wearing his porkpie hat from *The French Connection.*"

"Babe, let me roam the Porsche through this commune for millionaires to give you a chance to take it in. Holy shit, Sarah, the residences are all mini-estates with backyards facing the blue Mediterranean and magnificently landscaped."

"Allie, this is it. Look at the sunlight here, breathe in the sea air, and take in how peaceful it feels. I can't imagine finding a more desirable enclave to buy into."

She looked into his eyes. "I could be happy here, Allie." *I believe that I'm going to need a better selling point than just my happiness. I'll try another angle.*

"Allie, think about it. We're a lot closer to Israel from here—four months a year in Atlanta, four months in Paris and Cap Ferrat, four months in Jerusalem and Tel Aviv. That's a damn good life for us, Allie."

"I'm impressed with the bougainvillea-covered walls and the Mediterranean ambience, Sarah, but what do you know about this place? For example, who do we know here or hang out with? Do regular people and even some Jews live in these homes?"

"That's it, Allie. No one knows us. We can find peace and tranquility here."

The Porsche idled in front of the tony Cap Ferrat Inn; Allie cautioned that paradises can be extremely isolating.

"I doubt that, Allie. In fact, I bet that some Rothschilds live in Cap Ferrat. I'm sure that the bankers to the world will gladly welcome and integrate your $940 million into the local community and their banks."

He laughed. "Sarah, granted, it is beautiful, but so are a hundred other special enclaves that I can't get or keep holy in. And what am I going to talk about to the Rothschilds and their bankers, and please don't say money."

"Allie, it'd just be four months a year. Can't you do this for me?"

"Sarah, you'd kiss the devil's ass in Macy's window if it'd keep me from running, wouldn't you?

"You know it, pal. I'd blow the damn pope in the middle of Vatican Square on Easter Sunday if you'd stay out of the race."

"Just like Châtelet in Paris, pick out a property and buy it. Have a realtor manage the property for you. Your trust will cover this too. Maybe we'll find time one day to actually stay here for a while. Sarah, I'll buy you any home or thing you want, babe. I love you that much, but Atlanta is our home and the only one I need."

He floored the Porsche and didn't look back. She kept quiet until registering in the Loews Monte Carlo Hotel lobby. When he saw her about to complain, he pleaded for understanding.

"Unluckily for you, Sarah, I lived out this dream with Carole, who has the nicest house in California, certainly Malibu. I've OD'd on indulgence, opulence, and sensuality and am a different person now and require prayer in my life and great purpose to it. Your having given so much is why I took the past month to tour France with you, to make it up to you, if only a little bit."

Allie was crying and attracting stares from passersby.

"Sarah, I beg you to forgive me." His crying advanced to heavy sobbing. "I've used up my limit to give, babe, and have nothing left."

Whenever Allie cries like that, I know he is sincere, and I love him more for it. I've also let this scene go on for longer than it should and need to calm him down.

"Please, Allie, it's okay." She held him and stroked his hair. "I've gotten it out of my system. You can stop crying."

Cohen confessed through a stream of tears while the desk clerk hid her embarrassment.

"I know I'm selfish, Sarah, but this is a vacation for me and not a lifestyle. I'm guilt ridden living like a Chazer again and disgusted with myself and pray to the Redeemer to forgive me, but I love you so much, mon, that I've put my faith on the line and risk Hashem's judgment of my excess."

"Allie, please stop crying already. It's okay, I promise."

Cohen slowly regained control. "Honey, I know Cap Ferrat's stunning, but I'd be miserable there. And besides, I really haven't made up my mind yet, honest."

"Good, hey, Monaco looks like a fun place. I understand that the pool's on the roof. Let's go up and check it out. My tits need some color."

"Surprisingly, Sarah, the female hotel guests seem to be quite modest."

"I feel it, Allie, and it's inhibiting me from taking my top off."

"However, here comes sexy Italian film star Fabrianna Botticelli walking toward us topless. Her famous tits have about seven guys chewing on their towels."

Fabrianna sat down for an hour to talk to Allie and Sarah about supporting Doctors without Borders—in French, *Médecins sans Frontières*.

"It is my favorite nonprofit, Allie, so please help the organization because you *owe* me for making me put on my shirt. I bet most of the men around this pool *hate* you big-time for this." All three laughed merrily.

"I gladly give a million dollars," pledged Cohen, still laughing, "to a brave organization that I admire greatly and toast your new modesty."

Fabrianna laughed and then surprised Sarah.

"I'd like to cast you in a small but very important part in an upcoming film I'm producing. I start shooting a month from now. Please, you are perfect for this role of a high school principal who works with a younger undercover cop to solve a crime that happened in her school, and they fall in love. I must warn you, the script has an explicit sex scene between you and the young actor."

Allie smiled in amazement at Sarah, who answered, "I'm very flattered, Fabrianna, and I would really like to experience acting, but I unfortunately have a new home to move into and decorate and a son to start in a new school, so my schedule won't permit it. Sorry."

Allie teased Sarah with the Victor Hugo quote. "To dare is a form of wisdom, Sarah." He giggled, and the two women laughed.

"Excuse us, Fabrianna, but we have reservations at La Rascasse, a nice Provençal restaurant down by the marina. I will finally get to eat bouillabaisse tonight."

"We were there last night. Trust me, Allie, the dish is no big deal there, but Yves, La Rascasse's fantastic piano player, is unforgettable."

Allie and Sarah found out for themselves. "Fabrianna is right, Sarah. The bouillabaisse is overrated, but Yves is great and just serenaded us with Ray Charles's 'Georgia on My Mind,' the theme from *Gone with the Wind*, and now 'Dixie Moon,' done very cutely too."

A year later, Carla and Joel visited Monaco, looked for Yves and the cozy fish house on the marina, and discovered that it had been torn down and replaced by a charmless thirty-story condo tower. After dinner, Allie and Sarah played the slots at the Monte Carlo Casino. Sarah won two small bets in a row, and Allie leaned in.

"Sarah, I feel in my gut a third win in a row is coming. Let's bet the maximum amount."

"Sure, knock yourself out, pal."

She admired his audacity; Cohen increased their bet by six times, the maximum limit. The machine flashed all its lights, and a siren loudly blared their winning.

"Allie, I don't fucking believe it. We hit the $15,000 grand jackpot."

The manager stepped forward while the other players cheered the Cohens' good fortune. "Dr. and Mrs. Cohen," the manager announced to the crowd, "the casino is proud to provide a carriage ride back to your hotel and a cashier's check for your winnings. It is not every day that a Nobel Prize winner hits the grand jackpot. Please, let me take your picture for our publicity department."

Tina's flattering cover story appeared in the following week's *Paris Match*. Allie and Sarah returned to Paris, only to draw unwanted attention everywhere they went.

Allie called on the concierge for help. His brother-in-law fortunately managed a thirteenth-century Bourgogne chateau with a small inn that included a three-star Michelin restaurant deep in the heart of wine country. Allie and Sarah checked in, made love, and ate deliciously for four days in peace and splendor.

During this enchanting lull, a storm was gathering four thousand miles away. While the sun streamed through the Cohens' stained glass bedroom window, white lightning and black thunder cautiously jabbed inside and outside I-285, Atlanta's Perimeter Highway.

The second battle of Atlanta was delineating, the incompatibility arising from an amorphous white mass that incessantly swarmed in and around a powerful but contained black cell.

The drama lay in the black cell's willingness to accept an undesirable mitosis.

The outcome depended on the white mass's generosity in sharing the plasma of investment capital, political power, and adequate and desirable living space.

A flash point occurred upon the black cell perceiving the white mass to be smothering it back into containment, absorption, and irrelevance.

A happy ending was to be realized by convincing the black cell that the new arrangement would improve their condition and deliver on the promise. Far away in the Bourgogne countryside, Allie Cohen prayed to Adonai, blessed be He.

Dear Name, please make NDMA's eventual outcome fair and equitable to both the black and white communities. If not, Atlanta might be torn apart.

Not if you can stop that from happening, prophet.

Chapter 121

"It must have been the Lord," Allie told Sarah, "who commanded the contractors to finally complete our home in time for us to move in by the first of August. I marvel at how the Creator of the universe made the world in six days. I sure wish Adonai had been my general contractor."

"Well, Allie," Sarah rejoiced "after being held hostage for seven months living in a sky-high hotel room, God is also a rescuer. I'm very grateful for the small miracle of moving into my dream house."

"I appreciate your patience, babe, so here's a blank check to fashion your first *home beautiful*, no teacher-salary compromises anymore. Every interior designer worth his Guccis must be drooling over collaborating with our money to fill the nine rooms with tasteful furniture and art."

She continued the tongue-in-cheek tone. "Allie, my mom and sister-in-law Laurie have volunteered for the blood-and-guts mission of decorating the place."

"Some things are very important, Sarah." He smiled at her. "I'll typically shield myself from this big production. Two rabbis are helping me organize my home tabernacle. Excuse me, mon, I need to check if the water features are working correctly."

He thought for a while in front of the catchment, *Life at forty is as sweet and peaceful as I'd hoped.*

His new home was a veritable island of tranquility in a choppy ocean of tensions and unpredictable currents.

Two blissful weeks later in Cohen land, though, trouble surfaced. *A creeping feeling of déjà vu's appeared. It's welling up in me and lingering. My afternoon writing sessions are stale, and I fear writer's block is starting.*

He analyzed while riding on his bike trail. *I'm worried that my growing emptiness has mounted from a pattern of nice dinners with Sarah and Ari and, afterward, viewing a string of forgettable films.* He did another turn around the trail that followed inside the property line.

I am in possession, he contemplated to Yahweh, *of everything a man can want—a wonderful family, a fabulous home, more money that I can ever spend. Why should I, of all people, feel empty again?*

He finished his ride and put the bike away.

This is between Allie and Adonai. The Creator commands the prophet to search deeply before entrusting him with annointment.

Cohen sat on his beach the following day and searched his soul. He decided to look again to his two great strengths—family and chapel—but neither yielded any quick answers. Cohen wondered if maybe he was praying too much and becoming too regimented. Perhaps a change in schedule would reap benefits. He figured that a revision was easier to deal with than a crisis.

He switched writing until after Ari's bedtime; hopefully, that would lift the writer's block that had smothered his completion of his memoirs. Mitch Prager, his editor, offered to finish for him by mimicking Cohen's style to help meet the deadline, but Allie vetoed it. Memoirs weren't truly authentic, he felt, if someone else was even partially ghostwriting them.

Cohen needed an exciting project to lift him out of his deep funk. However, Judah Vision—his only cool, safe, and interesting venture—was shelved until Rick Samuels felt ready to leave WDDT.

Let me go boating on Lake Cohen and think about what to do next.

He pushed the pedal boat around the lake for a half hour to work the legs and then switched to the kayak for a half hour to focus on the upper body and then came back.

That was a nice workout but no answers. One by one, the lovely corners of my reserve are failing me, the walking and bike trail, now the lake. Let me try my soul restoration engine one more time, my tabernacle.

Cohen wrapped his tallit, bowed his head, and prayed, *Dear holy One, why should a man as blessed as I am feel so forsaken? Is it because I once had it all, and now I merely have everything? Please, Lord, help me, for I have been in the dark long enough.*

A metaphysical bolt of intelligence struck at Cohen, and a hundred mighty truths were revealed at once. There were no swirling colors or shrouds similar to the AlCoGlobalCorp Tower experience; this time, a direct blue and white light charged his spirit with kinetic intelligence and holiness. Yahweh purposely made Allie search for meaning; the hollowness forced him to look harder, listen better, and act more humbly.

Prophet, listen closely. The Lord trusts that you are finally an honorable witness and deserving to lead others out of the moral swamp. You will gird all foundations, bind all fissures, and heal the humans' wounds. Take your next step, prophet, for Hashem shines on your path.

Allie's revelations were instantly translated into earthly actions.

"I have a week left to file my registration fee. That's not much time to lay the groundwork for a campaign."

Rick called the next morning. "Allie, Dan Daniels and I are inviting you to do lunch with us today in his WDDT studio office. How about twelve thirty?"

Cohen accepted and set out at noon to drive over to the WDDT studio on an unbearably hot and humid July 23. Chilly streams of air blasted from the air conditioner vents at his exposed arms and face.

This is a good way to catch a summer cold, but I'm sweating like a pig. *Yecch, the first dog days are starting already. That means six to eight weeks of steamy days and feverish nights have started early this year. August is always a yucky and dangerous month to campaign, fevers in the blood and all that.*

The WDDT receptionist told Cohen to go straight into Daniels's office. *Poor news chief Terry Alexander has noticed me and stopped begging for a pay raise. Dan coldly turned him down, so now he's grinning like a damn fool to cover his embarrassment as he leaves the room.*

The notoriously tightfisted Daniels came out from behind his massive mahogany desk to greet Cohen, who noticed that Daniels looked taller, thinner, and more distinguished looking than he appeared on TV. Dan stuck his hand out to greet Cohen.

"Allie," said Dan as he vigorously shook Cohen's hand, "it's a pleasure to finally meet you."

"It's nice to finally meet you too, Dan."

Cohen sized him up. *This guy has built an innovative cable network, has amassed great wealth, and is an environmental advocate for protecting major wilderness areas under economic stress, very formidable man indeed.*

Initial talk centered on Dan's accounting of parlaying a small South Carolina radio station and ad agency into an unofficial fifth national TV network. Samuels entered the room trailing an elderly black waiter who wheeled in a rolling cart and began serving poached Georgia turbot and garden vegetables.

"WDDT," Rick described to Allie, "is becoming a viable production option to the Hollywood syndication cartels because its twenty-four-hour full signal and cable broadcaster covers North America with AM children's programs, afternoon soap operas, game shows, and pro sports. This is a great improvement over the original programming of sitcom reruns and old movies."

"That is an improvement," Cohen agreed. "But WDDT is still a highly leveraged empire, and the ratings plunge when the headlines fade."

Daniels looked at Rick and shrugged with his eyes.

You see what I mean about my mystique—manufacturing news events?

Cohen was tired of waiting for the real reason to break bread with Daniels.

"Dan, how about we get to the point of this meeting?"

Daniels did not want to appear too obvious. "I don't know what you mean, Allie."

"Yes, you do, Dan," urged Cohen, "because I already know Rick's latest gigs and don't own any WDDT stock. Sandy Forman says it's way overvalued."

Daniels ignored Cohen's little shot and steered the conversation to politics. "Okay, Allie, I'm bored with the broadcasting business, and that Walker crap a few days ago tore at my last great interest, news gathering. Recently, I've been giving some thought to running for public office. In fact, I just might take the plunge in the next year or two."

"Great." Cohen set Daniels up with "Start tomorrow and run for metro mayor, and I volunteer to be your campaign manager."

"Well." Daniels rambled when flustered. "I, uh, uhm."

"I'm serious Dan." Cohen rubbed it in. "You'd win in a minute. How about that—Dan Daniels, the first Metro Atlanta mayor."

"Enough, Allie. Actually, it's *you* whom I have in mind to be mayor. I was hoping that my political baptism was as your campaign manager."

"Dan, I think you'd make a much better mayor than me."

Cohen's smirk started to annoy Daniels, who was busy rationalizing.

"Being mayor, Allie, deals with too much minutiae and micromanagement for me. Frankly, I have in mind something a little more national and macro in scope, for example, the U.S. Senate or a White House run in four to eight years."

Cohen could not resist a dig. "Well, that's typically big thinking, Dan. I guess then that NDMA consolidation isn't all that important to you now, is it?"

"Please, Allie, NDMA's fallout has sufficiently threatened WDDT to ask you to lunch. Come on, I can't help it if I need a job that affects all Georgians, Americans, and maybe all humanity."

Cohen wanted to tell Daniels that the Peter Principle was a much greater problem than boredom but held his tongue. Instead, Allie needled Dan.

"Naturally, the job of metro mayor is good enough for me since no Jew could ever get elected senator from Georgia."

"Now let's be fair, Allie. You know damn well that I didn't say *or* think that."

"Perhaps, Dan, but you do prefer that I get stuck in a no-win, dead-end job and not you, am I right?"

I'm damned, Dan thought, *if I'm going to take any more of Cohen's crap.*

Dan appealed, "Christ, Allie, why do you keep busting my balls?"

"You're right," conceded Cohen. "Sorry, it's just that you power-structure guys are famous for slotting everybody for your own protection, and I'm the one you're giving the bum's rush to."

Daniels wasn't sure what he heard. "I don't understand. Are you turning me down or hedging or vaguely accepting?"

"I'm wavering, Dan."

Daniels, frustrated, begged, "Well, please make your mind up real soon. There's only eight days left. I promise to make winning so easy that you could campaign with your skullcap on. That's making it kosher, am I right?"

"It's true, Dan, that your resources and connections are awesome. Still, they can't reduce campaigning to a zero risk factor. Death can never be invalidated."

Cohen concluded the meeting with a strong message for Dan and Rick.

"I'll let you guys know in forty-eight hours, and don't call me. I'll call you. You know, you guys never even mentioned Teddy Hicks once. Poor slob, still fresh in the grave, and nobody remembers him already. I'll bet, though, that Hicks's wife hasn't forgotten. Shame on the both of you."

You did good, Allie, by saying what needed to be said.

Chapter 122

Cohen's pollster Ivan Terman learned from a friend that Mayor Mack Thomas felt slighted by Dan Daniels when he organized the business community into a low-profile political machine for Allie. Each below-the-radar effort to broaden support for Cohen clearly steamed Roger, Lesotho, and Eddie.

Southerners are one of the most conformist blocs of American voters. The powerful social engineering apparatus of the white power structure boldly scolded weak candidates to get out of the race and Cohen's way.

Terman's secret soundings analyzed Cohen's following as a mile wide and an inch thick, so the establishment instituted an advertising blitz to convince the public of Allie's infallibility.

Local columnists and editorial writers, even some conservatives, promoted the suddenly virtuous Cohen as the perfect choice, with two major points generally hyped: Cohen displayed great wisdom in conceiving NDMA, and he was a world figure capable of attracting new business to Atlanta. What more could you want?

Cohen didn't call Daniels within forty-eight hours, so Dan and Rick lured Allie over to his house for a friendly poker game. Cohen, in need of a fun diversion and who now and then enjoyed a friendly poker game with the guys, bought the pretense and suspected nothing as he steered up Samuels's nearly empty driveway.

Daniels's audacious scam of transporting the gathering in limos to clear the front of the house worked perfectly. Cohen knocked on the door. Rick and Naomi, his lovely blond wife of three years and a very successful interior decorator, greeted Allie and led him into the living room.

"Okay, Allie, let's play some poker."

Cohen observed the players. "I see the game, Rick, is politics, not cards."

Meldron Heatherly, CEO of Atlanta's biggest airline, shook his hands for all his thirty-thousand-plus employees. Sam Hill and David Edwards presided over major utilities and said "hello" as did Burton Childs, a former head of Coca-Cola, and McCoy Boulifant and Mervin Robbins, the two biggest bankers. R. Wilson Hardman and Nester Reade, two of the biggest real estate developers, saluted Cohen.

Phillip Mason, Marc Harris, and Townsend Mudd from the Metro Atlanta Chamber of Commerce shook hands with Allie. The rest of the gathering included major county commissioners, suburban city mayors, and major CEOs and entrepreneurs.

Dan and Rick introduced Allie to the well-heeled group of mostly taller older white men flushed with good whiskey.

Cohen fretted. *I feel like a burnt offering.* Allie looked for a surrogate candidate and spotted the still youthful-looking Teddy Fellman, Atlanta's first Jewish mayor and approached him.

"Mr. Fellman, have you given any thought to possibly running again?"

Fellman sighed. "My time passed, especially after losing to the first black mayor and running ads questioning Atlanta's future if he won. That didn't go down too well, if you remember."

He sighed again. The looks on about thirty faces agreed with Teddy, a very nice man who was widely loved and respected.

"Well, Teddy," complimented Cohen, "you're sure doing a great job boosting Buckhead these days."

Cohen asked Burton Childs, a beloved former Coca-Cola CEO and philanthropist, to take a shot. Childs asked Allie to step into the next room to share a secret with him. They both silently looked straight ahead until they entered the hall, and Burt wheeled around and bared his soul.

"I was arrested on a morals charge thirty years ago by a vice squad member posing as a male prostitute. I was since treated by a psychiatrist, married, and have two grown children and four adorable grandchildren. Sorry, Allie, I believe in letting my past stay past and firmly decline."

Allie shook Burt's hand and told him that he was brave to reveal that, and they returned to the living room. Cohen searched on.

Let's see. No religious leaders, right-wing ideologues, or racial extremists of any color. Damn, my choices do not abound with social giants capable of gaining the trust of 4 million Metro Atlantans, 5.5 million by 2010. It's looking like a white or black knight does not exist.

In a last-ditch attempt to recruit another fall guy, Cohen put superlawyer LaGrange Ringer on the spot.

"Mr. Ringer, you're certainly qualified. Why don't you go for it?"

The straight-talking Ringer, deputy secretary of the U.S. Department of Transportation during the Carter administration, firmly declined.

"Sorry, I can't afford government service anymore, Allie. I paid those dues once before, and that's enough. I got three kids in private universities at the same time now too and two weddings to prepare for."

Ringer paused to think for a second. "It's funny. The one thing from political life that bugged me the most," he shared from his Washington days, "was the press making a big deal over my Piedmont Driving Club membership. That's one annoyance, Cohen, I'm sure you'll be spared."

Allie laughed and quoted a hero. "You're right, like Groucho Marx, I wouldn't belong to a club that would have me as a member." The room rocked with laughter.

Cohen thought, *That old line wasn't that funny.*

Ringer turned salesman and recognized Allie's prejudice reduction treatment.

"Dr. Cohen, I can think of no better time to put that treatment of yours to widespread use, and I volunteer a political slogan too. 'Cohen possesses the life skills and solutions needed to thread the people together into a united seam for Atlanta's peace and prosperity.'"

"Thank you, Mr. Ringer, for your endorsement and catchy slogan. My educational process, though, is designed for eleven-year-olds who can't vote for seven years." Cohen turned from Ringer to address a problem surely to emerge during the heat of the campaign and election.

"Gentlemen, my warts are many in number and all graphically recorded by the media. How do you think that will play with more conservative whites? Think of the mud that will be slung at me. How can that be limited, if not avoided?"

"I think people today," Phillip Mason stated, "care more about whether a guy can do the job rather than personal behavior, especially in challenging times."

Cohen didn't buy that and glanced at Burt Childs, whose eyes showed agreement. Cohen scanned the room a final time, pulled at his shirt collar, squirmed in his seat, and took like what felt forever to speak.

"Gentlemen, thanks to Reagan's budget cuts, mayor's problems are worse than ever, and we have far fewer resources to attack them with."

The mayors and other elected officials who daily dealt with those gritty problems applauded.

"The rich, meanwhile, have gotten much richer, including me, and the poor have gotten poorer. In a nutshell, you guys are expecting me to keep together the game that works so well for us while the poor hurt. Remember, it's my ass that will be on the line."

"Allie," Dan Daniels proposed, "we will provide you with enormous power to create wholly new political structures with which to govern by. Any progressive reform you want, pal, you just name it."

Allie rolled his eyes—too much power was as dangerous as too little.

"Okay, I'll run, but everyone here is sworn to secrecy. I want to announce in my own way over the next couple of days. If I don't have your full cooperation, you can find yourselves another candidate."

From the tone of Cohen's voice, he'd assumed executive authority with the mission of centralizing and equalizing basic metrowide government services. Cohen's new lieutenants stood in line to shake his hand and confirm the historic birth of the Allie Cohen administration.

An hour later, Allie explained his decision to Sarah, who was not exactly thrilled by it.

"Are you fucking nuts? You're going to freak the whites and blacks out by wearing the tallit and tefillin all the time."

"Sarah, sweetie, please cool it with the stereotypes."

"Sorry, Allie, it helps me deal with the tempestuous nature of this election."

Cohen laughed and then pressed his head down into her cupped hands and wearily conceded her point.

"You're right, Sarah. What can I tell you but what's in store for our country and democracy if the best candidates don't stand up and lead?"

"Sorry, bub, I'm not swayed by your eloquence. In fact, you can stuff it. Why can't we mellow and go happily into middle age together just like the rest of our friends?"

"The holy One," Allie revealed, "has called upon me to run." He held her in his arms tightly.

"I have no will," Sarah begged, "to combat this power. I just want the little girl growing inside me to have a daddy."

Allie didn't want to deal with that and changed the subject.

"Can you believe it, Sarah? It's fifteen years today that we know each other."

"Good try, fool, but our anniversary of when we first met is tomorrow, the twenty-ninth."

"Please excuse me, Sarah. I'm embarrassed. The absentminded professor strikes again."

Allie drove right over to Neiman-Marcus at Lenox Mall to mollify her with expensive presents. Cohen picked out a fur jacket of white, gray, and black fox; a diamond-studded, gold bracelet; and dainty pearl earrings and presented them to Sarah later that evening.

"I hope you like your gifts, babe."

She smiled to radiate love to him. "They're all beautiful, Allie. I love them very much. Thank you."

Inside, though, she schemed. *I can't let him run and need to find a place that he always wanted to live. I know. I'm going to get him to move to San Francisco. Nope, Marin County across the Bay, that's better.*

Sarah, this location issue is among you, Allie, and the Almighty, and it will soon be settled once and for all.

Chapter 123

At 7:02 PM, Allie called Dan Daniels. "Dan, I want you to leak an inclined-to-run message during the 10:00 PM news."

"You got it, Allie, and I hope the official declaration ain't much longer."

I need to do something for Mack Thomas.

He searched several men's stores for an appropriate item and found nothing. *I think just paying Mack a personal visit is the best way of placating him.*

Allie motored downtown and, since he still had his ID card, parked in the Atlanta Public Schools lot. Cohen walked up the hill to the city hall's entrance, and halfway, he stopped to view the Atlanta skyline.

I have to say that the advance is dramatic. Fifteen years before, there were only clumps of tall buildings here and there. A fairly thick line of skyscrapers now stretches up Peachtree to north Buckhead. The central business district remains sterile, though, because few people live downtown, so the streets are devoid of life after the nighttime rush hour.

Farrah White, busy using the Xerox machine located on the mezzanine, spotted Cohen crossing the atrium in search of elevators or steps leading to the second floor. The secretary called out to her former teacher.

"Dr. Cohen, take the steps over there please." She pointed the way and waited for Allie to walk up the flight of stairs to access the mayor's office.

"You know, I was once a student of yours, but it was so long ago that I imagine that you wouldn't remember me anymore."

I'm nervous, she thought. *My old teacher Dr. Cohen is a famous man and a possible next boss too.*

She inhaled and breathed out deeply. Cohen's incredible recall matched the pretty face and her ample bosoms.

"Let's see, Farrah, uh, Farrah Wilson, right?"

She smiled while nodding yes. "Farrah," complimented Cohen, "you have become a lovely and radiant lady."

Farrah nearly levitated. "Oh, Dr. Cohen, you're still a charmer."

Then with her big almond-shaped eyes, she corrected, "My name now is Farrah White. I married Eddie right after graduation."

She brought Allie up-to-date on their lives.

"Eddie's done great, Dr. Cohen, and become one of the mayor's closest aides. He also runs a successful south-side youth training and employment center."

"Right, and it's going to run out of money in five months and maybe shut down."

"Yes, Dr. Cohen, two hundred young people will be added to the dropout list." She crossed her hands and looked down.

"I'm not going to let it happen, Farrah," he promised, "even if I have to reach into my own pocket. I like what Eddie's accomplishing with those kids, our most vulnerable young people."

"Thank you, Dr. Cohen, and God bless you for your support for the center."

"Farrah, please give Eddie my best wishes."

Cohen disappeared into the chamber.

Mack Thomas rose to shake hands with Allie and take stock of him. *I'm nearly a foot taller than Cohen, and that skullcap—well, in my opinion, it's not very cool to advertise your faith like that.*

Mack and Allie shook hands. "I see," Thomas commented, "that you're a much more religious man than your public image suggests."

"Mr. Mayor," Cohen answered cagily, "let's just say that I'm a born-again Jew like Jimmy Carter's becoming a born again Christian right before he ran for elective office."

"I understand. Please, Allie, call me Mack."

Allie smiled to show his pleasure at informality while Mack probed Cohen for any grudges held against Eddie White. "Hey, Allie, I heard that you taught social studies to both my secretary and her husband, who is a top aide of mine. I think it was about ten years ago when you were still at Bankhead High."

"Yes, Farrah and Eddie White. She was the better student."

Cohen worried that he sounded too negative. "Eddie has done extremely well, though, and I'm really happy for him and proud of him and Farrah too."

As far as I can tell, Cohen has wiped the slate clean. Mack got down to business. "Okay, Allie, what can I do for you?"

Man, I hate to cut political deals. He sighed before laying his cards on the table. "Mack, my intentions are such that perhaps it's better if I turn that question around and ask it to you."

I feel like telling Allie and all the white people behind him to get fucked. Mack felt slighted. *But I'm a politician too, so I'll just ease myself into this rocking chair, cup my hands, and wait for his proposal.*

"Mack, I guess you've heard the rumors that I may run for mayor—"

Thomas cut him off. "They aren't rumors, Allie. You *are* running. Lesotho was there when you filed and paid your fee this morning."

Cohen rubbed his trim beard with his fingers. Deal making for him was like getting his teeth pulled.

"Granted, Mack, it is official. Look, you've been a fine mayor and surely deserve the metro job—"

Thomas again interrupted Cohen, only this time he didn't hide his hurt feelings. "Except that I'm black and can't get elected because of the color of my skin. That's also why I wasn't the guest of honor at Rick Samuels's house the other night too, right?"

Allie squashed a chuckle out of respect.

"Mack, I understand that I'm your main obstacle to holding on to city hall. Please be fair, though, Mack. I didn't make this world or Atlanta. I'm just a schnook who got a thankless job thrust on him and now must get my act together quickly. If there's one thing worse than being the metro mayor, Mack, it's being a *bad* metro mayor."

"That's very true." Mack rocked back and forth. "That's very true."

"I need you, Mack, and am here today to urge you to run for metro council president. You have to be there to assure that black Atlantans get their 30 percent. We can make history together, Mack, so what do you say, man?"

"I say, Cohen, that you can sell monkey turds to an orangutan. Being the first metro council president, though, is a stepping stone to metro mayor."

Mack was aware of Cohen's reputation of splitting for greener pastures.

Cohen closed the deal with Mack. "I'm offering a gerrymandered metro district stretching from Five Points in the heart of Downtown Atlanta to just south of the airport in Hapeville. I acknowledge that you're a bit galled, Mack, but I feel this new south central Atlanta ward is in your best interest, especially with patronage jewels like the heart of downtown and the *airport* in your asset-packed district."

Airport patronage brought a smile to Mack's face, and then he turned serious. "Allie, what about places for Roger, Lesotho, and Eddie?"

"I envision Xeranga as an ombudsman or liaison and designate Wilcox to be the assistant prosecutor."

Thomas questioned, "Why assistant?"

"That plum, Mack, is my compromise with conservative whites. Chief of police and chief prosecutor are fair trade-offs for white support."

"You excluded all blacks from consideration. That's racism."

"No, that's politics. And according to Dan Daniels, since you took office, city hall has experienced an 81 percent blackanization."

"Well," Thomas admitted, "maybe my administration has been a bit preoccupied with black advances, but who can blame me when viewed against a hundred years of official Atlanta segregation?"

"Sorry, Mack, that's a cop-out. Your real preoccupation as an outsider has been building a black political machine for reelection instead of insuring full social justice."

Cohen pulled another Dan Daniels news item out of his pocket. "Mack, 68 percent of all Atlanta whites doubt that they'd be fairly judged for an opening at city hall on the basis of merit only."

I'm flirting, Thomas thought, *with strangling Dan Daniels.* But he pushed for Wilcox to head the prosecutor's office.

"Sorry," Cohen told Thomas. "How do you feel about Lucas Sanderson for prosecutor?"

"Man, Allie, ol' law and order Sanderson is unacceptable to the vast majority of black people."

"But you must admit," Allie cautioned, "that he is fair, and the blacks will sing another tune if the whites ask for someone worse."

"I get you. What are you going to do for Eddie?"

"I will out-of-pocket guarantee him his youth training and employment centers and expand it metrowide, but maybe it's time for Eddie to move up. Why not let somebody else run the program and make him a deputy in the housing authority or watershed bureau? He's a family man and needs some security. Nobody should have to live on shaky budgets or grants forever."

"Okay, those are good places for him."

"So, Mack, are you my council president?"

Thomas took a few seconds to think it over.

952

"Allie, I'm with you, but I resent the way the white power structure engineered away from the blacks and my team a quarter-billion-dollar budget, and don't forget that you're the dude they did it for."

"Mack," Cohen assured Thomas, "I'm dedicated to the black community getting its fair share of power and resources and plan to take care of most reasonable patronage needs."

"I like doing business with you, Cohen, but doubt you'll succeed with the next political kingpin you're planning to visit. Tell me, Allie, what magic phrases have you come up with to sweet-talk ol' E. Glenn Conway, 'the King of the 'Necks'?"

Don't worry, Allie, I have a surprising way into E. Glenn's hard heart, for he has a very sweet soft spot in him.

Chapter 124

I quake at the thought of driving to Kennesaw to cut a deal with the Prince of Cobb.

In need of spiritual advice on finding a common ground with an unyielding foe, Allie headed straight for his tabernacle to consult with Adonai and prayed long and hard for light to be shed on a difficult question.

How do I convince one of the most anti-Communist conservatives in the country that NDMA is good for him and his people who hate it like fucking poison? I know. I'll buy a sporty black Chevrolet pickup truck just to visit ol' E. Glenn. A sturdy F5 should hopefully warm Conway's reactionary heart, at the least put a nice smile on his tough-talking face.

Remember these two key lines, Allie. The F5 has more towing power. Also, the bigger the spread, the greater the need to move something—a pickup is invaluable.

Cohen turned onto Highway 41 and headed northward past Marietta, pronounced "May-ret-ta" in Cobb, a place Allie traditionally had difficulty trying to figure out without resorting to stereotyping the county. Cobb experienced enormous and erratic growth during the twenty years after integration. Continuous white flight and Lockheed's contracts-based military expansion fused a huge sprawl of middle-class subdevelopments full of very conservative white people.

In recent years, though, an in-migration of politically moderate professionals bought homes in the eastern sector made the schools better, and real estate values soared. Less growth in the western sector allowed a rural-minded faction to cling to power and provoke the traditional urban-rural schism.

J. B. Stoner lived in Marietta. The former publisher of the antiblack and anti-Semitic weekly, the *Thunderbolt*, blew up an exterior wall in Atlanta's oldest congregation, The Temple, in 1958. Stoner and accomplices, in 1959, planted a bomb in a black church in Birmingham that killed four little girls.

Stoner ran for governor of Georgia in 1973 and received seventy-three thousand votes; Cobb was his base. In 1979, Stoner was extradited to Alabama for the church-bombing crime and jailed under a state law that made it illegal to ignite dynamite near inhabited places.

Metro traffic congestion became so clogged during the 1960s that Atlanta started a public transportation system to ease the problem. Cobb County refused to join the Metropolitan Atlanta Rapid Transit System (MARTA) because blacks might ride buses and trains to Cobb, rob their home appliances and jewelry, and ride back to Atlanta with stolen goods in hand.

I think I can take the eastern half of the county pretty much for granted, Allie thought. *My problem in Cobb is striking a deal with the low-service, antitax fundamentalists loudly wedded to their tacky status quo. Gun racks and Confederate flags will forever adorn their trucks and jeeps, a reminder that Dixie lives on. Look away, look away, look away from Atlanta land.*

Allie passed Kennesaw Mountain, turned left on a nondescript country road, and traveled down it three miles as instructed by Conway's secretary. Five minutes passed.

I think it's that sprawling ranch house over there sitting on about twenty acres widely rumored to be a major center of mercenary training. According to Sandy Forman, E. Glenn was a CIA operative and left the company to train the antiterrorist platoons of three friendly Central American governments. That led to his becoming a wealthy arms dealer. A local journalist reported that Conway had howitzers, attack vehicles, and concussion bombs attached to a cruise missile. He liked to brag that he was the most ready man in America to repulse a commie invasion.

Allie believed him. Cohen parked his truck behind two other F5s lined up in the gravel driveway and stepped down from the cab. The wind nearly blew his skullcap off as he spotted Conway over in a nearby field.

There he is, probably improving the form of an anti-insurgency squad from South Africa, Chile, El Salvador, or other oppressive government.

Allie approached and formally greeted the intense E. Glenn, who did not extend his hand in return. *Conway believes this meeting to be a dirty business deal that he equates with stabbing his culture in the back. Frankly, me too.*

Allie looked into Conway's hard Baptist face and gulped. *This man is built to call a spade a nigger.*

E. Glenn expressed his position and, to put it mildly, was up front with Allie. "Cohen, I'm going to come right out and tell you that I hate your fucking guts and every goddamned thing you stand for. In my opinion, you're the type that's ruining this great country that used to stand for freedom and self-reliance, but I think that you'll find that I'm a reasonable man."

"Mr. Conway, if you don't mind, I think I can do without so much honesty." Conway laughed. *Good, E. Glenn has a sense of humor. That's a positive sign.* "I was wondering, Mr. Conway, how you acquired your colorful nickname."

Conway laughed again. "You mean King of the Rednecks?"

Cohen smiled and nodded yes. "About ten years ago, one of my ol' CIA buddies from the company attended a Fourth of July barbecue that I give every year for family and friends. The guy admired my spread. He knew about my money and political connections, and then he goes and says, 'Well, E. Glenn, you're practically King of the Rednecks.'"

Cohen laughed hard; E. Glenn liked that.

"Well, Rabbi, everyone started to laugh and make jokes about it. Obviously, the nickname stuck and probably helps me get about ten thousand more votes in each election. E. Glenn, 'King of the 'Necks.' I got to say it ain't hurt me none at all."

Cohen remembered. *Just the day before, E. Glenn was quoted claiming that he'd rather secede from the Union than have to join the lying Mack Thomas and the raping and robbing Atlanta blacks. Well, at least Conway isn't using the* n *word. He is what he is, a politician like me.* "Mr. Conway, despite what you may have heard about NDMA, let me clear that you could still remain the master of a slightly reduced dis—"

"Don't bullshit me, Cohen," E. Glenn interrupted, "because you know damn well that, from now on, there's only one master, and that's you sitting in the godforsaken Atlanta City Hall."

He pointed the index finger of his right hand at Cohen after the words *master* and *you*. Conway took time to spit tobacco juice, and a blustery wind caused a few drops to land on Allie's beige desert boots, so E. Glenn apologized.

"Sorry about that, Rabbi. I guess I'm losing my aim in my old age. Now about the NDMA crap you wrote, I don't like it one bit."

Allie said while staring at the disgusting tobacco juice stains on his shoes and knowing full well that he would have to throw them away as soon as he got home, "Please state your case, Mr. Conway."

"I swear that the goddamned country is going straight to hell. Lord knows that we got Communists in Washington for years, but now I got to take marching orders from them in Atlanta too. Jesus H. Rockefeller, each year they chip a little more freedom away from the good, hardworking Christian people of America."

Cohen asked Conway to please limit discussion to local issues, such as the value split between the eastern and western sectors over higher taxes for improving and expanding county services, especially education and transportation. Conway scratched his head as he looked downward and spoke.

"Rabbi, I understand perfectly that Cobb County is changing, and I'm not against all change or government for that matter too, but I do fear creeping bureaucratization, and even you have to admit that NDMA is another big step in that direction."

"Please, E. Glenn, you have to admit that NDMA will help Cobb with the cost of basic services. In my opinion, that's all local government should do—act like a business in delivering high-quality, low-cost services. You should be very proud, E. Glenn, that everybody says Cobb County provides very high-quality education, policing, and other basic services for the lowest tax rate of the five core counties."

"All right, Cohen, when you put it like that, maybe there is some good in the act, and possibly some of my county folk will benefit from it also. However, a hell of a vocal majority is already dead set against it and will fight Big Brother the whole hundred yards. Still, because of your fair and respectful compliment, I might consider going along if you promised not to carry out one of your so-called major objectives."

I can't believe my ears. Conway is offering to compromise. Allie happily responded, "Great, what's that?"

Allie's enthusiasm quickly waned when he heard E. Glenn's terms.

"Forget that dispersal-of-ghettos shit. Cobb County doesn't need any Mandingoes sticking their big salamis in our fine, virtuous white women."

Ah yes, the old fear of the black dick syndrome, Cohen thought, *the white man's irrational horror of a giant black cock entering a precious little white vagina—worse, their teenage daughter's. Yet I personally know three white women who have been brutally raped by black men.*

Conway surprised Cohen with a reasonable offer.

"Rabbi, I'll support NDMA if you'll shove that scattered-site-housing shit. That's my lone demand—no public housing projects full of poor blacks from Atlanta."

"Is that all?"

"Oh sorry, there is one more thing. I insist that you keep out pornography too, though a few titty bars like they have in Atlanta to attract the conventioneers are okay, but no scattered site whatsoever or dirty book and video stores, you hear me?"

Allie gratefully welcomed E. Glenn's cooperation. *I'm worried, though, that I'm paying too high a price for it and might lose trust from liberal blacks and whites, but compromise is the glue of U.S. politics, and E. Glenn seems to be meeting me more than halfway.*

Cohen's taking too much time to make up his mind, thought Conway.

"Come on, Rabbi, I don't have all day. Is it a deal or not?"

Allie decided. *If I'm going to do business with E. Glenn, then I have to make one thing clear.* "Mr. Conway," he declared, "I am not ordained, so please don't refer to me as *rabbi*. If you must be formal, please call me Doctor or Mister or preferably Allie or even Cohen."

"You're wearing a beanie, Cohen, ain't you?"

"One does not need to be a rabbi, Mr. Conway, to wear a yarmulke or *kippah*. Let's just say that I'm a little gung ho at the moment."

"Then you must be one of them aycids."

"Pardon me?" said Cohen dumbfounded by what Conway meant.

"You know, aycids, one of those Yahmees with them long scraggly beards, frock coats, and braids. How come you ain't wearing their garb too?"

Conway spit more tobacco juice but widely missed Cohen's shoes.

Allie corrected E. Glenn's pronunciation. "I think you mean Hasidic, ha-seed-ik."

"Yeah, how'd you say that, ha-sid-ik?"

He told E. Glenn, "Yes, that's pretty good."

"Cohen, I respect a religious man, even a Yahmee."

"Mr. Conway, I'd much prefer that you didn't use the term Yahmee. Please think of me as a born-again Jew seeking a personal relationship with his Lord."

"Do you believe in creationism, Cohen?"

"No, I don't, E. Glenn, because the Lord created Darwin."

Conway again scratched his head and smiled.

"Good reply, although I'm not sure you answered my question, but I guess that's the mark of a superior politician."

Cohen felt some warmth for Conway. "Please, E. Glenn, call me Allie."

Conway reciprocated. "Sure, and you can call me Glenn. I drop the E. for friends. It stands for Elmore, which I'm not so crazy about."

Allie extended his hand; Glenn shook it this time but demanded to hear Cohen verbally agree to his single condition.

"Well, Allie, what's it going to be? Are you going to blackanize Cobb County or aren't you?"

"Glenn, I promise to respect your local culture."

"That's not good enough, Allie. I'm still waiting to hear no mass blackanization."

Cohen's gut heaved from this sellout, but the three hardest words in Allie's vocabulary rattled from deep in his throat.

"It's a deal, Glenn, but I don't think blacks will or want to move to Cobb en masse. In fact, you're worrying about the wrong people and not preparing for the ones who are already showing up en masse."

Conway shook his head and hands to ask who.

"Glenn, Cobb's construction-oriented economy has attracted Mexican laborers by the tens of thousands. Large chunks of Cobb already sprout *mucho* Tex-Mex restaurants, and Spanish is heard regularly in those parts."

"You're right, Allie, Cobb hasn't responded as well as we should have. Cobb needs to get the schools and police ready to better serve our fast-growing Latino population."

"Check your demographics, Glenn. The Hispanic population is growing in Atlanta, DeKalb, and Gwinnett too. Developers and contractors love Hispanics as workers, so we have to do a better job reaching out and integrating them."

"You're right, Allie, and we'll talk some more about this. Hey, it's a kick seeing you climb into your truck." Conway wondered, "Allie, I'll bet you borrowed that F5 to impress me. That's my favorite pickup, you know."

I told you, Allie, that the F5 was his sweet spot.

"No, Glenn, I didn't. And yes, this is my truck. Glenn, we both have big spreads, and your property is probably three, four times the size of mine. Anyone with acreage knows that we all have to move something now and then, and pickups are invaluable."

"That's damn true, Allie. We all got to move something now and then."

"So I understand, Glenn, why you like the F5 so much too, best damn towing power in its class." Allie smiled at Glenn.

"Goddamn." Glenn slapped his thigh. "A Yahmee driving an F5 pickup, now who'da ever of thought it? You know, Cohen, you're all right in my book."

Masterfully done, prophet. The two main power brokers are lined up behind you.

Chapter 125

Farrah White shooed her children away from the dinner table to go do their homework so she and Eddie could talk quietly in the kitchen over coffee and dessert.

My husband is pensive, and I know why. She poured his cup and asked, "Why is your mind somewhere over Peachtree Street?"

White just said, "I don't know where my mind is right now."

He kept staring into space. A few seconds later, Eddie admitted, "I wasn't completely honest. I am bothered by something that you did or maybe didn't do."

Farrah knew very well what Eddie was hinting at.

"I'm sorry for not telling you that Allie Cohen met with the mayor yesterday."

He hugged her. "Baby, it's okay. I heard it was a good meeting, and I got the excellent news about Cohen's commitment to the training program. That's very cool, so I guess I got nothing to worry about now."

"Eddie, let's celebrate surviving this scary NDMA period. What about Alfredo's? I got a taste for veal *francese.*"

Eddie nixed her idea as premature and quoted, "Two birds in the bush ain't worth one in the hand."

"What's important, Eddie, is that your guys are looking out for you."

"You know, Farrah, I can shrug off Mack's becoming metro council president and Roger the assistant DA, but Cohen's grooming Lesotho for a special ombudsman role hurt a bit and made me a little jealous. I kind of hoped that the three of them would have waited until there was a defined role for me. Don't get me wrong, I'm thrilled about the commitment to the center and the other offers, but a lifetime can happen in six months. Farrah, babe?"

"Yeah, honey?"

"From now on, when you hear or see something, please let me know right away. Information is all I got, and you're my eyes and ears to the mayor's office."

"Sure, Eddie, but you always get so freaked out over this subject that I try to limit discussion to sure things. You ought to have more trust in your friends. They are looking out for you, you know."

"Trusting is hard for me, Farrah, and I need to work on it. It's good to have the water bureau or housing authority to fall back on."

Eddie asked her, "Baby, if I got so much respect, how come I ain't the ombudsman? I'll tell you why."

"I had a feeling you would."

"Because I'm a thick-lipped real-black type that's supposed to love organizing black losers."

"Lighten up, Eddie. Here, try one of these little éclairs from the Sit-In."

"Man, these are delicious, just ate three in a minute."

"That's enough, my man. These little cakes got some big damn calories. I don't want your stomach dunloppin' over your pants."

She gave him a hand job and put a smile on his face. Men are basically simple creatures.

Chapter 126

Two days later at Allie Cohen's Sit-In, the national, state, and local press corps contingents sat around drinking beer, coffee, or soft drinks.

The damn jaded reporters, thought Allie. *Many are smoking cigarettes outside in the parking lot while others are talking about who's sleeping with whom. They're supposed to be standing poised to record my historical announcement, but they're bopping around like a bunch of monkeys. Let me focus my attention on the television cameras to prevent the reporters from distracting me.*

The media characteristically gathered, shut up, and focused when the red light flashed.

"After much consideration, I have decided to run for the newly consolidated position of mayor of Metropolitan Atlanta. If elected, I swear to govern in the general welfare of all Metro Atlantans and implement NDMA guidelines in cooperation with the Metro Atlanta Oversight Committee or MAOC.

"I'm aware that I'm the author of this plan of improvement, but in no way should that imply that I have all the answers—I don't. I therefore welcome input from every sector of the body politic and vow to earn your trust.

"Please judge me not on preconceived notions but on my ability to solve problems and willingness to work hard to improve the quality of life for all Metro Atlantans. I ask for your cooperation and help so that a great city may continue to evolve.

"Step forward with me, and I pledge to advance Atlanta to world-class status. By accepting a few minor changes, we will surely prosper together in a favorable trade-off. You and I working together can help make the Atlanta region an even nicer place to live, work, play, and pray in. Thank you, and God bless Atlanta."

Mack Thomas watched Cohen's short televised speech at Lesotho and Sharon's Peeples Street condo in Atlanta's West End community. Xeranga nursed a St. Pauli Girl beer while reflecting aloud about what he'd just heard.

"Mack, am I nuts, or was that an acceptance speech? I mean, didn't it sound like the dude just took the oath of office for Chrissake?"

Mack laughed before answering, "The most amazing thing is Cohen sounded like the incumbent mayor, who's me."

"Do you think he can pull it off?" Lesotho waited for Mack's answer.

"Christ, only God knows," Mack concluded. "But if Cohen can't pull it off, I don't think I can either."

E. Glenn Conway watched also and caught Cohen in a sin of omission. *Jesus, Allie, you didn't say diddly-squat. Why didn't you tell the people about how all land sales will be temporarily frozen for fifty miles beyond the Perimeter Highway on January 1, 1989? Or tell 'em how MAOC will coerce the free market to develop inward toward the central city? You also didn't say a damn word about increasing tax rates in some areas or busing ghetto kids to magnet schools in the suburbs. For Chrissake, Cohen, you didn't say anything important at all.*

The business, Jewish, and black communities donated enough funds for Allie to outspend the opposition by a ten-to-one margin. While the other candidates were limited to yard signs, handbills, and a few last-minute TV ads, Cohen saturated the tube with multiple five-minute-long *messages from Allie.*

Each message framed another bold venture to make Atlanta exciting and great. The picture faded, and a toe-tapping melody left the viewer hopeful. "A new day's dawning, people. A new way's coming soon. Join hands with Allie to build Atlanta into the greatest city in the land."

Cohen kept a diary and log of his campaign; the first entry described media interest. "Two major television networks are broadcasting one-hour-long documentaries describing how Atlanta is coping with NDMA implementation. CBS's program emphasizes the business community's behind-the-scenes engineering of public attitudes to maintain the booming economic growth rates of recent years. ABC's documentary concentrates on the selling of me, Allie Cohen, and how other U.S. cities facing eventual NDMA adaptation are studying Atlanta's strategy and process.

"The primary race stayed surprisingly free of dirty politics until the last few days when red-faced Tom Wallace, an ultraconservative candidate from Acworth in northern Cobb County, ran ads focusing on my less-than-squeaky-clean past. Rick Samuels, my publicity consultant, responded to Wallace's desperate tactics by scheduling Sarah for a round of talk shows. My wonderful wife, in a series of interviews, spoke warmly of her teaching in both the inner-city and affluent suburban schools."

"My mission as First Lady of Atlanta," Sarah promised, "will be to equalize educational opportunity metrowide. We will achieve this by standardizing property taxation rates to adequately fund all public schools, as well as provide higher salaries along with more stringent requirements for hiring teachers and employment of innovative educational curricula."

The next diary entry read, "Sarah's appealing good looks and personal warmth won the hearts of viewers by candidly explaining how we overcame past problems and forged a terrific new life. Pollsters claim that the moment Atlantans fell in love with their new First Lady was when she announced that she'd give birth six months after I took office. Postelection analysts contend that her profamily remarks in the final hours caused my popularity to peak as the polls opened."

967

A landslide victory, Allie believed, was needed for a Jew to govern effectively, and he campaigned twelve hours a day to gain his mandate. Ivan Terman predicted that only the size of his victory was in question.

Still, I have to work harder to reach conservative working-class whites, my last pocket of deep resistance, and I will spend the last two days working the rural suburbs of Cobb, Gwinnett, and Clayton Counties to reach the pockets that are most mistrustful of my perceived liberal impulses.

Sarah questioned his strategy. "I'm not sure it's worth putting in all this time in areas that are almost openly hostile to you."

"The secret to reaching the evangelicals, Sarah, is to convince them that I view them just as their ministers do. They are the very rock and foundation of a society that does not show them the appreciation and respect they so richly deserve."

"Good luck with that line because it's exactly that type of victimhood thinking that keeps them out of the mainstream of life."

"That's true. You're right. Anyway, the line they like hearing best"—he laughed—"is 'You people are so hardworking and proud. A lot of you would starve to death before asking for a handout.' I tell you, mon, that line never fails to earn loud cheers and even louder whistles of approval."

"I'll bet, so shocking to hear that from them," she said sarcastically and then straightly, "but more shocking from you, my politician."

The following journal entry read, "Ari accompanied me to a speaking engagement at a megachurch in Woodstock. Afterward, during the ride home, Ari asked me, 'Dad, I kept hearing the word *conservative* used all night long. But to me, it felt like they were just being mean and tough to black people.'"

968

Allie smiled at Ari. "You're very perceptive for your age and so my son. Anyway, these people have not been well led by their politicians and ministers. They've been forever given simple answers about the complexities of modern life and told not to ask why or how come. Basically, Ari, they just want to hear me say that I like and care about them, and they don't expect much more than that."

The last campaign entry was "Election Day has finally come, and the Cohen campaign staff sits around the Sit-In, their political command center. They drink coffee; munch on Danish, doughnuts, or bagels; and continually update their estimate of how the cold and rainy weather might affect the metrowide turnout.

"Rick Samuels and Mike Schwartz press their noses against the wet and cold windowpane of the front door and draw back. 'Holy shit.' They warn, 'If the temperature drops any more, it'll start to ice over.'

"In Atlanta, a car-oriented city," Harvey Kartzman learned from a fender bender during freezing rain; "*ice storm* means that few will dare to leave home to vote."

Allie put his journal down. "The idea of postponing the election makes me nervous as hell. I'll pray to the Lord to please spare Atlanta an ice storm, our most dangerous weather condition."

He resumed writing his entry three hours later. "Amazingly, it quickly stopped raining and warmed up enough for Atlantans, in record numbers, to safely go to the voting booth and show that they deeply loved their city and region. I left the Sit-In shortly before sundown to go home and pray for a strong consensus. Afterward, I had a quiet dinner with Sarah and Ari and then retired to my study to listen to the election results and write my acceptance speech.

"Long lines and computer malfunctions delayed early projections until 10:00 PM, when—with only 6 percent of the precincts reporting—WDDT risked declaring me the winner with 81 percent of the vote.

"I ignored the media's bugging me to declare victory and didn't until eleven o'clock, when WSB-TV chanced projecting Mack Thomas the first metro council president with 59 percent. In many ways, the 30 percent of white Atlantans who voted for Mack Thomas, to me, are a greater triumph for the Atlanta electorate than my average Georgia landslide.

"My family and I made our grand entrance at the Sit-In several minutes past eleven thirty. The predominantly white and affluent north-side crowd, estimated by police at over five thousand, roared as I spoke with Sarah and Ari at my side. There was nothing remarkable about my speech except that I was giving it."

Allie uttered the usual generalities, that this was a people's victory, and thanked his campaign manager—David Sarasohn, who'd just received his MBA from Emory—and the many tireless workers. "I never could have won without their support." By midnight, he'd exhausted his supply of political clichés, and the crowd dissipated.

Thomas's supporters, in contrast, were first beginning to celebrate Mack's victory; Russell Holiday, a successful building contractor and the richest black man in Atlanta, honored Mack with an expensive bash at the in-again Polaris atop the blue domed Hyatt Regency.

Holliday toasted Thomas. "Today Atlanta's black community celebrates another great milestone, Mack Thomas's election as first metro council president. Let's give it up for Mack Thomas, a great black leader and humanitarian and one man whom I'm proud to call my dear friend."

Mack was a hero to his people on this special night and received a steady stream of well-wishers. Cohen sent his congratulations by video live from the Sit-In and celebrated Mack Thomas's victory as a great step forward for Atlanta. Mayor Cohen told the supporters of Metro Council President Thomas that he was honored to work with him in making Metro Atlanta the next great international city of the world.

Holliday and Marilyn Counts, a top-ranked newscaster, chatted with Ombudsman Xeranga, one of the three or four most powerful politicians in the new arrangement and who liked being the center of attention in a roomful of black VIPs.

"Lee," Counts asked, "what's the likely political agenda for the first ninety days of the new Cohen-Thomas administration?"

"Sorry, Marilyn. Like everyone else, I follow the mayor's lead, and we are all waiting for his agenda. Tonight is for celebration."

Twenty-five-year-old David Sarasohn, representing the Cohen camp, patiently waited his turn on the line to talk to Lee Xeranga and congratulate him. No one formed any lines at Eddie White's feet, and his insecurity rose.

Counts finished; White drifted by Sarasohn, who began talking to Lesotho.

"The mayor wants to expand the role of ombudsman to serve more than just black interests. He envisions your role as a liaison among the city hall, the metro council, and black and white West Side Atlantans. Well, Lee, do you have any problems with how the mayor wants to define your role?"

"Sarasohn," said Lesotho, liking what he was hearing, "tell the mayor that I could not design my function more ideally. But frankly, I don't think it's cool to say any more right now. In fact, why don't we finish discussing this over lunch tomorrow? Let's say you meet me at Trotter's about one o'clock, okay?"

Sarasohn smiled and said that sounded fine. Eddie approached David and self-consciously inquired if the mayor had made up his mind about the housing authority or the water bureau for him. Sarasohn's eyes lit up. "You know, Eddie, I think I have a better fit for you and prefer to recommend to Mayor Cohen a high-level job in MASS."

971

"Thank you, David, but what's MASS?"

"Metro Atlanta Sanitation Services. Garbage truck routes everywhere need reworking, new energy conservation methods will be employed, and snow removal systems need to be acquired. Frankly, Eddie, I think this is a very interesting agency and probably where the real action is. The more I think of it, I think MASS provides you a great metrowide chance to make a name for yourself, and I'm going to recommend you to the mayor."

Eddie vigorously shook Sarasohn's hand.

"David, I am genuinely interested and grateful. Thank you, and congratulate the mayor on his victory for me."

"You'll be hearing from me very soon, Eddie. In fact, why not join me and Lesotho at Trotter's tomorrow too? My treat."

David made Eddie's day with that invitation.

Allie sat in his study listening to the late Sunday night news and strategizing how to get the Cohen administration off to a fast and successful start. *The first step—the biggest party in Atlanta's history kicks off a weeklong inaugural. A busy weekend of gala events at the Omni, the World Congress Center, and Atlanta Stadium follow and precede a week of mini-inaugurals around town, one a day for each of the eight districts until I interact with all metro areas.*

Each day I'll schedule a morning town-hall-type meeting to hear NDMA praises or grievances and sponsor afternoon barbecues in area parks to formulate solutions and grand buffets and dance bands in the evening at selected Perimeter hotel ballrooms for the people to come together. I want these parties to be happy environments to generate formation of new political coalitions.

Sarah stuck her head in the doorway to inform Allie, "David Sarasohn dropped by and wants to talk. His parents are

972

thrilled he's working for you. Elena told me that death squads working for the Chilean secret police are targeting him so he can't go back and that a Brazilian software company specializing in agricultural applications wants to hire him after the campaign."

"David has great political instincts, whether it's in Chile or Atlanta, and the Brazilian offer sounds very exciting. Meanwhile, please send him right in, Sarah."

The cute blue-eyed David appeared. "Mayor Cohen, we've taken care of Mack, Lesotho, and Roger nicely. Are we doing enough for Eddie White? I think not and suggest that we reward him with a more important and better-paying position than the water bureau—deputy director of MASS or Metro Atlanta Sanitation Systems."

"All right, David, but does he have any experience in managing sanitation systems?"

"Yes, if being a garbageman counts, and that might be advantageous with the rank-and-file workers. Anyway, he has a history of surpassing expectations in every job he's had. There's a lot of innovation in sanitation today. Let's give him a chance to grow. I feel he could shine in this position."

"I appreciate your taking such an interest in Eddie White. That's how this administration is going to work—people from diverse backgrounds looking out for each other. Tell him he has the job."

"This is going to make Rev. William Walker very happy. This is good politics, boss."

Sorry, guys. Sarah's not going to see it as good politics, just politics as usual.

Chapter 127

Allie awoke the next morning to have breakfast with his family; instead, he found a note on the kitchen table from Sarah.

Dear Allie,

By the time you read this, Ari and I will be halfway to San Francisco. Last night, I overheard you and David trying to satisfy that big thug who threatened you years ago at Bankhead High.

I turned cold inside and out. The message I got was that if he didn't get what he hoped for, he might come after you.

Can't you see, honey? The hard rain has already begun to fall. You're only the mayor for a few days, and the people's demands are already too unrealistic to fulfill. Lord knows that unfulfilled expectations produce frustration and hate.

Guess who the grievances will be directed at. Since I do not wish to voluntarily become a widow, I'm off to Marin County.

Why Marin? Because I recall you saying many times how San Francisco was one of your favorite cities and that Marin had one of the best qualities of life anywhere. So I plan to buy the nicest home in the most beautiful and peaceful community.

I know that you will be on the first plane to the coast to bring us back and tell us that you made a commitment to the people of Atlanta. To that, I say fuck your commitment in the ear because my only goal is to live a long and comfortable life with my husband.

Of course, since I want you to find us so that I can talk you out of remaining mayor, I'll leave you with these two clues. When you get to San Francisco, take the ferry to Tiburon, the last stop. Then when you get off, call this number, 927-0344.

Love,
Sarah

Sarah, I need this chase like a hole in the head.

He got up from the table, groaning, "I've got a city, indeed a region, to run."

Allie phoned his office. "Heather, please have today's festivities canceled and rescheduled for tomorrow, and push everything else back a day. I'm riskily promising to return in twenty-four hours."

He was soon airborne in Dan Daniels's private jet and bound for San Francisco. Five hours later, he landed and ran through the airport to take a cab to the Embarcadero to catch the ferry to Tiburon. A bad rainstorm dumped sheets of rain just as the ferry began pulling away from the dock.

The darkening sky and choppy waters made Cohen feel like he was crossing the river Styx and might not make it to the other side. *Dear Yahweh, please forgive Sarah's reckless behavior and keep this damn ferry afloat.*

Don't worry, Allie, calm down.

He did when he heard the big boat dock at the pretty colony of Tiburon. Allie was desperate to find Sarah and Ari and stepped lively off the ferry. Cohen ran to a nearby pay phone and dialed the number Sarah furnished him.

It rang three times before a woman with a familiar voice picked up. "Jones Real Estate, who's calling please?"

Cohen almost said "the mayor of Atlanta" but, on second thought, just said, "Allie Cohen." He gave that voice a second thought. "Is this Jane Altman by some chance?"

A great old laugh from the past danced from the receiver. "My name is now Jane Altman Jones. I know what you're thinking, Allie. Old Janie married a gentile."

"Forgive me, Jane, but I'm much more interested in locating Sarah and Ari than discussing your husband's religion. Jane, I'm sure that you've heard that I'm now the mayor of Atlanta, and my wife, Sarah, ran off to San Francisco with my son and managed to somehow connect with you. So, Jane, while it is nice to speak to you, first, where are Sarah and Ari. And second, when are you coming to pick me up and take me to them?"

Jane sensed Allie was making a real effort not to be rude and informed him in a professional voice, "Sarah is hiding out in a magnificent residence somewhere in Marin, and I will be over in fifteen minutes to pick you up and personally show it to you." To her credit, Jane was on time.

"Jane, despite the insanity you're sharing with Sarah, it is good to see you again. You look healthy and happy and let your curly hair go frizzy."

"I'm glad to see you too, Allie." She hugged him warmly.

"I apologize for sounding like a real estate agent on the phone." In what sounded like a curious afterthought, she added, "I've only been selling houses for a year, but I am doing great."

They got into her green Volvo station wagon and drove up the road leading out of Tiburon and toward Route 101, Marin's main thoroughfare. Jane got around to explaining how she'd hooked up with her husband.

"It is okay, Janie," Cohen assured her. "You don't have to bother."

"Sorry, you need context. After majoring in dance therapy at Wisconsin, I moved to San Francisco. And unable to find a job, I met Raymond Jones, a native Californian. He proposed to me, and I figured I could always get a divorce, so I married him mostly to stay here, but now that I'm earning good money and have two beautiful and smart children, I'm making it work and really love Ray."

Allie patiently listened while she happily droned on, just days into his becoming consumed with the affairs of office. He had just gotten into daily management mode of a major city—making phone calls, chairing meetings, making speeches, and attending social events. At the moment, he was making chitchat with Jane about her eight-year-old daughter, Wanda, and six-year-old son, Jackie.

"Allie, I insist on giving you a short tour of scenic Marin before hooking up with Sarah."

They drove through the suburban wonderlands of Mill Valley and Larkspur and along the Pacific coast.

"We're in Bolinas now, a tiny town where a hard-core remnant of the 1960s counterculture relentlessly tears down the road signs to divert tourists coming to see them. Excuse me, Allie, but I still like to smoke pot. Bolinas brings it out in me."

She lit up a joint while steering the car in the direction of Mount Tamalpais. After toking on it for several seconds, she handed it to Cohen, who surprised her by passing on it. Jane was disappointed but soon got very stoned and quite sentimental.

"You know, Allie, of all the people from the old neighborhood, you've made it bigger than anyone else and, my god, of all things, the fucking mayor of Atlanta. Who would have thought?"

"Well," said the clearheaded Cohen, "I can, Jane, for I have three million people who are counting on me to put their new city together, so do you think we can curtail this tour a bit and take me straight to wherever Sarah is hiding out?"

"Okay, Allie, next stop, Kent Woodlands."

Jane headed north into the most lush and mountainous part of green Marin.

"I have to tell you, Allie, how I hooked up with Sarah. In typical small-world fashion, she picked my firm out of the yellow pages, and we became good friends instantly."

"That's nice."

Jane laughed and then told him that the well-shaded and winding road they just turned onto led to the top of a small mountain.

"We have now reached the apex of Kent Summit Estates and are parking in the four-car garage. Isn't this a fabulous home?"

Allie identified the style. "Jane, this is a Frank Lloyd Wright, isn't it?"

Jane nodded yes, entered the 3.5-acre compound listed at over $6 million, and led Allie around the side of the unique structure and into the elegantly landscaped and spacious backyard, where he spotted Sarah. She lay smugly outstretched in a chaise lounge nearby a kidney-shaped swimming pool, waiting for them.

Since the footsteps behind her could only be Jane's and Allie's, Sarah blindly greeted him. "Hey, chum, what do you think of my new home? Did you know that it was designed by Frank Lloyd Wright, your favorite architect?"

"That was back in college, Sarah. My favorite architect today is Lenny Meltzer."

"That's nice. Hey, look at that view. I did great, didn't I? I just know that you're going to love living here."

Allie brushed aside Sarah's irritating ambitions and knelt beside her to set her straight.

"Sarah, honey, please, no more nonsense. Come home with me, baby. I need you and love you and don't want to live without you."

Sarah interpreted his words. *Allie, if forced to return to Atlanta without me, will and me not liking that outcome will sweeten my tone and improve my salesmanship.*

Sarah emphasized with a sweep of her arm to the east. "Look at this palace, Allie, and look at that view of the mountains right over the roofline." The arm swept west. "Will you look at the ocean over there? It's nicer even than our Buckhead property, isn't it?" Sarah's right hand swept east again. "Didn't you always say that the Bay area is more beautiful and exciting than Atlanta? This is probably the most fabulous private homesite available in the whole country."

Cohen did not argue, nor did he bother to admire the property, the pretty vistas, or the small stream-fed lake.

He just stared at her with a fixed gaze that read, *Please cut the crap before I have to reschedule events again.*

"Sorry, Allie, I really love this place. This is my paradise." She jabbed her left thumb at herself twice while repeating, "My paradise."

Sarah turned to the vistas behind her; again, she swept her arm in a left-to-right arc to direct Allie's attention.

"Will you dig that great view of the city?" She pointed due south to the San Francisco skyline and continued moving westward. "There's the Golden Gate Bridge, the Pacific Ocean, and down below us are Marin's rolling green hills and beautiful valleys."

With the same enthusiasm and arm sweep, she described the fantastic house and its incomparable lines. "Look at Wright's angles, niches, and luxuriant streams of light from the unique windows."

He thought, *I can see Sarah capping her pitch.*

"Allie, despite the hefty price, mon, the property is a bargain as it's doubled in value every five years since it was built." Sarah was through; Allie had stoically listened.

"Please forget this dream and return home with me, and then add this place to your Châtelet and Cap Ferrat properties that you also didn't buy. Look, Sarah, Atlanta's our home. I've a big city to run, and I face a week of inaugural bashes beginning tomorrow. We must head to the airport in the next fifteen minutes or risk canceling another day of events."

Sarah pouted. Allie reasoned. "Money, this is a great dream at the wrong time of our lives. Maybe if we'd come here after Los Angeles instead of moving to New York, it might have worked. But it doesn't matter anymore, for I've been called on by the holy One, blessed be He, to make Atlanta work. I can't and won't apologize for that, so I'm begging you to come back with me. By the way, where's Ari?"

Sarah matter-of-factly explained, "The son of a famous movie director who lives next door liked Ari's looks and put him in a short film he's making with the father's guidance. Don't worry, Ari and the boy were fast friends, and the father is very nice."

She got up and huffily spoke while pacing around the pool.

"Allie, the danger to us is in Atlanta, come to grips with that. We're safe here or in Cap Ferrat or even in Israel, but you're a target in Atlanta. So if you don't get rid of the danger to you, Ari and I will live here. Prove to me that it's absolutely safe in Atlanta."

"Eddie White," Allie wearily responded, "is not a threat and should be given a chance to prove himself in an exciting new position. While it's true that Eddie was once a confused and troubled young man, he's turned his life around and become a solid citizen. Taking into account his fellow inner circle's rewards, he's probably right in expecting a similar-level job too."

"Allie, have you, for one minute, thought what happens if he fucks up? How he will act if you have to fire him? I'll tell you, he'll come to kill you. That's my dread."

"Sarah." Allie threw up his hands in frustration. "Must I promise you that nothing will ever happen to me?"

Sarah parried by reminding him, "Allie, I'm carrying your baby and fear rearing two children alone."

"Sarah, I'm damned if I do and damned if I don't. I admit it, I'm a target for all deranged whites and blacks, and the best security team cannot guarantee perfect safety. Still, the Redeemer has called upon me, and I must obey."

Cohen checked the time. "The moment of truth has arrived. Babe, either we leave now for my plane or I won't be in any shape tomorrow to perform my duties. Please, Sarah, don't force a trade-off between my family and city. I love you, money, and am praying that you and Ari will come home with me. So what are you going to do?"

"Allie, are you choosing your religion and Atlanta over your family?"

Allie turned that around. "Sarah, are you choosing a Frank Lloyd Wright home in fancy Kent Highlands in Marin County over my Orthodox faith and devotion to Adonai?"

Allie shook Sarah with that realization. *He's accusing me of taking the side of materialism against the Word and maybe the will of God too. I deeply believe in Adonai, Allie knows that, but I dare not tempt a judgment.* In a whisper of a voice, she gave in. "You're right, Allie. Let's go home."

They thanked Jane for everything, said goodbye to her, and went home to Atlanta, assumably with the issue settled before the eternal One, blessed be He.

Chapter 128

Allie's campaign week journal entry listed, "Rick Samuels, Mike Schwartz, Dan Daniels, and Sam Minkowitz take charge of my installation and organize two weeks of events designed to jump-start Metro Atlanta's consolidation.

"The inaugural plan is a smashing success. Eighteen thousand VIPs donate $1,000 each to enjoy Sarah and me, the metro commissioners, and entertainment stars at the world's biggest cocktail party held at the Omni. Thirty-four thousand more pay $250 to dance with us at the Georgia World Congress Center, and fifty-seven thousand citizens plunk down $25 to participate in a cultural extravaganza at Braves stadium."

"Atlantans outdid themselves during We Can Be Together Week. At first, whites and blacks and urban dwellers and suburbanites felt each other out like former combatants who'd just laid down their arms.

"Fortunately, the southern propensity to be friendly, enjoy favorite comfort foods, and drink beer in tune to lively music tore away the walls of mistrust. Metro Atlantans were brought together, formally introduced, hopefully to become neighbors.

"We Can Be Together Week helped us get the new configuration moving forward. The eight I-285 affairs were mini-inaugurals for each of the new districts. The multiple happenings helped us hit the ground running and give birth to a new and better Metro Atlanta.

"I was surprised to learn that the city's symbol, the phoenix, and slogan 'Resurgens Atlanta,' were still appropriate for an audacious people and region graced with an indomitable spirit. Ari and I came up with the marketing slogan 'Y'all pitch in' to encourage people to stay on track with their rendezvous with destiny."

Two weeks later, Allie had time for another journal entry.

"Ivan Terman's soundings suggest that the people like the way I'm on top of things and my firm and fair manner. I've surprised even myself with an ability to govern the office, chair a cabinet meeting, and control the bureaucracy.

"Quickly learning to say no when the MASS police threatened a slowdown on the job if I didn't renegotiate their contract won me the respect and admiration of some conservatives and businesspeople. Ivan Terman claims that I'm the most popular mayor in Atlanta history after one month.

"I think the real success story is Mack Thomas's deft handling of the metro council. White commissioners are finding his wielding of power to be fair and consistent. Lee Xeranga's also impressive with his political sensitivity and pragmatism."

The *Atlanta Journal-Constitution* published a six-part series on how NDMA was working. The newspaper introduced all the metro commissioners, and a tantalizing quote emerged from the magnolia mouth of good ol' boy Leroy Jennings of Clayton County, southeast metro district.

"At first, I was real worried that this African guy would be one big pain in the you-know-what. But so far, Lee's been a real pleasure to do business with. I've even come to like the guy. I guess that's what this is all about."

"I got to say that," E. Glenn Conway admitted, "NDMA is working better than I expected, and Thomas's and Xeranga's friendliness and fairness has been a nice surprise. Y'all know that was not easy for me, the King of the 'Necks, to say—after all, I have a reputation to protect."

When asked why NDMA was succeeding, Mayor Cohen repeatedly stated, "Our newly enlarged configuration, Metro

Atlanta, yields limitless chances to enhance opportunity and satisfy human desires and potential."

Allie did not often admit that he saw value in some aspects of Gestalt psychology. Life is a configuration of dots that the person arranges or connects with to satisfy personal needs and wants.

"Our aim," Cohen relentlessly preached, "is to encourage individual behavior to become more communitarian oriented. People should stop avoiding certain groups entirely by putting serious distance between them. Lifestyles established on primarily negative values are declared passé, if not taboo."

Cohen's next journal entry was "The cost of the election alone sent a ripple through the local economy. Renewed faith in the city's growth and future has fueled a surge of investment capital, resulting in record amounts of new construction projects.

"I addressed a real estate industry convention two days ago at the Georgia World Congress Center and told the gathering, 'Our resourceful business community recognizes that a freer marketplace has dawned. Developers, in particular, appreciate the end of overlapping or conflicting regulations, and a rigorous but fair centralized planning authority is designed to serve them with an easy walk-through process. The zoning board's mission facilitates intelligent, orderly land use and high-quality development.

"The Cohen administration is not antigrowth. We have dusted off the old-fashioned *village,* renamed it *new urbanism,* and declared it the preferred model over current suburban sprawl. I trumpet directed growth so our aim for Atlanta is to provide more of everything in a relatively compact and accessible infrastructure.'"

"Atlanta," Cohen said repeatedly in interviews, "has no reason to exist. The city's origin from intersecting railroads created a raison d'être of supplying instant gratification for whatever. The age of the car for satisfying our needs succeeded the railroad but must give way to a balanced regional transportation system."

In an interview with WDDT anchorman Ned Bryan, Cohen complained, "I'm starting to see some neighborhood groups that stand in the way of metro progress as elitist snobs. The Inman Park Community Self-Determination Committee (IPCSDC) made the mistake of standing in the way of progress that I believe in."

"What did IPCSDC do to annoy you?"

"The Interstate Insurance Company (IIC) applied for a building permit to construct a drive-in claims center. IPCSDC protested that the project was a tacky strip development that would marginally increase traffic flow in the area. *Marginally*, can you believe that? I mean, is that petty or what?"

"I agree. While you're at it, Mr. Mayor, is there anything else?"

"The neighborhood association also embarrassed me by leaking to the *AJC* that I awarded the city's fleet charter policy to IIC as a payoff for a substantial political contribution during the campaign. I resented what was widely viewed as a smear tactic but let it pass in the spirit of peaceful negotiations."

"It seems that it should have ended there."

"It didn't unfortunately. I graciously received IPCSDC leader Jan Duchon at my private residence and explained to him, 'IIC will employ seventeen people, pump over a million dollars a year into the local economy, and offer a useful service to the community that is known to reduce the trauma associated with car accidents.'"

"And that didn't satisfy them?"

"No. Duchon says to me, 'Cohen, you expressed a probusiness and growth philosophy. IPCSDC's mission is to preserve the quality of life in our neighborhood. For example, we prefer higher-quality development at that location like a fine restaurant or café with outdoor dining, not a drive-in claims center. Is anyone really wrong here?'"

"'Yes,' I told him because compromise is the American way. I saved the best part of my pitch for last, an expensive rendering of an attractive facility to serve the public, architecturally complementary with the neighborhood too. Duchon and IPCSDC were not impressed and rudely walked out."

"So your lesson, we gather, is that rudeness has no place in the conduct of business or government?"

"Yes, as well as silly and costly litigation in the courts. IPCSDC is taking its chances in court and will lose there too. The lesson to me is that interest groups have declared my political honeymoon over."

Cohen wrote a journal entry that evening. "The rest of the world has declared my honeymoon over too. The IRS sued Atlanta for $4.1 million in back taxes over a 1979 depreciation schedule for landfill equipment. Today a water main broke, leaving midtown very thirsty for eighteen hours, and a federal court increased EPA fines 300 percent for treatment plants leaking untreated sewage into the Chattahoochee River and Peachtree Creek after every rainstorm. This is a billion-dollar cleanup bond issue waiting to happen."

The following week's journal entry was "All the electricians today walked off the MARTA north line extension project to north Sandy Springs. A white cop accidentally shot a ten-year-old black boy in East Point, causing a street demonstration. Plus, a group of Baptist ministers from Conyers protested the inclusion of neon art in the Atlanta Airport they deem as erotic. I worry that the mounting ennui and minutiae might be causing me to lose sight of my original goals."

Eddie White started keeping his own journal too. He could not wait to get up in the morning to go to his job. Mayor Cohen expanded MASS's function to jointly work with the bureau of roads to tow illegally parked cars and with the police in responses to riots and insurrections.

Eddie quickly understood his role in this new MASS and tackled it like a man on a mission. Sharp young management teams eased him through the early transition period, and he was soon coordinating a few thousand workers and pieces of equipment through dozens of different routes each day all by himself.

Eddie in a journal entry:

"I feel the sanitation workers like and respect me because they see me as one of them. I was a garbageman and talk that up all the time. Making MASS work more efficiently, boosting productivity, or reducing or eliminating redundant costs fascinates me."

Yesterday Eddie met with a Georgia Tech management professor, a bank officer to finance equipment purchases, and a politician to satisfy his patronage needs. He has become an incessant brain-picker, a man on a mission to refine MASS's residential and commercial services.

Farrah wanted to add an entry to his journal.

"His intensity and single-mindedness of purpose has carried over into our homelife too. He bought a computer and spends so much time with his Mac that I'm complaining to friends of becoming a computer widow. Everyone keeps commenting on how he's grown into the job and is succeeding."

No one was more impressed than Mayor Cohen when, during a lull in his monthly meeting with the MASS leadership team, he saw Eddie reading an Israeli study of a new garbage disposal process and inquired about it.

"Mr. Mayor, the municipality of Ra'anana has this new composting process that eliminates the need for garbage dumps and landfills and saves a ton of money too. I'm looking at ways that we might adopt some of their processes to our own system."

"Go for it, Eddie. You're doing a great job, and your old teacher is proud as hell."

Farrah prayed daily for the best time of their lives to go on forever. *He is stroked and catered to by his doting staff. They even laugh at his corny jokes. May this lucky time last forever, and I don't mind at all his spending more time on his computer, going over routes or systems, than being with me.*

Eddie's doing so well, Farrah thought the next morning. *It calls for a celebration. I know. I'll treat him to lunch at the Georgia Plaza cafeteria across the street from city hall. They serve wine in cute little carafes.*

Eddie dominated conversation at lunch. "Farrah, I don't want to bore you by complaining of equipment breakdowns or idiot drivers who can't follow routes correctly, but I'll tell you this. MASS's new IBM computer system better cut costs by 10 percent like the salesman claims, or it's going back."

Farrah noticed that Eddie was so engrossed in his work that he'd hardly touched his salad or Chablis. *I can't believe my ears how he can ramble on and on about the virtues of biomass pellets and other energy stuff.*

"Dig it, Farrah. This process might supply up to 30 percent of all municipal government energy needs by 1992. That could result in an energy cost reduction of up to 12 percent for every citizen. Isn't that incredible?"

What's really incredible, thought Farrah, *is my husband's enthusiasm over biomass pellets. Is he the same old blood that I married years ago?*

It was after 1:00 PM, so they headed back to work. Eddie spoke in a stream-of-consciousness manner while walking across the street and into city hall.

"The best thing that's happened to me since being handed this job is that I don't feel real black anymore. I sense that all the people I meet now basically see me as the guy in charge and not some thick-lipped affirmative-action lottery winner."

"Ha ha! So how do you see yourself now?"

"As a pretty bright guy who just happens to be black. I guess my whole self-image has changed, hasn't it? I finally feel smart and capable of carrying on a conversation with almost anyone about anything."

He looked at his watch. "Hey, I almost forgot. I have to meet with a unit manager out in Douglasville in a half hour. I'll walk you back to your desk and then split."

Heather Meyers, Cohen's personal secretary, took off for lunch as soon as Farrah returned. The switchboard flashed before Mrs. White had a chance to sit down.

"Hello, Mayor Cohen's office."

"It's Harry Apollo, the governor of New York. May I please speak to Mayor Cohen."

990

Farrah cupped her hands over the receiver and told Eddie who it was. White's face wrinkled up in apprehension of what Apollo might want with Cohen. *I know better than to listen in but will chance it for Eddie's sake.*

Apollo, a moderate liberal, greeted Cohen. "Allie, how the hell are you?"

"I'm fine, Harry," said Allie and then thought, *I hardly know Apollo and wonder what the governor wants with me.*

The Whites out in the hall wanted to know too. *We met at a few cocktail parties when I was living in Manhattan, and we kibitzed a bit, that's all, yet the press has us as close. Go and figure.*

Farrah's stomach tensed when she heard Apollo say, "Allie, my pollsters are urging me to be visibly associated with a progressive southerner whose support for Israel and human dignity is unquestioned."

Farrah's stomach churned, and Eddie's faith in his future was on hold while Apollo laid out his presidential strategy to Cohen. "Allie, I need your help in winning over the Sun Belt to reindustrialize the rust belt north. I want to form the youngest and brightest government that's ever existed—technocrats, humanists, scientists, engineers, as few politicians as I can get away with."

Allie resisted adding inexperience to Apollo's ideal government.

"That sounds unrealistic, Harry, and to be up-front with you, I've been so busy trying to get a handle on this job that I haven't given any thought to national politics."

"Allie, Reagan's an old lox, and George Bush is a third term of him. We've got to get this country moving forward again. American needs real leadership, not government by public relations."

Cohen knew that Apollo stole that line from JFK, and although he liked the governor's rhetoric, Allie pressed Harry. "Please, Governor, get to the point."

Outside in the hall, Eddie and Farrah listened as if their paychecks hung in the balance.

"I know all about Judah Vision, Allie," the governor told Cohen. "If you sign on with me, I'll give you your own broadcast satellite to beam the Hebrew faith to Jews denied access to their religion and culture anywhere in the world starting with behind the Iron Curtain. They'll have to jam your broadcast to keep you out, if they can."

Harry Apollo is a terrific, if unprincipled, salesman who just made me an almost unrefusable offer. Allie weighed. *I'm turned on by Apollo's vision and turned off by the New Yorker's probable inability to win over his own party, forget the south.*

Out in the hall, the Whites awaited Cohen's decision, believing that the rest of their lives turned on a simple *yes* or *no* from him.

"Look, Harry, I appreciate the offer to globally transmit images of Jewish life, but I have a commitment to the people of Atlanta, and it's much too early to run out on it. Harry, the south won't go for you at all. Plus, you're running behind Dukakis in California, who has the nomination pretty much wrapped up. Hey, I'm too old to sign up for a doomed campaign, so sorry, Governor. Good luck with your candidacy though."

The Whites hugged each other and cheered. Farrah smiled as she put down the receiver.

"Man, Eddie, that was close. I was sure that Cohen was gonna take that Judah Vision offer. Wow, his own government satellite, I don't think I'd blame him if he took it. I finally understand what you mean by placing your faith in Cohen. The world just won't let that man stay in one place for any length of time, forget city hall."

"And let me hip you to this, Farrah," said Eddie, getting ready to leave for Douglasville. "We ain't out of the woods yet neither, not by a long shot."

"What do you mean, Eddie?"

"Imagine, Farrah, a Democratic candidate tendering the one irresistible position."

"What's that, my man?"

"Cohen's being appointed U.S. secretary of state or ambassador to the UN. For a Jew, Farrah, ending a garbage strike ain't the same thing as settling an Arab-Israeli war." Eddie turned and descended down the side stairwell.

Farrah worried. *I feel our lives are edging out into quicksand.*

Farrah, be mindful that you, more than Eddie, are the rock and foundation of the White family. Please, woman, force a smile and begin typing. Good, she did.

Chapter 129

Cohen wrote his first entry into his journal for convention preparation.

"We have spent the spring and summer of 1988 preparing the city for the Democratic National Convention invasion in early August to make Atlanta sparkle for this premium showcase. Public buildings are being cleaned up and tens of thousands of native flowers planted in downtown parks and along boulevard medians. MASS assistant director Eddie White, mainly responsible for the huge Spruce up the Big Peach program, has worked extremely hard and done a terrific job."

What Cohen did not know was that White worried the whole time. Eddie's own journal entry described a parallel reality.

"Cohen conceivably resigning at any moment hangs over my head and heart. I've worked closely with the mayor from April through June, and watching Cohen act as if he plans to be on the job for the next thirty years has stressed me.

"Last week, I experienced chest pains and entered Crawford Long Hospital to undergo an EKG series. Other than mild anxiety, the doctor tells me I'm fine. Go and figure."

As they left the hospital, Farrah looked up at the sky and murmured, "Lord, I know that you're punishing us for listening in on the phone call, aren't you? Before that Apollo call, my man was thriving. Now he's merely surviving. Please, God, I promise you that we've learned our lesson and will never do anything like that again."

We hear your prayers, Farrah. Trust me, you and Eddie are not being punished. This is in your head, for you have let guilt and fear get the better of you.

The Lord never answers my prayers though. Nothing changes. In his work, my man retains his bureaucrat's public face and continues to be good to me and the kids, but the joy has gone out of our lives. I can hardly return a smile to Mayor Cohen anymore.

The first wave of Democratic Party regulars and political technicians arrived in town. On what came to be called Black Monday, Farrah wasn't feeling well but dragged herself out of bed and to work. When she arrived, Heather was frantic.

"The mayor is planning a luncheon for the thirty top Democrats, and I haven't heard a word from the Sit-In's catering division."

"I'll take care of that, Heather," Farrah offered. "I've worked with catering a few times before."

Two hours later, the most powerful Democrats in the land filed past Farrah into the mayor's office to be fed corned beef, pastrami, or turkey sandwiches and sides provided by the Sit-In catering service.

Cohen greeted his guests one by one. *I'll mingle with the party establishment like a good mayor, host, and restaurant man should.*

All cheered Charley Moynihan, the Democratic national chairman, when he toasted. "This election is about the Democrats installing a government that cares about all the American people again, not just the rich white ones."

Meanwhile, out in the hall, Farrah typed away.

I know in my bones that the party is tempting Cohen away from Atlanta. Eddie always says my bones know immediately. Now how the hell can I get in there without looking too obvious? Eddie will go nuts on me if he has to read it in the newspapers like everybody else, but Heather is the mayor's personal secretary. She is at lunch though.

Farrah was almost witchlike in her bones, feeling the immediate future. The switchboard lit up. Farrah carefully picked up the receiver and heard an older woman's urgent voice.

"Hello, I must talk to Mayor Cohen immediately. It's a family emergency."

Farrah activated her official voice. "Would you please identify yourself and the nature of the emergency?"

"This is Rebecca Kartzman, the mayor's mother-in-law. Please tell the mayor that Mrs. Cohen's labor has started a few weeks earlier than expected. Harvey and I just dropped Sarah off in delivery, and she's doing well, so there's no need to worry. The only reason it's even an emergency is that the doctors predict a quick labor and birth, and the mayor wants to be there when the baby is born."

"Mrs. Kartzman," said Farrah, seizing the perfect opportunity to get inside the meeting, "I'm going to tell Mayor Cohen right this minute."

"Thank you very much. Knowing Allie, I think he'd be terribly disappointed if he ever missed such a blessed event."

"I believe so too," Farrah told Rebecca. "Excuse me, what hospital has Mrs. Cohen been checked into?"

Rebecca answered, "Northside Hospital."

"Congratulations, Mrs. Kartzman, on becoming a grandmother again."

"Thank you. That was sweet of you to say. Goodbye."

Farrah got up from her desk and entered the mayor's chambers as low profile as possible. Cohen was involved in a discussion with Ted Bell, who was quickly filling Allie in on all his changes and successes during the past couple of years.

"Mayor Cohen, my consultantship is booming, and I got engaged last weekend to a beautiful girl named Marlene Schwartz. I attribute all my new blessings to your helping me find myself in life."

"It's great to learn of all your good fortune. It couldn't happen to a nicer guy."

"Most of all, Mayor Cohen, you helped me come to terms with my dad's legacy, so I made it a mission the past year to get you appointed U.S. ambassador to the UN. The president likes that you won a Nobel Prize because of a tour he sponsored, so he finally agreed yesterday morning and needs you to start in two months. Is it possible to wrap up things in Atlanta quickly because ol' Dutch isn't remembering things too well these days? He could forget tomorrow what he agreed to today."

They both laughed. "Thank you, Ted, for all your efforts on my behalf, and let me give you a tentative yes, but I'll first have to talk with my wife, Sarah, and son, Ari, about living in New York again, though it shouldn't be a problem. The main thing, Ted, is that it's not going to be easy leaving Atlanta City Hall. There will be a lot of criticism. I know that your father is smiling down from heaven, Ted, at your great success."

Ted Bell emotionally hugged Allie; both men wiped a tear from their eye. Farrah self-consciously tapped the mayor on the shoulder just as Maryland U.S. senator Bob O'Connell joked, "Mayor Cohen, congratulations, you will serve as a true voice of reason in that August UN body."

Cohen sensed that was bad timing by both Bell and the senator, who was always blabbing away on WDDT. Farrah did not need to hear that either.

"Mayor Cohen, I have important news. Your mother-in-law called to say that Mrs. Cohen has gone into labor. She is doing well but expects you to be there as soon as you can."

Shouts of congratulations and mazel tov filled the room. Congressman Bill Bradley from Aurora, Colorado, asked Allie, "Mayor Cohen, do you have a preference?"

Allie beamed. "A little girl this time, Bill. I'm already blessed with a terrific son."

Cohen wrote in his second journal entry, "I excused myself, received a police escort to the hospital, and got there in time to witness the birth of seven-pound-eight-ounce Brenda Alicia Cohen. A pretty blond nurse cleaned Brenda up and placed the tiny pinkish bundle in my loving arms."

Brenda happily smiled at her daddy. Ari high-fived his dad and gave his new sister a little kiss. She smiled at her elder brother too.

Allie looked at Ari. "I think Brenda looks and smiles just like Mom."

Ari examined his sister. "I think so too. It's the way she wrinkles her lower lip."

"You're right, Ari. Anyway, I've waited so long for you, little Brenda, and were you ever worth it. I love you so much already and swear that I'm the happiest daddy in the world right now."

Ari added, "And I'm the happiest brother."

Allie kissed his son's cheek.

Sarah, groggy but smiling from within, joked, "And you're already preparing for when some seventeen-year-old punk drives up in a van and asks to take her out on a date."

"Hey, I remember what kind of animal I was at that age. I imagine they'll soon be hitting on li'l Brenda left and right. Need I repeat my famous slogan?"

Ari made a fist to imply that he, the big brother, would defend his sister's honor.

"Good boy, Ari, and yes, Allie, I remember your slogan well. 'A hard putz has no conscience.' I've always thought you're part Italian too." Sarah serenely chuckled before falling asleep.

Allie kissed his wife and told her, "I love you, Sarah, and thank you for giving me this magnificent gift of a beautiful baby girl."

At 5:00 PM, Cohen returned to city hall to sign a few documents; Ari spent the night with his grandparents. Farrah, finishing up typing, recognized her boss's footsteps, looked up from her word processor, and congratulated him.

"So you finally got that little girl you always wanted. I think that's wonderful, Mr. Mayor, and please tell Mrs. Cohen how happy I am for her too."

"Thank you, Farrah. That was sweet of you to say."

"That makes two fantastic things that happened to you today and on a Monday to boot."

Allie decided he needed to talk with Farrah about what Bell and the senator said. "Farrah, there's something I should explain to you."

She knew exactly what was on his mind and said it for him.

"I understand that you asking for Heather all the time spared me a conflict of interest. I might've heard something that could affect Eddie's career and put me in a funny situation, like today."

"That's perceptive."

She popped the big question. "Mr. Mayor, are you going to take the UN job?"

Cohen, with a poker face, admitted, "Probably, but it's all tentative until I sit down and talk with my family. That's all I can say at the moment."

"Who do you think would replace you as mayor?"

"Mack Thomas," Cohen explained, "would serve as interim mayor until a general election, but I speculate that if the suburbs manage to unite behind a single white candidate, Mack could be overwhelmed. I'm speculating. Don't take me too seriously. Mack might win for all we know."

Farrah recoiled a bit. Cohen ceased talking, sensing he'd made a mistake in alarming her.

"I'm a merit employee and vested," Farrah rambled. "I'm not affected by changes in administrations. They can come and go for all I care, but Eddie, Mr. Mayor, is a whole 'nother story."

"Farrah, it's risky to discuss this subject in the hallway. Give me ten minutes to make a phone call, and then walk in."

"I have plenty of time and will knock first before entering."

Chapter 130

The eternal One, perched over the Temple Mount, looked down at the two Muslim mosques that prominently occupy the skyline of east Jerusalem. The holy One, blessed be He, summoned me, Gabriel, His special angel, for an emergency meeting. The Creator began briefing me on the fate of the Dome of the Rock and Al-Aqsa Mosque that stand on the site of the First and Second Temples.

"Gabriel, I need you to perform a mission so important that, if you fail, it could lead to the end of Israel. There is no time to waste, so the special angel Eli will look after the prophet until you have saved Israel from an ultimate jihad."

"Lord, I'll be kind and just say that when Eli is referred to me as Your *special angel*, in today's educational vernacular, it means something very different."

"I know, Gabriel. Eli is My most limited angel and has failed Me on countless occasions, but he is such a sweet angel that I always give him another chance. The prophet is only hosting the Democratic National Convention and giving the nominee a parade down Peachtree. Even limited Eli can handle that. I hope."

"Master of the universe, what calamity is so urgent that You would place the prophet's safety at risk and in Eli's pathetic hands no less?"

"Gabriel, please be kind to Eli. He wants so badly to regain your trust and affection once more."

"I promise to try, Yahweh, but his incompetence makes it very hard. Now that I've said that, what concerns the Master of the universe?"

"Gabriel, do you recall how the Shin Bet stopped twenty-six young Israelis from elite families a few years ago from blowing up the Temple Mount to redeem Israel?"

"Yes, I remember, and the whole sordid affair was swept under the rug as expected."

"Sadly true. Anyway, the source of this problem is a school in Herzliya that many of Israel's leaders enroll their children in. Two charismatic gym teachers are dangerous fanatics who have dedicated their lives to destroying the two great mosques. Their aim is to reclaim the mount to build the Third Temple and fully redeem the Jewish people and the state of Israel."

"Are they planning to personally storm the mount and destroy the mosques themselves?"

"No, Gabriel, they train waves of students who join out of national pride and expect no punishment because of who their parents are. Not only did the two teachers influence the twenty-six but, ten years ago, these two former commandos and munitions experts also selected twelve other young male students to become the Golden Dome Dozen (GDD)."

"May I assume that the unit just finished their army duty and have been honed into a very self-sufficient commando unit?"

"Yes, exactly, the Golden Dome Dozen are positioned to attack in twenty-four hours."

"The attack is both ironic and moronic. The GDD believe they are on a mission for You, the Redeemer, but ignore the reality of threatening the survival of the nation they so blindly love."

"I know, and they should know too that they were already redeemed with the creation of their own state. Construction of a third temple is desirable, of course, but will not earn further consecration. Destruction of the two mosques, in fact, may cause Israel's end. Now hurry, Gabriel, and do what you do best."

"I assume You want me to invisibly sabotage them—cars don't start, core blasting components fail, communication systems go down, an outbreak of diarrhea, nausea, and knee injuries strike them all. I assure You, Hashem, I will use every trick in the book that I know to defeat these wayward Jews and am aware that there is no margin for error."

"Yes, My special angel will so invisibly stop this terrible mission that not even Shin Bet will know of it. Unfortunately, the two teachers have started training a second elite group of male students to become GDD II for a 1998 attack that the Shin Bet will stop, though the culprits won't be brought to justice either."

"Destruction of the mosque that Muhammad supposedly ascended to heaven on a winged horse, Name, would radicalize hundreds of millions of Muslims, even in moderate Islamic nations like India, Indonesia, and Turkey. A permanent global jihad would eventually exhaust and overwhelm Israel, who might resort to nuclear weapons to stave off the Muslim masses."

"Exactly, Gabriel. Now go and save Israel from twelve of its most devoted but misguided sons. Work your magic like a great broom sweeping away a nasty mess. I see concern in your face, Gabriel. What is the matter, My special angel?"

"My Lord, Tisha B'Av is upon us. Poor, simple Eli has always failed us on this most horrible of days in Jewish history, including the destruction of both temples."

"Forgive Me, Gabriel, if you think I put the prophet at risk. Life sometimes forces us to make tough decisions because our resources are stretched thinly at the moment from so many earthly problems. Please go and save Israel. We will both pray that Eli will keep the prophet safe."

"As You wish, God all knowing."

Gabriel turned his back on Hashem and flew away. A gray cloud formed over Adonai.

"Did I detect a note of sarcasm, even insolence, in Gabriel's voice?"

Chapter 131

Less than a mile away, MASS deputy director Eddie White coordinated dozens of high school kids earning community service hours in a final cleanup of Central City Park. C. K. Yang, White's able assistant, approached Eddie, who was standing on the park's Five Points corner. Cohen recruited Yang, a CPA and PhD systems analyst, to run MASS's computer operations.

Yang, a Georgia Tech graduate, spoke into his boss's ear.

"Mr. White, I randomly audited a printout for Garden World and found double billing to MASS and the bureau of the parks for $52,500 worth of shrubs and flowers that they outrageously delivered only half of."

"Good work, C. K. Do you think it's a fraud or a clerical error?"

"Fraud," Yang said. "The nursery's experiencing financial problems and allegedly took advantage of often sloppy controls associated with rushed efforts like Spruce up the Big Peach. Mr. White, we need to report this to the proper authority."

"C. K., it's close to five thirty. The city attorney's office is probably closed. The mayor, though, is scheduled to address the Democratic National Committee tonight, and Cohen usually works late when entertaining downtown in the evening."

"My car's parked right in the lot over there. Do you need a lift? It's so hot I swear that you can fry a fucking egg on Peachtree today."

Eddie laughed. "That's the first time I ever heard you curse, C. K. Yeah, it's hot as a motherfucker, all right. Ha ha! But it's only a half a mile over to city hall, so I'll walk the short distance, even in this goddamned sauna."

A few blocks away, Farrah knocked on Mayor Cohen's door and entered. Allie was busy wrapping up a call to Dan Daniels and motioned for her to sit down.

"All right, Dan, I'll expect your driver to pick me up at 8:00 PM sharp, and good luck with your speech too."

Allie put the receiver down and smiled at Farrah, her cue to complete what was on her mind. Farrah was visibly nervous but wasted little time in getting down to business.

"My husband loves his job, Mr. Mayor, and has no desire to find another one. I love my job too and feel the same way."

"I'm glad to hear that. You're both doing fine jobs."

He smiled and folded his hands. Farrah smiled and folded her hands.

"Mr. Mayor, I don't think you grasp the affect your personal decisions have on the fate of others, me and Eddie, for example. You, more than anybody, knows how far in life we have come since Bankhead High, and we're very worried about not being able to hold on to our gains."

"That's understandable, and of course, you guys know how proud of y'all I am." He continued to smile with folded hands.

"I predict that if you complete your first term in a good manner, you'll win a second term in an even bigger landslide. Why not stay with a sure thing and minimize disruption and uncertainty? More people than you can imagine are attached one way or another to your political decisions."

Cohen unfolded his hands and stopped smiling.

"I acknowledge that your concerns are normal, but the situation is far more complicated than merely keeping a lid on

1006

change. My becoming metro mayor, Farrah, was a freak political circumstance, and my popularity has probably peaked."

"I'm not so sure about that, Mr. Mayor."

"Look, after the convention, my job approval rating will steadily decline as the people of Atlanta tire of me. Here are some examples from the evening paper."

"I'm listening."

"Reagan is cutting federal aid to MARTA in half. This latest round of cuts will hammer the local economy with a fare increase and service reduction, which will dent daily ridership. The year's homicide rate is running ahead of last year's tragically high rate, and a record number of bars and restaurants along Peachtree Street were robbed in the past month, including the Sit-In. Last Thursday night, two punks broke in after closing and held up my seventy-two-year-old father-in-law with a sawed-off shotgun."

"I didn't know. That's awful."

Cohen concluded his spiel. "Now I'm going to read a letter from a bigot to the editor of the *AJC*. 'The mayor shouldn't wear his religion on his sleeve—and head—all the time. Cohen needs to realize that he is a Jew in a Christian nation and should behave accordingly. What are we to do if he closes city hall on a Jewish holiday and keeps it open on Christmas and Easter?' It's signed B. J. Travis, Snellville, Georgia. Now I ask you, Farrah, do I really need to deal with this stuff, which happens a lot more than you can ever imagine?"

Farrah bowed her head and concurred, "No, you do not."

"I'm not indispensable," Cohen reminded her. "Atlanta is a machine that nearly runs itself. Furthermore, Eddie's performance at MASS is rated excellent, and qualified minorities are badly needed by large organizations to show progress in meeting their hiring goals. Eddie has proved his ability and made a great place for himself. Please trust me on this."

That should have ended this discussion with her leaving. Wrong. Farrah started wiping tears from her eyes.

"It's funny. He's humming along in his work doing great, and then something a bit scary happens, and he starts to fall apart. If you leave soon, who will guarantee him a place if and when Mack goes down?"

Cohen was close to losing his patience.

"Farrah, please trust me on this. Everything will work out just fine. Eddie's most recent performance evaluation ranked him in superior status, ninety-seventh percentile, so please have faith, and the Lord will take care of you."

"Eddie doesn't have faith in himself, Mayor Cohen, so what does it matter if I or even the Lord does? I'm deeply concerned that Eddie will flip out on me if a future white mayor demotes or fires him. I beg you to do something to help us hold our ground."

"I feel sorry for you, Farrah, but honestly, I don't know what to do or tell you. I can't make my successor hire or staff Eddie, and as much as I'd like to help, it'd be unfair to stick a future mayor with him if he wasn't their choice."

Allie's choice of words bothered Farrah. "Sticking him on someone, eh? Do you still dislike him?"

"Of course, I don't and will overlook your mentioning it." *I'm done trying to make her see my side of the issue.* "Farrah, I'm proud of Eddie's success and will write a great letter of endorsement on his behalf. Eddie has sufficient boosters and connections to guarantee him a decent position even if Glenn Conway succeeds me as mayor. If you'll excuse me now, I have a speech to prepare for."

1008

Cohen turned his back to Farrah by swiveling his chair in a half circle and rehearsed an applause line.

Farrah resented Cohen. *He's patronizing me and just doesn't get it.*

She blankly rose from her chair and stared at Cohen for a few seconds and then mechanically removed her blouse and skirt and let each piece fall casually to the floor.

Cohen swiveled another 180 degrees to check if she'd left yet. The mayor's heart started racing.

Uh-oh, my secretary has stripped down to her bra and panties. Why the hell is she taking her clothes off? "Farrah!" he yelled at her. "What are you doing? Put your clothes back on right now, or I will write you up for sexual harassment and insubordination."

Farrah answered him in a soft and seductive voice, "Sexual harassment, wow, and insubordination too. That's not what they called it back in the day when you were my teacher. I used to throw my big titties out all the time to see if you'd look, and you always did. I think everyone called it *sexual attraction* back then, and I know I made you hard more than once."

"Farrah, you're acting and talking crazy. Now put your clothes on before I fire you."

She talked over him. "I talk and I talk, and you don't really hear me. Maybe you understand body language better."

A lump formed in Cohen's throat when she freed her large firm breasts and ever so slowly peeled off her panties. She then began trash-talking to try to turn him on.

"You must have stared at my tits all through U.S. history and International Relations. Here, touch my tits finally."

She placed his hands on her responsive nipples.

"Let's see if you're hard yet." She placed her hand on his penis. "Yeah, let me touch it."

She engulfed his face with her breasts while shoving her hand down his pants and began aggressively fondling him. Cohen, horny from a month with almost no sex, felt shame from his lust for Farrah's smoldering eroticism. His hands were busy exploring her whole body, and with each touch, his lust heightened.

Farrah encouraged Allie. "Now put your finger between my legs. Yeah, move it in and out, nice and slow. Yeah, ooh, you're making me so wet."

Cohen worried. *I'm beginning to have second thoughts.* "Farrah, we need to stop."

"Let me suck your cock." She was not to be denied, and he grew compliant to her fingers stroking his erect penis. Cohen closed his eyes as she put him in her mouth and moved her tongue up and down. "You like that. Sure you do."

She deep-throated him until he almost came; Cohen could not resist her.

"Stay in this job, and I'll suck and fuck you daily if you want." She put his penis inside her and rocked him reverse cowgirl for a few minutes. Cohen, again close to coming, abruptly stopped Farrah, compassionately touched her cheek, and gently counseled her.

"This is wrong, Farrah.We just broke a slew of commandments, so maybe if we stop now, the Lord will overlook our sins."

"I understand. You're right. We should stop."

"Let me cover your nakedness with my suit jacket."

He sweetly kissed her cheeks. The mayor's touching display of kindness released a flood of stored-up pain and remorse. Tears poured from her eyes.

Farrah put her head on Allie's shoulder and wept so hard that her body shook.

Cohen comforted Farrah by holding her in his arms and advised her by quoting from Macbeth.

"'If you can look into the seeds of time and say which grain will grow and which will not, speak then to me.' What I'm saying is that not only can't you control the future but the only real security you have also is your health and wits, so please do yourself a favor and stop creating so much ridiculous pressure. I order you to just take life one day at a time and try to do the best you can, okay?"

A knock on the door jolted Cohen into realizing that he and his secretary had better get dressed and fast too. A second later, Eddie White's unexpected voice boomed right through the door.

"Mayor Cohen, I just discovered an overbilling and need a directive from you to go after Garden World for fraud."

Before Cohen could react, Eddie opened the door. White walked in, stopped, and stared straight ahead in abject horror and shock; his world has fallen apart right before him. Tears quickly streamed from his eyes, and he cupped his hands over his mouth and rubbed it repeatedly. Finally, he spoke.

"What the fuck? My wife, Farrah, whom I love more than life itself, is in the arms of the mayor, who's holding a goddamned jacket around her naked body."

"Eddie, please." She begged him to listen to her, but he refused.

"You broke my fucking heart, Farrah, and I want to punch the shit out of both of you, only I can't decide which one to hit first."

White's hurt and anger drove him to wrap his powerful arms around his exploding head and roar like a bull elephant betrayed by his mate.

"Faaarrrrrrraaaaaahhhhhhh!" White's raw bleating made Farrah shake while Cohen prepared for an attack. Eddie again ferociously wailed her name at the top of his lungs.

"Faarrrraaaahhhh! Why did you do this?"

He wiped tears from his eyes with the back of his right hand.

"Eddie," Farrah nervously begged, "please, it's not what you think. If you'll only give me a minute to explain—"

"Fuck it, woman, ain't nothing to explain. You were either fucking the mayor or about to. What I don't understand is that you were my woman, my rock, the only thing in my life that I could count on since the goddamned eighth grade!"

"I made a mistake," Farrah confessed, "of foolishly using my body to save our positions. President Reagan has offered Mayor Cohen the UN job we both feared."

Eddie sarcastically condemned her. "So you were going to fuck the mayor to keep him from going to the UN to save my job. Now ain't that real helpful of you, you stupid bitch! Who the fuck wants a job that his wife fucked the boss to keep? Damn, I sure as hell don't!"

With that, White stepped forward toward his prone wife. Cohen watched the confrontation from behind his desk.

Oh, shit, he just slapped her hard enough to knock a man unconscious. She passed out instantly and hit the ground with a sickening thud. Fuck, now he's pointing a menacing finger at me.

"I accuse you of making Farrah screw you to keep her job. As soon as I leave here, I'm going to file $100 million sexual harassment case against you and the city if I first don't kill you with my bare hands."

Allie wondered how it had come to this. It didn't matter anymore; he had to save White from himself and tried his best.

"Eddie, please calm down before you do something stupid and ruin the rest of your life and mine. Now listen to me for crying out loud—"

"Dig that shit," Eddie cut him off. "He goes and fucks my old lady and tells me to listen. Well, eat shit."

"Damn you!" Cohen screamed. "I didn't fuck your wife. Now do you want to hear what happened or not?"

"No, I don't want to hear the shitty details! You've got some kind of balls, Cohen."

Farrah came back to life and tried again to stop Eddie from shattering their marriage and family. White rewarded his wife's reconciliation efforts with another crunching slap across the face, again knocking her out.

Perhaps it was better that she did not hear him angrily shout at her, "You stupid fucking whore bitch!"

After the assassinations of former San Francisco mayor George Moscone and city manager Harvey Milk, the APD City

Hall Security Task Force made Cohen keep a loaded pistol in his desk at all times. With White seemingly out of his mind with grief and the danger of a murderous attack creeping closer, Allie was forced to take the Glock pistol out of the drawer and point it at him.

White went berserk. "Motherfucker pulled a fucking gun on me. Man, now it's really personal! I'll get you, motherfucker, if it's the last thing I ever do!"

"And I'll give you one last chance, Eddie, to sit down and listen to common sense." Cohen's ultimatum boiled White's rage to insane proportions, and he lunged wildly to test the mayor's nerve.

"Eddie," said Cohen, laying down the law, "you may have sixty pounds on me, but that doesn't outweigh a bullet. Now unless you cool it and start listening to reason, I'm going to fucking shoot you."

White glared; Cohen further warned, "You're fucking with a guy, Eddie, who in an aerial dogfight shot down a Syrian MiG, so blowing your damn brains out from six feet away is rudimentary. Trust me on this."

Cohen aimed the gun at Eddie and held it straight with two hands poised to shoot.

White thought, *I got three options: leave and live to get even another day, die by gunfire, or scare the mayor into dropping his gun.*

Unfortunately, he chose the third. "You little Jew bastard, you don't have the motherfucking nerve to shoot me."

"You dumb dick," Cohen stonily responded to the slur, "that only makes my firing-away option that much easier."

The prophet's anger renders him unable to moderate his language and de-escalate the frightening situation. I will put a notion in Eddie's mind to cease and desist.

White remembered something. *Cohen had a real hot temper with the bad kids who wouldn't learn, and he* is *showing some fucking balls.*

Cohen drew on the Almighty's strength to give White one last chance.

"Okay, I'm going to count to three. And if you're not ready to listen, you'll not only be fired and banished but carried out on a fucking stretcher too."

Cohen started to call off the numbers. "One . . ."

White defiantly lurched forward. Cohen cocked the trigger; the sound stopped White in his tracks.

"Two." White glowered; Cohen stiffened. "Okay, fuck face, you had your chance. Get ready to die."

White venomously glared at Cohen and then turned his back and exited to fight another day. At the door, he stopped and set his terms with an insidious smirk on his face.

"One way or another, motherfucker, I'm gonna fucking kill you, so you better shoot me in the back on my way out, though I know you don't have the fucking guts to do it."

White is wrong. It is cowardly to shoot a man in the back. What would Gabriel do in this situation? Maybe Eddie, who does have a very good reason to be angry, is just blowing off steam and will calm down. It doesn't matter. I must protect the prophet, or Gabriel will never have anything to do with me again, for I have let him down so many times before on the eternal One's missions. I will relentlessly track Eddie White to make sure he does no harm to the prophet.

Chapter 132

Eddie disappeared into the night, leaving Farrah half-dead on the floor. Cohen, emotionally drained, slumped down in his chair and stared at the bruises on Farrah's pretty face.

How the hell did this all happen? And, Hashem, what do I do now? I guess I should tell the police and have them arrest Eddie before he can act out his threats. Maybe I should get some protection too. I do have two kids now. After this crap, it'd be great if I could start the UN job tomorrow.

Cohen suddenly remembered. *Oh no, Daniels will be here in an hour, and the last thing I need tonight is to speak to an arena full of politicians.*

Cohen called the DNC chief and worked out a deal just as Farrah opened her eyes and slowly struggled to her feet.

"All right, Charley," he said on speaker phone. "Let me get this straight. You're asking me to give the party's nominee a ticker-tape parade down Peachtree Street on August 7, the last day of the convention, and ride in my own vehicle too."

"Yes, Mr. Mayor, please provide two convertibles so the crowds can see the Democratic candidate and you, their popular mayor."

"I don't know, Charley, I don't like the idea of riding in an open-air convertible during lunchtime. My second child was just born, and I can't be so cavalier about my personal safety anymore."

Prophet, Eli begs you. Please don't ride in an open-air convertible. The threats and potential danger to you multiply terribly.

"You'll have full secret service protection," Moynihan promised. "Nothing will go wrong, Allie, I assure you. We're not going to let anything happen to the next U.S. ambassador to the UN."

"Yeah, that is if Reagan doesn't forget he agreed to it. Look, you're promising me nothing will go wrong? I don't buy that, and you shouldn't either, but I'll risk it for the good of the party."

Your decision, prophet, stresses me, so please reconsider for the Almighty's sake and mine. Yahweh and Gabriel forbid preemptive interventions on my part. I am disempowered because I simply made too many mistakes over the ages.

Cohen put the receiver down. "Farrah, do you need any medical attention? You look wobbly. I mean, you are leaning against the wall for support."

She declined. "No, I'll live."

"Here, put your clothes on already."

Cohen handed Farrah her underwear, and she let fly a wry dig while putting a leg through her panties.

"I see you didn't waste any time in taking the UN job."

An undercurrent of contempt in her voice offended Cohen. "Well, maybe you shouldn't have acted on your moronic idea of putting some moves on the mayor."

"You're right." She took responsibility. "All this trouble is my fault, isn't it?"

"Most but not all of it. I was part of the supporting cast. Whatever, start locating your husband, and then you need to get through to that bad actor that he's within an inch of destroying his life and your life too."

"I fear that I've lost him forever. It's quite obvious he doesn't want me anymore."

Allie somehow managed to keep knowledge of the incident from Sarah and also make it through the night. The next morning, he dragged himself from bed for a 6:00 AM tennis match with Rick Samuels.

The boys of summer were entering their middle years and now preferred tennis's slower pace, larger court, and being outdoors. One carryover was Allie's humiliating Rick and taunting his futility.

Cohen blasted scores of hard serves and passing shots by Rick's outstretched hands. Worse than enduring straight 6–2 losses and occasional crashes to the asphalt was Allie's merciless tongue.

"Whack, you lose again. Man, your body, Rick, looks like Yasser Arafat after an Israeli bombing raid."

"Thanks for the compliment."

"Come on, Rick, let's soak our bodies in the Jacuzzi."

"Tell me, Allie, why are you so hostile today?"

They rested their tired bodies in the huge hot tub. Cohen described the tumultuous events of the previous day. Rick listened and then shocked Cohen.

"Allie, I don't care if some big gorilla is after you. Christ, it's less than a year since you took office, or have you conveniently forgotten that?"

"Give me a break. The city machinery is working like a finely tuned engine. What's the big deal if I bug out for the UN?"

"What, are you stupid? You could tear the whole fucking city apart. Allie, if you pick up and run, I predict that the goon will not be the only person wanting to do you in."

Rick got it. *Allie appears to be hearing me, but he isn't going to follow my advice. In his mind, he's already reorganizing the UN.*

Rick opened his mouth several times to speak only to close it a second later. *Fuck it.*

"See you, Rick. I have to go home and daven."

The rays of the brilliant morning sun streamed through Sarah's bedroom window and stirred her from a restless sleep. *I had a horrible dream. Let me reach across the bed to tell it to Allie.*

Her hand felt only a pillow. *He must be in his chapel praying.*

A Technicolor neon sculpture fastened overhead to the ceiling bathed her white silk bathrobe in an iridescent light. Sarah washed her face, brushed her teeth, and then went looking for Allie. *Let's see if he's finished davening yet and is ready to have breakfast with me.*

Sarah found Allie in his conventicle. *He's wearing his customary garb but praying much more strenuously than he usually does, and I wonder why. The painful sounding psalms he's reciting are very emotional and affecting.*

Allie acknowledged her presence by gesturing with his head that he was almost done. Sarah waited patiently for him by sitting on a white couch embroidered with tiny blue Jewish stars set against a white area rug.

Allie's private tabernacle always makes me uncomfortable. I believe that a true place for prayer is a synagogue with a real congregation. Allie's claim that his tabernacle is kosher will never ring true to me.

Cohen put his prayer book away and came over to kiss his wife.

Sarah asked, "Why did this service take longer than usual?"

"It's Tisha B'Av," he answered in a measured voice, "the gravest of Jewish holidays."

"That's the holiday that it's best for Jews to not get out of bed that day, right?"

"Not quite. Jews are allowed to work if they fast and pray to Yahweh to protect them from another catastrophe, such as the destruction of the first two temples. Hey, why don't you and Ari join me in Central City Park to hear my speech? You can also take part in the parade up Peachtree Street too."

"Sorry, I've already made plans to visit my mother in the hospital. Ma's circulation problems are acting up again, so the doctor checked her into Piedmont Hospital last night to take some tests. I figured that a visit from her daughter and grandson will lift her spirit. Too bad Brenda is too young to come too."

"You're a good daughter, Sarah. Oh, I almost forgot. Tell Ari to tune in to WDDT at twelve thirty so he can watch his old man endorse the next president of the United States on national TV."

What is my husband doing being exposed like that on Tisha B'Av? Is he unnecessarily flirting with danger? "I'm worried, Allie. If this is such a tragic day, then why the hell are you speaking before thousands of people or riding in an open-air convertible up Peachtree?"

Sarah is still unaware of the Eddie White affair. If she were, she'd brain me with a lead pipe to keep me home. He placed his hands on her shoulders. "Mon, please don't worry. It's too late to call it off, and I promise you that nothing will happen."

"That promise is worthless, Allie, and you know it. Please cancel it for me. Christ, how could you be so dumb to schedule a parade on Tisha B'Av of all days?"

"Relax, babe, I just forgot. You're really making a big deal over nothing. Like New Year's Eve, it's just another day that people get all excited about. Remember, with the DNC Convention in town, the police have jailed every suspect and kook. Platoons of secret servicemen will be protecting me everywhere I go too."

"Yeah, like they did JFK."

Sarah, it is special angel Eli who promises you and Gabriel that I will not let anything happen to Allie, the prophet.

Chapter 133

"Please, Sarah," the mayor defended, "this is Atlanta and not Dallas. Look, money, I have to get to the office, so I better shower already."

He took Sarah in his arms and kissed her sexily. "I love you, babe."

After their lips parted, she kidded, "Thanks, that'll do a lot for my frustration."

"You'll live, money."

Sarah tried to seduce Allie away from his Tisha B'Av appointments. She stuck her hand between his thighs, rubbed his groin, and did her best Mae West imitation.

"Hey, big boy, let me give you a rise in your Levi's."

Allie winked at Sarah to suggest that Adonai might not approve of such talk in his tabernacle. He teasingly fondled her as they left the synagogue with the world's smallest congregation and then dropped a bombshell on her.

"Ted Bell secured the U.S. ambassador to the UN job for me. We have two months to move to New York, something you, Ari, and I will talk about over dinner tonight. I haven't told anyone yet, so please keep it a secret until then."

Sarah's eyes lit up. "Great, anything to get you out of this job, thank the Lord, even moving to New York again. You got my vote on that, pal. Thank you, Allie. I think this time around I prefer a brownstone. Ha ha!"

Farrah White lay in bed exhausted and close to a nervous breakdown.

I've hardly closed my eyes in the three days since Eddie disappeared.

She dragged herself out of bed and over to the front door to pick up the morning newspaper. Farrah frantically searched the paper's content for some news of her husband, found nothing again, called the police, and received the same tiresome report.

The APD are still looking for him. There's been an allpoints bulletin for three days and nothing so far. Jesus, I'm already late for work with a pile of typing on my desk waiting for me.

Farrah hurriedly dressed, gulped a cup of coffee, and raced over to city hall.

Thank god for Arvida. She sighed while ascending in the elevator. *She's been filling in like a champ during this time of crisis, taking real good care of her little brother too.*

Allie pulled into the city hall parking lot at the same time as Mack Thomas. They both got out and locked their vehicles. Cohen asked Thomas if the police had come up with any leads yet. Mack passed on a report that a man fitting Eddie's description was spotted in rural Spalding County, where he bought two handguns and a shotgun at a gun show.

"The Brady Bill," he then added, "does not cover private exchanges between sellers at gun shows, so no background checks were required."

Mack gave Allie a serious look. Cohen nodded to acknowledge the gravity of the situation.

"Mayor Cohen," Mack begged Allie, "please tell the Democratic National Committee to go straight to hell and to take their fucking parade with them too."

1023

Thomas did not see a DNC honcho waiting in the parking deck. The party operative was horrified at the thought of a last-minute cancellation and worried.

"Shit, the campaign's chemistry might be affected." The political technician mumbled, "We got to stop the ungluing of positive energies that are just starting to come together finally."

Mack threatened the operative, still unknown.

"What the fuck are you talking about? There's a man out there who's threatened to kill the mayor. Now do you get it, you dickhead, or do I have to fucking hit you to get through to you?"

"My name is Paul O'Malley for your information, and I don't like being threatened or called a dickhead. You hear me, asshole? That kind of language, you black motherfucker, will get you shot in my part of West Hartford."

"Well, excuse me, Mr. O'Malley, but we have a saying in the ghetto, 'Better a turkey than a dead pigeon.' If I were you, I'd postpone this parade until Eddie White's apprehended, that is, if you care more for the mayor's life than you do your damn campaign."

O'Malley, a tough former labor lawyer, reminded Mack that they were playing for big stakes, namely, the White House.

"Duh, risks come with the fucking territory." Thomas saw red when the sallow-looking O'Malley rudely paraphrased Harry Truman. "So, council president Thomas, if you can't stand the heat, get the fuck out of the goddamned kitchen."

Mack moved aggressively to attack the insensitive Yankee. Cohen jumped between Mack and O'Malley to physically restrain the metro council president from violently attacking the lout.

"Mack, we both know that O'Malley is a state-of-the-art political sleazeball. As bad as the dick is, he's not worth the shit you'll get from beating his fucking ass, though I'm very tempted to join you in kicking the crap out of him too."

Cohen's threat to join Thomas in kicking O'Malley's ass scared the operative to shut up. Mack calmed down too but not before scolding Cohen.

"If you had half a brain, Cohen, you'd tell O'Malley and the Democrats to go fuck themselves. You're obviously lusting after the goddamned UN job and risking the fate of the city too."

"The UN," Cohen responded, "has nothing to do with it. My administration simply cannot let one demented person hold us hostage. Our delaying everything is similar to caving in to the demands of a terrorist even before he submits them, and you know that if some nut wants to kill me bad enough, the whole damn army and navy can't stop them."

Please don't believe that for a minute, Allie, or even use the figure of speech because it makes the special angel Eli very anxious.

Mack remained adamant. "That's a load of crap, Cohen. All the DNC cares about is regaining the White House, and you're one little cog in their machine. Allie, I'm begging you to put off everything until tomorrow, and if you won't do it for me, then do it for Sarah, Ari, and your newborn daughter."

Allie said nothing; Mack, disgusted, walked away, muttering, "Cohen, you are the most stubborn motherfucker who ever lived."

Patrolman Johnny Epps, aged thirty-five and a former lineman for Hoke Smith High School, steered his motorcycle out of the Decatur Street Station and toward Central City Park. Epps, as usual, was assigned to the mayoral crowd control detail and expected to accompany the motorcade up Peachtree until its completion. He did not spot anything suspicious in the park area, so he checked out the enclosed drive-in facility of the adjacent Atlanta National Bank and Trust Building (ANBTB), a known haven for muggers preying on bank customers and employees. At 11:32 AM, Epps routinely glided his Harley-Davidson out of the late morning sunlight and into the ANBTB private throughway.

About twenty feet past the entrance, Patrolman Epps encountered darkness that obscured an inch-deep pool of motor oil. He suddenly skidded wildly, was almost out of control, and just missed a row of parked cars to his right.

Got to straighten out! Or I'm gonna fucking crash.

Unfortunately for Epps, the ten-year veteran's perfect driving record ended when his motorcycle smashed into the grille of a Lincoln Continental. The force of the collision hurled Epps from the Harley, and his body cut the air like a missile streaking just above the Lincoln's long, wide hood.

Epps blasted into the windshield helmet first, like a bowling ball leading a battering ram. His impact crumpled the safety glass; a dull, tinkling sound echoed off the walls. Johnny came to rest in the back seat amid shards of glass and to the cruel delight of a sinister figure crawling out from behind a nearby BMW.

A slightly smaller black male stripped off Epps's uniform and helmet and removed the firearm from its holster. He pushed the snub nose of the barrel hard up against Epps's ear, and fired into the drum.

The projectile tore a path through the victim's skull and brain and splattered the upholstery and windows. The next day, APD detectives recovered Epps's naked corpse from the stinking trunk of a rented Ford sedan, the one that had been seen in front of the rural gun show.

At 11:46 AM, Epps's impostor glided out of the throughway to patrol the waterfall area on the north side of Central City Park Plaza. The motorcade formed there and was to proceed up Peachtree Street from Five Points to the Peachtree Summit.

The impostor took his place in third position from the front of the line, turned off his motorcycle, and impatiently waited for the parade to start.

I have my eye on the impostor, Gabriel, and am tracking him closely.

Chapter 134

Cohen observed the crowd from his vantage point on the raised stage located across Peachtree Street from Central City Park and mulled over the sight before him.

The political advance specialists did their job well. A fairly large lunchtime crowd has congregated on the park mall as planned. I'm watching secretaries fold their neatly pressed dresses as nice southern girls usually do when they sit down to eat their delicate sandwiches.

College kids in tank tops and cutoffs whisked liberated Frisbees through the moist, heavy air. Here and there, businessmen in sagging summer weight suits delayed lunch to listen to their unusual mayor introduce the Democratic presidential candidate, Gov. Michael Dukakis of Massachusetts.

A local rockabilly band managed to pump up the crowd's adrenaline in spite of the blistering high noon sun and punishing humidity as bad a dog day afternoon as Cohen had experienced since moving south. Hundreds of convention delegates and a few thousand Atlantans gave Mayor Cohen a warm reception, no pun intended.

"I will waste no time in delivering my important message to Americans, a speech that deprograms Americans from the confusing doublespeak of the Reagan years by paraphrasing lines from Hannah Arendt's *Origins of Totalitarianism*. For eight years, President Reagan has cloaked himself in the image of FDR and undermined the New Deal at every opportunity. His lean, mean safety net has reduced Roosevelt's communitarian society to atomistic social Darwinism, the barest step above a dog-eat-dog society. I predict that someday the smart history teachers of the future will present the Reagan era as a neo–Gilded Age, a time when *caring* and *compassion* became *wimpy.*"

Laughter punctuated Cohen's delivery and helped him set up his finish with a flurry, the *four big bewares*: "Beware of sunny, smooth communicators who dangerously simplify complex problems so the masses will buy unworkable solutions. Beware of a movement that tells Americans that everything they say is possible when we know that none of it is true. Beware of a chief executive who bills himself as a guarantor of liberty yet doggedly chips away at our social and cultural freedoms. Beware of leadership that judges ideas with political litmus tests rather than by merit, common sense, reason, or public welfare.

"That is why I urge y'all to vote Democratic this November so that America may go forward once more. Thank you for listening, and I hope everyone enjoys the parade. Good day, goodbye, and God bless you."

I've reserved a WDDT studio, Cohen thought as he ended his address, *for later this evening to record my resignation speech. I appreciate the media's not picking up on the goodbye part yet.*

Allie smiled and waved to the crowd before gladly handing the microphone over to film star, political activist, and good friend Peter Bates. The audience enthusiastically clapped or cheered their mayor's speech and then warmly welcomed Bates, who introduced and endorsed the Democratic candidate.

Governor Dukakis is following Bates, Cohen thought. *Man, that's a hard act to follow.* Five minutes later: *I have to give Dukakis credit. He's working hard to impress the conservative southern audience with his moderate and pragmatic five-point program, and he isn't even breaking a sweat in this heat.*

Dukakis's five political promises included

1. balancing the budget,

2. correcting the trade imbalance,

3. governing fairly,

4. improving the nation's defenses,

5. more good jobs at good wages.

"Notably," said Cohen, "it's the south, so Dukakis ignored gun control."

Moynihan and Cohen went over the parade plans a last time.

"Charley, the motorcade starts at Five Points, Atlanta's busiest intersection, and arches up Peachtree Street to the Summit. High school and college marching bands, the south's contribution to American culture along with NASCAR, entertain the crowds lining the confetti-strewn streets."

Moynihan laughed; Cohen continued. "The cheering sea of white and black supporters will reach out to shake their politicians' hands as they wave to the crowds lining the street."

"Thank you, Mayor Cohen, for your colorful strategic analysis and this great turnout today. Mike Dukakis is grateful for all that you have done for him too."

A motorcycle patrolman with dark sunglasses assigned to guard Mayor Cohen's vehicle crawled along at five miles per hour. The cop controlled the bike with his left hand while his right hand rested against his gun. No one noticed his unbuckled holster, a safety violation carrying a hefty fine and one of the first rules taught to police academy rookies. I learned that fact from watching *Serpico* with Gabriel.

The late-model Cadillac Eldorado edged across the last ridge before the Peachtree Summit, the highest point in downtown. Cohen sat in the back, flanked by secret servicemen on both sides of him.

Allie looked to his right and saw something irregular, though he did not report it to his protectors. Johnny Epps, who regularly guarded him, was wearing a baggy uniform. Cohen found it hard to believe that Georgianne, his seamstress wife and a part-time preacher whose church Cohen once spoke at, let her husband out of the house dressed like that.

With the Summit up ahead and the secret service chief shouting orders to his men and him too, Cohen speculated. *I guess Johnny's lost weight dieting and Georgianne's been too busy to tailor his uniforms.*

The mayor strained to hear a directive being barked from Clint Murchison, the secret serviceman to his left who turned and started moving right.

White cursed Murchison. *Goddamn it, the fucking agent is shielding Cohen from my view, and I'm fast running out of time.*

Eddie's right index finger was on the gun's trigger, and he patiently waited for a clear view of his target. *That motherfucking agent keeps yakking away to the mayor, maybe about the weather for all I know. Goddammit, I only got a minute left until the motorcade reaches the corner of Peachtree Street and International Boulevard and where everyone will begin to scatter.*

Eddie began his assault by hugging the Cadillac and slowly raising his gun to get into position to shoot. Agent Murchison stepped out on the trunk to check out the rear flank, so I got positioned to make White drop his gun.

Thank god, Eddie mouthed, *that fucking agent is finally out of my line of fire.*

White summoned his courage to kill the prophet and die in a hail of gunfire. I prepared to knock the gun out of Eddie's hand before he could shoot.

I'm going to stop White right this second. Oh, Gabriel, the crowd—surging to get a closer look at the prophet—jostled a mother and caused her to lose control of her twin boys who are buckled into a double stroller. The precious blue-eyed towheads are rolling down International Boulevard, picking up speed, and heading straight into the path of a big oncoming truck. Hashem, I cannot save both the lives of the two children and the prophet. What do I do?

Five miles up Peachtree Street in Piedmont Hospital, young Ari Cohen finished an essay for a class assignment. The theme was each student's favorite sports hero; Ari chose Dale Murphy, the Atlanta Braves' slugging center fielder.

Okay, I finished up in time to watch my daddy on TV waving to the crowd.

Farrah White was in the curbside crowd searching for Eddie and recognized the motorcycle cop getting ready to shoot the mayor.

Oh my lord, I've been dreaming this horrible nightmare for the past three days in my sleep.

Fear and shame gripped Farrah as she tried to save her husband from his death mission by screaming with all the strength left in her battered body.

"Eddie, please don't do it! Eddie, for Arvida and Dennis's sake, please don't do it! They need their daddy!"

Eddie heard Farrah's pleas but coldly ignored her. Allie's eyes focused on a snub-nosed gun coming up at him.

Oh shit, the cop isn't Johnny Epps after all. It's Eddie.

I saved the twins from the truck in the nick of time, Gabriel, but now the startled crowd is reacting to gunfire by wildly dispersing. Most people in the shooting area are ducking for cover. Others with children are huddling and cowering.

APD officers have cordoned off the area to free the secret service to riddle the assassin's body with bullets while local police search for possible conspirators.

Secret service agent Murchison, Mayor Cohen's primary shield, testified at the inquiry.

"The mayor, in prophetlike manner, looked straight into the contorted face of his assassin and then looked to heaven with his arms raised toward the Lord. Mayor Cohen asked Adonai to please forgive Mr. White, for rage, hurt, and despair had so blinded him that he knew not what he was doing.

"I pulled my gun from its holster," described Murchison, "and saw the face of the fake cop. Mr. Eddie White's facial expression reflected anguish when Mayor Cohen calmly absolved him and rendered his final act in life meaningless. White's act was reduced to the work of a pathetic and misguided person.

"White—and pardon my language—aimed his gun at the mayor and mouthed, 'I hate you, motherfucker, for ruining my life, so get ready to pay your fucking *dues* just like I'm going tó pay mine.'

"White shot the mayor three times at close range from a left-to-right direction across the mayor's upper chest. The second pierced his heart. The force of the projectiles sliced into and through Cohen's flesh and drove him down into the back seat."

The agent cleared his throat and wiped a tear.

"The mayor lay there for a few moments, the sound of death expectorating up from his throat. The crowd lining the streets scattered to take cover from gunfire that was coming from the motorcade."

Murchison stopped to compose himself, wiped another tear from his eye, and then continued. "I cringed at the sight of the mayor lying down in his seat while the secret service detail grotesquely sliced up Mr. White's body with twenty-two bullets, three of which were mine. Pieces of White's thigh and cheek flesh were discovered in the street near his ripped-up body.

"His widow, Mrs. Farrah White, threw herself on her dead husband and screamed and sobbed uncontrollably. Since that moment, I've not been able to get that image out of my mind and am afraid I never will.

"Mayor Cohen"—Murchison stopped to compose himself again and wiped tears from both eyes—"Mayor Cohen feebly pressed both arms against the wounds to temporarily stop his bleeding. Despite my urging him to sit still and rest, he used his remaining seconds of consciousness to struggle to his feet."

At Piedmont Hospital, Ari watched his father rise on TV assumably to meet his Maker. *My mother and grandmother are crying hysterically. Mom just screamed about it being Tisha B'Av. I want to be strong and comfort Mom and Grandma, but the picture of my daddy wounded like that scares me, and I'm going to cry too.*

Agent Murchison stated Mayor Cohen's last words before he collapsed and died.

"Oh blessed One, I am sorry for all good works on earth that I have left undone. Please be generous with your grace."

A hundred thousand Americans watched Mayor Cohen's assassination live on television, millions more in the cable news replays. Allie lived past age forty-one and barely beat the jinx for the past three generations of Cohen males. Eddie White, in death, had become famous, if fleetingly.

Two days after the tragedy, a hundred thousand Atlantans wearing black armbands on their left sleeve marched down

Peachtree Street with candles in hand. Rick Samuels, Sam Minkowitz, Mike Schwartz, and Dan Daniels jointly organized Mayor Cohen's memorial service. Sixty thousand mourners filled the Braves stadium to honor Allie Cohen and all that he stood for.

Minkowitz introduced Carole Herman. "A dear friend of the family who needs no introduction wants to honor Allie's life with two memorial songs, 'A Day in the Life' by John Lennon and Bob Dylan's 'Blowing in the Wind.'"

Carole sang both songs so tenderly that the crowd lit candles to honor Allie's memory. She blew a kiss toward heaven, hugged and kissed Sarah and Ari, and held tiny Brenda for a few moments before leaving the stage in tears.

Interim mayor Mack Thomas concluded Allie Cohen's memorial service by quoting a refrain from an old Jesse Colin Young song.

"C'mon, people, now. Smile on your brother. Everybody, get together. Try to love one another right now."

Eleven months later, Sarah unveiled Allie's memorial stone. In accordance with his will, Lenny Meltzer's design was modest in size but engraved with words that Sarah heard in a dream the night before the funeral.

"He came and walked among us, yet too few saw or heard or cared."

In Washington DC, one of the first acts of the new president George H. W. Bush was repeal of NDMA. The Senate and House quietly attached the repeal to a general funding bill. The rider was trickily worded; Congress, by unanimously voting for the spending bill, invisibly opted to repeal the measure, and the media barely reported it.

Some pundits labeled it an aberration; the social experiment had come and gone, with few remembering that it even took place. Atlanta was its lone laboratory of application, and that was quickly undone and rolled back. The metropolitanization of Atlanta ceased and was dissolved; original boundaries were reinstated. Sprawl and decentralization became the norm again for the next twenty years as the suburbs resumed distancing themselves from the urban core. Mack Thomas did not run for mayor and retired from politics for a partnership in a lucrative law practice that specialized in municipal bond law.

Six months later, the Pew Foundation polled the nation on the influence and legacy of NDMA. One percent had heard of it, less than a half of a percent could identify its purpose, virtually no one cared that it had come and gone.

The Cohen family sometimes wondered if Allie had died for nothing. I do too, for though the prophet was widely beheld in life, he is only modestly exalted in death and with no discernable measure of awe.

Chapter 135

In the Creator's commissary, the eggs are never runny, and no one ever burns the toast or the bacon. Allie sat down to a heavenly breakfast with his grandpa Alvin and father, Barney, who introduced his son to the grandfather he'd never known.

Ma only said negative things about Alvin and clearly didn't like him. Allie recalled. *Dad never talked about him at all. Mom once said Alvin was too strict with Barney. He expected more from his elder son and punished him much worse than he did David.*

Tears formed in Grandpa Alvin's eyes as he hugged Allie and told him, "My greatest regret was watching your extraordinary life from the sidelines up here."

They all laughed. "My proudest moment was when you received the Nobel Peace Prize. My cronies all complained loudly that I badly abused my bragging rights."

"I'm happy," Allie deadpanned, "to finally meet you, Grandpa Alvin. I guess it's better late than never."

They all laughed heartily. Barney was thrilled to see his son again after thirty-three years of desperately missing him.

"It was my greatest pleasure," expressed Barney, "to have been your father, but I deeply regret having only ten years with you. Allie, you were my perfect son. No father ever enjoyed raising a boy more than I did you."

"I only have happy memories from my time with you, Dad. You and Mom gave Carla and me wonderful childhoods."

Tears streamed down Barney's cheeks.

"It's hard to describe, Allie, the joy and amazement I've received from all your successes in education, writing, business, movies, politics, and peace missions. I don't know how you achieved so much in just forty-one short years."

"Well, the passing of both you and Grandpa at age forty kind of shaped my attitude about my life expectancy prospects."

Barney and Alvin laughed so hard that their heads bobbled.

"The day Barney got run over and killed, I stopped believing that a long, secure, and safe life was in the cards for me."

They stopped laughing and became serious. "Allie," affirmed Alvin, "there is no Cohen male jinx. Chalk it up to major coincidence. The ten generations that came before Barney and me all lived to seventy years or more. Four of them reached eighty and one ninety."

"Well, whatever, I didn't take a day for granted and lived a frenetic life. I accomplished a great deal because I was always moving forward, and don't forget Hashem and Gabriel were also driving their prophet forward with new projects or destinations to go to."

Barney kvelled. "My proudest moment of all, Allie—even more than the Nobel Prize—was when you built the Sit-In and named the banquet room after me. It was a very smart move to open our dream of a great deli restaurant in Atlanta instead of New Jersey."

"Dad, what goes around comes around. In the end, we did it in New Jersey too. Joel, Carla's husband, will manage the newest Sit-In located in Livingston. In fact, the grand opening is this weekend. Sandy Forman and Harvey Kartzman think it's going to do very well despite serious competition from well-established brands."

Barney grew sentimental and sniffled.

"I miss my pretty Carla too, Allie. She always had such a zest for life." He wiped away a tear. "The best thing you ever did was to marry Sarah, a great wife with terrific parents, especially Harvey. I looked forward to getting to know him when he joins us up here. I also want to personally thank him for the Sit-In's success."

Alvin had twelve years with Barney, Barney ten years with Allie, and Allie eight years with Ari. All three loved watching Ari play Little League baseball at Murphey Candler Park that afternoon.

Alvin and Barney agreed that Ari looked a little more like Sarah but seemed just like Allie at the same age.

Alvin, Barney, and Allie eventually got around to discussing the president and Congress's repeal of NDMA. The three Cohens concluded in the fifth inning of the 1–0 shutout, which Ari was pitching and had knocked in the only run.

His dad and grandpa brought him down to earth with "You lived a very special life, son, and made a bit of a difference in the world, but as much as we hate to say it, kid, yes, you probably died for nothing. Think about it. Almost nobody remembers your greatest accomplishment in life."

A waxen Allie reflected on his death. *I so desperately miss Sarah, Ari, and Brenda that I question not diving to the floorboard instead of absolving poor Eddie White, I'd be down there having breakfast with my wife and kids.*

The eternal One sent me to act as a courier, and I approached and smiled at the three generations of Cohen men breaking bread and schmoozing together.

"Alvin and Barney, please excuse me, but I am the special angel Gabriel. The Master of the universe has summoned Allie for a conference, and I must escort him to his meeting with the Lord

Almighty. It was very nice to meet you, Alvin and Barney, and hope to see you guys again."

Alvin and Barney, dead for decades, had yet to be summoned by Adonai. Alvin kibitzed with Barney.

"We've been sitting here like rocks for ages, and the kid's here a day and already meets Yahweh. Go and figure."

Both laughed so hard that they slapped their thighs.

"That's our Allie," Barney added. "He's always been special."

A flash of light later, Allie and Gabriel stood before the holy One, who was perched over Atlanta and looking down at the city. Gabriel noticed that the brilliant glow that usually surrounded Adonai's aura appeared bleached, for Allie had no need to shield his eyes from the usual glare.

Hashem's fiercest protector asked the eternal One, "Why do You appear sapped to me today? What great weight has brought You to this wan state?"

"Thank you, Gabriel, for your concern."

The Lord's light brightened. "I have a mild fatigue from setting in motion countless peaceful human actions today. A velvet revolution will start tomorrow and sweep central Europe, tear down the Berlin Wall, and force the collapse of atheistic Soviet Communism. I can't wait for the day when the world is finally rid of this freedom-stealing and soul-killing system."

Cohen, the messenger, thanked the holy One.

"For the past forty years, the Cold War shaped every day of my life with the specter of nuclear war hanging over all of us." Cohen then apologized for not completing his mission.

"I am sorry, Adonai, that I failed You, all-knowing One."

The Name that no one dare say gently enveloped Allie to show him love. "You did not fail Me, Allie," reassured Hashem. "It is I who failed you. You did everything possible to alert the people. Your heart and soul rarely wavered from the path that was chosen for you. That is all a prophet can do and I to ask of you."

"Creator," Gabriel interjected, "I predicted at the outset that Allie might need you to shortcut the process. He might have succeeded if the Name had acted bolder."

The holy One, in a sarcastic tone, said, "Please, Gabriel, My special angel, enlighten the Name with your special wisdom."

Gabriel and Allie both looked at each other and laughed.

"Two points, please, Adonai." Hashem's fearless shield dared to lecture the holy One, blessed be He. "First, You did not have to enforce the forty-year rule. Second, You could have saved Allie from the bullets, even with Eli rescuing the twins."

"Yes, I, the Redeemer, could have but chose not to and for good reasons. My shield and protector, do you have any more to say to the Name?"

"Yes, holy One, Allie was starting up Judah Vision to message the world and was also headed to the UN, where he might have succeeded at exaltation and maybe even awe too, that is, if you hadn't cut short his time on earth."

"Gabriel, the people," the great Redeemer declared, "are still unworthy, though some strides were made during Allie's mission. For forty-one years, you have witnessed the measure of mankind's blind stupidity and sheer depravity. Surely, you do not think they deserve My deliverance. At least three decades of striving for a more divine perfection is necessary for Yahweh to even consider revisiting a final blessing."

Hashem's decision badly depressed Gabriel.

"The people are so thickheaded, Lord, that it will more likely take three centuries. It took the Chazers more than a hundred years to truly become Jews."

Allie rejoiced being in the presence of the Almighty and Gabriel and relished their frank exchanges. Cohen, inspired by Hashem and Gabriel, declared his great hope to become a second angelic shield for Hashem.

The newest angel asked the Name if there were any immediate plans for him. The Creator perked up; Allie shielded his eyes with an outstretched hand.

"For the time being, My new special angel—and Gabriel—will serve and protect My blessed souls in heaven."

The holy One surprised Allie by turning his question around.

"My son, is there anything that you might wish of Hashem?"

Adonai turned his light down; Cohen stepped forth.

"Yes, holy One, blessed be He. I wish for my son, Ari, to become the first Jewish president of the United States. Upon his growing into a fine young man and deciding on government for a career, I desire to return to the earth as his political adviser; marry Sarah, his mother; and finally enjoy my beautiful Brenda, my freckle-faced redheaded daughter, whom I smile at only from up here."

Gabriel informed Allie of the Lord's single bylaw.

"The Name only grants such wishes to those who provide major benefits to all mankind."

"Thank you, Gabriel, for that knowledge and you too, Master of the universe, for hearing my proposition. In light of the sacrifices I made, I believe I deserve the chance to reunite with my family. If Hashem grants me my wish, I promise an immense benefit unto all the peoples of the earth."

"Your sacrifice was indeed great, My son," Adonai acknowledged. "But to be truly deserving, the benefit must improve the lives of almost five and a half billion people. That is more than immense."

Gabriel nodded to Allie to begin.

Cohen illuminated the Almighty. "A Jewish U.S. president will keep the Jews of America and Israel safe and will be a light unto all the nations of the world."

"Yes, Allie, of course, for the Jews have always been a light unto the world, but this event is still far short of earthly transformation."

"I understand, Adonai. My hope is for Ari and me to prepare the world for a first coming in thirty years and without the stupid destruction of Armageddon. Instead of cataclysm and selective survival, humankind ushers in a golden age of peace and prosperity through love, friendship and cooperation."

Hashem's light shone on Allie, who bowed.

"Son, your vision is a true blessing for all the peoples of the earth, and thank you, my dear Allie."

"I am most grateful for the Creator's blessing my purpose, and I gloriously serve the eternal One's every request."

"For the next twenty years or until Ari is a grown man," Adonai directed, "and is ready to start changing America and the world, please join your father and grandfather to make the deli

1043

station in the commissary even more heavenly. The Name has guilty pleasures too, for there's nothing tastier than a good hot corned beef or pastrami sandwich on sour rye with a pickle and a scoop of New York potato salad."

Allie was beside himself with fantastic joy because the holy One's favorite food was the same as his.

"Dear Adonai," Cohen promised, "wait until Harvey, my father-in-law, and Max, my mother's husband, get here and join my dad in the kitchen. These guys really know how to pickle and brine corned beef and pastrami, also smoke lox and lake sturgeon."

"Little whitefish chubs too, Allie?" The holy One lit up like a sun.

Cohen's eyes opened widely and radiated such amazement that Gabriel filled him in. "Succulent smoked white fish is another of the Almighty's special comfort foods. Hashem annually shows His fondness for the prophet Jesus on Christmas Day by eating at a good Chinese restaurant, no pork or shellfish though. The Name that we dare not say, of course, may not consume tref."

"The Holy One," Gabriel giggled. "The holy One backed Moses's Ten Commandments and 613 laws and must set the example. The alternative is to endure Chazers."

Allie laughed and glowed with a joyful smile for the eternal One.

"Of course, Name, I promise you that the deli station in the commissary is going to go way past heavenly."

The eternal One's enhanced aura nearly blinded Allie and Gabriel.

"That will be My divine pleasure, Allie. And bless you, My son, for indulging the Creator's few pleasures."

"And bless You too, Name. I am Your holy, humble, and dedicated son who swears to avenge all who would do harm to Hashem and the souls in heaven. I shall perform the heavenly task the holy One has given me and await Your word and beckoning."

"Amen, My second angelic shield, for I have blessed you, My son."

The End

Printed in the United States
By Bookmasters